How to take a case before the

NATIONAL LABOR RELATIONS BOARD

How to take a case before the

NATIONAL LABOR RELATIONS BOARD

Fourth Edition Revised

by KENNETH C. McGUINESS

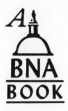

BNA
BOOK

THE BUREAU OF NATIONAL AFFAIRS, INC.—WASHINGTON, D.C.

The Bureau of National Affairs, Inc.
Washington, D.C. 20037

Library of Congress Cataloging in Publication Data

McGuinness, Kenneth C
    How to take a case before the National Labor Relations Board.

    Previous editions by L. G. Silverberg.
    Includes index.
    1. United States. National Labor Relations Board.   I. Silverberg, Louis G.   How to take a case before the National Labor Relations Board.   II. Title.
KF3372.M25   1975   344'.73'010269   74-32565
ISBN 0-87179-211-7

PRINTED IN THE UNITED STATES OF AMERICA

Contents

Charts, Tables, and Facsimiles

CHARTS

TABLES

FACSIMILES

Facsimile

Facsimile

Author's Preface

Constant changes in procedural rules and policies of the National Labor Relations Board have required the updating of this work. The Board is now compiling Volume 217 of its decisions. Nearly 60 volumes have been issued since the last revision of the text, adding again to the complexity of Board procedure.

The purpose of the book continues to be consistent with that of previous editions, including those originally prepared by Louis G. Silverberg. It provides a simple explanation of the procedural framework, both formal and informal, within which cases are processed before the Board. It makes no attempt to discuss Board substantive law, to analyze the wisdom or validity of Board procedures, or to suggest improvements or alternatives. The book instead concentrates on how to handle cases within existing rules and policies.

To the layman or lawyer inexperienced in Board matters, the text should provide a helpful guide through the intricacies of Board procedure. At the same time the explanations, tables, and citations are designed to provide the experienced labor lawyer or practitioner with ready reference to source materials and with checklists not published elsewhere in condensed form.

The necessity for a thorough grasp of procedure cannot be overemphasized. It is fundamental to the successful handling of cases before the Board and a significant advantage flows to the advocate who masters the Board's complicated procedural rules and policies.

A number of people deserve recognition for their assistance in preparing the final manuscript. The editorial comments of my colleague, Robert E. Williams, on new material were most valuable and consistent with his usual high standards. Lee Vincent, Joel Anderson, and Mike Balsamo of the NLRB's Washington staff were always helpful and cooperative in supplying forms, charts, diagrams, and other materials whenever called upon. Particularly deserving is Kevin McGuiness, who spent many long hours, often under trying circumstances, in research, verifying citations, and seeking out new source materials. My gratitude to them all.

Washington, D. C.   KENNETH C. MCGUINESS
May 1975

CHAPTER 1

What the Law Provides

Sec. 1–1. In general. Both the basic labor-management relations policy of the United States and the means adopted by Congress to carry out that policy are found in the National Labor Relations Act with its amendments. It is this statute which established the National Labor Relations Board and which, in turn, is administered by the Board.

The policy as set forth in the original Act (the Wagner Act) is a simple but sweeping declaration of purpose, stated in terms of eliminating the causes of obstructions to the free flow of commerce arising out of industrial strife and mitigating and eliminating such obstructions when they have occurred. Two methods of accomplishing the desired result were adopted— the encouragement of collective bargaining and the protection of the exercise by workers of full freedom of association, self-organization, and designation of representatives.[1] Both the purpose and the methods remain unchanged. Major amendments, the Labor Management Relations Act of 1947 (Taft-Hartley Act) and the Labor-Management Reporting and Disclosure Act of 1959 (Landrum-Griffin Act), have clarified the right to refrain from union activity, enhanced the protection afforded workers, included safeguards for the public, and improved the Board's organization and procedures.

The law in its present form, with more than 200 volumes of Board cases interpreting and applying its provisions, constitutes an exceedingly complex code of conduct for employers, employees, and unions. Its protection of the right of individuals to engage in, or refrain from, union activities sometimes seems more obscure than Congress intended, but its effect on labor-management relations has been profound.

The statute consists of five titles. (The full text appears in Appendix A, page 373.) The first, and most extensive, includes the establishment and function of the NLRB, the procedures for determining the exclusive bargaining agent of employees in a bargaining unit, and the conduct of employees, unions, and their agents which constitutes unfair labor practices. Title II establishes the Federal Mediation and Conciliation

Sec. 1.

Service and the procedures for handling national emergency disputes. Title III provides for suits by and against labor organizations. Title IV creates a now-defunct joint committee of Congress to study and report on labor relations problems, and Title V is limited to certain definitions and a saving and separability provision.

This discussion is concerned solely with those clauses of the statute, all in Title I, which are administered by the National Labor Relations Board. The substance of the principal provisions is set forth in this chapter. The portion of the statute which shapes the structure of the enforcing agency is treated in Chapter 2.

Sec. 1-2. Coverage of the Act—Types of business covered. Not everyone is subject to the provisions of the Act. The Board is given broad jurisdiction over all businesses whose materials, products, or services cross state lines or which affect the operations of other companies engaged in such activity.[2] However, the Board in its discretion may decline to assert jurisdiction provided that the standards which it uses are not more restrictive than those prevailing on August 1, 1959.[3] Businesses not covered by the Act are governed by state and local laws.

The statute empowers the Board to grant states and territories jurisdiction over cases involving industries which are engaged in or affect interstate commerce.[4] However, the Board has never exercised this power and ceded its jurisdiction because of the prerequisite that both the state's laws and their interpretation must be consistent with the federal law. No state has qualified.

Sec. 1-3. Coverage of the Act—Exempt employers. The statute specifically exempts the following employers from its coverage:[5]

1. The United States Government and the states, or any political subdivision of either;
2. Federal Reserve banks;
3. Wholly owned government corporations;
4. Any employer who is subject to the terms of the Railway Labor Act.
5. Labor organizations, except when acting as employers.

Sec. 1-4. Coverage of the Act—Exempt employees. The statute specifically exempts the following employees from its coverage:[6]

---

[2] NLRB v. Fainblatt, 306 U.S. 601, 4 LRRM 535 (1939); *see also* Mexican American Unity Council, Inc., 207 NLRB No. 128, 84 LRRM 1561 (1973).
[3] Sec. 14(c).
[4] Sec. 10(a).
[5] Sec. 2(2).
[6] Sec. 2(3).

1. Agricultural laborers;
2. Domestic servants;
3. Any individual employed by his parent or spouse;
4. Any individual employed by an employer who is subject to the Railway Labor Act;
5. Independent contractors;
6. Supervisors;
7. Government employees, Federal or State, including Government corporations and Federal Reserve Banks.

Sec. 1–5. Coverage of the Act—Supervisors, independent contractors, and agricultural laborers. The exemption of supervisors and independent contractors, and to a lesser extent agricultural laborers, has been most troublesome to the Board. The statute specifically states that it is not illegal for supervisors to organize; they are not, however, accorded the protections of the Act or the use of its election procedures.[7] A comprehensive definition of the term "supervisor" is found in the Act,[8] but the Board has also developed certain secondary tests of supervisory status.[9] (See also Sec. 8–10, page 140.)

Neither independent contractors nor agricultural employees are defined by the Act, and the Board has therefore been forced to evolve its own concept. In determining whether or not an individual is an independent contractor, the Board has consistently applied the common-law "right of control" test. If the recipient of the services in question has a right to control not only the result to be achieved but also the manner in which the work is to be performed, an employer relationship exists as a matter of law; otherwise, there exists an independent contractor relationship.[10] The Board has turned to interpretations of Section 3(f) of the Fair Labor Standards Act as its principal guideline in defining agricultural laborers.[11]

---

[7] Sec. 14(a); Packard Motor Co. v. NLRB, 330 U.S. 485, 19 LRRM 2397 (1947).
[8] Sec. 2(11).
[9] Textron, Inc., Bell Aerospace Co. Div., *sub nom.* NLRB v., 416 U.S. 267, 85 LRRM 2945 (1974), *aff'g and revs'g in part, reman'g* 82 LRRM 2753; *cf.* Chrysler Corp., 173 NLRB No. 160, 69 LRRM 1506 (1968) (confidential employees); North Arkansas Electrical Cooperative, 185 NLRB No. 83, 75 LRRM 1068 (1970) (managerial employees).
[10] National Freight Inc., 146 NLRB 144, 55 LRRM 1259 (1964); Pony Trucking, 198 NLRB No. 59, 81 LRRM 1249 (1972).
[11] Monterey County Bldg. & Constr. Trades Council, 142 NLRB 139, 52 LRRM 1535, *enf.,* NLRB v. Monterey County Bldg. & Constr. Trades Council, 335 F.2d 927, 57 LRRM 2023 (C.A. 9, 1964); Maneja v. Waialua Agricultural Co., 349 U.S. 254, 12 WH Cases 502; McElrath Poultry Co. v. NLRB, 86 LRRM 2687 (C.A. 5, 1974), *denying enforcement to* 84 LRRM 1295; *cf.* Victor Ryckebosch, Inc., 189 NLRB 40, 77 LRRM 1186 (1971), and cases cited therein, *rev'd,* 471 F.2d 20, 81 LRRM 2931 (C.A. 9, 1972). The Board has respectfully disagreed and adhered to its view until such time as the Supreme Court passes on the matter.

When dealing with employees in any of the foregoing categories particular care must be exercised to determine whether the exemptions apply.

Sec. 1–6. Access to the machinery of the Board—Data to be filed with the Secretary of Labor. The Landrum-Griffin Act requires the reporting of extensive information and financial data by unions.[12] Certain employers must also file reports. The data must be filed periodically with the Office of Labor-Management and Welfare-Pension Reports, a part of the U. S. Department of Labor.

The office has prepared necessary forms and instructions which may be used to make the required filings. Copies may be obtained from either its regional or area offices or by writing directly to its Washington office. (See Appendix G for directory of regional and area offices of the Office of Labor-Management and Welfare-Pension Reports.)

Since the passage of the 1959 amendments, filing of these reports does not affect the right of a party to invoke the Act. The only standard which a labor organization must meet before it has access to the Board's processes is that it conform to the definition of "labor organization" set forth in the Act, that is, it must be an organization representing employees for the purpose of dealing with the employer concerning grievances, labor disputes, wages, rates of pay, hours of employment, or conditions of work.[13]

Sec. 1–7. The prohibited unfair labor practices. The basic rights of employees which the statute seeks to guarantee are stated in Section 7. This provision declares:

> Employees shall have the right to self-organization, to form, join or assist labor organizations, to bargain collectively through representatives of their own choosing, and to engage in other concerted activities for the purpose of collective bargaining or other mutual aid or protection, and [employees] shall also have the right to refrain from any or all such activities. . . .

The Board and the courts have ruled that not all "union" or "concerted" activities are protected by Section 7. Among the activities held to be unprotected by the Act are:

---

[12]Sec. 9(f)(g)(h) of LMRA of 1947 required periodic filing of financial reports and non-Communist affidavits as a prerequisite to use of Board's processes. These provisions were deleted by LMRA of 1959.

[13]Sec. 2(5); *see also* NLRB v. Cabot Carbon Co., 360 U.S. 203, 44 LRRM 2204 (1959); NLRB v. Ampex Corporation, 442 F.2d 82, 77 LRRM 2072 (C.A. 7, 1971), *cert. denied,* 404 U.S. 939, 78 LRRM 2704 (1971).

1. Activity considered to be contrary to the legislative purpose of Congress; for example, a strike in violation of a collective bargaining agreement[14] or in violation of another federal statute;[15]
2. Activity aimed at the accomplishment of objectives which conflict with Board policy or Federal law; for example, to compel an employer to commit an unfair labor practice[16] or to violate another Federal law;[17]
3. Activity carried on in an "illegal" manner; for example, destruction of property,[18] sitdown strike,[19] mass picketing,[20] slowdown strike,[21] violence,[22] or "quickie"—intermittent and unannounced—strike;[23] and
4. Improper activity aimed at the destruction of the employer's market; for example, distribution of handbills attacking the quality of the company's product.[24]

The legal consequence of the finding that certain "concerted" activities are not protected by Section 7 is the freedom of the employer to:

1. Discharge or otherwise "discriminate" against the employees involved in that activity;[25] or
2. Decline to bargain with the union responsible for that activity.[26]

Section 7 is immediately followed by provisions which set forth employer and union unfair labor practices. These are broadly worded descriptions of conduct which is unlawful under the Act. (The employer unfair labor

[14]NLRB v. Sands Mfg. Co., 306 U.S. 332, 4 LRRM 530 (1939).
[15]Southern Steamship Co. v. NLRB, 316 U.S. 31, 10 LRRM 544 (1942).
[16]Ohio Ferro-Alloys Corp. v. NLRB, 213 F. 2d 646, 34 LRRM 2327 (C.A. 6, 1954).
[17]American News Co., 55 NLRB 1302, 14 LRRM 64 (1944); see also Claremont Polychemical Corp., 196 NLRB No. 75, 80 LRRM 1130 (1972).
[18]NLRB v. Indiana & Michigan Electric Co., 318 U.S. 9, 11 LRRM 763 (1943); Teamsters, Local 695 (Wisconsin Supply Corp.), 204 NLRB No. 139, 83 LRRM 1650 (1973).
[19]NLRB v. Fansteel Metallurgical Corp., 306 U.S. 240, 4 LRRM 515 (1939).
[20]Allen-Bradley Local No. 1111, United Electrical, Radio & Machine Workers of America v. Wisconsin Employment Relations Board, 315 U.S. 740, 10 LRRM 520 (1942); Burgreen Contracting Co., Inc., 195 NLRB No. 191, 79 LRRM 1700 (1972).
[21]Elk Lumber Co., 91 NLRB 333, 26 LRRM 1493 (1950); AAA Electric, Inc., 82 LRRM 2326 (C.A. 6, 1973), denying enforcement to 77 LRRM 1169.
[22]Artcraft Mantel & Fireplace Co., 174 NLRB No. 110, 70 LRRM 1113 (1969).
[23]Int'l Union, U.A.W.A., Local 232 v. Wisconsin Employment Relations Board, 336 U.S. 245, 23 LRRM 2361 (1949); New Fairview Hall Convalescent Home, 206 NLRB No. 108, 85 LRRM 1227 (1973).
[24]NLRB v. Local No. 1229, Int'l Brotherhood of Electrical Workers, 346 U.S. 464, 33 LRRM 2183 (1953).
[25]NLRB v. Fansteel Metallurgical Corp., 306 U.S. 240, 4 LRRM 515 (1939).
[26]Timken Roller Bearing Co. v. NLRB, 161 F.2d 949, 20 LRRM 2204 (C.A. 6, 1947); Artcraft Mantel and Fireplace Co., 174 NLRB No. 110, 70 LRRM 1294 (1969). It should be noted that the employers' right to decline to bargain lasts only as long as the illegal strike activity continues. See United Elastic Corp., 84 NLRB 768, 24 LRRM 1294 (1949); Dorsey Trailers Inc., 80 NLRB 478, 486, 23 LRRM 1112 (1948).

practices set forth in Section 8 (a) are diagrammed in Chart No. 1, pages 8–9. Certain union unfair labor practices found in Section 8 (b) are diagrammed in Charts No. 2 and 3, pages 10–13.)

Sec. 1–8. Employer unfair labor practices. It is an unfair labor practice for an employer:[27]

1. To interfere with, restrain or coerce employees in the exercise of the rights guaranteed in Section 7;
2. To dominate or interfere with the formation or administration of any labor organization or contribute financial or other support to it;
3. To encourage or discourage membership in any labor organization by discrimination in regard to hire or tenure or conditions of employment, with the one exception of the valid union shop;
4. To discharge or otherwise discriminate against an employee because he has filed charges or given testimony under the Act;
5. To refuse to bargain collectively with the majority representative of his employees; and
6. To enter into a "hot cargo" agreement with a union, that is, an agreement under which the employer promises not to do business with, or not to handle or otherwise deal in any of the products of, any other person.[28]

Sec. 1–9. Employer unfair labor practices—Discharges pursuant to a union-shop clause. The statute recognizes only one situation where it is legal for an employer to discharge an employee upon the request of a union because of nonmembership in the union.[29] Such discharge may be made pursuant to a union-shop agreement which binds all employees to become and remain members of the union 30 or more days after hire as a condition of continued employment. A discharge under such clause is permitted by the statute only if:

1. The union is both free from employer domination or employer assistance and is the majority-designated representative;
2. The union's authority to make such agreement has not been rescinded in a Board-conducted poll within one year preceding the effective date of the agreement;
3. The employer has reason to believe that membership was available to the employee on the same terms applicable to other members; and

---

[27]Sec. 8(a).
[28]Sec. 8(e).
[29]Sec. 8(a)(3).

4. The employer has reason to believe that membership was denied or terminated by the union only because of failure of the employee to offer to pay his dues or initiation fees.

Sec. 1–10. Employer unfair labor practices—Responsibility of the employer. As defined by the statute, an employer is responsible for unfair labor practices committed by any person acting as an agent, directly or indirectly.[30] "In determining whether any person is acting as an 'agent' . . . the question of whether the specific acts performed were actually authorized or subsequently ratified shall not be controlling."[31]

The fundamental rules which are used to determine responsibility for the acts of an "agent" follow:[32]

1. Authority to act as agent in a given manner will be implied whenever the conduct of the employer is such as to show that he actually intended to confer that authority;
2. The employer may be responsible for an act of his agent within the scope of the agent's general authority, or "scope of his employment," even though the employer has not specifically authorized or indeed may have specifically forbidden the act in question; and
3. The burden of proving the employer's responsibility is on the party asserting the agency relationship, both as to the existence of the relationship and as to the nature and extent of the agent's authority.

Thus, an employer has been found to have committed unfair labor practices because of the acts of a vice president,[33] treasurer,[34] superintendent,[35] manager,[36] personnel counselor,[37] bookkeeper,[38] foreman,[39] and leadman.[40] Agency has also been found and an employer ruled liable for the acts of a community businessmen's committee which included former owners of the employer.[41]

[30]Sec. 2(2).
[31]Sec. 2(13).
[32]Int'l Longshoremen's & Warehousemen's Union, Local 6, 79 NLRB 1487, 23 LRRM 1001 (1948).
[33]NLRB v. LaSalle Steel Co., 178 F.2d 822, 25 LRRM 2152 (C.A. 7, 1949).
[34]NLRB v. Republican Publishing Co., 174 F.2d 474, 24 LRRM 2052 (C.A. 1, 1949).
[35]NLRB v. Todd Co., Inc., 173 F.2d 705, 23 LRRM 2534 (C.A. 2, 1949).
[36]NLRB v. Beatrice Foods Co., 183 F.2d 726, 26 LRRM 2343 (C.A. 10, 1950).
[37]NLRB v. Olin Industries, Inc., 191 F.2d 613, 28 LRRM 2427 (C.A. 5, 1951).
[38]Joy Silk Mills, Inc., v. NLRB, 185 F.2d 732, 27 LRRM 2012 (C.A.D.C., 1950).
[39]NLRB v. LaSalle Steel Co., 178 F.2d 822, 25 LRRM 2152 (C.A. 7, 1949); Beaumont Steel Construction Co., 179 NLRB No. 77, 74 LRRM 1036 (1969).
[40]NLRB v. Norfolk Shipbuilding and Drydocking Corp., 172 F.2d 813, 23 LRRM 2312 (C.A. 4, 1949); Milgo Industrial, Inc., 203 NLRB No. 152, 83 LRRM 1280 (1973).
[41]The Colson Corp., 148 NLRB 827, 57 LRRM 1078 (1964).

Sections 8 (a) (1) (2) (3) (4) (5)

"It shall be an unfair labor practice for an EMPLOYER . . ."

1	**2**	**3**
To interfere with, restrain, or coerce employees in the exercise of the following rights:	To dominate or interfere with the formation or administration of a union, or to contribute financial or other support to it.	To discriminate in hiring, or any term or condition of employment, to encourage or discourage membership in a union (except as required under a valid union-security agreement.)
● to form, join, or assist a union		
● to bargain through representatives of their own choosing		
● to engage in concerted activities for mutual aid and protection		
● to refrain from such activity (except as required under a valid union security agreement.)		

CHART NO. 1. *The provisions of sections 8 (a) (1), (2), (3), (4), (5)*

SECTIONS 8(a) (1) (2) (3) (4) (5) – Contd.

4

To discriminate against an employee because he has filed charges or given testimony under the Act.

5

To refuse to bargain collectively with representatives of a majority of his employees in an appropriate unit.

Sections 8 (b) (1) (2) (3)

"It shall be an unfair labor practice for a LABOR ORGANIZATION

1 (A)	1 (B)	2
To restrain or coerce employees in the exercise of the following rights: ● to form, join, or assist a union ● to bargain through representatives of their own choosing ● to engage in concerted activities for mutual aid and protection ● to refrain from such activity (except as required under a valid union security agreement.)	To restrain or coerce an employer in the selection of his representatives for collective bargaining or handling grievances.	To cause or attempt to cause an employer to discriminate against an employee in hiring, or any term or condition of employment, to encourage or discourage membership in a union (except as required under a valid union security agreement.)

CHART NO. 2. *The provisions of sections 8 (b) (1), (2), (3)*

SECTIONS 8 (b) (1) (2) (3) – Contd.

OR ITS AGENTS... "

2

To cause or attempt
to cause an em-
ployer to discrim-
inate against an
employee who has
been denied mem-
bership in the
union, or whose
membership has
been terminated
on some grounds
other than failure
to pay dues and
fees uniformly
required of all
members.

3

To refuse to bargain
with an employer,
provided the union
is the valid repre-
sentative of a
majority of em-
ployees in an ap-
propriate unit.

Sections 8 (b) (4) (i) and (ii) (A), (B) and (C)

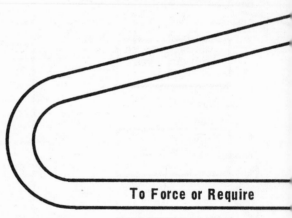

UNFAIR LABOR
PRACTICE FOR
LABOR
ORGANIZATION
OR ITS AGENTS

TO ENGAGE IN, INDUCE, OR ENCOURAGE

any individual employed by any
person engaged in commerce or in
an industry affecting commerce

or

TO THREATEN, COERCE, OR RESTRAIN

any person engaged in commerce or
in an industry affecting commerce

To Force or Require

The Statute assigns priority to the handling of such cases and directs that an injunction must be requested if there is reasonable cause to believe that they have merit

CHART NO. 3. *The provisions of Sections 8 (b) (4) (i) and (ii) (A), (B), and (C)*

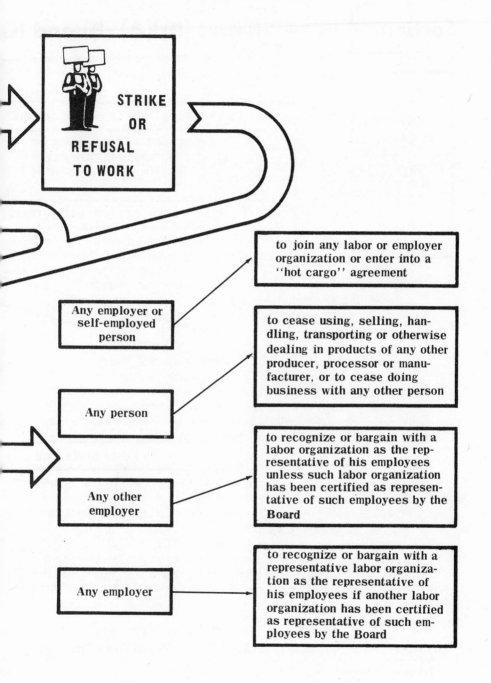

STRIKE
OR
REFUSAL
TO WORK

Any employer or self-employed person

to join any labor or employer organization or enter into a "hot cargo" agreement

Any person

to cease using, selling, handling, transporting or otherwise dealing in products of any other producer, processor or manufacturer, or to cease doing business with any other person

Any other employer

to recognize or bargain with a labor organization as the representative of his employees unless such labor organization has been certified as representative of such employees by the Board

Any employer

to recognize or bargain with a representative labor organization as the representative of his employees if another labor organization has been certified as representative of such employees by the Board

Furthermore, a successor employer, who acquires and continues his predecessor's business with the knowledge that the former employer had committed an unfair labor practice in the discharge of an employee, may be ordered by the Board to reinstate the employee with back pay.[42]

Sec. 1–11. Union unfair labor practices.   It is an unfair labor practice for a labor organization or its agents:[43]

1. To restrain or coerce employees in the exercise of the rights guaranteed in Section 7 or an employer in the selection of his representatives for the purposes of collective bargaining or the adjustment of grievances;
2. To cause or attempt to cause an employer to discriminate against an employee on account of his membership or nonmembership in a labor organization with the one exception of the valid union shop; (See discussion above, "Discharges pursuant to a union-shop clause," p. 6.)
3. To refuse to bargain collectively with an employer, provided the union is the majority-designated representative of the employees;
4. To encourage or engage in a strike or refusal to handle goods where an object of such activity is:
    (a) to require any employer or self-employed person to join a labor or employer organization or to enter into a "hot cargo" agreement;
    (b) to require any person to cease using, selling, handling or transporting the products of any other employer, or to cease doing business with any other person or to require some other employer to recognize or bargain with a labor organization which has not been certified by the Board as the representative of that other employer's employees; and
    (c) to require any employer to bargain with a labor organization where another labor organization has already been certified by the Board as the representative of his employees.
    (These complex provisions are usually referred to as the "secondary boycott" provisions. They are set forth in Sections 8 (b)(4)(A), (B) and (C) of the statute and are diagrammed in Chart No. 3, page 12.)
5. To encourage or engage in a strike in order to force an employer to assign work to members of a particular union or craft rather than to members of another union or craft;
6. To charge excessive or discriminatory initiation fees where a union shop is in effect;[44]

[42]Golden State Bottling Co., Inc., et al. v. NLRB, 414 U.S. 168, 84 LRRM 2839 (1973).
[43]Sec. 8(b).
[44]Television and Radio Artists (WBEN, Inc.), 208 NLRB No. 59, 85 LRRM 1256 (1974).

7. To cause or attempt to cause an employer to pay for work which is not to be performed. (This, the "featherbedding" provision, has been interpreted so narrowly that it has little practical application.[45])

8. To engage in picketing or threats of picketing where an object is either to organize employees or to force an employer to recognize or bargain with a union. (See Chapter 19 on picketing for organization or recognition.)

9. To enter into a "hot cargo" agreement with an employer.[46]

Sec. 1–12. Union unfair labor practices—Responsibility of the labor organization. The above provisions constitute unfair labor practices only when engaged in by "a labor organization or its agents"; employees or individuals cannot commit unfair labor practices unless they are acting as "agents" for the labor organization. Rules used to determine responsibility of a labor organization for the acts of an "agent" are the same as those set forth above in the discussion of "Responsibility of the employer," page 7. Application of these rules to specific situations has resulted in rulings that a union was responsible for the acts of a union attorney,[47] district representatives and officers,[48] president,[49] bargaining committee,[50] shop chairman,[51] business agent,[52] shop steward,[53] and a foreman with authority to enforce union "working rules."[54]

Sec. 1–13. Section 10(l) injunctions against labor organizations. The statute requires that the preliminary investigation of a charge alleging a violation of Sections 8(b)(4)(A), (B) or (C); Section 8(e); or Section 8(b)(7)

[45]American Newspaper Publishers Assn. v. NLRB, 345 U.S. 100, 31 LRRM 2422 (1953); NLRB v. Gamble Enterprises, Inc., 345 U.S. 117, 31 LRRM 2428 (1953).

[46]Sec. 8(e).

[47]NLRB v. Pacific Intermountain Express Co. and Int'l Brotherhood of Teamsters, Chauffeurs, Warehousemen & Helpers of America, Local No. 41, 228 F.2d 170, 37 LRRM 2226 (C.A. 8, 1955).

[48]NLRB v. United Mine Workers of America, District 31, 198 F.2d 389, 30 LRRM 2445 (C.A. 4, 1956).

[49]District 50, United Mine Workers of America, Tungsten Mining Local, 106 NLRB 903, 32 LRRM 1576 (1953).

[50]United Electrical, Radio & Machine Workers of America, Local 914 and United Rubber, Cork, Linoleum and Plastic Workers of America, Int'l Union, 106 NLRB 1372, 33 LRRM 1029 (1953).

[51]The Englander Co., Inc., 108 NLRB 38, 33 LRRM 1471 (1954).

[52]NLRB v. United Brotherhood of Carpenters & Jointers of America, Local No. 517, 230 F.2d 256, 37 LRRM 2623 (C.A. 1, 1956).

[53]NLRB v. United Hoisting Co., Inc., 198 F.2d 465, 30 LRRM 2507 (C.A. 3, 1952).

[54]NLRB v. Cement Masons Local No. 555, Operative Plasterers and Cement Masons Int'l, 225 F.2d 168, 36 LRRM 2426 (C.A. 9, 1955); for more recent examples, see Electrical Workers, IBEW, Local 3 (New York Telephone Co.), 81 LRRM 2483 (C.A. 2, 1972), *enf.* 78 LRRM 1431; Teamsters, Local 695 (Wisconsin Supply Corp.), 204 NLRB No. 139, 83 LRRM 1650 (1973); Teamsters, Local 326 (Eazor Express, Inc.), 208 NLRB No. 99, 85 LRRM 1415 (1974).

of the Act must be given top priority. The investigation is carried out by the Regional Office. The Act provides that if the officer or regional attorney to whom the matter is referred has reasonable cause to believe the charge has merit and complaint should issue, he is compelled—he has no discretion— to seek an injunction in the appropriate federal district court.[55] If the charging party is sustaining substantial and irreparable injury, a temporary restraining order will be requested to obtain interim relief prior to the court hearing on the injunction petition. In jurisdictional dispute cases arising under Section 8(b) (4)(D), the Section 10(*l*) procedures for injunctive relief may be used, but only where "appropriate" rather than in all cases. In practice, injunctions are uniformly sought where the jurisdictional dispute is interfering with the progress of the work.

Sec. 1–14. Section 10(j) injunctions against employers and unions. In addition to the mandatory injunctions referred to above, Section 10(j) authorizes the Board to seek a temporary or preliminary injunction in any unfair labor practice case after the General Counsel has instituted a formal proceeding, i.e., has issued a complaint.[56] This is sometimes called the discretionary injunction provision. Unlike Section 10*(l)*, it does not require that injunctive relief be sought, but only makes it possible for the Board to do so in cases where it is considered appropriate. The statute does not define any limits within which the discretion may or may not be used.

Responding to criticism of the infrequent occasions on which the Board has exercised its power to seek injunctions under Section 10(j), the Board in late 1961 began to make greater use of discretionary injunctions. However, the Board continues to look upon such injunctions as an extraordinary remedy which should be used sparingly in unfair practice cases and acts only in unusual circumstances. Consequently, the cases in which the Board has authorized the General Counsel to request such injunctions have been those where the effect of the alleged unfair labor practices was widespread, the public interest was seriously affected, the Board's processes were being interfered with, or the Board's ultimate remedy under the circumstances would have been clearly inadequate and the conduct was clear-cut and flagrant.

Injunctions under Section 10(j) have been sought to prevent an employer from attempting to cancel an existing contract,[57] from refusing to negotiate with a certified union,[58] from discharging employees for union activity and from interrogating and threatening employees.[59] The same provision has

[55]Sec. 10(1).
[56]Sec. 10(j).
[57]Kennedy v. Telecomputing Corp., 49 LRRM 2188 (D.C.S. Calif., 1961).
[58]Madden v. Alberto-Culver Co., 49 LRRM 2516 (D.C. N.Ill., 1961); Johnston v. Georgetown Steel Corp., 76 LRRM 2515 (D.C.S.C., 1970).
[59]Johnston v. Wellington Mfg. Div., 49 LRRM 2536 (D.C./W.S.C., 1961); Smith v. Old Angus, Inc. of Maryland, 81 LRRM 2936 (D.C. Md., 1972).

been used by the Board to compel both a union[60] and an employer to bargain collectively.[61]

The district court is empowered to grant such injunctive relief "as it deems just and proper."[62] Its action in denying or granting the Board's petition for injunctive relief is taken in an independent proceeding. It does not pass upon the ultimate merits of the unfair labor practices charged,[63] and its ruling in no way controls or binds the Board in its subsequent decision on the merits.[64] If the district court issues an injunction, it is dissolved upon issuance of the Board's decision, or upon court enforcement of the Board's order. However, in issuing an injunction, the district court has discretion to limit its duration to a term short of the Board's final decision.[65]

Neither discretionary nor mandatory injunctions may be obtained directly by the charging party. Only the Board, acting through the General Counsel, has this privilege.

Sec. 1–15. The duty to bargain. In its definition of what constitutes collective bargaining, the statute lays down certain rules which are binding upon both employers and labor organizations:[66]

1. They have the mutual obligation to meet at reasonable times and confer in good faith concerning wages, hours, and other conditions of employment;

2. They must execute a written contract incorporating any agreement reached if so requested by either party;

3. They are not compelled to agree to a proposal or require the making of a concession.

The employer is also under the obligation to furnish the union, upon request, with sufficient information to enable it to understand and

[60]Douds v. International Longshoremen, 241 F.2d 278, 39 LRRM 2682 (C.A. 2, 1957).
[61]Compton v. Sea-Land Service Inc., 53 LRRM 2016 (D.C.P.R., 1963); Humphrey v. NTRA-AARP Pharmacy, 84 LRRM 2599 (D.C.D.C., 1973). *See also* LeBus v. Manning, Maxwell, and Moore, Inc., 218 F. Supp. 702, 54 LRRM 2122 (D.C. W.La., 1963).
[62]Secs. 10(j) and 10(*l*). *See also* McLeod v. General Electric Co., 385 U.S. 533, 64 LRRM 2129 (1967), *sett'g aside judgment with direction of* 63 LRRM 2065; Boire v. Teamsters (Pilot Freight Carriers Inc.), 83 LRRM 2128 (C.A. 5, 1973), *aff'g* 81 LRRM 2888, *see also* 81 LRRM 2207.
[63]Douds v. Wine, Liquor & Distillery Workers Union, Local 1, 75 F. Supp. 447, 21 LRRM 2282 (D.C. S.N.Y., 1948).
[64]NLRB v. Denver Building and Construction Trades Council, 341 U.S. 675, 28 LRRM 2108 (1951).
[65]United Brotherhood of Carpenters and Jointers of America, District Council of Kansas City, Missouri v. Sperry, 170 F.2d 863, 23 LRRM 2040 (C.A. 10, 1948).
[66]Sec. 8(d).

intelligently discuss the issues raised in bargaining.[67] (See also Chapter 21, Strike Settlement Procedures.)

Sec. 1–16. Limitations on the Board's discretion in unfair labor practice cases. The statute strips the Board of any discretion in certain aspects of unfair labor practice case handling. For example, the Board must:

1. Refuse to issue a complaint upon a charge filed more than six months after the unfair labor practice has occurred;[68]
2. Apply the same rules of decision to company-assisted or company-dominated unions whether or not such unions are independent or affiliates of national labor organizations;[69]
3. Seek injunctions in Section 8(b)(4)(A), (B) or (C); 8(e) and 8(b)(7) cases as soon as the investigating officer finds merit in such charges; (For provisions of Sections 8(b)(4)(A), (B) and (C) see Chart No. 3, pages 12–13.)[70]
4. Give top priority to the handling of Section 8(b)(4)(A), (B) or (C); 8(e) or 8(b)(7) cases;[71]
5. Give priority to Section 8(a)(3) or 8(b)(2) cases over cases other than those given top priority under Sections 8(b)(4)(A), (B) or (C), 8(e) and 8(b)(7).[72]
6. Refuse to cede jurisdiction to any state whose labor relations law provisions or interpretations are not consistent with the Federal statute.[73]

Sec. 1–17. The various types of elections. The statute specifically provides for four different types of elections:[74]

1. The collective bargaining election, to determine the majority status of a labor organization. A petition for such election may be filed by a labor organization, a group of employees, an individual or by an employer.
2. The decertification election, to determine whether a certified or currently recognized labor organization still represents a majority of the employees. A petition for such election may be filed by a labor organization, a group of employees, or by an individual.

---

[67]Morris, THE DEVELOPING LABOR LAW (Washington, D.C.: BNA Books, 1971), 271–347 and cases cited therein.
[68]Sec. 10(b).
[69]Sec. 10(c).
[70]Sec. 10(l).
[71]*Ibid.*
[72]Sec. 10(m).
[73]Sec. 10(a).
[74]Sec. 9.

3. The deauthorization election, to determine whether the employees wish to remove the labor organization's authority to have a union-shop agreement. A petition for such election may be filed by a group of employees representing at least 30 percent of those covered by the agreement.
4. The national emergency election, to determine whether employees wish to accept the final offer of settlement made by their employer.[75] This election must be conducted between the sixtieth and seventy-fifth days after a federal district court has issued an injunction against a strike or lockout which imperils or threatens to imperil the national safety.

Sec. 1–18. The determination of the unit. The statute provides that "the Board shall decide in each case whether, in order to assure to employees the fullest freedom in exercising the rights guaranteed by this Act, the unit appropriate for the purposes of collective bargaining shall be the employer unit, craft unit, plant unit, or sub-division thereof."[76] Beyond this provision, the statute carries specific proscriptions concerning craft units, guards and professional employees.   (See Sec. 8–8, page 135.)

Sec. 1–19. The determination of unit—Craft units. The Board cannot decide that any craft unit is inappropriate for bargaining purposes on the ground that a different unit has been established by a prior Board determination, unless a majority of the employees in the proposed craft unit vote against separate representation.[77]

Sec. 1–20. The determination of unit—Guards. Guards may not be included in the same unit with other employees.[78] Furthermore, a union cannot be certified as exclusive bargaining representative for guards, if:

1. It admits to membership employees other than guards; or
2. It is affiliated "directly or indirectly" with a labor organization which admits to membership employees other than guards.[79]

The statute defines a guard as "any individual employed as a guard to enforce against employees and other persons rules to protect property of the employer or to protect the safety of persons on the employers premises."[80] (See Sec. 8–8, page 135.)

[75]Sec. 209(b).
[76]Sec. 9(b).
[77]Sec. 9(b)(2).
[78]Sec. 9(b)(3).
[79]*Ibid.*
[80]*Ibid.*

Sec. 1–21. The determination of unit—Professional employees. Professional employees may not be included in the same unit with other employees, unless a majority of the professionals first vote separately in favor of such inclusion.[81] The statute defines a professional employee as an employee engaged in work:[82]

1. Chiefly intellectual and varied in character, as opposed to routine mental or physical work;
2. Involving consistent exercise of discretion and judgment;
3. Requiring advanced scientific knowledge usually acquired by a prolonged course of specialized intellectual instruction in an institution of higher learning or hospital; and
4. Whose output cannot be standardized by time measurement.

Sec. 1–22. Unit clarification. The Board's Rules and Regulations also provide a means whereby either party to a bargaining unit, regardless of whether or not it has been formally established by NLRB representation procedures, may obtain a clarification of the unit by filing a petition for clarification,[83] in the absence of a question concerning representation.[84] A previous Board determination of the bargaining unit is conclusive only if it resolves the exact question upon which clarification is sought.[85] In practice, the Board applies to clarification petitions the same rules which require the dismissal of representation petitions filed during the certification year.[86] (See Sec. 6–8, page 90.)

Sec. 1–23. Limitations on the Board's discretion in election cases. The statute removes any and all discretion from the Board in certain areas involving election cases. For example the Board must:

1. Refrain from deciding that a craft unit is inappropriate for the reason that such decision was made earlier by the Board;
2. Refuse to find a unit of guards appropriate when other employees are included in the same unit;
3. Refuse to certify a union as bargaining agent for guards unless it, as well as its parent body, restricts its membership to guards;

---

[81]Sec. 9(b)(1). Leedom v. Kyne, 358 U.S. 184, 43 LRRM 2222 (1958).
[82]Sec. 2(12).
[83]Rule 102.60(b); *see also* Locomotive Firemen and Enginemen, 145 NLRB 1521, 55 LRRM 1177 (1964); Libbey-Owen Ford Co., 169 NLRB 126, 67 LRRM 1096 (1968); Libbey-Owen Ford Co., 189 NLRB No. 138, 76 LRRM 1805, 189 NLRB No. 139, 76 LRRM 1806 (1971).
[84]Gas Service Co., 140 NLRB 445, 52 LRRM 1037 (1963).
[85]Boston Gas Co., 136 NLRB 219, 49 LRRM 1742 (1962); West Virginia Pulp and Paper Co., 140 NLRB 1160, 52 LRRM 1196 (1963).
[86]Magma Copper Co., 115 NLRB No. 1, 37 LRRM 1255 (1956); Firestone Tire and Rubber Co., 185 NLRB No. 11, 74 LRRM 1761 (1970).

4. Refuse to place professional employees in a unit of other employees, unless the professionals are first given the opportunity to, and do, vote in favor of such inclusion;

5. Refrain from finding a unit appropriate for collective bargaining where the "controlling" factor is the extent to which the employees have been organized;

6. Refuse to conduct a collective bargaining or decertification election where either was conducted within the preceding twelve-month period;

7. Refuse to conduct a deauthorization election where one was conducted within the preceding twelve-month period;

8. Conduct a runoff election in which the ballot shall provide for a selection between the two choices receiving the largest and second largest number of votes in the original and inconclusive election.

Sec. 1–24. Types of cases. The National Labor Relations Board identifies 13 different types of cases based on the provisions of the Act involved. (See Chart 4, Types of Cases, page 22. Following is a brief description of each type and, in parentheses after each, the designations assigned by the Board:

1. An unfair labor practice charge filed by any person, usually an individual or a labor organization, against an employer alleging a violation of §§8(a)(1), (2), (3), (4) or (5) of the Act (CA case);

2. An unfair labor practice charge filed by any person, usually an employer or an individual, against a labor organization alleging a violation of §§8(b)(1), (2), (3), (5) or (6) of the Act (CB case);

3. An unfair labor practice charge alleging a violation of §§8(b) (4)(i)(ii), (A), (B) or (C) filed by any person, usually an employer, against a labor organization (CC case);

4. An unfair labor practice charge involving a jurisdictional dispute within the meaning of §8(b)(4)(D) filed by any person, usually an employer or a labor organization, (CD case);

5. An unfair labor practice charge involving §8(b)(7) filed by any person, usually an employer, against a labor organization (CP case);

6. An unfair labor practice charge involving §8(e) filed by any person, usually an employer, against an employer or labor organization or both (CE case);

7. A petition for a collective bargaining election filed by an individual, a group or a labor organization (RC case);

8. A petition for a collective bargaining election filed by an employer (RM case);

TYPES OF CASES   1. Charges o

CHARGE AGAINST EMPLOYER		CHARGE AGAINST
Section of the Act **CA**	Section of the Act **CB**	Section of the Act **CP**
8(a)(1) Interfere with, restrain, or coerce employees in exercise of their rights under Section 7 (to join or assist a labor organization or to refrain).	8(b)(1)(A) Restrain or coerce employees in exercise of their rights under Section 7 (to join or assist a labor organization or to refrain).	8(b)(7) To picket, cause, or threaten the picketing of any employer where an object is to force or require an employer to recognize or bargain with a labor organization as the representative of his employees, or to force or require the employees of an employer to select such labor organization as their collective bargaining representative, unless such labor organization is currently certified as the representative of such employees:
8(a)(2) Dominate or interfere with the formation or administration of a labor organization or contribute financial or other support to it.	8(b)(1)(B) Restrain or coerce an employer in the selection of his representatives for collective bargaining or adjustment of grievances.	
	8(b)(2) Cause or attempt to cause an employer to discriminate against an employee.	
8(a)(3) Encourage or discourage membership in a labor organization (discrimination in regard to hire or tenure).	8(b)(3) Refuse to bargain collectively with employer.	(A) where the employer has lawfully recognized any other labor organization and a question concerning representation may not appropriately be raised under Section 9(c),
8(a)(4) Discourage or otherwise discriminate against an employee because he has given testimony under the Act.	8(b)(5) Require of employees the payment of excessive or discriminatory fees for membership.	(B) where within the preceding 12 months a valid election under 9(c) has been conducted, or
8(a)(5) Refuse to bargain collectively with representatives of his employees.	8(b)(6) Cause or attempt to cause an employer to pay or agree to pay money or other thing of value for services which are not performed or not to be performed.	(C) where picketing has been conducted without a petition under 9(c) being filed within a reasonable period of time not to exceed 30 days from the commencement of such picketing.

Representati

9(c)(1)(A)(i) **RC**	9(c)(1)(B) **RM**	9(c)(1)(A)(ii) **RD**
Asserting the designation of filing party as bargaining agent.*	Alleging that one or more claims for recognition as exclusive bargaining agent have been received by employer.*	Asserting that the certified or recognized bargaining agent is no longer the representative.*

* This statement is not applicable if an 8(b)(7) charge is on file invol

CHART NO. 4. *Types of cases*

Unfair Labor Practices (C Cases)

LABOR ORGANIZATION		CHARGE AGAINST LABOR ORGANIZATION AND EMPLOYER
Section of the Act CC 8(b)(4) (i) To engage in, or induce or encourage any individual employed by any person engaged in commerce or in an industry affecting commerce to engage in, a strike or a refusal in the course of his employment to use, manufacture, process, transport, or otherwise handle or work on any goods or to perform any services; or (ii) To threaten, coerce or restrain any person engaged in commerce or in an industry affecting commerce, where in either case an object thereof is:	Section of the Act CD 8(b)(4)	Section of the Act CE 8(e) To enter into any contract or agreement (any labor organization and any employer) whereby such employer ceases or refrains or agrees to cease or refrain from handling or dealing in any product of any other employer, or to cease doing business with any other person.
(A) To force or require any employer or self-employed person to join any labor or employer organization or to enter into any agreement prohibited by Sec. 8(e).	(D) To force or require any employer to assign particular work to employees in a particular labor organization or in a particular trade, craft, or class rather than to employees in another trade, craft, or class, unless such employer is failing to conform to an appropriate Board order or certification.	
(B) To force or require any person to cease using, selling, handling, transporting, or otherwise dealing in the products of any other producer, processor, or manufacturer, or cease to doing business with any other person, or force or require any other employer to recognize or bargain with a labor organization as the representative of his employees unless such labor organization has been so certified.		
(C) To force or require any employer to recognize or bargain with a particular labor organization as the representative of his employees if another labor organization has been certified as the representative.		

Petitions (R cases)

9(e)(1) UD	9(b) UC	9(b) AC
Employees wish to rescind a union security clause.	Clarification of an existing bargaining unit.	Amendment of certification.

the same employer; however, the "R" designation applies.

9. A petition for an election filed by an individual, a group, or a labor organization challenging the current majority status of a labor organization (RD case);

10. A petition filed by an individual, a group, or a labor organization seeking an election to remove the authority of a labor organization to have a union-shop agreement (UD case);

11. A petition filed by a certified or currently recognized representative of a bargaining unit, or by an employer of employees in such a unit, to clarify the bargaining unit (UC case);

12. A petition filed by a certified representative of a bargaining unit, or by an employer of employees in such a unit, for amendment of the certification to reflect changed circumstances (AC cases);

13. A national emergency election conducted by the Board to determine whether or not employees wish to accept their employer's final offer of settlement (X case).

The foregoing explanation of the provisions of the law covers only its most important points. There are now literally thousands of Board decisions interpreting both the unfair labor practice and representation sections of the statute. These are found in more detail in the Labor Relations Expediter and, in full, in the Labor Relations Reference Manual.

CHAPTER 2

The Machinery of the National Labor Relations Board

Sec. 2–1. In general. The first National Labor Relations Board took office on August 27, 1935, shortly after the Wagner Act was passed. That law authorized establishment of the Board as the agency responsible for administration and enforcement of the Act. Congress gave little guidance as to the structure of the agency, however, and the Board, on its own initiative, established an administrative mechanism which made it prosecutor, judge, and jury.

The system aroused such criticism that, when Congress added major amendments to the original law as a part of the Labor Management Relations Act of 1947, a unique system for the administration of the statute was included. In effect, Congress retained the concept of a single enforcement agency but divided authority over it into two independent units—the Board and the Office of the General Counsel.

Both the statute and the legislative history show that the new office—that of the General Counsel—was created to perform the all-important preliminary functions of investigation and prosecution of unfair labor practice cases. The Board, on the other hand, was to restrict itself to quasi-judicial functions, operating essentially as a court and making decisions on the basis of a formal record. This organizational structure was left unchanged when Congress passed the Labor-Management Reporting and Disclosure Act of 1959 (Landrum-Griffin Act) except provision was made for the temporary filling of a vacancy in the Office of the General Counsel.

It is imperative that parties to NLRB proceedings understand the division of authority between the Board and the General Counsel. Not only does each have final authority in certain areas but the inter-relationship between the two entities frequently has some significance on the handling and outcome of a case.

While the Congressional intent of separation is clear, the failure of the language used to delineate fully the agency's work has led to sharp conflicts between the Board and the General Counsel as to which has authority in specific areas. To resolve these differences the Board adopted a statement in which it delegated various powers and functions to the General Counsel. There have been fluctuations in the scope of this delegation, but it is now reasonably well defined and complete. (The full text of the current delegation appears in Appendix C.)

Sec. 2–2. Functions and structure of the Agency. The Board more nearly resembles a court than a regulatory agency. Its principal function is judicial in character and it is wholly divorced from the investigation and prosecution of unfair labor practice charges. It has no authority over issuance of formal complaints and therefore rules only upon those unfair labor practice cases which the General Counsel decides to prosecute. The General Counsel has absolute authority over whether or not a complaint shall issue in a given proceeding and the scope of the complaint. There is no appeal from his refusal to prosecute and the Board has neither authority to require action on his part nor jurisdiction to hear an action brought by a charging party. The Board does have veto power over requests for Section 10(j) discretionary injunctions prior to the institution of court proceedings but, again, rules only on those requests which have first been approved by the General Counsel.

The Board has complete authority over representation matters. However, pursuant to the Labor-Management Reporting and Disclosure Act of 1959, the Board as of May 15, 1961, delegated its powers over these matters to the regional directors, retaining a right to review any of their decisions. (See Appendix D for full text of the Board's Delegation of Authority to regional directors in representation matters.) In practice the General Counsel exerts some influence on such cases through the indirect impact of his supervisory authority over the regional offices.

Sec. 2–3. Functions of the Board. More specifically the Board has five basic functions:

1. To prevent and remedy unfair labor practices committed by employers or labor organizations;[1]
2. To determine representatives for purposes of collective bargaining (delegated to the regional directors);[2]
3. To determine the authority of representatives to have union shop provisions in their collective bargaining agreements (delegated to the regional directors);[3]

[1]Sec. 10(a).
[2]Sec. 9(b) and (c).
[3]Sec. 9(e).

4. To determine jurisdictional disputes which have led to the filing of unfair labor practice charges;[4] and
5. To poll employees on their employer's last offer in "national emergency" situations.[5]

Sec. 2–4. Functions of the General Counsel. The General Counsel's responsibilities flow from both the provisions of the statute and the powers delegated to him by the Board.

Under the statute, he has two main functions:

1. To determine whether, when and upon what basis unfair labor practice charges shall be prosecuted.[6] He has the exclusive authority to prosecute a complaint;[7] his determination not to issue a complaint is not subject to Board or court review.[8]
2. To supervise all employees in the regional offices and all attorneys (except those serving as administrative law judges or legal assistants to Board members).[9] But the appointment, transfer, demotion or discharge of any regional director or of any officer-in-charge of a subregional office must have prior approval of the Board.

Under the terms of the agreement with the Board, the General Counsel is delegated authority to perform the following functions:

1. To apply to the courts for injunctions; however, the Board must give approval to all Section 10(j) discretionary injunctive proceedings;
2. To process all representation cases, subject to the Board's Rules and Regulations. (The full text of the Rules and Regulations appears in Appendix B.) Because the Board has formally delegated its representation powers under Section 9 to the regional directors, this means that the handling of the election cases is carried on by regional officials, supervised by the General Counsel; however, appeals from their rulings may be taken only to the Board, and not to the General Counsel;[10]
3. To seek compliance with the orders issued by the Board;
4. To apply to the appropriate courts for the enforcement of the Board's orders;

[4]Sec. 10(k).
[5]Sec. 209(b).
[6]Sec. 3(d).
[7]Bonwit Teller, Inc. v. NLRB, 197 F.2d 640, 30 LRRM 2305 (C.A. 2, 1952).
[8]Lincourt v. NLRB, 170 F.2d 306, 23 LRRM 2015 (C.A. 1, 1948); Newspaper Guild, Local 187 (Erie) (Times Publishing Co.) v. NLRB, 84 LRRM 2896 (C.A. 3, 1973), *denying enforcement to and reman'g* 80 LRRM 1364.
[9]Sec. 3(d).
[10]R. and R. Sec. 102.71.

5. To conduct employer's last offer elections in "national emergency" situations.

The Congressional scheme of separation of functions sometimes leads to a conclusion that there are, in reality, two wholly independent agencies. An organization chart gives this impression (see Chart No. 5, page 30) but the Board's participation in personnel actions involving regional directors and officers-in-charge, its delegation of functions to the General Counsel which may be, and has been, withdrawn from time to time, and its participation in budget and other administrative matters show that the NLRB is truly a single agency. Its unique feature is its two heads.

Sec. 2–5. Structure of the Board. The statute established a Board of five public members.[11] They are appointed for five-year terms by the President with Senate approval. The Board is authorized to delegate its powers to any three members.[12] Each member of the Board has a staff of about 25 legal assistants who serve that particular member. They assist in the review of transcripts of hearings and prepare drafts of opinions.[13] Because of the Board's volume of cases their role in the decisional process is extremely important.

The Board maintains its headquarters and staff in Washington. Attached to the Board are the offices of Executive Secretary, the Solicitor, the Director of Information and the Division of Judges.

Sec. 2–6. Executive Secretary. The Executive Secretary is the chief administrative officer of the Board. He plans and directs the functioning of the Board's decision-making process, ruling upon procedural questions, determining priorities in case handling, assigning cases to staffs of individual Board Members for analysis and presentation to panels of Board Members or the full Board, and conferring on behalf of the Board Members with unions, employers, and employees appearing as parties to cases. He also is responsible for issuing the decisions of the Board.

Sec. 2–7. Solicitor. The Solicitor is the Board's adviser on questions of law and policy.

Sec. 2–8. Director of Information. The Director of Information makes available to the public information concerning the activities of the Board and the status of cases. He advises the Board on matters of policy and

[11] Sec. 3(a).
[12] Sec. 3(b).
[13] Sec. 4(a).

public relations, and serves as its representative with the press. He also performs these functions on behalf of the Office of the General Counsel.

Sec. 2–9. Division of Judges. The Division of Judges consists of administrative law judges who conduct the hearings on unfair labor practice complaints. Formerly called trial examiners, these judges are independent of both the Board and the General Counsel. The statute forbids any review of the judges' findings or recommendations before issuance of their formal reports.[14] Furthermore, the administrative law judges are subject to the rules of the Civil Service Commission which govern appointment and tenure. For example, they are removable only after a hearing before that Commission.

Administrative law judges resemble federal district court judges. They are appointed, in effect, for life and act in a purely judicial capacity. They render the initial decision, yet have nothing to do with its disposition or consideration by the appellate body, the Board.[15] They are supervised by the Chief Administrative Law Judge, who has the final authority to designate which judge will conduct a hearing, to assign dates for such hearings, and to rule upon requests for extensions of time within which to file briefs, proposed findings, and conclusions.[16]

Sec. 2–10. Structure of the Office of the General Counsel. The statute provides a four-year term for the General Counsel, who is appointed by the President with Senate approval. The General Counsel maintains his headquarters and staff, except for the personnel in regional offices, in Washington. The Deputy General Counsel is accountable for the overall coordination of the General Counsel's organization, which consists of four main divisions: Division of Operations-Management, Division of Advice, Division of Enforcement Litigation, and Division of Administration. Each of the first three are supervised by an Associate General Counsel, while the fourth is headed by a Director of Administration.[17]

Sec. 2–11. Office of the General Counsel—Division of Operations–Management. The Associate General Counsel for the Division of Operations-Management supervises all field operations and is charged with the management of cases in all of the Washington divisions of the General Counsel. He is also responsible for developing systems to achieve effective integration of Washington and field case-processing activities.

[14]*Ibid.*
[15]*Ibid.*
[16]R. and R. Sec. 202.
[17]R. and R. Sec. 202.

NATIONAL LABOR RELATION:

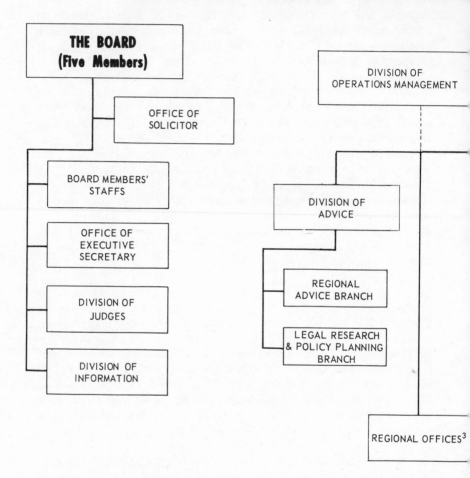

1 Exercise by General Counsel of authority and responsibility in certain matters, including that over personnel other than those responsible directly to the Board, and for all administrative functions of the agency, by delegation from the Board.

2 Division of Administration is also responsible directly to the Board for administrative support services required in the performance of Board functions.

3 Includes exercise by Regional Director of Board authority under Section 9 of the Act, in representation cases, by delegation from the Board.

CHART No. 5. *National Labor Relations Board organization chart*

BOARD ORGANIZATION CHART

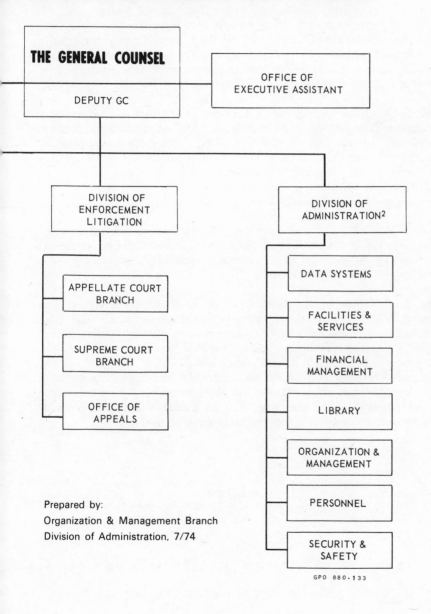

THE GENERAL COUNSEL

DEPUTY GC

OFFICE OF
EXECUTIVE ASSISTANT

DIVISION OF
ENFORCEMENT
LITIGATION

DIVISION OF
ADMINISTRATION[2]

APPELLATE COURT
BRANCH

SUPREME COURT
BRANCH

OFFICE OF
APPEALS

DATA SYSTEMS

FACILITIES &
SERVICES

FINANCIAL
MANAGEMENT

LIBRARY

ORGANIZATION &
MANAGEMENT

PERSONNEL

SECURITY &
SAFETY

Prepared by:
Organization & Management Branch
Division of Administration, 7/74

GPO 880-133

Sec. 2–12. Office of the General Counsel—Division of Advice. The Associate General Counsel for the Division of Advice oversees the functions of legal advice to regional offices, the injunction work of the district court branch, and the legal research and special project office. All questions involving mandatory or discretionary injunction proceedings are coordinated with the Special Counsel to the General Counsel for Priority Injunction Litigation, who serves as an expert advisor and counsel in the area of injunction cases which have statutory priority and are subject to mandatory proceedings in the U. S. district courts.

Sec. 2–13. Office of the General Counsel—Division of Enforcement Litigation. The Associate General Counsel for Enforcement Litigation is responsible for conduct of NLRB litigation seeking the enforcement or defense of Board orders in the U.S. courts of appeals and the United States Supreme Court, conduct of contempt litigation, and conduct of miscellaneous litigation in the federal and state courts to protect the Board's processes and functions.

Sec. 2–14. Office of the General Counsel—Division of Administration. The Director of Administration directs the administrative management, fiscal, and personnel work of the General Counsel. He also performs these functions on behalf of the Board.

Sec. 2–15. Office of the General Counsel—Regional Directors. The United States is divided into 31 regions for the purpose of administering the statute. Each region has an office which handles all cases arising in that area. (The locations of these offices and the areas they cover are set forth in Appendix E.) The staff in each office consists of a regional director, regional attorney, field examiners, and field attorneys. The regional director is the chief officer of the office. There are, at the present time, three sub-regional offices and nine resident offices. Each is under the direction of a supervisor who reports to the regional director of his region.

CHAPTER 3

Jurisdiction of the Board

Sec. 3–1. In general. The statute grants to the Board authority over all labor disputes, as defined in the Act, occurring "in commerce" or "affecting commerce." The Courts have construed this to mean that the Board's jurisdiction extends to the regulation of all such conduct as might constitutionally be regulated under the commerce clause, limited only by the rule of *de minimis.*[1]

Despite its extensive statutory grant of jurisdiction, the Board has never exercised its full authority. Instead it has considered only those cases which, in its opinion, have a substantial effect on commerce.[2] In approving this practice, the U.S. Supreme Court has noted that Congress left it to the Board to ascertain whether proscribed practices would in particular situations adversely affect commerce[3] and it has recognized that, even when the effect on interstate commerce is adequate to support jurisdiction, the Board sometimes properly declines to do so, when the policies of the Act would not be effectuated by its assertion of jurisdiction.[4]

Sec. 3–2. Jurisdictional standards. The Board's broad jurisdiction has brought within reach of its processes uncounted millions of employers, employees, and unions. In order to process its steadily increasing caseload with some degree of expedition, the Board has, over the years, evolved the concept of jurisdictional standards, expressed in terms of minimum annual dollar volume, to aid in determining whether it will effectuate the policies of the Act to assert jurisdiction over the labor dispute involved in a particular proceeding. This practice was given statutory recognition by the Labor-Management Reporting and Disclosure Act of 1959. There Congress stated that the Board might continue to decline jurisdiction over any labor dispute within its statutory jurisdiction, provided that it does not decline to assert jurisdiction over any labor dispute over which it would

[1]NLRB v. Fainblatt, 306 U.S. 601, 4 LRRM 535(1939).
[2]NLRB v. Denver Bldg. Trades Council, 341 U.S. 675, 28 LRRM 2108(1951).
[3]Polish National Alliance v. NLRB, 322 U.S. 643, 14 LRRM 700(1944).
[4]Guss v. Utah Labor Relations Board, 352 U.S. 817, 39 LRRM 2567(1957).

have asserted jurisdiction under the standards prevailing on August 1, 1959.[5]

Thus, the Board may expand but not contract its jurisdiction. In the same statute, Congress resolved the increasingly troublesome problem of conflicting federal and state jurisdiction by providing that the states may assert jurisdiction over labor disputes which the Board declines.[6]

Sec. 3–3. Jurisdiction–General standards. The Board's current jurisdictional standards are:

1. GENERAL NONRETAIL CONCERNS—Sales of goods to consumers in other states, directly or indirectly (called outflow), or purchases of goods from suppliers in other states, directly or indirectly (called inflow), of at least $50,000 per year.[7]

   DIRECT OUTFLOW is defined as goods shipped or services furnished by the employer outside his home state.

   INDIRECT OUTFLOW is defined as the sale of goods or services to users meeting any of the Board's jurisdictional standards, excepting the indirect outflow or indirect inflow standard.

   DIRECT INFLOW is defined as goods or services furnished the employer directly from outside the state.

   INDIRECT INFLOW is defined as goods or services which originated outside the state, but which the employer purchased from a seller or supplier within the state.

   In applying this standard, the Board will add direct and indirect outflow, or indirect and direct inflow; however, it will not add outflow and inflow.

2. RETAIL CONCERNS—An annual volume of business of at least $500,000, including sales and excise taxes.[8]

3. RETAIL AND MANUFACTURING COMBINED—Either the retail or the nonretail standard, when a single, integrated enterprise manufactures a product as well as sells it directly to the public.[9]

4. RETAIL AND WHOLESALE COMBINED—The nonretail standard, when a company is involved in both retail and wholesale operations.[10]

[5]Section 14(c)(1).
[6]Section 14(c)(2).
[7]Siemons Mailing Service, 122 NLRB No. 81, 43 LRRM 1056 (1958); American Home Systems, 200 NLRB No. 158, 82 LRRM 1183 (1972).
[8]Carolina Supplies and Cement Co., 122 NLRB No. 88, 43 LRRM 1062 (1958); Acme Paper Box Co., 201 NLRB No. 32, 82 LRRM 1333 (1973).
[9]Man Products Inc., 128 NLRB 546, 46 LRRM 1352 (1960); American Home Systems, 200 NLRB No. 158, 82 LRRM 1183 (1972).
[10]Pease Oil Co., 122 NLRB 344, 42 LRRM 1128 (1958); Dominick's Finer Foods Inc., 188 NLRB No. 138, 81 LRRM 2488 (C.A. 7, 1972), *enf.* 76 LRRM 1607.

5. INSTRUMENTALITIES, LINKS, AND CHANNELS OF INTERSTATE COMMERCE— An annual income of at least $50,000 from furnishing interstate transportation services or performing services valued at $50,000 or more for enterprises that meet any of the standards except indirect outflow or indirect inflow.[11]

6. NATIONAL DEFENSE—The enterprise has a substantial impact on national defense.[12]

7. TERRITORIES AND THE DISTRICT OF COLUMBIA—The normal standards as applied in the states are applicable to the Territories. Plenary jurisdiction is exercised in the District of Columbia.[13]

8. MULTIEMPLOYER BARGAINING ASSOCIATIONS—Regarded as a single employer in that the annual business of all members is totaled to determine whether any of the standards apply.[14]

9. MULTISTATE ESTABLISHMENTS—The annual business of all establishments is totaled to determine whether any of the standards apply.[15]

10. NONPROFIT ORGANIZATIONS—The same standards as if the organization is operated for profit.[16]

11. UNION EMPLOYERS—The appropriate nonretail standard.[17]

Sec. 3–4. Jurisdiction—Specific industries.   The Board's current jurisdictional standards for specific industries are:

1. APARTMENT PROJECTS—At least $50,000 in gross annual revenue.[18]

2. AUTOMOBILE DEALERS—Treated as retail operations, even if the dealer has a franchise from a national manufacturer.[19]

---

[11]HPO Service Inc., 122 NLRB 394, 43 LRRM 1127 (1958); Panorama Air Tour Inc., 204 NLRB No. 32, 83 LRRM 1276 (1973).
[12]Ready Mix Concrete and Materials Inc., 122 NLRB 318, 43 LRRM 1115 (1958); Trico Disposal Service, Inc., 191 NLRB No. 17, 77 LRRM 1330 (1971).
[13]Carribe Lumber and Trading Co., 148 NLRB 277, 56 LRRM 1506 (1946); Westchester Corp., 124 NLRB 194, 44 LRRM 1327 (1959); Contract Services Inc., 202 NLRB No. 42, 82 LRRM 1531 (1973); Van Camp Sea Food Co., 212 NLRB No. 76, 86 LRRM 1573 (1974).
[14]Siemons Mailing Service, 122 NLRB 81, 43 LRRM 1056 (1958); South Florida Taxi Assn., et al., 182 NLRB 1049, 74 LRRM 1238 (1970).
[15]Rodgers Lumber Co., 117 NLRB 1732, 40 LRRM 1063 (1957); Quality Courts Motels, Inc., 194 NLRB No. 169, 79 LRRM 1303 (1972).
[16]Drexel Home, 182 NLRB No. 151, 74 LRRM 1234 (1970); Visiting Nurses Assn., 187 NLRB No. 88, 76 LRRM 1096 (1971); NLRB v. Eugene Good Samaritan Center, 191 NLRB No. 14, 82 LRRM 3213 (C.A. 9, 1973), enf. 77 LRRM 1412.
[17]Chain Service Restaurant, 132 NLRB 960, 48 LRRM 1457 (1961); Civil Service Employees Assn., 181 NLRB No. 115, 73 LRRM 1475 (1970).
[18]Parkview Gardens, 166 NLRB No. 80, 65 LRRM 1492 (1967); Point East Condominiums Owners Assn., 193 NLRB No. 6, 78 LRRM 1107 (1971).
[19]Wilson Oldsmobile, 110 NLRB 534, 35 LRRM 1062 (1954).

3. BUILDING AND CONSTRUCTION—The appropriate jurisdictional standard in cases involving a single building trades employer or the multiemployer standard if the employer is part of a multiemployer bargaining association.[20]

4. COLLEGES, UNIVERSITIES, AND SECONDARY SCHOOLS—At least $1 million total annual income from all sources except those designated by the grantor as not available for operating costs. This applies to both profit and nonprofit institutions.[21]

5. COMMUNICATIONS—At least $100,000 annual gross volume of business for television, radio, telephone, or telegraph businesses.[22]

6. COUNTRY CLUBS—Treated as retail concerns.[23]

7. ENTERTAINMENT AND AMUSEMENT—Treated as retail concerns. The Board will not assert jurisdiction over horse and dog racing tracks.[24]

8. FEDERAL CREDIT UNIONS—At least $500,000 annual gross income from loans, deposits, and investment, or such related areas.[25]

9. GAMBLING CASINOS—At least $500,000 annual income.[26]

10. GUARD SERVICES—That companies furnishing plant guards to employers involved in interstate commerce are themselves subject to jurisdiction if the value of the services meets one of the Board's basic jurisdictional standards.[27]

11. HOSPITALS AND HEALTH-CARE INSTITUTIONS—Federal, state, and municipal hospitals are exempt, as are administrative employers in the health field. Under the 1974 amendments, the Board will assert jurisdiction over nursing homes, visiting nurse associations, and related facilities with gross revenues over $100,000 per year and over proprietary and nonprofit hospitals with gross revenues over $250,000 per year.[28]

[20]NLRB v. Denver Bldg. Trades Council, 341 U.S. 675, 28 LRRM 2108 (1951); Charles E. Forrester, 189 NLRB No. 80, 76 LRRM 1622 (1971).

[21]Cornell University 183 NLRB No. 41, 74 LRRM 1269 (1970); Windsor School Inc., 199 NLRB No. 54, 81 LRRM 1246 (1972).

[22]Raritan Valley Broadcasting System, 122 NLRB 90, 43 LRRM 1123 (1958); Athens TV Cable Inc., 160 NLRB No. 130, 63 LRRM 1111 (1966); Evans Broadcasting Corp., 179 NLRB No. 130, 72 LRRM 1508 (1969).

[23]Walnut Hills Country Club, 145 NLRB No. 9, 54 LRRM 1335 (1963); Yorba Linda Country Club, 199 NLRB No. 81, 81 LRRM 1302 (1972).

[24]The League of N.Y. Theatres Inc., 129 NLRB 1429, 47 LRRM 1210 (1961); Universal Security Consultants, 203 NLRB No. 111, 83 LRRM 1262 (1973); jurisdictional rule, 82 LRRM 1737.

[25]Lansing Federal Credit Union, 150 NLRB 1122, 58 LRRM 1195 (1965); Federal Credit Union, East Division, 193 NLRB No. 103, 78 LRRM 1305 (1971).

[26]El Dorado, Inc., 151 NLRB 579, 58 LRRM 1455 (1965)

[27]Burns Detective Agency, 110 NLRB 995, 35 LRRM 1179 (1954).

[28]Sec. 2(14) as amended; Butte Medical Properties, 168 NLRB No. 52, 66 LRRM 1259 (1967); University Nursing Homes Inc., 168 NLRB No. 53, 66 LRRM 1263 (1967); Ochsner Clinic v. NLRB 2565, 82 LRRM 2565 (C.A. 5, 1973), enf. 196 NLRB No. 4, 79 LRRM 1684; East Oakland Community Health Alliance, Inc., 218 NLRB No. 193, 89 LRRM 1372 (1975).

12. HOTELS AND MOTELS—At least $500,000 total annual volume of business, whether an establishment is residential or nonresidential.[29]

13. OFFICE BUILDINGS, SHOPPING CENTERS, AND PARKING LOTS—At least $100,000 total annual income, of which $25,000 or more is paid by other organizations which meet any of the standards, except the nonretail standard.[30]

14. POSTAL SERVICE—Full jurisdiction as provided in the Postal Reorganization Act of 1970.[31]

15. PRINTING, PUBLISHING, AND NEWSPAPERS—At least $200,000 total annual volume of business, and the employer must hold membership in or subscribe to interstate news services, publish nationally syndicated features, or advertise nationally sold products.[32]

16. PUBLIC UTILITIES—At least $250,000 total annual volume of business or $50,000 outflow or inflow, direct or indirect. This standard applies to retail gas, power, and water companies, as well as electric cooperatives. Wholesale utilities are subject to the general nonretail standards.[33]

17. RESTAURANTS—Treated as retail operations.[34]

18. SERVICE ESTABLISHMENTS—Treated as retail operations.[35]

19. SPORTS, PROFESSIONAL—Regarded as industries affecting interstate commerce and subject to jurisdiction.[36]

20. SYMPHONY ORCHESTRAS—At least $1 million total annual income, compiled from all sources except those designated by the donor as not available for operating costs.[37]

21. TAXICAB COMPANIES—At least $500,000 total annual volume of business.[38]

---

[29]Penn-Keystone Realty Corp., 191 NLRB No. 105, 77 LRRM 1600 (1971); Holiday Inn Southwest, 202 NLRB No. 14, 82 LRRM 1664 (1973).
[30]Mistletoe Operating Co., 122 NLRB 1534, 43 LRRM 1333 (1958); Carol Management Corp., 133 NLRB 1126, 48 LRRM 1782 (1961); Air Lines Parking Inc., 196 NLRB No. 154, 80 LRRM 1179 (1972).
[31]United States Postal Service, 208 NLRB No. 144, 85 LRRM 1212 (1974).
[32]Belleville Employing Printers, 122 NLRB 350, 43 LRRM 1125 (1958); George S. Roberts and Sons, Inc., 78 LRRM 2874 (C.A. 2, 1971), enf. in part 188 NLRB No. 51, 76 LRRM 1337.
[33]Sioux Valley Empire Electrical Assn., 122 NLRB 92, 43 LRRM 1057 (1958); Tri-County Electrical Membership Corp., 145 NLRB 810, 55 LRRM 1057 (1958), enf. 343 F.2d 60, 58 LRRM 2704 (C.A. 4, 1965).
[34]Bickford's Inc., 110 NLRB 190, 35 LRRM 1341 (1954); Furusato Hawaii, Ltd., 192 NLRB No. 18, 77 LRRM 1668 (1972).
[35]Claffery Beauty Shoppes, 110 NLRB 620, 35 LRRM 1709 (1954); OK Barber Shop, 187 NLRB No. 115, 76 LRRM 1178 (1971).
[36]American League, 180 NLRB No. 30, 72 LRRM 1545 (1969).
[37]Jurisdiction rule, 82 LRRM 1519; NLRB Rules and Regulations § 1032, LRX 4095 (1973).
[38]Red and White Airway Cab Co., 123 NLRB 83, 43 LRRM 1392 (1959); Buffalo Cab Co. Inc., 189 NLRB No. 66, 80 LRRM 2093 (C.A. 5, 1972), enf. 76 LRRM 1848.

22. TRANSIT COMPANIES—At least $250,000 total annual volume of business.[39]

Sec. 3–5. Jurisdiction refused—By its definitions of "employer" and "employee," the statute prevents the Board from asserting jurisdiction over certain employers and certain employees.[40] (See Chapter 1.). However, the Board also refuses jurisdiction over the following areas as a matter of policy.

1. FOREIGN COMMERCE—The Board will refuse jurisdiction in cases where the employer enjoys a close relationship with a foreign government, even if the subsidiary employees normally would come under the NLRB jurisdiction.[41]
2. FOREIGN SHIPPING—The Supreme Court has held that although foreign vessels are temporarily in U. S. ports, the Taft-Hartley Act does not apply to labor disputes of foreign crews, overruling the Board's policy of asserting jurisdiction if the foreign flagship's U. S. contracts "outweighed" its foreign contracts.[42]
3. LOCAL EDUCATIONAL INSTITUTIONS—The Board will not assert jurisdiction if it is evident that an educational institution's activities were essentially local in nature, despite the argument that the institution meets the appropriate monetary standard.[43]
4. POLITICAL SUBDIVISIONS—The Board has held that public bodies created directly by the state and governed by state officials appointed by the state or by election by voters of a state-created district are exempt from its jurisdiction.[44]

Sec. 3–6. Jurisdictional standards—Rules of application. In applying the dollar-volume standards, the Board has developed certain rules of application. The most important of these are:

1. The Board has held that there is no need for a separate showing of legal jurisdiction if the employer does enough interstate business to

[39]Charleston Transit Company, 123 NLRB 1296, 44 LRRM 1123 (1959); Buffalo Cab Co. Inc., 189 NLRB No. 66, 80 LRRM 2093 (C.A. 5, 1972), *enf.* 76 LRRM 1848.
[40]Sections 2(2) and (3).
[41]RCA Oms. Inc., 202 NLRB No. 42, 82 LRRM 1757 (1973); Contract Services Inc., 202 NLRB No. 156, 82 LRRM 1757 (1973).
[42]Benz v. Compania Naviera Hidalgo, S.A., 325 U.S. 138, 39 LRRM 2636 (1957); McCulloch v. Sociedad Nacional de Marineros, 372 U.S. 10, 53 LRRM 2425 (1963); Navios Corp. Maritime Union, 62 LRRM 2128 (C.A. 3, 1966), *aff'g* 58 LRRM 2040.
[43]Center for Urban Education, 189 NLRB No. 125, 77 LRRM 1065 (1971); *cf.* Allen & O'Hara Developments, 210 NLRB No. 41, 86 LRRM 1126 (1974).
[44]City of Austell Natural Gas System, 186 NLRB No. 144, 75 LRRM 1327 (1970); Lewiston Orchards Irrigation District, 186 NLRB No. 121, 75 LRRM 1430 (1970); City Public Service Board, San Antonio, 197 NLRB No. 48, 80 LRRM 1332 (1972); Ohio Inns, Inc., 205 NLRB No. 102, 84 LRRM 1005 (1973).

satisfy the NLRB's indirect inflow or outflow tests. However, when the standards involved are exclusively in terms of gross dollar volume of business, proof of legal jurisdiction is necessary in that an employer may do the required volume of business within the confines of a single state.[45]

2. The Board will assert jurisdiction in any proceeding where the record establishes legal jurisdiction, irrespective of a showing that the applicable standard is met, if the employer, after being afforded proper opportunity, fails to cooperate in the production of necessary commerce information.[46]

3. Secondary boycotts—When asserting jurisdiction in secondary-boycott cases, the NLRB views the primary employer as the one with whom the union has a direct dispute and the secondary employer as the one whose employees the union is trying to "induce" to stop handling the primary's goods. If necessary for the application of jurisdiction, the NLRB will consider the operations of the primary and the secondary employer together. When considering the secondary employer's operations, the Board will consider the entire business of the secondary employer with the primary employer at the location affected by the boycott. If the secondary employer meets jurisdictional standards, the Board will assert authority, regardless of whether or not the primary employer satisfies the standards. Finally, if more than one secondary employer is involved, jurisdiction will be asserted as long as one or more of the secondary employers meets the standards.[47]

Sec. 3–7. Jurisdictional standards—Computing jurisdictional amount. In applying its jurisdictional standards the Board normally determines business volume on the basis of the employer's past experience for the most recent calendar or fiscal year preceding the Board's hearing, rather than on the basis of future operations.[48] But, if annual figures are not available, those for a period of less than one year may be projected to obtain annual volume.[49]

[45]Southern Dolomite, 129 NLRB 1342, 47 LRRM 1173 (1961); Wurster, Bernardi, and Emmons, Inc., 192 NLRB No. 121, 78 LRRM 1050 (1971).
[46]Tropicana Products, Inc., 122 NLRB 121, 43 LRRM 1077 (1958); Quality Courts Motel, Inc., 194 NLRB 169, 79 LRRM 1303 (1972).
[47]International Brotherhood of Teamsters, Local 554, 110 NLRB 1769, 35 LRRM 1281 (1954); Euclid Foods, Inc., 118 NLRB 130, 40 LRRM 1135 (1957); Electrical Workers, IBEW, Local 257 (Osage Neon Plastics), 176 NLRB No. 56, 71 LRRM 1246 (1969).
[48]Aroostock Federation of Farmers, Inc., 114 NLRB 538, 36 LRRM 1611 (1955).
[49]United Mine Workers of America, District 2, 96 NLRB 1389, 29 LRRM 1043 (1951); Drug and Hospital Union, Local 119 v. McLeod (666 Cosmetics, Inc.), 80 LRRM 2503 (D.C. N.Y., 1972), see also 79 LRRM 2610.

Sec. 3–8. Jurisdictional standards—Advisory opinions. Even with the published standards it is sometimes difficult to predict whether or not the Board will assert jurisdiction. In recognition of this fact, procedures have been established whereby parties to a dispute before a State court or agency, or the court or agency itself, may petition the Board for an advisory opinion on jurisdiction.[50] These opinions are advisory only.

Sec. 3–9. Jurisdictional standards—Declaratory opinions. Also, the General Counsel may petition the Board and obtain a declaratory order disposing of jurisdictional issues where both a charge and a petition relating to the same employer are pending in a regional office.[51] Unlike the advisory opinions, these orders are final. The procedural requirements for both advisory opinions and declaratory orders are set forth in the Board's Rules and Regulations.

[50]R. and R., Sec. 102.98–102.104.
[51]R. and R., Sec. 102.105–102.110.

CHAPTER 4

Selecting a Bargaining Agent

Sec. 4–1. Representation proceedings. Representation proceedings—the right to select or reject a bargaining agent—are the heart of the National Labor Relations Act. Section 7 guarantees to employees the right to form, join, or assist labor organizations, to bargain collectively through representatives of their own choosing, and to engage in other concerted activities for the purpose of collective bargaining or other mutual aid or protection. Section 9 sets forth the procedures which employees may use to exercise the right to select, or reject, a union representative by means of secret ballot elections.

For nearly 25 years, a large proportion of the Board's workload was devoted to resolving issues raised in representation proceedings. As the Board's caseload grew, the representation matters became increasingly burdensome. Recognizing the routine nature of many of these cases and the relative stability of the Act's interpretation in this area, Congress, as a part of the 1959 amendments, authorized the Board to delegate the bulk of its authority over election cases to the regional directors.[1]

Sec. 4–2. Delegation to the regional directors. The Board waited until May 15, 1961,[2] to exercise this authority and today the regional directors play the leading role in representation case processing. (See Chart No. 6, page 42). This was accomplished by a formal delegation (Appendix D) in which the Board gave authority to the regional directors to:

1. Decide whether a question concerning representation exists;
2. Determine the appropriate collective bargaining unit;
3. Direct an election;
4. Certify the results of the election; and
5. Make findings and issue rulings on objections and challenged ballots.

[1]Section 3(b).
[2]Appendix G.

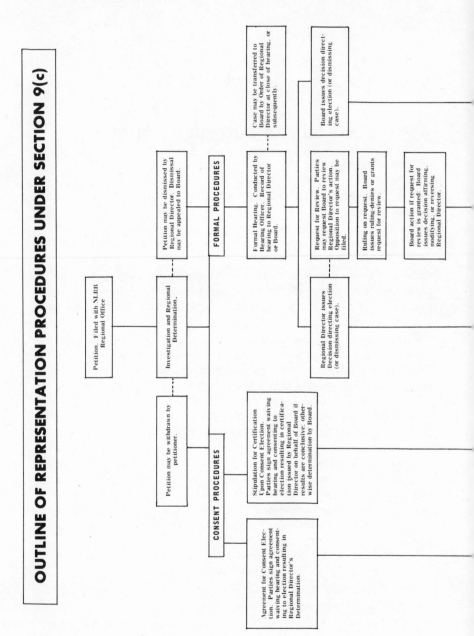

CHART NO. 6. *Outline of representation procedures under section 9 (c)*

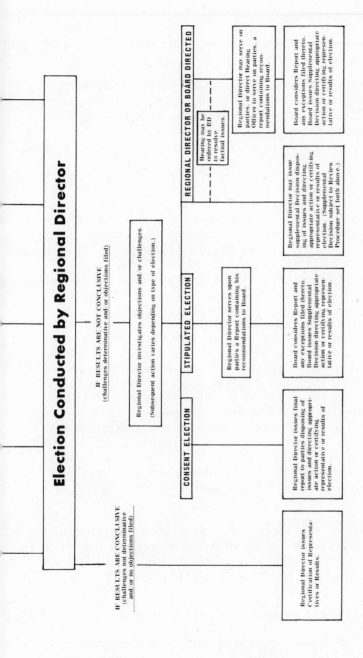

Election Conducted by Regional Director

IF RESULTS ARE NOT CONCLUSIVE
(challenges determinative and or objections filed)

Regional Director investigates objections and or challenges.

(Subsequent action varies depending on type of election.)

IF RESULTS ARE CONCLUSIVE
(challenges not determinative
and or no objections filed)

CONSENT ELECTION

Regional Director issues final report to parties disposing of issues and directing appropriate action or certifying representative or results of election.

STIPULATED ELECTION

Regional Director serves upon parties a Report containing his recommendations to Board.

Board considers Report and any exceptions filed thereto. Board issues Supplemental Decision directing appropriate action or certifying representative or results of election.

Regional Director issues Certification of Representatives or Results.

REGIONAL DIRECTOR OR BOARD DIRECTED

Hearing may be ordered by RD to resolve factual issues.

Regional Director may serve on parties, or direct Hearing Officer to serve on parties, a report containing recommendations to Board.

Board considers Report and any exceptions filed thereto. Board issues Supplemental Decision directing appropriate action or certifying, representative or results of election.

Regional Director may issue supplemental Decision disposing of issues and directing appropriate action or certifying representative or results of election. (Supplemental Decision subject to Review Procedure set forth above.)

Prepared by:
Organization & Methods Branch
Division of Administration—7/61

The Board retained a limited form of review, as suggested by the statute, to assure uniform and consistent application of its interpretation of applicable law and policy. Thus, review by the Board from the regional director's decision may be sought only upon the following four grounds.[3]

1. Where a substantial question of law or policy is raised because of the absence of or the departure from officially reported Board precedent;
2. Where the director's decision on a substantial factual issue is clearly erroneous and such error prejudicially affects the rights of a party;
3. Where the conduct of the hearing or any ruling in connection with the proceeding has resulted in prejudicial error;
4. Where there are compelling reasons for reconsideration of an important Board rule or policy.

A representation case may also reach the Board through transfer by the director at any time prior to reaching his decision.[4] (See Facsimile No. 1, page 45.) This privilege is rarely used by the directors except for novel issues of law or policy. Until a transfer is made, it is presumed that the director will decide the case. After transfer the Board considers the case in the same manner as if review had been granted.

Sec. 4–3. Election stays and waivers. Further action on the part of the director is not stayed by the filing of a request for review or by the granting of review, unless otherwise ordered by the Board.[5] Thus the director ordinarily proceeds immediately with election arrangements, including issuance of Notice of Election, and attempts to set the election date within 30 days after issuance of the Direction of Election. But in order to allow time for the Board to rule on any request for review, elections are not scheduled until at least 25 days after the decision unless the parties waive the right to request review. Waiver allows an immediate election after issuance of the Direction of Election, but all parties must waive, and the Excelsior list requirement must be met.[6] (See Section 9.2, page 155.) In practice many elections are not scheduled until more than 30 days after the Direction issues.

Section 4–4. Propriety of delegation. The propriety of the Board's delegation of authority over representation cases under the amendment to Section 3(b) is now well established. The authority is exercised as a part of the Board's function to interpret the Act, subject to review by the courts.[7]

[3]R. and R. Sec. 102.67(c).
[4]R. and R. Sec. 102.67(h).
[5]R. and R. Sec. 102.67(g).
[6]R. and R. Sec. 102.67(f).
[7]Wallace Shops Inc., 133 NLRB 16, 48 LRRM 1564 (1961); NLRB v. Magnesium Casting Co., 427 F.2d 114 (C.A. 1), 74 LRRM 2234 (1970).

FORM NLRB-4481
(1-67)

UNITED STATES OF AMERICA
BEFORE THE NATIONAL LABOR RELATIONS BOARD

Case No.

ORDER TRANSFERRING REPRESENTATION CASE
TO THE NATIONAL LABOR RELATIONS BOARD

IT IS HEREBY ORDERED, pursuant to Section 102.67 of the National Labor Relations Board Rules and Regulations, that the above-entitled matter be and it hereby is transferred to and continued before the Board in Washington, D. C.

Subject to the provisions of Section 102.67 (i)* of the aforementioned rules and regulations, briefs may be filed with the Executive Secretary, National Labor Relations Board, Washington, D. C., 20570, on or before

By direction of the Regional Director for Region

Dated _____   _____
                                                                (Signature)

                                                                _____
                                                                (Title)

*(i) If any case is transferred to the Board for decision after the parties have filed briefs with the regional director, the parties may, within such time after service of the order transferring the case as is fixed by the regional director, file with the Board eight copies of the brief previously filed with the regional director. Such copies shall be printed or otherwise legibly duplicated: Provided, however, That carbon copies of typewritten matter shall not be filed and if submitted will not be accepted. No further briefs shall be permitted except by special permission of the Board. If the case is transferred to the Board before the time expires for the filing of briefs with the regional director and before the parties have filed briefs, such briefs shall be filed as set forth above and served in accordance with subsection (b) of this section, within the time set by the regional director. If the order transferring the case is served on the parties during the hearing, the hearing officer may, prior to the close of the hearing and for good cause, grant an extension of time within which to file a brief with the Board for a period not to exceed an additional 14 days. Requests for extension of time in which to file a brief with the Board under authority of this section not addressed to the hearing officer during the hearing shall be filed in writing with the Board and copies thereof shall immediately be served on the other parties and the regional director. Requests for extension of time shall be received by the Board not later than 3 days before the date such briefs are due in Washington, D. C. A copy of any such request shall be served immediately on the other parties and the regional director and shall contain a statement that such service has been made. No reply brief may be filed except upon special leave of the Board.

GPO 921-997

FACSIMILE NO. 1
*Order transferring representation case
to the National Labor Relations Board*

CHAPTER 5

The Petition for an Election

Sec. 5–1. In general. The law provides that the labor organization designated by a majority of employees in an appropriate bargaining unit shall be the exclusive bargaining agent for those employees.[1] The NLRB's function in such representation proceedings is to ascertain and certify the bargaining representative chosen by the employees in the appropriate unit.

Sec. 5–2. Method of determining majority status. The "preferred" and, today, the most widely used method of determining a union's status as bargaining representative of a group of employees is direct use of the NLRB's election procedures.But there are two other methods by which bargaining status may be established. One is voluntary recognition by an employer after a union claims majority status. The propriety of this technique is well established where the employer has no reasonable doubt of the employees' preference for the union and recognition is not granted to assist a particular union at the expense of a rival.

The other method of establishing majority status is Board-ordered recognition without an election.[2] This may occur where a union secures authorization cards or other indication of employee interest from a majority of the employees, demands recognition, and the employer refuses and concurrently engages in pervasive unfair labor practice activity which makes it impossible for the employees to express their free and uncoerced choice in a secret ballot election.[3]

It is the election, or representation, procedures with which we are concerned here for, in addition to wide use, an election must be conducted by the National Labor Relations Board before a certification of a labor organization's exclusive bargaining status can be issued.[4]Bargaining status obtained through voluntary recognition places the same duty on the

---

[1]Sec. 9(a).
[2]NLRB v. Gissel Packing Co., 395 U.S. 575, 596, 71 LRRM 2481, 2488 (1969); *see also* NLRB v. Ship Shape Maintenance Co., 81 LRRM 2865 (C.A.D.C., 1972), *enf. in part* 189 NLRB No. 58, 77 LRRM 1137; Steel-Fab Inc., 212 NLRB No. 25, 86 LRRM 1474 (1974).
[3]*Ibid. See also* Linden Lumber Div., Summer Co., 190 NLRB No. 116, 77 LRRM 1305 (1971).
[4]General Box Co., 82 NLRB 678, 23 LRRM 1589 (1949).

employer to bargain in good faith as that arising after an NLRB-conducted election, but certain advantages are obtained by a union which wins an election.

Sec. 5–3. Benefits of NLRB certification. Following are some of the benefits enjoyed by one or both of the parties to the labor-management relationship when a union has been certified by the Board or the regional director:

1. The employer is obligated to bargain with the certified union for at least one year, absent unusual circumstances.[5]The one year has been interpreted by the Board to mean one year of good faith bargaining rather than a calendar year.[6]Unusual circumstances, according to the Supreme Court, are a schism within the certified union, its defunctness, or "a radical fluctuation in the size of the bargaining unit within a short period of time."[7]

2. Where the parties have not yet signed an agreement, any petition for an election filed within a year of certification will be dismissed, again absent unusual circumstances.[8]

3. The parties are virtually assured that their contractual relationship will not be disturbed by an NLRB-directed election if their contract was signed within a year of the issuance of certification and the contract contains no unlawful provisions.[9] However, where the contract is due to expire within the certification year, the Board has entertained a timely petition for an election filed within that year.[10]

4. A certification is added "insurance" against a strike by an outside union, as it is illegal under Section 8(b)(4)(C) of the Act for one union to exert pressure for recognition on behalf of employees for whom a rival union has received Board certification. (See Chart No. 3, pages 12–13, and Chapter 19, Recognition and Organizational Picketing.)

[5]Ray Brooks v. NLRB, 348 U.S. 96, 35 LRRM 2158 (1954); U.S. Eagle Inc., 202 NLRB No. 74, 82 LRRM 1561 (1973).
[6]Mar-Jac Poultry Inc., 136 NLRB 785, 49 LRRM 1854 (1962); LaMar Hotel, 137 NLRB 1271, 50 LRRM 1366 (1962); Gebhardt Vogel Tanning Co., 154 NLRB No. 68, 60 LRRM 1037 (1965); Town and Country, 194 NLRB No. 176, 79 LRRM 1163 (1972).
[7]Morris, THE DEVELOPING LABOR LAW (Washington, D.C.: BNA Books, 1971), p. 164; cf. Kentucky News Incorporated, 165 NLRB 777, 65 LRRM 1600 (1962); NLRB v. Burns International Security Service, 404 U.S. 99, 78 LRRM 2463 (1971); NLRB v. Siegler Corp., 305 F. 2d 670, 50 LRRM 2676 (C.A. 9, 1962), enf. 129 NLRB 1098, 47 LRRM 1138.
[8]Aleo Mfg. Co., 109 NLRB 1297, 34 LRRM 1554 (1954); Joe Pistocco Auto Service, Inc., NLRB No. 16–RM–146, 40 LRRM 1368 (1957).
[9]F.J. Kress Box Co., 97 NLRB 1109, 29 LRRM 1212 (1952); Pine Transportation Inc., 197 NLRB No. 43, 80 LRRM 1334 (1972).
[10]Ludlow Typograph Co., 108 NLRB 1463, 34 LRRM 1249 (1954).

5. A union with a certification may try to get other unions to strike in sympathy with it if the company will not honor the certification and bargain.[11](Note that a sympathy strike for any other reason is likely to be an unlawful secondary boycott.)
6. If a union is certified as bargaining agent for employees doing a certain type of work and the employer gives this type of work to employees belonging to another union, the certified union may strike to compel the employer to honor the certification.[12] Without a certification, a strike to force the employer to assign work to members of one union rather than another may be illegal.

Sec. 5–4. The petition—Necessity. The authority for NLRB action in election proceedings is found in Section 9 of the Act.[13]Before it may act, however, a petition must be filed. Neither the Board nor the General Counsel is empowered to determine the bargaining representative or to investigate a claim of majority status on its own initiative.[14]The petition is a formal request addressed to the NLRB to determine whether or not a majority of employees in a bargaining unit wish to be represented by a particular labor organization for the purposes of collective bargaining.

Sec. 5–5. The petition—Who may file. The statute provides that a petition for an investigation and certification of representatives may be filed by:

1. Any individual, an employee, or group of employees acting on behalf of employees;[15]
2. A labor organization acting on behalf of employees;[16]or
3. An employer, but only when one or more individuals or labor organizations present to him a claim to be recognized as the exclusive bargaining representative.[17]

Sec. 5–6. Individual petitions. An individual who files a petition, supported by a substantial number of employees, need only show that he is seeking representative status for the purpose of collective bargaining.[18]Since

---

[11]Sec. 8(b)(4)(B).
[12]Sec. 8(b)(4)(D).
[13]Sec. 9(c) and Sec. 3(b).
[14]Sec. 9(c)(1).
[15]Sec. 9(c)(1)(A).
[16]*Ibid.*
[17]Sec. 9(c)(1)(B).
[18]The Hoffman Packing Co., Inc., 87 NLRB 601, 25 LRRM 1182 (1949).

a supervisor cannot represent employees for bargaining purposes, the Board will dismiss petitions filed by supervisors.[19]

Sec. 5–7. Employer petitions. An employer may file a petition when he is confronted with a demand for recognition.[20]If this occurs, no formal recognition request is necessary and the employer's good faith in questioning the union's claim is assumed.[21]The employer's right to file a petition when a union is currently recognized or certified is more limited. Thus, the Board has ruled that an employer may file an election petition in the following situations:

1. The union asks for a meeting to negotiate an agreement;
2. The union pickets for recognition or organization (see Chapter 19);
3. The employer can demonstrate by objective considerations that an incumbent certified union has lost its majority status. These considerations may be submitted in confidence and determined administratively by the regional director.[22]

The employer may not file a petition if:
1. The petition is filed after a contract is signed;[23]
2. The employer's doubt as to majority status of an incumbent union rests on a mere change in ownership of the employer;[24]
3. The employer cannot show reasonable grounds for doubting an incumbent union's majority status.[25]

Sec. 5–8. Union petitions. A labor organization may petition for an election in one of three circumstances:

1. Where the employer has not recognized it as exclusive bargaining representative, and the union seeks such recognition. In such case, a formal demand for recognition need not precede the filing of the petition.[26]

[19]Kennecott Copper Corp., 98 NLRB 75, 29 LRRM 1300 (1952); cf. Buckeye Village Market Inc., 175 NLRB No. 46, 70 LRRM 1529 (1969).
[20]Sec. 9(c)(1)(B).
[21]Continental Southern Corp., 83 NLRB 668, 24 LRRM 1127 (1949).
[22]United States Gypsum Co., 157 NLRB No. 60, 61 LRRM 1384 (1966); United States Gypsum Co., 161 NLRB 601, 63 LRRM 1308 (1966); North Hempstead Telephone Answering Service, 63 LRRM 1116 (N.Y. Bd., 1966); NLRB Field Manual 11042.
[23]Pazan Motor Freight, Inc., 116 NLRB 1568, 39 LRRM 1045 (1956); Cleveland Pneumatic Tool Co., 135 NLRB 815, 49 LRRM 1585 (1962).
[24]Maintenance, Inc., 148 NLRB 1299, 57 LRRM 1129 (1964); NLRB v. Burns Int'l. Security Service, 406 U.S. 272, 80 LRRM 2225 (1972); Ranch-Way, Inc., 203 NLRB No. 118, 83 LRRM 1197 (1973), suppl'g 183 NLRB No. 116.
[25]United States Gypsum Co., 157 NLRB No. 60, 61 LRRM 1384 (1966).
[26]Advance Pattern Co., 80 NLRB 29, 23 LRRM 1022 (1948); Swalley Printing Co., NLRB No. 10–RC–5156, 50 LRRM 1116; Gray Drug Stores, Inc., 197 NLRB No. 105, 80 LRRM 1449 (1972).

2. Where the union, despite its recognition by the employer and the negotiation of a collective bargaining agreement, files a petition for an election in order to obtain the benefits of a certification.[27](See page 48, "Benefits of NLRB Certification.")

3. Where two or more labor organizations file a joint petition for an election in which they seek certification as the joint representative for a single group of employees. Authorization may be in the name of any of the petitioners, and the authorization cards do not have to stipulate whether or not the employees desire joint or individual representation.[28] If a joint representative is certified, the employer may insist that they bargain jointly.[29]

Sec. 5–9. Union petitions and internal union matters. Where the qualifications, character, or internal matters of a union have been urged as a reason for dismissal of a union's petition for an election, the Board has repeatedly held: "Absent certain statutory limitations, the choice of the bargaining representative rests upon the desires of the employees."[30]Accordingly, to cite several examples, the Board has refused to dismiss a union's petition where the following allegations were made:

1. The petitioner was not a "labor organization" because a United States District Court found that it had been "fraudulently chartered" as part of an intraunion dispute.[31]

2. The petitioner had no local charter in the state as required by state law.[32]

3. The state law prohibited representation of nurses by labor organizations, such as petitioner, whose constitutions contain strike provisions.[33]

4. The petitioner was a foreign labor organization.[34]

5. The petitioner was employer-dominated.[35]

---

[27]General Box Co., 82 NLRB 678, 23 LRRM 1589 (1949); Montgomery Ward and Co., 137 NLRB 346, 50 LRRM 1137 (1962); McGraw Edison Co., National Electric Coil Div., 199 NLRB No. 133, 81 LRRM 1439 (1972).
[28]NLRB v. National Truck Rental Co., Inc., 239 F.2d 422, 38 LRRM 2781 (C.A.D.C., 1956); Hamburg Industries, Fidelity Service, and Industrial Technical Service, 193 NLRB No. 13, 78 LRRM 1130 (1971); Pharmaseal Laboratories, 199 NLRB No. 37, 81 LRRM 1215 (1972).
[29]Swift and Co., 115 NLRB 752, 37 LRRM 1392 (1956); Jackson Manor Nursing Home, 194 NLRB No. 152, 79 LRRM 1166 (1972); cf. Midway Lincoln Mercury, 180 NLRB No. 10, 72 LRRM 1575 (1969).
[30]Auto Transports, Inc., 100 NLRB 272, 30 LRRM 1272 (1952).
[31]Imperial Reed & Rattan Furniture Co., 117 NLRB 495, 39 LRRM 1259 (1957).
[32]General Shoe Corp., 109 NLRB 618, 34 LRRM 1396 (1954).
[33]Consolidated Vultee Aircraft Corp., 108 NLRB 591, 34 LRRM 1044 (1954).
[34]Hamilton Bros., Inc., 133 NLRB 868, 48 LRRM 1740 (1961).
[35]Bi-States Co., 117 NLRB 86, 39 LRRM 1180 (1957).

6. The petitioner was a religious organization with restrictive membership, and not primarily a labor organization.[36]

7. The petitioner was incompetent to represent the employees because of its inexperience in the industry.[37]

8. The petitioner could not represent technical employees or clerical employees because it also represents production and maintenance employees.[38]

9. The petitioner could not represent office clerical employees because it also represents over-the-road truck drivers.[39]

10. The petitioner, a local union, could not be certified as representative for a nationwide group of employees.[40]

11. The petitioner, a national union, could not be certified as representative for a local group of employees.[41]

12. The local petitioner's parent union requested withdrawal of the petition.[42]

13. The charter of the local petitioner had been revoked by its international union.[43]

14. The petitioner's constitution and bylaws prohibited it from representing the employees covered by the petition.[44]

15. The petition covered black employees and the petitioner's policies allegedly discriminated against blacks.[45]However, the Board has held that it will not make its representation procedures available to a labor organization that discriminates racially when acting as a statutory bargaining representative and that unions which exclude employees from membership on racial grounds or which classify or segregate members on racial grounds, may not obtain or retain a certification.[46]

16. Certification of the petitioner would impede settlement of jurisdictional disputes in the construction industry.[47]

[36]Berghuis Construction Co., 116 NLRB 1297, 38 LRRM 1463 (1956).
[37]Jacksonville Linen Service, 89 NLRB 1354, 26 LRRM 1108 (1950).
[38]Solar Aircraft Co., 116 NLRB 200, 38 LRRM 1217 (1956); NLRB v. Swift & Co., 292 F.2d 561, 48 LRRM 2695 (C.A. 1, 1961), enf. 46 LRRM 1319.
[39]Auto Transports, Inc., 100 NLRB 272, 30 LRRM 1272 (1952).
[40]National Van Lines, 117 NLRB 1213, 39 LRRM 1408 (1957).
[41]New Castle Products, Inc., 99 NLRB 811, 30 LRRM 1134 (1952).
[42]Sheller Mfg. Corp., Dryden Rubber Division, 110 NLRB 1652, 35 LRRM 1353 (1954).
[43]Awning Research Institute, 116 NLRB 505, 38 LRRM 1294 (1956).
[44]F.C. Russell Co., 116 NLRB 1015, 38 LRRM 1389 (1956).
[45]Pacific Maritime Assn., 110 NLRB 1647, 35 LRRM 1299 (1954); 112 NLRB 1280, 36 LRRM 1193 (1955).
[46]Hughes Tool Co., 147 NLRB 1573, 56 LRRM 1289 (1964); see also Sec. 10-2, page 187, for further discussion. Bekins Moving and Storage Co., 211 NLRB No. 7, 86 LRRM 1323 (1974); Grants Furniture Plaza, 213 NLRB No. 80, 87 LRRM 1175 (1974); Bell & Howell Co., 213 NLRB No. 79, 87 LRRM 1172 (1974).
[47]The Heating, Piping & Air Conditioning Contractors, Cincinnati Master Plumbers Assn., 110 NLRB 261, 34 LRRM 1634 (1954).

17. The petitioner is engaging in a jurisdictional dispute.[48]
18. A jurisdictional award covers the employees involved in the petition.[49]
19. The petitioner had agreed with the State Labor Federation to divide employees covered by the petition among various other unions.[50]
20. The petitioner, by filing the petition, was seeking to help another union avoid its commitments under a no-raiding agreement.[51]
21. The petition violated either the no-raiding provision of the AFL-CIO constitution,[52] or the AFL Internal Disputes Plan,[53] and an appeal was pending before the president of the AFL-CIO.[54]
22. The petitioner's constitution, bylaws, and other internal documents discriminated against women, but the Board recently adopted a procedure for testing this issue after election.[55]
23. The petitioner had underworld connections.[56]

Although the Board has refused to dismiss petitions involving disputes between affiliated unions, it has taken steps to delay the processing of petitions which involve either: (1) AFL-CIO affiliates; or (2) IUD members.

Sec. 5–10. AFL-CIO affiliates. The Board takes the following action whenever a petition is filed in a case involving at least two affiliates of the AFL-CIO, one of which has either been recognized by the employer for at least one year or has been certified by the NLRB as collective bargaining agent for the employees involved:

1. The regional director sends immediate notification of the fact of filing to the presidents of the AFL-CIO and of the parent international unions involved, to all parties involved, and to the Board's Executive Secretary.
2. The regional director undertakes the customary informal investigation of the merits of the petition.
3. If the petitioner is an affiliate of the AFL-CIO, the regional director delays any necessary formal notice (i.e., issuance of notice of a

---

[48]Miron Building Products Co., 116 NLRB 1406, 39 LRRM 1002 (1956).
[49]Assn. of Motion Picture Producers, Inc., 88 NLRB 521, 25 LRRM 1349 (1950).
[50]Olin Mathieson Chemical Corp., 114 NLRB 948, 37 LRRM 1073 (1955).
[51]Mason Can Co., 115 NLRB 105, 37 LRRM 1246 (1956).
[52]Victor Mfg. and Gasket Co., 133 NLRB 1283, 49 LRRM 1031 (1961); cf. Plough Inc., 203 NLRB No. 58, 83 LRRM 1086 (1973).
[53]S.G. Adams Co., 115 NLRB 1012, 37 LRRM 1469 (1956).
[54]*Ibid.*
[55]American Mailing Corp., 197 NLRB No. 33, 80 LRRM 1294 (1972); Alden Press Inc., 212 NLRB No. 91, 86 LRRM 1605 (1974).
[56]Hotel Properties d/b/a Landmark Hotel and Casino, 194 NLRB No. 139, 79 LRRM 1067 (1972).

hearing) for a period of 30 days from the date of the above notification.

4. If the petitioner is not an affiliate of the AFL-CIO, the regional director may, in his discretion, delay formal action as above, including but not limited to those situations where the petitioner voluntarily requests a delay to permit operation of the no-raiding machinery.

5. At the expiration of the 30-day period the case will be processed in accordance with normal procedures unless an active proceeding under the AFL-CIO no-raid agreement has been initiated.

Sec. 5–11. IUD members. The Board will take the following action whenever a petition for an election is filed in a case in which two or more members of the Industrial Union Department of the AFL-CIO (IUD) are involved:

1. The regional director sends immediate notification of the fact of filing to the Director of the IUD, AFL-CIO.

2. The regional director continues to process the case without interruption.

3. If the IUD program overlaps that of the AFL-CIO, both procedures are followed, including delaying processing of the petition as outlined in Sec. 5–10, No. 3, page 53. For example, if one of the IUD unions is an incumbent union with an established bargaining relationship, the procedures of both AFL-CIO affiliates and IUD members are involved. The appropriate notice is given to all parties and, if necessary, the case is delayed for a period of 30 days.[57]

Sec. 5–12. Filing the petition—Where to file. The petition is filed with the NLRB regional office in whose area the bargaining unit of employees is located. (The location of these offices and the areas they cover are set forth in Appendix E.) If the proposed unit exists in two or more regions, the petition may be filed in any one of these regions.[58] Assistance in the preparation of the petition will be furnished by the regional office upon request. If a petition is filed through the mails, it is suggested, though it is not required, that it be sent by registered or certified mail.

Sec. 5–13. Filing the petition—Timeliness. In addition to statutory requirements, the Board has fashioned through its decisions a number of policies that limit the conditions under which a petition may be filed. Accordingly, when a party decides to petition for an election and

[57]NLRB Field Manual 11050.–11054.3.
[58]R. and R. Sec. 102.60; National Van Lines, 117 NLRB 1213, 39 LRRM 1408 (1957).

certification of representatives, the petition should be filed as early as possible within the time period allowed by the Board. For contract-bar doctrines, see Sec. 5–14, page 56.)

Following are some of the basic restrictions which make timeliness of filing a petition significant:

1. *The statutory bar.* The Board will not conduct an election where a valid election has been held in the same unit in the preceding 12 months. The valid election may have been conducted either by the Board[59] or a state agency.[60]

2. *Policies.*

A. *The certification year.* The Board will not conduct an election where it has issued a certification covering the same unit in the proceeding 12 months, absent unusual circumstances. This 12-month period runs from the date of certification, not from the date of balloting.[61]

B. *Extensions.* The Board has extended the one-year certification period, and in some instances refused to conduct an election until the employer has fulfilled its duty to bargain in good faith for a total of 12 months, excluding from its computation those periods when the employer failed to bargain.[62]

C. *Fluctuating workforce.* The Board usually conducts elections during the period of peak employment in industries whose workforce fluctuates due to the seasonal nature of their business. If the peak has passed, the Board will hold the election at or about the next seasonal peak.[63]

D. *Filing dates.* Despite an existing agreement, the Board will direct an election where the petition for an appropriate unit is filed before the expiration or renewal date of the contract, provided that the petition is filed not less than 60 days and not more than 90 days before the expiration or renewal date of the contract.[64] Petitions filed on the sixtieth day will be considered untimely.[65] If the petition is filed outside those

[59]Sec. 9(c)(3); Fullana Construction Co., Inc., 104 NLRB 1109, 32 LRRM 1211 (1953).
[60]Olin Mathieson Chemical Corp., 115 NLRB 1501, 38 LRRM 1099 (1956); Modern Litho Plate Corp., 134 NLRB 66, 49 LRRM 1110 (1961); We Transport Inc., 198 NLRB No. 144, 81 LRRM 1010 (1972).
[61]Ray Brooks v. NLRB, 348 U.S. 96, 35 LRRM 2158 (1954) and cases cited therein; Rockwell Valves Inc., 115 NLRB 236, 37 LRRM 1271 (1956).
[62]Mar-Jac Poultry Inc., 136 NLRB 785, 49 LRRM 1854 (1962); LaMar Hotel, 137 NLRB 1271, 50 LRRM 1366 (1962); Town and Country, 194 NLRB No. 176, 79 LRRM 1163 (1972).
[63]Cleveland Cliffs Iron Co., 177 NLRB 668, 39 LRRM 1319 (1957); Bardo Prods. Co., 117 NLRB 313, 39 LRRM 1220 (1957).
[64]Leonard Wholesale Meats, 136 NLRB 1000, 49 LRRM 1901 (1962); Penn-Keystone Realty Corp., 191 NLRB No. 105, 77 LRRM 1600 (1971).
[65]Hemisphere Steel Products Inc., 131 NLRB 56, 47 LRRM 1595 (1961).

time limits, no election will be directed[66] unless the contract has expired. (See Chart 7, pages 57–59, Table Showing Timely Filing of Petitions.)

E. *Absence of certification.* In cases where there is no outstanding certification of a union, the Board will accept and process petitions filed during the last 60 days of the 12-month period, but will not direct the election until the 12 months have expired. The 12-month period in cases involving the absence of certification runs from the date of election in the earlier election and not from the date of the Board's determination of election results.[67]

F. *Invalid elections.* The Board will direct an election within 12 months of a previous election where that election, whether conducted by the NLRB or a state agency, was invalid.[68]

Sec. 5–14. Filing the petition—Contract-bar doctrines. The Board generally will not direct an election where a valid contract is in existence.[69] Such a contract must be in writing and signed[70] by the parties before the petition is filed.[71] It must (a) provide for exclusive bargaining;[72] (b) cover an appropriate bargaining unit; (c) provide terms and conditions of employment;[73] and (d) extend for a definite and reasonable term.[74]

1. *Duration.* The Board considers a contract of three years duration or less as a reasonable term; contracts for longer time periods operate as a bar to rival petitions only for the first three years.[75]

If during the term of a contract the parties agree on an amendment or a new contract with a terminal date after the terminal date on the existing contract, the amendment or new contract will be "premature." This premature extension will not bar an otherwise timely petition. This doctrine does not apply to contracts executed during the 60-day insulated period

[66]Leonard Wholesale Meats, 136 NLRB 1000, 49 LRRM 1901 (1962); The National Cash Register Co., 201 NLRB No. 120, 82 LRRM 1353 (1973).
[67]Mallinckrodt Chemical Works, 84 NLRB 291, 24 LRRM 1253 (1949); Kolcast Industries, Inc., 117 NLRB 418, 39 LRRM 1242 (1957); Bendix Corp., 179 NLRB No. 18, 72 LRRM 1264 (1969).
[68]NLRB v. Capital Transit Co., 221 F.2d 864, 35 LRRM 2500 (C.A.D.C., 1955); Southern Minnesota Supply Co., 116 NLRB 968, 39 LRRM 1367 (1956).
[69]Polar Ware Co., 139 NLRB 1006, 51 LRRM 1452 (1962); Road Materials Inc., 193 NLRB No. 130, 78 LRRM 1448 (1971).
[70]Pittsburgh Plate Glass Co., 118 NLRB 961, 40 LRRM 1296 (1957); Peter Paul Inc., 204 NLRB No. 57, 83 LRRM 1310 (1973).
[71]Highway Transport Association, 116 NLRB 1718, 39 LRRM 1078 (1956); Pharmaseal Laboratories, 199 NLRB No. 37, 81 LRRM 1215 (1972); Peter Paul Inc., 204 NLRB No. 57, 83 LRRM 1310 (1973).
[72]The Dover Ceramic Co., 115 NLRB 1040, 37 LRRM 1488 (1956).
[73]Consolidated Cement Corp., 117 NLRB 492, 39 LRRM 1262 (1957); Tom's Monarch Laundry and Cleaning Co., 168 NLRB No. 39, 66 LRRM 1277 (1967).
[74]Nash-Kelvinator Corp., 110 NLRB 447, 35 LRRM 1074 (1954).
[75]General Cable Corp., 139 NLRB 1123, 51 LRRM 1444 (1962); Penn-Keystone Realty Corp., 191 NLRB No. 105, 77 LRRM 1600 (1971).

FORM NLRB-4645
(4-72)

TABLE SHOWING TIMELY FILING OF PETITIONS

CONTRACT EXPIRATION DATE *	PETITION TIMELY IF FILED ON OR BETWEEN DATES	CONTRACT EXPIRATION DATE *	PETITION TIMELY IF FILED ON OR BETWEEN DATES	CONTRACT EXPIRATION DATE *	PETITION TIMELY IF FILED ON OR BETWEEN DATES	CONTRACT EXPIRATION DATE *	PETITION TIMELY IF FILED ON OR BETWEEN DATES
January	Oct 4 – Nov 2	**February**	Nov 4 – Dec 3	**March**	Dec 2 – Dec 31	**April**	Jan 2 – Jan 31
1	Oct 4 – Nov 2	1	Nov 4 – Dec 3	1	Dec 2 – Dec 31	1	Jan 2 – Jan 31
2	Oct 5 – Nov 3	2	Nov 5 – Dec 4	2	Dec 3 – Jan 1	2	Jan 3 – Feb 1
3	Oct 6 – Nov 4	3	Nov 6 – Dec 5	3	Dec 4 – Jan 2	3	Jan 4 – Feb 2
4	Oct 7 – Nov 5	4	Nov 7 – Dec 6	4	Dec 5 – Jan 3	4	Jan 5 – Feb 3
5	Oct 8 – Nov 6	5	Nov 8 – Dec 7	5	Dec 6 – Jan 4	5	Jan 6 – Feb 4
6	Oct 9 – Nov 7	6	Nov 9 – Dec 8	6	Dec 7 – Jan 5	6	Jan 7 – Feb 5
7	Oct 10 – Nov 8	7	Nov 10 – Dec 9	7	Dec 8 – Jan 6	7	Jan 8 – Feb 6
8	Oct 11 – Nov 9	8	Nov 11 – Dec 10	8	Dec 9 – Jan 7	8	Jan 9 – Feb 7
9	Oct 12 – Nov 10	9	Nov 12 – Dec 11	9	Dec 10 – Jan 8	9	Jan 10 – Feb 8
10	Oct 13 – Nov 11	10	Nov 13 – Dec 12	10	Dec 11 – Jan 9	10	Jan 11 – Feb 9
11	Oct 14 – Nov 12	11	Nov 14 – Dec 13	11	Dec 12 – Jan 10	11	Jan 12 – Feb 10
12	Oct 15 – Nov 13	12	Nov 15 – Dec 14	12	Dec 13 – Jan 11	12	Jan 13 – Feb 11
13	Oct 16 – Nov 14	13	Nov 16 – Dec 15	13	Dec 14 – Jan 12	13	Jan 14 – Feb 12
14	Oct 17 – Nov 15	14	Nov 17 – Dec 16	14	Dec 15 – Jan 13	14	Jan 15 – Feb 13
15	Oct 18 – Nov 16	15	Nov 18 – Dec 17	15	Dec 16 – Jan 14	15	Jan 16 – Feb 14
16	Oct 19 – Nov 17	16	Nov 19 – Dec 18	16	Dec 17 – Jan 15	16	Jan 17 – Feb 15
17	Oct 20 – Nov 18	17	Nov 20 – Dec 19	17	Dec 18 – Jan 16	17	Jan 18 – Feb 16
18	Oct 21 – Nov 19	18	Nov 21 – Dec 20	18	Dec 19 – Jan 17	18	Jan 19 – Feb 17
19	Oct 22 – Nov 20	19	Nov 22 – Dec 21	19	Dec 20 – Jan 18	19	Jan 20 – Feb 18
20	Oct 23 – Nov 21	20	Nov 23 – Dec 22	20	Dec 21 – Jan 19	20	Jan 21 – Feb 19
21	Oct 24 – Nov 22	21	Nov 24 – Dec 23	21	Dec 22 – Jan 20	21	Jan 22 – Feb 20
22	Oct 25 – Nov 23	22	Nov 25 – Dec 24	22	Dec 23 – Jan 21	22	Jan 23 – Feb 21
23	Oct 26 – Nov 24	23	Nov 26 – Dec 25	23	Dec 24 – Jan 22	23	Jan 24 – Feb 22
24	Oct 27 – Nov 25	24	Nov 27 – Dec 26	24	Dec 25 – Jan 23	24	Jan 25 – Feb 23
25	Oct 28 – Nov 26	25	Nov 28 – Dec 27	25	Dec 26 – Jan 24	25	Jan 26 – Feb 24
26	Oct 29 – Nov 27	26	Nov 29 – Dec 28	26	Dec 27 – Jan 25	26	Jan 27 – Feb 25
27	Oct 30 – Nov 28	27	Nov 30 – Dec 29	27	Dec 28 – Jan 26	27	Jan 28 – Feb 26
28	Oct 31 – Nov 29	28	Dec 1 – Dec 30	28	Dec 29 – Jan 27	28	Jan 29 – Feb 27
29	Nov 1 – Nov 30	**29	Dec 2 – Dec 31	29	Dec 30 – Jan 28	29	Jan 30 – Feb 28
30	Nov 2 – Dec 1			30	Dec 31 – Jan 29	30	Jan 31 – Mar 1
31	Nov 3 – Dec 2			31	Jan 1 – Jan 30		

* "Contract Expiration Date" is last effective date of contract. A contract "to" or "until" a date does not include that date and the last effective date is the preceding day.

** Leap Year Adjustment — Add one day to each of the petition timely dates when contract expires March 1 - April 29 inclusive.
Add one day to first of the petition timely dates when contract expires April 30 - May 28 inclusive.

CHART NO. 7. *Timely filing of petitions*

TABLE SHOWING TIMELY FILING OF PETITIONS

CONTRACT EXPIRATION DATE*	PETITION TIMELY IF FILED ON OR BETWEEN DATES	CONTRACT EXPIRATION DATE*	PETITION TIMELY IF FILED ON OR BETWEEN DATES	CONTRACT EXPIRATION DATE*	PETITION TIMELY IF FILED ON OR BETWEEN DATES	CONTRACT EXPIRATION DATE*	PETITION TIMELY IF FILED ON OR BETWEEN DATES
**May 1	Feb 1 – Mar 2	June 1	Mar 4 – Apr 2	July 1	Apr 3 – May 2	August 1	May 4 – Jun 2
May 2	Feb 2 – Mar 3	June 2	Mar 5 – Apr 3	July 2	Apr 4 – May 3	August 2	May 5 – Jun 3
May 3	Feb 3 – Mar 4	June 3	Mar 6 – Apr 4	July 3	Apr 5 – May 4	August 3	May 6 – Jun 4
May 4	Feb 4 – Mar 5	June 4	Mar 7 – Apr 5	July 4	Apr 6 – May 5	August 4	May 7 – Jun 5
May 5	Feb 5 – Mar 6	June 5	Mar 8 – Apr 6	July 5	Apr 7 – May 6	August 5	May 8 – Jun 6
May 6	Feb 6 – Mar 7	June 6	Mar 9 – Apr 7	July 6	Apr 8 – May 7	August 6	May 9 – Jun 7
May 7	Feb 7 – Mar 8	June 7	Mar 10 – Apr 8	July 7	Apr 9 – May 8	August 7	May 10 – Jun 8
May 8	Feb 8 – Mar 9	June 8	Mar 11 – Apr 9	July 8	Apr 10 – May 9	August 8	May 11 – Jun 9
May 9	Feb 9 – Mar 10	June 9	Mar 12 – Apr 10	July 9	Apr 11 – May 10	August 9	May 12 – Jun 10
May 10	Feb 10 – Mar 11	June 10	Mar 13 – Apr 11	July 10	Apr 12 – May 11	August 10	May 13 – Jun 11
May 11	Feb 11 – Mar 12	June 11	Mar 14 – Apr 12	July 11	Apr 13 – May 12	August 11	May 14 – Jun 12
May 12	Feb 12 – Mar 13	June 12	Mar 15 – Apr 13	July 12	Apr 14 – May 13	August 12	May 15 – Jun 13
May 13	Feb 13 – Mar 14	June 13	Mar 16 – Apr 14	July 13	Apr 15 – May 14	August 13	May 16 – Jun 14
May 14	Feb 14 – Mar 15	June 14	Mar 17 – Apr 15	July 14	Apr 16 – May 15	August 14	May 17 – Jun 15
May 15	Feb 15 – Mar 16	June 15	Mar 18 – Apr 16	July 15	Apr 17 – May 16	August 15	May 18 – Jun 16
May 16	Feb 16 – Mar 17	June 16	Mar 19 – Apr 17	July 16	Apr 18 – May 17	August 16	May 19 – Jun 17
May 17	Feb 17 – Mar 18	June 17	Mar 20 – Apr 18	July 17	Apr 19 – May 18	August 17	May 20 – Jun 18
May 18	Feb 18 – Mar 19	June 18	Mar 21 – Apr 19	July 18	Apr 20 – May 19	August 18	May 21 – Jun 19
May 19	Feb 19 – Mar 20	June 19	Mar 22 – Apr 20	July 19	Apr 21 – May 20	August 19	May 22 – Jun 20
May 20	Feb 20 – Mar 21	June 20	Mar 23 – Apr 21	July 20	Apr 22 – May 21	August 20	May 23 – Jun 21
May 21	Feb 21 – Mar 22	June 21	Mar 24 – Apr 22	July 21	Apr 23 – May 22	August 21	May 24 – Jun 22
May 22	Feb 22 – Mar 23	June 22	Mar 25 – Apr 23	July 22	Apr 24 – May 23	August 22	May 25 – Jun 23
May 23	Feb 23 – Mar 24	June 23	Mar 26 – Apr 24	July 23	Apr 25 – May 24	August 23	May 26 – Jun 24
May 24	Feb 24 – Mar 25	June 24	Mar 27 – Apr 25	July 24	Apr 26 – May 25	August 24	May 27 – Jun 25
May 25	Feb 25 – Mar 26	June 25	Mar 28 – Apr 26	July 25	Apr 27 – May 26	August 25	May 28 – Jun 26
May 26	Feb 26 – Mar 27	June 26	Mar 29 – Apr 27	July 26	Apr 28 – May 27	August 26	May 29 – Jun 27
May 27	Feb 27 – Mar 28	June 27	Mar 30 – Apr 28	July 27	Apr 29 – May 28	August 27	May 30 – Jun 28
May 28	Feb 28 – Mar 29	June 28	Mar 31 – Apr 29	July 28	Apr 30 – May 29	August 28	May 31 – Jun 29
May 29	Mar 1 – Mar 30	June 29	Apr 1 – Apr 30	July 29	May 1 – May 30	August 29	Jun 1 – Jun 30
May 30	Mar 2 – Mar 31	June 30	Apr 2 – May 1	July 30	May 2 – May 31	August 30	Jun 2 – Jul 1
May 31	Mar 3 – Apr 1			July 31	May 3 – Jun 1	August 31	Jun 3 – Jul 2

* "Contract Expiration Date" is last effective date of contract. A contract "to" or "until" a date does not include that date and the last effective date is the preceding day.

** Leap Year Adjustment — Add one day to each of the petition timely dates when contract expires March 1 – April 29 inclusive.
Add one day to first of the petition timely dates when contract expires April 30 – May 28 inclusive.

CHART NO. 7. *Second page*

TABLE SHOWING TIMELY FILING OF PETITIONS

CONTRACT EXPIRATION DATE*	PETITION TIMELY IF FILED ON OR BETWEEN DATES	CONTRACT EXPIRATION DATE*	PETITION TIMELY IF FILED ON OR BETWEEN DATES	CONTRACT EXPIRATION DATE*	PETITION TIMELY IF FILED ON OR BETWEEN DATES	CONTRACT EXPIRATION DATE*	PETITION TIMELY IF FILED ON OR BETWEEN DATES
September 1	Jun 4 – Jul 3	October 1	Jul 4 – Aug 2	November 1	Aug 4 – Sep 2	December 1	Sep 3 – Oct 2
2	Jun 5 – Jul 4	2	Jul 5 – Aug 3	2	Aug 5 – Sep 3	2	Sep 4 – Oct 3
3	Jun 6 – Jul 5	3	Jul 6 – Aug 4	3	Aug 6 – Sep 4	3	Sep 5 – Oct 4
4	Jun 7 – Jul 6	4	Jul 7 – Aug 5	4	Aug 7 – Sep 5	4	Sep 6 – Oct 5
5	Jun 8 – Jul 7	5	Jul 8 – Aug 6	5	Aug 8 – Sep 6	5	Sep 7 – Oct 6
6	Jun 9 – Jul 8	6	Jul 9 – Aug 7	6	Aug 9 – Sep 7	6	Sep 8 – Oct 7
7	Jun 10 – Jul 9	7	Jul 10 – Aug 8	7	Aug 10 – Sep 8	7	Sep 9 – Oct 8
8	Jun 11 – Jul 10	8	Jul 11 – Aug 9	8	Aug 11 – Sep 9	8	Sep 10 – Oct 9
9	Jun 12 – Jul 11	9	Jul 12 – Aug 10	9	Aug 12 – Sep 10	9	Sep 11 – Oct 10
10	Jun 13 – Jul 12	10	Jul 13 – Aug 11	10	Aug 13 – Sep 11	10	Sep 12 – Oct 11
11	Jun 14 – Jul 13	11	Jul 14 – Aug 12	11	Aug 14 – Sep 12	11	Sep 13 – Oct 12
12	Jun 15 – Jul 14	12	Jul 15 – Aug 13	12	Aug 15 – Sep 13	12	Sep 14 – Oct 13
13	Jun 16 – Jul 15	13	Jul 16 – Aug 14	13	Aug 16 – Sep 14	13	Sep 15 – Oct 14
14	Jun 17 – Jul 16	14	Jul 17 – Aug 15	14	Aug 17 – Sep 15	14	Sep 16 – Oct 15
15	Jun 18 – Jul 17	15	Jul 18 – Aug 16	15	Aug 18 – Sep 16	15	Sep 17 – Oct 16
16	Jun 19 – Jul 18	16	Jul 19 – Aug 17	16	Aug 19 – Sep 17	16	Sep 18 – Oct 17
17	Jun 20 – Jul 19	17	Jul 20 – Aug 18	17	Aug 20 – Sep 18	17	Sep 19 – Oct 18
18	Jun 21 – Jul 20	18	Jul 21 – Aug 19	18	Aug 21 – Sep 19	18	Sep 20 – Oct 19
19	Jun 22 – Jul 21	19	Jul 22 – Aug 20	19	Aug 22 – Sep 20	19	Sep 21 – Oct 20
20	Jun 23 – Jul 22	20	Jul 23 – Aug 21	20	Aug 23 – Sep 21	20	Sep 22 – Oct 21
21	Jun 24 – Jul 23	21	Jul 24 – Aug 22	21	Aug 24 – Sep 22	21	Sep 23 – Oct 22
22	Jun 25 – Jul 24	22	Jul 25 – Aug 23	22	Aug 25 – Sep 23	22	Sep 24 – Oct 23
23	Jun 26 – Jul 25	23	Jul 26 – Aug 24	23	Aug 26 – Sep 24	23	Sep 25 – Oct 24
24	Jun 27 – Jul 26	24	Jul 27 – Aug 25	24	Aug 27 – Sep 25	24	Sep 26 – Oct 25
25	Jun 28 – Jul 27	25	Jul 28 – Aug 26	25	Aug 28 – Sep 26	25	Sep 27 – Oct 26
26	Jun 29 – Jul 28	26	Jul 29 – Aug 27	26	Aug 29 – Sep 27	26	Sep 28 – Oct 27
27	Jun 30 – Jul 29	27	Jul 30 – Aug 28	27	Aug 30 – Sep 28	27	Sep 29 – Oct 28
28	Jul 1 – Jul 30	28	Jul 31 – Aug 29	28	Aug 31 – Sep 29	28	Sep 30 – Oct 29
29	Jul 2 – Jul 31	29	Aug 1 – Aug 30	29	Sep 1 – Sep 30	29	Oct 1 – Oct 30
30	Jul 3 – Aug 1	30	Aug 2 – Aug 31	30	Sep 2 – Oct 1	30	Oct 2 – Oct 31
		31	Aug 3 – Sep 1			31	Oct 3 – Nov 1

*"Contract Expiration Date" is last effective date of contract. A contract "to" or "until" a date does not include that date and the last effective date is the preceding day.

CHART NO. 7. *Third page*

preceding the terminal date of the old contract, after the terminal date, or at a time when the existing contract could bar an election due to other contract-bar provisions.[76]

2. *Unlawful clauses* The Board has tempered its contract-bar doctrine in the areas of union security, checkoff, racial discrimination, and hot cargo, in an attempt to strike a balance between the need for industrial stability and the employees' right to choose bargaining representatives.

A. *Union security.* If a contract contains an unlawful union security clause, it will be classified no bar by the Board. However, if the clause is eliminated by a proper rescission or amendment and the inclusion of a provision "clearly deferring the effectiveness" of the stipulation, the contract will be "cured."[77]

B. *Checkoff.* A checkoff clause does not jeopardize the contract's ability to act as a bar unless it is illegal on its face, or has been held illegal in an unfair labor practice proceeding or in court in an action brought by the Attorney General.[78]

C. *Hot cargo.* Although a provision may violate Section 8(e), it will not prevent the contract from acting as a bar. Unlike a union-security clause, a hot-cargo provision is not considered to restrain the selection of a collective bargaining agent.[79]

3. *Expanding units.* The following rules are used by the Board to determine whether or not elections should be held in an expanding unit, despite the presence of a valid contract.[80]

A. *Prehire agreements.* A contract will not bar an election if it was executed before the employees were hired or prior to a substantial increase in employee number. Such an increase occurs if over 70 percent of the personnel are hired after the contract's execution, or there is a change in over 50 percent of the job classifications.[81]

B. *Relocation and consolidation.* A contract will not bar an election if the change, coupled with a major personnel change, is in the nature rather than the size of operations involving (1) a merger of two or more

---

[76]Deluxe Metal Furniture Co., 121 NLRB 995, 42 LRRM 1470 (1958); Penn-Keystone Realty Corp., 191 NLRB No. 105, 77 LRRM 1600 (1971); Union Carbide Corp., 190 NLRB No. 40, 77 LRRM 2894 (1971).

[77]Keystone Coat, Apron, and Towel Supply Co., 121 NLRB 880, 42 LRRM 1456 (1958); NLRB v. News Syndicate Co., 365 U.S. 695, 47 LRRM 2916 (1961); NLRB v. International Typographical Union, 365 U.S. 705, 47 LRRM 2920 (1961); Peabody Coal Co., 197 NLRB No. 152, 80 LRRM 1550 (1972).

[78]Keystone Coat, Apron, and Towel Supply Co., 121 NLRB 880, 42 LRRM 1456 (1958); Gary Steel Supply Co., 144 NLRB 470, 54 LRRM 1082 (1963); General Electric Co., 173 NLRB No. 83, 69 LRRM 1395 (1968).

[79]Food Haulers Inc., 136 NLRB 394, 49 LRRM 1774 (1962).

[80]General Extrusion Co., 121 NLRB 1165, 42 LRRM 1508 (1958).

[81]West Penn Hat and Cap Corp., 165 NLRB 77, 65 LRRM 1417 (1967); Mishara Construction Co., 171 NLRB No. 80, 68 LRRM 1120 (1968); National Cash Register Co., 201 NLRB No. 120, 82 LRRM 1353 (1973).

operations into a completely new operation;[82] (2) a renewal of operations at the same location after an undetermined amount of time; or (3) a renewal of operations at a new location after a time lapse.[83]

4. *Purchasers.* A contract will bar an election during its term, despite a change in ownership. The successor employer may not doubt its obligation to or the majority status of the incumbent union.[84]

5. *Accretions.* The Board uses the following guidelines to judge whether or not a new operation should come under the coverage of the existing plant's contract, thereby barring an election:

A. The degree of interchange among employees;

B. Geographic proximity;

C. Integration of operations;

D. Integration of machinery and product lines;

E. Centralized administrative control;

F. Similarity of working skills, conditions, and functions;

G. Common control over labor relations;

H. Collective bargaining history;

I. The size and number of employees at the facility to be acquired as compared with the existing operation.

If the contract contains an "accretion" clause covering future acquisitions, the Board will treat any related dispute as either a question of contract interpretation or a question of whether or not an accretion exists.[85]

6. *Schism.* A contract will not bar an election if a schism develops, a situation that stems from either (1) an intra-union dispute over basic policy questions or (2) employee action that results in the deterioration of the bargaining representative to the point where an election is necessary for the restoration of stability. Only Communism and corruption have been considered schismatic by the Board in the past.[86]

7. *Defunctness.* If the union has become defunct, the contract with the employer will not act as a bar. Defunctness exists where the union no

[82]National Car-loading Corp., 167 NLRB 116, 66 LRRM 1166 (1967); General Electric Co., 170 NLRB 153, 67 LRRM 1561 (1968); General Electric Co., 185 NLRB No. 4, 74 LRRM 1710 (1970).
[83]Slater Sys. Maryland, Inc., 134 NLRB 865, 49 LRRM 1294 (1961); Rheem Mfg. Co., 188 NLRB No. 67, 76 LRRM 1311 (1971).
[84]William J. Burns International Detective Agency, Inc., 406 U.S. 272, 80 LRRM 2225 (1972), aff'g 77 LRRM 2081; Eklund's Sweden House Inn, Inc., 203 NLRB No. 56, 83 LRRM 1173 (1973).
[85]Morris, THE DEVELOPING LABOR LAW, p. 175; Public Service Co. of New Hampshire, 190 NLRB No. 68, 77 LRRM 1129 (1971); cf. Remington Rand Div. of Sperry Rand Corp., 190 NLRB No. 92, 77 LRRM 1240 (1971).
[86]Aleo Mfg. Co., 109 NLRB 1297, 34 LRRM 1554 (1954); Hershey Chocolate Corp., 121 NLRB 901, 42 LRRM 1460 (1958); Allied Chemical Corp., Specialty Chemical Division, Baker and Adamson Works, 196 NLRB No. 77, 80 LRRM 1026 (1972).

longer is an effective labor organization and is unwilling to "fulfill its responsibilities in administering the contract."[87]

Sec. 5–15. Filing the petition—What to file. The petition for an election must be in writing and signed. It must either be notarized or must contain a declaration by the person signing it that its contents are true and correct to the best of his knowledge.[88] Blank forms are obtainable at NLRB regional offices and should be used. (See Facsimile No. 2, p. 63.) In filing the petition, one original and four copies must be submitted to the appropriate regional office.

Sec. 5–16. Filing the petition—Contents. The petition form, in brief, contains the name and address of the party filing the petition, the name and address of the employer's establishment, a description of the unit claimed to be appropriate, the approximate number of employees involved, and the names of all labor organizations which claim to represent the employees.

The Board has held that the petition was valid where blanks were left unanswered,[89] or where the petition contained such technical defects as failure to indicate either the number of employees supporting the petition or that a request for recognition has been made to the employer.[90] While the validity of the petition is usually upheld where the defects are cured at the subsequent hearing,[91] it is better practice to fill out the form completely and special care should be taken to show the employer's name accurately. The Board has ruled that the petitioner has the duty to indicate any claims by other unions, of which he may be aware, to represent the same employees.[92] Where the petitioner has withheld such information, the Board has set aside the election.[93]

Sec. 5–17. Filing the petition—Description of unit. In filling out the petition, particular care should be taken in describing the desired unit of employees; inaccurate or ambiguous language may: (a) invite argument as to the employees covered and thus block the possibility of complete agreement on a consent election; (b) lead to intervention from other labor organizations; (c) render the unit inappropriate under the provisions of the statute or the Board's rulings; or (d) provide a basis for challenging ballots.

---

[87]Hershey Chocolate Corp., 121 NLRB 901, 42 LRRM 1460 (1958); Aircraft Turbine Service Inc., 173 NLRB No. 110, 69 LRRM 1406 (1968); Loree Footwear Corp., 197 NLRB No. 61, 80 LRRM 1339 (1972).
[88]R. and R. Sec. 102.60.
[89]Petco Corp., 98 NLRB 150, 29 LRRM 1311 (1952).
[90]Padgett Printing and Lithographing Co., 101 NLRB 144, 31 LRRM 1024 (1952).
[91]NLRB v. National Truck Rental Co., Inc., 239 F.2d 422, 38 LRRM 2781 (C.A.D.C., 1956).
[92]Somerville Iron Works, Inc., 117 NLRB 1702, 40 LRRM 1073 (1957).
[93]*Ibid.*

The petitioner's description of the bargaining unit should include sufficient detail to make identification of the group as simple as possible. Also, the classifications of employees to be excluded from the unit should be specified. For example, where a unit of "production and maintenance employees" is sought, the petitioner should also indicate such exclusions as "all guards, professional employees and supervisors as defined in the Act." However, a petition will not be dismissed because it fails to list such exclusions.[94]

Sec. 5–18. Showing of interest by petitioner. If the petition is filed by an employer, neither he nor the labor organization is required to submit information as to employee interest in the union involved.[95] It is sufficient for the employer's petition to be based on a request for recognition. No formal demand is required; for example, picketing for the purpose of obtaining recognition is equal to a demand on which the employer may base his petition.[96]

If the petition is filed by an employee, or group of employees, or a labor organization—and the petitioner is not a party to a current or a recently expired contract—it must be accompanied by a showing that at least 30 percent of the employees in the appropriate unit desire the union to be their bargaining agent or wish to have an NLRB election to make such a determination.[97]

The Act does not specifically require the showing of interest by a petitioning labor organization. The Board adopted the requirement as an administrative matter, to determine for itself whether or not further proceedings are warranted. Accordingly, the Board and the courts have repeatedly held that the showing of interest may not be questioned by any of the parties as a matter of right.[98] Thus, the showing submitted by the petitioning labor organization is always held in confidence by the Board,[99] and no party has the right to litigate such questions as: the adequacy of

[94]Sealed Power Corp., NLRB No. 7–RC–2109, 32 LRRM 1186 (1953).
[95]Hooker Electrochemical Co., 116 NLRB 1393, 38 LRRM 1482 (1956).
[96]Indegro Inc., 117 NLRB 386, 39 LRRM 1238 (1957).
[97]Statements of Procedure Sec. 101.18(a); Esso Standard Oil Co., 124 NLRB 1383, 45 LRRM 1020 (1959); Chrysler Corp., NLRB No. 7–RC–8185, 65 LRRM 1692 (1967).
[98]NLRB v. T.I. Case Co., 201 F.2d 597, 31 LRRM 2330 (C.A. 9, 1953).
[99]The Midvale Co., 114 NLRB 372, 36 LRRM 1575 (1955).

Form NLRB-502
(11-64)

Form Approved.
Budget Bureau No. 64-R002.14

UNITED STATES OF AMERICA
NATIONAL LABOR RELATIONS BOARD

PETITION

DO NOT WRITE IN THIS SPACE	
CASE NO	
DATE FILED	

INSTRUCTIONS.—Submit an original and four (4) copies of this Petition to the NLRB Regional Office in the Region in which the employer concerned is located.
If more space is required for any one item, attach additional sheets, numbering item accordingly.

The Petitioner alleges that the following circumstances exist and requests that the National Labor Relations Board proceed under its proper authority pursuant to Section 9 of the National Labor Relations Act.

1. Purpose of this Petition *(If box RC, RM, or RD is checked and a charge under Section 8(b)(7) of the Act has been filed involving the Employer named herein, the statement following the description of the type of petition shall not be deemed made.)*

(Check one)

☐ RC–CERTIFICATION OF REPRESENTATIVES—A substantial number of employees wish to be represented for purposes of collective bargaining by Petitioner and Petitioner desires to be certified as representative of the employees.

☐ RM–REPRESENTATION (EMPLOYER PETITION)—One or more individuals or labor organizations have presented a claim to Petitioner to be recognized as the representative of employees of Petitioner.

☐ RD–DECERTIFICATION—A substantial number of employees assert that the certified or currently recognized bargaining representative is no longer their representative.

☐ UD–WITHDRAWAL OF UNION SHOP AUTHORITY—Thirty percent (30%) or more of employees in a bargaining unit covered by an agreement between their employer and a labor organization desire that such authority be rescinded.

☐ UC–UNIT CLARIFICATION—A labor organization is currently recognized by employer, but petitioner seeks clarification of placement of certain employees: *(Check one)* ☐ In unit not previously certified ☐ In unit previously certified in Case No.

☐ AC–AMENDMENT OF CERTIFICATION—Petitioner seeks amendment of certification issued in Case No.

Attach statement describing the specific amendment sought.

2. NAME OF EMPLOYER		EMPLOYER REPRESENTATIVE TO CONTACT	PHONE NO.

3. ADDRESS(ES) OF ESTABLISHMENT(S) INVOLVED *(Street and number, city, State, and ZIP Code)*

4a. TYPE OF ESTABLISHMENT *(Factory, mine, wholesaler, etc.)*	4b. IDENTIFY PRINCIPAL PRODUCT OR SERVICE

5. Unit Involved *(In UC petition, describe PRESENT bargaining unit and attach description of proposed clarification.)*

Included

Excluded

6a. NUMBER OF EMPLOYEES IN UNIT:	
PRESENT	
PROPOSED (BY UC/AC)	

6b. IS THIS PETITION SUPPORTED BY 30% OR MORE OF THE EMPLOYEES IN THE UNIT?

FACSIMILE NO. 2
Form of petition used in election, decertification, union-shop deauthorization, unit clarification, and amendment of certification cases

☐ YES ☐ NO
*Not applicable in
R.M, U.C, and AC

(If you have checked box RC in 1 above, check and complete EITHER item "a or "b, whichever is applicable)

7a. ☐ Request for recognition as Bargaining Representative was made on .... and Employer
(Month, day, year)
declined recognition on or about................. *(If no reply received, so state)*
(Month, day, year)

7b. ☐ Petitioner is currently recognized as Bargaining Representative and desires certification under the act.

8. Recognized or Certified Bargaining Agent *(If there is none, so state)*

NAME .... AFFILIATION

ADDRESS .... DATE OF RECOGNITION OR CERTIFICATION

9. DATE OF EXPIRATION OF CURRENT CONTRACT, IF ANY *(Show month, day, and year)* | 10. IF YOU HAVE CHECKED BOX UD IN 1 ABOVE, SHOW HERE THE DATE OF EXECUTION OF AGREEMENT GRANTING UNION SHOP *(Month, day, and year)*

11a. IS THERE NOW A STRIKE OR PICKETING AT THE EMPLOYER'S ESTABLISH-MENT(S) INVOLVED? YES ...... NO ...... | 11b. IF SO, APPROXIMATELY HOW MANY EMPLOYEES ARE PARTICIPATING?

11c. THE EMPLOYER HAS BEEN PICKETED BY OR ON BEHALF OF .... A LABOR
(Insert name)

ORGANIZATION, OF .... SINCE ....
(Insert address) *(Month, day, year)*

12. ORGANIZATIONS OR INDIVIDUALS OTHER THAN PETITIONER (AND OTHER THAN THOSE NAMED IN ITEMS 8 AND 11c), WHICH HAVE CLAIMED RECOGNITION AS REPRESENTATIVES AND OTHER ORGANIZATIONS AND INDIVIDUALS KNOWN TO HAVE A REPRESENTATIVE INTEREST IN ANY EMPLOYEES IN THE UNIT DESCRIBED IN ITEM 5 ABOVE. (IF NONE, SO STATE.)

NAME	AFFILIATION	ADDRESS	DATE OF CLAIM *(Required only if Petition is filed by Employer)*

I declare that I have read the above petition and that the statements therein are true to the best of my knowledge and belief.

....
(Petitioner and affiliation, if any)

By... ....
(Signature of representative or person filing petition) *(Title, if any)*

Address ....
(Street and number, city, State, and ZIP Code) *(Telephone number)*

WILLFULLY FALSE STATEMENT ON THIS PETITION CAN BE PUNISHED BY FINE AND IMPRISONMENT (U.S. CODE, TITLE 18, SECTION 1001)

GPO 894-283

petitioner's showing of interest,[100] timeliness of submission,[101] currency of dates,[102] authenticity,[103] or subsequent revocation of authorizations.[104]

The Board relaxed the 30 percent showing of interest where a petition was filed pursuant to the Board's invitation after it had denied the petitioner's motion for clarification of the unit because of the age (20 years) of the certification.[105]

During a strike situation, the petition should be accompanied by a showing of interest of 30 percent of the number employed at the time the strike began. This 30 percent may come from the strikers, the nonstrikers, the replacements, or any combination thereof.[106]

As a practical matter, few unions file petitions without a showing of interest well above the Board's requirements. A survey conducted by the Board showed that petitioning unions won elections in only 19 percent of the cases where they had authorization cards from 30 percent to 50 percent of the employees but they won 52 percent of the elections where they had 50 percent to 70 percent of the cards and 74 percent where they had cards from more than 70 percent of the employees.[107]

Sec. 5–19. Showing of interest by intervenors. A union's showing of interest governs the extent to which it will be permitted to participate in the case. The 30 percent requirement applies only to a petitioning union and to another union asking to intervene which urges the adoption of a different appropriate unit from that sought by the petitioner. A union seeking to intervene in order to block a consent election or participate fully in the hearing must submit designations of at least 10 percent of the employees in the unit claimed by the petitioner. And a union which seeks limited intervention for the purpose of having its name on the ballot is permitted to do so by showing interest on the part of only one employee in the unit claimed to be appropriate. (Also, see Chapter 7.) All authorization cards by intervening unions must be dated prior to the close of the hearing or execution of a consent election agreement.

Sec. 5–20. Types of designation. The Act makes no requirement as to the form of evidence necessary to show interest in a labor organization.[108] Usually it consists of authorization cards signed by the employee and dated

[100]Morganton Full Fashioned Hosiery Co., 102 NLRB 134, 31 LRRM 1288 (1953); Modern Plastics Corp., 169 NLRB 716, 67 LRRM 1261 (1968).
[101]Wyman-Gordon Co., 117 NLRB 75, 39 LRRM 1176 (1957); Rappahannock Sportswear Co., Inc., 163 NLRB 703, 64 LRRM 1417 (1967).
[102]The Cleveland Cliffs Iron Co., 117 NLRB 668, 39 LRRM 1319 (1957).
[103]Barber-Colman Co., 130 NLRB 478, 47 LRRM 1373 (1961); Riviera Manor Nursing Home, 200 NLRB No. 53, 81 LRRM 1411 (1972), *suppl'g* 76 LRRM 1832.
[104]Reliable Mailing Service Co., 113 NLRB 1263, 36 LRRM 1459 (1955).
[105]F.W.D. Corporation, 138 NLRB 386, 51 LRRM 1042 (1962); Pickands, Mather and Co., Interlake Steamship Co. Div., 178 NLRB No. 20, 72 LRRM 1008 (1969), *aff'g* 70 LRRM 177.
[106]Field Manual 11022.3.
[107]Address by Chairman Frank W. McCulloch, Aug. 7, 1962.
[108]Lebanon Steel Foundry v. NLRB, 130 F.2d 404, 10 LRRM 760 (C.A.D.C., 1942).

at the time they are signed; this is the form preferred by the Board. In addition to such authorization cards, the Board has accepted: (1) lists of signatures; (2) applications for union membership;[109] and (3) cards expressing a desire for an election and certification of the petitioning union.[110]

Sec. 5–21. Adequacy of showing of interest. In passing upon the sufficiency of a petitioner's submitted showing of interest, the Board has ruled in these basic areas:

1. Undated authorization cards will be rejected;[111] they will not be counted, whether or not they are accompanied by dated cards.[112]
2. It is the better practice to submit cards which name the petitioning party.[113]
3. Authorization cards which name an organizing committee acting on behalf of a petitioning district and local are accepted as evidence of interest.[114]
4. Authorization cards which name the petitioner's parent organization are accepted as evidence of petitioner's interest,[115] and are added to those cards which designate the petitioning affiliate.[116]
5. Authorization cards signed before the petitioner transferred affiliation to another international are not accepted as evidence of the employees' interest in the new affiliation;[117] the Board requires the petitioner to make a new showing.
6. Authorization cards signed before the name of the petitioning local was changed to that of another local of the same international are accepted as evidence of a showing of interest.[118]
7. Authorization cards signed before the local petitioner's international union was expelled from the AFL-CIO are accepted as evidence of a showing of interest.[119]
8. Where a joint petition is filed by more than one union, it is immaterial whether the authorization cards indicate desire for individual or joint

---

[109]NLRB v. Somerset Shoe Co., 111 F.2d 681, 6 LRRM 706 (C.A. 1, 1940).
[110]Potomac Electric Power Co., 111 NLRB 553, 35 LRRM 1527 (1955).
[111]A. Werman and Sons, Inc., 114 NLRB 629, 37 LRRM 1021 (1955).
[112]Jefferson City Cabinet Co., NLRB No. 10–RC–3600; administrative decision, Jan. 14, 1957, 39 LRRM 1160 (1957).
[113]Olin Mathieson Chemical Corp., 114 NLRB 948, 37 LRRM 1073 (1955).
[114]Cab Service and Parts Corp., 114 NLRB 1294, 37 LRRM 1181 (1955).
[115]United States Gypsum Co., 118 NLRB 20, 40 LRRM 1120 (1957).
[116]NLRB v. Bradford Dyeing Association, 310 U.S. 318, 6 LRRM 684 (1940).
[117]Mohawk Business Machines Corp., 118 NLRB 168, 40 LRRM 1145 (1957).
[118]Atlantic Mills Servicing Corp. of Cleveland, Inc., 118 NLRB 1023, 40 LRRM 1305 (1957).
[119]Louisiana Creamery, Inc., 120 NLRB 170, 41 LRRM 1456 (1958).

representation; all the cards are accepted and counted in support of the joint petition.[120]

9. Authorizations to revoke checkoff are rejected as evidence of a showing of interest in support of an individual's petition to rescind union shop authority.[121]

10. In seasonal industries, it is sufficient to submit a showing of 30 percent of those currently employed in the unit at the time the petition is filed; it is not necessary to submit a 30-percent showing of those employed at the peak of the season.[122]

11. Where a union's petition is dismissed because of an inadequate showing of interest, it may file a new petition supported by the required number of authorization cards.[123] The petitioner in this situation may use the same authorization cards provided the petition is timely and the authorization cards are still current.

12. A valid contract with an employer covering all or part of the employees in the bargaining unit sought may be used as the showing of interest by the union signatory to the agreement.

The petitioner should always remember that, where the Board finds appropriate a unit other than the one sought in the petition, the showing of interest originally submitted may be inadequate in the new unit. This may mean either a dismissal of the petition,[124] or a later request for submission of an additional showing of interest.[125]

To avoid either result, the petitioner should submit its fullest showing of interest in any possible alternative unit which the petitioner, the employer or another union may be seeking. Where the alternative units are smaller than the one set forth in the petition, the showing of interest should be broken down so as to indicate the support in the smaller (e.g., craft) unit or units.

Sec. 5–22. Attack on showing of interest.   As indicated before, parties cannot, as a matter of right, attack the petitioner's showing of interest.[126] Furthermore, NLRB hearing officers are under instructions not to permit litigation of the showing of interest in a representation hearing,[127] and the Board's Rules and Regulations provide no administrative procedure whereby it may be contested by a party. However, the Board has conducted

[120]Vanadium Corp. of America, 117 NLRB 1390, 40 LRRM 1010 (1957); St. Louis Independent Packing Co., 169 NLRB 1106, 67 LRRM 1338 (1968).
[121]Valencia Baxt Express, Inc., 24–UD–21, 49 LRRM 1446 (1962).
[122]Bordo Products Co., 117 NLRB 313, 39 LRRM 1220 (1957).
[123]U.S. Rubber Co., 91 NLRB 293, 26 LRRM 1477 (1950).
[124]E.I. duPont de Nemours and Company, 116 NLRB 286, 38 LRRM 1242 (1956).
[125]E.I. duPont de Nemours and Company, 117 NLRB 1048, 39 LRRM 1381 (1957).
[126]NLRB v. T.I. Case Co., 201 F.2d 597, 31 LRRM 2330 (C.A.9, 1953); Adelphi University, 195 NLRB No. 107, 79 LRRM 1545 (1972).
[127]Louisiana Creamery, Inc., 120 NLRB 170, 41 LRRM 1456 (1958).

special investigations and held collateral hearings into the nature of the showing of interest (e.g. whether the authorization cards were fraudulent).[128] To obtain such an investigation a party must submit data (e.g., affidavits) which are of sufficient weight to cast doubt on the reliability of the petitioner's showing of interest.[129] This data will not be accepted as evidence at the representation hearing, but should be submitted to the regional director[130] or to the Board in Washington.[131] If the investigation discloses that the remaining valid showing of interest falls below the required 30 percent, the petition will be dismissed.[132] However, if the remaining valid showing of interest satisfies the 30 percent interest requirement the petition will ordinarily be processed but the invalid portion of the showing may be turned over to the United States Attorney for possible prosecution under the United States Code.[133]

Sec. 5–23. 48-hour rule. Where the employer files the petition for an election, as stated above no showing of interest is required but he must submit to the regional office proof of demand by the labor organization for recognition. This proof must be submitted along with the petition or within 48 hours. This proof may consist of a letter from the union containing the demand, an affidavit of an oral demand, or other evidence which establishes the raising of a question concerning representation. Otherwise, the petition is subject to dismissal.

Where an individual, a group of employees or a labor organization files the petition for an election, the showing of interest also must be submitted along with the petition or within 48 hours of the filing, "but in no event later than the last day on which the petition might timely be filed."[134] Upon the failure to produce the data within the 48 hours, the petition is subject to dismissal. However, upon a showing of good cause, the regional director may grant one extension of time up to 10 days, within which the data may be submitted. For example, the designations may not be readily available because the employees are scattered over a large area.

Neither the Act nor the Rules and Regulations require completion of the Board's investigation of the showing of interest before the hearing. Accordingly, the Board has ruled that some authorization cards submitted more than 48 hours after filing of the petition—before the opening of the hearing or at the hearing—may be accepted.[135]

---

[128]Globe Iron Foundry, 112 NLRB 1200, 36 LRRM 1170 (1955); cf. American Beauty Baking Co., 198 NLRB No. 50, 81 LRRM 1228 (1970); M.P.C. Restaurant Corp., 198 NLRB No. 13, 81 LRRM 1457 (1970).
[129]*Ibid.*
[130]Royal Jet, Inc., 113 NLRB 1064, 36 LRRM 1477 (1955).
[131]Globe Iron Foundry, 112 NLRB 1200, 36 LRRM 1170 (1955).
[132]Columbia Records, 125 NLRB 1161, 45 LRRM 1244 (1959).
[133]Title 18 U.S.C., Section 1001.
[134]Statements of Procedure Sec. 101.17.
[135]Channel Master Corp., 114 NLRB 1486, 37 LRRM 1196 (1955).

CHAPTER 6

Prehearing Handling of the Election Petition

Sec. 6–1. In general. Immediately upon the docketing of a petition for a representation election, a written notification of its filing is sent by the regional director to the employer and to all labor organizations who either: (1) claim to represent any employees in the unit described in the petition; or (2) have an interest in the disposition of the case.

Sec. 6–2. Letter to the parties. The notification contains a copy of the petition and the name of the Board agent to whom the case has been assigned. The letter may ask recipients to submit:

1. Copies of any existing or recently expired contracts.
2. Documentary material—such as letters—which bear upon the question concerning representation.
3. The names of any parties who should be informed of the proceeding. (See Facsimiles No. 3–6A, pages 72–81.)

Employers are ordinarily asked to submit:

1. A payroll list covering the employees in the requested bargaining unit. Unless this list is submitted, the petitioner's estimate of the number of employees involved will be viewed as accurate, and those who designate the union as their bargaining agent will be considered as within the unit. The payroll list should be of those employees employed as of the date of the petition; the names should be in alphabetical order and accompanied by their appropriate job classification. During a strike situation, the payroll list as of the date of the start of the strike will be requested, as will lists for all other dates on which additional employees join the strike. This list is used by the regional office to check the union's showing of interest, and it should not be confused with the Excelsior list.[1] (See Sec. 6–3, page 82.)

[1] NLRB Field Manual 11024.4.

T-6(4/9/73)

NATIONAL LABOR RELATIONS BOARD

REGION 12

Room 706, Federal Building, 500 Zack Street, P.O. Box 3322

Tampa, Florida 33601   Telephone 228-7711

Gentlemen:

A petition for certification as collective bargaining representative of certain of
your employees has been filed with this office, pursuant to the Labor Management
Relations Act, as amended. A copy of the petition is enclosed. Should you desire
further information before a Board agent communicates with you, telephone or write
the office to which the case is being assigned, referring to the above case name
and number.

Any party to this proceeding may be represented by counsel or other representative,
and notification thereof may be made on the enclosed Notice of Appearance (Form
NLRB-4701) and mailed promptly to this office. Also, if desired, enclosed Form
NLRB-4813 may be executed and likewise mailed by an <u>authoritative official</u> of any
party to this proceeding for the purpose of designating counsel or representative,
who is entering appearance in the party's behalf, as agent to receive <u>exclusive</u>
service of documents as mentioned in Form 4813. However, if in addition to counsel
or representative, the party wants to receive service of such documents for <u>direct</u>
information, Form 4813 should not be filed. Enclosed Form NLRB-4812 explains some
basic representation case procedures.

When determined that it is appropriate to conduct an election, our role is to determine whether or not a majority of the non-supervisory employees within an appropriate
bargaining unit desire to be represented by the participating labor organization.
Such determination is normally made by our conduct of a secret ballot vote among the
concerned unit employees, and we encourage parties to mutually permit us, through our
consent election procedure which is explained in Form NLRB-4812, to conduct a secret
ballot vote, thereby affording the employees an opportunity to freely express their
preference. Such consent procedure eliminates any need for a hearing, which involves
both time and expenses for all concerned. It is hoped that when appropriate, this
matter can be so handled.

In order that we may check the sufficiency of the required proof of interest submitted in support of the petition, you are requested to furnish us with an alphabetized list, with job titles, of all non-supervisory employees <u>solely</u> within the
unit set forth in the petition. <u>Prompt</u> submission is urged and in no event may
timely submission be made later than 96 hours (Mon-Fri) preceding the date of any
scheduled hearing. The list should be dated and reflect the payroll period ending
on or immediately preceding the petition filing date, contain full available names
and not just initials, and should be submitted to the assigned Board office
indicated herein below.

FACSIMILE NO. 3
*Form of letter to employer when representation petition
filed by union or employees*

T-6

-2-

If there is an existing or recently expired collective bargaining contract covering any or all of the employees encompassed by the petition, a copy should be submitted. Should labor organizations other than the petitioner claim to represent any of the employees in petitioner's proposed unit, please furnish their names and addresses and facts relating thereto.

It has been our experience when a representation petition is filed, that it is helpful to the employees if an early announcement thereof is made, together with an explanation of rights, responsibility and Board procedures. Observation has likewise shown the desirability of informing employers and unions of their obligation to refrain from conduct which would impede employees' freedom of choice.

Accordingly, you are requested to post the enclosed Notice to Employees (NLRB-666) in conspicuous places in areas where employees, such as those described in the enclosed petition, work and to inform me whether they have been posted and if additional copies are needed. Copies of this Notice are being made available to the labor organization(s) involved. If an election is not conducted pursuant to this petition, the posted Notice should be removed.

In the event an election is hereafter conducted, the Board will require that a second list be filed by the employer with the undersigned, containing the names and addresses of all eligible voters. To be timely, such list when requested must be filed within 7 days from the date of either the direction of election or approval of election agreement. In accordance with established Board policy, this eligibility list will be made available to all parties to the case.

Your cooperation in bringing this matter to an early conclusion will be appreciated.

Very truly yours,

Harold A. Boire

Harold A. Boire
Regional Director

Enclosures

cc:

Case Assigned to	Telephone Number	Address

FACSIMILE NO. 3. *Second page*

NATIONAL LABOR RELATIONS BOARD

REGION 12

Room 706, Federal Building, 500 Zack Street

Tampa, Florida 33602   Telephone 228-7711

Gentlemen:

A petition has been filed with this office by the above-named
employer, pursuant to the provisions of the Labor Management
Relations Act, as amended. A copy of the petition is enclosed.

The case is being assigned to a staff member of the office shown
below, who will communicate with you as early as feasible. Any
inquiries, in the meantime, should be directed to the office shown
below to which the case is being assigned, and all communications
should refer to the above case name and number.

Attention is called to the right of any party to be represented by
counsel or other representative in a proceeding before the National
Labor Relations Board and the courts. Such designation should be
made on the enclosed Notice of Appearance (Form NLRB-4701) and mailed
promptly to this office.

It has been our experience that, by the time a petition such as this
one has been filed, employees may have questions about what is going
on and what may happen. At this point, it is not known what disposition will be made of the petition, but experience has shown that an
explanation of rights, responsibilities and Board procedures can be
helpful to the employees covered by the petition. The Board believes
that employees should have readily available information about their
rights and the proper conduct of employee representation elections.
Likewise, it feels that employers and unions should be apprised of
their responsibilities to refrain from conduct which could impede
employees' freedom of choice.

FACSIMILE NO. 4.
Form of letter to union when representation petition
filed by employer (RM)

T-8(a)

- 2 -

Accordingly, the employer is being requested to post the enclosed
Notice to Employees in conspicuous places in areas where employees
such as those described in the enclosed petition work, and to
advise me whether they have been posted. The employer is being
alerted to remove such posted Notice, in the event an election is
not conducted pursuant to this petition.

Your cooperation in bringing this matter to an early conclusion will
be appreciated. Should you make inquiry regarding this case, please
refer to the case name and number, addressing your letter to the
office shown below.

Very truly yours,

Harold A. Boire

Harold A. Boire
Regional Director

Enclosures

Case assigned to	Telephone Number	Address

FACSIMILE NO. 4. *Second page*

T-8

NATIONAL LABOR RELATIONS BOARD

REGION 12

Room 706, Federal Building, 500 Zack Street

Tampa, Florida   33602   Telephone 228-7711

Gentlemen:

The petition which you filed in the above-captioned case, pursuant to
the provisions of the Labor Management Relations Act, as amended, is
being assigned to a staff member who will communicate with you as
soon as feasible. A copy of the petition is attached. In accordance
with Section 101.17 of the Board's Statements of Procedure, as amended,
the petitioning employer must supply within 48 hours after filing,
proof of demand for recognition by the labor organization named in the
petition and, in the event said labor organization is the incumbent
representative of the unit involved, a statement of the objective
considerations demonstrating reasonable grounds for believing that
said labor organization has lost its majority status.

Attention is called to the right of any party to be represented by
counsel or other representative in a proceeding before the National
Labor Relations Board and the courts. Such designation should be
made on the enclosed Notice of Appearance (Form NLRB-4701) and mailed
promptly to this office.

In the event an election, either directed or by mutual agreement, is
hereafter conducted, the Board will require that a list of names and
addresses of all eligible voters be filed by the employer with the
undersigned, who will in turn make it available to all parties to the
case. To be timely such list, when required upon the approval of an
election agreement or direction of an election, must be filed with
the undersigned within 7 days from the date of such approval or
direction.

FASCIMILE No. 5
*Form of letter to employer when representation petition
filed by employer (RM)*

T-8

- 2 -

It has been our experience when a representation petition is filed, that it is helpful to the employees if an early announcement thereof is made, together with an explanation of rights, responsibility and Board procedures. Observation has likewise shown the desirability of informing employers and unions of their obligation to refrain from conduct which would impede employees' freedom of choice.

Accordingly, you are requested to post the enclosed Notice to Employees in conspicuous places in areas where employees such as those described in the enclosed petition work, and to advise me whether they have been posted, and if additional copies are needed. Copies of this Notice are being made available to the labor organization involved. In the event an election is not conducted pursuant to this petition, you are requested to remove the posted Notice.

Your cooperation in bringing this matter to an early conclusion will be appreciated. Should you make inquiry regarding this case, please refer to the case name and number, addressing your letter to the office shown below.

Very truly yours,

Harold A Boire

Harold A. Boire
Regional Director

Enclosures

Case assigned to	Telephone Number	Address

FACSIMILE NO. 5. *Second page*

T-7(a) (6/28/73)

NATIONAL LABOR RELATIONS BOARD

REGION 12

Room 706, Federal Building, 500 Zack Street, P.O. Box 3322

Tampa, Florida 33601   Telephone 228-7711

Gentlemen:

A petition for decertification of your organization has been filed with
this office, pursuant to the Labor Management Relations Act, as amended.
A copy of the petition is enclosed. This matter is being assigned to a
staff member of the office shown below, who will communicate with you as
early as feasible.

In the meantime, you are requested to furnish us with a statement of your
position. If there is any current contract which you claim to be a bar,
please submit a copy thereof. Such submission should be made, preferably,
to the office to which the case is being assigned and should refer to the
above case name and number.

Any party to this proceeding may be represented by counsel or other representative, and notification thereof may be made on the enclosed Notice of
Appearance (Form NLRB-4701) and mailed promptly to this office.

Also, if desired, enclosed Form NLRB-4813 may be executed and likewise
mailed by an authoritative official of any party to this proceeding for
the purpose of designating counsel or representative, who is entering
appearance in the party's behalf, as agent to receive exclusive service
of documents as mentioned in Form 4813. However, if in addition to counsel
or representative, the party wants to receive service of such documents for
direct information, Form NLRB-4813 should not be filed. Enclosed Form
NLRB-4812 explains some basic representation case procedures.

When determined that it is appropriate to conduct an election, our role is
to determine whether or not a majority of the non-supervisory employees
within the bargaining unit desire to continue to be represented by the
present bargaining representative. Such determination is normally made by
our conduct of a secret ballot vote among the concerned unit employees, and
we encourage parties to mutually permit us, through our consent election
procedure which is explained in Form NLRB-4812, to conduct a secret ballot
vote, thereby affording the employees an opportunity to freely express their

FACSIMILE NO. 6.
*Form of letter to union when petition for
decertification (RD) has been filed*

T-7(a) (6/28/73)

-2-

preference.   Such consent procedure eliminates any need for a hearing,
which involves both time and expense for all concerned.   It is hoped
that when appropriate, this matter can be so handled.

It has been our experience when a representation petition is filed, that
it is helpful to the employees if they have knowledge of the Board's
procedures as well as their rights, and the responsibilities of the employer
and the union to respect such rights, and that the union and employer be
informed of such obligation.

Accordingly, the employer is being requested to post the enclosed Notice
to Employees in conspicuous places in areas where employees as described
in the enclosed petition work, and to inform me whether they have been
posted.   In the event an election is not conducted pursuant to this petition
the employer is being asked to then remove the posted Notice.

Your cooperation will be appreciated, so that this matter can be brought
to an early conclusion.

Very truly yours,

Harold A. Boire

Harold A. Boire
Regional Director

Enclosures

cc:

Case assigned to	Telephone number	Address

FACSIMILE NO. 6. *Second page*

T-7 (6/29/74)

NATIONAL LABOR RELATIONS BOARD

REGION 12

Room 706, Federal Building, 500 Zack Street, P.O. Box 3322

Tampa, Florida 33601   Telephone 228-2641

Gentlemen:

A petition for decertification of representative has been filed with this office,
pursuant to the provisions of the Labor Management Relations Act, as amended. A
copy of the petition is attached.

This case is being assigned to a staff member of the office shown below who will communicate with you at an early date. However, in the meantime, to expedite our investigation, you are requested to submit the following information.

1. An alphabetized list of the full available names (not just initials) of
    unit employees, with job titles or classifications, for the payroll period
    ending on or immediately preceding the filing date of the petition, which
    list is used to check the sufficiency of Petitioner's proof of interest.
    Prompt submission thereof is requested and to be timely it must be sub-
    mitted and received no later than 96 hours (Mon.-Fri.) preceding the date
    of any scheduled hearing.

2. All correspondence, contracts and board certification, if any, bearing
    upon the question of representation. This would include correspondence
    with the Petitioner and any current or recently expired contracts with
    the recognized or certified representative covering any of the employees
    in the unit set forth in the petition.

3. Names and addresses of any other organizations which have or claim an
    interest in the unit covered by this petition.

Any party to this proceeding may be represented by counsel or other representative, and notification thereof may be made on the enclosed Notice of Appearance (Form
NLRB-4701) and mailed promptly to this office.

Also, if desired, enclosed Form NLRB-4813 may be executed and likewise mailed by an
authoritative official of any party to this proceeding for the purpose of designating
counsel or representative, who is entering appearance in the party's behalf, as agent
to receive exclusive service of documents as mentioned in Form 4813. However, if in
addition to counsel or representative, the party wants to receive service of such
documents for direct information, Form 4813 should not be filed. Enclosed Form NLRB-
4812 explains some basic representation case procedures.

FACSIMILE NO. 6A.
*Form of letter to employer when petition
for decertification (RD) has been filed*

T-7 (6/29/74

- 2 -

It has been our experience when a representation petition is filed, that it is helpful to the employees if an early announcement thereof is made, together with an explanation of rights, responsibility and Board procedures. Observation has likewise shown the desirability of informing employers and unions of their obligation to refrain from conduct which would impede employees' freedom of choice.

Accordingly, you are requested to post the enclosed Notice of Employees (NLRB-666) in conspicuous places in areas where employees, such as those described in the enclosed petition, work and to inform me whether they have been posted and if additional copies are needed. Copies of this Notice are being made available to the labor organization(s) involved. If an election is not conducted pursuant to this petition, the posted Notice should then be removed.

In the event an election is hereafter conducted, the Board will require that a second list be filed by the employer with the undersigned, containing the names and addresses of all eligible voters. To be timely, such list when requested must be filed within 7 days from the date of either the direction of election or approval of election agreement. In accordance with established Board policy this eligibility list will be made available to all parties to the case.

Your cooperation in bringing this matter to an early conclusion will be appreciated.

Very truly yours,

Harold A. Boire
Regional Director

Enclosures

cc:

Case assigned to	Telephone Number	Address

FACSIMILE NO. 6A. *Second page*

2. Data showing the nature of the company's business and its volume of operations for jurisdictional purposes. (See Facsimile No. 7, page 83.)
3. A position on the appropriateness of the bargaining unit requested and whether or not the employer is willing to consent to an election.

Included in the initial letters to the parties is a request that they post a notice to employees (See Facsimile No. 8, page 84.) containing information about employee rights and the proper conduct of employee representation elections. This is a request only and failure to post the notice is not considered sufficient cause to set aside the election.

The letters also include Form 4701 (see Facsimile No. 9, page 86), which is used to notify the Agency of a party's desire to be represented by counsel, Form 4814 (see Facsimile No. 10, page 87), which is used to designate a representative as the agent for service of documents,[2] and Form 4812, a brief statement of representation case procedures (see Facsimile No. 11, page 88.)

Sec. 6–3. Excelsior lists. The letter also advises the employer that he is required to furnish to the regional director a list of the names and addresses of all eligible voters in the event that an election is directed or a consent-election agreement is approved. This list, generally referred to as the Excelsior list, must be filed with the regional director within seven days of the direction of or agreement to an election.[3] The names and addresses should be listed in a systematic manner (i.e., alphabetically, by clock or card numbers, either as a whole unit or by departments or units). The list will be used as the voting list and should be kept up to date.[4] (See Sec. 9–2, page 155.)

Sec. 6–4. The Board agent's investigation. In his investigation, the Board agent will seek to determine:

1. Whether the employer's operations affect commerce within the meaning of the statute.
2. The appropriateness of the unit of employees for the purposes of collective bargaining.
3. The existence of a question concerning representation.
4. Where a labor organization is petitioning for the election, whether the labor organization has been designated by at least 30 percent of the employees.

[2]NLRB Field Manual 11000.7.
[3]NLRB Field Manual 11002.
[4]NLRB Field Manual 11312.3; Excelsior Underwear Inc., 156 NLRB No. 111, 61 LRRM 1217 (1966); NLRB v. Wyman-Gordon Co., 394 U.S. 759, 70 LRRM 3345 (1969), *revs'g and remand'g* 68 LRRM 2483.

GENERAL COMMERCE QUESTIONNAIRE

1.   The exact name of the company _____

2.   Is it a corporation, partnership, an individual doing business under a trade
name, or other type of ortanization? If a corporation, please give the State in which
incorporated.   If a partnership, please give the name and address of each partner and
his share of interest in the business.   If an individual, please give his name and
address and the name under which he is doing business.

_____

_____

3.   Location of headquarters or principal office or place of business.

_____

4 (a) If the company is affiliated with other companies, please give the names and
locations, and nature of affiliation, such as parent company, or subsidiary.

_____

      (b) Is the company a member of an Employer Association? _____ If so, give names
of Associations. _____

5.   The type and location of all plants, projects, or businesses operated by the
company _____

_____

6.   The materials purchased to be used or handled by the company at the operation
involved in this purchasing _____

7.   The products manufactured, goods or merchandise handled, or a brief description
of operations or service performed at the operation involved in this proceeding.

_____

8 (a) A reasonable estimate of the value of materials, supplies, or merchandise used
or handled during the past 12-month period _____

      (b) The approximate percentage thereof shipped to you directly from outside the
State _____

9 (a) A reasonable estimate of the value of goods or merchandise sold, service rendered, or products manufactured, processed, or sold by the establishment during the
past 12-month period (that is, the gross revenues of the establishment).

_____

      (b) The approximate percentage thereof sold or shipped or destined to points out-
side the State _____

10.   Has the company done any work for or furnished materials or parts to any other
companies apparently engaged in interstate commerce? _____
If so, give dollar value of such services or materials furnished during the past 12-
month period. _____

11.   Do any of your operations have any connection with the defense program, or do
you service any other company engaged in the defense program? _____

_____

_____
      (date)

_____   _____
      (signature)   (title)

FACSIMILE NO. 7.
General commerce questionnaire

Form NLRB 666
(7–72)

★NOTICE TO EMPLOYEES

FROM THE

National Labor Relations Board

A PETITION has been filed with this Federal agency seeking an election to determine whether certain employees want to be represented by a union.

The case is being investigated and NO DETERMINATION HAS BEEN MADE AT THIS TIME by the National Labor Relations Board.   IF an election is held Notices of Election will be posted giving complete details for voting.

It was suggested that your employer post this notice so the National Labor Relations Board could inform you of your basic rights under the National Labor Relations Act.

YOU HAVE THE RIGHT under Federal Law

- To self-organization

- To form, join, or assist labor organizations

- To bargain collectively through representatives of your own choosing

- To act together for the purposes of collective bargaining or other mutual aid or protection

- To refuse to do any or all of these things unless the union and employer, in a state where such agreements are permitted, enter into a lawful union security clause requiring employees to join the union.

It is possible that some of you will be voting in an employee representation election as a result of the request for an election having been filed.   While NO DETERMINATION HAS BEEN MADE AT THIS TIME, in the event an election is held, the NATIONAL LABOR RELATIONS BOARD wants all eligible voters to be familiar with their rights under the law IF it holds an election.

FACSIMILE NO. 8.
Notice to employees (Form 666)

The Board applies rules which are intended to keep its elections fair and honest and which result in a free choice. If agents of either Unions or Employers act in such a way as to interfere with your right to a free election, the election can be set aside by the Board. Where appropriate the Board provides other remedies, such as reinstatement for employees fired for exercising their rights, including backpay from the party responsible for their discharge.

NOTE:

The following are examples of conduct which interfere with the rights of employees and may result in the setting aside of the election.

- Threatening loss of jobs or benefits by an Employer or a Union

- Misstating important facts by a Union or an Employer where the other party does not have a fair chance to reply

- Promising or granting promotions, pay raises, or other benefits, to influence an employee's vote by a party capable of carrying out such promises

- An Employer firing employees to discourage or encourage union activity or a Union causing them to be fired to encourage union activity

- Making campaign speeches to assembled groups of employees on company time within the 24-hour period before the election

- Incitement by either an Employer or a Union of racial or religious prejudice by inflammatory appeals

- Threatening physical force or violence to employees by a Union or an Employer to influence their votes

Please be assured that IF AN ELECTION IS HELD every effort will be made to protect your right to a free choice under the law. Improper conduct will not be permitted. All parties are expected to cooperate fully with this agency in maintaining basic principles of a fair election as required by law. The National Labor Relations Board as an agency of the United States Government does not endorse any choice in the election.

NATIONAL LABOR RELATIONS BOARD
an agency of the
UNITED STATES GOVERNMENT

THIS IS AN OFFICIAL GOVERNMENT NOTICE AND MUST NOT BE DEFACED BY ANYONE

FACSIMILE NO. 8. Second page

Form NLRB-4701
(7-68)

National Labor Relations Board
NOTICE OF APPEARANCE

CASE NO.

TO: (Check one box only)1/

/ / Regional Director   / / Executive Secretary   / / General Counsel
                            National Labor   National Labor
                            Relations Board   Relations Board
                            Washington, D. C. 20570   Washington, D. C. 20570

The undersigned hereby enters his appearance as representative of _____

in the above-captioned matter.

Signature of representative (please sign in ink)	Representative's name, address, zip code (print or type)	
Date		
	Area Code	Telephone Number

1/ If case is pending in Washington and Notice of Appearance is sent to the General Counsel or the Executive Secretary, a copy should be sent to the Regional Director of the Region in which the case was filed so that his records will reflect the appearance.

GPO 927-003

FASCIMILE NO. 9.
Notice of appearance (Form 4701)

Form NLRB-4813
(7-72)

National Labor Relations Board

NOTICE OF DESIGNATION OF REPRESENTATIVE
AS AGENT FOR SERVICE OF DOCUMENTS

CASE NO.

TO: Regional Director,

I, the undersigned party, hereby designate my representative, whose name and address appears below and who has entered an appearance on my behalf in this proceeding, as my agent to receive exclusive service of all documents and written communications relating to this proceeding, including complaints and decisions and orders, but not including charges, amended charges, subpoenas, directions of election or notices of election, and authorize the National Labor Relations Board to serve all such documents only on said representative. This designation shall remain valid until a written revocation of it signed by me is filed with the Board.

Signature of party (please sign in ink)	Representative's name, address, zip code (print or type)	
Title		
Date	Area Code	Telephone Number

GPO 933-911

FASCIMILE NO. 10.
*Notice of designation of representative as agent
for service of documents (Form 4813)*

FORM NLRB-4812
(1-73)

NATIONAL LABOR RELATIONS BOARD

NOTICE: PARTIES INVOLVED IN A REPRESENTATION PETITION SHOULD BE AWARE OF THE FOLLOWING PROCEDURES:

Right to be represented by counsel

Any party has the right to be represented by counsel or other representative in any proceeding before the National Labor Relations Board and the courts. In the event you wish to have a representative appear on your behalf, please have your representative complete Form NLRB-4701, Notice of Appearance, and forward it to the respective regional office as soon as counsel is chosen.

Designation of representative as agent for service of documents

In the event you choose to have a representative appear on your behalf, you may also, if you so desire, use Form NLRB-4813 to designate that representative as your agent to receive exclusive service on your behalf of all formal documents and written communications in the proceeding, excepting decisions directing an election and notices of an election, and further excepting subpoenas, which are served on the person to whom they are addressed. If this form is not filed, both you and your representative will receive copies of all formal documents. If it is filed copies will be served only upon your representative, and that service will be service upon you under the statute. The designation once filed shall remain valid unless a written revocation is filed with the Regional Director.

Investigation of petition

Immediately upon receipt of the petition, the regional office conducts an impartial investigation to determine if the Board has jurisdiction, whether the petition is timely and properly filed, whether the showing of interest is adequate, and if there are any other interested parties to the proceeding or other circumstances bearing on the question concerning representation.

Withdrawal or dismissal

If it is determined that the Board does not have jurisdiction or that other criteria for proceeding to an election are not met, the petitioner is offered an opportunity to withdraw the petition. Should the petitioner refuse to withdraw, the Regional Director dismisses the petition and advises the petitioner of the reason for the dismissal and of the right to appeal to the Board.

Agreement and conduct of election

Upon the determination that the criteria are met for the Board to conduct a secret ballot election to resolve the question concerning representation, the parties are afforded the opportunity to enter into a consent election agreement. There are two forms: An Agreement for Consent Election provides that the parties accept the final determination of the Regional Director; a Stipulation for Certification Upon Agreement for Consent Election provides for the right of appeal to the Board on postelection matters. The secret ballot election will be conducted by an agent of the NLRB under the terms of the agreement and the parties shall have the right to observe and certify to the conduct of the election.

Hearing

If there are material issues which the parties cannot resolve by agreement, the Regional Director may issue a notice of hearing on the petition. At the hearing, all parties will be afforded the opportunity to state their positions and present evidence on the issues.

Scheduling of a hearing does not preclude the possibility of a consent election agreement. Approval of an agreement will serve as withdrawal of the notice of hearing.

Names and addresses of eligible voters

Upon approval of an election agreement, or upon issuance of a direction of election, the employer will be required to prepare a list of the names and addresses of eligible voters. The employer must file the eligibility list with the Regional Director within 7 days after approval of the election agreement, or after the Regional Director or the Board has directed an election. The Regional Director then makes the list available to all other parties. The employer is advised early of this requirement so that he will have ample time to prepare for the eventuality that such a list becomes necessary. (This list is in addition to list of employees in the proposed unit and their job classifications to be used to verify the showing of interest by a union.)

FACSIMILE NO. 11.
Statement of representation case procedures

5. Where an employer is the petitioner, whether a demand for collective bargaining rights has been made upon him.
6. If a strike is currently taking place, all pertinent data, including date of commencement of the strike, nature of the strike, number of employees, and whether strikers have been replaced.[5]

Frequently the Board agent will rely on telephone consultation, the information submitted in response to the director's initial letter, or personal contact with individual parties, but he may arrange joint conferences of the parties. These informal conferences are intended to determine the respective positions of the parties and to secure pertinent information. After full investigation, the petition may be disposed of informally, or the regional office may institute formal proceedings.

Sec. 6–5. Amendment of petition. Although the Board's Rules and Regulations make no provision for the amendment of a petition, the petitioner may do so at any point during the investigation. A petition may be amended, using the regular petition form, in one of two ways:

1. By restating in the "amended petition" the original contents together with the desired changes; or
2. By stating in the "amended petition" the changes that are to be made in the original petition.

As in the instance of the original petition, it is perfectly proper for the petitioner to ask the assistance of the Board agent in the preparation of the amendment.

The Board has held that a petitioner may amend its unit request at any time before the close of the hearing.[6] In the event that the petitioner seeks a unit larger than the one originally requested, at least a 30 percent showing of support in the larger unit is required.[7]

Sec. 6–6. Informal disposition of the petition. A petition may be disposed of before a formal hearing in three ways:

1. Withdrawal of the petition by the petitioning party.
2. Dismissal of the petition by the regional director.
3. Adjustment by consent of the parties to an election.

---

[5]Sec. 9(c)(3).
[6]Cohn Goldwater Manufacturing Co., 103 NLRB 399, 31 LRRM 1531 (1953); Peabody Coal Co., 197 NLRB No. 152, 81 LRRM 1156 (1972).
[7]Carbide and Carbon Chemicals Corp., 88 NLRB 437, 25 LRRM 1341 (1950); Long Stores Inc., 129 NLRB 1495, 47 LRRM 1221 (1961).

Sec. 6–7. Withdrawal of a petition. The petitioner may on its own motion ask to withdraw the petition. Or, the Board agent may request that the withdrawal be made because, among other possible reasons:

1. The desired unit is not appropriate.
2. A written contract blocks further investigation at that time.
3. The petitioning union has failed to submit an adequate showing of interest.[8]
4. Further processing of the petition is blocked by unresolved unfair labor practice charges.[9] (See also Sec. 7–3, page 107.)

Where the petitioner seeks to withdraw the petition, a form for that purpose will be supplied. (See Facsimile No. 12, page 91.) Prior to the close of the formal hearing a petition may be withdrawn only with the consent of the regional director.[10] The case is closed as soon as the withdrawal is approved by the regional director.

Where the petitioner's request to withdraw the petition is denied, another procedure is followed. (See page 146, "Disclaimer and Withdrawal of Petition.") (For further discussion of withdrawal, see Chapter 8.)

Sec. 6–8. Dismissal of a petition. If a petition is not withdrawn, as requested by the Board agent, the regional director will dismiss the petition.[11] The regional director thereupon will send a letter to the parties informing them of his action. (See Facsimile No. 13, page 92.) This letter will state the grounds for the regional director's dismissal of the petition. Unless the petitioning party takes a timely appeal, the case is closed at this point.

The petitioning party has 10 days from receipt of the regional director's letter in which to appeal from his action. This is done by filing a request for review with the National Labor Relations Board in Washington, D. C.; eight copies must be filed and a copy sent to the regional director and to each of the other parties within the same 10 days. The request for review should contain a complete statement setting forth the facts and reasons upon which the appeal is based. It may be granted by the Board upon one or more of the following grounds only: (1) a substantial question of law is raised due to the absence of, or departure from, Board precedent; (2) there are compelling reasons for reconsideration of NLRB policy; (3) the request for review is accompanied by documentary evidence previously submitted to the regional director raising serious doubts as to the regional director's

---

[8]Statements of Procedure Sec. 101.18(b) and (c).
[9]R. and R., Sec. 102.75; Surprenant Mfg. Co. v. Alpert, 318 F.2d 396, 53 LRRM 2405 (1963); E. and R. Webb, Inc., 194 NLRB No. 176, 79 LRRM 1163 (1972).
[10]R. and R. Sec. 102.60.
[11]R. and R. Sec. 102.71 (as amended February 10, 1975).

NLRB 601
(7-57)

UNITED STATES OF AMERICA.
NATIONAL LABOR RELATIONS BOARD

WITHDRAWAL REQUEST

In the matter of _____ _____
                        (Name of case)   (Number of case)

This is to request withdrawal of the (petition) (charge) in the above case.

_____
(Name of Party Filing)

By _____
                (Name of Representative)

_____
(Title)

Date _____

Withdrawal request approved

_____
(Date)

_____
Regional Director,
National Labor Relations Board.

FACSIMILE NO. 12.
Form for requesting withdrawal of petition or charge

NATIONAL LABOR RELATIONS BOARD

Date

Petitioner

Re: Case Name
Case Number

Gentlemen:

The above-captioned case, petitioning for an investigation and certification/decertification of representatives under Section 9 (c) of the National Labor Relations Act, has been carefully investigated and considered.

As a result of the investigation, it appears that, because (it would not effectuate the purposes of the Act to assert jurisdiction herein/the petitioner has failed to submit evidence of designation as bargaining agent of a substantial number of employees involved/the unit of employees for which petitioner seeks to act as bargaining agent / seeks decertification_/ is inappropriate for collective bargaining purposes/etc.), further proceedings are not warranted at this time. I am, therefore, dismissing the petition in this matter.

Pursuant to the National Labor Relations Board Rules and Regulations, you may obtain a review of this action by filing a request for such a review with the National Labor Relations Board, Washington, D. C. 20570. A copy of such request for review must be served upon each of the other parties to the proceeding, including the undersigned. This request must contain a complete statement setting forth the facts and reasons upon which it is based. The request (original and six copies) should be filed within ten (10) days from the date of receipt of this letter, except that the Board may, upon good cause shown, grant special permission for a longer period within which to file.

Very truly yours,

Regional Director

cc: Other parties

Board

FACSIMILE NO. 13.
*Form of letter sent by regional director
informing the parties of his dismissal of the petition*

factual findings; (4) the regional director's action is, on its face, arbitrary or capricious; or (5) the petition raises issues which can best be resolved upon the basis of a record developed at a hearing.[12]

Where the petitioner desires an extension of time in which to file an appeal, a request should be addressed to the Board in Washington with copies to the other parties. The request addressed to the Board must be accompanied by proof of service upon the other parties.[13]

When the request for review is received by the Board in Washington, notice of its receipt will be sent to all interested parties by the Board's Executive Secretary. (See Facsimile No. 14, page 94.) Likewise, when the appeal has been decided by the Board, all parties will be notified of the action taken.

The Board may deny the request for review, which closes the case, or may grant review and: (1) reverse the regional director and order further processing of the case; or (2) uphold the regional director's dismissal of the case, stating the grounds for its action and citing appropriate Board precedents. (See Facsimile No. 15, page 95.)

Sec. 6–9. Adjustment by consent to an election. If the investigation discloses that the requirements for an election have been met, the Board agent will attempt to persuade the parties to adjust the representation dispute by agreeing to use the Board's informal election machinery. There are two types of informal adjustment:

1. The agreement for consent election.[14]
2. The stipulation for certification upon consent election.[15]

Both types of informal adjustment may be entered into by the parties at any stage of an election case before issuance of the regional director's decision in the matter. Either type of adjustment becomes effective only upon approval by the regional director. Prior to such approval, any party may insist upon changes in the terms of the adjustment or withdraw entirely. After approval by the regional director, another procedure applies. (See page 146, "Disclaimer and Withdrawal of Petition.")

The date of a representation election is often a most significant factor in the success or failure of a union organizing campaign. A vote at the peak of the drive is most desirable from the union's point of view and the filing of the petition is usually timed with this in mind. The employer, on the other hand, frequently tries to delay the election, both to gain time to persuade the employees they are better off without the union and to let the inherent

---

[12]*Ibid.*
[13]*Ibid.*
[14]R. and R. Sec. 102.62(a).
[15]R. and R. Sec. 102.62(b)

NATIONAL LABOR RELATIONS BOARD

Washington, D.C. 20570

Date

Petitioner

Re: Case Name
Case Number

Dear _____:

This will acknowledge receipt of your Request for Review of the Regional Director's dismissal of the petition in the above case. The Board will carefully consider your appeal and you will be advised subsequently of its decision.

Very truly yours,

Associate Executive Secretary

cc: Regional Director

Other parties

FACSIMILE No. 14.
Form of letter sent by the Board to all parties
advising them of receipt of an appeal

NATIONAL LABOR RELATIONS BOARD

Washington, D.C. 20570

Date

Petitioner

Re: Case Name
     Case Number

Dear _____:

    The Board has carefully considered your Request for Review of the Regional Director's dismissal of the petition in the above case and decided that as the unit requested by the Appellant did not include all the employees performing similar work in other departments of the Employer, the Regional Director was warranted in dismissing the petition on the ground that the unit sought was inappropriate. See (appropriate case citation).

Very truly yours,

Associate Executive Secretary

cc: Regional Director

    Other parties

FACSIMILE NO. 15.
Form of letter sent by the Board informing all parties
of its refusal to reverse a regional director's dismissal of petition

difficulty of sustaining interest in any such program take its toll. These are the tactical considerations which weigh heavily on the decision of whether or not to consent to an election.

Prior to the delegation of representation matters to the regional directors, a party could delay an election for several months by refusing to consent to an election. A formal hearing was thereby required and the case automatically transferred to the Board in Washington for decision. The delegation has substantially reduced the effectiveness of this technique. In fiscal 1973, for example, the regional directors issued their decisions, on the average, only 20 days after the close of hearing. Because of the approvals required and the Excelsior list requirements, it is rarely possible to hold a consent election earlier than three weeks after the petition is filed. On the other hand, most regional directors will approve dates for consent elections up to approximately two months after the filing date.

Other factors to be considered in deciding whether or not to consent to an election are:

1. Avoidance of employee resentment sometimes caused by what appears to be a party's effort to delay or avoid the bargaining process.
2. Saving the time and expense of a formal and public hearing.
3. Psychological advantages flowing from the practice of resolving disputes (including representation issues) by direct negotiation and agreement.
4. Advantage to the employer of resolving the problem quickly where rival unions are organizing and there is disruption in the plant.
5. Possibility of compromising differences over the scope of the bargaining unit, unit status of particular employees, and voter eligibility.
6. The effect of the new Board rule that bargaining will be ordered on the basis of authorization cards, despite the union's loss of an election in those cases where there are meritorious objections filed in the representation case.[16] (In the case of the agreement for consent election, the regional director will have final authority as to whether such objections are meritorious.)

Under both types of informal adjustment the parties agree that:

1. The employer is engaged in commerce, as illustrated by a brief statement of the commerce facts.
2. An appropriate unit exists and precisely what that unit covers.
3. An election shall be conducted at a certain date, time, and place.
4. A specific payroll shall be used to determine eligibility.

[16]NLRB v. Gissel Packing Co., 395 U.S. 575, 71 LRRM 2481 (1969).

5. As soon after the election as possible, the votes shall be counted and tabulated. Upon the conclusion of the counting, each party will be served with a tally of ballots.

Sec. 6–10. The agreement for consent election. The terms of the agreement for consent election are set forth in printed forms available at the Board's regional offices. (See Facsimile No. 16, page 98.) Under the terms of the consent agreement, in addition to those specified above, the parties agree that:

1. They waive their right to any hearing at any stage of the proceeding.[17]
2. The rulings of the regional director on all questions relating to the election (for example, eligibility to vote, validity of challenges and objections) shall be final and binding.[18] The Board cannot entertain any objections to the regional director's rulings unless they are arbitrary and capricious.[19] The Board itself has said: "In the absence of fraud, misconduct, or such gross mistakes as imply bad faith on the part of the regional director, we deem his determination to be final in consent elections, even though we might have reached a different conclusion."[20]
3. If challenged ballots are sufficient in number to affect the results of the count, the regional director shall conduct an investigation and rule upon the challenged ballots.
4. If objections to the conduct of the election are filed with the regional director and the other parties within five days of the issuance of the tally of ballots, the regional director shall conduct an investigation and rule upon the objections.
5. If the regional director finds that the objections to the conduct of the election have merit, he may: (a) set aside the results of the election; and (b) conduct a new election at a date, time, and place to be determined by him.[21]
6. The regional director shall issue to the parties a certificate of results— where a majority of the employees have voted against representation—or a certification of representatives—where a labor organization has received at least a majority of the valid ballots cast. (See Facsimiles No. 38 and 39, pages 202–203.) In either event, the

---

[17]NLRB v. Saxe-Glassman Shoe Corp., 209 F.2d 238, 31 LRRM 2271 (C.A. 1, 1953).
[18]Buffalo Arms, Inc. v. NLRB, 224 F.2d 105, 36 LRRM 2229 (C.A. 2, 1955); Delta Drilling Co., 169 NLRB 617, 67 LRRM 1251 (1968); Sports Coach Corp. of America, 203 NLRB No. 24, 83 LRRM 1152 (1973).
[19]*Ibid.*
[20]McMullen Leavens Co., 83 NLRB 948, 24 LRRM 1175 (1949).
[21]NLRB v. W. S. Hatch Co., 82 LRRM 2662 (C.A. 9, 1973), *enf.* 77 LRRM 1477.

NLRB-651
(12-61)

UNITED STATES OF AMERICA
NATIONAL LABOR RELATIONS BOARD

AGREEMENT FOR CONSENT ELECTION

Pursuant to a Petition duly filed under Section 9 of the National Labor Relations Act as amended, and subject to the approval of the Regional Director for the National Labor Relations Board (herein called the Regional Director), the undersigned parties hereby waive a hearing and AGREE AS FOLLOWS:

1. SECRET BALLOT.—An election by secret ballot shall be held under the supervision of the said Regional Director, among the employees of the undersigned Employer in the unit defined below, at the indicated time and place, to determine whether or not such employees desire to be represented for the purpose of collective bargaining by (one of) the undersigned labor organization(s). Said election shall be held in accordance with the National Labor Relations Act, the Board's Rules and Regulations, and the applicable procedures and policies of the Board, provided that the determination of the Regional Director shall be final and binding upon any question, including questions as to the eligibility of voters, raised by any party hereto relating in any manner to the election, and provided further that rulings or determinations by the Regional Director in respect of any amendment of any certification resulting therefrom shall also be final.

2. ELIGIBLE VOTERS.—The eligible voters shall be those employees included within the Unit described below, who were employed during the payroll period indicated below, including employees who did not work during said payroll period because they were ill or on vacation or temporarily laid off, employees in the military services of the United States who appear in person at the polls, employees engaged in an economic strike which commenced less than twelve (12) months before the election date and who retained their status as such during the eligibility period and their replacements, but excluding any employees who have since quit or been discharged for cause and employees engaged in a strike who have been discharged for cause since the commencement thereof, and who have not been rehired or reinstated prior to the date of the election, and employees engaged in an economic strike which commenced more than 12 months prior to the date of the election and who have been permanently replaced. At a date fixed by the Regional Director, the parties, as requested, will furnish to the Regional Director, an accurate list of all the eligible voters, together with a list of the employees, if any, specifically excluded from eligibility.

3. NOTICES OF ELECTION.—The Regional Director shall prepare a Notice of Election and supply copies to the parties describing the manner and conduct of the election to be held and incorporating therein a sample ballot. The parties, upon the request of and at a time designated by the Regional Director, will post such Notice of Election at conspicuous and usual posting places easily accessible to the eligible voters.

4. OBSERVERS.—Each party hereto will be allowed to station an equal number of authorized observers, selected from among the nonsupervisory employees of the Employer, at the polling places during the election to assist in its conduct, to challenge the eligibility of voters, and to verify the tally.

5. TALLY OF BALLOTS.—As soon after the election as feasible, the votes shall be counted and tabulated by the Regional Director, or his agent or agents. Upon the conclusion of the counting, the Regional Director shall furnish a Tally of Ballots to each of the parties. When appropriate, the Regional Director shall issue to the parties a certification of representatives or of results of election, as may be indicated.

6. OBJECTIONS, CHALLENGES, REPORTS THEREON.—Objections to the conduct of the election or conduct affecting the results of the election, or to a determination of representatives based on the results thereof, may be filed with the Regional Director within 5 days after issuance of the Tally of Ballots. Copies of such objections must be served upon the other parties at the time of filing with the Regional Director. The Regional Director shall investigate the matters contained in the objections and issue a report thereon. If objections are sustained, the Regional Director may in his report include an order voiding the results of the election and, in that event, shall be empowered to conduct a new election under the terms and provisions of this agreement at a date, time, and place to be determined by him. If the challenges are determinative of the results of the election, the Regional Director shall investigate the challenges and issue a report thereon. The method of investigation of objections and challenges, including the question whether a hearing should be held in connection therewith, shall be determined by the Regional Director, whose decision shall be final and binding.

7. RUN-OFF PROCEDURE.—In the event more than one labor organization is signatory to this agreement, and in the event that no choice on the ballot in the election receives a majority of the valid ballots cast, the Regional Director shall proceed in accordance with the Board's Rules and Regulations.

8. COMMERCE.—The Employer is engaged in commerce within the meaning of Section 2 (6) (7) of the National Labor Relations Act.

16—47668—7

FACSIMILE NO. 16.
First page of form of agreement for consent election

9. WORDING ON THE BALLOT.—Where only one labor organization is signatory to this agreement, the name of the organization shall appear on the ballot and the choice shall be "Yes" or "No." In the event more than one labor organization is signatory to this agreement, the choices on the ballot will appear in the wording indicated below and in the order enumerated below, reading from left to right on the ballot, or if the occasion demands, from top to bottom. (If more than one union is to appear on the ballot, any union may have its name removed from the ballot by the approval of the Regional Director of a timely request, in writing, to that effect.)
First.

Second.

Third.

10. PAYROLL PERIOD FOR ELIGIBILITY.—

11. DATE, HOURS, AND PLACE OF ELECTION.—

12. THE APPROPRIATE COLLECTIVE BARGAINING UNIT.—

If Notice of Representation Hearing has been issued in this case, the approval of this agreement by the Regional Director shall constitute withdrawal of the Notice of Representation Hearing heretofore issued.

        (Employer)

By ....
     (Name and title)   (Date)

Recommended:

    (Board Agent)   (Date)

Date approved ....

        Regional Director,
National Labor Relations Board.

Case No. ....

    (Name of Organization)

By ....
   (Name and title)   (Date)

   (Name of other Organization)

By ....
   (Name and title)   (Date)

GPO 937-446

FACSIMILE No. 16. *Second page*

regional director's certification has the same force and effect as if issued by the Board in Washington, D.C.[22]
7. Any rulings by the regional director in respect to any amendment of the certification shall be final.[23]

As to the subsequent effect to be given to consent election agreements in other proceedings, courts and the Board have ruled:

1. A consent election agreement does not constitute settlement of earlier unfair labor practices.[24]
2. A consent election agreement does not bar further action by the Board against earlier unfair labor practices.[25]
3. Certifications based on consent elections are not controlling on later unit determinations to be made by the Board or the regional director.[26]
4. Bargaining history based on a consent election agreement is not controlling on later unit determinations to be made by the Board or the regional director.[27]

Sec. 6–11. Difference between consent and directed election. From the foregoing it is apparent that the effect of the consent agreement is, with two exceptions, like that of the directed election after a hearing. Thus, in both instances, the regional director rules on all questions relating to the election, investigates and rules upon challenged ballots and objections to conduct of the election, and certifies the results. Also, neither the consent nor the directed election constitutes settlement of earlier unfair labor practices or bars further action on such practices. The principal exception is found in the scope of review of the director's action. In the case of the consent election, the Board or a court will consider only those actions of the director which are arbitrary and capricious. In the case of directed elections, as more fully explained in the discussion of requests for review (see page 143), rulings will be set aside if erroneous. The other exception is that, while the Board has been known to change a unit determination in subsequent proceedings, it ordinarily follows a determination made after a hearing in a prior matter.

Sec. 6–12. Stipulation for certification upon consent election. The terms of the stipulation for certification upon consent election differ chiefly from those of the consent election agreement in that:

[22]R. and R. Sec. 102.62(a).
[23]R. and R. Sec. 102.62(a).
[24]Fairfield Engineering Co. v. NLRB, 168 F.2d 67, 22 LRRM 2056 (C.A. 6, 1948).
[25]The Wallace Corp. v. NLRB, 323 U.S. 248, 15 LRRM 697 (1944).
[26]International Minerals and Chemical Corp., 113 NLRB 53, 36 LRRM 1249 (1955).
[27]Humble Oil and Refining Co., 115 NLRB 1485, 38 LRRM 1114 (1956).

1. In the stipulation for certification, the parties agree to waive their rights to any hearing before the election; in the consent election agreement, the parties waive any possible hearing.
2. In the stipulation for certification, the parties agree that the Board in Washington, D.C., shall finally determine all questions relating to the election (for example, validity of challenges and objections to the conduct of the election);[28] in the consent election agreement, the parties agree that the regional director shall make the final and binding decisions on such matters.

The terms of the stipulation for certification upon consent election are set forth in printed forms which are available at the NLRB field offices. (See Facsimile No. 17, pages 102–103.)

Under the terms of a stipulation for certification, post-election procedures are similar to those followed in contested cases where the regional director or the Board orders that the election be conducted, but final determination is made by the Board rather than the regional director. These procedures are discussed in Chapter 10, "Post-Election Procedures."

---

[28]Knapp-Sherrill Co. v. NLRB, 488 F.2d 655, 85 LRRM 2289 (C.A. 5, 1974), enf. 82 LRRM 1381.

FORM NLRB-652
(5-72)

UNITED STATES OF AMERICA
NATIONAL LABOR RELATIONS BOARD

STIPULATION FOR CERTIFICATION UPON CONSENT ELECTION

Pursuant to a Petition duly filed under Section 9 of the National Labor Relations Act, as amended, and subject to the approval of the Regional Director for the National Labor Relations Board (herein called the Regional Director), the undersigned parties hereby AGREE AS FOLLOWS:

1. SECRET BALLOT.—An election by secret ballot shall be held under the supervision of the said Regional Director, among the employees of the undersigned Employer in the unit defined below, at the indicated time and place, to determine whether or not such employees desire to be represented for the purpose of collective bargaining by (one of) the undersigned labor organization(s). Said election shall be held in accordance with the National Labor Relations Act, the Board's Rules and Regulations, and the applicable procedures and policies of the Board.

2. ELIGIBLE VOTERS.—The eligible voters shall be those employees included within the Unit described below, who were employed during the payroll period indicated below, including employees who did not work during said payroll period because they were ill or on vacation or temporarily laid off, and employees in the military services of the United States who appear in person at the polls, also eligible are employees engaged in an economic strike which commenced less than twelve (12) months before the election date and who retained their status as such during the eligibility period and their replacements, but *excluding* any employees who have since quit or been discharged for cause and employees engaged in a strike who have been discharged for cause since the commencement thereof, and who have not been rehired or reinstated prior to the date of the election, and employees engaged in an economic strike which commenced more than twelve (12) months prior to the date of the election and who have been permanently replaced. At a date fixed by the Regional Director, the parties, as requested, will furnish to the Regional Director, an accurate list of all the eligible voters, together with a list of the employees, if any, specifically excluded from eligibility.

3. NOTICES OF ELECTION.—The Regional Director shall prepare a Notice of Election and supply copies to the parties describing the manner and conduct of the election to be held and incorporating therein a sample ballot. The parties, upon the request of and at a time designated by the Regional Director, will post such Notice of Election at conspicuous and usual posting places easily accessible to the eligible voters.

4. OBSERVERS.—Each party hereto will be allowed to station an equal number of authorized observers, selected from among the nonsupervisory employees of the Employer, at the polling places during the election to assist in its conduct, to challenge the eligibility of voters, and to verify the tally.

5. TALLY OF BALLOTS.—As soon after the election as feasible, the votes shall be counted and tabulated by the Regional Director, or his agent or agents. Upon the conclusion of the counting, the Regional Director shall furnish a Tally of Ballots to each of the parties.

6. POST-ELECTION AND RUN-OFF PROCEDURE.—All procedure subsequent to the conclusion of counting ballots shall be in conformity with the Board's Rules and Regulations.

7. RECORD.—The record in this case shall be governed by the appropriate provisions of the Board's Rules and Regulations and shall include this stipulation. Hearing and notice thereof, Direction of Election, and the making of Findings of Fact and Conclusions of Law by the Board prior to the election are hereby expressly waived.

8. COMMERCE.—The Employer is engaged in commerce within the meaning of Section 2(6) of the National Labor Relations Act, and a question affecting commerce has arisen concerning the representation of employees within the meaning of Section 9(c). *(Insert commerce facts.)*

FACSIMILE NO. 17.
First page of form of stipulation for certification
upon consent election in a representation case

9. WORDING ON THE BALLOT.—Where only one labor organization is signatory to this agreement, the name of the organization shall appear on the ballot and the choice shall be "Yes" or "No." In the event more than one labor organization is signatory to this agreement, the choices on the ballot will appear in the wording indicated below and in the order enumerated below, reading from left to right on the ballot, or if the occasion demands, from top to bottom. *(If more than one union is to appear on the ballot, any union may have its name removed from the ballot by the approval of the Regional Director of a timely request, in writing, to that effect.)*

First.

Second.

Third.

10. PAYROLL PERIOD FOR ELIGIBILITY.—

11. DATE, HOURS, AND PLACE OF ELECTION.—

12. THE APPROPRIATE COLLECTIVE BARGAINING UNIT.—

If Notice of Representation Hearing has been issued in this case, the approval of this stipulation by the Regional Director shall constitute withdrawal of the Notice of Representation Hearing heretofore issued.

.... | ....
(Employer) | (Name of Organization)

.... | ....
(Address) | (Address)

By .... | By ....
(Name and Title)   (Date) | (Name and Title)   (Date)

Recommended:

.... | ....
(Board Agent)   (Date) | (Name of other Organization)

Date approved ....

.... | ....
Regional Director, | (Address)
National Labor Relations Board. |

Case No. .... | By ....
| (Name and Title)   (Date)

GPO 868-313

FACSIMILE No. 17. *Second page*

CHAPTER 7

The Representation Hearing

Sec. 7–1. Notice of hearing. If the parties cannot agree on one of the informal methods of determining the union's majority status, the regional director takes formal action by serving a notice of hearing on all interested parties. (See Facsimile No. 18, page 106.)[1]

The notice of hearing fixes the time and place of the hearing. There is no formal requirement as to the minimum number of days' notice the regional director must give to the parties, but he usually will attempt to give the parties at least five days.

Accompanying the notice of hearing will be a copy of the representation petition; a copy of National Labor Relations Board Form 4669, which replaces the hearing officer's opening statement (Facsimile No. 19, page 108; and a supplemental notice (Facsimile No. 20, page 110, which informs the parties: (1) they may still settle upon an informal adjustment of the case; and (2) they must follow a specified procedure to obtain a postponement of the hearing.

In seeking a postponement of the hearing, a party must:

1. Submit the request in writing to the regional director.
2. Set forth reasons, in detail, for the request.
3. Suggest alternative dates for any rescheduled hearing.
4. Obtain the positions of all other parties and set them forth in the request; where possible, the party requesting the postponement should secure the agreement of the other parties.
5. Serve copies of the request simultaneously on all other parties.

Before ruling upon a request for postponement of hearing, the regional director usually waits until all parties have had an opportunity to inform him of their position. His ruling is served on all parties.

Sec. 7–2. Consolidated cases. The regional director, acting for the General Counsel, may consolidate any pending cases, or sever cases which

[1]R. and R. Sec. 102.63

FORM NLRB-852
(4-72)

UNITED STATES OF AMERICA

BEFORE THE NATIONAL LABOR RELATIONS BOARD

Case No.

NOTICE OF REPRESENTATION HEARING

The Petitioner, above named, having heretofore filed a Petition pursuant to Section 9(c) of the National Labor Relations Act, as amended, 29 U.S.C. Sec. 151 et seq., copy of which Petition is hereto attached, and it appearing that a question affecting commerce has arisen concerning the representation of employees described by such Petition,

YOU ARE HEREBY NOTIFIED that, pursuant to Sections 3(b) and 9(c) of the Act, on the day of   , 19   , at

a hearing will be conducted before a hearing officer of the National Labor Relations Board upon the question of representation affecting commerce which has arisen, at which time and place the parties will have the right to appear in person or otherwise, and give testimony.

Signed at   on the   day of   , 19

Regional Director, Region
National Labor Relations Board

GPO 928-054

FACSIMILE NO. 18.
Notice of representation hearing

already have been consolidated.[2] The regional director may take this action either upon his own motion or upon the request of any party.

Sec. 7–3. Blocking charges. As a matter of policy, the Board will consider an unfair labor practice charge as blocking the processing of an election petition when:

1. A charge of unfair labor practices (other than a violation of Section 8(e)[3] is pending;[4]
2. That charge affects some or all of the employees involved in the election case; and
3. The charging party is also a party to the election case.

The Board will proceed if an unfair labor practice charge has been dismissed by the regional director even though an appeal from that dismissal is pending before the General Counsel.[5]

The Board will also proceed with the election case to its completion in certain section 8(a) and (b) cases if the charging party will execute a "Request to Proceed" and file it with the regional director.[6] (See Facsimile No. 21, page 111.) In the "Request to Proceed" the charging party waives any right to urge the illegal acts set forth in the charge as a basis for objections to any election based upon conduct occurring prior to the filing of the petition.

The Board will not honor a "Request to Proceed" where the charge alleges: (1) company domination of a labor organization,[7] or (2) bad faith bargaining by either the employer or the union. Whenever charges alleging violations of these sections of the statute[8] are pending, no action will be taken on the election case until final disposition of the charges.

Also, the Board has ruled that a copy of the "Request to Proceed" need not be served upon any other party;[9] and the request cannot affect in any way the processing or the merits of the unfair labor practice case.[10]

After an election petition is blocked by a pending unfair labor practice charge and the parties have been so notified by the Board, any party may

[2]R. and R. Sec. 102.72 (b) and (d); Great Atlantic and Pacific Tea Co., 116 NLRB 1463, 39 LRRM 1017 (1956); NLRB v. LaSalle Steel Co. 178 F.2d 829, 25 LRRM 2152 (C.A. 7, 1949); Port Huron Area School District, 63 LRRM 1109 (Mich. Bd., 1966).
[3]Holt Bros., 146 NLRB No. 45, 55 LRRM 1310 (1964); Templeton v. Dixie Color Printing Co., Inc., 77 LRRM 2392 (C.A. 5, 1971), vac'g and reman'g 74 LRRM 2206, 2319.
[4]Edward J. Schlachter Meat Co., Inc., 100 NLRB 1171, 30 LRRM 1418 (1952); Dufresne v. McCann Steel Co., 78 LRRM 2331 (D.C. Tenn., 1971); Bishop v. NLRB, 502 F.2d 1024, 87 LRRM 2524 (C.A. 5, 1974).
[5]Stewart-Warner Corp., 112 NLRB 1222, 36 LRRM 1176 (1955).
[6]Sears Roebuck & Co., 104 NLRB 311, 32 LRRM 1086 (1953).
[7]Edward J. Schlachter Meat Co., Inc., 100 NLRB 1171, 30 LRRM 1418 (1952).
[8]Sections 8(a)(2), 8(a)(5), and 8(b)(3).
[9]Wilson & Co., Inc., 81 NLRB 504, 23 LRRM 1383 (1949).
[10]Aerovox Corp., 104 NLRB 246, 32 LRRM 1078 (1953).

Form NLRB-4669
(1-68)   (R Cases)

STATEMENT OF STANDARD PROCEDURES IN FORMAL HEARINGS HELD
BEFORE THE NATIONAL LABOR RELATIONS BOARD PURSUANT TO
PETITIONS FILED UNDER SECTION 9 OF THE
NATIONAL LABOR RELATIONS ACT, AS AMENDED

The hearing will be conducted before a hearing officer of the National Labor Relations Board.

Parties may be represented by an attorney or other representative and present evidence relevant to the issues.

An official reporter will make the only official transcript of the proceedings and all citations in briefs or arguments must refer to the official record. After the close of the hearing, one or more of the parties may wish to have corrections made in the record. All such proposed corrections, either by way of stipulation or motion, should be forwarded to the Regional Director or to the Board in Washington (if the case is transferred to the Board) instead of to the hearing officer, inasmuch as the hearing officer has no power to make any rulings in connection with the case after the hearing is closed. All matter that is spoken in the hearing room will be recorded by the official reporter while the hearing is in session. In the event that any of the parties wish to make off-the-record remarks, requests to make such remarks should be directed to the hearing officer and not to the official reporter.

Statements of reasons in support of motions or objections should be as concise as possible. Objections and exceptions may upon appropriate request be permitted to stand to an entire line of questioning. Automatic exceptions will be allowed to all adverse rulings.

Five copies of all pleadings submitted during the hearing are to be filed with the hearing officer.

The sole objective of the hearing officer is to ascertain the respective positions of the parties and to obtain a full and complete factual record upon which the duties under Section 9 of the National Labor Relations Act may be discharged by the Regional Director or the Board. It may become necessary for the hearing officer to ask questions, to call witnesses, and to explore avenues with respect to matters not raised by the parties. The services of the hearing officer are equally at the disposal of all parties to the proceedings in developing the material evidence.

After close of hearing, any party who desires to file a brief may do so in the appropriate manner described below.

1.   Briefs filed with the Regional Director:

       Unless transfer of the case to the Board is announced prior to close of hearing, the brief should be filed in duplicate with the Regional Director. A typed brief with a carbon copy is acceptable. A copy must also be served upon each of the other parties and proof of such service must be filed with the Regional Director at the time the briefs are filed.

       The briefs shall be filed within 7 days after the close of the hearing unless an extension of time is granted by the hearing officer. As to any extension of time for filing briefs, the hearing officer is empowered to grant an extension not to exceed an additional 14 days upon request made before the hearing closes and for good cause.

FACSIMILE NO. 19.
*First page of statement of standard procedures
in representation case hearings (Form 4669)*

THE REPRESENTATION HEARING

Any request for an extension of time made after the close of the hearing must be received by the Regional Director not later than 3 days before the date the briefs are due. Such request must be in writing and copies must be served immediately upon each of the other parties.

2. Briefs filed with the Board in Washington, D. C.

    a. If transfer of case to Board is announced at the hearing:

        Eight copies of a brief, legibly printed or mimeographed, double-spaced, must be filed with the Board in Washington, D. C. Carbon copies of typewritten matter will not be filed and if submitted will not be accepted. A copy must also be served upon each of the other parties. Proof of such service must be filed with the Board simultaneously with the briefs.

        The briefs shall be filed within 7 days after the close of hearing unless an extension of time is granted by the hearing officer. As to any extension of time requested at the hearing, the hearing officer is empowered to grant an extension not to exceed an additional 14 days upon request made for good cause.

        Any request for an extension of time made after the close of hearing must be received by the Board in Washington not later than 3 days before the date the briefs are due. Such requests must be in writing and copies must be served immediately upon each of the other parties.

    b. Transfer of case to Board effected after close of hearing:

        Pursuant to Section 102.67 of the Board's Rules and Regulations, the Regional Director may at any time after the close of hearing and before decision, transfer a case to the Board for decision. The order transferring the case will fix a date for filing briefs in Washington.

        If briefs have already been filed with the Regional Director, the parties may file 8 copies of the same brief with the Board in the same manner as set forth in "a" above, except that service on the other parties is not required. No further briefs shall be submitted except by special permission of the Board.

        If the case is transferred to the Board before the time expires for filing of briefs with the Regional Director and before the parties have filed briefs, such briefs shall be filed as set forth in "a" above.

        Requests for extension of time shall be received by the Board not later than 3 days before the date such briefs are due in Washington, D. C. A copy of any such request shall be served immediately on each of the other parties and the Regional Director and shall contain a statement that such service has been made. No reply brief may be filed except upon special leave of the Board.

GPO 874-642

FACSIMILE NO. 19. *Second page*

FORM NLRB-4338
(7-72)

NATIONAL LABOR RELATIONS BOARD
N O T I C E

Case No. _____

The issuance of the notice of formal hearing in this case does not mean that the matter cannot be disposed of by agreement of the parties. On the contrary, it is the policy of this office to encourage voluntary adjustments. The examiner or attorney assigned to the case will be pleased to receive and to act promptly upon your suggestions or comments to this end. An agreement between the parties, approved by the Regional Director, would serve to cancel the hearing.

However, unless otherwise specifically ordered, the hearing will be held at the date, hour, and place indicated. Postponements *will not be granted* unless good and sufficient grounds are shown *and* the following requirements are met:

(1)   The request must be in writing. An original and two copies must be served on the Regional Director;

(2)   Grounds therefor must be set forth *in detail;*

(3)   Alternative dates for any rescheduled hearing must be given;

(4)   The positions of all other parties must be ascertained in advance by the requesting party and set forth in the request; and

(5)   Copies must be simultaneously served on all other parties *(listed below),* and that fact must be noted on the request.

Except under the most extreme conditions, no request for postponement will be granted during the three days immediately preceding the date of hearing.

GPO 861-472

FACSIMILE NO. 20
Supplemental notice regarding postponements
of representation case hearings (Form 4338)

FORM NLRB-4551
(10-62)

UNITED STATES OF AMERICA
NATIONAL LABOR RELATIONS BOARD

REQUEST TO PROCEED

In the matter of _____ _____
(Name of Case)   (Number of Case)

The undersigned hereby requests the Regional Director to proceed with the above-captioned representation case, notwithstanding the charges of unfair labor practices filed in Case No. _____.

It is understood that the Board will not entertain objections to any election in this matter based upon conduct occurring prior to the filing of the petition.

Date _____

By _____
                _____
                (Title)

FACSIMILE No. 21.
Form of request to proceed

obtain a review of the Board's action by filing a request with the NLRB in Washington, D.C. Grounds for review are limited to the following: (1) a substantial question of law is raised due to the absence of, or departure from, Board precedent; (2) there are compelling reasons for reconsideration of NLRB policy; (3) the request for review is accompanied by documentary evidence previously submitted to the regional director raising serious doubts as to the regional director's factual findings; (4) the regional director's action is, on its face, arbitrary or capricious; or (5) the petition raises issues which can best be resolved upon the basis of a record developed at a hearing.[11]

The same rules that apply to the filing of other requests for review in representation matters also govern the filing of a review of the Board's action in cases involving blocking charges. (See Sec. 6–8, page 90.)

Sec. 7–4. Prehearing motions. All motions made by the parties before the opening of the hearing must be filed with the regional director.[12] Motions should state briefly the action requested and the grounds for such request. (For example, if the moving party desires to intervene, a statement should be made of the grounds upon which the party claims an interest in the proceeding.) Copies of motions must be served immediately upon each of the parties.

The regional director may rule upon all motions filed with him, serving a copy of his ruling upon each of the parties, or he may refer the motion to the Board agent hearing the matter.

The regional director's rulings on motions to revoke subpoenas become part of the record at the hearing only upon request of the aggrieved party. Otherwise, all prehearing motions and rulings automatically become part of the record at the hearing.[13]Prehearing rulings by the regional director (other than dismissals of petitions) may not be appealed directly to the Board but may be considered by the Board in connection with a request for review of the regional director's decision.[14]

Sec. 7–5. Conduct of the hearing. The representation hearing usually is conducted in the region where the election petition originated and, with rare exceptions, is open to the public.

A verbatim transcript is made by an official reporter retained by the NLRB regional office; this constitutes the official record of the hearing. Copies may be purchased by the parties but must be ordered from the

---

[11]R. and R. Sec. 102.71(b); NLRB Field Manual 11730–11730.9; Surprenant Mfg. Co. v. Alpert, 318 F.2d 396, 53 LRRM 2405 (1963); E. and R. Webb, Inc., 194 NLRB No. 176, 79 LRRM 1163 (1972).
[12]R. and R. Sec. 102.65(a).
[13]R. and R. Sec. 102.65(c).
[14]R. and R. Sec. 102.65(c).

official reporter. A copy is also placed in the regional office formal file. Although available to parties and the public, its use is discouraged and the regional director will not permit removal of the transcript from the office. All citations and references made in briefs and motions must refer to the official record.

Sec. 7–6. Opening statement. The officer presiding over the hearing may be a Board attorney, field examiner, or administrative law judge. Information formerly included in an opening statement of the hearing officer is now enclosed with the notice of hearing. (See Facsimile No. 19, page 108.)

Sec. 7–7. Right of parties. At the hearing the parties are given full opportunity to present their respective positions and to produce data in support of their contentions. Each party has the power to call, examine, and cross-examine witnesses.

Sec. 7–8. Applications for subpoenas. Subpoenas are available to any party. They are obtained by filing a written application with the regional director if made before the opening of the hearing, or with the hearing officer at the hearing.[15] The application need not name either the witness or the documents sought. Also, notice of such application need not be communicated to the other parties.[16] The regional director or the hearing officer, as the case may be, must furnish the subpoenas requested. (See Facsimile Nos. 22 and 23, pages 114 and 115.)

If the person against whom the subpoena is issued does not intend to comply, he has five working days from the date of service within which to petition the regional director to revoke. Upon receipt of such petition, the regional director or hearing officer will give immediate notice to the party upon whose request the subpoena was issued.[17]

The regional director or hearing officer may revoke the subpoena, among other reasons, on the ground that the subpoena seeks evidence which does not relate to any matter under investigation; or the subpoena does not describe with sufficient particularity the evidence sought.

The regional director or hearing officer is required to make a statement of the reasons for his ruling.[18]

Failure to file a timely petition to revoke a subpoena may bar the party

[15]R. and R. Sec. 102.66(c).
[16]*Ibid;* Playskool, Inc., et al.; NLRB v., 74 LRRM 2662 (C.A. 7, 1970).
[17]R. and R. Sec. 102.66(c).
[18]*Ibid.*

NLRB-32
(11-55)

SUBPOENA

UNITED STATES OF AMERICA
NATIONAL LABOR RELATIONS BOARD

To _____

_____

Request therefor having been duly made by _____

_____

whose address is _____ _____ _____
　　　　　　　　　　　　　　(Street)　　　　　(City)　　　　(State)
YOU ARE HEREBY REQUIRED AND DIRECTED TO APPEAR before _____

_____ *of the National Labor Relations Board,*

at _____

in the City of _____

on the _____ *day of* _____, 19____, *at* _____ *o'clock* ____ *m.*

of that day, to testify in the Matter of _____

_____

_____

_____

A-　244027

In testimony whereof, the seal of the National Labor Relations Board is affixed hereto, and the undersigned, a member of said National Labor Relations Board, has hereunto set his hand and authorized the issuance hereof.

Issued at_____

this _____ day of _____, 19____

NOTICE TO WITNESS.—Witness fees for attendance, subsistence, and mileage, under this subpoena are payable by the party at whose request the witness is subpoenaed. A witness appearing at the request of the General Counsel of the National Labor Relations Board shall submit this subpoena with the voucher when claiming reimbursement.

FACSIMILE NO. 22.
*Form of subpoena used where testimony
is sought from the party to be served*

NLRB–31
(3-66)

SUBPOENA DUCES TECUM

UNITED STATES OF AMERICA
NATIONAL LABOR RELATIONS BOARD

To

Request therefor having been duly made by

whose address is

YOU ARE HEREBY REQUIRED AND DIRECTED TO APPEAR BEFORE
of the National Labor Relations Board,
at
in the City of
on the   day of   , 19   , at   o'clock   m.
of that day, to testify in the Matter of

And you are hereby required to bring with you and produce at said time and place the following books, records, correspondence, and documents:

B- 69701

In testimony whereof, the seal of the National Labor Relations Board is affixed hereto, and the undersigned, a member of said National Labor Relations Board, has hereunto set his hand and authorized the issuance hereof.

Issued at
this   day of   , 19

NOTICE TO WITNESS.—Witness fees for attendance, subsistence, and mileage, under this subpoena are payable by the party at whose request the witness is subpoenaed. A witness appearing at the request of the General Counsel of the National Labor Relations Board shall submit this subpoena with the voucher when claiming reimbursement.
16—62497-2

FACSIMILE NO. 23.
Form of subpoena used where testimony
and documents are sought from the party to be served

from making a subsequent attack on that subpoena, compelling him to produce the desired data.[19]

The petition to revoke a subpoena, any answer filed thereto, and the regional director's ruling on the petition become part of the record only upon request of the aggrieved party.[20]

Sec. 7–9. Appearances. Any party has the right to appear at a hearing in person, by counsel, or by other representatives. The NLRB does not prescribe rules of admission to practice before it or its hearing officers, and parties are not required to be represented by attorneys. Misconduct of an aggravated character on the part of any attorney or other representative may cause the Board to refuse the offender permission to practice further before it.[21]

Sec. 7–10. Sequence of the hearing. Usually the hearing follows this sequence:

1. The hearing officer notes for the record the appearances on behalf of the parties.
2. The hearing officer places in the record the so-called "formal papers." These consist of the petition, the notice of hearing, any prehearing motions and the rulings thereon, and affidavits of service.
3. Factual agreements—on such matters as the status of the labor organization or the operations of the company—are then placed in the record by stipulation.
4. If the size of the unit is a contested issue, the petitioner will be asked to proceed with relevant testimony. Other parties then produce direct testimony. Witnesses called by any party are subject to cross-examination.
5. The same procedure is followed on other contested issues.
6. At the conclusion of the hearing, the parties are entitled, upon request, to engage in oral argument.[22]

Sec. 7–11. Function of the hearing officer. The hearing officer who conducts the hearing is an agent of the regional director.[23] As the hearing is considered to be part of the investigation, it is his function to assure that the record includes a full presentation of factual material upon which the regional director or the Board, as the case may be, can decide the issues involved.[24]

---

[19]NLRB v. Stanley Gemalo, 130 F. Supp. 500, 35 LRRM 2577 (D.C.S.N.Y., 1955); Sprague, C.H. and Son Co., 74 LRRM 2641 (C.A. 1, 1970), *enf. as modified* 70 LRRM 1577.
[20]R. and R. Sec. 102.65(c).
[21]R. and R. Sec. 102.38, 102.44, 102.66.
[22]R. and R., Sec. 102.66(e).
[23]Rochester Metal Products, 94 NLRB 1779, 28 LRRM 1289 (1951).
[24]Altamont Knitting Mills, Inc., 101 NLRB 525, 31 LRRM 1103. (1952).

The hearing officer has authority to call, examine, and cross-examine witnesses and to call for documentary evidence for introduction into the record. Indeed, the Board has ruled that it is not improper for a hearing officer to develop "most of the evidence" on a critical issue by examination of witnesses, where the parties have failed to call their own witnesses.[25]

The hearing officer has the power to limit the testimony to relevant issues. Thus, he can stop examination of witnesses[26] or refuse to permit a line of testimony which produces no evidence.[27] Although leading questions may be asked of witnesses, the hearing officer may stop such questioning where the practice is being abused.[28]

The hearing officer is empowered[29] and required[30] to rule on all motions (except motions to dismiss the petition) referred to him or made at the hearing. Any motion to dismiss the petition must be referred by the hearing officer to the regional director or the Board, as the case may be.[31]

The hearing officer may, in his discretion, postpone the hearing or adjourn it to a later date or to a different place. He may do this either by oral announcement at the hearing or in writing.[32]

Sec. 7–12. Rules of evidence. Technically, representation hearings are nonadversary investigatory proceedings. As might be expected, however, the issues are often vigorously contested. The statute does not set forth rules of evidence to be used in representation proceedings but the Board, through its Rules and Regulations, states that the rules of evidence prevailing in the courts shall not be controlling.[33] Thus, the Board has repeatedly overruled objections which raise technicalities concerning the presentation of evidence.[34] Furthermore, it has been held that the provisions of the Administrative Procedure Act do not apply to the conduct of representation hearings.[35]

Sec. 7–13. Stipulations at hearings. From time to time in the course of the hearing—either on or off the record—the hearing officer may try to obtain all-party stipulations. These are factual agreements on issues

[25]United States Smelting, Refining & Mining Corp., 116 NLRB 661, 38 LRRM 1314 (1956); Allis-Chalmers Mfg. Co., Inc., 180 NLRB No. 41, 72 LRRM 1241 (1969).
[26]Ravenna Arsenal, Inc., 98 NLRB 1, 29 LRRM 1283. (1952).
[27]Sears Roebuck & Co., 112 NLRB 559, 36 LRRM 1060.(1955).
[28]Altamont Knitting Mills, Inc., 101 NLRB 525, 31 LRRM 1103 (1950).
[29]R. and R. Sec. 102.65(a).
[30]Father & Son Shoe Stores, Inc., 117 NLRB 1479, 40 LRRM 1032 (1957).
[31]R. and R. Sec. 102.65(a).
[32]R. and R. Sec. 102.64(b).
[33]R. and R. Sec. 102.66 (a).
[34]Jerome E. Mundy Co., 116 NLRB 1487, 39 LRRM 1019 (1956).
[35]International Union of Operating Engineers, Local No. 148 v. International Union of Operating Engineers, Local No. 2, 173 F.2d 557, 23 LRRM 2517 (C.A. 8, 1949); Bricklayers Union v. NLRB, 82 LRRM 2746 (C.A. D.C., 1973), enf. 79 LRRM 1432.

pertinent to the hearing, undertaken to narrow the contested issues and to shorten the hearing. The regional director or Board, as the case may be, will not be bound by any stipulation that is inconsistent with the statute or Board policy. Thus, contrary to all-party stipulations, the Board has excluded guards[36] and supervisors[37] from agreed-upon units. Likewise, the parties' stipulation that an employer is engaged in commerce within the meaning of the Act and that the Board should exercise jurisdiction is not binding. The Board may still determine whether assertion of jurisdiction would be contrary to its policy.[38] (See Chapter 3.)

Although the language of a stipulated unit may not in all respects be that usually employed by the Board, the regional director or Board, as the case may be, will decline to disturb the agreed-upon unit, as long as it does not violate Board policy.[39] The Board has ruled, however, that stipulated units even though not contrary to law or policy, do not establish Board policy with respect to unit composition.[40]

When entering into stipulations covering the composition of a unit, parties should make sure that they are acquainted with the duties of the employees who are to be included in or excluded from the unit. Referring to its well-established "policy of honoring concessions made in the interest of expeditious handling of representation cases,"[41] the regional director or Board, as the case may be, will refuse to reopen a record on the post-hearing plea of a party's oversight or lack of knowledge at the time it entered into the stipulation.[42]

Sec. 7–14. Amendment of petition. The petitioner may move during the hearing to amend the petition. It is the Board's settled policy to allow the parties to litigate all issues raised by such an amendment which have not been fully litigated previously.[43]

A petition amended during the hearing does not constitute a new petition, where:

1. The amendment merely particularizes the composition of the unit.[44]

[36]Colonial Shirt Corp., 114 NLRB 1214, 37 LRRM 1136(1959); Wallace-Murray Corp., 192 NLRB No. 160, 78 LRRM 1046 (1971).
[37]Central Cigar & Tobacco Co., 112 NLRB 1094, 36 LRRM 1151((1955); Loral Corp., 200 NLRB No. 153, 82 LRRM 1368 (1972); cf. Textron Inc. v. NLRB, 82 LRRM 2753 (C.A.2, 1973).
[38]East Newark Realty Corp., 115 NLRB 483, 37 LRRM 1328(1956).
[39]Hoffman Hardware Co., 112 NLRB 982, 36 LRRM 1140(1955).
[40]The Eavey Co., 115NLRB 1779, 38 LRRM 1177(1956).
[41]New York Shipping Assn., 109 NLRB 1075, 34 LRRM 1492 (1954).
[42]Stanley Aviation Corp., 112 NLRB 461, 36 LRRM 1028 (1955); Cruis Along Boats Inc., 128 NLRB 1019, 46 LRRM 1419 (1960); Sport Coach Corporation of America, 203 NLRB No. 24, 83 LRRM 1152 (1973).
[43]The DeLaval Separator Co., 97 NLRB 544, 29 LRRM 1124 (1951).
[44]Blatz Brewing Co., 94 NLRB 1277, 28 LRRM 1182 (1951).

2. The categories of employees involved in the amended petition are covered in the original petition.[45]
3. The petition is amended so as to seek, in the alternative, separate units rather than the single unit originally requested.[46]

Where the petition is amended during the hearing to embrace a substantially larger unit, the Board has ruled:

1. The petitioner is required to submit the required showing of interest in the larger unit;[47] and
2. The amended petition will not be dismissed if no party was prejudiced and if no valid collective bargaining agreement was executed by the company and another union between the time of filing the original petition and the amendment.[48]

Sec. 7–15. Motions before hearing officer. All motions made at the hearing must be made in writing or stated on the record.[49] If in writing, an original and four copies must be filed, and a copy served immediately upon each of the other parties.[50] The motion should state briefly the relief sought and the grounds for such motion.

As stated above, the hearing officer must rule on every motion, except a motion to dismiss the petition.[51] A motion to dismiss, which may be made in writing or orally,[52] must be referred to the regional director or the Board.

Motions are filed with the hearing officer during the hearing, with the regional director before and after the hearing and, if the case is transferred to the Board, with that body after the transfer takes place. The regional director or the Board, as the case may be, will consider such motions when considering the entire record of the proceeding.[53]

Rulings of the hearing officer may be made orally on the record or in writing.[54] If in writing, a copy will be served on each party. All motions, rulings, and orders become part of the record, except rulings on motions to revoke subpoenas.[55] The petition to revoke a subpoena, any answer filed,

---

[45] The Rauland Corp., 97 NLRB 1333, 29 LRRM 1258 (1952).
[46] Crossett Paper Mills, Division of Crossett Lumber Co., 98 NLRB 542, 29 LRRM 1396 (1952).
[47] Carbide & Carbon Chemicals Corp., 88 NLRB 437, 25 LRRM 1341 (1950).
[48] Cohn Goldwater Mfg. Co., 103 NLRB 399, 31 LRRM 1531 (1953); see also Hyster Co., 72 NLRB 937, 19 LRRM 1238 (1947).
[49] R. and R. Sec. 102.65(a).
[50] Ibid.
[51] R. and R. Sec. 102.65(a).
[52] Valley Concrete Co., 88 NLRB 519, 25 LRRM 1354 (1950).
[53] R. and R. Sec. 102.65(a).
[54] Ibid.
[55] R. and R. Sec. 102.65(c).

and a ruling thereon become part of the record only upon specific request of the aggrieved party.[56]

Sec. 7–16. Appeals from hearing officer. All rulings by the hearing officer are ultimately considered when the entire record is considered by the regional director or the Board.[57] In limited instances, rulings by the hearing officer may be appealed during the hearing by special permission of the director.[58] A party seeking to appeal a ruling by the hearing officer should:

1. Request the regional director for special permission to appeal, indicating why such early appeal is being sought and why appeal cannot be postponed.
2. State the ruling from which appeal is being taken, with supporting data to show why the ruling should be reversed.
3. Serve a copy of its request and supporting data upon each of the other parties.[59]

Sec. 7–17. Types of issues excluded from hearing. The Board has devised, through many decisions, procedural rules with respect to the types of evidence which will not be permitted to be introduced at representation hearings. Following are some basic areas in which testimony will not be received in the representation hearing:

1. The adequacy of the showing of interest submitted by a union.[60]
2. Allegations that authorization cards were procured by fraud, misrepresentation, or coercion,[61] or that they have been revoked,[62] or that they are stale,[63] or that supervisors influenced or participated in the union's acquisition of a showing of interest.[64]
3. The manner, method, or procedure employed by the Board in determining the showing of interest.[65]

[56]R. and R. Sec. 102.66(c).
[57]R. and R. Sec. 102.65(c).
[58]*Ibid.*
[59]*Ibid.*
[60]A. Werman & Sons, Inc., 114 NLRB 629, 37 LRRM 1021 (1955).
[61]Standard Cigar Co., 117 NLRB 852, 39 LRRM 1332 (1957); American Beauty Baking Co., 198 NLRB No. 50, 81 LRRM 1228 (1972), *suppl'g* 74 LRRM 1209.
[62]Reliable Mailing Service Co., 113 NLRB 1263, 36 LRRM 1459 (1955); General Dynamics Corp., 175 NLRB No. 155, 71 LRRM 1116 (1969).
[63]The Cleveland Cliffs Iron Co., 117 NLRB 668, 39 LRRM 1319 (1957).
[64]Georgia Kraft Co., 120 NLRB 806, 42 LRRM 1066 (1958); Southeastern Rubber Mfg. Co., Inc., 173 NLRB No. 119, 69 LRRM 1434 (1968); Adelphi University, 195 NLRB No. 107, 79 LRRM 1545 (1972).
[65]Pacific Gas & Electric Co., 97 NLRB 1397, 29 LRRM 1256 (1952).

4. Alleged commission of unfair labor practices by one of the parties, unless such matters are material to the question of whether a question concerning representation exists.[66]
5. The meaning of a contract's provisions, where the contract's language is clear and unambiguous.[67]
6. The practices of the contracting parties under union-security or checkoff clauses regardless of the contract's ambiguity.[68]
7. The eligibility of employees for union membership.[69]
8. The extent to which economic strikers have been replaced.[70]

Sec. 7–18. Oral argument. Any party is entitled, upon request, to a reasonable period for oral argument at the close of the hearing before the hearing officer.[71] Such oral argument will be included in the stenographic report of the hearing.

Sec. 7–19. Briefs. Parties have the right to file briefs with the regional director or the Board, as the case may be, within seven days after the close of the hearing.[72] However, the hearing officer is empowered to grant an additional 14 days for the submission of briefs, provided that the request for an extension of time is made before the close of the hearing.[73] Such request and supporting reasons must be stated on the record. The right to file briefs is announced by the hearing officer at the close of the oral argument.

Formerly, information with respect to filing briefs was announced by the hearing officer at the close of the hearing. This is now included in Form 4669 which is mailed to the parties with the notice of hearing. (See Facsimile No. 26, pages 134.)

Sec. 7–20. Payment of witnesses. Witness fees and mileage are paid by the party at whose request witnesses appear.[74] These fees are in the amount paid for like services in the federal courts. (See "Payment of Witnesses," page 278 for amounts.)

Sec. 7–21. Conduct at the hearing. The Board's rules covering the conduct of parties at the representation hearing are the same as in the unfair labor practice hearing, except that the hearing officer is substituted

[66]Foothill Electric Corp., 120 NLRB 1350, 42 LRRM 1184 (1958).
[67]Reading Hardware Corp., 85 NLRB 610, 24 LRRM 1446 (1949); see also Knife River Coal Mining Co., 96 NLRB 1, 28 LRRM 1474 (1951).
[68]Paragon Products Corp., 134 NLRB 662, 49 LRRM 1160 (1961).
[69]Northern Redwood Lumber Co., 88 NLRB 272, 25 LRRM 1307 (1950).
[70]Eastern Camera & Photo Corp., 140 NLRB 569, 52 LRRM 1068 (1963).
[71]R. and R. Sec. 102.66(e).
[72]R. and R. Sec. 102.67(a) and (i).
[73]Ibid.
[74]R. and R. Sec. 102.66(g).

for the administrative law judge. These rules are set forth on page 279 under "Conduct at the Hearing."

Sec. 7–22. Hearing officer's report. Shortly after the close of the hearing, the hearing officer submits a report to the regional director or the Board, as the case may be.[75] It consists of an analysis of the issues presented at the hearing and a summary of the evidence. The statute prohibits the hearing officer from including any recommendations in the report.[76] The Board has repeatedly ruled that the report is an administrative document and is therefore not available for inspection by any of the parties.[77]

Sec. 7–23. Intervention. The statute does not provide any standards or procedures whereby a labor organization may intervene in a representation case started by another labor organization, by an employer, by an individual, or by a group of employees. The Board's Rules and Regulations, however, state that intervention will be permitted to an interested person "to such extent and upon such terms as . . . (it) may deem proper."[78]

Sec. 7–24. Who may intervene. According to the Board's administrative practices and decisions, a union demonstrates sufficient interest to be permitted intervention where:

1. The union is party to a current contract[79] or to a recently expired contract[80] covering the employees involved;
2. The union has been certified[81] or is the currently recognized representative of the employees involved;
3. The union demanded recognition by the employer, and that demand was the basis on which the employer filed the petition;[82]
4. The union submits some timely showing of interest, "of any percentage," among the employees involved—for example, signed and dated authorization cards;[83]
5. A representative of the union (international) signed the contract between its affiliate (local) and the employer;[84]

---

[75]R. and R. Sec. 102.66(f).
[76]Sec. 9(c)(1).
[77]Radio Corporation of America, 89 NLRB 699, 26 LRRM 1022 (1950).
[78]Sec. 102.65(b).
[79]Pacific Metals Co., Ltd., 91 NLRB 696, 26 LRRM 1558 (1950).
[80]Soldwedel Co., 113 NLRB 225, 36 LRRM 1292 (1955).
[81]Vicksburg Hardwood Co., 62 NLRB 44, 16 LRRM 180 (1945).
[82]P. R. Mallory & Co., Inc., 89 NLRB 962, 26 LRRM 1079 (1950).
[83]Beneke Corp., 109 NLRB 1191, 34 LRRM 1537 (1954).
[84]Electric Products Co., 89 NLRB 218, 25 LRRM 1540 (1950); Manhattan College, 195 NLRB No. 23, 79 LRRM 1253 (1972).

6. The union (international) administers, through a trustee, the affairs of an affiliate which has a current contract with the employer.[85]

However, if a union seeks to be heard solely on the issue of unit, intervention may be permitted where it has no representation among the employees involved, but where:

1. The union represents another unit in the plant involved;[86]
2. The union has a substantial number of collective bargaining agreements in the industry involved;[87]
3. The union wishes to make certain that an appropriate unit, to which all parties agreed, is not defined so as to include employees represented by it;[88]
4. The union's only concern is to disaffirm any interest in the unit sought by the petitioner.[89]

An order permitting withdrawal of a petition with prejudice to filing of another petition for six months is a time limitation applicable only to a petitioner; it does not serve as a bar to intervention. Accordingly, an interested union is permitted to intervene in a hearing even though less than six months have elapsed since withdrawal with prejudice of its petition for the same bargaining unit.[90]

The regional director or the Board will deny intervention to:

1. A group of employees who do not wish any union to represent them.[91]
2. Individual employees who do not seek to function as bargaining representative.[92]
3. A union found by the Board to be company-dominated and which was ordered disestablished.[93]

Sec. 7-25. Extent of participation by intervening union. Where a union's status as intervenor is based on a showing of designations among the employees, the extent of its participation in the case is determined by

[85]The Great Atlantic and Pacific Tea Co., 120 NLRB 656, 42 LRRM 1022 (1958).
[86]Georgia Kraft Co., 120 NLRB 806, 42 LRRM 1066 (1958).
[87]Pacific Gas and Electric Co., 91 NLRB 615, 26 LRRM 1577 (1950).
[88]General Box Co., 82 NLRB 678, 23 LRRM 1589 (1949).
[89]The Fort Industry Co., 87 NLRB 1579, 25 LRRM 1278 (1949).
[90]California Furniture Shops, Ltd., 115 NLRB 1399, 38 LRRM 1080 (1956); Food Mart, 162 NLRB 1420, 64 LRRM 1197 (1967).
[91]Central Carolina Farmers Exchange, Inc., 115 NLRB 1250, 38 LRRM 1039 (1956).
[92]Alaska Salmon Industry, Inc., 82 NLRB 1395, 24 LRRM 1039 (1949).
[93]Brown Express, 80 NLRB 753, 23 LRRM 1135 (1948).

the number of designations submitted. The Board has established the following rules to govern participation:

1. A union can intervene only for the purpose of appearing on the ballot in the unit petitioned by another union, if its showing of interest is less than 30 percent.[94] The Board does not require a minimum showing of any particular percentage for an intervening union to appear on the ballot.[95]

2. An intervening union can both oppose the unit sought by the petitioner and seek its own unit, if its showing of interest is at least 30 percent of the employees in the latter unit.[96] Thus, an intervenor must submit: (a) at least a 30 percent showing in the craft unit, if it seeks to sever a craft unit from the petitioner's industrial unit;[97] or (b) a 30 percent showing in a unit which is substantially larger than that sought by the petitioner.[98] Accordingly, if the issue of an appreciably different unit is raised by an intervenor which has at least a 30 percent showing in its desired unit, it need not file a separate petition for that unit.[99]

3. An intervening union can block a consent election agreed to by the other parties, if its showing of interest is at least 10 percent of the employees in the agreed-upon unit.[100] Where the intervenor has less than a 10 percent showing (it may be only one or two designations), it will be permitted a place on the ballot provided it accepts the terms of the consent election agreement.[101]

4. Where an intervening union is party to a consent election agreement and the petitioning union withdraws from that agreement, the intervenor must submit a showing of at least 30 percent before the election will be conducted.[102]

5. The intervenor must have a showing of at least 30 percent to successfully oppose withdrawal of a petition, unless the petition was filed by an employer.[103] Where the petition was filed by an employer and the employer seeks withdrawal, the intervenor may obtain the election originally sought without submitting any showing of interest.[104]

---

[94]Comwel Co., 88 NLRB 810, 25 LRRM 1404 (1950).
[95]Beneke Corp., 109 NLRB 1191, 34 LRRM 1537 (1954).
[96]Boeing Airplane Co., 86 NLRB 368, 24 LRRM 1624 (1949).
[97]Ibid.
[98]Electric Auto Lite, 87 NLRB 129, 25 LRRM 1079 (1949).
[99]Tennessee Coach Co., 88 NLRB 253, 25 LRRM 1321 (1950); Tin Processing Corp., 80 NLRB 1369, 23 LRRM 1253 (1948).
[100]17 NLRB Ann. Rep. 31, fn. 19.
[101]Ibid.
[102]Dierks Paper Company, 120 NLRB 290, 41 LRRM 1490 (1958).
[103]International Aluminum Corp., 117 NLRB 1221, 39 LRRM 1407 (1957).
[104]Ibid.

Sec. 7–26. How to intervene. A motion for intervention must be filed by any person who desires to intervene in a representation proceeding. The motion must state the grounds upon which an interest is claimed in the proceeding.[105]

When the motion for intervention is filed before the opening of the hearing, it must be filed in writing with the regional director.[106] If filed at the hearing, it must be filed in writing with the hearing officer, or stated orally on the record.[107]

If the motion is made in writing, addressed to either the regional director or the hearing officer, the moving party must:

1. File an original and four copies of the motion; and
2. Serve a copy immediately upon each of the other parties to the proceeding.[108]

The regional director or the hearing officer, as the case may be, is empowered to permit intervention ". . . to such extent and upon such terms as he may deem proper,"[109] and the intervenor thereupon becomes a party to the proceeding. It is within the Board's discretion whether to entertain an appeal from the hearing officer's ruling. The procedure for appeal is the same as set forth on page 120, under "Appeals from hearing officer."

If the motion for intervention is filed after the transfer of the case to the Board, it must be filed in writing with the Board in Washington.[110] The requirements for this type of filing are set forth on page 129, under "Copies of Documents Submitted to Board."

Sec. 7–27. Timeliness of intervention. The Board has fashioned a number of rules which make it essential that motions for intervention and supporting data be filed in timely fashion; otherwise, the moving party may be injured. Accordingly, when a labor organization decides to intervene in a representation case, it should file the motion for intervention as early as possible.

Following are some of the basic Board rules which stress timeliness:

1. Where a labor organization files a motion for intervention with a regional director, it must submit evidence of interest. This evidence

[105] R. and R. Sec. 102.65(b).
[106] R. and R. Sec. 102.65 (a).
[107] *Ibid.*
[108] *Ibid.*
[109] R. and R. Sec. 102.65(b).
[110] R. and R. Sec. 102.65(a).

must be submitted along with the motion or within 48 hours. In the absence of any submitted data, the labor organization has no standing in the case.

2. If the union seeking intervention files its evidence of interest more than 48 hours later and after a consent election agreement has been approved by the regional director or after the hearing has closed, the union will not be permitted to participate in the case. However, its name may be added to the ballot in a consent election if the parties to the consent election agreement agree to the addition.

3. Where a consent election is to be held, the showing of interest necessary for an intervenor to participate must have been acquired and dated not later than the date of the consent election agreement.[111] However, the Board has denied intervention where the intervening union withdrew from the representation proceeding prior to signing of the stipulation between the employer and the petitioning union and the motion to intervene was filed five days before the date of the election.[112] The extent of the intervenor's participation will be determined by the number of such timely designations. (See page 123 under "Extent of participation by intervening union.")

4. The showing of interest on which an intervenor may rely in order to participate in a proceeding must be acquired and dated before the close of the hearing.[113] Thus, after the hearing, the Board: (a) permits intervention to a union which has not received notice of the hearing, where the union submits a showing of interest as of the time of the hearing;[114] and (b) denies a motion to intervene where there is not evidence of any interest acquired by the union before the hearing closed.[115]

The Board permits two exceptions to the rule that an intervening union's showing of interest must have been acquired before the close of the hearing: (a) where the representation proceeding was delayed by filing of unfair labor practice charges and the original petitioner was, by its own practices, in part responsible for such delay; and (b) where a labor organization claims to be the authorized successor of the contracting labor organization.[116]

A motion to intervene after the close of hearing will be denied where authorization cards are falsely dated. Thus, the Board has denied intervention where investigation revealed that certain authorization cards,

[111]Stationers Corp., 99 NLRB 240, 30 LRRM 1057 (1952).
[112]Trane Co., 137 NLRB 1506, 50 LRRM 1434 (1962).
[113]Metropolitan Life Insurance Co., 90 NLRB 935, 26 LRRM 1294 (1950).
[114]United Boat Service Corp., 55 NLRB 671, 14 LRRM 48 (1944).
[115]Arrow Mill Co., 92 NLRB No. 166 (not reported), 27 LRRM 1224 (1951).
[116]Bull Insular Line, Inc., 107 NLRB 674, 33 LRRM 1224 (1954).

although dated prior to the hearing, were actually signed after close of the hearing.[117]

The Board has granted intervention after issuance of decision directing an election and placed the intervening union on the ballot where: (a) some of the intervenor's members were included in the unit; (b) the intervenor had not been aware of either the petition or the inclusion of its members in the unit; and (c) the intervenor immediately filed a request for intervention and submitted a timely and adequate showing of interest.[118]

[117]Miller Container Corp., 115 NLRB 509, 37 LRRM 1344 (1956).
[118]Southeastern Illinois Gas Co., Division of United Cities Gas Co. 119 NLRB 1665, 41 LRRM 1366 (1958).

CHAPTER 8

Posthearing Procedures, Withdrawals, and Disclaimers in Representation Cases

Sec. 8–1. Copies of documents submitted to regional director or Board. After the close of the hearing, the entire record in the case is forwarded to the regional director or, upon issuance by the regional director of an order transferring the case, to the Board in Washington. The record includes: the petition, notice of hearing, motions, rulings, the stenographic report of the hearing, stipulations, and exhibits.[1]

There are certain established requirements for all formal documents—for example, motions and briefs—which are submitted for consideration:

1. If a brief or motion is filed with the regional director, an original and one copy must be presented; or, if the case is before the Board, eight copies must be filed.
2. Such documents may be typewritten if filed with the regional director; however, only printed or legibly duplicated (not typewritten) copies are accepted by the Board.
3. Copies must be served upon all other parties and proof of such service filed with the documents.[2]

Sec. 8–2. Extensions of time to file briefs. Requests for further time to file a brief—in addition to the seven days after the close of the hearing plus the 14 days which the hearing officer may grant[3]—should be addressed to the regional director, or if the case has been transferred to the Board, to the Board's Executive Secretary. The need for the extension must be explained. Such requests should be:

1. Served immediately upon other parties; and

[1] R. and R. Sec. 102.67(a), (h), and (i).
[2] *Ibid.*
[3] *Ibid.*

2. Made no later than three working days before the date the briefs are due.[4]

Neither the regional director nor the Board will consider evidence which is submitted for the first time in the brief and which has not been produced at the hearing.[5]

Parties do not have the right to file a reply brief, but they may be filed upon receipt of special permission.[6] Special leave must also be obtained by an organization desiring to present its views as an amicus curiae, but such leave is usually granted.[7]

Sec. 8–3. Posthearing motions. All motions filed after the close of the hearing must be filed directly with the regional director or the Board, as the case may be. Such motions should briefly state the order or relief sought and the grounds therefor.[8] Any party, including the regional director, may file an answer to a motion. The answer should be filed promptly in the same form and manner as other documents.[9]

Sec. 8–4. Oral argument. Any party desiring to argue orally before the regional director or the Board may address a request to the regional director or the Board after the close of the hearing and before issuance of the decision.[10] The regional director usually permits oral argument where, in his opinion, the case involves matters on which he may wish to hear contentions more fully developed than those set forth in written briefs. Due to the large volume of cases, permission is rarely granted by the Board. In order to increase the number of oral arguments heard, the Board has instituted a policy of holding regular hearings the first Monday of each month for cases which, in its opinion, involve a basic policy question or a question whose resolution may be precedent setting.[11]

Neither the right of the regional director nor that of the Board to order oral argument is dependent on a request from the parties. Either may set a date for hearing oral argument at their discretion in a case before them for decision.

Whenever request for oral argument is granted, all parties are served with a notice of hearing. (See Facsimile No. 24, page 131.) The regional director's notice of hearing for oral argument is similar in style.) The oral

---

[4]*Ibid.*
[5]Swift & Co., 117 NLRB 61, 39 LRRM 1166 (1957).
[6]R. and R. Sec. 102.67(a) and (i).
[7]United States Gypsum Co., 118 NLRB 20, 40 LRRM 1120 (1957).
[8]R. and R. Sec. 102.65(a).
[9]Westinghouse Electric Corp., 108 NLRB 556, 34 LRRM 1039 (1954).
[10]R. and R. Sec. 101.21(b).
[11]NLRB Press Release (R–1175), October 1970.

UNITED STATES OF AMERICA
BEFORE THE NATIONAL LABOR RELATIONS BOARD

Petitioner

Other parties

                                        Case No.

NOTICE OF HEARING

PLEASE TAKE NOTICE that pursuant to authority vested in
the National Labor Relations Board under the National Labor Relations
Act, as amended, a hearing will be held before the National Labor
Relations Board on Monday, November 25, 1974, at 10:00 a.m., or
soon thereafter as the Board may hear you in the Hearing Room,
1717 Pennsylvania Avenue, N. W., Washington, D. C., for the purpose
of oral argument, in the above-entitled matter. Argument will be
limited to one-half hour for the General Counsel and the Charging
Party, to be divided or shared between them; one-half hour for the
Respondents, to be divided or shared between them; and one-half
hour for the amicus intervenors, to be divided or shared between
them.

Dated, Washington, D. C., November 1, 1974.

By direction of the Board:

_____
Executive Secretary

FACSIMILE No. 24.
*Sample of a notice of hearing
setting oral argument before the Board*

argument is conducted in the regional office if before the regional director or in Washington if before the Board. Each party to the proceeding is entitled to 30 minutes' argument. Request for additional time may not be granted unless timely application is made in advance of oral argument. It is not unusual for persons who have filed amicus curiae briefs to be permitted to argue orally.

Sec. 8–5. The regional director's or Board's decision.   The decision by the regional director or the Board is made on the basis of the entire written record. The decision may either:

1. Direct that an election be held; or
2. Dismiss the petition.

The decision is a formal document setting forth the facts of the case, the issues, the contentions of the parties, and a determination of the issues with supporting reasons. As a matter of policy, neither the regional director nor the Board will decide hypothetical questions raised by the parties. Thus the Board has refused to rule on the possible unit placement of employees who might assume new duties.[12] Also, the Board sometimes leaves the unit placement of small numbers of fringe employees undetermined. In such cases the decision states that the employees in question will vote subject to challenge. The Board then resolves their status only if the challenged ballots are determinative or on a post-election motion to clarify the unit.

Since representation matters have been delegated to the regional directors, the Board's cases ordinarily involve novel or difficult questions of law or fact. Its decisions, with rare exceptions, are published in printed volumes of Board cases.

Sec. 8–6. Precedent for regional director's decision.   A decision issued by a regional director contains the same information found in the Board decision, but it determines no substantial question of law or policy and must rely on precedents found in the Board's officially published cases. The director's decisions are not published in the Board's reporting system, but they are available for public inspection at the regional office. They are not used as precedents. (See Facsimile No. 25, page 133, for a regional director's decision directing an election, and Facsimile No. 26, page 134 for a regional director's decision dismissing the petition because of an inappropriate unit.)

Sec. 8–7. Substance of regional director's or Board's direction of election.
The direction of election whether issued by the regional director or the Board:

[12]Kolcast Industries, Inc., 8–RC–3005, Aug, 9, 1957 (not reported).

UNITED STATES OF AMERICA
BEFORE THE NATIONAL LABOR RELATIONS BOARD

DECISION AND DIRECTION OF ELECTION

Upon a petition duly filed under Section 9(c) of the National Labor Relations Act, a hearing was held before a hearing officer of the National Labor Relations Board. The hearing officer's rulings made at the hearing are free from prejudicial error and are hereby affirmed.

Pursuant to the provisions of Section 3(b) of the Act, the Board has delegated its powers in connection with this case to the undersigned Regional Director.

Upon the entire record in this case, the Regional Director finds:

1. The Employer is engaged in commerce within the meaning of the Act and it will effectuate the purposes of the Act to assert jurisdiction herein.

2. The labor organization(s) involved claim(s) to represent certain employees of the Employer.

3. A question affecting commerce exists concerning the representation of certain employees of the Employer within the meaning of Section 9(c)(1) and Section 2(6) and (7) of the Act.

4. The following employees of the Employer constitute a unit appropriate for the purposes of collective bargaining within the meaning of Section 9(b) of the Act:

DIRECTION OF ELECTION

An election by secret ballot will be conducted by the undersigned Regional Director among the employees in the unit found appropriate at the time and place set forth in the notice of election to be issued subsequently, subject to the Board's Rules and Regulations. Eligible to vote are those in the unit who were employed during the payroll period immediately preceding the date below, including employees who did not work during that period because they were ill, on vacation, or temporarily laid off. Also eligible are employees engaged in an economic strike which commenced less than 12 months before the election date and who retained their status as such during the eligibility period and their replacements. Those in the military services of the United States may vote if they appear in person at the polls. Ineligible to vote are employees who have quit or been discharged for cause since the designated payroll period and employees engaged in a strike who have been discharged for cause since the commencement thereof, and who have not been rehired or reinstated before the election date, and employees engaged in an economic strike which commenced more than 12 months before the election date and who have been permanently replaced. Those eligible shall vote whether (or not) they desire to be represented for collective-bargaining purposes by

Dated _____   _____

at _____   Regional Director, Region

FACSIMILE NO. 25.
Sample form of a regional director's decision directing an election

FORM NLRB-4479
(11-63)

UNITED STATES OF AMERICA
BEFORE THE NATIONAL LABOR RELATIONS BOARD

THE COOLEY CONTAINER CORPORATION   1/
                                          Employer

and

LOCAL 94, UNITED METAL PRODUCTS, MACHINERY, AND RELATED EQUIPMENT
WORKERS OF AMERICA, AFL-CIO   Petitioner

CASE NO. 30-RC-4104

DECISION AND ORDER

Upon a petition duly filed under Section 9(c) of the National Labor Relations Act, a hearing was held before a hearing officer of the National Labor Relations Board. The hearing officer's rulings made at the hearing are free from prejudicial error and are hereby affirmed.

Pursuant to the provisions of Section 3(b) of the Act, the Board has delegated its powers in connection with this case to the undersigned Regional Director.

Upon the entire record in this case, the Regional Director finds:

1. The Employer is engaged in commerce within the meaning of the Act and it will effectuate the purposes of the Act to assert jurisdiction herein.

2. The labor organization(s) involved claim(s) to represent certain employees of the Employer.

3. No question affecting commerce exists concerning the representation of certain employees of the Employer within the meaning of Section 9(c)(1) and Section 2(6) and (7) of the Act, for the following reasons:

The Petitioner seeks a unit of two truck drivers while the Employer contends that an over-all unit of seven applicator-truckers is appropriate.

The Employer is engaged in the sale and installation of home improvements, including siding, roofing and storm windows. In addition to the seven applicator-truckers, there are 15 employees engaged almost enclusively in applying siding and roofing. The two employees sought to be represented by the Petitioner are classified as applicator-truckers. Applicator-truckers deliver materials to the job site from the Employer's and distributors' warehouses, start jobs and answer complaints of customers after completion of the job, performing whatever repair work is necessary.

The Petitioner contends that the two employees it seeks to represent are primarily engaged in trucking and delivery duties. Although the record reveals that these two employees spend more time on deliveries than the other five applicator-truckers, it is equally clear that the great majority of their time, like that of the other applicator-truckers, is spent in applying siding and roofing. The record also reveals that these two employees work together with the other applicator-truckers on siding and roofing. All seven applicator-truckers are subject to the supervision of the Employer's president and are eligible to participate in the Employer's health insurance program. As the two applicator-truckers do not have such special and distinct interests as to outweigh their community of interest with the other five applicator-truckers, it is found that the unit sought is inappropriate. 2/ Accordingly, the Employer's Motion to Dismiss is granted.

---

1. The name of the Employer appears as amended at the hearing.
2. Sylvania Electric Products, Inc., 135 NLRB 768, 769-770; Kalamazoo Paper Box Corp., 136 NLRB 134; Tops Chemical Company, 137 NLRB 736,737.

ORDER

IT IS HEREBY ORDERED that the petition(s) filed herein be, and it (they) hereby is, (are), dismissed.

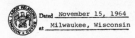

Dated November 15, 1964   /s/
at Milwaukee, Wisconsin   Regional Director for the Thirtieth   Region.

FACSIMILE No. 26.
Sample form of a regional director's decision dismissing the petition because of an inappropriate unit

1. Sets forth the bargaining unit to be voted.
2. Designates the union or unions whose names are to appear on the ballot.
3. Specifies the employee categories eligible to vote.
4. States that the election shall be conducted by the regional director within an appropriate time.

If the decision is issued by the regional director, despite the Board's Statements of Procedure the election will normally not be scheduled to be held sooner than the 25th day after the date of his decision. This policy is followed to permit the Board to rule on any request for review which may be filed.[13] However, if the parties desire an early election after the regional director's decision and direction of election, the right to request review may be waived.[14] (See Facsimile No. 27, page 136, for Waiver.) If the decision and direction of election is issued by the Board, it states that the election shall be conducted by the regional director not later than 30 days after the date of the direction of election.

The regional director or the Board will issue a direction of election even though:
1. An appeal from a regional director's dismissal of unfair labor practices is pending before the General Counsel.[15]
2. A current economic strike exists.[16]
3. A request is made to have the issues resolved under the union's Internal Disputes Plan.[17]

Sec. 8–8. Appropriate bargaining unit. The description of the appropriate bargaining unit is the most common issue in a representation case; however, the large number of Board and court precedents reflect the difficulty and complexity of this subject. The Supreme Court has said that: "The issue as to what unit is appropriate is one for which no absolute rule of law is laid down by statute . . . The decision of the Board, if not final, is rarely to be disturbed."[18] Following are the basic rules, as provided by the Act:

1. The unit shall be that which assures employees the fullest freedom in exercising the rights guaranteed by the Act, and shall be an employer unit, craft unit, plant unit, or subdivision thereof.[19] (See Secs. 1–18 through 1–22, beginning on page 19.)

[13]Statements of Procedure, Sec. 101.21(d).
[14]R. and R. Sec. 102.67(f).
[15]Steward Warner Corp., 112 NLRB 1222, 36 LRRM 1176 (1955); see Sec. 7–3, page 107.
[16]Shipowners' Association of the Pacific Coast, 100 NLRB 1250, 30 LRRM 1434 (1952).
[17]Pollock Paper Corp., 115 NLRB 231, 37 LRRM 1272 (1956).
[18]Packard Motor Car Co. v. NLRB, 330 U.S. 584, 19 LRRM 2397 (1949); Pan American Petroleum Corp., 77 LRRM 2641 (C.A. 10, 1971), enf. 72 LRRM 1283.
[19]Sec. 9(b).

FORM NLRB-4480
(5-61)

UNITED STATES OF AMERICA

NATIONAL LABOR RELATIONS BOARD

WAIVER

IN THE MATTER OF _____   _____
                        (Name of case)   *(Number of case)*

PURSUANT TO SECTION 102.67 OF THE RULES AND REGULATIONS OF THE NATIONAL LABOR RELATIONS BOARD,
THE UNDERSIGNED HEREBY WAIVES ITS RIGHT TO REQUEST REVIEW OF THE REGIONAL DIRECTOR'S _____ IN THE

_____   _____
(Name of document or applicable documents)

_____   OR   ☐ CHECK IF DOCUMENT
(Date of Document)   NOT YET ISSUED.

ABOVE CAPTIONED MATTER.

_____
(Name of Party)

BY _____
(Name of Representative)

_____
(Title)

DATE _____

FACSIMILE NO. 27.
*Waiver of right to request review
of regional director's decision*

2. The unit is inappropriate if it includes both professional and nonprofessional employees, unless a majority of the professional employees vote for inclusion in such a unit.[20]

3. A craft unit cannot be found inappropriate on the ground that a different unit has been established by a prior Board determination unless a majority of the employees in the proposed craft unit vote against separate representation.[21]

4. A unit is inappropriate if it includes, in a unit of production and maintenance workers, plant guards, and a plant-guard union may not be certified if it takes persons other than guards into membership or is affiliated directly or indirectly with a union that represents persons other than guards.[22]

5. A unit's appropriateness is not controlled by the extent to which the employees have organized.[23]

The following factors, fashioned by Board and court decisions, are also used to determine whether or not a bargaining unit is appropriate:[24]

1. A community of interest among the employees concerning wages, hours, and working conditions.[25]

2. Geographical and physical proximity. Although there is no mathematical formula for determining when such integration ends and separation begins, the Board has used the Standard Metropolitan Statistical Area to determine a unit's appropriateness.[26]

3. A history of collective bargaining, proving that a workable relationship exists between the employer and the bargaining unit, and that there is a community of interests within the unit itself.[27]

4. Employee desires for a bargaining unit, as demonstrated by the results in a self-determination election (the Globe doctrine).[28]

---

[20]Sec. 9(b)(1). Bell Aerospace Co., Division of Textron, 196 NLRB No. 127, 80 LRRM 1099 (1972), denying reconsideration of 77 LRRM 1265; Hudson Waterway Corp. and Seatrains Lines, 193 NLRB No. 58, 78 LRRM 1257 (1971).
[21]Sec. 9(b)(2).
[22]Sec. 9(b)(3); Beyerl Chevrolet Inc., 199 NLRB No. 24, 82 LRRM 1075 (1972).
[23]Sec. 9(c)(5).
[24]For further discussion see Abodeely, THE NLRB AND THE APPROPRIATE BARGAINING UNIT (Philadelphia: University of Pennsylvania Press, 1971).
[25]Continental Baking Co., 99 NLRB 777, 782, 30 LRRM 1119 (1952); Continental Can Co., 171 NLRB No. 99, 68 LRRM 1155 (1968).
[26]Sav-On Drugs, Inc., 138 NLRB 1032, 51 LRRM 1153 (1962); Drug-Fair Community Drug Co., 180 NLRB No. 94, 73 LRRM 1065 (1970).
[27]Meijer Supermarkets, Inc., 142 NLRB No. 69, 53 LRRM 1081 (1963); Eaton Mfg. Co., 121 NLRB 813, 42 LRRM 1447 (1958); see also Buckeye Village Market, Inc., 175 NLRB No. 46, 70 LRRM 1529 (1969).
[28]The Globe Machine and Stamping Co., 3 NLRB 294, 1–A LRRM 122 (1937); Pittsburgh Plate Glass Co. v. NLRB, 313 U.S. 146, 8 LRRM 425 (1941); Black and Decker Mfg. Co., 147 NLRB 825, 828, 56 LRRM 1302 (1964); Libbey-Owens Ford Glass Co., 169 NLRB No. 2, 67 LRRM 1096 (1968).

5. Similarity to employer administrative or territorial divisions.[29]
6. Functional integration of the employer's operations,[30] and the frequency of employee interchange.[31]

Single-location units of multilocation operations are appropriate if the requested unit maintains a substantial degree of autonomy, even though there is considerable centralization of authority and integration between the various facilities. The Board uses the same guidelines for proving autonomy that it takes into account in questions of accretion.[32] (See Sec. 5–14, page 56.).

A homogeneous and identifiable bargaining unit which is not plantwide or storewide is appropriate if it can be characterized by the following three factors: the employees within the unit are under separate supervision; they perform substantially all their work tasks in buildings or areas physically separated from those in which the bulk of the remaining employees work; and they are not integrated, to any substantial degree, with other employees in the performance of their ordinary duties.[33]

The Board has also ruled that a unit must be *an* appropriate unit, although it does not have to be *the most* appropriate for bargaining.[34] While the courts do not have the authority to find a unit more appropriate than one found by the regional director or the Board,[35] they may set aside a regional director's or Board's determination if it is arbitrary or capricious.[36]

The appropriateness of a multiemployer bargaining unit depends upon the voluntary consent of all parties to the agreement and upon the history of collective bargaining. When establishing such a unit, it is necessary to demonstrate that all of the employer members "intend to be bound in future collective bargaining by group rather than individual action."[37] Participation as a member of a multiemployer unit may be shown by demonstrating that the employer has participated in negotiations covering

[29]Paxton Wholesale Grocery Co., 123 NLRB 316, 43 LRRM 1424 (1959); Sav-On Drugs, Inc., 138 NLRB 1032, 51 LRRM 1153 (1962).
[30]Potter Aeronautical Corp., 155 NLRB 1077, 60 LRRM 1473 (1965); Sears Roebuck and Co., 172 NLRB No. 132, 68 LRRM 1469 (1968).
[31]Meijer Supermarkets, Inc., 142 NLRB 513, 53 LRRM 1081 (1963); Gerber Productions Co., 172 NLRB No. 195, 69 LRRM 1017 (1968).
[32]Frisch's Big Boy Ill-Mar, 147 NLRB 551, 56 LRRM 1246 (1964); Twenty-First Century Restaurant of Nostrand Avenue Corp., licensee of McDonald's Corp., 192 NLRB No. 103, 78 LRRM 1015 (1971); Gray Drug Stores Inc., 197 NLRB No. 105, 80 LRRM 1449 (1972).
[33]Levitz Furniture Co. of Santa Clara, 192 NLRB No. 13, 77 LRRM 1579 (1971); John Wanamaker, Philadelphia, Inc., 195 NLRB No. 82, 79 LRRM 1378 (1972); J. C. Penny Co., Store 1302, 196 NLRB No. 67, 80 LRRM 1071 (1972), 196 NLRB No. 63, 80 LRRM 1027 (1972).
[34]A. S. Beck Shoe Corp., 92 NLRB 1457, 27 LRRM 1268 (1951); Jackson Manor Nursing Home, 194 NLRB No. 152, 79 LRRM 1166 (1972).
[35]NLRB v. Smythe, 212 F. 2d 664, 34 LRRM 2108 (C.A. 5, 1954).
[36]Pittsburgh Plate Glass Co. v. NLRB, 313 U.S. 146, 8 LRRM 425 (1941).
[37]Morris, THE DEVELOPING LABOR LAW (Washington: BNA Books, 1971), pp. 236–245.

the unit for a period of no less than one year[38] and has adopted the resulting agreements.[39]

Sec. 8–9. NLRB craft severance policies. Frequently, the Board is asked to rule on the appropriateness of a craft unit which has petitioned to be separated from the rest of the industrial unit for collective bargaining purposes. In all such cases involving the issue of craft severance, the Board will examine the following factors:

1. Whether or not the proposed unit consists of a distinct and homogeneous group of skilled journeymen craftsmen performing the functions of their craft on a nonrepetitive basis, or of employees constituting a functionally distinct department, working in trades or occupations for which a tradition of separate representation exists.
2. The history of collective bargaining of the employees sought at the plant involved, and at other plants of the employer, with emphasis on whether the existing patterns of bargaining are productive of stability in labor relations, and whether such stability will be unduly disrupted by the destruction of the existing patterns of representation.
3. The extent to which the employees in the proposed unit have established and maintained their separate identity during the period of inclusion in a broader unit, and the extent of their participation or lack of participation in the establishment and maintenance of the existing pattern of representation and the prior opportunities, if any, afforded them to obtain separate representation.
4. The history and pattern of collective bargaining in the industry involved.
5. The degree of integration of the employer's production processes, including the extent to which the continued normal operation of the production processes is dependent upon the performance of the assigned functions of the employees in the proposed unit.
6. The qualifications of the union seeking to "carve out" a separate unit, including that union's experience in representing employees like those involved in the severance action.[40]

Sec. 8–10. Excluded employees. The Board has also developed special rules pertaining to the exclusion of specific types of employees from bargaining units. For example:

[38]Miron Building Products Co., 116 NLRB 194, 39 LRRM 1002 (1956).
[39]Quality Limestone Products, Inc., 143 NLRB 589, 53 LRRM 1357 (1963).
[40]Mallinckrodt Chemical Works, 162 NLRB 387, 64 LRRM 1011 (1966). *See also* Towmotor Corp., 187 NLRB No. 138, 76 LRRM 1193 (1971); Dow Chemical Co., 202 NLRB No. 6, 82 LRRM 1594 (1973).

1. *Confidential employees.* Confidential employees should be excluded from rank-and-file bargaining units if, in their normal course of duties, they have access to confidential information that relates to the labor relations policies of their employer.[41]

2. *Clerical employees.* Clerical employees are categorized as either office clerical, considered to be "white collar" office workers, or plant clerical, considered to have interests similar to those involved in production. In practice, office clerical employees are frequently excluded from a rank-and-file bargaining unit while plant clericals are usually included.[42]

3. *Managerial employees.* Managerial employees are defined as those who formulate, determine, and effectuate management policies and are excluded from a rank-and-file bargaining unit.[43]

4. *Supervisory employees.* Supervisory employees are defined as "individuals . . . having authority in the interest of the employer, to hire, transfer, suspend, lay off, recall, promote, discharge, assign, reward, or discipline other employees, or responsibility to direct them, or to adjust their grievances, or effectively to recommend such action, if in connection with the foregoing the exercise of such authority is not of a merely routine or clerical nature, but requires the use of independent judgment."[44] They are excluded from a rank-and-file bargaining unit.[45]

Sec. 8–11. Eligibility to vote. The usual direction of election will state that the following employees in the appropriate unit are eligible to vote:

1. Employees who were employed during the payroll period immediately preceding the date of the direction of election, provided they are still employed at the time of the election.[46]

2. Employees who did not work during the above payroll period because they were ill, on vacation, or temporarily laid off.[47]

---

[41]Swift and Co., 124 NLRB 899, 44 LRRM 1527 (1959); Air Line Pilots Assn., 185 NLRB No. 114, 75 LRRM 1196 (1970).
[42]For rules to determine office clerical status see Vulcanized Rubber Co., 129 NLRB 1256, 47 LRRM 1175 (1961); for similar rules for plant clericals see Swift and Co., 131 NLRB 1143, 48 LRRM 1219 (1961).
[43]Illinois State-Journal-Register, Inc. v. NLRB, 412 F.2d 37, 71 LRRM 2668 (C.A. 7, 1969), *enf.* 69 LRRM 1028; General Dynamics Corporation, 213 NLRB No. 124, 87 LRRM 1705 (1974).
[44]Sec. 2(11).
[45]Mid-State Fruit, Inc., 186 NLRB No. 11, 75 LRRM 1281 (1970); *see also* Chapter 1 and cases cited therein.
[46]Walterboro Mfg. Corp., 106 NLRB 1383, 33 LRRM 1028 (1953).
[47]Wright Manufacturing Co., 106 NLRB 1239, 32 LRRM 1655 (1953); Sangamo Electric Co., 110 NLRB 1, 34 LRRM 1587 (1954); NLRB v. Atkinson Dredging Co., 329 F.2d 158, 55 LRRM 2598 (C.A. 4, 1964), *cert. denied,* 377 U.S. 965, 56 LRRM 2416; Staiman Bros., 81 LRRM 2133 (C.A.3, 1972), *denying enforcement to* 77 LRRM 1189.

3. Employees engaged in an economic strike who are not entitled to reinstatement, having been permanently replaced, in any election within 12 months of the start of the strike.[48]
4. Employees who are entitled to reinstatement (unfair labor practice strikers) in any election regardless of the 12-month limitation.[49]
5. Replacements employed on a permanent basis prior to the voting-eligibility cutoff dates. If a strike starts after the direction of election, replacements can vote if they are employed on the day of the election.[50] However, if the strike begins before the direction of election, replacements are subject "to the general rules specifying eligibility both at the time of the direction of election and an election day."[51]
6. Employees in the military service who appear in person at the polls.

The Board has ruled that the following employees in the appropriate unit are ineligible to vote:

1. Employees who have quit or been discharged for cause and have not been rehired or reinstated prior to the date of election.[52]
2. Employees, as shown by objective evidence, who have abandoned interest in their struck jobs.[53]
3. Replacements for those striking employees who are entitled to reinstatement.[54]

In special situations the payroll period immediately preceding the regional director's issuance of the notice of hearing will be used for eligibility purposes. For example, this has been done where, at the time of the direction of election:

1. A plant does not have a representative number of employees because of its seasonal operations.[55]
2. All employees in the unit have been laid off because of lack of work.[56]

---

[48]The Act, Sec. 9(c)(B)(3); Laidlaw Corp., 171 NLRB 1366, 68 LRRM 1252 (1968); Wahl Clipper Corp., 195 NLRB No. 104, 79 LRRM 1433 (1972).
[49]Kellburn Mfg. Co., 45 NLRB 322, 11 LRRM 142 (1942); cf. Roylyn, Inc., 178 NLRB No. 33, 72 LRRM 1043 (1969).
[50]Tampa Sand and Material Co., 137 NLRB 1549, 50 LRRM 1438 (1962); Macy's Missouri-Kansas Div., 173 NLRB No. 232, 70 LRRM 1039 (1969).
[51]Greenspan Engraving Corp., 137 NLRB 1308, 50 LRRM 1380 (1962).
[52]Stainless Welded Products, Inc., 104 NLRB 204, 32 LRRM 1042 (1953); Choc-ola Bottlers, Inc. v. NLRB, 83 LRRM 2204 (C.A. 7, 1973), denying enforcement to 80 LRRM 1256.
[53]W. Wilton Wood, Inc., 127 NLRB 1675, 46 LRRM 1240 (1960); Laidlaw Corp., 414 F.2d 99, 71 LRRM 3054; (1969); Harlem Rivers Consumers Cooperative Inc., 191 NLRB No. 48, 77 LRRM 1883 (1971).
[54]Lock Joint Tube Co., 127 NLRB 1146, 46 LRRM 1170 (1960); Tampa Sand and Material Co., 137 NLRB 1549, 50 LRRM 1438 (1962).
[55]Nephi Processing Plant, Inc., 107 NLRB 647, 33 LRRM 1211 (1953).
[56]Raphael G. Wolff Studios, 104 NLRB 508, 32 LRRM 1102 (1953).

In interpreting the above rules, the Board has laid down these basic considerations:

1. "The essential element in determining an employee's eligibility to vote is his status on the eligibility payroll date and on the date of the election."[57] It is of no significance that an individual employed on those dates intended to quit, or actually did quit, or became a supervisor shortly after the election.[58]

2. Strikers are presumed to be "economic strikers" unless they are found by the Board to be on strike because of unfair labor practices on the part of the employer.[59]

3. Economic striker status is forfeited if it is shown that the employer has eliminated his job for economic reasons, or that the employee was discharged or refused reinstatement for misconduct rendering him unsuitable for reemployment.[60]

4. Laid-off employees who have reasonable expectation of reemployment in the foreseeable future are eligible to vote.[61]

5. Seasonal, casual, or temporary employees are not eligible to vote unless they have a reasonable expectation of reemployment and a substantial interest in working conditions at the employer's place of business.[62]

6. Regular part-time, as distinguished from temporary or casual, employees may vote.[63]

7. Temporarily transferred employees may vote.[64]

[57]Gulf States Asphalt Co., 106 NLRB 1212, 32 LRRM 1643 (1953); Business Aviation Inc., 202 NLRB No. 151, 82 LRRM 1710 (1973).
[58]Personal Products Corp., 114 NLRB 959, 37 LRRM 1079 (1955); Electronic Computer Corp., 98 NLRB No. 164 (not reported); Business Aviation Inc., 202 NLRB No. 151, 82 LRRM 1710 (1973); cf. Roy N. Lotspeich, 204 NLRB No. 61, 83 LRRM 1380 (1973), suppl'g 199 NLRB No. 166, 81 LRRM 1527.
[59]Bright Foods, Inc., 126 NLRB 553, 45 LRRM 1343 (1960).
[60]W. Wilton Wood, Inc., 127 NLRB 1675, 46 LRRM 1240 (1960).
[61]NLRB v. Jesse Jones Sausage Co., 309 F. 2d 664, 51 LRRM 2501 (C.A. 4, 1962); Tomadur, Inc., 196 NLRB No. 128, 80 LRRM 1755 (1972), suppl'g 73 LRRM 1289; Sierra Lingerie Co., 191 NLRB No. 148, 77 LRRM 1573 (1971).
[62]William E. Locke, 137 NLRB 1610, 50 LRRM 1469 (1962); S. Martinelli and Co., 99 NLRB 43, 30 LRRM 1031 (1952); for seasonal employees, there are occasional special time limitations, see Median Inc., 200 NLRB No. 145, 82 LRRM 1037 (1972); Hondo Drilling Co., N.S.L., 164 NLRB No. 67, 65 LRRM 1094 (1967); Mademoiselle Shoppe Inc., 199 NLRB No. 147, 82 LRRM 1022 (1972); Knapp-Sherrill Co. v. NLRB, 488 F.2d 655, 85 LRRM 2289 (C.A. 5, 1974), enf. 82 LRRM 1381.
[63]Providence Pub. Market Co., 79 NLRB 1482, 23 LRRM 1011 (1948); Tol-Pac, Inc., 128 NLRB 1439, 46 LRRM 1485 (1960); Food Fair Stores, Inc., 120 NLRB 1669, 42 LRRM 1242 (1958); Lee, Henry, Co., 194 NLRB No. 196, 79 LRRM 1159 (1972); Kraftco Corp., Kraft Foods Div., 198 NLRB No. 94, 81 LRRM 1176 (1972).
[64]Huntley Van Buren Co., 122 NLRB 957, 43 LRRM 1229 (1959); du Pont, E. I., de Nemours &Co. Inc., 210 NLRB No. 51, 86 LRRM 1155 (1974).

8. All issues as to voting eligibility of strikers and replacements are deferred until after the election for disposition by way of challenged ballots.[65]
9. Employees allegedly discharged in violation of the Act are permitted to vote subject to challenge. If the number of challenged ballots could affect the result of the election, the Board will resolve them after completion of the unfair labor practice proceeding.[66]
10. Employees found by the Board to be discriminatorily discharged are eligible to vote, even though the unfair labor practice case is pending before a court of appeals.[67]
11. Employees will not be deprived of their right to vote on the grounds that they are probationary employees,[68] minors,[69] Indians,[70] aliens,[71] or illiterate.[72]

Sec. 8–12. Appeal of regional director's decision in election cases. The parties may appeal from a regional director's decision by filing a request for review with the Board. The Board may deny the request and refuse to consider the appeal except in one instance. Prior to the close of the hearing parties, as a matter of right, may take an appeal to the Board from the regional director's dismissal of a petition.[73] (See Sec. 6–8, "Dismissal of a Petition," page 90.)

Sec. 8–13. Regional director's decisions—Grounds for review. In all other cases the request for review may be based on four grounds only:[74]

1. That a substantial question of law or policy is raised because of the absence of or the departure from officially reported Board precedent.
2. That the regional director's decision on a substantial factual issue is clearly erroneous on the record and such error prejudicially affects the rights of a party.
3. That the conduct of the hearing or any ruling made in connection with the proceeding has resulted in prejudicial error.
4. That there are compelling reasons for reconsideration of an important Board rule or policy.

---

[65]Bright Foods, Inc., 126 NLRB 553, 45 LRRM 1343 (1960).
[66]Hunt Theater Corp., 113 NLRB 167, 36 LRRM 1277 (1955); Tampa Sand and Material Co., 137 NLRB 1549, 50 LRRM 1438 (1962); Pacific Tile and Porcelain Co., 137 NLRB 1358, 50 LRRM 1394 (1962); Gary Aircraft Corp., 193 NLRB No. 21, 78 LRRM 1535 (1971).
[67]Ohio Ferro Alloys Corp., 107 NLRB 504, 33 LRRM 1184 (1953).
[68]Sheffield Corp., 123 NLRB 1454, 44 LRRM 1155 (1959).
[69]NLRB v. New Era Die Co., Inc., 118 F. 2d 500, 8 LRRM 551 (C.A. 3, 1941).
[70]Simplot Fertilizer Co., 107 NLRB 1211, 33 LRRM 1357 (1954).
[71]Cities Service Oil Co. of Pennsylvania, 87 NLRB 324, 25 LRRM 1112 (1949).
[72]Albion Malleable Iron Co., 104 NLRB 225, 32 LRRM 1084 (1953).
[73]R. and R. Sec. 102.71.
[74]R. and R. Sec. 102.67(c).

Requests for review (eight copies) must be filed with the Board in Washington within 10 days from the date of the regional director's decision or order.[75] Copies must be served on all parties including the regional director.[76] The request must set forth reasons for seeking review in sufficient detail for the Board to rule without having to research the case record.[77] Any party may file a statement opposing the request within seven days of being served with the request.[78] It is important to recognize that the facts available for the Board's consideration are restricted to those included in the request and the statement in opposition.

The regional director's action is not stayed by the filing of a request for review unless otherwise ordered by the Board. Thus, the regional director may proceed immediately to make any necessary arrangements for an election, including the issuance of a notice of election.[79]

If the Board rejects the request for review, the parties will receive a telegram from the Associate Executive Secretary of the Board in Washington stating:

"It is hereby ordered that the petitioner's request for review of the regional director's decision and direction of election be, and it hereby is, denied as it raises no substantial issues warranting review. By direction of the Board."

Sec. 8–14. Regional director's decisions—Denial of review. Denial of a request for review amounts to Board approval of the regional director's action. It precludes relitigating any such issues in any related subsequent unfair labor practice proceeding.[80] On receipt of the Board's telegram the regional director will proceed with the holding of the election.

Sec. 8–15. Regional director's decisions—Granting of review. On the other hand if the Board decides to grant the request for review, the parties will receive a telegram from the Associate Executive Secretary stating:

"It is hereby ordered that request of the employer for review of regional director's decision and direction of election be, and it hereby is, granted as it raises substantial issues warranting review. The election is hereby stayed pending decision on review. By direction of the Board."

On the granting of a request for review the parties, within seven days after issuance of the order granting review, may file briefs (eight copies) with the Board. The Board will consider the entire record in the light of the grounds relied upon for review. (Any request for review may be withdrawn

---

[75]R. and R. Sec. 102.67(b).
[76]*Ibid.*
[77]R. and R. Sec. 102.67(d).
[78]R. and R. Sec. 102.67(e).
[79]Statements of Procedure, Sec. 101.21(d).
[80]R. and R. Sec. 102.67(f).

with the permission of the Board.)[81] The Board proceeds upon the record, or after oral argument or the submission of briefs or upon further hearing, as it may determine, to decide the issues referred to it or to review the decision of the regional director. It will then direct a secret ballot of the employees, dismiss the petition, affirm or reverse the regional director's order in whole or in part, or make such other disposition of the matter as it deems appropriate.[82]

Sec. 8–16. Regional director's decisions—Reconsideration by the regional director.

Although the Board's rules do not currently provide for motions for reconsideration in representation cases, such motions are sometimes honored. Also, a regional director may, in his discretion, treat a request for review as a motion for reconsideration. In either event, if the regional director feels that a change in his original decision is warranted, he may take whatever action is appropriate. If the regional director decides to treat a request for review as a motion for reconsideration, he will notify the Board and it will suspend action on the pending request until such time as the regional director advises the Board that further proceedings are being handled in the region or that the Board should resume consideration of the request for review. A regional director will entertain a motion for reconsideration filed with him but its filing will not toll the running of the time in which a request for review must be filed with the Board. However, if the director amends his decision in response to the motion the time for filing the request for review will not begin to run until the issuance of the amended decision.

Sec. 8–17. Motion for reconsideration of Board's decision.

All motions for reconsideration filed after the Board's decision on the request for review should be filed directly with the Board with a copy to each of the parties. Any party may file an answer to a motion for reconsideration. Neither the filing of a motion for reconsideration of a decision and direction of election nor an answer will delay the election arrangements. Until ordered otherwise by the Board the regional director will proceed with the holding of the election as directed.

Sec. 8–18. Disclaimer and withdrawal of petition.

In addition to the direction of election, consent election procedures, and dismissal, representation petitions may be disposed of in two other ways: by disclaimer or withdrawal. Thus, a party who has filed a representation petition or intervened in a pending case sometimes decides it does not wish to proceed. In that event the petitioner, whether an employer, or a union, or the

---

[81]R. and R. Sec. 102.67(g).
[82]R. and R. Sec. 102.67(j).

intervening union, files a request for withdrawal with the regional director. When an employer has filed a petition or a group of individual employees seeks to decertify a union, the union may submit a disclaimer of interest which has the same effect as a request for withdrawal.

A request for withdrawal of petition may be granted, with or without prejudice to the filing of a new petition, or it may be denied. A disclaimer of interest may be accepted or rejected. Following are the various conditions and procedures to be observed in this regard:

A petition may be withdrawn:

1. At any time before the close of hearing, only with the consent of the regional director with whom the petition was filed;[83] and
2. After the close of hearing, only with the consent of the regional director, or if the case was transferred to the Board, only with the consent of the Board.[84]

Sec. 8–19. Withdrawal of petition before hearing. Upon investigation of a petition, the NLRB agent may request that withdrawal be made, or the petitioner may on its own motion ask to withdraw. (For a statement of the procedures at this point, see page 90 under "Withdrawal of a Petition.") The regional director may grant the request for withdrawal without prejudice to the later filing of a new petition at any time.[85] The case is closed as soon as the withdrawal is approved by the regional director.[86]

Sec. 8–20. Withdrawal of petition after election agreement. The following rules apply where, after an election agreement—consent or stipulated—has been approved by the regional director, the *union* requests withdrawal of its petition and no inconsistent action by the union is involved:

1. The election will be cancelled, whether or not the employer objects.
2. Withdrawal will be granted with prejudice to the filing of a new petition by the union for a period of six months from the date of the regional director's letter, unless good cause is shown to the contrary.[87] (For a statement of what constitutes "good cause," see page 152 under "Proceedings within six months.")
3. Where, in addition to the petitioning union, another union is party to the election agreement, the election will be held if the intervening union submits an interest showing of at least 30 percent, or a recent

[83]R. and R. Sec. 102.60.
[84]*Ibid.*
[85]Wyman-Gordon Co., Ingalls Shepard Division, 117 NLRB 75, 39 LRRM 1176 (1957).
[86]Petco Corp., 98 NLRB 150, 29 LRRM 1311 (1952).
[87]19 NLRB Ann. Rep. 19.

contract covering the unit involved. The regional director may give the intervening union a reasonable amount of time to obtain and submit its additional designations; the showing of interest need not antedate the date of approval of the election agreement. If the intervening union submits the required showing the petitioning union will be dropped from the ballot "with six months prejudice to the filing of a new petition unless good cause be shown" to the contrary, and the election will be held in accordance with the agreement. This standard applies regardless of whether an employer approves or objects to the withdrawal.[88]

The following rules apply where, after an election agreement—consent or stipulated—has been approved by the regional director, the *employer* requests withdrawal of his petition and no inconsistent action by the union is involved:

1. The election will be cancelled and the withdrawal request will be granted without prejudice to the filing of a new petition if the union or unions involved do not oppose the request.
2. The withdrawal request will be denied and the election will be held as scheduled if the union or unions involved oppose the employer's request for withdrawal.

After the conduct of a valid consent election, a request for withdrawal of the petition will not be granted.

Sec. 8–21. Withdrawal of petition at hearing.   A request for withdrawal of petition may be made at the hearing, as part of the record. The hearing officer has no authority to approve such request;[89] he must refer the request to the regional director. If the regional director approves the request for withdrawal of petition, he will do so without prejudice to the filing of a new petition and he will withdraw the notice of hearing. The case is closed at this point.

Sec. 8–22. Withdrawal of petition after hearing.   After close of the hearing, a request for permission to withdraw a petition should be addressed to the regional director, or to the Board in Washington if the case has been transferred there.[90] A request made after close of the hearing, whether required to be addressed to the regional director or the Board, may

---

[88]Thiokol Chemical Corp., 114 NLRB 21, 36 LRRM 1508 (1955); *cf.* Victorville Lime Rock Co., 107 NLRB 1145, 33 LRRM 1335 (1954).
[89]Norfolk Coca-Cola Bottling Works, Inc., 88 NLRB 462, 24 LRRM 1646 (1949).
[90]R. and R. Sec. 102.60.

be made before[91] or after[92] issuance of the decision. As in the case of withdrawals after approval of a consent agreement, the request will be granted only with prejudice. The Board has denied as "untimely" a union's request for withdrawal where it was filed after the conduct of a valid Board-ordered election,[93] and the same rule would apply to an election ordered by a regional director.

An employer's request for withdrawal of its petition after close of the hearing will be denied if opposed and the union need not submit a showing of interest to obtain the election.[94]

A union's withdrawal request at this stage will be denied where:

1. An intervening union opposes such request, desires to proceed to an election, and demonstrates at least a 30 percent showing of interest in the unit.[95] In such an instance, however, the petitioner is permitted to withdraw from the election with prejudice to filing a new petition within six months.[96]

2. The union is engaged in action inconsistent with its stated desire to withdraw both its petition and interest in representing the employees. The Board has repeatedly ruled that the attempted withdrawal, to be granted, must be "clear and unequivocal" and the union must not be "currently engaged in conduct inconsistent" with withdrawal of its claim of majority representation.[97] Examples of union conduct "inconsistent" with claimed withdrawal are:

(a) Picketing for recognition.[98]

(b) Threatening to strike for recognition.[99]

(c) Demanding that the employer bargain.[100]

(d) Continuing both to negotiate with the employer and to engage in so-called "organizational" picketing.[101]

(e) Picketing for adoption of union wage and employment standards.[102]

[91]Consolidated Rendering Co., 117 NLRB 1784, 40 LRRM 1090 (1957).
[92]Thiokol Chemical Corp., 114 NLRB 21, 36 LRRM 1508 (1955).
[93]Munsingwear, Inc., NLRB No. 18–RC–3107, 40 LRRM 1303 (1957).
[94]International Aluminum Corp., 117 NLRB 1221, 39 LRRM 1407 (1957).
[95]Carpenter Baking Co., 112 NLRB 288, 36 LRRM 1003 (1958).
[96]Ibid.
[97]New Pacific Lumber Co., 119 NLRB 1307, 41 LRRM 1290 (1958); Martino's Complete Home Furnishings, 145 NLRB 604, 55 LRRM 1003 (1963).
[98]Capitol Market No. 1, 145 NLRB 1430, 55 LRRM 1173 (1964); Holiday Inn of Providence-Downtown, 179 NLRB No. 58, 72 LRRM 1321 (1969); Denny's Restaurant, Inc., 186 NLRB No. 21, 75 LRRM 1284 (1970).
[99]Standard Automotive Mfg. Co., 109 NLRB 726, 34 LRRM 1426 (1954).
[100]Casey-Metcalf Machinery Co., 114 NLRB 1520, 37 LRRM 1208 (1955).
[101]V & D Machinery Embroidery Co., 107 NLRB 1567, 33 LRRM 1432 (1954).
[102]Francis Plating Co., 109 NLRB 35, 34 LRRM 1278 (1954).

(f) Demanding that the employer sign a contract and union members refusing to load trucks on employer's refusal to sign.[103]

(g) Urging its contract as a bar to the proceeding.[104]

Whenever a union is permitted to withdraw a petition—after the close of the hearing or after issuance of the direction of election—the following condition is always applied: The regional director will not entertain a new petition from the withdrawing union for a period of six months from the date of the NLRB order, unless good cause is shown to the contrary.[105] The grant of permission to withdraw the petition will contain language substantially as follows:

"It is hereby ordered that the petitioner's request to withdraw petition be, and it hereby is granted with prejudice to its filing a new petition for a period of six months from the date of this order unless good cause is shown to the contrary."[106]

There is only one possibility for a union to withdraw its petition after issuance of a decision and direction of election without prejudice to filing a new petition at any time: Where the decision and direction of election finds an appropriate unit substantially different from the one sought in the petition and orders an election, the regional director or the Board may provide that the petition may be withdrawn without prejudice upon application to the regional director.[107]

Where a union seeks to withdraw from a runoff election, the request will be granted with prejudice to the filing of a new petition for a period of one year from the date of the decision and direction of election.[108]

Whenever a petitioner files a new petition after expiration of the six-month period or the one-year period, as the case may be, a new showing of interest is required; a current 30 percent showing of interest among the employees in the unit must be submitted.[109]

Sec. 8–23. Disclaimer.   Where either an employer has filed the petition or an individual or group of employees seeks to decertify the union, the latter may terminate the proceeding by making a "clear and unequivocal" disclaimer of interest in representing the employees involved.[110] The disclaimer must be made known to all interested parties. The rules applied to disclaimers are substantially the same as those used for withdrawals.

[103]McAllister Transfer, Inc., 105 NLRB 751, 22 LRRM 1348 (1948).
[104]3 Beall Brothers 3, 110 NLRB 685, 35 LRRM 1086 (1954).
[105]Sears, Roebuck & Co., 107 NLRB 716, 33 LRRM 1233 (1954).
[106]*Ibid.*
[107]American Potash & Chemical Corp., 117 NLRB 1508, 40 LRRM 1038 (1957).
[108]Pittsburgh Steamship Division of United States Steel Corp., 106 NLRB 1248, 32 LRRM 1659 (1953).
[109]General Dynamics Corp., 175 NLRB No. 155, 71 LRRM 1116 (1969).
[110]Plough, Inc., 203 NLRB No. 50, 83 LRRM 1086 (1973).

The NLRB neither provides nor requires any special form for the making of a disclaimer of interest. Usually the disclaimer merely states that the undersigned union waives or disclaims any right to represent the described employees or the employees involved in a designated NLRB case.

Sec. 8–24. Disclaimer before hearing. The regional director may dismiss the petition without prejudice on the basis of a union's valid and unequivocal disclaimer filed: (a) before the opening of the hearing; or (b) before his approval of an election agreement, consent or stipulated.

A union which has filed a disclaimer cannot block the making of an election agreement.

Sec. 8–25. Disclaimer at hearing. A disclaimer of interest may be filed during the hearing. The hearing officer will refer it to the regional director. If the regional director accepts the disclaimer as valid and unequivocal, he will: (a) instruct the hearing officer to adjourn the hearing indefinitely; (b) withdraw the notice of hearing; and (c) dismiss the petition without prejudice.

The Board has held that the failure of a union to appear at the hearing does not constitute a disclaimer.[111]

Sec. 8–26. Disclaimer after election agreement. The following rules apply where a union's valid and unequivocal disclaimer is filed after the regional director's approval of an election agreement, consent or stipulated:

1. The election will be cancelled, whether or not the petitioner—the employer, or the individual or group of employees seeking decertification—objects; and
2. The petition will be dismissed with prejudice, with these conditions attached: (a) the petition will be reinstated, upon request of the petitioner, if the union should make a claim for recognition by the employer within six months from the date of the regional director's letter; and (b) any petition filed by the disclaiming union within those six months will not be entertained, unless good cause is shown to the contrary.[112] (For a statement of what constitutes "good cause," see page 152 under "Proceedings within six months.")

Sec. 8–27. Disclaimer after hearing. After the close of hearing, a disclaimer of interest should be addressed to the regional director or, if the case has been transferred, to the Board. The regional director or the Board, as the case may be, will refuse to dismiss the petition and will regard the

[111]Central Optical Co., 88 NLRB 246, 15 LRRM 1318 (1950).
[112]19 NLRB Ann. Rep. 19.

union's disclaimer ineffective where the union is engaged in action which is inconsistent with its stated disclaimer of interest. The union's disclaimer, to be effective, must be "clear and unequivocal" and not "inconsistent" with its actions.[113] Some examples of inconsistent behavior by unions which unsuccessfully sought to terminate election proceedings are set forth on page 149, under "Withdrawal of petition after hearing." In addition to these examples, the Board has held ineffective a union's disclaimer following an employer petition in view of a history of earlier, repeated disclaimers which were submitted as soon as the employer petitions were filed.[114]

Sec. 8–28. Action on disclaimer. Whenever a disclaimer is accepted as valid and unequivocal, the regional director or the Board will:

1. Dismiss the petition.[115]
2. Advise the disclaiming union that any petition filed by it within six months from the date of the order will not be entertained, unless good cause is shown to the contrary.[116]
3. State that the petition will be reinstated, upon request of the petitioner, if the union should make a claim for recognition by the employer within six months from the date of the order.[117]
4. Include in the order a determination that the disclaiming union is no longer the exclusive representative of the employees involved if the petition was filed by an individual or group of employees seeking decertification of the union.[118]

Following is a sample of an order dismissing a petition for decertification:

It is hereby ordered that the petition for decertification filed by John Doe, petitioner herein, be, and it hereby is, dismissed on the basis of said disclaimer of representation by Local (union); and

It is determined that the above-named union, having disclaimed its interest, is no longer the exclusive representative of the employees in the unit involved in this proceeding.

---

[113]Holiday Inn of Providence-Downtown, 179 NLRB No. 58, 72 LRRM 1321 (1969); Denny's Restaurant Inc., 186 NLRB No. 21, 75 LRRM 1284 (1970).
[114]Shepherd Machinery Co., 115 NLRB 736, 37 LRRM 1379 (1956).
[115]Old Angus Restaurant, 165 NLRB 675, 65 LRRM 1367 (1967); Autohaus-Brugger Inc., 173 NLRB No. 32, 69 LRRM 1274 (1968).
[116]Richmond Motor Car Dealers Assn., 116 NLRB 1761, 39 LRRM 1088 (1956).
[117]Campos Dairy Products, Ltd., 107 NLRB 715, 33 LRRM 1233 (1954).
[118]Little Rock Road Machinery Co., 107 NLRB 715, 33 LRRM 1232 (1954).

Moreover, the parties are advised the regional director will not entertain a petition filed by the union within six months from the date of this order, unless good cause is shown to the contrary.

In the event that the union, purporting to represent the employees in the unit involved in this proceeding, makes a claim upon the employer within six months from the date of this order, the regional director will entertain a motion by the petitioner requesting reinstatement of the petition.[119]

An order dismissing an employer's petition on the basis of a disclaimer contains substantially the same language. The Board has dismissed an employer's petition and revoked a union's certification where the union: (a) disclaimed all interest in any employees on the payroll; and (b) restricted its claim to representation solely to strikers.[120]

Sec. 8–29. Proceedings within six months. As noted above, in certain cases of union disclaimer of interest or withdrawal of petition, the official action will carry the limitation that "any petition filed within six months (from that action) will not be entertained unless good cause is shown to the contrary." When a union files a new petition within that six-month period, the regional director will determine whether "good cause," in fact, exists; this determination may go one of two ways.

1. If the regional director decides that "good cause" exists, he will issue a notice of hearing. The issue will be considered at the hearing and, based on facts brought out there, he may change his decision. If not and an appeal is taken, the Board may ultimately decide whether or not the regional director's determination was correct.[121]
2. If the regional director determines that "good cause" does not exist, he will dismiss the petition. The petitioning union may thereupon seek review of the dismissal by appealing to the Board,[122] in the manner set forth on page 90, under "Dismissal of a petition."

What constitutes sufficient "good cause" to entertain a petition within the prohibited period of six months is not stated comprehensively by the Board; instead, it judges each case individually. However, the following are some examples of what the Board may consider good cause:

1. The disclaimer or withdrawal of the original petition was made because of the expansion or contraction of the unit.

[119]*Ibid.*
[120]Hygienic Sanitation Co., 118 NLRB 1030, 40 LRRM 1308 (1957).
[121]R. and R. Sec. 102.67(c); Agawam Food Mart Inc., 162 NLRB 1420, 64 LRRM 1197 (1967).
[122]R. and R. Sec. 102.71.

2. The union did not wish to proceed to an election on the original petition in the presence of an outstanding complaint of unfair labor practices.
3. The employer has agreed to a consent election at the request of the petitioning union.

The Board has ruled that withdrawal of a petition with prejudice to filing of another petition for six months applies only to a petitioner; it does not apply to an intervening union. Accordingly, an interested union is permitted to intervene in an election proceeding even though less than six months have elapsed since withdrawal with prejudice of its petition for the same bargaining unit.[123]

---

[123]California Furniture Shops, Ltd., 115 NLRB 1399, 38 LRRM 1080 (1956).

CHAPTER 9

The Election

Sec. 9–1. In general. If representation cases are the heart of the Act, the core of those proceedings is the election, and it is here that the NLRB exercises enormous power. Control of the conduct of the election rests in the NLRB alone.[1] It has been repeatedly held that the Board has a "wide degree of discretion in establishing the procedure and safeguards necessary to insure the fair and free choice of bargaining representatives by employees."[2]

Sec. 9–2. Employee eligibility list (Excelsior list). Within seven days after the director approves a consent election agreement or after an election has been directed (except expedited elections— see Chapter 19), the employer must file with the regional director an election eligibility list, known as the Excelsior list, containing the names and home addresses of all eligible voters. The list is immediately made available to all unions involved in the case. Failure to furnish the list is sufficient basis to set aside the election.[3]

Sec. 9–3. Preelection conference. The actual planning and conduct of the election are the responsibility of the regional director. After the direction of election issues, a Board agent will arrange an informal conference of all parties. The purpose of this conference is to settle the details of the election.

The holding of a preelection conference is solely within the discretion of the regional director. It is not required by the Board's Rules and Regulations. Accordingly, any objection to an election based on the Board agent's failure to hold a preelection conference will be overruled.[4]

[1]NLRB v. Waterman Steamship Corp., 309 U.S. 206, 5 LRRM 682 (1940).
[2]NLRB v. A.J. Tower Co., 329 U.S. 324, 19 LRRM 2128 (1946).
[3]Excelsior Underwear, Inc., 156 NLRB No. 111, 61 LRRM 1217 (1966); Nathan's Famous of Yonkers, 186 NLRB 131, 75 LRRM 1321 (1970); American Petrofina Company of Texas, 203 NLRB No. 158, 83 LRRM 1252 (1973).
[4]Eisner Grocery Co., 116 NLRB 976, 38 LRRM 1376 (1956).

The parties at the conference will be called upon to consider such matters as: time of election, place of election, eligibility list, places on the ballot, and election observers. The Board agent will attempt to secure agreement among the parties on all the details of the election. Consequently, parties should go to the preelection conference with their positions on such details carefully prepared. In a directed election, the regional director has final authority to determine any question incidental to the arrangements of the election. Furthermore, it is the Board's "long established policy, absent unusual circumstances, not to interfere with the regional director in the exercise of his discretion in making arrangements with respect to the conduct of elections and the counting of ballots."[5]

A party's participation in the checking of an eligibility list does not constitute a final and binding agreement as to eligibility; that party remains free to challenge voters at the election whose names appear on or were omitted from the eligibility list.[6] However, any objections to the election based on errors in the eligibility list will be overruled; challenges at the election are the only means whereby errors in the eligibility list may be attacked.[7]

Parties should particularly exercise the greatest care in checking the eligibility list for either erroneous appearances or omissions of names before entering into a written and signed agreement listing those eligible to vote. Such agreement will be the sole basis on which any later questions of eligibility will be resolved. It is the Board's stated policy:

> Where the parties enter into a written and signed agreement which expressly provides that issues of eligibility resolved therein shall be final and binding upon the parties, the Board will consider such an agreement, and only such an agreement, a final determination of the eligibility issues treated therein unless it is, in part or in whole, contrary to the Act or established Board policy.[8]

Thus, where a probationary employee was excluded from eligibility by terms of a pre-election agreement, and such exclusion was contrary to established Board policy, the Board rejected the agreement as controlling and ordered the employee's ballot to be opened and counted.[9]

If the check of the eligibility list discloses that the number of challenges to be raised is significant, consideration should be given to withdrawal of

[5]Independent Rice Mill, Inc., 111 NLRB 536, 35 LRRM 1509 (1955).
[6]Lloyd A. Fry Roofing Co., 118 NLRB 312, 40 LRRM 1188 (1957); Laymon Candy Co., 199 NLRB No. 65, 81 LRRM 1504 (1972).
[7]Calcor Corp, 106 NLRB 539, 32 LRRM 1498 (1953); Olson Bodies, Inc., 73 LRRM 2202 (C.A. 2, 1970), enf. 68 LRRM 1031; cf. Neuhoff Bros. Packers, Inc., 62 LRRM 2380 (C.A. 5, 1966), enf. 59 LRRM 1761.
[8]Norris-Thermador Corp., 119 NLRB 1301, 41 LRRM 1283 (1958).
[9]Westlake Plastics Co. and Crystal-X Corp., 119 NLRB 1434, 41 LRRM 1326 (1958).

the regional director's approval of the election agreement or to reconvening the parties for clarification.[10]

Sec. 9–4. Time of election. The date of the election, if it is a regional director's direction of election, will generally be held between the 25th and 30th day after the date of his decision. However, if the direction of election is issued by the Board in Washington, the date of election may be at any time within 30 days from the date of direction of election. Where necessary, the Board will amend its direction of election so as to grant an extension of time to hold the election.[11]

An election may not be held sooner than 10 days after the regional director has received the list of names and addresses of the eligible voters. Where the parties jointly wish a prompt election, presumably the employer will make the list available in less than seven days. If the parties are pressing for an early election, the 10-day period can be provisionally calculated from the date it is estimated the list will arrive in the regional office.[12]

The particular day selected for the election usually will be one when substantially all eligible employees will have an opportunity to vote. Thus, to insure such opportunity, NLRB elections may even be conducted on holidays.[13] Paydays are frequently used because absenteeism is at a minimum.

In a seasonal industry, if the plant is not at or near peak operation at the time of issuance of the direction of election, the regional director has authority to schedule the election at or near the peak. And, eligibility to vote may be determined by employment during the payroll period immediately preceding the date of the regional director's issuance of the notice of election.[14]

As discussed earlier, the regional director will not conduct an election when an unfair labor practice charge affecting some or all of the employees involved in the election is pending unless a "request to proceed" is filed.[15] (See Sec. 7–3, Blocking charges, page 107.) As a matter of policy the regional director will conduct the election where the charge of unfair labor practices has been dismissed by the regional director but is pending on appeal before the General Counsel.[16]

Where the Board has issued a decision and order against an employer in an unfair labor practice proceeding, the direction of election will provide

[10]NLRB Field Manual 11094, 11312.4.
[11]Simplot Fertilizer Co., 107 NLRB 1217, 33 LRRM 1357 (1954).
[12]NLRB Field Manual 11302.1.
[13]Cities Service Oil Co. of Pennsylvania, 87 NLRB 324, 25 LRRM 1112 (1949).
[14]H. A. Rider & Sons, 117 NLRB 517, 39 LRRM 1269 (1957).
[15]Surrat v. NLRB, 463 F.2d 378, 80 LRRM 2804 (C.A. 5, 1972), *aff'g* 78 LRRM 2115.
[16]Ekco Products, Inc., 116 NLRB 134, 38 LRRM 1206 (1956).

that the election will not be held until the employer has complied completely with the affirmative provisions of that order.[17]

Sec. 9–5. Voting hours.   The voting hours—during, before or after working hours—will be arranged so that all eligible employees on all shifts will have adequate opportunity to vote. Split voting schedules, where the polls are kept open only long enough for employees on a shift to vote and are reopened for a later shift or shifts, are commonly used. Also, voting is often conducted at one plant and the polls then moved to another plant in multiemployer or multiplant bargaining unit situations.

Sec. 9–6. Place of election.   The polling place is determined with a view to easy accessibility to the voters. The regional director usually endeavors to have the election conducted on company property but not in areas where supervisors can observe the balloting.

The Board will deny any request that it, rather than the regional director, determine the place for conducting the election. However, in denying such requests, the Board has stated that a party can raise the issue as an objection to the election.[18]

Sec. 9–7. Form of the ballot.   In an election involving only one labor organization, the ballot will provide the employees the opportunity to vote on the question: "Do you wish to be represented for purposes of collective bargaining by (name of union)?" Spaces are provided for voting "yes" or "no." (See Facsimile No. 28, page 159.)

In an election involving two or more labor organizations, each will be asked to designate its choice of positions on the ballot. Unless they agree on definite positions, the place of each union's name on the ballot is determined by lot (for example, by the toss of a coin). The ballot will afford a choice of representation by any of the labor organizations or by none. (See Facsimile No. 29, page 160.)

In an election to determine whether or not a group of employees wishes to be severed from a larger unit, the ballot will not provide for a "neither" or "no union" choice.[19] The ballot will afford only a choice between the contending labor organizations, and will carry this language: "This ballot is to determine the collective bargaining representative for the unit in which you are employed." (See Facsimile No. 30, page 161.)

---

[17]S. B. Whistler and Sons, Inc., 92 NLRB No. 197 (not reported).
[18]Manchester Knitted Fashions, Inc., 108 NLRB 1366, 34 LRRM 1214 (1954); J. P. Stevens and Co., Inc., 167 NLRB 266, 66 LRRM 1024 (1967).
[19]American Tobacco Co., Inc., 115 NLRB 218, 37 LRRM 1263 (1956).

UNITED STATES OF AMERICA

National Labor Relations Board

OFFICIAL SECRET BALLOT

FOR CERTAIN EMPLOYEES OF

THE COOLEY CONTAINER CORPORATION

Do you wish to be represented for purposes of collective bargaining by -

LOCAL 94, UNITED METAL PRODUCTS, MACHINER, AND RELATED
EQUIPMENT WORKERS OF AMERICA,
AFL-CIO

MARK AN "X" IN THE SQUARE OF YOUR CHOICE

YES ☐   NO ☐

DO NOT SIGN THIS BALLOT. Fold and drop in ballot box.
If you spoil this ballot return it to the Board Agent for a new one.

FACSIMILE NO. 28.
*Sample of ballot used in a collective bargaining election
involving only one union*

UNITED STATES OF AMERICA

National Labor Relations Board

OFFICIAL SECRET BALLOT

FOR CERTAIN EMPLOYEES OF

THE COOLEY CONTAINER CORPORATION

This ballot is to determine the collective bargaining representative, if any, for the unit in which you are employed.

MARK AN "X" IN THE SQUARE OF YOUR CHOICE

[Name of Union A]	[Name of Union B]
☐	☐

DO NOT SIGN THIS BALLOT. Fold and drop in ballot box. If you spoil this ballot return it to the Board Agent for a new one.

FACSIMILE No. 29.
Sample of ballot used in a collective bargaining election involving more than one union

UNITED STATES OF AMERICA

National Labor Relations Board

OFFICIAL SECRET BALLOT

FOR CERTAIN EMPLOYEES OF

THE COOLEY CONTAINER CORPORATION

This ballot is to determine the collective bargaining representative, if any, for the unit in which you are employed.

MARK AN "X" IN THE SQUARE OF YOUR CHOICE

[Name of Union A]	NEITHER	[Name of Union B]
☐	☐	☐

DO NOT SIGN THIS BALLOT. Fold and drop in ballot box. If you spoil this ballot return it to the Board Agent for a new one.

FACSIMILE No. 30.
Sample of ballot used in "severance" election

Several petitioning unions may appear jointly as a single choice on the ballot.[20]

Should a union request the use of a shortened name on the ballot, whether or not the matter was raised initially at a hearing, the regional director may permit the use of the shortened name if by so doing there is no possibility of the voters being misled. If used, the full name must be used with the shortened name appearing in parentheses below.

Sec. 9–8. The notice of election. Official notices of election are usually posted in the plant at least three days before the election. These notices are intended to inform all eligible voters concerning the details of the election. (See Facsimile No. 31, page 163. Also see page 198 for special notices in rerun elections.)

The employer will be asked to post copies of the notice which will be supplied to him by the NLRB regional office. Posting places include regular bulletin boards, time-card racks, and rest rooms. The labor organizations may also be given copies of the notice of election for such posting as they wish to make.

An employer's failure to post the notices may be reason to set aside the election if the regional director finds that the polling was not adequately publicized and interested employees were thereby prevented from voting.[21] However, an employer's refusal to post notices of the election cannot operate to invalidate an election; in such circumstances, NLRB agents will undertake to publicize the date, place, and hours of the election.[22]

The notice of election usually contains a sample copy of the ballot. Defacement or markings of the posted sample ballots does not require the regional director to set aside the election.[23] However, the Board has warned that where one of the parties is responsible for the defacement or marking of the sample ballot, the election may be set aside.[24]

When the sample ballot on the NLRB's posted notice of election is marked or defaced, it should be removed and replaced. Extra copies will be supplied by the regional office.

Sec. 9–9. Preelection propaganda. The Board has repeatedly declared that, as a general rule, it will not censor or police preelection campaign propaganda of the parties.[25] However, the Board has imposed limitations

[20]The Transport Co. of Texas and Transport Co., Inc., 111 NLRB 884, 35 LRRM 1611 (1955).

[21]F. H. Vahsling, Inc., 114 NLRB 1451, 37 LRRM 1194 (1955); c.f. Kilgore Corp., 209 NLRB No. 134, 85 LRRM 1615 (1974), enf. den. NLRB v. Kilgore Corporation, —F.2d–, 88 LRRM 2833 (C.A. 6, 1975).

[22]The Falmouth Co., 115 NLRB 1533, 38 LRRM 1124 (1956).

[23]Rheem Mfg. Corp., 114 NLRB 404, 36 LRRM 1600 (1955); cf. Marketing Services, 192 NLRB No. 162, 78 LRRM 1266 (1971).

[24]Murray Chair Co., 117 NLRB 1385, 40 LRRM 1009 (1957); Mademoiselle Shoppe, Inc., 199 NLRB No. 147, 82 LRRM 1022 (1972).

[25]United Aircraft Corp., 103 NLRB 102, 31 LRRM 1437 (1953).

NOTICE OF ELECTION

UNITED STATES OF AMERICA ★ NATIONAL LABOR RELATIONS BOARD

PURPOSE OF THIS ELECTION

This election is to determine the representative, if any, desired by the eligible employees for purposes of collective bargaining with their employer. (See printed portion of this Notice of Election for description of eligible employees.) A majority of the valid ballots cast will determine the results of the election.

SECRET BALLOT

The election will be by SECRET ballot under the supervision of the Regional Director of the National Labor Relations Board. Voters will be allowed to vote without interference, restraint, or coercion. Electioneering will not be permitted at or near the polling place. Violations of these rules should be reported immediately to the Regional Director or his agent in charge of the election. Your attention is called to Section 12 of the National Labor Relations Act:

ANY PERSON WHO SHALL WILLFULLY RESIST, PREVENT, IMPEDE, OR INTERFERE WITH ANY MEMBER OF THE BOARD OR ANY OF ITS AGENTS OR AGENCIES IN THE PERFORMANCE OF DUTIES PURSUANT TO THIS ACT SHALL BE PUNISHED BY A FINE OF NOT MORE THAN $5,000 OR BY IMPRISONMENT FOR NOT MORE THAN ONE YEAR, OR BOTH.

An agent of the Board will hand a ballot to each eligible voter at the voting place. Mark your ballot in secret in the voting booth provided. DO NOT SIGN YOUR BALLOT. Fold the ballot before leaving the voting booth, then personally deposit it in a ballot box under the supervision of an agent of the Board.

A sample of the official ballot is shown at the center of this Notice.

ELIGIBILITY RULES

Employees eligible to vote are those described under VOTING UNIT in this Notice of Election, including employees who did not work during the designated payroll period because they were ill or on vacation or temporarily laid off, and also including employees in the military service of the United States who appear in person at the polls. Employees who have quit or been discharged for cause since the designated payroll period and who have not been rehired or reinstated prior to the date of this election are not eligible to vote.

CHALLENGE OF VOTERS

An agent of the Board or an authorized observer may question the eligibility of a voter. Such challenge MUST be made before the voter has deposited his ballot in the ballot box.

AUTHORIZED OBSERVERS

Each of the interested parties may designate an equal number of observers, this number to be determined by the Regional Director or his agent in charge of the election. These observers (a) act as checkers at the voting place and at the counting of ballots, (b) assist in the identification of voters, (c) challenge voters and ballots, and (d) otherwise assist the Regional Director or his agent.

INFORMATION CONCERNING ELECTION

The Act provides that only one valid representation election may be held in a 12-month period. Any employee who desires to obtain any further information concerning the terms and conditions under which this election is to be held or who desires to ask any question concerning the holding of an election, the voting unit, or eligibility rules may do so by communicating with the Regional Director or his agent in charge of the election.

RIGHTS OF EMPLOYEES

Under the National Labor Relations Act, employees have the right:

- To self-organization
- To form, join, or assist labor organizations
- To bargain collectively through representatives of their own choosing
- To act together for the purposes of collective bargaining or other mutual aid or protection
- To refuse to do any or all of these things unless the union and employer, in a State where such agreements are permitted, enter into a lawful union security clause requiring employees to join the union.

It is the responsibility of the National Labor Relations Board to protect employees in the exercise of these rights.

The Board wants all eligible voters to be fully informed about their rights under Federal law and wants both Employers and Unions to know what is expected of them when it holds an election.

The following are examples of conduct which interfere with the rights of employees and may result in the setting aside of the election:

- Threatening loss of jobs or benefits by an Employer or a Union
- Misstating important facts by a Union or an Employer where the other party does not have a fair chance to reply
- Promising or granting promotions, pay raises, or other benefits, to influence an employee's vote by a party capable of carrying out such promises.
- An Employer firing employees to discourage or encourage union activity or a Union causing them to be fired to encourage union activity
- Making campaign speeches to assembled groups of employees on company time within the 24-hour period before the election.
- Incitement by an Employer or a Union of racial or religious prejudice by inflammatory appeals
- Threatening physical force or violence to employees by a Union or an Employer to influence their votes

The National Labor Relations Board protects your right to a free choice

Improper conduct will not be permitted. All parties are expected to cooperate fully with this agency in maintaining basic principles of a fair election as required by law. The National Labor Relations Board is an agency of the United States Government and does not endorse any choice in the election.

NATIONAL LABOR RELATIONS BOARD
an agency of the
UNITED STATES GOVERNMENT

SAMPLE

WARNING: THIS IS THE ONLY OFFICIAL NOTICE OF THIS ELECTION AND MUST NOT BE DEFACED BY ANYONE

FACSIMILE NO. 31.
Notice of election (Form 707)

on certain techniques used in campaigning; these involve: (1) false or misleading propaganda; (2) threats of reprisal or promises of benefit; (3) appeals to racial prejudice; and (4) propaganda which interferes with the voters' free choice because of its form or timing.[26]

Sec. 9–10. False or misleading election propaganda. Board decisions establish certain basic tests for determining whether an election should be set aside on the basis of misrepresentations in a party's campaign propaganda. These tests have been summarized as follows:

1. *Substantiality.* Was the misrepresentation enough of a departure from the truth to be likely to have influenced the voters' choice?
2. *Materiality.* Was the subject matter of the misrepresentation closely enough related to election issues to influence the voters?
3. *Timing.* Did the opposing party have the adequate opportunity to reply to the misrepresentation prior to the election?
4. *Source.* Did the misrepresentation come from a party in a position to have special knowledge of the subject matter, so that voters would be likely to rely on, or unable to check, its accuracy?
5. *Voters' independent knowledge.* Did the misrepresentation relate to a matter about which the voters lacked independent knowledge, thus precluding a finding that they were able to evaluate the claim for themselves?[27]

It is generally said that each of these questions must be answered in the affirmative in order for a misrepresentation to result in invalidation of the election. However, the application of the foregoing criteria to specific campaign statements often involves difficult questions of interpretation.[28] Broadly speaking, the Board's task is to determine not merely whether false statements have been made, but whether such statements "in fact" constituted an interference with the employees' free choice.[29]

Sec. 9–11. Campaign statements containing threats or promises. Although Section 8(c) of the Act protects the right of employers and unions to express any views, argument, or opinion, this protection has been held to be available only in unfair labor practice cases. It does not prevent such statements from being used as a basis for setting aside representation

[26]Williams, Janus, and Huhn, NLRB REGULATION OF ELECTION CONDUCT (Philadelphia: University of Pennsylvania Press, 1974).
[27]Williams, Janus, and Huhn, *supra;* Morris, THE DEVELOPING LABOR LAW (Washington, D.C.: BNA Books, 1971), Chapter 5, p. 63 *et seq.*
[28]Compare Modine Mfg. Co., 203 NLRB No. 17, 83 LRRM 1133 (1973), with Medical Ancillary Services, Inc., 212 NLRB No. 80, 86 LRRM 1598 (1974) (dissenting opinion of Member Penello).
[29]Southwestern Portland Cement Co. v. NLRB, 407 F.2d 131, 70 LRRM 2536 (C.A. 5, 1969), *cert. den.*, 396 U.S. 820 , 72 LRRM 2431.

elections.[30] Moreover, Section 8(c) specifically excludes from protection any statements containing threats of reprisal or force or promises of benefit.

In practice, an employers' preelection statements regarding the possible consequences of unionization are likely to be ruled objectionable unless they are carefully phrased as mere predictions, and not as threats or promises.[31] The Board considers such factors as (1) whether the suggested consequences are demonstrably probable and (2) whether such consequences lie beyond the control of the employer. If there is any implication that action is to be taken for anti-union reasons rather than reasons of economic necessity, the election is likely to be set aside.

Applying these criteria, the Board has invalidated elections because of:

1. "Veiled" or "implied" threats of plant closure or relocation if the union won the election;[32]
2. Exaggerated predictions of loss of business, job security, or benefits;[33]
3. Repeated references to the inevitability of strikes if the union were selected;[34]
4. Statements indicating that the employer would bargain "from scratch";[35]
5. Declarations of an intent to contest the union's certification through the courts if the employees voted in favor of representation.[36]

The Board has also set aside elections where the employer assembled employees for a preelection showing of a movie that portrayed strike violence and people being stoned when they entered a plant.[37] Recently, however, the Board ruled that the showing of the same film, without other illegal or objectionable conduct accompanying it, was an insufficient basis for setting an election aside.[38]

Sec. 9–12. Preelection appeals to racial prejudice. In deciding whether appeals to racial prejudice warrant setting aside the election, the Board

[30]Dal-Tex Optical Co., 137 NLRB 1782, 50 LRRM 1489 (1962); General Shoe Corp., 77 NLRB 124, 21 LRRM 1337 (1948).
[31]Williams, Janus, and Huhn, *supra* note 26, pp. 62–92; NLRB v. Gissel Packing Co., 395 U.S. 575, 71 LRRM 2481 (1969).
[32]Lake Catherine Footwear, Inc., 133 NLRB 443, 48 LRRM 1683 (1961); State Supply Warehouse Co., 206 NLRB No. 36, 84 LRRM 1233 (1973).
[33]Aerona Mfg. Corp., 118 NLRB 461, 40 LRRM 1196 (1957). *But compare* Allied/Egry Business Systems, Inc., 169 NLRB 514, 67 LRRM 1195 (1968)
[34]Boaz Spinning Co., Inc., 177 NLRB 788, 71 LRRM 1506 (1969).
[35]General Industries Electronics Co., 146 NLRB 1139, 56 LRRM 1015 (1964). *But see* Monroe Mfg. Co., 200 NLRB No. 71, 82 LRRM 1042 (1972) (dissenting opinion of Chairman Miller).
[36]Lord Baltimore Press, 142 NLRB 328, 53 LRRM 1019 (1963).
[37]Plochman and Harrison-Cherry Lane Foods, Inc., 140 NLRB 130, 51 LRRM 1558 (1962).
[38]Hawesville Rolling Mill, Nat'l Aluminum Div. of Nat'l Steel Corp., 204 NLRB No. 42, 83 LRRM 1305 (1973).

holds that the test is whether the party making the racial appeal limits himself to setting forth truthfully the other party's position on matters or whether, instead, he is deliberately seeking to overstress and exacerbate racial feelings by irrelevant, inflammatory appeals. The burden is on the party making use of a racial message to establish that it was truthful and germane, and where there is doubt as to whether the total conduct of such party is within the permissible limits, such doubt is resolved against him.[39] The Board has ordered a new election based upon the employer's distribution of various forms of literature stressing appeals and arguments against unionization upon racial consideration,[40] however, the Board has denied a new election where an employer's letter circulated to the employees was temperate in tone and told them of certain facts concerning union expenditures to help eliminate segregation.[41]

Sec. 9–13. Form and timing of campaign speech and propaganda. As indicated, some preelection propaganda may be ruled objectionable not because of its content, but because of the time, place, or manner of its presentation. Thus, the Board has sustained objections based upon:

1. *"Captive audience" speeches on the eve of the election.* Neither party may make election speeches to massed assemblies of employees within 24 hours before the scheduled time for starting the election. However, this rule does not apply to the distribution of campaign literature on or off the job site prior to the election, nor will it prohibit the use of any other legitimate campaign propaganda or media, including campaign speeches on or off company premises during the 24 hour period if employee attendance is voluntary and on the employees' own time.[42]

2. *Electioneering or other conduct near the polls.* Electioneering in and around the voting place is forbidden. The NLRB agent, where necessary, will indicate the forbidden area to cover approximately a circle whose diameter is 200 feet with the polling place in the center.

The Board has found the following types of electioneering objectionable, and elections were set aside where:

---

[39]Sewell Mfg. Company, 138 NLRB 66, 50 LRRM 1532 (1962).
[40]Sewell Mfg. Company, 140 NLRB 220, 51 LRRM 1611 (1962).
[41]Allen-Morrison Sign Company, 138 NLRB 73, 50 LRRM 1535 (1962); *cf.* Archer Laundry Co., 150 NLRB 1427, 58 LRRM 1212 (1965); Baltimore Luggage Co., 162 NLRB No. 113, 64 LRRM 1145 (1967); Mohawk Bedding Co., 204 NLRB No. 1, 83 LRRM 1317 (1973).
[42]Peerless Plywood Co., 107 NLRB 427, 33 LRRM 1151 (1953); Honeywell, Inc., 162 NLRB 323, 64 LRRM 1002 (1966); Southland Cork Co., 146 NLRB 906, 55 LRRM 1426 (1964), *enf. in part,* 342 F.2d 702, 58 LRRM 2555 (1965); Shop Rite Foods, Inc., 195 NLRB No. 14, 79 LRRM 1231 (1972).

(a) In defiance of the NLRB agent's order, a union distributed handbills in the "no electioneering" area during voting hours in full view of voters entering the booths.[43]

(b) A sound truck could be clearly heard within 30 feet of the polling place, and it broadcast while the polls were open.[44]

The Board has held the following activities not sufficient basis for setting aside elections:

(c) The wearing of stickers, buttons and similar insignia by voters and observers which, by their size or nature, do not constitute electioneering;[45] however, such identifications are discouraged by NLRB agents.

(d) The distribution of noncoercive handbills in front of the plant on election day;[46] or

(e) The mere presence of union representatives at or near the polling area.[47]

Also, the Board has ruled that, "regardless of the content of the remarks exchanged," prolonged conversation by representatives of either the employer or the union with prospective voters in the polling area "constitutes conduct which, in itself," will invalidate an election.[48]

3. *Questioning, polling, or surveillance of employees.* An employer's attempt to obtain information about employees' union activities will be grounds to invalidate the election if carried out under circumstances tending "to instill in the minds of employees fear of discrimination."[49] In determining whether an employer's preelection meetings or interviews with employees have had such a tendency, the Board looks to such factors as the size of the group of employees involved and the location of the meetings. Meetings with individuals or small groups of employees, or sessions conducted in a "locus of managerial authority"—i.e., a company office or isolated location

---

[43]Continental Can Co., 80 NLRB 785, 23 LRRM 1126 (1948).
[44]Alliance Ware, Inc., 92 NLRB 55, 27 LRRM 1040 (1950).
[45]Electric Wheel Co., 120 NLRB 1644, 42 LRRM 1244 (1958); Laney and Duke Storage Warehouse Co., Inc., 63 LRRM 2552 (C.A. 5, 1966), *enf. in part* 58 LRRM 1389.
[46]Lloyd A. Fry Roofing Co., 108 NLRB 1297, 34 LRRM 1185 (1954).
[47]Pacific Maritime Assn., 112 NLRB 1280, 36 LRRM 1193 (1955).
[48]Michelm, Inc., 170 NLRB No. 46, 67 LRRM 1395 (1968); Star Expansion Indus. Corp., 170 NLRB No. 47, 67 LRRM 1400 (1968); Harold W. Moore and Son, 173 NLRB No. 191, 70 LRRM 1002 (1968); Lincoln Land Moving and Storage, Inc., 197 NLRB No. 160, 80 LRRM 1489 (1972); Mead Corp., 189 NLRB No. 36, 76 LRRM 1563 (1971).
[49]NLRB v. West Coast Casket Co., 205 F.2d 902, 32 LRRM 2353 (C.A. 9, 1953). *See generally* Williams, Janus, and Huhn, *supra* note 26, pp. 167–194.

away from the employees' normal work stations or meeting places—will generally be deemed election interference.[50]

Interrogation or polling of employees about their union sentiments is often held to constitute coercion and election interference. However, such questioning is permissible if the following safeguards are present: (1) The purpose of the questioning is to determine the truth of a union's claim of majority, (2) this purpose is communicated to the employees, (3) assurances against reprisal are given, (4) any polling is conducted by secret ballot, and (5) the employer has not engaged in unfair labor practices or otherwise created a coercive atmosphere.[51]

Company surveillance of employees' organizing activities or union meetings has been held to constitute election interference, as well as an unfair labor practice.[52] Conduct calculated to create the impression that management has had union activities under surveillance is treated similarly.[53] The mere presence of a company official or agent at a place where union meetings are being conducted, however, is not objectionable in the absence of evidence showing an improper purpose.[54]

4. *Visiting voters' homes.* Systematic preelection visits to employees' homes by employer representatives afford a ground for invalidating the election regardless of whether the employer's actual remarks to the employees are coercive in character.[55] Home visits by union representatives, however, are considered unobjectionable as long as they are not accompanied by any actual threats or coercion.[56]

5. *Reproduction of official ballots.* The Board will set aside any election in which a party distributes a document purporting to be a copy of the official ballot unless it is completely unaltered in form and content and marked "sample." The Board has thus stated the rule:

. . . it will not permit the reproduction of any document purporting to be a copy of the Board's official ballot, other than one completely unaltered in form and content and clearly marked sample on its face, and upon objection validly filed, will set aside the results of any election in which the successful party has violated this rule.[57]

[50]General Shoe Corp., 97 NLRB 499, 29 LRRM 1113 (1951); Peoples Drug Stores, Inc., 119 NLRB 634, 41 LRRM 1141 (1957); Marshall Durbin & Co., 179 NLRB 1027, 72 LRRM 1563 (1969).
[51]Struksnes Construction Co., 165 NLRB 1062, 65 LRRM 1385 (1967); Griffith Ladder Corp., 159 NLRB 175, 62 LRRM 1383 (1966).
[52]Shovel Supply Co., 118 NLRB 315, 40 LRRM 1189 (1957); General Electric Wiring Devices, Inc., 182 NLRB 876, 74 LRRM 1224 (1970).
[53]Phelps Dodge Corp., 177 NLRB 531, 71 LRRM 1385 (1969).
[54]Atlanta Gas Light Co., 162 NLRB 436, 64 LRRM 1051 (1966).
[55]Peoria Plastic Co., 117 NLRB 545, 39 LRRM 1281 (1957).
[56]Plant City Welding and Tank Co., 119 NLRB 131, 41 LRRM 1014 (1959).
[57]Allied Electric Products, Inc., 109 NLRB 1270, 34 LRRM 1538 (1954).

Accordingly, the Board has found a violation of this rule sufficient ground for setting aside the election even though the party distributing the ballot had no improper motive, and the ballot differed from the official ballot in color, type, size and placement of the world "sample."[58] Likewise, violation of the rule will not be excused on the ground that the reproduced ballot was surrounded by propaganda material;[59] no employees were misled;[60] another party to the election engaged in similar conduct;[61] the party which distributed the ballot sought to neutralize its effect by subsequently distributing a circular stating the Board is "absolutely neutral" in the election.[62] In one case a reproduction of one-half of the facsimile of the ballot which contained no reference to the Government, the Board, or the NLRB agents and did not contain the phrase "Official Sample Ballot" caused the setting aside of an election.[63]

Sec. 9–14. Other objectionable preelection conduct. Certain other preelection conduct will support objections to the election if it occurs under circumstances from which the Board can infer probable interference with the voters' choice.

1. *Granting or withholding benefits.* When an employer raises wages or confers other benefits on employees during the pendency of an election petition, the Board will find election interference unless the change was based upon (1) established past practice, (2) justifiable economic considerations, or (3) independent industry or corporate policy.[64] It is the employer's burden to show such justification by affirmative evidence. An employer who withholds or postpones scheduled benefits during the preelection period may also be found to have interfered with the vote.[65] The key question in both situations is whether the circumstances made it clear that the employer's action was prompted by legitimate business considerations.

2. *Waiver of initiation fees by union.* The Supreme Court recently held that a union interfered with an NLRB election when it offered to waive initiation fees for all employees who signed union "recognition

---

[58]Wallace & Tiernan, Inc., 112 NLRB 1352, 36 LRRM 1189 (1955).
[59]Hughes Tool Co., 119 NLRB 739, 41 LRRM 1169 (1957).
[60]Superior Knitting Corp. and Alto Manufacturing Corp., 112 NLRB 984, 36 LRRM 1133 (1955).
[61]The Wilmington Casting Co., 110 NLRB 2114, 35 LRRM 1364 (1954).
[62]The De Vilbiss Co., 114 NLRB 945, 37 LRRM 1061 (1955).
[63]Paula Shoe Company, Inc., 121 NLRB 673, 42 LRRM 1419 (1958).
[64]International Shoe Co., 123 NLRB 682, 43 LRRM 1520 (1959); Domino of California, Inc., 205 NLRB No. 123, 84 LRRM 1540 (1973).
[65]Great Atlantic & Pacific Tea Co., 101 NLRB 1118, 31 LRRM 1189 (1952). *Cf.*, NLRB v. Big Three Industrial Gas, 441 F.2d 774, 77 LRRM 2120 (C.A. 5, 1971).

slips" before the election.[66] The Court reasoned that this practice permitted the union "to buy endorsements and paint a false portrait of employee support" during the campaign.[67] The Board permits initiation-fee waivers, however, where applicable to those who join the union after the election as well as those who join before.[68]

3. *Company favoritism or assistance of competing union.* An employer may not properly attempt to aid a union in its election campaign or to manipulate employee sentiment in favor of one competing union rather than another. Accordingly, the Board has set aside elections where:

(a) The employer favored one union by denying its competitors equal opportunities to campaign;[69]

(b) The employer treated the supporters of a disfavored union in a discriminatory manner;[70]

(c) The employer dominated or assisted one union in violation of Section 8(a)(2);[71]

(d) The employer made speeches implying that it would deal more favorably with one union than with its rival;[72]

(e) The employer executed a contract with one of the competing unions after an election had been directed;[73]

(f) The company official or supervisor engaged in solicitation in favor of a union.[74]

These rules do not, however, prohibit an employer from making a simple, noncoercive declaration to the effect that he would prefer that his employees choose a particular union.[75]

4. *Third party interference.*   Conduct by persons or organizations other than the union and employer participating in an election can sometimes taint the results so that the election will be set aside. This can occur when (1) the "third party" acts as an agent of one of the parties,[76] (2) the party being aided by the third person's conduct is aware of such activity and fails to disavow it,[77] or (3) the third party's

---

[66]NLRB v. Savair Mfg. Co., 84 LRRM 2929 (1973).
[67]*Id.,* 84 LRRM at 2930.
[68]B. F. Goodrich Co., 209 NLRB No. 182, 85 LRRM 1529 (1974).
[69]LaPointe Machine Tool Co., 113 NLRB 172, 36 LRRM 1273 (1965).
[70]The Murry Co., 49 NLRB 1225, 12 LRRM 212 (1943); Red Ball Motor Freight, Inc., 157 NLRB 1237, 61 LRRM 1522 (1966).
[71]Weather Seal, Inc., 161 NLRB 1226, 63 LRRM 1428 (1966).
[72]Hudson Sharp Machine Co., 107 NLRB 32, 33 LRRM 1042 (1953).
[73]Johnson Transport Co., 106 NLRB 1105, 32 LRRM 1621 (1953); Krambo Food Stores, Inc., 120 NLRB 1391, 42 LRRM 1188 (1958). *But see* G & H Towing Co., 168 NLRB 589, 66 LRRM 1343 (1967).
[74]Stevenson Equipment Co., 174 NLRB 865, 70 LRRM 1302 (1969); Talladega Cotton Factory, Inc., 91 NLRB 470, 26 LRRM 1517 (1950).
[75]Rold Gold of California, Inc., 123 NLRB 285, 43 LRRM 1421 (1951).
[76]Goodyear Clearwater Mill No. 2, 102 NLRB 1329, 31 LRRM 1447 (1953).
[77]H.I. Siegel, Inc., 165 NLRB 493, 65 LRRM 1505 (1967).

conduct creates a "general atmosphere of fear," in the community which renders impossible the rational, uncoerced selection of a bargaining representative.[78]

Sec. 9–15. Preelection interference. In 1961, the Board established the doctrine that conduct that is an unfair labor practice under the Act is also viewed as violative of the Board's election rules, hence capable of having the election set aside.[79]

Sec. 9–16. Election observers. The Board's Rules and Regulations provide: "Any party may be represented by observers of his own selection, subject to such limitations as the regional director may prescribe." When arrangements are being made for the election, the NLRB agent will inform the company and each labor organization whose name is to appear on the ballot that each may appoint an equal number of election observers. The number of observers is dependent on the circumstances of the election (for example, the number of voters involved and the number of voting places required). The NLRB agent usually will determine the number after consulting the parties.

The parties are not entitled to observers as a matter of right,[80] except in the case of a consent election.[81] Nor can a nonunion group of employees insist upon being represented by its observers.[82]

A party can refuse or fail to avail itself of the opportunity to be represented by an observer. Where a party is thus not represented by an observer at the election:

1. The responsibility to challenge voters on behalf of the absent party does not shift to the NLRB agent.[83]
2. The absent party's postelection objections to any votes cast will be rejected.[84]

It is the Board's policy that observers must be nonsupervisory employees,[85] unless the parties agree otherwise. Beyond this, the Board has

---

[78]P.D. Gwaltney Jr. & Co., Inc., 74 NLRB 371, 20 LRRM 1172 (1947); Monarch Rubber Co., Inc., 121 NLRB 81, 42 LRRM 1294 (1958).
[79]Dal-Tex Optical Co., 137 NLRB 1782, 50 LRRM 1489 (1962).
[80]Semi-Steel Casting Co. of St. Louis v. NLRB, 160 F.2d 388, 19 LRRM 2458 (C.A. 8, 1947).
[81]Breman Steel Co., 115 NLRB 247, 37 LRRM 1273 (1956).
[82]Semi-Steel Casting Co. of St. Louis v. NLRB, *supra* note 80.
[83]Balfre Gear & Mfg. Co., 115 NLRB 19, 37 LRRM 1223 (1956).
[84]The Association of Motion Picture Producers, Inc., 88 NLRB 1097, 25 LRRM 1446 (1950).
[85]Worth Food Market Stores, Inc., 103 NLRB 259, 31 LRRM 1527 (1953); Wilkinson Mfg. Co., 79 LRRM 2682 (C.A. 8, 1972), *enf. in part* 76 LRRM 1862; Mountain States Tel. and Tel. Co., 207 NLRB No. 87, 84 LRRM 1483 (1973).

repeatedly prohibited "persons closely identified with an employer," even though they are nonsupervisory employees, from acting as observers.[86] The following types of individuals have been disqualified to act as observers:

1. Nonemployee union official.[87]
2. Employer's attorney.[88]
3. Wife of company president.[89]
4. Office manager.[90]

The Board has qualified as observers: (1) on behalf of an employer, employees who work in the industrial relations department;[91] and (2) on behalf of a union, an employee whose discharge was the subject of a pending unfair labor practice charge.[92] An employee who is eligible to vote does not lose his right to vote because he has been designated and acts as an election observer.[93]

Before the conduct of the election, the authorized observers will be called together by the NLRB agent and given their instructions and assignments. The observers usually are given a detailed list of instructions as to their conduct during the election. (See Facsimile No. 32, page 173.) Generally the authorized observers will be asked to:

1. Act as checkers at the voting place and at the counting of ballots.
2. Assist in the identification of voters.
3. Challenge voters.
4. Otherwise assist the NLRB agent.

While engaged in their duties at the voting place, election observers, as a matter of right, may keep lists of names of voters whose ballots they intend to challenge.[94] However, the official eligibility list is the only list which observers may use to record those who have or have not voted.[95]

Sec. 9–17. Mechanics of voting.   The actual polling is always conducted and supervised by NLRB agents.[96] They will arrange the physical layout of the polling place (for example, the voting booths, the checking tables, and

[86]International Stamping Co., 97 NLRB 921, 29 LRRM 1158 (1951).
[87]Columbia Broadcasting System, Inc., 70 NLRB 1368, 18 LRRM 1450 (1946); E-Z Davies Chevrolet, 68 LRRM 2228 (C.A. 9, 1968), enf. 63 LRRM 1453.
[88]Peabody Engineering Co., 95 NLRB 952, 28 LRRM 1391 (1951).
[89]Wiley Mfg. Inc., 93 NLRB 1600, 27 LRRM 1623 (1951).
[90]Watkins Brick Co., 107 NLRB 500, 33 LRRM 1176 (1953).
[91]Northrop Aircraft, Inc., 106 NLRB 23, 32 LRRM 1390 (1953).
[92]Soerens Motor Co., 106 NLRB 1388, 33 LRRM 1021 (1953).
[93]Kroder-Reubel Co., 72 NLRB 240, 19 LRRM 1155 (1947).
[94]Bear Creek Orchards, 90 NLRB 286, 26 LRRM 1204 (1950); Tom Brown Drilling Co., 172 NLRB No. 133, 68 LRRM 1473 (1968).
[95]Milwaukee Cheese Co., 112 NLRB 1383, 36 LRRM 1225 (1955).
[96]Statements of Procedure Sec. 101.19(a) (2).

FORM NLRB-722
(1-73)

UNITED STATES OF AMERICA
NATIONAL LABOR RELATIONS BOARD

INSTRUCTIONS TO ELECTION OBSERVERS

DUTIES *(General):*

1. Act as checkers and watchers.
2. Assist in identification of voters.
3. Challenge voters and ballots.
4. Otherwise assist agents of the Board.

THINGS TO DO *(Specific):*

1. Identify voter.
2. Check off the name of the person applying to vote. One check before the name by one organization. One check after the name by the other organization or the Company.
3. See that only one voter occupies a booth at any one time.
4. See that each voter deposits a ballot in the ballot box.
5. See that each voter leaves the voting room immediately after depositing his ballot.
6. Report any conflict as to the right to vote to the agent of the Board at your table.
7. Remain in the voting place until all ballots are counted in order to check on the fairness of the count, if ballots are counted at that time. If they are not counted immediately, you will be informed as to when and where ballots will be counted.
8. Report any irregularities to the Board agent as soon as noticed.
9. Challenge voters only for good cause.
10. Wear your observer badge at all times during the conduct of the election.
11. BE ON TIME. *(One-half hour before the time for the opening of the polls.)*

THINGS NOT TO DO *(Specific):*

1. Give any help to any voter. Only an agent of the Board can assist the voter.
2. Electioneer any place during the hours of the election.
3. Argue regarding the election.
4. Leave the polling place without the agent's consent.
5. Use intoxicating liquors.
6. Keep any list of those who have or have not voted.

As an official representative of your organization, you should enter upon this task with a fair and open mind. Conduct yourself so that no one can find fault with your actions during the election. You are here to see that the election is conducted in a fair and impartial manner, so that each eligible voter has a fair and equal chance to express himself freely and in secret.

NATIONAL LABOR RELATIONS BOARD

FACSIMILE NO. 32.
Instructions to election observers (Form 722)

the ballot box; portable voting booths are furnished by the regional director). Approximately 350 to 400 voters per hour can be handled at one election table according to the following voting procedure, which is substantially followed in all of the NLRB regional offices:

The voter enters the polling place at a designated entrance. He appears before an election table behind which the authorized observers are seated; they have before them the official voting register. The prospective voter identifies himself by name and whatever badge number the voting register may carry. After the observers have checked off his name as eligible to vote, the employee will be handed a ballot by the NLRB agent.

The voter is then directed to an unoccupied voting booth. Only one voter is allowed in the booth at any one time; no one is permitted to go into the booth with him. If there are isolated instances—not enough to affect the results of the election—where more than one employee is in the booth at the same time, the election will not be set aside.[97]

Each voter marks his ballot in the privacy of the booth. Where the booths are so arranged that employees can be observed while they mark their ballots, the Board will set aside the election.[98]

The voter is not to put any mark on the ballot other than the "X" in the desired box; any other mark may void the ballot. After he marks the ballot, the voter folds it and drops it into the ballot box. No one is allowed to touch the marked ballot except the voter himself. After dropping the ballot in the box the employee leaves the voting area. A marked ballot dropped elsewhere and found later (for example, in the booth) will be considered void and will not be counted.[99]

Sec. 9–18. Challenging a voter. Any authorized election observer or NLRB agent has the right to challenge a voter.[100] A party's mere participation in the preelection compilation and checking of the eligibility list does not constitute an agreement that wipes out the right to challenge ballots at the election.[101]

The NLRB agent will give the observers an opportunity to challenge voters. Observers generally will base their challenge on the ground that an employee is ineligible to vote because he is not included in the specified unit; for example, the voter may be challenged because he is stated to be a supervisory employee.

The NLRB agent must challenge any individual whose name is not on the eligibility list; failure to do so where such an unchallenged vote might have affected the result of the election is sufficient to have the election set

---

[97]Machinery Overhaul Co., Inc., 115 NLRB 1787, 38 LRRM 1168. (1956)
[98]The Royal Lumber Co., 118 NLRB 1015, 40 LRRM 1304 (1957).
[99]F. J. Stokes Corp., 117 NLRB 951, 39 LRRM 1338 (1957).
[100]R. and R. Sec. 102.69(a).
[101]O.E. Szekely and Associates, Inc., 117 NLRB 42, 39 LRRM 1151 (1957); Fisher-New Center Co., 184 NLRB No. 92, 74 LRRM 1609 (1970).

aside. The Board agent will not make challenges on behalf of the parties, whether or not such parties have observers present.[102]

The challenge must be made before the voter is given a ballot. The NLRB agent will not accept a challenge after the ballot is cast or after the close of the election.[103]

A party cannot remedy failure to make timely challenges by filing objections to the conduct of the election on the basis of the unchallenged votes. Such objections will be overruled as postelection challenges.[104] A party's statement at the opening of the polls that it challenged each and every voter does not constitute a proper challenge; each voter has to be challenged individually as he presents himself for a ballot.[105]

When a prospective voter is challenged, the NLRB agent will indicate on a stub of an envelope the reasons stated for the challenge, the identity of the challenger, and the name, classification, and badge or clock number of the voter. The challenged voter is then given a ballot and the envelope. He is instructed to mark his ballot, insert it into the envelope, seal the envelope, and drop it into the ballot box. The challenged ballot envelopes are segregated from the other ballots at the time of the count. (See Facsimile No. 33, page 176, for sample of Challenged Ballot Envelopes.)

A party may withdraw challenges before the ballots are counted.[106] If the number of challenged ballots is sufficient to affect the results of the election, and only then, the eligibility of the challenged voters will be determined. (The procedure for determination of challenges is set forth on page 192 under "Investigation of Challenged Ballots.")

Sec. 9–19. Certification on conduct of election. It is the policy to close the polls at the time set forth in the notice of election, no sooner[107] or later.[108] After the polls are closed the ballot box will be sealed by the NLRB agent in the presence of the authorized observers. The NLRB agent will then ask them to sign a certification on the conduct of the election. This certificate declares that the election was fairly conducted and that the secrecy of the ballot was preserved. (See Facsimile No. 34, page 179.)

---

[102]NLRB Field Manual 11338; Knox Metal Products, Inc., 75 NLRB 277, 21 LRRM 1038 (1947); Schwartz Bros., Inc. v. NLRB, 82 LRRM 2376 (C.A. D.C., 1973), enf. 78 LRRM 1499.
[103]NLRB v. A.J. Tower Co., 329 U.S. 324, 19 LRRM 2128 (1946).
[104]Oppenheim Collins & Co., 108 NLRB 1257, 34 LRRM 1180 (1954).
[105]William R. Whittaker Co., Ltd., 94 NLRB 1151, 28 LRRM 1150 (1951).
[106]Sears Roebuck and Co., 117 NLRB 522, 39 LRRM 1278 (1957).
[107]Repcal Brass Manufacturing Co., 109 NLRB 4, 34 LRRM 1277 (1954).
[108]Glauber Water Works, 112 NLRB 1462, 36 LRRM 1224 (1955); cf. Westchester Plastics of Ohio, Inc., 69 LRRM 2507 (C.A. 6, 1968), enf. 65 LRRM 1275.

CHALLENGED BALLOT

Secret ENVELOPE

IDENTIFICATION STUB
PUT ADDITIONAL INFORMATION ON
THE BACK OF THIS STUB

NAME_____

CLOCK NO._____UNIT_____

JOB CLASS_____

COMPANY_____

POLLING PLACE_____

DATE_____

REASON FOR CHALLENGE_____

_____

CHALLENGED BY_____

BOARD AGENT_____

FACSIMILE NO. 33.
Copy of challenged-ballot envelope

The signing of the certificate does not deprive a party of the right to file objections;[109] nor can the fact that all parties signed the certificate prevent the regional director or Board from setting aside the election.[110]

Sec. 9-20. Mailed ballots. Mail ballots will be used by the regional director in special situations; for example, where employees are scattered over a wide geographic area. The regional director has broad discretion in determining the method by which such an election shall be conducted.[111] Specific provision in the direction of election for mail balloting is not essential, and the omission of such provision is not a valid basis for an objection to the conduct of an election.[112] Furthermore, it is within the regional director's discretion to determine whether only a part of the election shall be conducted by mail.[113]

The procedures for handling of mail balloting are as follows:

1. The date by which the mailed ballots must be returned to the regional office is fixed by the regional director. In those instances in which voting is done partly by mail and partly manually, the mail deadline will be set to precede the manual voting.
2. The NLRB regional office mails to each eligible voter: (a) one ballot; (b) a postage-free return addressed envelope, to which is attached a stub with a space for the voter's signature; and (c) a notice of the election and instructions to the voter. (See Facsimile No. 35, page 180.) Where the regional director deems it necessary, he may address the mail ballots to individual employees in care of the employer, rather than to their homes.[114]
3. At the time scheduled for the count, the closed and returned envelopes are treated in the same manner as votes in a manual election, being checked off against the eligibility list by the NLRB agent and authorized observers.
4. The stubs with the identifying signatures are detached from those envelopes which contain unchallenged votes. Mail ballots with no signatures affixed to the envelopes will be declared void and will not be counted.[115]
5. The unmarked envelopes are shuffled, and their ballots are extracted.
6. The mail ballots are mixed with ballot box votes, if any, and counted.
7. As in manual elections, authorized observers participate in checking eligibility and counting the ballots.

[109]F.J. Stokes Corp., 117 NLRB 951, 39 LRRM 1338 (1957).
[110]The Royal Lumber Co., 118 NLRB 1015, 40 LRRM 1304 (1957).
[111]Shipowners' Association of the Pacific Coast, 110 NLRB 479, 35 LRRM 1077 (1954).
[112]Simplot Fertilizer Co., 107 NLRB 1211, 33 LRRM 1357 (1954).
[113]Ibid.
[114]Pacific Gas and Electric Co., 89 NLRB 938, 26 LRRM 1056 (1950); Groendyke Transport Inc., 64 LRRM 2270 (C.A. 10, 1967), reman'g 60 LRRM 1174.
[115]Northwest Packing Co., 65 NLRB 890, 17 LRRM 249 (1945).

Sec. 9–21. Counting the ballots. In most elections the ballots are counted immediately after the closing of the polls. As in the actual conduct of the election, the NLRB agent has the assistance of the authorized observers in counting the ballots. Unlike the rule prevailing at the polling place, supervisory employees, executives, and any other persons designated by the parties may observe the counting.

Sec. 9–22. Counting the ballots—Opening the ballot box. The ballot boxes are opened and the ballots counted in the presence of the observers representing all parties. The ballots are handled only by the NLRB agent; the tallies are made by the authorized observers. They, in addition to the NLRB agent, may question the validity of a ballot. Absent agreement among the observers as to the validity of a ballot or as to the intention of a voter's mark on a ballot, the NLRB agent is empowered to make the determination. However, any party may press its disagreement with the agent's determination by filing timely objections. (The procedure for filing such objections is set forth on page 187, under "Postelection Procedures.")

An unmarked ballot will be considered void and will not be counted as a vote.[116] Likewise, a write-in vote on the ballot will not be counted.[117]

Sec. 9–23. Counting ballots in self-determination elections. A majority of the valid votes cast in an election determines the result.[118] However, the Board has set up special procedures for the segregation, pooling, and counting of ballots in self-determination elections involving: (1) severance of a group of employees from a larger grouping, e.g., where one union is seeking a unit of craftsmen only and another union seeks a unit which includes production workers as well as craftsmen; (2) residual groups where only a portion of an appropriate unit has been represented; and (3) professional employees. In each instance, the smaller group's ballots are segregated, and counted before those in the larger grouping.

Sec. 9–24. Severance election. In a severance election (for example, involving a craft):

1. Failure of any union to receive a majority of votes of the craft employees will not lead to a runoff election.[119] Instead, the ballots of the craft employees will be pooled with those of the employees in the larger group, and all the ballots will be covered in one count.[120] If a majority in the group sought to be severed do not vote for the union

---

[116]Vulcan Furniture Mfg. Corp., 214 F.2d 369, 34 LRRM 2449 (C.A. 5, 1954); Drever Heat Treating, Inc., NLRB No. 5-RC-6292, 70 LRRM 1315 (1969).
[117]Woodmark Industries, Inc., 80 NLRB 1105, 23 LRRM 1209 (1948); Columbus Nursing Home Inc., 188 NLRB No. 131, 76 LRRM 1417 (1971).
[118]NLRB v. Vulcan Furniture Mfg. Corp., 214 F.2d 369, 34 LRRM 2449 (C.A. 5, 1954).
[119]Sutherland Paper Co., 114 NLRB 211, 36 LRRM 1545 (1955).
[120]Ibid.

NLRB-750
(5-1-45)

UNITED STATES OF AMERICA
NATIONAL LABOR RELATIONS BOARD

CERTIFICATION ON CONDUCT OF ELECTION

Name of employer .... Case No. ....

Date of election .... Place ....

The undersigned acted as agents of the Regional Director and as authorized observers, respectively, in the conduct of the balloting at the above time and place.

WE HEREBY CERTIFY that such balloting was fairly conducted, that all eligible voters were given an opportunity to vote their ballots in secret, and that the ballot box was protected in the interest of a fair and secret vote.

For

For the Regional Director, Region

For

For

FACSIMILE No. 34.
Form for certification on conduct of election

UNITED STATES OF AMERICA
NATIONAL LABOR RELATIONS BOARD

NOTICE OF ELECTION OF REPRESENTATIVE
and
INSTRUCTIONS TO ELIGIBLE EMPLOYEES VOTING BY
UNITED STATES MAIL

NOTICE OF ELECTION

An election by secret ballot is being conducted under the supervision of the Regional Director of the National Labor Relations Board among the eligible voters to determine the representative, if any, desired by them for the purpose of collective bargaining with the employer named on the enclosed ballot. Your name appears on the list of those who are eligible to vote in this election.

PLEASE SEE THE OTHER SIDE OF THIS PAGE FOR AN IMPORTANT STATEMENT CONCERNING YOUR RIGHTS UNDER FEDERAL LAW AND HOW THE NLRB PROTECTS YOUR RIGHT TO A FREE CHOICE AND A FAIR ELECTION.

An OFFICIAL BALLOT and a RETURN-ADDRESSED SECRET ENVELOPE are enclosed. To vote by mail, carry out the following instructions:

INSTRUCTIONS TO ELIGIBLE EMPLOYEES VOTING BY UNITED STATES MAIL
(Read Carefully)

FROM THE TIME YOU OPEN THE ENVELOPE CONTAINING THE BALLOT, YOU SHOULD CONSIDER YOURSELF IN THE SAME POSITION AS THOUGH IN A VOTING BOOTH IN A MANUALLY CONDUCTED ELECTION. YOU SHOULD THEREFORE FOLLOW THE INSTRUCTIONS BELOW AND DROP YOUR BALLOT IN THE UNITED STATES MAIL BEFORE DISCUSSING IT WITH ANYONE. Read the official ballot carefully. *Ignore the instruction on the ballot to* "Fold and drop in ballot box," as this does not apply to persons who vote by mail. Mark an "X" in the square of your choice. Fold the ballot and put it in the envelope addressed to the National Labor Relations Board. Seal this envelope. *Sign your name (do not print it) on the outside of the envelope* in the space provided after the word "Signature." Deposit this envelope, which requires no postage, in the United States mail *so that your ballot will be RECEIVED at the place shown on the return envelope not later than*

_____
(Date)

This is a secret ballot election. YOUR BALLOT WILL BE VOID AND WILL NOT BE COUNTED *UNLESS* you:

1. Mark on the ballot only in the place provided for marking; *do not* identify yourself on the ballot.

2. Return the ballot in the same envelope which you received for that purpose.

3. Sign your name in your *own* handwriting on the outside of that envelope after the word "Signature," so that your name can be checked against the eligibility list.

After your name is checked against the eligibility list the detachable part of the envelope, the stub upon which your name appears, will be removed and destroyed. The remaining section of the envelope containing the ballot will be mixed with all other ballot sections before it is opened by agents of the Board and your ballot removed, thus insuring secrecy.

If you have any question about this election you can contact the Regional Director or his agent at the address below.

NATIONAL LABOR RELATIONS BOARD

Form NLRB–4175
(7–72)

FACSIMILE NO. 35.
First page of notice of election and voting instructions
to employees voting by mail (Form 4175)

RIGHTS OF EMPLOYEES

Under the National Labor Relations Act, employees have the right:

- To self-organization
- To form, join, or assist labor organizations.
- To bargain collectively through representatives of their own choosing
- To act together for the purposes of collective bargaining or other mutual aid or protection
- To refuse to do any or all of these things unless the union and employer, in a state where such agreements are permitted, enter into a lawful union security clause requiring employees to join the union.

It is the responsibility of the National Labor Relations Board to protect employees in the exercise of these rights.

The Board wants all eligible voters to be fully informed about their rights under Federal law and wants both Employers and Unions to know what is expected of them when it holds an election.

If agents of either Unions or Employers interfere with your right to a free, fair, and honest election, the election can be set aside by the Board. Where appropriate the Board provides other remedies, such as reinstatement for employees fired for exercising their rights, including backpay from the party responsible for their discharge.

The following are examples of conduct which interfere with the rights of employees and may result in the setting aside of the election:

- Threatening loss of jobs or benefits by an Employer or Union
- Misstating important facts by a Union or an Employer where the other party does not have a fair chance to reply
- Promising or granting promotions, pay raises, or other benefits, to influence an employee's vote by a party capable of carrying out such promises
- An Employer firing employees to discourage or encourage union activity or a Union causing them to be fired to encourage union activity
- Making campaign speeches to assembled groups of employees on company time after ballots are scheduled to be dispatched by the regional office
- Incitement by either an Employer or a Union of racial or religious prejudice by inflammatory appeals
- Threatening physical force or violence to employees by a Union or an Employer to influence their votes

The National Labor Relations Board protects your right to a free choice

Improper conduct will not be permitted. All parties are expected to cooperate fully with this agency in maintaining basic principles of a fair election as required by law. The National Labor Relations Board as an agency of the United States Government does not endorse any choice in the election.

NATIONAL LABOR RELATIONS BOARD
an agency of the
UNITED STATES GOVERNMENT

GPO : 1972 O - 473-205

FACSIMILE NO. 35. *Second page*

seeking severance, the votes will be pooled with those in the more comprehensive group and counted as follows: Votes for the union seeking severance will be counted among the valid votes cast, but will not be counted for or against the union seeking the more comprehensive unit.[121]

2. If no election is simultaneously conducted in the more comprehensive group and if a majority of the employees in the voting group (the craft group) do not vote for the union seeking severance, these employees will remain a part of the existing unit and the regional director will issue a certification of results to that effect.[122]

3. If the union seeking the production unit specifically asks that the craft group be excluded from the overall unit and there is no contrary bargaining history, the votes of the craftsmen will not be pooled if they reject separate representation.[123]

Sec. 9–25. Residual groups.   In an election involving a residual group, different rules are followed. Where an incumbent union asks to represent a residual group in addition to an existing unit, the Board refuses to allow a self-determination election in the residual group, holding a single election among employees in both groups.[124] But when Union A petitions for both an existing unit and a residual group and Union B is interested in the former unit only, the Board orders the ballots counted separately. If Union B wins in the existing unit it is entitled to represent that unit and Union A's representation is limited to the residual group. But if Union B loses, all ballots are pooled and Union A's bargaining status is determined by the tally of all ballots.[125]

Sec. 9–26. Professional groups.   In directing a self-determination election for professional employees, the Board provides that they vote on whether they: (a) wish to be included with nonprofessionals; and (b) desire representation by either union, or by none.

If a majority of the professional employees vote in favor of inclusion, their votes will be pooled and counted with the votes of the nonprofessional group. If a majority of the professional employees vote against inclusion, they will not be included with nonprofessionals and their votes will be counted separately to determine their representative, if any.[126]

[121]American Potash & Chemical Corp., 107 NLRB 1418, 33 LRRM 1380 (1954).
[122]Standard Oil Co., 118 NLRB 1099, 40 LRRM 1322 (1957).
[123]Balléntine Packing Co., Inc., 132 NLRB 923, 48 LRRM 1451 (1961).
[124]D. V. Displays Corp., 134 NLRB 568, 49 LRRM 1199 (1961).
[125]Felix Half & Brother, Inc., 132 NLRB 1523, 48 LRRM 1528 (1961).
[126]Westinghouse Electric Corp., 116 NLRB 1545, 39 LRRM 1039 (1956).

Sec. 9–27. Determining validity of disputed ballots. In counting and determining the validity of disputed ballots, the NLRB agent is bound by the following rules:

1. An improperly marked ballot is void and not counted.[127]
2. A ballot is invalid if its markings either identify the voter[128] or give "rise to the possibility of revealing the identity of the voter."[129]
3. A ballot is valid if the voter's intent is clearly indicated, even though the ballot is marked with obscenity,[130] irregular scribbling;[131] erasures, or blots.[132]

If any party disagrees with the NLRB agent's ruling on the validity of a ballot, it may file a timely objection after the count.[133] (The procedure for filing such objections is set forth in Chapter 10.)

Sec. 9–28. Tally of ballots. After the tallies have been tabulated, the authorized observers will be asked to sign a tally of ballots. This document includes both the results of the count and a statement that the counting and tabulating were accurate. (See Facsimiles No. 36 and 37, pages 184 and 185.) After the tally has been signed by the authorized observers, the NLRB agent will serve a copy of it upon each designated representative of the parties.[134]

The signing of the tally of ballots does not deprive a party of the right to file objections.[135]

---

[127]Semi-Steel Casting Co. of St. Louis v. NLRB, 160 F.2d 388, 19 LRRM 2458 (C.A. 8, 1947); Spaulding Fibre Co. v. NLRB, 83 LRRM 2650 (C.A. 2, 1973) *denying enforcement to* 82 LRRM 1076.

[128]Eagle Iron Works, 117 NLRB 1053, 39 LRRM 1379.

[129]George K. Garrett Co., Inc., 120 NLRB 484, 41 LRRM 1519 (1958); Liberty Coach Co., Inc., *sub nom.* Electrical Workers, IUE v. NLRB, 71 LRRM 2991 (C.A. D.C., 1969), *enf. in part* 68 LRRM 1511; Knapp-Sherrill Co., 196 NLRB No. 106, 80 LRRM 1467 (1972).

[130]*Ibid.*

[131]Belmont Smelting and Refining Works, Inc., 115 NLRB 1481, 38 LRRM 1104 (1956); F. Strauss and Sons, Inc., 195 NLRB No. 112, 79 LRRM 1560 (1972).

[132]American Cable and Radio Corp., 107 NLRB 1090, 33 LRRM 1324 (1954); Schapiro and Whitehouse, Inc., 61 LRRM 2289 (C.A. 4, 1966), *denying enforcement to* 57 LRRM 1094.

[133]George K. Garrett Co., Inc., 120 NLRB 484, 41 LRRM 1519 (1958).

[134]Statements of Procedure, Sec. 101.19(a)(3).

[135]General Plywood Corp., 79 NLRB 1458, 23 LRRM 1017.

FORM NLRB-760
(5-73)

UNITED STATES OF AMERICA
NATIONAL LABOR RELATIONS BOARD

| Date Filed |

Case No. _____

Date issued _____

Type of Election:
(Check one:)

☐ Stipulation

☐ Board Direction

☐ Consent Agreement

☐ RD Direction

Incumbent Union *(Code)*

*(If applicable
check either
or both:)*

☐ 8(b) (7)

☐ Mail Ballot

TALLY OF BALLOTS

The undersigned agent of the Regional Director certifies that the results of the tab-
ulation of ballots cast in the election held in the above case, and concluded on the date
indicated above, were as follows:

1. Approximate number of eligible voters _____

2. Void ballots _____

3. Votes cast for _____

4. Votes cast for _____

5. Votes cast for _____

6. Votes cast against participating labor organization(s) _____

7. Valid votes counted (sum of 3, 4, 5, and 6) _____

8. Challenged ballots _____

9. Valid votes counted plus challenged ballots (sum of 7 and 8) _____

10. Challenges are (not) sufficient to affect the results of the election.

11. A majority of the valid votes counted plus challenged ballots (item 9) has (not)
been cast for:

_____

For the Regional Director

_____

The undersigned acted as authorized observers in the counting and tabulating of
ballots indicated above. We hereby certify that the counting and tabulating were fairly
and accurately done, that the secrecy of the ballots was maintained, and that the results
were as indicated above. We also acknowledge service of this tally.

For_____   For_____

_____   _____

_____   _____

For_____   For_____

_____   _____

_____   _____

FACSIMILE No. 36.
Tally of ballots (Form 760)

FORM NLRB-4168
(10-70)

UNITED STATES OF AMERICA

NATIONAL LABOR RELATIONS BOARD

Case No .————————————

Date Issued ————————————

Type of Election:

(Check one)   (Also check box
☐ Consent Agreement   below where appropriate)
☐ Stipulation   ☐ 8 (b) (7)
☐ Board Direction
☐ RD Direction

REVISED TALLY OF BALLOTS
(Counting of Challenged Ballots)

The undersigned agent of the Regional Director certifies that the results of counting the challenged ballots directed to be counted by the

on   and the addition of these ballots to the original Tally of

Ballots, executed on   , were as follows:

	ORIGINAL TALLY	CHALLENGED COUNTED	FINAL TALLY
Approximate number of eligible voters . . .	_____		
Void ballots	_____		
Votes cast for:	_____	_____	_____
Votes cast for:	_____	_____	_____
Votes cast for:	_____	_____	_____
Votes cast against participating labor organization(s)	_____	_____	_____
Valid votes counted	_____		_____
Undetermined challenged ballots	_____		_____
Valid votes counted plus challenged ballots	_____		_____
Sustained challenges (voters ineligible) . .			_____

The remaining undetermined challenged ballots, if any, shown in the Final Tally column are (not) sufficient to affect the results of the election.

A majority of the valid votes plus challenged ballots as shown in the Final Tally column has (not) been cast for_____

For the Regional Director

The undersigned acted as authorized observers in the counting and tabulating of ballots indicated above. We hereby certify that this counting and tabulating, and the compilation of the final tally, were fairly and accurately done, and that the results were as indicated above. We also acknowledge service of this Tally.

FOR_____   FOR_____

FOR_____   FOR_____

GPO 902.026

FACSIMILE NO. 37.
Revised tally of ballots (Form 4168)

CHAPTER 10

Postelection Procedures

Sec. 10–1. Objections. For many years the Board's Rules and Regulations have provided that objections may be raised as to either: (1) the manner in which the election was held; or (2) conduct which affected the results of the election.[1] The applicable procedures are the same for both types of objections. If the objections are found to have merit, the election will be set aside and a new one will be conducted.[2]

Sec. 10–2. Objections claiming racial discrimination. Recently, a new basis for objections was added when the NLRB sustained an objection claiming that a union which won an election practiced invidious racial discrimination. The Board held that such objections will be considered only if:

1. The objections are filed within five days after the election and are served on all parties.
2. The discrimination is allegedly practiced by the union winning the election. The objections will be considered by the Board before the issuance of certification and, if they are found to have merit, the union will not be certified as a bargaining representative.[3]

Although the scope of the Board's holding has not been fully determined,[4] it will be applied in cases of sex discrimination.[5] Also, the NLRB has not yet specified what degree or form of invidious discrimination will be sufficient to warrant withholding certification.[6]

[1]Sec. 102.69(a). For a study of postelection objections, see Williams, Janus, and Huhn, NLRB REGULATION OF ELECTION CONDUCT (Philadelphia: University of Pennsylvania Press, 1974).
[2]Statements of Procedure Sec. 101.19(a) (4).
[3]Bekins Moving and Storage Co., 211 NLRB No. 7, 86 LRRM 1323 (1974); Mansion House Center Management Corporation, 85 LRRM 2769 (C.A. 8, 1974), enf. 79 LRRM 1279 (1972).
[4]Emporium and Western Addition Community Org., 192 NLRB No. 173, 77 LRRM 1669, rev'd 485 F.2d 917, 83 LRRM 2738 (C.A.D.C., 1973). The Board is currently seeking certiorari with the Supreme Court.
[5]Alden Press, 212 NLRB No. 91, 86 LRRM 1605 (1974).
[6]Bekins Moving and Storage Co., 211 NLRB No. 7, 86 LRRM 1323 (1974).

Sec. 10–3. Objections—Who may file.   Objections may be filed only by the following: the employer involved, the petitioner (which may be an individual), and any labor organization or individual whose name appeared on the ballot as a choice.[7] Thus, a party is not prevented from filing objections against misconduct because:

1. It also has engaged in misconduct.[8]
2. It is not aggrieved by the misconduct.[9]

The Board has refused to entertain objections filed by such "nonparties" as:

1. A "neither committee" which claimed representation among the employees in the voting unit.[10]
2. An intervening union whose name was withdrawn from the ballot before the election.[11]

A party may withdraw its objections without prejudicing its rights under charges of unfair labor practices based on the misconduct.[12]

Sec. 10–4. Objections—When to file.   The regional director will refuse to consider any objections unless they are timely filed. To be timely:

1. Objections must be filed with the regional director, in quadruplicate, within five working days after the tally of ballots has been furnished.
2. Copies of the objections must be served immediately upon each of the other parties.
3. Proof of service upon the other parties must be submitted to the regional director.[13]

All of the foregoing conditions must be met even though there are challenged ballots in sufficient numbers to affect the results of the election.[14]

The Board has repeatedly warned that parties will be "held to strict

---

[7]R. and R. Sec. 102.69(a); NLRB Field Manual 11392.3.
[8]The Wilmington Casting Co., 110 NLRB 2114, 35 LRRM 1364 (1954); see also Zatco Metal Products Co., 173 NLRB No. 6, 69 LRRM 1231 (1968).
[9]Legion Utensils Co., 103 NLRB 875, 31 LRRM 1586 (1953).
[10]Wilson and Co., Inc., 82 NLRB 405, 23 LRRM 1575 (1949).
[11]Warwick Mfg. Corp., 107 NLRB 1, 33 LRRM 1040 (1953).
[12]Calcasieu Paper Co., Inc., 99 NLRB 794, 30 LRRM 1131 (1952).
[13]R. and R. Sec. 102.69(a); Hughes Tool Co., 197 NLRB No. 17, 80 LRRM 1479 (1972).
[14]Ibid.

compliance" with the rules for filing objections.[15] Following are some of the basic rulings which concern the requirement of filing objections with the regional director within five days after the tally has been furnished:

1. The five working days start running from the date that the tally of ballots has been furnished.[16] Furnished means the date of receipt of the tally by a party, either in person from the NLRB agent or by mail.[17] Usually the tallies are handed to the parties immediately after the ballots are counted at the close of the election.
2. Date of "filing" with the regional director means date of receipt of the objections at the NLRB regional office during working hours and not the date they are deposited in the mail[18]
3. The Board has rejected objections filed in person 20 minutes after the close of business on the last day for filing.[19]
4. One court, in passing upon the five-day requirement, found a "fatal defect" in a party's objections to an election because the objections were received by the regional director on the sixth day.[20]
5. However, more recently the Board has ruled objections received on the sixth day were to be accepted and considered on their merits where: (a) the party took every precaution necessary to assure delivery by the post office within the five-day period; and (b) the delay in receiving the objections was not attributable to the party.[21]

When a regional director rules that objections are not timely, they will be rejected and returned to the filing party. A request for leave to appeal the rejection may be filed in the same manner as for other final rulings of the regional director. (See Sec. 8–12, page 143.)

Sec. 10–5. Service of objections. Care must also be exercised in the requirement that copies of the objections are to be served immediately upon each of the other parties. The Board has ruled that:

1. The date of service is the day on which the objections are deposited in the mail.[22]

---

[15]General Box Co., 115 NLRB 301, 37 LRRM 1286 (1956); *cf.* Zinke's Foods, Inc., *sub nom.* Retail Clerks, Local 1401 v. NLRB, 79 LRRM 2984 (C.A.D.C., 1972), *enf.* 75 LRRM 1211; *see also* Wilson-Sinclair Co., 191 NLRB No. 62, 77 LRRM 1438 (1971).
[16]Jacksonville Journal Co., 117 NLRB 360, 39 LRRM 1229 (1957); Van Tran Electric Corp., 78 LRRM 2575 (C.A. 6, 1971), *enf.* 76 LRRM 1148.
[17]General Box Co., 115 NLRB 301, 37 LRRM 1286 (1956).
[18]General Electric Co., 103 NLRB 108, 31 LRRM 1506 (1953).
[19]Smithfield Packing Co., Inc., 112 NLRB 940, 36 LRRM 1117 (1955).
[20]NLRB v. Conlon Bros. Mfg. Co., 187 F.2d 329, 27 LRRM 2407 (C.A. 7, 1951).
[21]Rio de Oro Uranium Mines, Inc., 119 NLRB 153, 41 LRRM 1057 (1957); KLAS-TV, 197 NLRB No. 178, 80 LRRM 1479 (1972).
[22]Audubon Cabinet Co., 117 NLRB 861, 39 LRRM 1327 (1957).

2. Where a party mails copies of its objections to the other parties on the same day it has filed them with the regional director, this constitutes "immediate service" which is timely.[23]

3. Where a party mails copies of its objections to the other parties two days after they were filed with the regional director, this is not considered "immediate service," and the objections are rejected as untimely.[24]

4. Where a party fails to serve a copy upon one of the parties the objections are rejected.[25]

There is one exception to the strict rules of timeliness: The regional director will consider objections, regardless of their timeliness, where they involve an election irregularity attributable to an NLRB agent.[26]

Sec. 10–6. Sufficiency of objections.   The Rules and Regulations provide that objections must contain a short statement of the reasons for the objections.[27] Objections that fail to supply the reasons will be rejected.[28] To be accepted, objections: (a) must "identify the nature of the misconduct" on which they are based; and (b) the misconduct must warrant setting aside the election.[29] Thus, objections will be rejected where they contain merely:

1. A general conclusion of interference with the election, without specific content or substance.[30]

2. A promise that a bill of particulars will be filed within a few days.[31]

Sec. 10–7. Subject matter of objections.   There are many decisions that limit the subject matter of objections which the Board will consider. Objections will be overruled involving: (1) contentions held to be in the nature of postelection challenges; (2) misconduct which occurred before certain cutoff dates; (3) misconduct by the party filing the objections; and (4) unfair labor practice questions.

---

[23]Fisher Products Co., 114 NLRB 161, 36 LRRM 1528 (1955).
[24]General Time Corp., 112 NLRB 86, 35 LRRM 1716 (1955).
[25]General Electric Co., 103 NLRB 110, 31 LRRM 1505 (1953); Boatten Pontiac Corp., 163 NLRB 680, 64 LRRM 1466 (1967).
[26]General Electric Co., 118 NLRB 805, 40 LRRM 1263 (1957); Kerona Plastics Extrusion Co., 196 NLRB No. 179, 80 LRRM 1231 (1972).
[27]Sec. 102.69(a); Lindsley Industries of Sarasota, Inc., 199 NLRB No. 83, 81 LRRM 1274 (1972).
[28]Don Allen Midtown Chevrolet, Inc., 113 NLRB 879, 36 LRRM 1461 (1955).
[29]Atlantic Mills Serving Corp. of Cleveland, Inc., 120 NLRB 1284, 42 LRRM 1158 (1958); Gooch Packing Co., Gooch Blue Ribbon Meats Div., 79 LRRM 2864 (C.A. 5, 1972), remand'g 76 LRRM 1453.
[30]Don Allen Midtown Chevrolet, Inc.,113 NLRB 879, 36 LRRM 1461 (1955).
[31]Progressive Brass Foundry Co., Inc., 114 NLRB 963, 37 LRRM 1072 (1955); Wilson-Sinclair Co., 191 NLRB No. 62, 77 LRRM 1438 (1971).

Under the basic ground rules limiting the above four areas, objections will be overruled involving:

1. Appropriateness of the unit;[32] or ineligibility or eligibility of persons to vote;[33] (Note: Questions of eligibility are handled by challenges but the validity of a ballot may be raised in an objection.[34])

2. Misconduct which occurred before the date of filing of the petition, rather than before the date of the direction of election,[35] or the execution of the election agreement,[36] as was formerly the case;

3. Misconduct by the objecting party;[37]

4. Allegations of company domination,[38] or conduct "wholly identical" with the subject matter of unfair labor practice charges dismissed by the General Counsel.[39] (Where a complaint has been issued by the General Counsel, the Board may hold a consolidated hearing on both the objections and the complaint.[40] In such a consolidated case, the Board may decline to pass upon the objections if: (a) it finds unfair labor practices; and (b) more than one year will have elapsed from the date of election to the end of the period in which notices are to be posted pursuant to the Board's order; in such instance, the Board will dismiss the petition for the election without prejudice to the filing of a new petition.)[41]

Sec. 10–8. Investigation of objections. If the objections are properly filed and served, the regional director assigns them for investigation by an NLRB agent, who may or may not be the person who conducted the election.[42]

It has been held repeatedly that a party filing objections is obligated to furnish evidence in support of such objections. Unless such evidence is supplied, the regional director is not required to pursue the investigation,[43] and the objections can be overruled.[44] The evidence must be submitted at

[32]Burrus Mills, Inc., 116 NLRB 1257, 38 LRRM 1452 (1956).
[33]NLRB v. A. J. Tower Co., 328 U.S. 324, 19 LRRM 2128 (1946).
[34]George K. Garrett Co., Inc., 120 NLRB 484, 41 LRRM 1519 (1958).
[35]Ideal Electric and Manufacturing Co., 134 NLRB 1275, 49 LRRM 1316 (1961); R. Dakin and Co., 191 NLRB No. 65, 77 LRRM 1467 (1971), suppl'g 73 LRRM 1447.
[36]Goodyear Tire & Rubber Co., 138 NLRB 453, 51 LRRM 1070 (1962).
[37]Talladega Cotton Factory, Inc., 91 NLRB 470, 26 LRRM 1517 (1950); Camp Milling Co. Inc., 109 NLRB 471, 34 LRRM 1360 (1954).
[38]Shipowners' Association of the Pacific Coast, 110 NLRB 479, 35 LRRM 1077 (1954).
[39]Times Square Stores Corp., 79 NLRB 361, 22 LRRM 1373 (1948).
[40]The Deming Co., 107 NLRB 1100, 33 LRRM 1327 (1954).
[41]Baird-Ward Printing Co., 108 NLRB 815, 34 LRRM 1090 (1954).
[42]NLRB v. Huntsville Manufacturing Co., 203 F.2d 430, 31 LRRM 2637 (C.A. 5, 1953).
[43]Audobon Cabinet Co., Inc., 119 NLRB 349, 41 LRRM 1085 (1957).
[44]NLRB v. Huntsville Manufacturing Co., 203 F.2d 430, 31 LRRM 2637 (C.A. 5, 1953); Amax Aluminum Extrusion Products, Inc., 73 LRRM 2780 (C.A. 5, 1970), enf. 70 LRRM 1417.

"the time of filing or forthwith upon request from the regional director";[45] the objecting party cannot take the position that such evidence should be produced only at a hearing.[46]

The regional director's jurisdiction in making the investigation is not limited to objections raised by parties.[47] Where the investigation ". . . uncovers matter relating to the conduct of an NLRB agent or the functioning of NLRB processes sufficient to cause the election to be set aside, the regional director will consider such matter even if not within the scope of the objections."[48] This rule is observed regardless of the objecting party's: (a) change of position concerning its own objections;[49] or (b) failure to follow the established procedure for filing objections.[50] If it appears to the regional director that substantial factual issues exist, a hearing may be ordered. In the case of stipulated elections this automatically transfers the case to the Board.[51]

Sec. 10–9. Investigation of challenged ballots. If challenged ballots are sufficient in number to affect the result of the election, a Board agent will conduct a special investigation into the merits of the individual challenges. The reasons for the challenge will have been given and marked on the challenge envelope during the balloting. A ballot may not be challenged after the election. The party making the challenge may be called upon to furnish information in support of the challenge during the investigation. As in the case of objections, if substantial factual issues exist, a hearing may be ordered.

Sec. 10–10. Report on objections and challenges. After completion of the investigation, the course which the regional director will follow depends on whether the election was held pursuant to (1) a directed election (by the regional director or the Board); or (2) a stipulated consent election agreement; or (3) a consent election agreement.

1. In the case of a directed election:

The regional director may (a) issue a report on objections and/or challenges with specific recommendations as to their disposition; (b) issue such a report and forward it to Washington; or (c) issue a supplemental decision disposing of the objections and/or challenges

---

[45]Atlantic Mills Servicing Corp of Cleveland, Inc., 120 NLRB 1284, 42 LRRM 1158 (1958).
[46]Adler Metal Products Corp., 114 NLRB 170, 36 LRRM 1533 (1955).
[47]Belk's Department Store of Savannah, Ga., Inc., 98 NLRB 280, 29 LRRM 1325 (1952).
[48]Richard A. Glass Co., 120 NLRB 914, 42 LRRM 1087 (1958); cf. Thomas Industries, Inc., Thomas Products Co., Div., 169 NLRB 706, 67 LRRM 1237 (1968), denying reconsideration to 66 LRRM 1147.
[49]Tidelands Marine Services, Inc., 116 NLRB 1222, 38 LRRM 1444 (1956).
[50]Edward J. Schlachter Meat Co., 100 NLRB 1171, 30 LRRM 1418 (1952).
[51]R. and R. Sec. 102.69(c); 102.69(h).

himself in an appropriate manner.[52] If the regional director follows either course (a) or (b), the parties have the right to file exceptions to the report within 10 days with the regional director or the Board, as the case may be, as provided by the Board's rules and regulations;[53] however, if the director himself disposes of the matter, the rights of the parties are limited to a request for review of the supplemental decision under the four grounds provided in the Board's rules and regulations.[54] (See "Grounds for Review," page 144.)

2. In the case of a stipulated election:

The stipulated election agreement provides that the Board, rather than the regional director, shall make the final determination of postelection issues. The regional director investigates all objections and challenges which may be in issue and issues a report in which he makes specific recommendations to the Board with respect to the disposition of the objections or challenges. The parties have a right to file exceptions to this report with the Board within 10 days. Unlike requests for review where the Board has discretion over whether or not to entertain the requests and they are granted on limited grounds only, the exceptions are considered by the Board on their merits and will be sustained if supported by the record, regardless of the director's recommendations. The director's report is omitted if a hearing was ordered.[55]

3. In the case of a consent election:

In a consent election, the regional director has final authority over all issues which may arise. Objections and challenges arising under the consent election are investigated by the regional director after which he issues a report making a final determination with respect to the issues. This disposition is final with no right of appeal. However, if the action of the regional director is arbitrary or capricious, the NLRB may consider a motion to set aside the director's decision.[56] The Board's determination is subject to review in the courts.[57]

Sec. 10–11. Exceptions to report on objections and/or challenges. In the event exceptions to a regional director's report on objections or challenges are filed, a request for further time to file exceptions—in addition to the 10 days—should be addressed to the Board's Executive Secretary or the

[52]R. and R. Sec. 102.69(c).
[53]*Ibid.*
[54]R. and R. Sec. 102.67(c).
[55]R. and R. Sec. 102.62(b); 102.69(c); 102.70; Statements of Procedure Sec. 101.19(b).
[56]R. and R. Sec. 102.62(a).
[57]NLRB v. Staiman Brothers, 81 LRRM 2133 (C.A. 3, 1972), *denying enforcement to* 189 NLRB No. 44, 77 LRRM 1189.

regional director, as the case may be. The request for extension of time should be:

1. Served immediately upon all other parties.
2. Made no later than three working days before the date the exceptions are due.[58]

Sec. 10–12. Who may file exceptions.   The Board has repeatedly ruled that only parties are entitled to file exceptions. Thus, the Board has held:

1. A party may file exceptions to a report on objections even though that party did not file objections.[59]
2. As a general rule, individual employees[60] and economic strikers[61] may not file exceptions.

However, in some instances, the Board has permitted individual employees to file exceptions and has limited them to matters directly relating to the employees' interests. Thus, the Board permitted intervention of employees, who did not claim to represent any employees for bargaining purposes, for the limited purpose of filing exceptions to that part of the report on objections which concerned their exclusion from the election.[62]

The Board has held repeatedly that objections will be overruled "unless the exceptions advert to specific substantial evidence contraverting the regional director's conclusions."[63]

Sec. 10–13. Content of the exceptions.   The exceptions should contain a complete statement of the supporting facts and reasons.[64] Any data subsequently submitted will be rejected as untimely.[65] Also, the Board, or the regional director, will reject:

1. Objections to an election raised for the first time in the exceptions.[66]
2. Evidence submitted as part of the exceptions, where such evidence was not submitted in support of the objections and was not newly discovered.[67]

---

[58]R. and R. Sec. 102.69(c).
[59]Westinghouse Electric Corp., 119 NLRB 1858, 41 LRRM 1424 (1958).
[60]H. O. Canfield Co., 80 NLRB 1027, 23 LRRM 1195 (1948).
[61]Dadourian Export Corp., 80 NLRB 1400, 23 LRRM 1286 (1948).
[62]Shoreline Enterprises of America and Shoreline Packing Corp., 114 NLRB 716, 37 LRRM 1048 (1955).
[63]Adler Metal Products Corp., 114 NLRB 170, 36 LRRM 1533 (1955).
[64]R. and R. Sec. 102.69(g) (as amended February 10, 1975).
[65]Radio Corporation of America, 90 NLRB 1989, 26 LRRM 1416 (1950).
[66]Jo-Art Mfg. Co., 116 NLRB 1889, 39 LRRM 1117 (1956).
[67]General Electric Co., 115 NLRB 306, 37 LRRM 1296 (1956).

3. Contentions in the exceptions which were the subject of an unfair labor practice charge which the General Counsel dismissed on appeal.[68]

If no exceptions are filed, the matter will ordinarily be decided forthwith upon the record;[69] but a hearing may be ordered instead.[70]

Where exceptions are taken only to some of the regional director's recommendations, the remaining recommendations to which no exceptions are taken[71] will automatically be adopted.

Sec. 10–14. Right to hearing on exceptions. The filing of timely exceptions does not guarantee a hearing.[72] According to the Rules and Regulations, one of two things may be done after such exceptions are filed:[73]

1. If exceptions do not raise substantial and material factual issues, the matter may be decided upon the record, without a hearing. Thus, the Board has ruled that it may deny a request for hearing where: (a) the report on objections contains all necessary evidence;[74] or (b) even if a conflict in evidence is involved.[75]
2. If exceptions raise substantial and material factual issues, a notice of hearing may be issued. Several courts have ruled that this means the Board must order a hearing when "substantial questions are raised as to the validity of an election,"[76] but the Board, as a practical matter, has very broad discretion in this area.[77]

Sec. 10–15. Hearing on exceptions. The notice of hearing will be served on all parties by the regional director. The hearing may be conducted by either an NLRB agent from a regional office or an administrative law judge from Washington. It will be conducted in the same manner as the original hearing on the petition.[78] (See "The Representation Hearing",page 105.)

---

[68]Westchester Broadcasting Corp., 95 NLRB 1057, 28 LRRM 1418 (1951).
[69]R. and R. Sec. 102.69(c).
[70]Paramount Cap Mfg. Co., 115 NLRB 747, 37 LRRM 1418 (1956).
[71]Flight Enterprises, Inc., 119 NLRB 1442, 41 LRRM 1326 (1958).
[72]International Shoe Co., 87 NLRB 479, 25 LRRM 1133 (1949).
[73]R. and R. Sec. 102.69(c).
[74]A. D. Julliard and Co., 110 NLRB 2197, 35 LRRM 1401 (1954).
[75]Gastonia Combed Yárn Corp., 109 NLRB 585, 34 LRRM 1404 (1954).
[76]NLRB v. Poinsett Lumber and Mfg. Corp., 221 F.2d 121, 35 LRRM 2736 (C.A. 4, 1955); NLRB v. Bata Shoe Co., 377 F.2d 821, 826, 65 LRRM 2318 (C.A. 4, 1967), cert. den., 389 U.S. 917, 66 LRRM 2370 (1967); Howell Refining Co. v. NLRB, 400 F.2d 213, 69 LRRM 2032 (C.A. 5, 1968), denying enforcement to 164 NLRB 512, 65 LRRM 1199.
[77]Rockwell Manufacturing Company, Kearney Division, 330 F.2d 795, 55 LRRM 2868 (C.A. 7, 1964).
[78]R. and R. Sec. 102.69(d).

For example, as in the instance of the original hearing, parties may file briefs, as a matter of right, after conclusion of the hearing. (The procedure for the filing of briefs is the same as that set forth in Sec. 7–19, page 121.)

Also, as in an unfair labor practice hearing, after a witness has testified any party may call for and obtain any statement in the possession of the Board signed or otherwise approved by the witness.[79] (See Sec. 16–7, page 269.)

When objections to an election or challenges and an unfair labor practice complaint cover the same ground, consideration of the exceptions and the complaint may be consolidated for the purpose of the hearing.[80] In such instances, an attempt will be made to apply: (a) the procedures for hearings in election cases to those parts of the hearing involving the objections or challenges; and (b) the procedures for hearings in unfair labor practice cases to those parts involving the complaint. (The latter type of hearing is described beginning on page 265.)

After the close of the hearing, if held at the instance of the Board, the entire record in the case will be forwarded to the Board in Washington. Otherwise it is turned over to the regional director. (This procedure is not followed where the hearing was consolidated to cover both an unfair labor practice complaint and objections. Then the administrative law judge issues a decision after the close of the hearing.) The record includes: the notice of hearing, motions, rulings, the stenographic report of the hearing, stipulations, exhibits, objections to the conduct of the election, the report on such objections, the report on challenged ballots, exceptions to such reports, the record previously made in the case, and the hearing officer's report, if any.[81]

Sec. 10–16. Report on exceptions. The order directing that a hearing be held will usually state that the hearing officer's report shall: (a) resolve questions involving credibility of witnesses; (b) make findings of fact; and (c) make recommendations as to the disposition of the challenges or objections.[82] Thus, the Board has ruled that, while a hearing officer cannot make recommendations after the original hearing before the election, the hearing officer may do so after the hearing on exceptions.[83]

As a matter of right, the parties have 10 days from the date of issuance of the report on exceptions in which to take exception to it.[84] The exceptions should be filed with the Board in Washington, or the regional director, as the case may be, and copies served upon all other parties. If the hearing was

[79]R. and R. Sec. 102.118.
[80]R. and R. Sec. 102.33(b).
[81]R. and R. Sec. 102.69(f).
[82]R. and R. Sec. 102.69(d).
[83]Talladega Cotton Factory, Inc., 91 NLRB 470, 26 LRRM 1517 (1950).
[84]R. and R. Sec. 102.69(d).

consolidated—to cover both an unfair labor practice complaint and objections or challenges—parties have 20 days in which to file exceptions.[85]

If no exceptions are filed to the report, the matter may be decided forthwith upon the record.[86]

Sec. 10–17. Decision on challenged ballots. Decision as to both objections and challenges is made on the basis of the entire written record. Challenged ballots need not be ruled upon where the outcome of the election would not be affected either way.[87] Where a conclusive election may result from opening and counting a group of challenged ballots, the Board or the regional director may refuse to rule upon an additional group of challenged ballots.[88]

If challenged ballots are ruled to be the votes of ineligible voters, these ballots remain unopened and are not counted. If they are ruled to be the votes of eligible voters, the regional director opens and counts such ballots and issues a revised tally of ballots. (See Facsimile No. 34, p. 179, revised tally of ballots.) Where only one challenged ballot is involved and it is ruled to be the vote of an eligible voter, it is opened and counted, even though the secrecy of the vote is destroyed.[89]

The counting procedures are the same as those at the original count. (See page 178.) Any party may file objections with the regional director to the revised tally within three days after receiving it.[90]

If timely objections are filed to the revised tally, the procedures that follow are the same as those in regard to objections filed after the election. (See page 187.) If timely objections are not filed, and the results of the election are decisive, the regional director will issue a certification.[91]

Sec. 10–18. Decision on objections. In rendering a decision on objections to the conduct of the election or conduct affecting the results of the election, the Board or the regional director, may:

1. Overrule the objections, and a certification will be issued if the results of the election are conclusive: or
2. Sustain the objections, in whole or in part, and set aside the election.[92]

A decision sustaining objections and setting aside an election:

---

[85]R. and R. Sec. 102.46.
[86]R. and R. Sec. 102.69(d).
[87]Marlin-Rockwell Corp. v. NLRB, 116 F.2d 586, 7 LRRM 353 (C.A. 2, 1941); Carlisle Paper Box Co., 68 LRRM 2831 (C.A. 3, 1968), *enf.* 67 LRRM 1132.
[88]S & S Corrugated Paper Machinery Co., Inc., 89 NLRB 1363, 26 LRRM 1112 (1950).
[89]Davison Chemical Co., 115 NLRB 786, 37 LRRM 1417 (1956).
[90]R. and R. Sec. 102.69(g).
[91]*Ibid.*
[92]Statements of Procedure, Sec. 101.19(b) and 101.21(c).

1. If made by the regional director is subject to the request for review procedures (see page 143).
2. If made by the Board is not reviewable by a court.[93]
3. May be based on findings of objectionable incidents which are not unfair labor practices.[94]
4. May be based on findings of objectionable conduct committed by others than the parties to the proceeding.[95]

Sec. 10–19. Rerun elections.   The decision setting aside the election will direct a new election, a rerun, to be conducted by the regional director. The order will indicate that the rerun is to be conducted either: (a) within a specific period from the date of the order; (b) at a date to be determined by the regional director; or (c) at a time to be decided by the Board when it is advised by the regional director that a fair election can be conducted.[96]

Sec. 10–20. Notices in rerun elections.   Notices to be posted informing employees of the details of the rerun election may include a paragraph explaining why the election was set aside.[97] Consequently, if requested by a party or if deemed warranted by the regional director, the notice will include language reading substantially as follows:

NOTICE TO ALL VOTERS. The election conducted on (date), was set aside because the National Labor Relations Board found that certain conduct of the (employer, union, third party, Board agent) interfered with the employees' exercise of a free and reasoned choice. Therefore, a new election will be held in accordance with the terms of this Notice of Election. All eligible voters should understand that the National Labor Relations Act, as amended, gives them the right to cast their ballots as they see fit, and protects them in the exercise of this right, free from interference by any of the parties.

Sec. 10–21. Voting eligibility in rerun election.   All other aspects and procedures of a rerun election are the same as those of the original election, with one exception: the voting eligibility date of the rerun election will be different from that used in the original election.[98] The decision ordering a rerun election will designate as the voting eligibility date either:

---

[93]Bonwit Teller, Inc. v. NLRB, 197 F.2d 640, 30 LRRM 2305 (C.A. 2, 1952).
[94]NLRB v. Shirlington Supermarket, Inc., 224 F.2d 649, 36 LRRM 2485 (C.A. 4, 1955).
[95]Diamond State Poultry Co., 107 NLRB 3, 33 LRRM 1043 (1953); Monarch Rubber Co., 121 NLRB 81, 42 LRRM 1294 (1958).
[96]Lewittes & Sons, Inc., 40 NLRB 43, 9 LRRM 381 (1942).
[97]The Lufkin Rule Co., 147 NLRB 341, 56 LRRM 1212 (1964).
[98]Buffalo Arms, Inc., 114 NLRB 950, 37 LRRM 1079 (1955); Pickands, Mather and Co., Interlake Steamship Co. Div., 178 NLRB No. 20, 72 LRRM 1008 (1969), aff'g 70 LRRM 1177.

1. The last full payroll period preceding the date of the decision ordering the rerun;[99] or
2. If the decision is made by the regional director and no review is granted, the last full payroll period preceding the date of issuance of the notice of election.

If objections are filed and the regional director or Board sets aside the rerun election, another rerun election can be held. However, if the results of the rerun are not decisive—that is, no single choice received a majority of the valid votes cast—no runoff will be conducted if the original election was either: (a) a runoff election; or (b) a "severance" election. (The procedures applicable to the runoff election are set forth below, starting with the next paragraph; the "severance" election is described on page 158, under "Form of the Ballot," and on page 178, under "Counting of Ballots.")

Sec. 10–22. Runoff election. A runoff election is conducted only where: (a) the ballot in the original election contained three or more choices; and (b) no single choice received a majority of the valid votes cast. Thus, there can be no runoff where the original ballot provided for: (1) a "yes" and "no" choice in a one-union election; or (2) a "severance" election.

If an election results in no one choice receiving a majority of the valid votes cast, where the ballot provides for at least three choices (that is, for two labor organizations and "neither"), the regional director must conduct a runoff election.[100] This requirement is automatic; a party need not petition for a runoff election.

The runoff will be conducted as soon as practicable after the original election, but not during the period in which objections to the original election may be filed. If timely objections are filed, a runoff will not be conducted until they have been resolved.

As stated above, only one runoff election can be conducted in any single representation proceeding.[101] However, a runoff, if it is set aside, can be rerun.[102]

Sec. 10–23. Voting eligibility in runoff election. Eligibility to vote in the runoff election (unlike the rerun election) is limited to employees who: (a) were eligible to vote in the original election; and (b) are employed in an eligible category on the date of the runoff election.[103] Thus, the original eligibility date has been retained for a runoff election even where

[99]Pennington Bros., Inc., 98 NLRB 965, 29 LRRM 1455 (1952).
[99]R. and R. Sec. 102.70(a); Georgia-Pacific Corp., 195 NLRB No. 132, 79 LRRM 1698 (1972); cf. Tullahoma Concrete Pipe Co., Inc., 168 NLRB 555, 66 LRRM 1325 (1967).
[101]Ibid.
[102]R. and R. Sec. 102.70(e).
[103]R. and R. Sec. 102.70(b).

substantial employee turnover had occurred since that date.[104] However, where a runoff election had been set aside and the number of employees in the unit had increased substantially since the date of that election, the Board has ordered a current payroll period to establish eligibility to vote in the rerun, runoff election.[105]

Sec. 10–24. Voter's choices in runoff elections.   The ballot in the runoff election will provide for a selection between the two choices receiving the largest and second largest number of valid votes cast in the original election.[106] For example:

1. Where one labor organization received the least number of valid votes cast and the choices on the original ballot were between "Union A," "Union B," and "neither union," the remaining labor organization and a "no" choice will appear on the runoff ballot.
2. Where each of the two labor organizations received more votes than the "neither" choice, the two labor organizations will be the only choices on the runoff ballot.
3. Where each of two choices received an equal number of votes which was larger than the number of votes cast for the third choice, the third choice will be dropped from the runoff ballot.
4. Where each of two choices received an equal number of votes and the third choice received none, and not all of the eligible voters had cast valid votes, the third choice will be dropped from the runoff ballot.[107]

Sec. 10–25. Tie votes.   The following rules apply in other instances involving tie votes in the original election:[108]

1. The regional director will certify the results of the original election and will not conduct a runoff or a rerun election where:
   (a) Two or more choices received an equal number of votes;
   (b) The remaining choice received no votes; and
   (c) All eligible voters cast valid votes.[109]
2. The regional director will declare the original election a nullity, set it aside, and conduct a rerun, with the same choices as on the original ballot, where:
   (a) All choices received an equal number of votes; or

---

[104]Cone Brothers Contracting Co. v. NLRB, 235 F.2d 37, 38 LRRM 2318 (C.A. 5, 1956).
[105]United Aircraft Corp., 103 NLRB 878, 31 LRRM 1592 (1953).
[106]R. and R. Sec. 102.70(c).
[107]W. Shanhouse Sons, Inc., 100 NLRB 604, 30 LRRM 1328 (1952).
[108]R. and R. Sec. 102.70(d).
[109]U.S. Rubber Co., 83 NLRB 378, 24 LRRM 1087 (1949).

(b) Two choices received an equal number of votes, and the third choice received a greater number of votes.[110]
3. The voting unit or group in a rerun election resulting from a tie vote remains the same as that in the original election but the eligibility of employees changes as in any other rerun election.

Sec. 10–26. Runoff election results. If the rerun election results in another nullity, the regional director will dismiss the petition. If the rerun election is otherwise not conclusive, the regional director will conduct a runoff election according to one of the four examples set forth above.

A labor organization which is eliminated from the runoff ballot by the results of the first election may participate in a proceeding involving objections to the runoff election.[111] Any objection to the runoff election will be rejected as untimely which is based on conduct which occurred before the original election and to which no objections had been filed.[112]

Sec. 10–27. Types of certification. The end product of a representation proceeding is a certification, which can be issued only after an election.[113] There are two main types of certifications:

1. CERTIFICATION OF REPRESENTATIVE, issued after an election in which a majority of employees voted for representation by a labor organization. (See Facsimile No. 38, page 202.)
2. CERTIFICATION OF RESULTS OF ELECTION, issued after an election in which a majority of employees voted against representation. (See Facsimile No. 39, page 203.)

The Board will issue a variation on the above certifications which is patterned to meet specialized situations. For example: Certificate of Results of Election, issued after a severance or self-determination election in which a majority of the group (e.g., craft) did not vote for the union seeking severance, and no election was simultaneously held in the more comprehensive group (e.g., production and maintenance). (See Facsimile No. 40, page 205.)

The Board will issue a certification of representative only where, in the words of the statute, "the majority of the employees"[114] have cast their ballots in favor of a labor organization. The Board and the courts have repeatedly held that the phrase "the majority of the employees" means

---

[110]United States Gypsum Co., 81 NLRB 1129 (1949).
[111]The American Tobacco Co., 93 NLRB 1323, 27 LRRM 1568 (1951).
[112]National Petro-Chemicals Corp., 107 NLRB 1610, 33 LRRM 1443 (1954); Sonoco Products Co., 69 LRRM 2037 (C.A. 9, 1968), *denying enforcement to* 65 LRRM 1405; Singer Co., 161 NLRB 956, 63 LRRM 1381 (1966); Logan Co., 171 NLRB No. 83, 68 LRRM 1141 (1968); Owens-Corning Fiberglas Corp., 179 NLRB No. 39, 72 LRRM 1289 (1969).
[113]Ray Brooks v. NLRB, 348 U.S. 96, 35 LRRM 2158 (1954).
[114]Sec. 9(a).

FORM NLRB-4279
(3-72)   RC-RM-RD

UNITED STATES OF AMERICA
NATIONAL LABOR RELATIONS BOARD

TYPE OF ELECTION

(Check one)   (Also check box
below where
☐ Consent Agreement   appropriate)

☐ Stipulation   ☐ 8(b)(7)

☐ Board Direction

☐ RD Direction

Case No.

CERTIFICATION OF REPRESENTATIVE

An election having been conducted in the above matter under the supervision of the Regional Director of the National Labor Relations Board in accordance with the Rules and Regulations of the Board; and it appearing from the Tally of Ballots that a collective bargaining representative has been selected; and no objections having been filed to the Tally of Ballots furnished to the parties, or to the conduct of the election, within the time provided therefor;

Pursuant to authority vested in the undersigned by the National Labor Relations Board, IT IS HEREBY CERTIFIED that a majority of the valid ballots have been cast for

and that, pursuant to Section 9(a) of the National Labor Relations Act, as amended, the said labor organization is the exclusive representative of all the employees in the unit set forth below, found to be appropriate for the purposes of collective bargaining in respect to rates of pay, wages, hours of employment, or other conditions of employment.

UNIT:

Signed at
On the   day of   19

On behalf of

NATIONAL LABOR RELATIONS BOARD

Regional Director, Region
National Labor Relations Board

GPO 478-598

FACSIMILE NO. 38.
*Certification of representation in election
won by labor organization (Form 4279)*

FORM NLRB-4280
(2-66)

UNITED STATES OF AMERICA
NATIONAL LABOR RELATIONS BOARD

TYPE OF ELECTION

(Check one)

☐ Consent Agreement

☐ Stipulation

☐ Board Direction

☐ RD Direction

(Also check box
below where
appropriate)

☐ 8(b)(7)

Case No.

CERTIFICATION OF RESULTS OF ELECTION

An election having been conducted in the above matter under the supervision of the Regional Director of the National Labor Relations Board in accordance with the Rules and Regulations of the Board; and it appearing from the Tally of Ballots that no collective bargaining representative has been selected; and no objections having been filed to the Tally of Ballots furnished to the parties, or to the conduct of the election, within the time provided therefor;

Pursuant to authority vested in the undersigned by the National Labor Relations Board,

IT IS HEREBY CERTIFIED that a majority of the valid ballots has not been cast for any labor organization appearing on the ballot, and that no such organization is the exclusive representative of all the employees, in the unit herein involved, within the meaning of Section 9(a) of the National Labor Relations Act, as amended.

Signed at
On the   day of   , 19

_____
Regional Director, Region
National Labor Relations Board

GPO 861-496

FACSIMILE NO. 39.
*Certification of results in election lost
by labor organization (Form 4280)*

majority of the valid votes cast, not a majority of those eligible to vote.[115] Thus, a labor organization may be certified which received less than a majority of those eligible to vote, but more than one-half of the valid votes actually cast.

However, the Board has ruled that it need not automatically issue a certification in every instance where a labor organization is designated by a majority of the valid votes cast: "The Board may refuse to certify a successful union where, upon its own motion or other proper procedures, the legality of any stage in the representation proceeding is called into question."[116] Thus certification has been withheld where the number of employees in the unit was reduced to one after the election.[117] Here, the Board held that it would be contrary to policy to certify a representative for a one-man unit.

In all instances of valid elections involving only one labor organization—the ballot affording choices of "yes" and "no"—a certification of results of election will always be issued where the labor organization fails to receive a majority of the valid ballots cast. Thus, where such election results in a tie vote, an equal number of valid votes having been cast for and against the labor organization—and challenges, if any, have been resolved—the Board will issue a certification of results of election.[118]

Sec. 10–28. Significance of certification. The certification of representative is merely a determination that a majority of employees in an appropriate unit have selected a particular labor organization as their exclusive bargaining representative.[119] It is not affected by change in ownership of the employing entity.[120] (For a discussion of the importance of certification, see page 48 under "Benefits of Board Certification.") The Board has ruled that the certification is not a jurisdictional award:

It is true that such certification presupposes a determination that the group of employees involved constitutes an appropriate unit for collective bargaining purposes, and that in making such determination the Board considers the general nature of the duties and work tasks of such employees. However, unlike a jurisdictional award, this determination by the Board does not freeze the duties or work tasks of the employees in the unit found appropriate.

Thus, the Board's unit finding does not preclude the employer from adding to, or subtracting from, the employee's work assignments. While

---

[115]Semi-Steel Casting Co. of St. Louis v. NLRB, 160 F.2d 388, 19 LRRM 2458 (C.A. 8, 1947).
[116]Worthington Pump and Machinery Corp., 99 NLRB 189, 30 LRRM 1052 (1952).
[117]Cutter Laboratories, 116 NLRB 260, 38 LRRM 1241 (1956).
[118]John W. Thomas Co., 111 NLRB 226, 36 LRRM 1444 (1955); see also Tullahoma Concrete Pipe Co., Inc., 168 NLRB 555, 66 LRRM 1325 (1967).
[119]Miron Building Products Co., Inc., 116 NLRB 1406, 39 LRRM 1002 (1956); Dawes Laboratories, Inc., 164 NLRB 935, 65 LRRM 1178 (1967).
[120]NLRB v. Alberto Armato and Wire & Sheet Metal Specialty Co., 199 F.2d 800, 31 LRRM 2089 (C.A. 7, 1952).

UNITED STATES OF AMERICA

NATIONAL LABOR RELATIONS BOARD

* * * * * * * * * * * * * * * * *
*
* $\Box$ Consent Agreement
*
* $\Box$ Stipulated
*
*   Case No. $\Box$ Board Direction
*
* $\Box$ RD Direction
*
* * * * * * * * * * * * * * * * *

CERTIFICATE OF RESULTS OF ELECTION

An election having been conducted in the above matter by the undersigned Regional Director of the National Labor Relations Board in accordance with the Rules and Regulations of the Board, among:

And no objections having been filed to the Tally of Ballots furnished to the parties, or to the conduct of the election, within the time provided therefor;

Pursuant to authority vested in the undersigned by the National Labor Relations Board,

IT IS HEREBY CERTIFIED that a majority of the valid ballots has not been cast for a union seeking to represent the above-named employees in a separate unit. Accordingly, $\overline{/}$ name of production and maintenance union $\overline{/}$ may continue to bargain for these employees as part of the existing $\overline{/}$ production and maintenance $\overline{/}$ unit which it currently represents.

Signed at

On the   day of   , 19

Regional Director for   Region
National Labor Relations Board

FACSIMILE No. 40.
*Certification of results issued by regional director
after a "severance" election, severance voted down, and
no election conducted in larger group*

that finding may be determined by, it does not determine, job content; nor does it signify approval, in any respect, of any work task claims which the certified union may have made before the Board or elsewhere.[121]

Sec. 10–29. Duration of certification. As for the vitality of a certification—how long is its duration—the Board and courts have repeatedly held: The certification identifies the union's status as exclusive bargaining representative with certainty and finality for a reasonable period of time, customarily for one year after date of certification, and indefinitely thereafter until such status is shown to have ceased.[122] Thus, an employer, absent unusual circumstances, must bargain with a certified union during the year following the date of certification even though: (a) the union loses a majority of employees from membership;[123] or (b) opposing petitions for elections are pending or may be filed with the Board.[124] The Board has ruled that the same effect is to be given to certifications issued by state agencies after secret ballot elections as to Board certifications.[125]

The vitality of a certification is not extended or affected in any way where the Board issues a certificate that a currently recognized representative may continue to bargain for a group of employees which, in a "severance" or self-determination election, has voted against severance from the existing unit.[126]

Sec. 10–30. Who issues certification. The same force and effect attach to a certification regardless of whether it is issued by a regional director or by the Board in Washington.[127]

The regional director will issue certifications in all cases where the election was held pursuant to an Agreement for Consent Election. In elections held pursuant to a Stipulation for Certification Upon Consent Election (1) the certification will be issued by the regional director where no objections are filed and challenges are not determinative of the results; (2) the certification will be issued by the Board where objections are filed or challenges are determinative of results, except that the regional director will issue a certification after the opening and counting of challenged ballots pursuant to a direction of the Board.

In elections directed by the regional director or the Board, certification will be issued (1) by the regional director where no objections are filed and challenges are not determinative; (2) by the regional director in a

[121]The Plumbing Contractors Assn. of Baltimore, Md., Inc., 93 NLRB 1081, 27 LRRM 1514 (1951).
[122]Ray Brooks v. NLRB, 348 U.S. 96, 35 LRRM 2158 (1954); see also Abrams v. Carrier Corp., 75 LRRM 2736 (C.A. 2, 1970), reman'g 75 LRRM 2724.
[123]Ray Brooks v. NLRB, 348 U.S. 96, 35 LRRM 2158 (1954).
[124]NLRB v. Henry Heide, Inc., 219 F.2d 46, 35 LRRM 2378 (C.A. 2, 1955).
[125]Bluefield Produce & Provision Co., 117 NLRB 1660, 40 LRRM 1065 (1957).
[126]B. F. Goodrich Chemical Co., 84 NLRB 429, 24 LRRM 1275 (1949).
[127]R. and R. Secs. 102.54(a), 102.61(b) and 102.61(c).

supplemental decision based on his administrative investigation or hearing, where there are objections and/or challenges; (3) by the Board where the regional director's report transferred the case to the Board; and (4) by the regional director after opening and counting challenged ballots pursuant to his own direction or that of the Board.

Sec. 10–31. Clarification of bargaining units and amendment of certifications. The Board has repeatedly held that its certifications are subject to reconsideration,[128] that it may police its certifications by amendment, clarification,[129] and even by revocation.[130] However, the Board has held that motions to clarify bargaining units which raise the problem of resolving work assignment disputes are not properly matters for consideration in representation proceedings.[131]

Clarification of an existing bargaining unit is requested by filing a petition on the same form used in representation election cases.[132] (See Facsimile No. 2, page 64.) The petition may be filed only where no question concerning representation exists. Formerly the Board refused to clarify units where there was no prior NLRB certification despite the existence of a bargaining unit.[133] Both certified and uncertified units may be clarified under the current procedures. (See Sec. 1–24, page 21.)

Sec. 10–32. Who may file petition to clarify. The petition to clarify may be filed by the labor organization currently recognized or certified as bargaining representative of the employees in a bargaining unit or by the employer involved. Neither a rival union nor individual employees are authorized to file.

Sec. 10–33. Contents of the petition to clarify. The petition form calls for substantially the same information as required in petitioning for an election (see "Filing the Petition," page 62) except that a description of the proposed clarification, the number of employees in the unit before and after the clarification, the job classifications affected and the number of employees in each, and a statement of reasons for clarification must be included.[134]

---

[128]Worthington Pump and Machinery Corp., 99 NLRB 189, 30 LRRM 1052 (1952).
[129]The Bell Telephone Co. of Pennsylvania, 118 NLRB 371, 40 LRRM 1179 (1957).
[130]Metal Workers Union, 147 NLRB No. 166, 56 LRRM 1289 (1964).
[131]Ingersoll Products Division of the Borg-Warner Corporation, 150 NLRB 912, 58 LRRM 1168 (1965).
[132]R. and R. Sec. 102.60(b).
[133]The Bell Telephone Co. of Pennsylvania, 118 NLRB 371, 40 LRRM 1179 (1957).
[134]R. and R. Sec. 102.61(d).

Sec. 10–34. Limitations on clarification. Clarification of a bargaining unit is usually sought to resolve the unit placement of disputed classifications of employees. A petition for clarification must not raise a question of representation. In other words, such a petition cannot be used in the place of an election petition when the object is to add a classification of employees that had been deliberately omitted from the unit.[135] However, a petition to clarify will not be dismissed even though the Board has not ruled on the appropriateness of the bargaining unit and no certification exists.[136] Also, a previous Board determination of the bargaining unit is conclusive only if it resolves the exact question upon which clarification is sought.[137]

Sec. 10–35. Amendment of certification. Any party may file a petition for amendment to reflect changed circumstances, such as changes in the name or affiliation of the labor organization involved or the name or location of the employer involved, if the bargaining unit is covered by certification and there is no question concerning representation.[138]

Ambiguity in the description of the unit or a change in duties of certain employees in the unit should now be handled by a petition to clarify rather than to amend. The practical difference is not significant, as the same form is used for both petitions and they are processed in the same manner, except that the petition to amend may be used only when there is an outstanding certification.

Sec. 10–36. Who may file petition to amend. Either the certified bargaining representative or the employer may file a petition to amend a certification. Such a petition cannot be filed by a currently recognized bargaining agent who is not certified.

Sec. 10–37. Contents of the petition to amend. The petition to amend a certification includes information similar to that found in the representation petition (see "Filing the Petition," page 62) and the same form is used. (See Facsimile No. 3, page 72.) The details of the desired amendment and the reasons for its adoption must be shown.[139]

---

[135]Morris, THE DEVELOPING LABOR LAW (Washington D.C.: BNA Books, 1971); Lufkin Foundry and Machine Co., 174 NLRB No. 90, 70 LRRM 1262 (1969); *cf.* Westinghouse Electric Co., 173 NLRB No. 43, 69 LRRM 1332 (1968); Libbey-Owens-Ford Glass Co., 202 NLRB No. 15, 82 LRRM 1417 (1973).
[136]Locomotive Firemen and Enginemen, 145 NLRB 1521, 55 LRRM 1177 (1964).
[137]Boston Gas Co., 136 NLRB 219, 49 LRRM 1742 (1962); West Virginia Pulp and Paper Co., 140 NLRB 1160, 52 LRRM 1196 (1963).
[138]Statements of Procedure, Sec. 101.17.
[139]R. and R. Sec. 102.61(e).

Sec. 10–38. Investigation of petition to clarify or amend. After a petition to clarify or to amend has been filed, the regional director has wide latitude in its consideration. He may conduct whatever investigation he believes appropriate and may then:

1. Issue a decision without a hearing.
2. Prepare and serve a notice of hearing on all parties directly affected.
3. Take any other action he deems appropriate.[140]

If a hearing is ordered, the hearing and posthearing procedures are, insofar as applicable, identical with those used in representation cases.[141] An exception is made, however, in cases arising out of a unit or certification which resulted from a consent election agreement. In those instances the regional director's action on the petition is final and provision for review of his decisions do not apply. Also, petitions dismissed without a hearing are treated as a decision of the director and any Board review must be obtained by use of the request for review procedure (see "Appeal of Regional Director's Decisions in Election Cases," page 143) rather than that used for dismissal of representation petitions (see "Dismissal of a Petition," page 90). Review will not be granted in cases arising out of consent election agreements.

The rules are not clear as to the procedure for handling petitions to clarify or amend where the certification involved resulted from a Stipulation for Certification Upon Consent Election. The rules say that petitions may be filed to clarify an existing bargaining unit or to amend a certification, without reference to Stipulations for Certification Upon Consent Election,[142] but the hearing and posthearing procedures to be used do not apply to such cases.[143] Until the point is clarified, the regional director should be consulted before proceeding. If a petition is not proper, a motion to the Board would be used.

The Board has held that amendment of the certification does not amount to a new certification, recertification, or extension of the old certification.[144] This does not appear to be changed by the current rules and it would seem logical that it would apply to clarifications as well as amendments.

Sec. 10–39. Revocation of certification. A regional director has the authority to revoke a certification on a motion by one of the parties, or on his own initiative, if he feels that revocation is appropriate in a given

---

[140]R. and R. Sec. 102.63(b).
[141]*Ibid.*
[142]R. and R. Sec. 102.60(b).
[143]R. and R. Sec. 102.63(b).
[144]National Carbon Co., 116 NLRB 488, 38 LRRM 1284 (1956).

situation.[145] Where the certification arose out of an agreement for consent election, the regional director's action on revocation will be final. However, if the certification arose from a directed or a stipulated election, the regional director's action shall be final, subject to the right of the parties to request review by the Board. For example, a certification may be revoked[146] where the certified labor organization:

1. Represents members only.[147]
2. Denies equal representation and membership in the union to employees in the unit because of race.[148]
3. Excludes from contract coverage certain employees in the unit.[149]
4. Denies claim to represent any employees on the payroll, making this denial as a reason why the employer's petition for an election should be dismissed.[150]

Sec. 10–40. Court review of certification.   A regional director or Board certification, unlike a final order issued in an unfair labor practice proceeding, is not subject to direct review by a court.[151] However, the certification may be reviewed as part of the review of an unfair labor practice order based upon that certification.[152] Mere consolidation of a representation case with an unfair labor practice case does not afford court review of the certification where the unfair labor practice order is not based on the certification.[153]

However, some courts have held that a certification may be directly reviewed where:

1. There is a showing of unlawful action by the Board and resulting injury.[154]

---

[145]NLRB Field Manual 11478.3; Uyeda (Udaco Mfg. Co.) v. Brooks, 62 LRRM 2831 (C.A. 6, 1966), revs'g and reman's 57 LRRM 2275.
[146]Ray Brooks v. NLRB, 348 U.S. 96, 35 LRRM 2158 (1954).
[147]Pittsburgh Plate Glass Co., 111 NLRB 1210, 35 LRRM 1658 (1955).
[148]Hughes Tool Co., 147 NLRB No. 166, 56 LRRM 1289 (1964); see also Sec. 10–2, page 000.
[149]A. O. Smith Corp., 119 NLRB 621, 41 LRRM 1153 (1957).
[150]Hygienic Sanitation Co., 118 NLRB 1030, 40 LRRM 1308 (1957); other examples: National Federation of Labor, Inc. (Carpenters, District Council of Miami and Vicinity), 160 NLRB 961, 63 LRRM 1050 (1966); Douglas Oil Co., 197 NLRB No. 42, 80 LRRM 1351 (1972).
[151]American Federation of Labor v. NLRB, 308 U.S. 401, 5 LRRM 670 (1940).
[152]Pittsburgh Plate Glass Co. v. NLRB, 313 U.S. 146, 8 LRRM 425 (1941).
[153]Big Lake Oil Co. v. NLRB, 146 F.2d 967, 15 LRRM 937 (C.A. 5, 1945).
[154]Inland Empire District Council, Lumber and Sawmill Workers Union v. Millis, 325 U.S. 697, 16 LRRM 743 (1945).

2. The Board has acted in excess of its delegated powers and contrary to a specific prohibition in the Act.[155]
3. A substantial constitutional question is raised.[156]
4. Questions of great national interest because of their international complexion are present.[157]

[155]Leedom v. Kyne, 358 U.S. 184, 43 LRRM 2222 (1958); cf. Boire v. Greyhound, 376 U.S. 473, 55 LRRM 2694 (1964); cf. Local 714, IBT v. Madden (Harco Aluminum, Inc.), 57 LRRM 2284 (D.C. N.Ill., 1964); Templeton v. Dixie Color Printing Co., 444 F.2d 1064, 77 LRRM 2392 (C.A. 7, 1971); U.A.W. (Thomas Engine Corp.) v. NLRB, 317 F. Supp. 1162 (D.C. D.C.),; Dufresne v. McCann Steel Co., 78 LRRM 2331 (D.C. Tenn., 1971); Commorato v. McLeod, 78 LRRM 2741 (D.C.N.Y., 1971).
[156]Fay v. Douds, 172 F.2d 720, 23 LRRM 2356 (C.A. 2, 1949).
[157]McCulloch v. Sociedad Nacional, 372 U.S. 10, 52 LRRM 2425 (1963); cf. Office Employees, Local 153 v. Miller, 83 LRRM 2788 (D.C. N.Y., 1973).

CHAPTER 11

The Decertification Case

Sec. 11–1. In general. An election to determine whether a certified or currently recognized labor organization continues to represent a majority of the employees is called a decertification proceeding. The discussion covering certification elections in the proceeding chapters also applies to the decertification case, except to the extent indicated in this chapter.

Sec. 11–2. Who may file. The statute provides that a decertification petition may be filed by:

1. Any individual, an employee, or group of employees acting on behalf of employees; or
2. A labor organization acting on behalf of employees.[1]

To cite several examples, a petition for decertification filed by an individual has been processed in the following circumstances:

1. The petitioner was not an employee of the particular employer involved.[2]
2. The petitioner was an officer of the union.[3]
3. The petitioner was a labor relations consultant.[4]
4. The petitioner died subsequent to filing, and the employees involved asked that the processing of the petition be continued.[5]

An employer or his agent cannot file a petition for decertification.[6] Instead, an employer who questions a union's majority status must file a representation (RM) petition. (See Sec. 5–7, page 50, and Facsimile No. 2,

---

[1]Sec. 9(c)(1)(A); *cf.* Litton Industries, Automated Business Systems Div., 189 NLRB No. 32, 76 LRRM 1549 (1971).
[2]Clackamas Logging Co., 113 NLRB 229, 36 LRRM 1287 (1955).
[3]Morse and Morse, Inc., 83 NLRB 383, 24 LRRM 1085 (1949); *cf.* Kansas Color Press, Inc., 69 LRRM 2176 (C.A. 10, 1968), *vac'g and reman'g* 62 LRRM 1243.
[4]Armco Drainage & Metal Products, Inc., 116 NLRB 1260, 38 LRRM 1457 (1956).
[5]Northwestern Photo Engraving Co., 106 NLRB 1067, 32 LRRM 1589 (1953).
[6]Sperry Gyroscope Co., 136 NLRB 294, 49 LRRM 1766 (1962).

page 64.) If the union loses the election, the practical result is the same. Thus a petition for decertification was dismissed where the petitioner was:

1. A leadman with supervisory powers.[7]
2. A supervisor, even though it was contended that he was compelled to be a member of the union.[8]
3. A confidential employee to whom the employer entrusted secret labor relations information.[9]

Sec. 11–3. Dismissal.   A dismissal of a petition for decertification is not reviewable in court,[10] and such dismissal does not amount to recertification of the incumbent union.[11]

A petition for decertification will not be considered where the labor organization: (a) has never been certified; and (b) is not currently recognized by the employer.[12] A petition for decertification will be entertained where the labor organization either: (a) has been certified; or (b) is currently recognized by the employer. Thus, the Board has refused to dismiss a decertification petition in view of a union's certification although the employer stated it no longer recognized the union.[13] The fact that the certification is more than one year old will not bar a petition for decertification.[14]

A dismissal of a petition for decertification—because the union has never been certified and is not being currently recognized by the employer—is without prejudice to the filing of a representation petition by the employer, any person, or union.[15]

Frequently, a decertification petition is dismissed on the basis of the Board's "blocking charge" policy which halts representation proceedings while an unfair labor practice charge is pending. (See Sec. 7–3, page 107.) However, a decision to dismiss a petition on this basis is not final and the

---

[7]Bethlehem Steel Co., Shipbuilding Div., 111 NLRB 185, 35 LRRM 1437 (1955); Suburban Homes Corp., 173 NLRB No. 80, 69 LRRM 1402 (1968); Custom Bronze and Aluminum Corp., 197 NLRB No. 67, 80 LRRM 1369 (1972).
[8]Laris Motor Sales, Inc., 104 NLRB 1106, 32 LRRM 1199 (1953).
[9]Star Brush Mfg. Co., Inc., 100 NLRB 679, 30 LRRM 1335 (1952).
[10]Vane A. Cameron and Raymond G. Franks v. NLRB, 207 F.2d 775, 33 LRRM 2133 (C.A. 6, 1953); Grissom v. NLRB, 84 LRRM 2517 (D.C. La., 1973).
[11]World Publishing Co., 109 NLRB 355, 34 LRRM 1345 (1954).
[12]Coca-Cola Bottling Co. of Pottsville, 97 NLRB 503, 29 LRRM 1111 (1951); however, see Gem International, Inc. v. Hendrix 80 LRRM 3302 (D.C. Mo., 1972).
[13]Cross Paper Products Corp., 88 NLRB 1037, 25 LRRM 1438 (1950).
[14]Federal Shipbuilding and Drydock Co., 76 NLRB 413, 21 LRRM 1191 (1948); United States Steel Corp., American Bridge Div., 156 NLRB 1216, 61 LRRM 1237 (1966).
[15]Queen City Warehouses, Inc., 77 NLRB 268, 22 LRRM 1012 (1948).

courts have granted relief to employees where it was felt that the "blocking charge" practice was undermining the employees' right to representation.[16]

Sec. 11–4. Unit for decertifications. In filling out the petition form, it should be remembered that the same unit principles apply in decertification proceedings as in the other representation proceedings,[17] with one exception: A decertification proceeding will not be permitted to take a "severance" or self-determination vote by any group such as craft,[18] technical,[19] or professional employees.[20] Accordingly, a decertification election will be held only in an established unit. Therefore, the description of the unit in the petition should always follow the lines of the established unit.

Sec. 11–5. Hearing. The conduct of the hearing in a decertification case is the same as in other representation proceedings. This includes the general rule that evidence of unfair labor practices will not be received in a decertification hearing. Thus, evidence will not be admitted if it concerns employer participation in the institution of the proceeding, whether such evidence pertains to showing of interest or to employer responsibility for filing of the petition.[21] However, the Board has indicated that such activity may be the basis for timely objections to an election.[22]

Sec. 11–6. Results of election. The certifications issued after decertification elections are the same as those issued in other representation proceedings (see Facsimiles No. 38 and 39, pages 202, 203), with one exception: In a decertification election among a unit of guards involving a union which admits to membership employees other than guards, a certificate of results will issue regardless of the outcome of the tally; a certification of representative will not issue if the union should be designated by a majority of the valid votes.[23]

A certificate of results of election—certifying that the union is no longer the bargaining representative—will always be issued where the union fails

[16]Coffey's Transfer Co., 115 NLRB 888, 37 LRRM 1430 (1956); Templeton v. Dixie Color Reprinting Co., Inc., 444 F.2d 1064, 1070, 77 LRRM 2392 (C.A. 5, 1971), vac'g and reman'g 74 LRRM 2206, 2319; Commarato v. McLeod, 78 LRRM 2741 (D.C.N.Y., 1971); Dufresne v. McCann Steel Co., 78 LRRM 2331 (D.C.Tenn., 1971); Surrat v. NLRB, 463 F.2d 378, 80 LRRM 2804 (C.A. 5, 1972), aff'g 78 LRRM 2115.
[17]General Electric Co., 103 NLRB 403, 31 LRRM 1533 (1953); Food Fair Stores, Inc., 204 NLRB No. 23, 83 LRRM 1257 (1973).
[18]Campbell Soup Co., 111 NLRB 234, 35 LRRM 1453 (1955).
[19]Menasco Manufacturing Co., 111 NLRB 604, 35 LRRM 1526 (1955).
[20]Westinghouse Electric Co., 103 NLRB 403, 31 LRRM 1341 (1956); also applicable to plant units, see General Electric Co., 180 NLRB No. 162, 73 LRRM 1193 (1970); Duke Power Co., Lee Steam Station, 191 NLRB No. 41, 77 LRRM 1417 (1971).
[21]Union Mfg. Co., 123 NLRB 1633, 44 LRRM 1189 (1959); Typographical Union v. McCulloch, 222 F. Supp. 154, 54 LRRM 2276 (D.C.D.C., 1963).
[22]Sperry Gyroscope Co., 136 NLRB 294, 49 LRRM 1766 (fn. 4) (1962).
[23]The Hoover Co., 90 NLRB No. 265, 26 LRRM 1435 (1950).

to receive a majority of the valid ballots cast. Thus, where a decertification results in a tie vote, the union will receive a certificate of results just as if a majority had voted to decertify it.[24]

[24]Best Motor Lines, 82 NLRB 269, 23 LRRM 1557 (1949).

CHAPTER 12

The Union-Shop Deauthorization Referendum

Sec. 12–1. In general. The most stringent form of union security clause permissible under the National Labor Relations Act, as amended, is one which binds all employees in the appropriate bargaining unit to become and remain members of the union 30 days (or some longer period) after the date of hire or the date the contract becomes effective, whichever is later.[1] The closed shop, requiring union membership as a condition of obtaining and retaining employment, which was proper under the Wagner Act, is banned completely. Moreover, today an employer may not discriminate against an employee for nonmembership in the union if the employee tenders the periodic dues and initiation fees uniformly required by the union.[2]

According to the statute,[3] a union enters into a valid union-shop agreement if the following conditions are satisfied:

1. The union is the exclusive bargaining representative of the employees in an appropriate bargaining unit.

2. During the year preceding the effective date of the agreement, the union's authority to make a union-shop agreement was not rescinded in a Board-conducted referendum.

3. The contracting union must be free from employer domination or assistance within the meaning of section 8(a)(2).

4. The agreement must contain an appropriate 30-day grace period for all employees who are not members of a union when it takes effect. The required grace period in the building and construction industry is seven days.

[1] Sec. 8(a)(3).
[2] *Ibid.*
[3] Sec. 8(a)(3); Sec. 8(f).

While the statute permits the union shop, it also specifically provides that employees covered by such a provision may vote to rescind their bargaining agent's authority to make a union shop agreement.[4]

A deauthorization petition will be entertained where there is any form of union-security agreement, including an agency shop,[5] regardless of its legality under the Act.[6]

Sec. 12–2. Who may file.   A union-shop deauthorization petition may be filed by:

1. An employee or group of employees acting in behalf of 30 percent of the employees in the appropriate bargaining unit;[7] or

2. Thirty percent of the employees in the appropriate bargaining unit.[8]

Sec. 12–3. Timeliness of filing.   A petition for deauthorization can be filed only if there is in existence a union-security agreement between the employer and the union, or an extension of such agreement.[9] (The normal contract-bar principles, pursuant to which the Board dismisses representation petitions filed in the face of valid contracts, are not applied by the Board to deauthorization cases.)[10] In the absence of a union-security agreement, the Board will dismiss the deauthorization petition.[11]

Where a representation case or an unfair labor practice case is pending and it involves some or all of the same employees, a deauthorization petition will not be processed. Instead, it will be suspended until disposition is made of the other case. If investigation of the pending representation case should reveal a question concerning representation and a collective bargaining election is to be held, the deauthorization petition will be dismissed.

The statute prohibits the conduct of a deauthorization referendum in any unit or part of a unit in which a valid referendum was conducted in the preceding 12 months.[12] However, conduct of a representation election within the preceding 12 months does not preclude a deauthorization election.[13]

---

[4]Sec. 9(e)(1).
[5]Monsanto Chemical Company, 147 NLRB 49, 56 LRRM 1136 (1964).
[6]Andor Co., Inc., 119 NLRB 925, 41 LRRM 1184 (1957).
[7]R. and R. Sec. 102.83.
[8]Sec. 9(e)(1)
[9]*Haley Canning* Co., 107 NLRB 928, 33 LRRM 1272 (1954).
[10]Andor Co., Inc., 119 NLRB 925, 41 LRRM 1184 (1957).
[11]Wakefield's Deep Sea Trawlers, Inc., 115 NLRB 1024, 37 LRRM 1480 (1956).
[12]Sec. 9(e)(2).
[13]Monsanto Chemical Company, 147 NLRB 49, 56 LRRM 1136 (1964).

Sec. 12–4. Description of unit. In filling out the petition form (Facsimile No. 3, page 72) the unit should be described as nearly as possible in the terms used to define the unit in the union-security agreement. The Board will dismiss a deauthorization petition if the described unit is not coextensive with the unit covered by the union-security agreement.[14]

After investigation, a Board agent will attempt to secure either a consent or stipulated election agreement, if the requirements for the referendum are met. If the parties refuse to consent, the regional director may direct an election without a hearing. A notice of hearing is issued if the case involves questions requiring resolution by the regional director or the Board in Washington.[15]

Sec. 12–5. Referendum ordered by regional director. The regional director will order a deauthorization referendum[16] held on the basis of an investigation only where:

1. The petitioner has made the 30 percent showing within a unit covered by a union-security agreement.
2. The parties have refused to enter into a referendum agreement— consent or stipulated.
3. No questions are involved in the case which require decision by the regional director or the Board in Washington.[17]

As soon as the regional director decides to order a referendum, a letter is written to the parties informing them of his decision, supplying copies of the notice, and inviting their cooperation. (See Facsimile No. 41, page 220.)

Sec. 12–6. Eligibility list. Parties should take the utmost care in checking the eligibility list. In this type of poll, the statutory term "majority" means a majority of those eligible to vote, and not a majority of those actually voting.[18]

Sec. 12–7. Hearing and election procedures. The hearing and election procedures are substantially the same as those followed in representation cases.[19] (See Chapters 7, 8, and 9 and flow chart No. 6, page 42, on representation elections under Section 9(c).) The only additional procedure in the union-shop deauthorization referendum is that the regional director

---

[14]Hall-Scott, Inc., 120 NLRB 1364, 42 LRRM 1175 (1958); Roman Containers, Inc., 190 NLRB No. 47, 77 LRRM 1105 (1971).
[15]R. and R. Sec. 102.85.
[16]*Ibid.*
[17]Truth Tool Co., 111 NLRB 642, 35 LRRM 1519 (1955).
[18]Sec. 8(a) (3); Southwest Engraving Co., 198 NLRB No. 99, 81 LRRM 1069 (1972).
[19]Bi Mart Co. et al., NLRB No. 36–UD–88, 70 LRRM 1564 (1969); Sierra Electric Inc., 176 NLRB No. 63, 71 LRRM 1254 (1969).

NATIONAL LABOR RELATIONS BOARD

Date_____

Petitioner

Employer

Union

Re:

Gentlemen:

On the basis of the investigation made to date in the above matter, it appears appropriate now to conduct a secret ballot to determine whether or not certain of the employees of _____(employer)_____ wish to withdraw the authority of _____(union)_____ to require, under its agreement with their employer, that membership in the union be a condition of employment.

Accordingly, pursuant to Section 9 (e) (1) of the National Labor Relations Act, as amended, and Section 102.85 of the Board's Rules and Regulations, an election by secret ballot will be conducted as provided in the enclosed Notice of Election.

Additional copies of the Notice of Election are being herewith furnished the employer herewith for posting in conspicuous places throughout the plant.

Your cooperation will be appreciated.

Very truly yours,

_____
Regional Director

FACSIMILE NO. 41.
*Form of letter sent to parties when regional director
has decided to conduct a deauthorization referendum*

may direct an election without a hearing.[20] The postelection procedures—where either the regional director or the Board has ordered the referendum—are also the same as in elections in representation cases. (See Chapter 10.)

Sec. 12–8. Form of the ballot. The proposition to be voted on in a deauthorization referendum is stated on the ballot: "Do you wish to withdraw the authority of your bargaining representative to require under its agreement with the employer that membership in the union be a condition of employment." (See Facsimile No. 42, page 222.)

Sec. 12–9. Results of election. As indicated above, the decisive majority in a deauthorization referendum is a majority of the employees eligible to vote, not a majority of the valid votes cast. The Board will not conduct a runoff of any deauthorization referendum.[21] The regional director or the Board, as the case may be, will issue a certificate of results.[22] (See Facsimile No. 43, page 223.) An affirmative vote for deauthorization has an immediate effect; it invalidates the union-security clause of an existing agreement.[23] Furthermore, where an affirmative vote is cast for deauthorization, the union cannot enter into a valid union-shop agreement for a period of one year from the date of the certificate of results.[24]

---

[20]Statement of Procedures, Sec. 101.29.
[21]*Ibid.*
[22]Potters v. Shore, 70 LRRM 2649 (D.C. Pa., 1970).
[23]Monsanto Chemical Co., 147 NLRB 49, 56 LRRM 1136 (1964); Local 714, IBT v. Madden (Harco Aluminum, Inc.), 57 LRRM 2284 (D.C.N.Ill., 1964); Penn Cork and Closures, Inc., 64 LRRM 2855 (C.A. 2, 1967), *enf.* 61 LRRM 1037; W.P. Thrie and Sons, 165 NLRB 167, 65 LRRM 1205 (1967).
[24]Sec. 8(a)(3).

UNITED STATES OF AMERICA

National Labor Relations Board

OFFICIAL SECRET BALLOT

FOR CERTAIN EMPLOYEES OF

Do you wish to withdraw the authority of your bargaining representative to require, under its agreement with the Employer, that membership in the Union be a condition of employment?

MARK AN "X" IN THE SQUARE OF YOUR CHOICE

YES   NO

DO NOT SIGN THIS BALLOT. Fold and drop in ballot box.
If you spoil this ballot return it to the Board Agent for a new one.

FACSIMILE No. 42.
Form of union-shop deauthorization ballot

UNITED STATES OF AMERICA

NATIONAL LABOR RELATIONS BOARD

```
* * * * * * * * * * * * * * * * * * * * * * * * *
In the Matter of                              *
                                              *
                                              *
                                              *
                                              *    Case No.
                                              *
                                              *
                                              *
                                              *
* * * * * * * * * * * * * * * * * * * * * * * * *
```

CERTIFICATE OF RESULTS OF ELECTION

Following the filing of a petition, pursuant to Section 9 (e) of the National Labor Relations Act, as amended, an election was conducted herein under the direction and supervision of the undersigned Regional Director for the National Labor Relations Board. No objections were filed to the conduct of the election, or to the Tally of Ballots.

Pursuant to the authority vested in the undersigned by the National Labor Relations Board,

IT IS HEREBY CERTIFIED that a majority of employees eligible to vote have (not) voted to withdraw the authority of (Name of union)

to require, under its agreement with the Employer, that membership in such labor organization be a condition of employment, in conformity with Section 8 (a) (3) of the Act, as amended.

Signed at   this   day of

_____
Regional Director for_____ Region
National Labor Relations Board

FACSIMILE No.43.
*Form of certification of results issued by regional director
after union-shop deauthorization referendum*

CHAPTER 13

The Unfair Labor Practice Charge and Investigation

Sec. 13–1. In general. The National Labor Relations Board has the exclusive power to prevent employers and labor organizations from engaging in unfair labor practices. It is not empowered to move against individuals unless it can be demonstrated that such individuals acted as agents of an employer or a labor organization. Neither the Board nor the Office of the General Counsel has the authority to investigate alleged unfair labor practices on its own initiative.[1] Only the filing of a charge can "provide the spark which starts the machinery of the Act running."[2]

Sec. 13–2. Contents of the charge. Appropriate forms on which to file charges may be obtained at any NLRB regional office. Three types of forms are available. The first is used to allege unfair labor practices on the part of an employer (see Facsimile No. 44, page 226); the second for unfair labor practices by a labor organization or its agents (see Facsimile No. 45, page 227); and the third is a special charge used to attack "hot cargo" contracts[3] (see Facsimile No. 46, page 228).

The contents of the charge are not specified in the Act,[4] and there is no requirement that the Board's forms be used. If not used, all information requested on the forms must be included and, unless there is a statute-of-limitations problem, the regional office will ask that the charge be refiled on the Board forms.

In addition to the information describing the parties and the alleged unfair labor practices, the charge must:

---

[1]National Licorice Co. v. NLRB, 309 U.S. 350, 6 LRRM 674 (1940).
[2]American Shuffleboard Co. v. NLRB, 190 F.2d 898, 28 LRRM 2489 (C.A. 3, 1951).
[3]Sec. 8(e).
[4]Consumers Power Co. v. NLRB, 113 F.2d 38, 6 LRRM 849 (C.A. 6, 1940).

```
FORM NLRB-501
   (2-67)
                                                            Form Approved
                                                            Budget Bureau No. 64-R001.12

                         UNITED STATES OF AMERICA
                       NATIONAL LABOR RELATIONS BOARD

                         CHARGE AGAINST EMPLOYER

INSTRUCTIONS: File an original and 4 copies       DO NOT WRITE IN THIS SPACE
of this charge with NLRB                           Case No.
regional director for the region in which the
alleged unfair labor practice
occurred or is occurring.                          Date Filed
```

1. EMPLOYER AGAINST WHOM CHARGE IS BROUGHT

a. Name of Employer	b. Number of Workers Employed

c. Address of Establishment (Street and number, city, State, and ZIP code)	d. Employer Representative to Contact	e. Phone No.

f. Type of Establishment (Factory, mine, wholesaler, etc.)	g. Identify Principal Product or Service

h. The above-named employer has engaged in and is engaging in unfair labor practices within the meaning of section 8(a), subsections (1) and _____ (List subsections) _____ of the National Labor Relations Act, and these unfair labor practices are unfair labor practices affecting commerce within the meaning of the Act.

2. Basis of the Charge (Be specific as to facts, names, addresses, plants involved, dates, places, etc.)

By the above and other acts, the above-named employer has interfered with, restrained, and coerced employees in the exercise of the rights guaranteed in Section 7 of the Act.

3. Full Name of Party Filing Charge (If labor organization, give full name, including local name and number)

4a. Address (Street and number, city, State, and ZIP code)	4b. Telephone No.

5. Full Name of National or International Labor Organization of Which It Is an Affiliate or Constituent Unit (To be filled in when charge is filed by a labor organization)

6. DECLARATION

I declare that I have read the above charge and that the statements therein are true to the best of my knowledge and belief.

By _____   _____
  (Signature of representative or person filing charge)   (Title, if any)

Address _____
    (Telephone number)   (Date)

WILLFULLY FALSE STATEMENTS ON THIS CHARGE CAN BE PUNISHED BY FINE AND IMPRISONMENT (U.S. CODE, TITLE 18, SECTION 1001)

☆ GPO 473-109

FACSIMILE NO. 44.
Form of charge against employer (Form 501)

FORM NLRB-508
(4-73)

Form Approved
O.M.B. No. 64-R0003

UNITED STATES OF AMERICA
NATIONAL LABOR RELATIONS BOARD

CHARGE AGAINST LABOR ORGANIZATION OR ITS AGENTS

INSTRUCTIONS: File an original and 3 copies of this charge and an additional copy for each organization, each local and each individual named in item 1 with the NLRB regional director for the region in which the alleged unfair labor practice occurred or is occurring.

DO NOT WRITE IN THIS SPACE
Case No.
Date Filed

1. LABOR ORGANIZATION OR ITS AGENTS AGAINST WHICH CHARGE IS BROUGHT

a. Name	b. Union Representative to Contact	c. Phone No.

d. Address (Street, city, State and ZIP code)

e. The above-named organization(s) or its agents has (have) engaged in and is (are) engaging in unfair labor practices within the meaning of section 8(b), subsection(s) ———(List Subsections)——— of the National Labor Relations Act, and these unfair labor practices are unfair labor practices affecting commerce within the meaning of the Act.

2. Basis of the Charge (Be specific as to facts, names, addresses, plants involved, dates, places, etc.)

3. Name of Employer	4. Phone No.

5. Location of Plant Involved (Street, city, State and ZIP code)	6. Employer Representative to Contact

7. Type of Establishment (Factory, mine, wholesaler, etc.)	8. Identify Principal Product or Service	9. No. of Workers Employed

10. Full Name of Party Filing Charge

11. Address of Party Filing Charge (Street, city, State and ZIP code)	12. Telephone No.

13. DECLARATION

I declare that I have read the above charge and that the statements therein are true to the best of my knowledge and belief.

By ————————————————————   ————————————————
      (Signature of representative or person making charge)   (Title or office, if any)

Address ————————————————————
                        (Telephone number)   (Date)

WILLFULLY FALSE STATEMENTS ON THIS CHARGE CAN BE PUNISHED BY FINE AND IMPRISONMENT (U.S. CODE, TITLE 18, SECTION 1001)

GPO 863-327

FACSIMILE NO. 45.
Charge against labor organization or its agents (Form 508)

FORM NLRB-509
(12-65)

Form Approved
Budget Bureau No. 64-R009.2

UNITED STATES OF AMERICA
NATIONAL LABOR RELATIONS BOARD
CHARGE ALLEGING UNFAIR LABOR PRACTICE UNDER SECTION 8(e) OF THE ACT

INSTRUCTIONS: File an original and 3 copies of this charge, and an additional
copy for each organization, each local and each individual named in item 1 with
the NLRB regional director for the region in which the alleged unfair labor
practice occurred or is occurring.

Case No.

Date Filed

1. CHARGE FILED AGAINST: Employer and Labor Organization ☐   Employer ☐   Labor Organization ☐

a. Name of Labor Organization (Give full name, including local name and number)	b. Union Representative to Contact	c. Phone No.

d. Address (Street and number, city, State and ZIP code)

e. Name of Employer	f. Employer Representative to Contact	g. Phone No.

h. Location of Plant Involved (Street, city, State and ZIP code)

i. Type of Establishment (Factory, mine, wholesaler, etc.)	j. Identify Principal Product or Service	k. No. of Workers Employed

The above-named labor organization or its agents, and/or employer has (have) engaged in and is (are) engaging in unfair labor practices within the meaning of section 8(e) of the National Labor Relations Act, and these unfair labor practices are unfair labor practices affecting commerce within the meaning of the Act.

2. Basis of the Charge (Be specific as to facts, names, plants involved, dates, places, etc.)

3. Full Name of Party Filing Charge (If labor organization, give full name, including local name and number)

4a. Address (Street and number, city, State and ZIP code)	4b. Telephone No.

5. Full Name of National or International Labor Organization of Which It Is an Affiliate or Constituent Unit (To be filled in when charge is filed by a labor organization)

6. DECLARATION

I declare that I have read the above charge and that the statements therein are true to the best of my knowledge and belief.

By _____   _____
     (Signature of representative or person filing charge)   (Title, if any)

Address _____
                                  (Telephone number)   (Date)

WILLFULLY FALSE STATEMENTS ON THIS CHARGE CAN BE PUNISHED BY FINE AND IMPRISONMENT (U.S. CODE, TITLE 18, SECTION 1001)

☆ U.S. GOVERNMENT PRINTING OFFICE : 1973—728-617/1311 3-1

FACSIMILE NO. 46.
Charge alleging unfair labor practice under Sec. 8(e) of the Act

1. Contain a declaration by the person signing that its contents are true to the best of his knowledge; or
2. Be sworn to before a notary public or a Board agent.[5]

The charge form, in brief, calls for the name and address of the party against whom the charge is made, the name and address of the charging party, the subsections of the Act alleged to have been violated, and a statement of the facts constituting the alleged unfair labor practices. Although the Board's blank form carries the instruction, "be specific as to facts, names, addresses, etc.," both the Board and the courts have ruled that:

1. A charge is intended neither to frame the issues nor to constitute proof.[6]
2. A charge is not invalid if it fails to particularize and specify each unfair labor practice with precision.[7] Board agents, when asked for assistance in framing the charge, uniformly suggest that it be made in the general language of the statute.[8] However, care should be taken to set forth dates and names where material, as in discharge or refusal-to-bargain situations.

Other basic items to be kept in mind in filling out the charge forms are:

1. The charge should not include statements in the nature of evidence. Required factual information, whether in affidavit form or a fact statement, furnished in support of the charge may be supplied separately. If quoted or incorporated by reference, it must be served on the party charged along with the charge form.
2. Where more than one party has participated in the commission of the alleged unfair labor practice, the Board cannot issue an order against an employer or a labor organization unless it is named in the charge.[9] But it is not mandatory to file charges against all the wrongdoers.[10] The charging party may elect to bring charges against one or more of them. For example, in a case where an employee is discharged by his employer at the request of a union, pursuant to an allegedly illegal contract—the employee may choose to file a charge against the employer, or against the union, or against both. Also, either or both parties to an illegal "hot cargo" contract may be charged.

---

[5]R. and R. Sec. 102.11; NLRB v. Sue-Ann Mfg. Co., 211 F.2d 91, 33 LRRM 2580 (C.A. 5, 1954).
[6]NLRB v. Indiana & Michigan Electric Co., 318 U.S. 9, 11 LRRM 763 (1943).
[7]NLRB v. Kingston Cake Co., 191 F.2d 563, 28 LRRM 2571 (C.A. 3, 1951).
[8]Kansas Milling Co., v. NLRB, 185 F.2d 413, 27 LRRM 2048 (C.A. 10, 1950).
[9]NLRB v. Hopwood Retinning Co., Inc., 98 F.2d 97, 2 LRRM 650 (C.A. 2, 1938).
[10]The Radio Officers' Union of the Commercial Telegraphers Union v. NLRB, 347 U.S. 17, 33 LRRM 2417 (1954).

Sec. 13–3. Assistance in filing a charge. If the person desiring to file a charge needs assistance in its preparation, he may call upon the NLRB's regional office for aid. These requests are entirely proper and are particularly helpful to persons unfamiliar with the law or in complex cases. The assistance will be given by either an NLRB attorney or a field examiner.

Sec. 13–4. Where to file a charge. The charge is filed with the regional office in whose area the alleged unfair labor practices have occurred. A charge which alleges such practices in two or more regions may be filed with the regional director for any of such regions. (The areas covered by the regional offices are set forth in Appendix E.)

In filing the charge with the regional office, one original and four copies must be submitted, together with one additional copy for each charged party.[11] The charge may be filed in person or by mail. If filed through the mails, the Rules and Regulations suggest that it be sent by registered or certified mail. However, it has been judicially held that service of the charge by regular mail does not invalidate the service.[12]

Sec. 13–5. Service of charge. The regional director, as a matter of course, will serve copies of the charge upon the charged parties; however, he assumes no responsibility for compliance with the requirement that such service must be made. If a regional director has served the charges in timely fashion, the proceeding is not invalidated because the charging party has failed to do so.[13] Where the six-month statute of limitations is significant, the charging party should serve the party against whom the charge is made as soon as it files its charges with the NLRB regional office. (See "When to File a Charge," page 232.)

Sec. 13–6. Who may file a charge. Any person—an individual, an employer, or a labor organization—may file a charge alleging unfair labor practices.[14]

In a variety of situations parties have attacked the validity of Board proceedings because of: (1) the identity of the person or organization filing the charge; or (2) the motivation or character of the person or organization making the charge. Following are some of the situations in which the Board and the courts have ruled on these issues:

1. On the issue of identity of the charging party, the Supreme Court has ruled that the type of person or organization making the charge, or

---

[11]R. and R. Sec. 102.11.
[12]Olin Industries, Inc., Winchester Repeating Arms Co. Division v. NLRB, 192 F.2d 799, 29 LRRM 2117 (C.A. 5, 1951).
[13]General Motors Corp. v. NLRB, 222 F.2d 349, 36 LRRM 2093 (C.A. 5, 1955).
[14]R. and R. Sec. 102.9.

the relationship between such person or organization and the individuals involved in the acts complained of, are not limited by the Act.[15] Thus, for example, it has been held that unfair labor practice proceedings may be maintained where the charges are filed by:

(a) An attorney, on behalf of individual employees.[16]

(b) An attorney, on behalf of a labor organization.[17]

(c) An individual, in effect a "stranger," who is not an employee.[18]

(d) A discriminatorily discharged employee, on behalf of himself and other employees similarly discharged.[19]

(e) An individual, on behalf of a labor organization, even though he is not authorized to file the charge.[20]

(f) An employer who is not a member of an employer association in a case where rights of members of that association are involved.[21]

(g) A labor organization which is not the majority representative.[22]

(h) A labor organization which has no members in the employ of the charged company.[23]

(i) A labor organization, against another labor organization, where both parties are affiliated with the same parent federation.[24]

(j) A party to a primary dispute, where the charge alleges an illegal secondary boycott.[25]

2. On the issue of motivation or character of the charging party, the Supreme Court has said that "dubious character, evil or unlawful motives, or bad faith of the informer cannot deprive the Board of its jurisdiction to conduct the inquiry."[26] Thus, the courts have held that the Board's power to process an unfair labor practice case was not affected where, it was claimed, the charging party itself had engaged in misconduct;[27] had filed the charge in bad faith and for unlawful motives;[28] or to further objectives of the Communist Party.[29] It would

---

[15]NLRB v. Pennsylvania Greyhound Lines, Inc., 303 U.S. 261, 2 LRRM 599 (1938).
[16]NLRB v. New Hyden Coal Co., 228 F.2d 68, 37 LRRM 2185 (C.A. 6, 1955).
[17]NLRB v. Braswell Motor Freight Lines, 209 F.2d 622, 33 LRRM 2459 (C.A. 5, 1954).
[18]NLRB v. Indiana & Michigan Electric Co., 318 U.S. 9, 11 LRRM 763 (1943).
[19]Southern Furniture Mfg. Co. v. NLRB, 194 F.2d 59, 29 LRRM 2392 (C.A. 5, 1952).
[20]McComb Mfg. Co., 95 NLRB 596, 28 LRRM 1351 (1951).
[21]Heating, Piping and Air Conditioning Contractors New York City Assn., Inc., 102 NLRB 1646, 31 LRRM 1482 (1953).
[22]NLRB v. Pennsylvania Greyhound Lines, Inc., 303 U.S. 261, 2 LRRM 599 (1938).
[23]NLRB v. General Shoe Corp., 192 F.2d 504, 29 LRRM 2112 (C.A. 6, 1951).
[24]Local 404, International Brotherhood of Teamsters, Chauffeurs, Warehousemen & Helpers of America, 100 NLRB 801, 30 LRRM 1360 (1952).
[25]Wine, Liquor & Distillery Workers Union, Local 1, 78 NLRB 504, 22 LRRM 1222 (1948).
[26]NLRB v. Indiana & Michigan Electric Co., 318 U.S. 9, 11 LRRM 763 (1943).
[27]Ibid.
[28]NLRB v. Fred P. Weissman Co., 170 F.2d 952, 23 LRRM 2131 (C.A. 6, 1948).
[29]NLRB v. Fulton Bag & Cotton Mills, 180 F.2d 68, 25 LRRM 2215 (C.A. 10, 1950).

follow that a party to an illegal "hot cargo" contract may attack the validity of the contract by charging the other party to the agreement.

However, the Supreme Court has also said that the Board has discretion to consider the motivation and character of the charging party:[30]

While we hold that misconduct of the union would not deprive the Board of jurisdiction, this does not mean that the Board may not properly consider such misconduct as material to its own decision to entertain and proceed upon the charge. The Board has wide discretion in the issue of complaints. . . . It is not required by the statute to move on every charge; it is merely enabled to do so.

It may decline to be imposed upon or to submit its process to abuse. The Board might properly withhold or dismiss its own complaint if it should appear that the charge is so related to a course of violence and destruction, carried on for the purpose of coercing an employer to help herd its employees into the complaining union, as to constitute an abuse of the Board's process.

And, in a later case, a court of appeals stated:[31]

There is considerable evidence which would have justified the Board in refusing to entertain and proceed upon the charges . . . because of bad faith and unlawful motives on the part of the (charging) union, but . . . this is a matter within the discretion of the Board.

Sec. 13–7. When to file a charge.   The statute requires that the charge be filed with the Board's office and served upon the charged party within six months of the unfair labor practice.[32] If this deadline is not met, the charge will not be processed.[33]

It is the responsibility of the charging party to serve a copy of the charge upon each of the parties against whom the charge is made.[34] Such service should be made as soon as the charge is filed with the regional office. It has been repeatedly held that the date for tolling the six-month limitation is the date on which the charge is served upon the charged party, where such service was made after the charge was filed with the Board's office.[35] This does not mean that the charge must be filed with the Board's office before it can be served upon the charged party.[36]

---

[30]NLRB v. Indiana & Michigan Electric Co., 318 U.S. 9, 11 LRRM 763 (1943).
[31]NLRB v. Fred P. Weissman Co., 170 F.2d 952, 23 LRRM 2131 (C.A. 6, 1948).
[32]Sec. 10(b).
[33]NLRB v. Textile Machine Works Inc., 214 F.2d 929, 34 LRRM 2535 (C.A. 3, 1954); Asko, Inc., 202 NLRB No. 30, 82 LRRM 1498 (1973).
[34]R. and R. Sec. 102.14.
[35]Luzerne Hide and Tallow Co., 89 NLRB 989, 26 LRRM 1076 (1950). Section 102.113(a) of the Board's rules provide that "The date of service shall be the day when the matter served is deposited in the United States mail, or is delivered in person, as the case may be."
[36]The Baltimore Transfer Co. of Baltimore City, Inc., 94 NLRB 1680, 28 LRRM 1241 (1951).

Sec. 13–8. Six-month statute of limitations. Where the alleged unfair labor practice occurred more than six months before filing and service of the charge, a violation cannot be found by the Board. However, where the unfair labor practice is of a continuing nature and extends into the six-month period, the illegal acts occurring within that period can be found to be violations. Here are a few examples:

1. The execution of a contract containing an illegal union-security clause more than six months before filing and service of the charge is not a violation. However, the continuation and enforcement of the same contract within that period have been found violative of the Act.[37]
2. The continuation of domination and interference with an employee committee within the six-month period has been held illegal.[38]
3. The Board cannot order reinstatement of discharged strikers to their former jobs where the discharges occurred more than six months before filing and service of the charge, even though they applied for their old jobs within that period. However, a court has upheld the Board's order of reinstatement of those discharged strikers who, within six months of the filing and service of the charge, had applied for "a job" or "any job" or "employment"—in effect, new employment—and were discriminatorily refused such employment.[39]
4. A court has also upheld the Board's finding that the six-month period begins when the facts of an employer's discriminatory hiring policy first became known to an applicant for employment.[40]
5. A hot-cargo contract entered into prior to the six-month period will be found unlawful, if reaffirmed during that period.[41]

The courts have repeatedly held: "The six-month limitation refers only to acts that occur before the charge and does not prohibit the inclusion (in the complaint) of similar or related acts happening after the charge."[42]

Sec. 13–9. Supporting data. At the time the charge is filed with the NLRB's regional office, the charging party should be prepared to submit the following information: (1) an affidavit or statement in writing setting

[37]Paul W. Speer, Inc., 98 NLRB 212, 29 LRRM 1319 (1952).
[38]Sharples Chemicals, Inc., 100 NLRB 20, 30 LRRM 1225 (1952).
[39]NLRB v. Textile Machine Works, Inc., 214 F.2d 929, 34 LRRM 2535 (C.A. 3, 1954); see also Lee A. Consaul Co., 81 LRRM 2580 (C.A. 9, 1972), denying enforcement to 192 NLRB No. 170, 78 LRRM 1379.
[40]NLRB v. Shawnee Industries, Inc., 333 F.2d 221, 56 LRRM 2567 (C.A. 10, 1964).
[41]Los Angeles Mailers' Union, No. 9, I.T.U. (Hillbro Newspaper Printing Co.), 135 NLRB 1132, 49 LRRM 1659 (1962), enf. 311 F.2d 121, 51 LRRM 2359 (C.A. D.C., 1962).
[42]NLRB v. Anchor Rome Mills, 228 F.2d 775, 37 LRRM 2367 (C.A. 5, 1956); Painters, New York District Council No. 9 (Westgate Painting and Decorating Corp.), 79 LRRM 2145 (C.A. 2, 1971), enf. 75 LRRM 1465; cf. NLRB v. McCready and Sons, Inc., 83 LRRM 2674 (C.A. 6, 1973), denying enforcement to 79 LRRM 1212.

forth in detail the charging party's version of the relevant facts, including names, dates, and places; (2) the names and addresses of possible witnesses and other persons who may have knowledge of facts supporting the charging party; and (3) any documents or other evidence available to the charging party that support the charge. If a novel theory of law is involved, it is advisable to include an explanation and analysis of appropriate authorities as an aid to the regional office in its investigation and consideration of the case.

Sec. 13–10. 72-hour rule. If the charging party does not submit the above data at the time the charge is filed, the NLRB agent may indicate that he has 72 hours to do so. If this deadline is not met, the charge is subject to dismissal. However, upon a showing of good cause, the regional director may extend the time within which the data may be submitted. For example, the indicated evidence may not be readily available to the charging party except through subpoena. Another example of "good cause" would be the unavailability of witnesses because of their great distance from the Board's regional office.

Thus the 72-hour rule means, in effect, that a charge will be dismissed:

1. If the charging party fails, without good cause, to submit supporting evidence which he either has in his possession or is able to obtain.

2. If the regional office feels that the charge is frivolous or unsupported.

Sec. 13–11. Amendment of charge. Although the Act makes no provision for the amendment of a charge, the Board and the courts have recognized the power of the charging party to do so.[43] A charge may be amended, using the regular charge form, in one of two ways:

1. By restating in the "amended charge" the original charges together with the desired changes; or

2. By stating in the "amended charge" the changes that are to be made in the original charge.

As in the instance of the original charge, it is proper for the charging party to ask the assistance of the NLRB agent in the preparation of the amendment. Whenever an amended charge is filed, a copy should be served upon each of the parties against whom the amended charge is made.

Amendment of the charge does not constitute a withdrawal of either the original charge or an earlier amendment.[44]

[43]Brown Equipment & Mfg. Co., 100 NLRB 801, 30 LRRM 1360 (1952).
[44]NLRB v. Star Beef Co., 193 F.2d 8, 29 LRRM 2190 (C.A. 1, 1951).

The amended charge may allege new unfair labor practices which occurred after the original charge and within the six-month period before the filing and service of the amended charge.[45]

The Board and the courts have held that the six-month limitation does not have to be met by the amended charge where the original charge has been timely filed and served, and the amended charge: (a) is "a restatement of an original charge";[46] (b) merely particularizes the allegations of an original charge;[47] (c) is based on a like fact situation as that contained in the original charge;[48] (d) "defines more precisely" the allegations in the original charge;[49] or (e) "relates back" to the same unfair labor practice alleged in the original charge.[50]

However, the Board and the courts have also held that where an amended charge raises "a new and separate cause of action," that amended charge must independently satisfy the six-month limitation as to filing and service.[51] Thus, the courts have dismissed unfair labor practices based on occurrences subsequent to the original charge and more than six months before the filing and service of the amended charge;[52] courts have also found "an entirely new and different cause of action" where the amended charge relied on these occurrences to introduce for the first time either an allegation of bad faith bargaining[53] or a new company to be charged.[54]

Sec. 13–12. Charges receiving priority. The statute assigns priorities to the processing of various unfair labor practice cases.[55] Thus, in each NLRB regional office, priority over all other cases will be given to the investigation of charges in the following order: (1) Sections 8(b)(4)(A), (B) and (C); (2) Section 8(b)(4)(D); (3) Section 8(b)(7); (4) Section 8(e); (5) Section 8(a)(3); and (6) Section 8(b)(2).

In cases involving Sections 8(b)(4)(A), (B), (C); Sections 8(b) (7), and Section 8(e), if the regional director has reasonable cause to believe there has been a violation as alleged, it is mandatory under Section 10(l) that an injunction be sought in the U.S. District Court. Although not mandatory,

[45]Philip Carey Mfg. Co., 140 NLRB 1103, 52 LRRM 1184 (1963).
[46]Mason & Hughes, Inc., 86 NLRB 848, 25 LRRM 1019 (1949).
[47]NLRB v. Gaynor News Co., 197 F.2d 719, 30 LRRM 2340 (C.A. 2, 1952).
[48]Ibid.; Mason-Rust, 179 NLRB No. 71, 72 LRRM 1372 (1969).
[49]NLRB v. Gaynor News Co., 197 F.2d 719, 30 LRRM 2340 (C.A. 2, 1952); Stafford Trucking, Inc., 64 LRRM 2086 (C.A. 7, 1966), enf. 60 LRRM 1121; NLRB v. IUOE, Local 925, 80 LRRM 2398 (C.A. 5, 1972), enf. in part, reman'g in part 76 LRRM 1856.
[50]NLRB v. R. H. Osbrink Mfg. Co., 218 F.2d 341, 35 LRRM 2291 (C.A. 9, 1954); El Cortez Hotel, 67 LRRM 2716 (C.A. 9, 1968), enf. 63 LRRM 1182.
[51]Knickerbocker Mfg. Co., Inc., 109 NLRB 1195, 34 LRRM 1551 (1954); Central Power and Light Co., 74 LRRM 2269 (C.A. 5, 1970), enf. 69 LRRM 1329; McGraw-Edison Co., Speed Queen Div., 192 NLRB No. 142, 78 LRRM 1148 (1971).
[52]Indiana Metal Products Corp. v. NLRB, 202 F.2d 613, 31 LRRM 2490 (C.A. 7, 1953).
[53]NLRB v. I.B.S. Mfg. Co., 210 F.2d 634, 33 LRRM 2583 (C.A. 5, 1954).
[54]NLRB v. McCarron Co., 206 F.2d 543, 32 LRRM 2455 (C.A. 3, 1953).
[55]Sec. 10(1) and 10(M).

an injunction under Section 10(1) may also be sought by the regional director where a violation of Section 8(b) (4)(D) is charged and such relief is appropriate. Ordinarily this means when there is a work stoppage. In other cases the Board has discretionary power under Section 10(j) to seek injunctive relief.

Sec. 13–13. Notice to the charged party. Upon receipt of a charge by the NLRB's regional office, it is docketed and assigned a number. The regional director will send a copy, via registered mail, to the party against whom the charge is made. The copy of the charge is accompanied by (1) a statement of procedure as to how the charge will be handled (see Facsimile No. 47, page 237); (2) a form for notifying the Agency of a party's desire to be represented by counsel (See Facsimile No. 9, page 86); and (3) a form designating a representative as the agent for service of documents (see Facsimile No. 10, page 87.) There will also be a letter which gives the name of the agent to whom the case has been assigned. The letter asks the charged party to submit:

1. His version of the facts and circumstances surrounding the alleged unfair labor practices.[56]
2. If the charged party is an employer, data showing the nature of the company's business operations, a "commerce questionnaire." (See Facsimile No. 7, page 83.)

Sec. 13–14. Investigation of the charge. The NLRB agent commences his investigation as quickly as possible after the case is assigned to him. Priority cases are given preference but, currently, each regional director attempts to have investigations completed with sufficient speed to enable him to reach a decision as to disposition of all charges within 30 days after filing.

The investigation consists of interviews with parties and witnesses by one or more NLRB agents. Written statements are normally requested from all witnesses. The investigation is not limited to witnesses suggested by the parties but may include anyone the agents feel may shed light on the charges. Joint conferences of the parties may sometimes be arranged. The charging party ordinarily assists the NLRB agent in every way possible in the investigation. In part this is an attempt to persuade the regional director the case has merit but, also, lack of cooperation is sufficient reason for the director to summarily dismiss the charge for lack of cooperation.

The case of the party charged is somewhat different. Those who practice before the Board have widely varying views as to the extent they will cooperate in the investigation when they represent the party charged. No

---

[56]Statements of Procedure, Sec. 101.4; Madden v. Masters, Mates and Pilots, Inc., 166 F.Supp. 862, 42 LRRM 2664 (D.C. N.Ill., 1958), *cert. denied,* 358 U.S. 909, 43 LRRM 2209 (1958).

FORM NLRB-4541
(2-72)
NATIONAL LABOR RELATIONS BOARD

NOTICE: PARTIES INVOLVED IN AN UNFAIR LABOR PRACTICE CHARGE SHOULD BE AWARE OF THE FOLLOWING
PROCEDURES:

Right to be represented by counsel

Any party has the right to be represented by counsel or other representative in any proceeding before the National
Labor Relations Board and the courts. In the event you wish to have a representative appear on your behalf,
please have your representative complete Form NLRB-4701, Notice of Appearance, and forward it to the respective
regional office as soon as counsel is chosen.

Designation of representative as agent for service of documents

In the event you choose to have a representative appear on your behalf, you may also, if you so desire, use
Form NLRB-4813 to designate that representative as your agent to receive exclusive service on your behalf of
all formal documents and written communications in the proceeding, excepting charges and amended charges, and
further excepting subpoenas which are served on the person to whom they are addressed. If this form is not filed,
both you and your representative will receive copies of all formal documents, including complaints, orders and
decisions. If it is filed copies will be served only upon your representative, and that service will be considered
service on you under the statute. The designation once filed, shall remain valid unless a written revocation is
filed with the Regional Director.

Impartial investigation to determine whether charge has merit

Immediately upon receipt of a charge, the regional office conducts an impartial investigation to obtain all the
facts which are material and relevant to the charge. In order to determine whether the charge has merit, the
Region interviews the available witnesses. Your active cooperation in making witnesses available and stating
your position will be most helpful to the Region.

The Region seeks evidence from all parties. Naturally, if only the charging party cooperates in the investigation, a situation results whereby the evidence presented by the charging party may warrant the issuance of a
complaint, in the absence of any explanation from the party charged with having violated the law. Where evidence
of meritorious defenses is made available a number of cases are withdrawn or dismissed. Your active cooperation
will result in disposing of the case at the earliest possible time, whether the case has merit or not.

If the charge lacks merit, charging party has opportunity to withdraw

If it is determined that the charge lacks merit, the charging party is offered the opportunity to withdraw it. Should
the charging party refuse to withdraw the charge, the Regional Director dismisses the charge, advising the charging
party of its right to appeal the dismissal to the General Counsel.

If the charge has merit, the matter may be voluntarily adjusted

If the Regional Director determines that the charge has merit, all parties are afforded an opportunity to settle the
matter by voluntary adjustment. It is the policy of this Office to explore and encourage voluntary adjustments
before proceeding with litigation, before the Board and Courts, which is both costly and time consuming. The
Regional Director and the members of his staff are always available to discuss adjustment of the case at any
stage and will be pleased to receive and act promptly upon any suggestions or comments concerning settlement.

Voluntary adjustments after issuance of complaint

If settlement is not obtained, the Regional Director will issue a complaint which is the basis for litigating the
matter before the Board and Courts. However, issuance of a complaint does not mean that the matter cannot still
be disposed of by voluntary adjustment by the parties. On the contrary, at any stage of the proceeding the Regional
Director and his staff will be pleased to render any assistance in arriving at an appropriate settlement, thereby
eliminating the necessity of costly and time consuming litigation.

GPO 926-190

FACSIMILE NO. 47.
Statement of procedures in handling unfair labor practice charges

single rule applies in every case. The principle to be kept in mind is that the NLRB agent is acting as an impartial investigator at this stage of the case. If his investigation discloses no merit to the charges, the case will be withdrawn or dismissed. A refusal to cooperate means that this decision will be based on facts developed primarily from the charging party and his witnesses. When it is recognized that a substantial majority of charges filed are found to be without merit as a result of the investigation, it is obviously to the advantage of the party charged that the regional director have an accurate understanding of facts favorable to that party.

On the other hand, if a complaint issues, the impartial investigator becomes the prosecutor. Any information turned over to him during the investigation may be used against the party charged with violating the Act.

If the legal issues involved in the case are either novel or complex, parties should submit their views of the law to the regional office, orally or in writing or both. Frequently, it is advisable to ask for a meeting with the regional director and his principal advisors. In the pressure of other work or of meeting case-handling deadlines, facts and legal principles which a party feels are significant may be overlooked by the NLRB agent responsible for the investigation. Personal contact with the supervisory staff avoids such omissions.

In particularly difficult cases, such contacts should be made with the General Counsel in Washington. These cases are referred by the regional director to the General Counsel for "advice." Parties are often not informed of the referral but, where the regional director does not make final disposition of a charge within 30 days after it is filed, it has usually been sent in for advice. (See "Oral Argument Before General Counsel," page 241, for procedure to be used.)

Upon completion of the investigation, the case may be disposed of informally, or the regional office may institute formal proceedings.

Sec. 13–15. Informal disposition of a charge.   A charge may be disposed of informally in three ways:

1. Withdrawal by the charging party.
2. Dismissal by the regional director.
3. Adjustment by the parties.

Sec. 13–16. Withdrawal of a charge.   Where the investigation reveals no violation of the statute or a lack of jurisdiction by the Board, the NLRB agent will ask the charging party to withdraw its charge. If withdrawn, the party charged with the violation is immediately notified by the regional office and the case is closed.

Also, a charging party, on his own initiative, may ask to withdraw the charge. However, pursuant to the Board's rules, a "charge may be withdrawn, prior to the hearing, only with the consent of the regional director with whom such charge was filed."[57]

Therefore, before the director grants any request for withdrawal, a Board agent will look into the reasons for such request; he is under instructions to view violations of the statute as a public concern, and not as a private matter. An adjustment by the parties which does not remedy the indicated unfair labor practices, or which is contrary to the public interest, may not be accepted as basis for withdrawal of a charge.[58] For example the Board will not recognize a private settlement in which an employer attempts to buy release from unfair labor practice charges by payment of money, nor will withdrawal be permitted where the investigation has disclosed violent conduct by the party charged.

Once the charge is withdrawn with the consent of the regional director, it cannot be revived; it is as if that charge had never been filed.[59] Accordingly, where a charge is refiled, the six-month limitation applies with respect to the date of the refiling and not the filing date of the charge which was withdrawn.[60]

Sec. 13–17. Dismissal of a charge. If a charge is not withdrawn when requested by the NLRB agent, the regional director will refuse to issue a formal complaint; thus, in effect, he dismisses the charge. The regional director notifies the parties of his action by letter. (See Facsimile No. 48, page 240.) This letter states the reasons for his action, frequently in general terms, e.g., insufficiency of evidence, but a more detailed summary report will be included if requested by the charging party. The letter may also cite specific Board rulings. Unless the charging party takes a timely appeal, the case is closed at this point.

Sec. 13–18. Appeal from the dismissal. The charging party has 10 days from the receipt of the regional director's letter in which to appeal from his action.[61] Such appeal should be addressed to the General Counsel in Washington, D.C., with a copy to the regional director. A copy need not be served on the other parties. The General Counsel advises other interested parties of the filing of the appeal but not of its contents.

The appeal should contain a complete statement setting forth the facts and reasons upon which the appeal is based. It is, in effect, a part of the investigation, for the power of the regional director to act on the charge

[57]Sec. 102.9.
[58]NLRB v. Oertel Brewing Co., 197 F.2d 59, 30 LRRM 2236 (C.A. 6, 1952); Retail Clerks Local 1288 (Ničkels Pay-Less Stores of Tulare County, Inc.), 163 NLRB 817, 69 LRRM 1433 (1967).
[59]NLRB v. Electric Furnace Co., 327 F.2d 373, 55 LRRM 2398 (C.A. 6, 1964).
[60]Olin Industries, Inc., 97 NLRB 130, 29 LRRM 1071 (1951).
[61]R. and R. Sec. 102.19.

NATIONAL LABOR RELATIONS BOARD

Date:

Charging party
Address

Re: Name and Number of Case

Gentlemen:

The above-captioned case charging a violation under Section 8 of
the National Labor Relations Act as amended, has been carefully investigated and considered.

As a result of the investigation, it appears that, because
[there is insufficient evidence of violation] or [a summary report
setting forth the reasons for dismissal will be included here in the
dismissal letter if the charging party desires it], further proceedings
are not warranted at this time. I am, therefore, refusing to issue
complaint in this matter.

Pursuant to the National Labor Relations Board Rules and Regulations
(Section 102.19) you may obtain a review of this section by filing a
request for such review with the General Counsel of the National Labor
Relations Board, Washington, D. C. 20570, and a copy with me. This
request must contain a complete statement setting forth the facts
and reasons upon which it is based. The request must be received by
the General Counsel in Washington, D. C., by the close of business on
(month-day-year). Upon good cause shown, however, the General Counsel
may grant special permission for a longer period within which to file.
A copy of any such request should be submitted to me.

Very truly yours,

_____
Regional Director

cc: General Counsel,
       National Labor Relations Board
       Washington, D. C. 20570

       Respondent
       Address

FACSIMILE NO. 48.
Form of letter sent by regional director
informing the parties of his refusal to issue a complaint

rests entirely on his capacity as an agent of the General Counsel. In fact it is not uncommon for the regional office to be asked to supply further information or to reinvestigate particular aspects of the case as a part of the consideration on appeal.

Sec. 13–19. Oral argument before General Counsel. The appeal is processed by the General Counsel's staff in Washington and is decided on the record forwarded by the regional director, the information in the appeal itself, and any facts or argument submitted by the party charged. While parties are not encouraged to present their positions to the General Counsel personally, a party wishing to do so may request an appointment. Where this is done, the party will, at a minimum, have an opportunity to present his views of the facts and the law to high-ranking members of the General Counsel's staff. Though referred to as "oral arguments" these are, in fact, informal discussions. Other parties are not present but, where one party is granted such argument, other parties are then given a similar opportunity. In complex cases, a personal interview with the General Counsel or his staff is frequently well worth the time and expense involved. The General Counsel has final authority over issuance of the complaint and is not limited in any way by the action of the regional director.

After a review of the case, the General Counsel may reverse the regional director and direct that an unfair labor practice complaint be issued or may uphold the regional director's refusal to proceed—thereby dismissing the case. The General Counsel's refusal to issue is final; it is not subject to court review. However, the charging party may file a motion for reconsideration of the decision if it states with particularity the error requiring reconsideration and it is filed within 10 days of the service of the decision.[62]

Appeal to the General Counsel from the regional director's refusal to issue a complaint will not serve to stop the processing of a representation or a decertification case while that appeal is pending.[63] Thus, the regional director will conduct an election while an unfair labor practice appeal is pending before the General Counsel even though the party appealing is a union appearing on the election ballot.[64] (See Sec. 7–3, page 107.)

---

[62]R. and R. Sec. 102.19(c).
[63]Langenberg Hat Co., 116 NLRB 198, 38 LRRM 1216 (1956).
[64]Autotyre Division of Ekco Products Co., 116 NLRB 134, 38 LRRM 1206 (1956).

CHAPTER 14

Settlement of the Unfair Labor Practice
Charge

Sec. 14–1. In general. If investigation reveals merit in a charge, the NLRB agent will normally attempt to secure an adjustment that will remedy the unfair labor practices without the necessity of further proceedings. However, the Board has held that the General Counsel is not required to seek this adjustment before issuing a complaint.[1] There are two types of settlements:

1. The informal settlement, which is a simply stated agreement wherein the charged party undertakes to remedy the unfair labor practices. Its terms are subject to the approval of the regional director.
2. The formal settlement, which is usually in the form of a signed stipulation wherein provision is made for remedy of the unfair labor practices and the issuance of a cease and desist order by the Board in Washington. It may also provide for the entry of a court decree enforcing the Board's order.

Sec. 14–2. Informal settlement. The informal settlement—the most frequent type of adjustment—is used where the party charged with the violation has no history of illegal conduct and there appears to be little likelihood of a repetition of the violation. It may contain a "nonadmission" clause wherein the respondent agrees to the settlement without admitting that he has committed the alleged unfair labor practices.[2]

Sec. 14–3. Informal settlement after complaint issues. Formerly, the General Counsel rarely agreed to an informal settlement after a complaint had issued. The policy was adopted to encourage informal adjustments early in the handling of the case. Under current practice, however, informal

---

[1]Dairylee, Inc., 149 NLRB 829, 57 LRRM 1427 (1964).
[2]Southwest Chevrolet Corp., 194 NLRB No. 157, 79 LRRM 1156 (1972); Smith Company of Calif., 200 NLRB No. 106, 82 LRRM 1269 (1972).

settlements are authorized as readily after issuance of the complaint as before.

The informal settlement usually is reduced to writing on a form prepared and made available by the regional office. (See Facsimile No. 49, page 245.) The settlement agreement is subject to the approval of the regional director. It always provides for withdrawal of the charge by the charging party as soon as the accused party complies with the terms of the agreement. The regional office is under instructions not to close a case without proof of such compliance. If the party charged with the violation should fail to perform its obligations set forth in the settlement agreement, the regional director may proceed to issue a complaint.[3]

Where a charge alleges unfair labor practices committed by more than one named party (e.g., by an employer and a union), any one of the charged parties may enter into a settlement agreement concerning itself, without affecting the rights of any other party charged with an unfair labor practice.[4] However, in the event a complaint issued against the other party is dismissed by the Board or a court, the party settling will be required to pay the full amount of any back pay or other financial liability involved.

Sec. 14–4. Appeal from informal adjustment. The charging party cannot block an informal settlement where the regional office accepts as sufficient the remedial action offered by the party charged with the violation. Where the charging party objects to such adjustment, the settlement agreement is signed only by the accused party and the regional director, and the charge is dismissed as provided by the agreement. The charging party may then take an appeal to the General Counsel, within 10 days of the date of the letter of dismissal. (The procedure for appeal is the same as that set forth on page 239 under "Appeal from the dismissal.")

It has been held that in a situation where all parties sign the informal agreement (e.g., the employer, the union, and the regional director), the employees affected cannot obtain court review of that agreement.[5] However, a court recently held that an informed settlement is a final order entitling the charging party to court review.[6] (See also page 250, "Settlement After Complaint Issues.")

In a case where the employer is alleged to have illegally assisted or dominated a labor organization, that labor organization also signs the agreement. Or, it may sign and submit a separate statement in which it

[3]MPO-TV of Calif., Inc., 197 NLRB No. 134, 81 LRRM 1223 (1972); Guy F. Atkinson Co., Bingham-Williamette Co. Div., 199 NLRB No. 188, 81 LRRM 1377 (1972); Fox River Pattern Inc., 199 NLRB No. 12, 81 LRRM 1596 (1972).
[4]NLRB v. Newspaper and Mail Deliverer's Union of New York, 192 F.2d 654, 29 LRRM 2136 (C.A. 2, 1951).
[5]Stanley Anthony v. NLRB, 204 F.2d 832, 32 LRRM 2247 (C.A. 6, 1953).
[6]ILGWU Local 415-475 v. NLRB, 501 F.2d 823, 86 LRRM 2851 (C.A. D.C., 1974).

Form NLRB-4775 N: :B-/ 7'.
(6-71)

UNITED STATES OF AMERICA
NATIONAL LABOR RELATIONS BOARD

In the Matter of

SETTLEMENT AGREEMENT

The undersigned Charged Party and the undersigned Charging Party, in settlement of the above matter, and subject to the approval of the Regional Director for the National Labor Relations Board, HEREBY AGREE AS FOLLOWS:

POSTING OF NOTICE — Upon approval of this Agreement, the Charged Party will post immediately in conspicuous places in and about its plant/office, including all places where notices to employees/members are customarily posted, and maintain for a period of at least 60 consecutive days from the date of posting, copies of the Notice attached hereto and made a part hereof, said Notices to be signed by a responsible official of the Charged Party and the date of actual posting to be shown thereon. In the event this Agreement is in settlement of a charge against a union, the union will submit forthwith signed copies of said Notice to the Regional Director who will forward them to the employer whose employees are involved herein, for posting, the employer willing, in conspicuous places in and about the employer's plant where they shall be maintained for a period of at least 60 consecutive days from the date of posting.

COMPLIANCE WITH NOTICE — The Charged Party will comply with all the terms and provisions of said Notice.

BACKPAY — The Charged Party will make whole the employees named below by payment to each of them of the amount set opposite his or her name.

REFUSAL TO ISSUE COMPLAINT — In the event the Charging Party fails or refuses to become a party to this Agreement, then, if the Regional Director in his discretion believes it will effectuate the policies of the National Labor Relations Act, he shall decline to issue a Complaint herein (or a new Complaint if one has been withdrawn pursuant to the terms of this Agreement), and this Agreement shall be between the Charged Party and the undersigned Regional Director. A review of such action may be obtained pursuant to Section 102.19 of the Rules and Regulations of the Board if a request for same is filed within 10 days thereof. This Agreement is contingent upon the General Counsel sustaining the Regional Director's action in the event of a review. Approval of this Agreement by the Regional Director shall constitute withdrawal of any Complaint(s) and Notice of Hearing heretofore issued in this case.

PERFORMANCE — Performance by the Charged Party with the terms and provisions of this Agreement shall commence immediately after the Agreement is approved by the Regional Director, or, in the event the Charging Party does not enter into this Agreement, performance shall commence immediately upon receipt by the Charged Party of advice that no review has been requested or that the General Counsel has sustained the Regional Director.

NOTIFICATION OF COMPLIANCE — The undersigned parties to this Agreement will each notify the Regional Director in writing what steps the Charged Party has taken to comply herewith. Such notification shall be given within 5 days, and again after 60 days, from the date of the approval of this Agreement. In the event the Charging Party does not enter into this Agreement, initial notice shall be given within 5 days after notification from the Regional Director that no review has been requested or that the General Counsel has sustained the Regional Director. Contingent upon compliance with the terms and provisions hereof, no further action shall be taken in the above case.

(Charged Party)	(Charging Party)
By:	By:
(Name and Title)	(Name and Title)
Date:	Date:
Recommended:	Approved:
(Date)	(Date)
By:	By:
Board Agent	Regional Director
	National Labor Relations Board

FACSIMILE NO. 49.
Settlement agreement form (Form 4775)

surrenders any rights it may have in the proceeding. Likewise, where the informal agreement provides that the charged party shall cease giving effect to any or all provisions of a contract, efforts will be made by the Board agent to have the other party to that contract either sign the settlement agreement or surrender any rights it may have in the proceeding. Where the interested party—that is, either the illegally assisted or dominated labor organization or the other party to the affected contract—refuses either to join in the settlement agreement or to waive its rights, the regional director will issue a formal complaint and proceed to a hearing.

Sec. 14–5. Notice to employees of informal settlement. All settlement agreements provide for notice to the employees of the action taken by the charged party to remedy the specific unfair labor practices. While there is some give and take as to the terms of a settlement, it is most unusual to find any deviation from the notice-posting requirements. In the case of unfair labor practices committed by a labor organization, such notices may be:

1. Posted at the union's meeting hall.
2. Mailed to the employees against whom the unfair labor practices were committed.
3. If the employer is willing, posted at the place of employment. In the case of unfair labor practices committed by an employer, the notices usually are posted prominently at the place of business.

Various types of prepared notices are available at the regional offices; each notice is worded to fit the particular unfair labor practice. (See Facsimiles No. 50 and 51, pages 247, 248.) Notices are usually posted for 60 days.

Sec. 14–6. Effect of informal settlement. The regional office will police the terms of the settlement agreement to see if they are being observed. When the regional director is satisfied that all the terms have been performed—usually after the expiration of the notice-posting period—he will notify the parties that he is closing the case. However, this notification will state that continued observance of the terms of the informal settlement is a condition of the case remaining closed.

A pending representation case will be partially processed while the terms of the settlement agreement are being performed. For example, a hearing may be held, or the regional director or the Board may issue a direction of election. However, an election will not be held until terms of the agreement have been performed and the notice-posting period has expired.

Where an informal agreement provides for bargaining in settlement of charges of refusal to bargain or bad faith bargaining, such settlement is not

FORM NLRB–4726
(4–71)

NOTICE TO MEMBERS

POSTED BY ORDER OF THE
NATIONAL LABOR RELATIONS BOARD
AN AGENCY OF THE UNITED STATES GOVERNMENT

Pursuant to agreement, and in order to effectuate the policies of the National Labor Relations Act, as amended, we hereby notify our members that:

WE WILL NOT engage in or induce or encourage the employees of (the employer whose employees were induced to boycott the charging party) to engage in a strike or concerted refusal in the course of their employment to transport or otherwise handle or work on any goods, articles, materials, or commodities, or to perform any services where an object thereof is: (1) to force or require the said (the employer whose employees were induced to boycott the charging party) to cease handling, transporting, or otherwise dealing in the products of (the name and address of charging party), or to cease doing business with said (the name of charging party); (2) to force or require the said (the name of charging party) to recognize or bargain with (the union involved) as representative of its employees when (the union involved) has not been certified as a representative of such employees under the provisions of Section 9 of the Act.

_____
(Name of respondent union)

Dated _____ By _____
                            (Representative)   (Title)

_____

THIS IS AN OFFICIAL NOTICE AND MUST NOT BE DEFACED BY ANYONE

This notice must remain posted for 60 consecutive days from the date of posting and must not be altered, defaced, or covered by any other material. Any questions concerning this notice or compliance with its provisions may be directed to the Board's Office,

FACSIMILE No. 50.
Example of notice used in settlement of union unfair labor practice

FORM NLRB-4722
(10-70)

NOTICE TO
EMPLOYEES

POSTED PURSUANT TO A SETTLEMENT AGREEMENT
APPROVED BY A REGIONAL DIRECTOR OF THE
NATIONAL LABOR RELATIONS BOARD
AN AGENCY OF THE UNITED STATES GOVERNMENT

PURSUANT TO AGREEMENT, AND IN ORDER TO EFFECTUATE THE POLICIES OF
THE NATIONAL LABOR RELATIONS ACT, AS AMENDED, WE HEREBY NOTIFY OUR
EMPLOYEES THAT:

WE WILL NOT discriminate against our employees by
terminating them in order to discourage membership in
GENERAL TEAMSTERS, CHAUFFEURS AND HELPERS, LOCAL UNION
NO. 249 AFFILIATED WITH INTERNATIONAL BROTHERHOOD OF
TEAMSTERS, CHAUFFEURS, WAREHOUSEMEN AND HELPERS OF
AMERICA or any other union.

WE WILL reinstate [named employees] with backpay.

WE WILL bargain collectively with GENERAL TEAMSTERS,
CHAUFFEURS AND HELPERS, LOCAL UNION NO. 249 AFFILIATED
WITH INTERNATIONAL BROTHERHOOD OF TEAMSTERS, CHAUFFEURS,
WAREHOUSEMEN AND HELPERS OF AMERICA, as the exclusive
collective-bargaining representative of our employees
in the unit of

All regular truckdrivers employed at the
[name of company] terminal; excluding all
office clerical employees, guards, professional
employees and supervisors as defined in the
National Labor Relations Act, as amended.

WE WILL NOT change the jobs or working conditions of those
drivers without notifying and consulting that union.

                          [NAME OF COMPANY]_____
                                (Employer)

Dated _____   By_____
                          (Representative)   (Title)

THIS IS AN OFFICIAL NOTICE AND MUST NOT BE DEFACED BY ANYONE

This notice must remain posted for 60 consecutive days from the date of posting and must not be altered, defaced,
or covered by any other material. Any questions concerning this notice or compliance with its provisions may be directed
to the Board's Office,

FACSIMILE NO. 51.
Example of notice used in settlement of employer unfair labor practice

automatically equal to a certification that allows the parties one year in which to negotiate a contract free from rival claims and petitions.[7] However, the Board, with court approval, has held:[8]

A settlement agreement containing a bargaining provision, if it is to achieve its purpose, must be treated as giving the parties thereto a reasonable time in which to conclude a contract.

We therefore hold that after providing in the settlement agreement that it would bargain with the union, the respondent (employer) was under an obligation to honor that agreement for a reasonable time after its execution without questioning the representative status of the union.

Accordingly, the Board has held that a settlement agreement and a contract entered into pursuant to that settlement bars a rival union's petition for an election which was filed shortly before the settlement.[9] Also, the Board has ruled that a petition for decertification was timely filed and ordered an election, where it was filed one month after the settlement agreement; the Board there found that a reasonable time for bargaining had elapsed, the terms of the settlement agreement had been fully performed, and the regional director had reported that the employer had bargained in good faith.[10]

While it is the Board's policy to honor the settlement agreements to which its agents are parties, the Board will go behind a settlement agreement where unfair labor practices continue after its execution, where that agreement is breached,[11] or where there is no "meeting of the minds";[12] in the former two circumstances, the Board litigates the presettlement as well as the postsettlement violation."[13]

Sec. 14–7. Formal settlement. If investigation of a charge reveals a flagrant violation of the statute, violence, or the likelihood of repeated violations, the NLRB agent attempts to secure a formal adjustment. This type of adjustment—usually embodied in a settlement stipulation—is made simultaneously with or immediately after the issuance of the complaint and notice of hearing by the regional director. (See Facsimiles No. 52 and 53, pages 251, 254.)

The settlement stipulation is subject to the approval of the Board in Washington.[14] The Board cannot change it in any aspect; it can merely

[7]Ruffalo's Trucking Service, Inc., 114 NLRB 1549, 37 LRRM 1201 (1955).
[8]Poole Foundry and Machine Co. v. NLRB, 192 F.2d 740, 29 LRRM 2104 (C.A. 4, 1951); *see also* Frank Becker Towing Co., 151 NLRB 466, 58 LRRM 1434 (1965).
[9]Dick Brothers Inc., 110 NLRB 451, 35 LRRM 1016 (1954).
[10]Ruffalo's Trucking Service Inc., 114 NLRB 1549, 37 LRRM 1201 (1955).
[11]The Wallace Corp. v. NLRB, 323 U.S. 248, 15 LRRM 697 (1944); Arrow Specialities, Inc., 76 LRRM 2351 (C.A. 8, 1971), *enf.* 72 LRRM 1025; NLRB v. San Francisco Labor Council, 82 LRRM 3079 (C.A. 9, 1973), *enf.* 77 LRRM 1593.
[12]IATSE, Local 659, 197 NLRB No. 134, 81 LRRM 1223 (1972).
[13]Radio Station KHMO, 102 NLRB 26, 31 LRRM 1280 (1953).
[14]Tennessee Packers, Inc., 67 LRRM 2669 (C.A. 6, 1968), *reman'g* 63 LRRM 1190.

approve or reject it. If the settlement is rejected, the case is sent back to the regional office and it is processed as if no agreement had been executed. Ordinarily, the stipulation is signed by all parties and contains:

1. A statement of jurisdictional facts.
2. A waiver of the right to a public hearing and to further proceedings.
3. A statement of the facts constituting the unfair labor practices.
4. Consent to the issuance of a specific Board order.

Frequently, the settlement stipulation further states the consent of the parties to the entry of a court-of-appeals decree enforcing the terms of the Board order. The consent order is the equivalent of a court order entered after a contested hearing.[15] In some instances the General Counsel may insist on the provision for a consent decree before agreeing to the proposed settlement; such insistence, it has been held, is within his discretion.[16]

A formal adjustment thus involves the issuance of a cease-and-desist order by the Board, whereas an informal settlement does not.[17] Violation of a formal settlement stipulation leads to court enforcement of the Board's order. In those cases where the settlement stipulation provides for an entry of a court decree, nonperformance of the terms of the settlement will ordinarily lead to a petition by the Board that the offending party be held in contempt of court.

Sec. 14–8. Settlement after complaint issues.   Where a formal settlement has been agreed upon by the regional director and the party charged after issuance of complaint, the charging party is urged to sign the settlement stipulation, as some cases have upheld the right of the charging party to insist upon a hearing once a complaint has issued.[18] Nevertheless, if the party charged agrees to take action which will effectuate the policies of the Act, the settlement is often consummated without the participation of the charging party.

Sec. 14–9. Settlements without Board participation.   Whether executed before or after complaint issues, the Board is not bound by a settlement

[15]Pittsburgh Plate Glass Co. v. NLRB, 313 U.S. 146, 8 LRRM 425 (1941).
[16]Gimbel Brothers, Inc., 100 NLRB 870, 30 LRRM 1365 (1952).
[17]Successful Creations, Inc., 202 NLRB No. 33, 82 LRRM 1505 (1973).
[18]Marine Engineers Beneficial Assn. v. NLRB, 202 F.2d 546, 31 LRRM 2454 (C.A. 3, 1953), *cert. denied*, 346 U.S. 819, 32 LRRM 2750 (1953); Local 112, Industrial Workers v. Rothman, et al., 209 F.Supp. 295, 51 LRRM 2259 (D.C. D.C., 1962); Textile Workers of America, AFL-CIO v. NLRB, 48 LRRM 2718 (C.A. D.C., 1961); Leeds and Northrup Co. v. NLRB, 61 LRRM 2283 (C.A. 3, 1966); Terminal Freight Coop. Assn. v. NLRB, 78 LRRM 2097 (C.A. 3, 1971), *see also* 72 LRRM 2989; Concrete Materials of Georgia, Inc. v. NLRB, 440 F.2d 61, 76 LRRM 2832 (C.A. 5, 1971); NLRB v. Oil, Chemical and Atomic Workers, 82 LRRM 3159 (C.A. 1, 1973).

DS-655

Houston, Texas

UNITED STATES OF AMERICA
BEFORE THE NATIONAL LABOR RELATIONS BOARD

TEXTILE WORKERS UNION OF
AMERICA, AFL-CIO/CLC

and

PLASTECO, INC.

DECISION AND ORDER
Statement of the Case

On October 7, 1974, Textile Workers Union of America,
AFL-CIO/CLC, herein called Respondent; Plasteco, Inc., herein called the
Charging Party; and the General Counsel of the National Labor Relations Board
entered into a Settlement Stipulation, subject to approval of the Board,
providing for the entry of a consent order by the Board and a consent judgment
by any appropriate United States Court of Appeals. The parties waived all
further and other procedure before the Board to which they may be entitled
under the National Labor Relations Act, as amended, and the Rules and Regulations of the Board, and Respondent waived its right to contest the entry of
a consent judgment or to receive further notice of the application therefor.

Pursuant to the provisions of Section 3(b) of the National Labor
Relations Act, as amended, the National Labor Relations Board has delegated
its authority in this proceeding to a three-member panel.

The aforesaid Settlement Stipulation is hereby approved and made a
part of the record herein, and the proceeding is hereby transferred to and
continued before the Board in Washington, D.C., for the entry of a Decision
and Order pursuant to the provisions of the said Settlement Stipulation.

Upon the aforesaid Settlement Stipulation and the entire record
in the proceeding, the Board makes the following:

Findings of Fact

1. The business of the Charging Party

Charging party is, and has been at all times material herein, a
corporation duly organized under and existing by virthe of the laws of the
State of Texas, having its principal office and place of business at Houston,
Texas, where it is engaged in the business of the production and sale of
plexiglass products.

Charging Party, in the operations of its business described
immediately above, during the preceding 12 months, said period being
representative of its operations at all times material herein, sold and
shipped goods valued in excess of $50,000 directly to customers located outside
the State of Texas from its Houstan, Texas operations.

FACSIMILE NO. 52.
*First page of example of settlement stipulation
of union unfair labor practice*

DS-655

The Charging Party and the Respondent admit, and we find, that the Charging Party is an employer engaged in commerce within the meaning of Section 2(6) and (7) of the Act.

2. The labor organization involved

Textile Workers of America, AFL-CIO/CLC, is a labor organization within the meaning of Section 2(5) of the Act.

ORDER

Upon the basis of the above findings of fact, the Settlement Stipulation, and the entire record in the proceeding, and pursuant to Section 10(c) of the National Labor Relations Act, as amended, the National Labor Relations Board hereby orders that:

The Respondent, Textile Workers Union of America, AFL-CIO/CLC, its officers, agents, and representatives, shall:

1. Cease and desist from:

(a) Committing acts of physical violence upon the persons of non-striking employees of Plasteco, Inc., with, including, but not limited to, fists, hard objects, and/or vehicles.

(b) Committing acts of physical violence upon the property of non-striking employees of Plasteco, Inc. and the property of employees hired as strike replacements of Plasteco, Inc.

(c) Committing acts of physical violence upon the persons and/or property of employees of employers doing business with Plasteco, Inc. with, including, but not limited to, hard objects, projectiles, and/or vehicles.

(d) Threatening to commit acts of physical violence on the persons, families, homes, and/or property of non-striking employees of Plasteco, Inc. hired as strike replacements by Plasteco, Inc. and employees of employers doing business with Plasteco, Inc.

(e) In any other manner restraining and coercing the employees of Plasteco, Inc., Houston, Texas, in the exercise of their rights guaranteed by Section 7 of the National Labor Relations Act, as amended.

2. Take the following affirmative action which the National Labor Relations Board finds will effectuate the policies of the National Labor Relations Act, as amended:

(a) Notify members of Respondent and other persons acting in concert of participation with members of Respondent in connection with the strike that Respondent is engaging in, at Plasteco, Inc., Houston, Texas, a meeting at which time Respondent will read aloud the attached Notice to Employees and Members, and instruct the members of Respondent and/or other persons to comply with said Notice.

- 2 -

FACSIMILE No. 52. *Second page*

DS-655

(b) Post in conspicuous places in the business offices,
meeting halls, and other places where they customarily post notices to
their members, signed copies of the attached Notice to Employees and
Members. Copies of said Notice, on forms provided by the Regional Director
for Region 23, after being duly signed by authorized representatives of
the Respondent, shall be posted immediately upon receipt thereof, and be
maintained by it for a period of 60 consecutive days thereafter in conspicuous
places, including all places where such notices to members are customarily
posted. Reasonable steps shall be taken by the Respondent to insure that
said notices are not altered, defaced, or covered by any other material.

(c) Mail, on or before October 10, 1974, copies of the
attached Notice to all striking employees at Plasteco, Inc. There will be
no other documents or correspondence mailed with the Notice.

(d) Sign and mail sufficient copies of said Notice to the
Regional Director for Region 23 for posting by Plasteco, Inc., if willing,
in all places where notices to its employees are customarily posted.

(e) Notify the Regional Director for Region 23, in writing,
within 10 days from the date of this Order, what steps the Respondent has
taken to comply herewith.

Dated, Washington, D.C.,

_____
Edward B. Miller,   Chairman

_____
John H. Fanning,   Member

_____
John A. Penello,   Member

NATIONAL LABOR RELATIONS BOARD

(SEAL)

FACSIMILE NO. 52. *Third page*

DS-658
San Carlos, Calif.

UNITED STATES OF AMERICA
BEFORE THE NATIONAL LABOR RELATIONS BOARD

BAY CITY SCREW & BOLT CO.

and   Case 20-CA-9231

INTERNATIONAL LONGSHOREMEN'S AND
WAREHOUSEMEN'S UNION, LOCAL 6

DECISION AND ORDER

Statement of the Case

On October 10, 1974, Bay City Screw & Bolt Co., herein called
Respondent; International Longshoremen's and Warehousemen's Union, Local 6,
herein called the Union; and the General Counsel of the National Labor
Relations Board entered into a Settlement Stipulation, subject to approval
of the Board, providing for the entry of a consent order by the Board and
a consent judgment by any appropriate United States Court of Appeals. The
parties waived all further and other procedure before the Board to which
they may be entitled under the National Labor Relations Act, as amended,
and the Rules and Regulations of the Board, and Respondent waived its right
to contest the entry of a consent judgment or to receive further notice of
the application therefor.

Pursuant to the provisions of Section 3(b) of the National Labor
Relations Act, as amended, the National Labor Relations Board has delegated
its authority in this proceeding to a three-member panel.

The aforesaid Settlement Stipulation is hereby approved and made
a part of the record herein, and the proceeding is hereby transferred to
and continued before the Board in Washington, D.C., for the entry of a
Decision and Order pursuant to the provisions of the said Settlement
Stipulation.

Upon the basis of the aforesaid Settlement Stipulation and the
entire record in the proceeding, the Board makes the following:

Findings of Fact

1. The business of the Respondent

At all times material herein, Respondent has been an Illinois
corporation with a place of business located in San Carlos, California,
where it has been engaged in the non-retail sale of screws and bolts.

During the past 12 months, Respondent, in the course and conduct
of its business operations, sold and shipped products valued in excess of
$50,000 from its San Carlos, California, facility directly to purchasers
located outside the State of California.

Respondent admits, and we find, that it is an employer engaged in
commerce and in operations affecting commerce within the meaning of
Section 2(2), (6), and (7) of the Act.

2. The labor organization involved

International Longshoremen's and Warehousemen's Union, Local 6,
is a labor organization within the meaning of Section 2(5) of the Act.

FACSIMILE No. 53.
First page of example of settlement stipulation
of employer unfair labor practice

DS-658

ORDER

Upon the basis of the above findings of fact, the Settlement Stipulation, and the entire record in the proceeding, and pursuant to Section 10(c) of the National Labor Relations Act, as amended, the National Labor Relations Board hereby orders that:

The Respondent, Bay City Screw & Bolt Co., its officers, agents, successors, and assigns, shall:

1. Cease and desist from:

(a) Intimidating, restraining and coercing employees by threatening to close its plant if its employees designated or selected the Union as their collective-bargaining agent.

(b) Interrogating its employees regarding their union activities.

(c) Issuing warning letters to its employees, thereby making them subject to imminent discharge, because of their membership in or activities on behalf of the Union or because they engaged in other concerted activities for the purpose of collective bargaining or other mutual aid or protection.

2. Take the following affirmative action which the National Labor Relations Board finds will effectuate the policies of the National Labor Relations Act, as amended:

(a) Remove the warning letters issued to employees Charles Metz and Michael F. Capone from their personnel files.

(b) Post immediately in conspicuous places in Respondent's plant, copies of the attached Notice to Employees. Copies of the said Notice, on forms provided by the Regional Director for Region 20, shall, after being duly signed by the Respondent's authorized representative, be posted immediately upon receipt thereof and maintained for 60 consecutive days thereafter in conspicuous places, including all places where notices to employees are customarily posted. Reasonable steps shall be taken by the Respondent to insure that said Notices are not altered, defaced, or covered by any other material.

(c) Notify the Regional Director for Region 20, in writing, within 10 days from the date of this Order, what steps Respondent has taken to comply herewith.

Dated, Washington, D.C.,

_____
Edward B. Miller, Chairman

_____
John H. Fanning,   Member

_____
John A. Penello,   Member

NATIONAL LABOR RELATIONS BOARD

(SEAL)

-2-

FACSIMILE NO. 53. *Second page*

agreed to by the parties in which it does not participate, e.g., a strike settlement initiated by a municipal government which the Board neither participated in nor approved.[19] A proceeding before the Board is a "public proceeding" and the Board is consequently not concerned with the settlement of private rights.[20]

---

[19]Plumbers and Pipefitters Union (Astrove Plumbing and Heating Corp.), 152 NLRB 1093, 59 LRRM 1234 (1965).
[20]Phelps Dodge Corp. v. NLRB, 313 U.S. 177, 8 LRRM 439 (1941).

CHAPTER 15

The Unfair Labor Practice Complaint-
Prehearing Procedures

Sec. 15–1. Issuance of a complaint. If investigation discloses that a charge has merit and if efforts to settle the case are unsuccessful, the regional director, on behalf of the General Counsel, takes formal action for the first time in the proceeding. He does this by serving on all "parties" a complaint and a notice of hearing. The "parties," for the purpose of this service, include: the party against whom the charge was filed, the charging party, any party to a contract alleged to be unlawful,[1] any allegedly company-assisted or-dominated labor organization, and, in a "jurisdictional dispute" case, every labor organization involved. Employees affected by these proceedings and company-assisted or-dominated labor organizations are not, as a matter of right, necessary parties.[2] In the service of the complaint, the charges need not be attached.[3]

There is no fixed period of time in which a complaint must issue.[4] The six-month limitation applies only to the filing and service of a charge and not to the issuance of a complaint. However, regional directors are currently issuing complaints about 51 days after the filing of the charge.

Sec. 15–2. Contents of the complaint. The complaint must contain: (1) a clear and concise statement of the facts upon which assertion of jurisdiction by the Board is predicated; and (2) a clear and concise description of the acts which are claimed to constitute unfair labor practices, including, where known, the approximate dates and places of such acts and the names of respondent's agents or other representatives by whom committed. A well-drafted complaint should be "bill of particulars proof."[5]

---

[1]Consolidated Edison Co. of New York, Inc. v. NLRB, 305 U.S. 197, 3 LRRM 646 (1938).
[2]National Licorice Co. v. NLRB, 309 U.S. 350, 6 LRRM 674 (1940).
[3]Peerless Yeast Co., 86 NLRB 1098, 25 LRRM 1023 (1949).
[4]NLRB v. Jay Co., Inc. 227 F.2d 416, 34 LRRM 2589 (C.A. 9, 1954).
[5]R. and R. Sec. 102.15; Bob's Casing Crews, Inc., 80 LRRM 2090 (C.A. 5, 1972), enf. 78 LRRM 1060, see also 74 LRRM 2753; Western Commercial Transport, 201 NLRB No. 10, 82 LRRM 1366 (1973).

The contents of the charge do not limit the scope of the complaint. "Courts have not hesitated to sustain allegations in Board complaints which were considerably wider in scope than the language contained in the charge."[6] The discretion of the General Counsel has been upheld where the Board and the courts have found a sufficient legal relationship between the subject matter of the charge and the allegation of the complaint.[7] Thus, the courts have held that the General Counsel, in issuing complaints, may include allegations not specifically enumerated in a timely charge, where such allegations: (a) merely "elaborate the charge with particularity";[8] (b) "are of the same general nature" or part of a continuing pattern;[9] (c) involve "similar or related acts";[10] or (d) are "fairly embraced" within the general terms of the charge.[11]

One court has warned, however, that the complaint is improper ". . . if it gets so completely outside of the situation which gave rise to the charge that it (the Board) may be said to be initiating the proceeding on its own motion . . ."[12]

Sec. 15–3. Amendment to complaint.   Prior to issuance of a Board order, a complaint may be amended: (1) before the commencement of the hearing by the regional director who issued the complaint; (2) during the hearing and before transfer to the Board by the administrative law judge; and (3) after transfer to the Board by the NLRB.[13] If the amendment to the complaint involves the naming of a newly charged party, the charge must be amended as well;[14] otherwise, a complaint may be amended without amending the charge.[15] Private parties cannot amend the complaint.[16]

Sec. 15–4. Consolidation of cases.   Consolidation of proceedings lies within the discretion of the General Counsel or the Board.[17] Thus,

[6]NLRB v. Globe Wireless, Ltd., 193 F.2d 748, 29 LRRM 2319 (C.A. 9, 1951); cf. Luxaire, Inc., 67 LRRM 2813 (C.A. D.C., 1968), enf. 65 LRRM 1327; Thompson Bros. Coal Co., Inc., 192 NLRB No. 5, 77 LRRM 1589 (1971); United Aircraft Corp., 192 NLRB No. 62, 77 LRRM 1785 (1971).
[7]NLRB v. Kingston Cake Co., 191 F.2d 563, 28 LRRM 2571 (C.A. 3, 1951).
[8]NLRB v. Westex Boot & Shoe Co., 190 F.2d 12, 28 LRRM 2220 (C.A. 5, 1951).
[9]NLRB v. Kohler Co., 220 F.2d 3, 35 LRRM 2606 (C.A. 7, 1955).
[10]NLRB v. Anchor Rome Mills, 228 F.2d 775, 37 LRRM 2367 (C.A. 5, 1956); Springfield Garment Mfg. Co., 152 NLRB 1043, 59 LRRM 1248 (1965).
[11]NLRB v. Talladega Cotton Factory, Inc., 213 F.2d 209, 34 LRRM 2196 (C.A. 5, 1954).
[12]NLRB v. Kohler Co., 220 F.2d 3, 35 LRRM 2606 (C.A. 7, 1955).
[13]R. and R. 102.17, as amended August 9, 1972.
[14]NLRB v. Hopwood Retinning Co., Inc., 98 F.2d 97, 2 LRRM 650 (C.A. 2, 1938).
[15]Consolidated Edison Co., of New York v. NLRB, 305 U.S. 197, 3 LRRM 646 (1938); Russell-Newman Mfg. Co., Inc., 70 LRRM 2502 (C.A. 5, 1969), enf. in part 66 LRRM 1257.
[16]Sunbeam Plastics Corp., 144 NLRB 1010, 54 LRRM 1174 (1963).
[17]NLRB v. Seamprufe, Inc., 186 F.2d 671, 27 LRRM 2216 (C.A. 10, 1951); Operating Engineers, Local 925 (J. L. Manta, Inc.), 80 LRRM 2398 (C.A. 5, 1972), enf. in part, reman'g in part 76 LRRM 1856.

prejudice to the parties has not been found in the consolidation of proceedings: (1) against an employer and a labor organization involving discrimination against the same employees;[18] (2) against unions affecting employees of two employers;[19] and (3) involving an unfair labor practice complaint and objections to an election.[20]

Sec. 15–5. The answer. The statute provides that the party against whom the complaint is issued "shall have the right to file an answer."[21] The Board rules state that the answer "shall" be filed within 10 days of the service of the complaint.[22] The answer should contain a simple statement of the facts which constitute the grounds of defense. It should specifically treat with every one of the facts alleged in the complaint, either by denial, admission, or explanation. If the party charged with the violation has no knowledge of certain allegations in the complaint, he should so state in his answer; such statement will operate as a denial. The Board has held that a general denial is sufficient to satisfy the requirements of the Rules and Regulations.[23]

If no answer is filed, or if certain allegations are not answered, the Board may consider those unanswered allegations as true, and it can so find.[24]

An original and four copies of the answer should be filed with the regional director who issued the complaint.[25] Immediately upon filing the answer, the party charged with the violation must serve a copy on each of the other parties. The original copy of the answer must be signed by the party or by his attorney.

Sec. 15–6. Notice of hearing. A notice of hearing usually is part of the formal complaint when it is served upon the parties. The notice of hearing fixes the time and place of the hearing before an administrative law judge.

The hearing date is set at least 10 days after the time of the receipt of the complaint and, in most cases, much later.

Sec. 15–7. Postponement of hearing. The Board's rules provide for the postponement of the hearing, either on the regional director's own motion

---

[18]The North Electric Mfg. Co., 84 NLRB 136, 24 LRRM 1221 (1949).
[19]NLRB v. United Mine Workers of America, District 31, 198 F.2d 389, 30 LRRM 2445 (C.A. 4, 1952).
[20]NLRB v. Dal-Tex Optical Co., Inc., 310 F.2d 58, 51 LRRM 2608 (C.A. 5, 1962); Dove Mfg. Co., 61 LRRM 2200 (C.A. 9, 1966), enf. as modified 55 LRRM 1154.
[21]Sec. 10(b).
[22]R. and R. Sec. 102.20.
[23]Graniteville Co., Sibley Division, 96 NLRB 456, 28 LRRM 1538 (1951).
[24]Liquid Carbonic Corp., 116 NLRB 795, 38 LRRM 1361 (1956); Plycoma Veneer Co., 196 NLRB No. 146, 80 LRRM 1222 (1972); South Burlington Mechanical and Electrical Contractors, Inc., 203 NLRB No. 127, 83 LRRM 1431 (1973).
[25]R. and R. Sec. 102.21.

or on "good cause" shown by any party.[26] Postponement of the opening date of a hearing is initiated by a request addressed to the regional director. In making such request, the petitioning party should keep in mind the following:

1. The request must be in writing.
2. Grounds for the request should be specified.
3. Alternative dates for any rescheduled hearing should be given.
4. Positions of all other parties must be ascertained in advance by the requesting party and set forth in the request.
5. Copies of the request must be simultaneously served on all other parties and that fact noted on the request.

To expedite the grant of the request for postponement, the party seeking the extension of time should, wherever possible, obtain the agreement of the other parties. Except in emergency situations, no request for postponement will be granted during the three days immediately preceding the date of hearing.

Sec. 15–8. Adjustments after complaint.   The issuance of a complaint and notice of hearing does not mean that the parties are foreclosed from making settlement agreements or adjustments. The settlement procedures described in Chapter 14 apply.

In addition, all parties may enter into a stipulation whereby they waive the right to a hearing, stipulate the facts, and agree that an administrative law judge may issue a decision upon the basis of the submission. Where this is done, the parties may specifically reserve the right to submit briefs to the administrative law judge. Such a stipulation does not in any way affect the parties' right to take to the Board any exceptions they may wish to file to the administrative law judge's decision. The stipulation is submitted in duplicate to the Chief Administrative Law Judge at the Washington headquarters of the Board.

Another alternative is a stipulation whereby the case is presented directly to the Board in Washington. This is accomplished by an agreement in which the parties stipulate the facts, waive their right to a hearing and to a administrative law judge's decision, and agree that the Board may rule upon the basis of the submission. In addition, the parties may ask the Board to set a time for the filing of briefs. This stipulation does not bind the parties to accept the Board's decision; the right to appeal to the appropriate court of appeals remains unaffected. Such a submission is made by filing an original and seven copies with the Board's executive secretary in Washington.

[26]R. and R. Sec. 102.16.

Sec. 15–9. Prehearing motions. All motions made by the parties before the opening of the hearing must be filed with the regional director.[27] The motion should state briefly the action requested and the grounds for such request. The moving party must file an original and four copies of each motion with the regional director, and serve a copy upon each of the other parties.

The regional director rules on all prehearing motions which concern:

1. Extension of time in which to file the answer.
2. Postponement of the hearing date.
3. Intervention in the hearing.

The regional director has the discretion either to rule on a motion to intervene or to refer it to the administrative law judge for a ruling.[28] All other motions will be referred by the regional director to an administrative law judge for ruling. Where the administrative law judge rules on a motion before the opening of the hearing, his ruling must be in writing and must be served on all parties.[29]

Sec. 15–10. Prehearing application for a deposition. Application for a deposition, if made before the opening of the hearing, must be filed with the regional director.[30] It should set forth both the reasons why, when, and where such deposition should be taken and the matters concerning which it is expected the witness will testify. It should be served upon the regional director at least seven days before the time it is desired that the deposition be taken. The regional director may grant such application only if, in the exercise of his discretion, he finds "good cause" has been shown;[31] for example, "good cause" may be found in the unavailability of a witness, either due to illness or great distance from the place of hearing.

If the application is granted and an Order and Notice of Deposition is issued, the procedure followed is identical to that used when an administrative law judge grants a similar application. (See page 276.)

Sec. 15–11. Motions for summary judgment. If no answer is filed or the answer is defective, counsel for the General Counsel usually files a motion for summary judgment, asking that the allegations of the complaint be decided without a hearing. The original and seven copies of the motion are filed with the Board. Motions for summary judgment are also used in

[27]R. and R. Sec. 102.24.
[28]R. and R. Sec. 102.29.
[29]R. and R. Sec. 102.25.
[30]R. and R. Sec. 102.30(a).
[31]NLRB v. Globe Wireless, Ltd., 193 F.2d 748, 29 LRRM 2319 (C.A. 9, 1951).

refusal-to-bargain cases involving tests of the validity of a representation proceeding.[32]

Sec. 15–12. Prehearing applications for subpoenas. Applications for subpoenas, if filed before the opening of the hearing, must be filed with the regional director (see Facsimiles No. 22 and 23, pages 114, 115). The regional director may issue a subpoena before the issuance of the unfair labor practice complaint;[33] his refusal to issue a subpoena is not reviewable in court.[34] Notice of such application need not be communicated to the other parties.[35]

If the person served with the subpoena does not intend to comply, he must, within five days after the date of service of the subpoena, petition the regional director to revoke. Failure to file such timely petition may bar the party from making a subsequent attack on a subpoena compelling him to produce the desired data.[36] Upon receipt of such petition, the regional director:[37]

1. Gives immediate notice of the petition to revoke to the party upon whose request the subpoena was issued.
2. Refers the petition to the administrative law judge or the Board for ruling.

The administrative law judge or the Board, as the case may be, must revoke the subpoena if:

1. The subpoena seeks evidence which does not relate to any matter under investigation.
2. The subpoena does not describe with sufficient particularity the evidence sought.
3. The subpoena is invalid for any other reason sufficient in law. If any person refuses to comply with a subpoena issued upon the request of a private party, the Office of the General Counsel may institute proceedings to enforce that subpoena in the appropriate district

---

[32]R. and R. Sec. 102.24; Hamilton Electronics Co. v. NLRB, 83 LRRM 2543 (C.A. 4, 1973), *enf.* 79 LRRM 1592; United Steelworkers, Local 4102, 199 NLRB No. 20, 81 LRRM 1188 (1972); NLRB v. Aaron Convalescent Home, 83 LRRM 2473 (C.A. 6, 1973), *enf.* 194 NLRB No. 114, 79 LRRM 1235.
[33]Link v. NLRB, 330 F.2d 437, 55 LRRM 2977 (C.A. 4, 1964).
[34]Laundry Workers International Union, Local 221 v. NLRB, 197 F. 2d 701, 30 LRRM 2270 (C.A. 5, 1952).
[35]R. and R. Sec. 102.31(a).
[36]NLRB v. Stanley Gemalo, 130 F. Supp. 500, 35 LRRM 2577 (D.C. S.N.Y., 1955).
[37]R. and R. Sec. 102.31(b); Kayser-Roth Hosiery Co., Inc., 78 LRRM 2130 (C.A. 6, 1971), *enf. in part* 76 LRRM 1231.

court.[38] However, the Office of the General Counsel, by starting such action, does not assume the responsibility of prosecuting the matter before the court; the responsibility rests with the party who wants the subpoena enforced.[39] (See page 277 for further discussion of subpoena enforcement.)

[38]Wyman-Gordon Co. v. NLRB, 394 U.S. 759, 70 LRRM 3345 (1969), *revs'g and reman'g* 68 LRRM 2483; NLRB v. International Typographical Union, 76 F.Supp. 895, 21 LRRM 2483 (D.C. S.N.Y., 1948); Gyrodyne Co., 203 NLRB No. 164, 83 LRRM 1350 (1973), *suppl'g* 68 LRRM 1124.
[39]R. and R. Sec. 102.31(d).

CHAPTER 16

The Unfair Labor Practice Hearing

Sec. 16–1. In general. The function of the General Counsel in an unfair labor practice case is divided into three distinct parts. The first, discussed in Chapter 13, is the investigatory stage where his role is that of impartial investigator, weighing the facts which rebut, as well as those which support, charges which have been filed. Once he determines that the facts warrant issuing an unfair labor practice complaint, his status shifts from investigator to prosecutor. It is this function which he performs as the case is heard by an administrative law judge and finally decided by the Board. The third role of the General Counsel is that of the Board's lawyer after the Board's decision and order has issued. It is his duty to obtain compliance with that order and, if not accomplished by voluntary action of the wrongdoer, the General Counsel represents the Board before the courts of appeals and the Supreme Court to enforce the order.

Prior to issuance of the complaint, the General Counsel—through his agents in the regional office—has full control over the case. Once the complaint issues, his authority begins to change. Until the opening of the hearing before an administrative law judge he continues to rule on minor matters, such as a change in the hearing date, requests for subpoenas, motions to intervene, and settlements. When the hearing starts, however, control over the case passes to the Board, acting through the administrative law judge, and the General Counsel and his agents are merely one of the parties. For example, after the opening date of the hearing and before the case is transferred to the Board, a charge may be withdrawn only with the consent of the administrative law judge.[1]

Sec. 16–2. Pretrial conference. The administrative law judge, upon joint request of the parties involved or his own initiative, will conduct a prehearing conference prior to or shortly after the opening of the hearing. The objectives of the conference are: (1) to avoid surprise and obfuscation by clarifying the issues and theories of the complaint and answer; (2) to simplify the issues and eliminate the taking of evidence on relevant matters

[1]R. and R. Sec. 102.9.

about which there is no dispute; and (3) to provide the parties another opportunity to negotiate a settlement at a conference conducted by the administrative law judge.[2]

Sec. 16–3. The hearing. The hearing usually is open to the public and conducted in the region where the charge originated. A verbatim transcript is made by an official reporter retained by the Board; this constitutes the official record of the hearing. If any party desires to purchase copies of the transcript, he makes his own arrangement with the reporter. The regional office obtains one copy, which is technically available to all parties, but its use by other than Board personnel is discouraged. All citations and references made in briefs and motions must refer to the official record. However, any party, as a matter of right, may bring in a private reporter to record the hearing.[3]

Sec. 16–4. Conduct of the hearing. An explanation of the mechanics of the hearing is enclosed with the complaint. (Facsimile No. 54, page 267.) The presiding officer is an administrative law judge sent from Washington (or San Francisco in the case of hearings in the Far West) by the Chief Administrative Law Judge. Parties are not entitled to advance notice of this designation.[4]

Responsibility for prosecution of the complaint rests on the General Counsel, who is customarily represented by an attorney from the regional office which issued the complaint. Charging parties and respondents are usually represented by counsel, but the Board does not prescribe rules of admission for practice before it or its administrative law judges, and parties sometimes use their own employees or professional consultants.

Sec. 16–5. Sequence of the hearing. The hearing, in general, follows the usual sequence of a trial in court. A brief opening statement is made by counsel for the General Counsel, the prosecutor, followed by a similar statement made by respondent, the defendant. The latter's statement is often reserved until after the Government's case has been presented. Counsel for the General Counsel then introduces into evidence the formal documents. These include the notice of hearing, the complaint, the charge upon which the complaint is based, affidavits and proof of service, the answer, and any written motions and rulings made before the opening of the hearing.

[2]NLRB Field Manual Sec. 10381.1.
[3]Inland Steel Co. v. NLRB, 109 F.2d 9, 5 LRRM 821 (C.A. 7, 1940); Marriott Corp., 72 LRRM 2564 (C.A. 4, 1969), enf. in part 69 LRRM 1181; cf. Daisy Originals, Inc. of Miami, 187 NLRB No. 15, 75 LRRM 1561 (1970).
[4]Fant Milling Co., 117 NLRB 1277, 39 LRRM 1395 (1957).

FORM NLRB-4668
(1-73)   (C CASES)

SUMMARY OF STANDARD PROCEDURES IN FORMAL HEARINGS HELD BEFORE THE
NATIONAL LABOR RELATIONS BOARD IN UNFAIR LABOR PRACTICE PROCEEDINGS
PURSUANT TO SECTION 10 OF THE NATIONAL LABOR RELATIONS ACT, AS AMENDED

The hearing will be conducted by an Administrative Law Judge of the National Labor Relations Board. He will preside at the hearing as an independent, impartial trier of the facts and the law and his decision in due time will be served on the parties. His headquarters are either in Washington, D.C. or San Francisco, California.

At the date, hour, and place for which the hearing is set, the Administrative Law Judge, upon the joint request of the parties, will conduct a "prehearing" conference, prior to or shortly after the opening of the hearing, to assure that the issues are sharp and clear-cut; or he may, on his own initiative, conduct such a conference. He will preside at any such conference, but he may, if the occasion arises, permit the parties to engage in private discussions. The conference will not necessarily be recorded, but it may well be that the labors of the conference will be evinced in the ultimate record -- for example, in the form of statements of position, stipulations, and concessions. Except under unusual circumstances, the Administrative Law Judge conducting the prehearing conference will be the one who will conduct the hearing; and it is expected that the formal hearing will commence or be resumed immediately upon completion of the prehearing conference. No prejudice will result to any party unwilling to participate in or to make stipulations or concessions during any prehearing conference.

(This is not to be construed as preventing the parties from meeting earlier for similar purposes. To the contrary, the parties are encouraged to meet prior to the time set for hearing in an effort to narrow the issues.)

Parties may be represented by an attorney or other representative and present evidence relevant to the issues.

An official reporter will make the only official transcript of the proceedings, and all citations in briefs and arguments must refer to the official record. The Board will not certify any transcript other than the official transcript for use in any court litigation. Proposed corrections of the transcript should be submitted, either by way of stipulation or motion, to the Administrative Law Judge for his approval.

All matter that is spoken in the hearing room while the hearing is in session will be recorded by the official reporter unless the Administrative Law Judge specifically directs off-the-record discussion. In the event that any party wishes to make off-the-record statements, a request to go off the record should be directed to the Administrative Law Judge and not to the official reporter.

Statements of reasons in support of motions and objections should be specific and concise. The Administrative Law Judge will allow an automatic exception to all adverse rulings, and, upon appropriate order, an objection and exception will be permitted to stand to an entire line of questioning.

FACSIMILE NO. 54.
*First page of statement of standard procedures
in unfair labor practice hearings (Form 4668)*

All exhibits offered in evidence shall be in duplicate. Copies shall also be supplied to other parties. If a copy of any exhibit is not available at the time the original is received, it will be the responsibility of the party offering such exhibit to submit the copy before the close of hearing. In the event such copy is not submitted, and the filing thereof has not for good reason shown been waived by the Administrative Law Judge, any ruling receiving the exhibit may be rescinded and the exhibit rejected.

Any party shall be entitled, upon request, to a reasonable period at the close of the hearing for oral argument, which shall be included in the stenographic report of the hearing. In the absence of a request, the Administrative Law Judge may himself ask for oral argument, if at the close of the hearing he believes that such argument would be beneficial to his understanding of the contentions of the parties and the factual issues involved.

Any party shall also be entitled upon request made before the close of the hearing, to file a brief or proposed findings and conclusions, or both, with the Administrative Law Judge who will fix the time for such filing.

Attention of the parties is called to the following requirements laid down in Section 102.42 of the Board's Rules and Regulations with respect to the procedure to be followed before the proceeding is transferred to the Board:

No request for an extension of time within which to submit briefs or proposed findings to the Administrative Law Judge will be considered unless received by the Chief Administrative Law Judge in Washington, D. C. (or in cases under the San Francisco, California branch office of the Division of Judges, the Presiding Judge in charge of such office) at least 3 days prior to the expiration of time fixed for the submission of such documents. Notice of request for such extension of time must be served simultaneously upon all other parties, and proof of such service furnished to the Chief Administrative Law Judge or Presiding Judge as the case may be. All briefs or proposed findings filed with the Administrative Law Judge must be submitted in triplicate, and may be in typewritten, printed, or mimeographed form, with service upon the other parties.

In due course the Administrative Law Judge will prepare and file with the Board his decision in this proceeding, and will cause a copy thereof to be served upon each of the parties. Upon filing of the said decision, the Board will enter an order transferring this case to itself, and will serve copies of that order, setting forth the date of such transfer, upon all parties. At that point, the Administrative Law Judge's official connection with the case will cease.

The procedure to be followed before the Board from that point forward, with respect to the filing of exceptions to the Administrative Law Judge's Decision, the submission of supporting briefs, requests for oral argument before the Board, and related matters, is set forth in the Board's Rules and Regulations, Series 8, as amended, particularly in Section 102.46, and following sections. A summary of the more pertinent of these provisions will be served upon the parties together with the order transferring the case to the Board.

Adjustments or settlements consistent with the policies of the Act reduce government expenditures and promote amity in labor relations. Upon request, the Administrative Law Judge will afford reasonable opportunity during the hearing for discussions between the parties if adjustment appears possible, and may himself suggest it.

GPO 941-789

FACSIMILE NO. 54. *Second page*

Evidence is then presented in support of the allegations in the complaint, followed by that in defense and, in turn, by rebuttal. The administrative law judge, the counsel for the General Counsel, and representatives of all parties to the proceeding have the right to call, examine, and cross-examine witnesses.[5] At the conclusion of presentation of evidence the parties may engage in oral argument, but it has become common for the parties to waive oral argument and to submit written briefs as permitted by the rules.[6] Proposed findings and conclusions may be submitted to the administrative law judge, but this is rarely done.

Sec. 16–6. Rules of evidence.   According to the statute, the hearing shall, "so far as practicable, be conducted in accordance with the rules of evidence applicable in the district courts of the United States under the rules of procedure for the district courts."[7] The Federal Rules of Civil Procedure provide that whenever a statute or rule of the state in which the hearing is held favors the reception of evidence, that statute or rule shall govern rather than the federal rule of evidence, if the latter is narrower.[8] As might be expected, there is considerable variation in the latitude with which different administrative law judges apply these rules. The Board rarely reverses an administrative law judge because of his rulings on the admissibility of evidence.

The statute provides that evidence of conduct occurring more than six months before the filing and service of the charge cannot support a finding of unfair labor practice.[9] However, such evidence may be received at the hearing as background for the purpose of throwing light on occurrences which fall within the six-month period.[10]

Sec. 16–7. Documentary evidence.   In addition to calling witnesses and presenting oral testimony, all parties have the right to introduce into the record documentary evidence to the extent permitted by the administrative law judge.[11] Such exhibits must be introduced in the form of an original and one copy. The administrative law judge may grant a motion to substitute copies for originals of letters and documents already received in evidence.[12]

Sec. 16–8. Documents in possession of the Board or General Counsel. The Board's rules prohibit its personnel from producing or testifying about "any files, documents, reports, memoranda, or records of the

[5]R. and R. Sec. 102.38.
[6]R. and R. Sec. 102.42.
[7]Sec. 10(b).
[8]Rule 43(a).
[9]Sec. 10(b).
[10]NLRB v. Lundy Mfg. Corp., 316 F.2d 921, 53 LRRM 2106 (C.A. 2, 1963).
[11]R. and R. Sec. 102.38; Fontaine Truck Equipment Co., 193 NLRB No. 30, 78 LRRM 1191 (1971); cf. R-W Service System, Inc., 193 NLRB No. 100, 78 LRRM 1409 (1971).
[12]United Packinghouse Workers of America, 89 NLRB 310, 25 LRRM 1556 (1950).

Board," in response to a subpoena or otherwise, without the written consent of the Board or the General Counsel, whichever has control over the subject matter. Where a motion for the production of such documents (usually those in the General Counsel's file) is made in the course of the hearing and is denied by the administrative law judge, request for the material may be addressed to the General Counsel in Washington. If the General Counsel refuses to make the material available, permission to appeal from the administrative law judge's ruling may be asked of the Board in Washington.

Parties are entitled as a matter of right to obtain copies of pretrial statements in one situation: Where a witness called by counsel for the General Counsel has testified, opposing counsel may ask for and obtain a copy of any written, pretrial statement made by that witness. Such request, however, is inappropriate if made during either the General Counsel's examination of his witness or after the witness has been excused. The request should be made just prior to cross-examination of the witness.[13] If the counsel for the General Counsel then refuses to furnish the statement, the administrative law judge must strike the entire testimony of that witness.[14]

Sec. 16–9. The function of the administrative law judge. As presiding officer, the administrative law judge is responsible for the orderly conduct of the hearing and the preservation of the parties' rights at the hearing. The opening statement which he formerly made, setting forth the manner in which the hearing is conducted, is now served on the parties with the complaint. (See Facsimile No. 54, page 267.)

The administrative law judge also is charged with the duty of seeing that a complete record is made and that all pertinent facts are elicited. "The [judge] is not required to sit idly by and permit a confused or meaningless record to be made."[15] Accordingly, the administrative law judge has the authority to examine and cross-examine witnesses and, on his own motion, may call witnesses to the stand.

The Board has admonished its administrative law judges:[16]

It is appropriate . . . for the administrative law judge to direct the hearing so that it may be confined to material issues and conducted with all expeditiousness consonant with due process. . . . However, the

---

[13]R. W. Hughes Construction Company, Inc., 150 NLRB 455, 58 LRRM 2005 (1964); Al Ortale Rambler, 152 NLRB 1136, 59 LRRM 1326 (1965); American Rubber and Plastics Corp., 200 NLRB No. 127, 82 LRRM 1001 (1972).
[14]R. and R. Sec. 102.118; Jencks v. U.S., Ra-Rich Manufacturing Corp., 121 NLRB 700, 42 LRRM 1403 (1958); Harvey Aluminum, Inc., 139 NLRB 151, 51 LRRM 1288 (1962).
[15]NLRB v. Bryan Mfg. Co., 196 F.2d 477, 30 LRRM 2008 (C.A. 7, 1963).
[16]Indianapolis Glove Co., 88 NLRB 986, 25 LRRM 1424 (1950).

administrative law judge must guard against expediting a hearing by limiting either party in the full development of its case.

Again there is considerable variation in the approach of the individual administrative law judges, and a litigant sometimes faces the uncomfortable necessity of insisting on the right to full presentation of his case despite the obvious interest of the administrative law judge in expediting the hearing. In rare instances, where the administrative law judge has exceeded his authority and improperly limited a party, the Board and the courts have either: (a) remanded the case for rehearing[17] or (b) cured the error by accepting as true rejected offers of proof.[18]

The administrative law judge's findings on the credibility of a witness, based on his observation of the witness, are given great weight by the Board; they will not be overturned unless they are contrary to the clear preponderance of all the evidence in the record.[19]

The powers exercised by the administrative law judge, between the time he is designated and the time the case is transferred to the Board, are described by the Board's rules thus:[20]

1. To administer oaths and affirmations;
2. To grant applications for subpoenas;
3. To rule upon petitions to revoke subpoenas;
4. To rule upon offers of proof and receive relevant evidence;
5. To take or cause depositions to be taken;
6. To regulate the course of the hearing and, if necessary, to exclude persons or counsel from the hearing for contemptuous conduct, and to strike all related testimony of witnesses refusing to answer any proper question;
7. To hold conferences for the settlement or simplification of the issues by consent of the parties, but not to adjust cases;
8. To dispose of procedural requests, including motions referred to the administrative law judge by the regional director and motions to amend pleadings; also to dismiss complaints or portions of complaints; and to order hearings reopened or consolidated prior to issuance of administrative law judge decisions;
9. To make and file decisions in conformity with Section 8 of the Administrative Procedure Act, Public Law 89–54, U.S.C., Sec. 557.
10. To call, examine, and cross-examine witnesses, and to introduce into the record documentary or other evidence;

[17]Wheeler v. NLRB, 314 F.2d 260, 52 LRRM 2183 (C.A. D.C., 1963).
[18]Coca-Cola BQttling Co. of St. Louis, 95 NLRB 284, 28 LRRM 1309 (1951); Bethlehem Steel Co. v. NLRB, 120 F.2d 641, 8 LRRM 962 (C.A. D.C., 1941).
[19]Poinsett Lumber & Mfg. Co., 147 NLRB 1197, 56 LRRM 1381 (1964).
[20]R. and R. Sec. 102.35; Jefferson Stores, Inc., 201 NLRB No. 101, 82 LRRM 1316 (1973).

11. To request the parties at any time during the hearing to state their respective positions concerning any issue in the case or theory in support thereof; and

12. To take any other action necessary under the foregoing and authorized by the published Rules and Regulations of the Board.

Sec. 16–10. Function of counsel for the General Counsel. Counsel representing the General Counsel at the hearing has the task of presenting evidence to prove the allegations of the complaint; he always has the burden of proving a violation of the Act.[21] He is responsible for the manner and order in which the evidence is elicited in support of the complaint.

Sec. 16–11. Function of counsel for the charging party. Counsel for the party filing the charges is entitled to participate in the hearing,[22] and is entitled to examine witnesses and to introduce evidence on his own behalf as long as it does not jeopardize the prosecution of the complaint. It is to his advantage to work closely with, and in support of, the counsel for the General Counsel. He is ordinarily most effective when he concentrates on assisting the General Counsel's office in getting the facts. The manner and degree of participation in the hearing by the representative for the charging party should be carefully worked out with the counsel for the General Counsel. The prime responsibility for proving the case rests with the latter and the charging party who tries to "take over" from counsel for the General Counsel usually meets resistance from both that individual and the administrative law judge.

Sec. 16–12. Function of counsel for the accused party. The party charged with unfair labor practices has the full right to call and cross-examine witnesses, and to present documentary material in support of its case.

Sec. 16–13. Intervention at the hearing. Any person desiring to intervene in the case may make a request in writing before the hearing, or orally at the hearing.[23] (The procedure to be followed in the filing of a prehearing motion for intervention is set forth on page 261, under "Prehearing Motions.") The administrative law judge will rule upon such request during the hearing, permitting intervention to such extent and upon such terms as he may deem proper. Thus, legitimate interest in the proceeding is found and the motion to intervene granted where the moving party is signatory to a contract which is being attacked. A motion to

---

[21]NLRB v. Miami Coca-Cola Bottling Co., 222 F.2d 341, 36 LRRM 2153 (C.A. 5, 1955).
[22]Spector Freight System Inc., 141 NLRB 1110, 52 LRRM 1456 (1963).
[23]R. and R. Sec. 102.29.

intervene has also been granted to an employers' association where one of its members was the party charged with the unfair labor practices,[24] and to an employee in a refusal-to-bargain case where an issue of possible misrepresentation by a union agent in obtaining authorization cards was raised.[25] Such motions have been denied to: (a) a group of employees who had filed the petition in an earlier decertification proceeding;[26] and (b) a union signatory to a contract where the contract was not being attacked and the union would not be the subject of any remedial order.[27]

Sec. 16–14. Amendment of complaint. The General Counsel may move during the hearing to have the complaint amended;[28] no other party, including the charging party, is empowered to seek amendment of the complaint.[29] The administrative law judge's grant of such a motion must afford the affected party freedom from surprise and ample opportunity to defend and litigate the additional matters.[30] The administrative law judge may also grant a motion to amend the complaint and to reopen the hearing—after the original hearing has been closed and before his decision has been issued—to adduce evidence on matters which occurred after the close of the original hearing.[31] (See Sec. 15–3, page 258).

Sec. 16–15. Motions before the administrative law judge. All motions made at the hearing may be made in writing or stated on the record.[32] Motions made after the close of the hearing, but before the issuance of his decision, should be addressed to the administrative law judge, care of the Chief Administrative Law Judge, in Washington, or the associate chief administrative law judge in San Francisco, as the case may be, and copies served on the other parties.[33]

Rulings by the administrative law judge, if made during the hearing, will be stated orally for the record. In all other instances, the administrative law judge's rulings are made in writing and served on all the parties.

On motion made during the hearing, the administrative law judge may exercise his authority:

1. To grant the General Counsel's motion to dismiss a complaint.[34]

[24]Sterling Furniture Co., 94 NLRB 32, 28 LRRM 1007 (1951).
[25]Gary Steel Products Corp., 144 NLRB 1160, 54 LRRM 1211 (1963).
[26]Sanson Hosiery Mills, Inc., 92 NLRB 1102, 27 LRRM 1201 (1950).
[27]Consolidated Builders, Inc., 99 NLRB 972, 30 LRRM 1165 (1952).
[28]R. and R. Sec. 102.17.
[29]Sunbeam Plastics Corp., 144 NLRB 1010, 54 LRRM 1174 (1963).
[30]NLRB v. Dinion Coil Co., Inc., 201 F.2d 484, 31 LRRM 2223 (C.A. 2, 1952).
[31]International Longshoremen's and Warehousemen's Union, 90 NLRB 1021, 26 LRRM 1314 (1950).
[32]R. and R. Sec. 102.24.
[33]R. and R. Sec. 102.25.
[34]Swan Fastener Corp., 95 NLRB 503, 28 LRRM 1343 (1951).

2. To deny the General Counsel's motion to dismiss a complaint.[35]
3. To dismiss the complaint at the close of the General Counsel's presentation, before both sides have presented evidence.[36]
4. To deny a joint motion of the charging and charged parties to dismiss the complaint.[37]

Sec. 16–16. Appeals from the administrative law judge's ruling. All rulings by the administrative law judge are subject to review by the Board in Washington. Such review may be sought by a party at any of three stages:

1. During the hearing.
2. After the close of the hearing and before the issuance of the administrative law judge's decision.
3. After issuance of the administrative law judge's decision.

As a matter of right, a party may appeal from the administrative law judge's ruling after he has issued his decision by including the ruling in the exceptions to the administrative law judge's decision filed with the Board.[38]

However, the Board, in its discretion, may entertain an appeal from an administrative law judge's ruling when such appeal is made before the issuance of the administrative law judge's decision.[39] Where a party seeks to appeal a ruling at such an early stage—for example, during the hearing—it should:

1. Request the Board for special permission to appeal, indicating why such early appeal is being sought and why appeal cannot be postponed until issuance of the administrative law judge's decision;
2. State the ruling from which appeal is being taken, with supporting data to show why the administrative law judge's ruling should be reversed by the Board; and
3. Serve a copy upon each of the other parties.

In only one instance can parties appeal to the Board as a matter of right from an administrative law judge's ruling before issuance of his decision: where the administrative law judge has granted a motion to dismiss a

---

[35]General Maintenance Engineers, Inc., 142 NLRB 295, 53 LRRM 1034 (1963); Electrical Workers, IBEW, Local 1986 (Asplundh Tree Expert Co.), 161 NLRB 1397, 63 LRRM 1474 (1966).
[36]Cherry Rivet Co., 97 NLRB 1303, 29 LRRM 1237 (1952).
[37]Local 450 International Union of Operating Engineers, 117 NLRB 1301, 39 LRRM 1410 (1957).
[38]R. and R. Sec. 102.46.
[39]R. and R. Sec. 102.26.

complaint in its entirety.[40] Such request for review by the Board must be filed with the Board within 10 days from the date of the dismissal; otherwise the case will be closed. The General Counsel, as any other party, is entitled to ask the Board for review of the administrative law judge's dismissal of the complaint.[41]

Sec. 16–17. Stipulations at hearing. The General Counsel may enter into a stipulation with the party against whom the charge was filed, even though the charging party refuses to join in the stipulation. However, the charging party is entitled to introduce evidence either to contradict or to explain parts of the stipulation.[42]

The parties' stipulation that an employer is engaged in commerce within the meaning of the Act and that the Board should exercise jurisdiction is not binding on the Board; the Board may still determine whether assertion of jurisdiction would be contrary to its policy.[43] Stipulations as to jurisdictional facts, however, will be accepted by the Board.

Sec. 16–18. Official notice of proceedings. The administrative law judge may take official notice of proceedings before the Labor Board in other cases. If done, he must so state either on the record or in his decision, and the parties must be given an opportunity to show the contrary of any fact of which he took official notice.[44]

Sec. 16–19. Representation matters at hearing. The Board and the courts have held that a representation proceeding and a subsequent unfair labor practice case based on that proceeding "are really one."[45] Accordingly, issues relating to the validity of a Board certification resulting from a representation proceeding and decided in that proceeding may not be tried again in a later unfair labor practice hearing.[46] Thus, in an unfair labor practice hearing, the administrative law judge will reject evidence on any issue which has been litigated in a prior representation case where that evidence was available at the time of the earlier proceeding and even though no hearing was held during the processing of the representation case.[47]

[40]R. and R. Sec. 102.27.
[41]Collins Baking Co., 83 NLRB 599, 24 LRRM 1104 (1949).
[42]International Union, United Automobile, Aircraft, and Agricultural Implement Workers of America v. NLRB, 231 F.2d 237, 37 LRRM 2744 (C.A. 7, 1956).
[43]East Newark Realty Corp., 115 NLRB 483, 37 LRRM 1328 (1956).
[44]International Longshoremen's and Warehousemen's Union, Local 10, 102 NLRB 907, 31 LRRM 1416 (1953).
[45]Pittsburgh Plate Glass Co., v. NLRB, 313 U.S. 146, 8 LRRM 425 (1941); Smith Company, 200 NLRB No. 106, 82 LRRM 1270 (1972).
[46]*Ibid.*
[47]National Carbon Co., A Division of Union Carbide and Carbon Corp., 110 NLRB 2184, 35 LRRM 1413 (1954); Neuhoff Bros., Packers Inc., 154 NLRB No. 40, 59 LRRM 1761 (1965).

Furthermore, the Board has held that the administrative law judge lacks the authority to make a unit finding contrary to the earlier determination made by the Board in the representation proceeding.[48]

Sec. 16–20. Separation of witnesses.   Any party at the hearing may ask the administrative law judge to exclude prospective witnesses from the hearing room. In addition to counsel, at least one representative for each party is usually allowed to remain in the hearing room.[49] The Board has ruled that individuals who filed charges[50] and employees involved in discriminatory discharges[51] are entitled to remain in the hearing room during the taking of the entire testimony.

Sec. 16–21. Depositions.   Application for a deposition, if made during a hearing or after a hearing but before transfer of the case to the Board, must be filed with the administrative law judge.[52] The procedure followed is like that used for prehearing depositions except the administrative law judge acts on the application rather than the regional director. (See "Prehearing Application for a Deposition," page 261.) Thus, the application must set forth the reasons why, when, and where the deposition should be taken, and the matters concerning which it is expected the witness will testify. It should be served on the administrative law judge at least seven days before the date it is desired that the deposition be taken. The application is granted only if, in the exercise of his discretion, the administrative law judge finds "good cause" has been shown; for example the unavailability of a witness due to illness or distance from the place of hearing.

If the administrative law judge grants the application, he will issue an Order and Notice of Deposition and serve it on all parties. This Order and Notice will set forth:

1. The name of the witness.
2. The time and place of the testimony.
3. The name of the officer before whom the witness is to testify.

All parties must be permitted to examine and cross-examine witnesses.[53] Objections to questions or evidence must be made at the time of the examination; otherwise they are considered to be waived. The transcript of

[48]Kearney & Trecker Corp., 101 NLRB 1577, 31 LRRM 1255 (1952).
[49]Progressive Mine Workers of America v. NLRB, 187 F.2d 298, 27 LRRM 2334 (C.A. 7, 1951).
[50]Globe Wireless, Ltd., 88 NLRB 1262, 25 LRRM 1460 (1950).
[51]Jacques Power Saw Co., 85 NLRB 440, 24 LRRM 1412 (1949).
[52]R. and R. Sec. 102.30(a).
[53]R. and R. Sec. 102.30(c).

the testimony must be signed by the witness, or some explanation for the lack of signature must be indicated by the officer.

An original and two copies of the transcript will be sent by the officer taking the deposition to the administrative law judge. The administrative law judge rules upon the admissibility of all or any part of the deposition.[54]

Sec. 16–22. Subpoenas. Any party desiring a subpoena during the course of the hearing must file its request with the administrative law judge.[55] Notice of such application need not be communicated to the other parties. The Board's rules state that the application must be made in writing, but there is no requirement that the application either name the person whose testimony is desired or describe the documents sought to be presented.[56]

The party requesting a subpoena should state the type desired. There are two types:

1. The subpoena ad testificandum which requires the party served to appear for the sole purpose of giving testimony. (See Facsimile No. 19, page 108.)
2. The subpoena duces tecum which requires the party served to appear both to give testimony and to present certain documents named in the subpoena. (See Facsimile No. 20, page 110.) This type of subpoena should be served on the individual having custody of the documents desired, not merely on a company or a union.

The issuance of the subpoena is mandatory "upon application of any party."[57] Inasmuch as counsel for the General Counsel is "a party" to the proceeding, he, too, can secure the issuance of a subpoena by the administrative law judge.[58]

If the person against whom the subpoena is issued does not intend to comply, he has five days after the date of service of the subpoena to petition the administrative law judge to revoke.[59] Upon receipt of such written petition, the administrative law judge gives immediate notice to the party upon whose request the subpoena was issued.

Sec. 16–23. Petition to revoke subpoena. In ruling upon the petition to revoke the subpoena, the administrative law judge is required to make a

[54]R. and R. Sec. 102.30(d).
[55]R. and R. Sec. 102.31(a).
[56]*Ibid.*
[57]NLRB v. Central Oklahoma Milk Producers Assn., 285 F.2d 495, 47 LRRM 2294 (C.A. 10, 1960).
[58]NLRB v. Lewis Food Co., 357 U.S. 10, 42 LRRM 2209 (1958).
[59]R. and R. Sec. 102.31(b).

statement of the reasons for his decision. The Board's Rules provide that the subpoena shall be revoked if, in the administrative law judge's opinion:

1. The subpoena seeks evidence which does not relate to any matter under investigation.[60]
2. The subpoena does not describe with sufficient particularity the evidence sought.
3. The subpoena is invalid for any other reason sufficient in law.

The petition to revoke, any answer filed by the party seeking the subpoena, and the administrative law judge's ruling—unlike all other motions and rulings at the hearing—do not automatically become part of the official record of the case. They become part of the record only upon the request of the party who is aggrieved by the ruling.[61]

Failure to petition for revocation within the five days may bar the party from making a subsequent attack on a subpoena compelling him to produce the desired data.[62]

If any person refuses to comply with a subpoena which was issued upon the request of a private party, proceedings to enforce may be brought in the appropriate court.[63] Although enforcement must be instituted by the General Counsel, he acts routinely upon the request of the private party unless enforcement would be clearly inconsistent with the law and the policies of the Act. However, the General Counsel, by starting such action, does not assume the responsibility of prosecuting the matter before the court; the responsibility rests with the party who wants the subpoena enforced.[64]

Although it does not appear in its published decisions, the Board has ruled that refusal to honor a subpoena justifies the use of secondary evidence to prove the fact in question and that such refusal may preclude his later introduction of evidence respecting the issue.[65]

Sec. 16–24. Payment of witnesses. Witnesses who are subpoenaed to appear before the administrative law judge are entitled to fees and expenses for mileage equal to those paid witnesses in the federal courts;[66] i.e., $20 for each day they are required to appear, 10 cents per mile to and from the hearing, and, where required by travel distance to be away from home

[60]NLRB v. Playskool, Inc., et al., 74 LRRM 2662 (C.A. 7, 1970).
[61]R. and R. Sec. 102.31(b).
[62]NLRB v. Stanley Gemalo, 130 F.Supp. 500, 35 LRRM 2577 (D.C. S.N.Y., 1955).
[63]NLRB v. International Typographical Union, 76 F.Supp. 895, 21 LRRM 2483 (D.C. S.N.Y., 1948); see also Chapter 15, footnote 38, page 263.
[64]R. and R. Sec. 102.31(d).
[65]Plant City Welding & Tank Co., 123 NLRB 1146, 44 LRRM 1072 (1959); Southeastern Galvanizing Corp., Inc., 130 NLRB 123, 47 LRRM 1261 (1961).
[66]R. and R. Sec. 102.32.

overnight, an additional $16 per day. Witness fees and mileage are paid by the party at whose request the witnesses appear.[67]

Sec. 16–25. Conduct at the hearing.   Any objection with respect to the conduct of the hearing, including any objection to the introduction of evidence, may be stated orally or in writing. The objection should be accompanied by a statement of the grounds on which it is based. Both are included in the record of the hearing. Objections are not considered waived by further participation in the hearing.[68] Exception need not be taken to each adverse ruling upon objection as automatic exceptions are allowed.

If the administrative law judge rules any question to be improper, the witness need not answer it. If the administrative law judge rules the question to be proper and the witness still refuses to answer, the administrative law judge may, in his discretion, strike from the record all testimony previously given by the witness on related matters.[69]

Sec. 16–26. Misconduct at the hearing.   The Board's rules provide that misconduct at the hearing may be ground for the administrative law judge to exclude the offender from the hearing.[70] For example, an administrative law judge, with subsequent court approval, excluded counsel for one party from a hearing because of his contemptuous conduct in the hearing room.[71] Likewise, the administrative law judge may eject a witness from the hearing room in order to maintain order.[72]

In cases of "misconduct of an aggravated character," when engaged in by an attorney or other representative of a party, the Board may suspend or disbar the offender from further practice before it.[73]

The Board may initiate the disciplinary action on its own motion,[74] but the rules provide for "due notice and hearing" before the imposition of any discipline.[75] Such action has rarely been taken by the Board, but representatives were suspended from practice before the Board, or any of its agents, after a finding of "misconduct of an aggravated character in the following instances:"

1. A union representative was suspended for a period of six months; during a hearing recess period he had made threatening statements,

---

[67]NLRB Field Manual 11780. These fees do not apply in Alaska.
[68]R. and R. Sec. 102.41.
[69]R. and R. Sec. 102.44(c).
[70]Sec. 102.44(a).
[71]NLRB v. Weirton Steel Co., 135 F.2d 494, 12 LRRM 693 (C.A. 3, 1943).
[72]Wertheimer Stores Corp., 107 NLRB 1434, 33 LRRM 1398 (1954).
[73]R. and R. Sec. 102.44(b).
[74]Robert S. Cahoon, 106 NLRB 831, 32 LRRM 1568 (1953).
[75]R. and R. Sec. 102.44(b).

including threats of violence to the individual who had initiated the proceeding.[76]

2. An attorney was suspended for a period of 90 days; during the course of the hearing he had assaulted opposing counsel.[77]

Sec. 16–27. Claim of bias or prejudice. At any time before the administrative law judge issues his decision, any party may request him to withdraw from the case on grounds of personal bias or prejudice.[78] The party making such request should submit an affidavit to the administrative law judge setting forth in detail the matters alleged to constitute grounds for disqualification. This affidavit should be filed promptly upon the discovery of the alleged facts. Again, such affidavits are rarely filed.

If, in the opinion of the trial examiner, the affidavit is filed with due diligence and is sufficient on its face, he will disqualify himself and immediately withdraw from the case. If he does not disqualify himself and withdraw, he shall so rule on the record and give the grounds for his ruling. This ruling, as is the case with all others made by the administrative law judge, is subject to appeal to the Board.[79]

Sec. 16–28. Oral argument. Any party is entitled, upon request, to a reasonable period for oral argument at the close of the hearing before the administrative law judge.[80] Such arguments are included in the stenographic report of the hearing. Oral argument should be used only if the party does not desire to file a written brief. If made, the argument should be confined to the points on which clarification appears to be necessary. The essential facts should be emphasized, arguments as to credibility of witnesses made, and the legal principles involved pointed out.

Sec. 16–29. Briefs and proposed findings. In most cases, a more effective argument can be made by means of a written brief. Such briefs, as well as proposed findings, may be filed as a matter of right upon request made prior to the close of the hearing. The importance of an effective brief cannot be overemphasized. At the close of the hearing, all facts upon which the case will be decided are a part of the record, but they have not yet been organized into a coherent story. The party who carefully and accurately marshalls the facts in his brief to the administrative law judge will often

---

[76]Herbert J. Nichol, 111 NLRB 447, 35 LRRM 1489 (1955).
[77]Robert S. Cahoon, 106 NLRB 831, 32 LRRM 1568 (1953).
[78]R. and R. Sec. 102.37.
[79]R. and R. Sec. 102.37; Bob's Casing Crews, Inc., 80 LRRM 2090 (C.A. 5, 1972), enf. 78 LRRM 1060, see also 74 LRRM 2753; Tonkawa Refining Co., 79 LRRM 2103 (C.A. 10, 1971), enf. 76 LRRM 1269.
[80]R. and R. Sec. 102.42.

find the case being considered, in substantial part, from his statement of those facts.

A party's treatment of the law is equally important. Most administrative law judges are thoroughly versed in the application of the Act, but it is a complex law, subject to many interpretations, and a well-reasoned legal argument will carry great weight.

The brief should be concise. Long briefs containing repetitious factual statements, implausible legal arguments, or personal attacks on the Board, the administrative law judge, or opposing counsel are apt to receive little consideration.

The brief may be typewritten, mimeographed, or printed.[81] A copy must be served on each party. Three copies of the brief and a statement of service upon the other parties should be filed with the administrative law judge.[82]

The administrative law judge fixes the time, not to exceed 35 days from the close of the hearing, for the filing of briefs. Requests for extensions of time in which to file must be addressed to the Chief Administrative Law Judge in Washington, or Associate Chief Administrative Law Judge in San Francisco, as the case may be. Such requests if reasonable, are usually given favorable consideration. If one extension is granted, requests for additional time will be denied except in unusual circumstances. Notice of a request for extension of time must be served upon all other parties, and proof of such service should accompany the request.[83]

[81]R. and R. Sec. 102.46(j).
[82]R. and R. Sec. 102.42.
[83]*Ibid.*

CHAPTER 17

Unfair Labor Practice Posthearing
Procedures

Sec. 17–1. Substance and functions of the administrative law judge's decision. After the close of the hearing and the submission of briefs, if any, the administrative law judge prepares his decision based upon his consideration of all of the evidence, the briefs, and his own analysis of the applicable law. The decision contains the administrative law judge's findings of fact and conclusions of law, as well as the reasons for his determinations on all material issues. He also makes recommendations as to what action should be taken in the case.

The administrative law judge may recommend dismissal or uphold the complaint, in whole or in part. If he sustains the complaint, or any part of it, the administrative law judge recommends that the accused party cease and desist from the unlawful acts found and take action to remedy their effects.

While the administrative law judge's findings are entitled to be given great weight, his decision is not conclusive on the Board.[1] Thus, the Board is not bound by the administrative law judge's conclusions of fact or law.[2] However, because of the administrative law judge's opportunity to observe the demeanor of the witnesses, the Board usually accepts his credibility determinations and findings of fact,[3] and will not overturn them unless a preponderance of relevant evidence convinces the Board his resolution is incorrect.[4]

---

[1]Universal Camera Corp. v. NLRB, 340 U.S. 474, 27 LRRM 2373 (1951); Webster Outdoor Advertising Co., *sub nom.* Sign and Pictorial Local 1175, BPDP, 72 LRRM 2274 (C.A. D.C., 1969), *denying review of* 67 LRRM 1589.
[2]NLRB v. Chauffers, Teamsters, Warehousemen & Helpers Local Union No. 135, 212 F.2d 216, 34 LRRM 2058 (C.A. 7, 1954).
[3]Standard Dry Wall Products, Inc., 91 NLRB 544, 26 LRRM 1531 (1950), *enf.*, 188 F.2d 362, 27 LRRM 2631 (C.A. 3, 1954); Chamin Paper Products Co., 186 NLRB No. 89, 75 LRRM 1389 (1970).
[4]Poinsett Lumber and Mfg. Co., 147 NLRB 1197, 56 LRRM 1381 (1964); Mary Anne Bakeries, 164 NLRB 207, 65 LRRM 1071 (1967).

The administrative law judge's decision performs two important functions for the parties:

1. It affords the respondent an opportunity for immediate and voluntary compliance without the necessity of a Board order or a possible court decree.
2. It serves to define the issues to be argued before the Board in cases where any of the parties differ with the administrative law judge's appraisal of the case.

Copies of the administrative law judge's decision are filed with the Board in Washington and served upon each of the parties. Immediately upon receipt of the administrative law judge's decision, the Executive Secretary of the Board enters an order transferring the case to the Board. (See Facsimile No. 55, page 285.) The record of the case, as transferred to the Board, consists of: the charge, the complaint and notice of hearing, the answer, any amendments to the foregoing documents, motions, rulings, orders, the stenographic report of the hearing, stipulations, exhibits, documentary evidence, depositions, and the administrative law judge's decision. Even rejected exhibits are included in a rejected exhibit file. Thus, everything considered by the administrative law judge in his handling of the case is forwarded to the Board except the parties' briefs to the administrative law judge and motions and rulings on revocation of subpoenas which the moving party has not asked to be made a part of the record. If exceptions, cross-exceptions, or answering briefs are subsequently filed, these too become a part of the record before the Board.[5]

In cases where the General Counsel has exercised his discretion to seek an injunction and such injunction has issued but the administrative law judge recommends dismissal in his decision, the General Counsel will so advise the appropriate district court.[6] Discretion then lies with the district court as to whether it will modify or terminate the injunction.[7]

Sec. 17–2. Compliance with the administrative law judge's decision. The party against whom the complaint was issued may comply with the recommendations made in the administrative law judge's decision. All communications concerning such compliance should be addressed to the regional director who issued the complaint. In fact, immediately upon receipt of the administrative law judge's decision, the regional director sends out a letter in which he offers assistance to achieve early compliance.

[5]R. and R. Sec. 102.45.
[6]R. and R. Sec. 102.94(b).
[7]Evans v. International Typographical Union, 81 F. Supp. 675, 22 LRRM 2576 (D.C. S. Ind., 1948).

FORM NLRB-1405
(8-72)

UNITED STATES OF AMERICA
BEFORE THE NATIONAL LABOR RELATIONS BOARD

Case

ORDER TRANSFERRING PROCEEDING TO THE
NATIONAL LABOR RELATIONS BOARD

A hearing in the above-entitled proceeding having been held before a duly designated Administrative Law Judge and the Decision of the said Administrative Law Judge, a copy of which is annexed hereto, having been filed with the Board in Washington, D. C.,

IT IS HEREBY ORDERED, pursuant to Section 102.45 of National Labor Relations Board Rules and Regulations, that the above-entitled matter be, and it hereby is, transferred to and continued before the Board.

Dated, Washington, D. C.,

By direction of the Board:

_____
John C. Truesdale
Executive Secretary

NOTE: *Communications concerning compliance with the Decision of the Administrative Law Judge should be with the Director of the Regional Office issuing the complaint.*

Attention is specifically directed to the excerpts from the Rules and Regulations appearing on the page attached hereto.

Exceptions to the Decision of the Administrative Law Judge in this proceeding must be received by the Board in Washington, D. C., on or before

FACSIMILE No. 55.
Form of order transferring a case to the Board (Form 1405)

(See Facsimile No. 56, page 287.) However, such a letter will not be sent in any case where the Office of the General Counsel disagrees in whole or in part with the decision and intends to file exceptions to the decision with the Board.

If compliance with the administrative law judge's decision occurs and if no exceptions to the decision are filed, the Board normally will close the case, thereby ending the entire proceeding. However, even in the absence of exceptions and despite compliance, the Board may issue an order adopting as its own the decision and recommendations of the administrative law judge. The Board may take this step in any case where it feels that such decision is "necessary in order to effectuate the policies of the Act."[8]

Sec. 17–3. Failure to file exceptions to administrative law judge's decision. If no exceptions to the administrative law judge's decision are filed within 20 days after the case is transferred to it, the Board will automatically adopt the decision as its own.[9] The administrative law judge's decision thus acquires the force and effect of an order of the Board. In such cases the Board rarely seeks enforcement in the court of appeals but, where it does, it acts as if the parties have waived all objections for all purposes.[10] Accordingly, the Board will ask the court of appeals to issue a decree enforcing the Board's decision without considering the merits of the case.

Where the Board seeks such automatic enforcement of its decision, the court may concern itself only with two questions: (a) whether the party against whom the order issued was subject to the Act; and (b) whether the Board had jurisdiction to issue the order.[11] Beyond that, failure to file exceptions to the administrative law judge's decision is conclusive as to all issues, and the court will automatically enforce the Board's order.[12] Thus, for example, the court will not consider objections that:

1. There is no substantial evidence to support the Board's findings.[13]
2. The Board's remedial order is invalid.[14]
3. Exceptions were made orally during a telephone conversation with a Board employee.[15]

These cases are the exception. In most instances, the parties comply with the administrative law judge's decision or file exceptions.

---

[8]Statements of Procedure, Sec. 101.12(c).
[9]R. and R. Sec. 102.48(a).
[10]*Ibid.*
[11]NLRB v. Holger Hansen and Hansen Mfg. Co., 220 F.2d 733, 35 LRRM 2675 (C.A. 1, 1955).
[12]NLRB v. Pugh and Barr, Inc., 194 F.2d 217, 29 LRRM 2382 (C.A. 4, 1952).
[13]NLRB v. George Noroian Co., 193 F.2d 172, 29 LRRM 2201 (C.A. 9, 1951).
[14]NLRB v. Puerto Rico Steamship Assn., 211 F.2d 274, 33 LRRM 2755 (C.A. 1, 1954).
[15]NLRB v. Mooney Aircraft, 310 F.2d 565, 51 LRRM 2615 (C.A. 5, 1962).

NATIONAL LABOR RELATIONS BOARD

Regional Office

Respondent
Address

Re: Name and no. of case

Gentlemen:

You have recently received the Decision of Administrative Law Judge
_____ in the above case. Pursuant thereto, you are required to
notify me within 20 days of the receipt of that document what steps you have
taken or will take to comply.

Further litigation in this matter can be avoided by complying promptly and
completely with the Administrative Law Judge's recommendations. Compliance
Officer _____ will assist you in effecting compliance. If you have
any questions, please write or telephone Mr. _____.

I am enclosing _____ copies of the notice you will need in order to comply
with the terms of the recommended order. Please sign and date these; post
an appropriate number; and return three signed and dated copies with a
covering letter stating exactly when and where you posted other copies.

Pursuant to Section 102.48(a) of the Board's Rules and Regulations, failure
to file timely exceptions will automatically result in the Administrative
Law Judge's Decision becoming the Decision and Order of the Board.

/As soon as you offer reinstatement to the discriminatee(s) please
advise us and we shall assist you in computing back pay./

/If and when the charging union requests bargaining meetings, it
would be appreciated if you would keep a complete file of all correspondence and memoranda so that the character of the bargaining may be
evaluated if it becomes necessary to do so./

At the end of the posting period please advise me that the notices were
continuously and conspicuously posted. If and when you have fully complied
with the affirmative terms of the Administrative Law Judge's Decision, and
there are no reported violations of its negative provisions, we shall
notify you that your case has been "closed" on compliance.

Very truly yours,

Regional Director

FACSIMILE NO. 56.
*Form of letter sent by regional director regarding compliance
with the decision of the administrative law judge*

Sec. 17–4. Copies of documents submitted to the Board. The Board's rules set forth certain requirements which apply to all formal documents—motions, exceptions and briefs—which are submitted for its consideration:

1. Eight copies of formal documents must be presented.[16]
2. Such copies must be either printed or legibly duplicated; carbon copies of typewritten matter will not be accepted.[17]
3. Copies must be served upon all other parties, and proof or statement of such service given to the Board.[18]

Sec. 17–5. Motions. All motions filed after the issuance of the administrative law judge's decision must be filed with the Board in Washington.[19]

Sec. 17–6. Intervention. The Board's rules do not provide for intervention after the issuance of the administrative law judge's decision. However, the Board on occasion has entertained motions and granted permission for such intervention. Thus, for example, the Board granted permission to intervene where: (a) an employer sought to intervene in order to file exceptions to an administrative law judge's findings which related to its agreement with the union involved in the proceeding;[20] and (b) an international union sought to intervene in a proceeding involving one of its locals in order to file exceptions so as to protect "interests of the international and all of its other subordinate locals."[21]

Intervention for the purpose of filing an amicus curiae brief in important cases, particularly by trade associations or parent labor organizations, is more common. In some instances, the Board solicits such briefs where it is considering adoption of a new policy.

Sec. 17–7. Withdrawal of charge after issuance of administrative law judge's decision. A charge may be withdrawn after issuance of the administrative law judge's decision only if the Board consents to grant such motion.[22] Upon withdrawal of the charge, the complaint will be dismissed.

The Board has permitted withdrawal of charges where no party objected and the alleged unfair labor practices have ceased.[23] It has refused to permit withdrawal of charges where:

[16]Sec. 102.46(j).
[17]*Ibid.*
[18]*Ibid.*
[19]R. and R. Sec. 102.47.
[20]Newspaper and Mail Deliverers' Union of New York and Vicinity, 101 NLRB 589, 31 LRRM 1105 (1952).
[21]Honolulu Star-Bulletin, Ltd., 123 NLRB 395, 43 LRRM 1449 (1959).
[22]R. and R. Sec. 102.9.
[23]Voice of Alabama, Inc., 80 NLRB 1390 (1948).

1. The unfair labor practices have not been remedied, even in the absence of objections from any party.[24]
2. The General Counsel has objected.[25]

Sec. 17–8. Severance after issuance of administrative law judge's decision. Where, in a consolidated proceeding against more than one party, one of the parties complies fully with the recommendations of the administrative law judge's decision, the Board may sever the proceeding.[26] The case against the complying party usually will be closed; the case against the remaining party will continue to be processed. This sometimes occurs where an employer and a union are charged by an individual with maintaining an illegal hiring arrangement. If the remedy includes back pay, the complying party will be required to pay half the amount due. However, the case is not closed and, if the noncomplying party prevails on appeal, the Board will look to the complying party for the balance of the back pay.

Sec. 17–9. Exceptions to the administrative law judge's decision. As a matter of right any party—including the General Counsel—may file exceptions to the administrative law judge's decision, or to any other part of the record or proceedings;[27] it should not be overlooked that exceptions may be filed to any rulings made prior to or during the hearing. Eight copies of the exceptions must be filed with the Board within 20 days—or within any further period as the Board may allow—from the date of service of the order transferring the case to the Board. Copies of the exceptions must be served immediately upon all other parties and the regional director.

Parties should comply strictly with these filing requirements. For example, the Board has ruled that no timely exceptions were filed where: (a) only one copy of the exceptions was filed with the Board, or it was in summary form;[28] and (b) a party failed to serve a copy of its exceptions upon the regional director.[29] The Board is sometimes more lenient than its published decisions indicate, particularly when dealing with those inexperienced in handling Board matters, and one court refused summary enforcement of the Board's order where exceptions filed one day late due to extraordinary circumstances had been rejected by the Board.[30] Neverthe-

[24]Yawman & Erbe Mfg. Co., 89 NLRB 881, 26 LRRM 1052 (1950).
[25]International Longshoremen's and Warehousemen's Workers Union, 90 NLRB 1021, 26 LRRM 1314 (1950).
[26]Atlantic Freight Lines, Inc., 117 NLRB 464, 39 LRRM 1256 (1957).
[27]R. and R. Sec. 102.46(a).
[28]Whitlock Corp., 103 NLRB 909, 31 LRRM 1597 (1953); Pat Izzi Trucking Co., 149 NLRB 1097, 57 LRRM 1474 (1964).
[29]Franklin County Sugar Co., 100 NLRB 228, 30 LRRM 1256 (1952).
[30]NLRB v. Marshall Maintenance Corp., 320 F.2d 641, 53 LRRM 2895 (C.A. 3, 1963); Teleservice Co. of Wyoming Valley, 149 NLRB 1053, 57 LRRM 1413 (1964).

less, there is no reason to jeopardize one's case by carelessness in following the rules for filing.

The Board's rules require that each exception:

1. Shall set forth specifically the questions of procedure, fact, law, or policy to which exceptions are taken.
2. Shall identify that part of the administrative law judge's decision to which objection is made.
3. Shall designate by precise citation of page the portions of the record relied upon (line citations are no longer required).
4. Shall state the grounds for the exceptions and shall include the citation of authorities unless set forth in a supporting brief.

Any exception which fails to comply with these requirements may be disregarded.[31]

The Board's rules provide: "No matter not included in a statement of exceptions may thereafter be urged before the Board, or in any further proceedings."[32] The Act states: "No objection that has not been urged before the Board . . . shall be considered by the court, unless the failure or neglect to urge such objection shall be excused because of extraordinary circumstances."[33] Accordingly, the utmost care should be taken in the analysis of the administrative law judge's decision and the drafting of the statement of exceptions; the exceptions must be specific in order to preserve the points for consideration by the court of appeals.[34] The courts have repeatedly held that they cannot consider objections which have not been urged before the Board.[35]

Sec. 17–10. Briefs. As a matter of right each party may file a brief in support of its statement of exceptions.[36] The brief shall contain no matter not included within the scope of the exceptions and shall contain the following:

1. A concise statement of the case containing all that is material to the consideration of the questions presented.
2. A specification of the questions involved and to be argued.
3. The argument, presenting clearly the points of fact and law relied upon in support of the position taken on each question, with specific

---

[31]Sec. 102.46(b); Hunter Metal Industries, Inc., 155 NLRB No. 41, 60 LRRM 1342 (1965); American Federation of Unions, 205 NLRB No. 100, 84 LRRM 1142 (1973).
[32]Sec. 102.46(h).
[33]Sec. 10(3).
[34]NLRB v. Cheney California Lumber Co., 327 U.S. 385, 17 LRRM 819 (1946).
[35]NLRB v. Star Beef Co., 193 NLRB F.2d 8, 29 LRRM 2190 (C.A. 1, 1951); cf. NLRB v. Goldblatt, 286 F.2d 665, 47 LRRM 2365 (1961).
[36]R. and R. Sec. 102.46(a).

page reference to the transcript and the legal or other material relied upon.[37]

4. An index if over 20 pages in length.

The brief to the Board, like that to the administrative law judge, should be concise. Care should be taken to correct factual errors or misplaced emphasis in the administrative law judge's decision. Discussion of applicable law should both present the party's view of the case and specifically meet conflicting theories found in the decision.

Incorporation by reference of the brief to the administrative law judge is not recommended. That brief is directed to a single individual who heard the case and observed the witnesses. A brief to the Board must interest and persuade the Board members and their legal assistants, none of whom will have previously participated in the case and all of whom will be working from the formal written record. Moreover, the Board members themselves rarely read the record but must rely for both the facts and the law on briefs of the parties and memoranda prepared by their legal assistants. Their time is limited. Short, accurate briefs which avoid repetition and irrelevancies are more likely to be read and digested.

The brief in support of exceptions should be filed and served at the same time and in the same manner as the exceptions, but as a separate document.[38]

It should be kept in mind that, as a matter of right, a party who is satisfied with the administrative law judge's decision may file a brief in support.[39]

Sec. 17–11. Answering brief. Whenever exceptions are filed, any party may, within 10 days, file an answering brief limited to questions raised in the exceptions and/or may file cross-exceptions relating to any portion of the administrative law judge's decision. The answering brief must present clearly the points of fact and law relied upon in support of the position taken on each question.[40] Comments made above with respect to the brief in support of exceptions are equally applicable here. Cross-exceptions may be filed only by a party who has not previously filed exceptions. A supporting brief may be filed along with the cross-exceptions.[41]

Sec. 17–12. Cross-exceptions and answering brief. Frequently the administrative law judge will dismiss certain allegations in a complaint and sustain others. When this occurs a party may find that, for all practical

[37]R. and R. Sec. 102.46(c).
[38]R. and R. Sec. 102.46(a) and (j).
[39]R. and R. Sec. 102.46(a).
[40]R. and R. Sec. 102.46(d).
[41]R. and R. Sec. 102.46(e).

purposes, he has won his case, even though he disagrees with the administrative law judge's findings on minor issues. As a result, if the opposing party does not file exceptions, the party who won may not be interested in taking the case to the Board by filing exceptions with respect to the minor issues. At the same time, he may be uncertain as to whether the loser will file exceptions, in which event the winner would want to file a brief in support of the administrative law judge's decision and exceptions to the minor issues lost.

When faced with this set of circumstances, the winning party may do nothing until the time for filing exceptions has expired. If the loser files exceptions, the winner may then file cross-exceptions to the portion of the decision which he considers adverse and file a brief in support of these cross-exceptions. In other words, the filing of exceptions by either party serves to keep the entire matter alive and thus enables the other party to protect his position by filing cross-exceptions to any portion of the decision. Moreover, although a brief in support of the decision must be filed within the 20-day time limit for filing exceptions, if such a brief is not filed by the winner and exceptions are filed by the loser, the winner can file a reply brief which, from a practical standpoint, would serve the same purpose as the brief in support.

Whenever any party files cross-exceptions, any other party may file within 10 days an answering brief to the cross-exceptions. The answering brief must be limited to the questions raised in the cross-exceptions.[42]

Sec. 17–13. Oral argument. Any party desiring to argue orally before the Board should address a written request to the Board's executive secretary simultaneously with the filing of its statement of exceptions or cross-exceptions.[43] It is within the Board's discretion whether or not to grant the request.[44] Although there have been many comments, including some from the Board members themselves, about the desirability of more oral arguments, pressure of the Board's workload has kept the number to a small fraction of the Board's caseload. As a rule, the Board has granted the request only where the case involves:

1. A basic policy question.
2. A question whose resolution may be precedent-setting.
3. Matters on which the Board may wish to hear arguments more fully developed than those set forth in written briefs.

[42]R. and R. Sec. 102.46(f).
[43]R. and R. Sec. 102.46(i).
[44]NLRB v. Luzerne Hide & Tallow, 188 F.2d 439, 27 LRRM 2537 (C.A. 3, 1951).

Whenever the Board grants a party's request for oral argument, all parties are served with a notice of hearing. (See Facsimile No. 24, page 131.) The oral argument is usually conducted before the Board in Washington. Each party to the proceeding is entitled to 30 minutes' argument. Request for additional time may not be granted unless timely application is made in advance of oral argument.

Sec. 17–14. Reopening of record after administrative law judge's decision.
Although neither the Act nor the Board's rules provide that parties may request reopening of the record after issuance of the administrative law judge's decision and before issuance of the Board's decision, the Board has authority to order the record reopened, and it has entertained motions filed for this purpose. It has then ruled on the basis of whether or not material evidence sought to be introduced was known and available at the time of hearing.[45] The Act does provide for the possible reopening of the record after the issuance of the Board's decision and after its submission to a court.[46]

Sec. 17–15. The Board's decision and order. If exceptions are filed to the administrative law judge's decision, the Board makes its decision on the basis of the entire written record.[47] However, where exception is taken to a factual finding of the administrative law judge, the Board, in determining whether the finding is contrary to a preponderance of the evidence, may limit its consideration to such portions of the record as are specified in the exceptions, the supporting brief, and the answering brief.[48] The Board is precluded from consulting the administrative law judge or any agent of the General Counsel.[49]

The Board may delegate its powers to a panel of three members.[50] Where two of four participating Board members disagree with a finding of an administrative law judge, the latter's finding is left unchanged.[51]

The statute requires the Board to base its findings "upon the preponderance of the testimony taken."[52] The Board, with judicial approval, has taken the position that it may take official notice of findings in proceedings before it in other matters, even absent a request from the

[45]R. and R. Sec. 102.48(b); A. M. Andrews Co., 112 NLRB 626, 36 LRRM 1093 (1955).
[46]Sec. 10(e).
[47]R. and R. Sec. 102.48(b).
[48]R. and R. Sec. 102.48(c).
[49]Sec. 4(a) of Act and Sec. 101.12 Statements of Procedure.
[50]Sec. 3(b) of Act.
[51]The Newton Co., 112 NLRB 465, 36 LRRM 1054 (1955).
[52]Sec. 10(c) of Act.

parties, provided the parties are given an opportunity to show the contrary of any fact of which the Board has taken notice.[53]

Sec. 17–16. Board's decision and order—Effect of administrative law judge's decision. The Board is not bound by the administrative law judge's decision.[54] The Board's decision may adopt, modify, or reject the findings, conclusions, and recommendations of the administrative law judge.[55] For example, courts have held:

1. The Board's decision may add to the administrative law judge's recommendations any order which the Board deems warranted by the evidence.[56]
2. The Board may make findings as to matters litigated at the hearing but not considered by the administrative law judge.[57]
3. The Board is not required to make a specific ruling on each and every exception to the administrative law judge's decision where the Board's decision adopts the findings of the administrative law judge and informs the party of its rulings on exceptions.[58]
4. If the Board rejects the administrative law judge's findings, it must state the basis for its disagreement, not merely that it disagrees.[59]

Sec. 17–17. Form of Board decisions. The Board's decision and order may take one of two forms:

1. Where the Board adopts the findings and conclusions of the administrative law judge, the Board may issue a "short form" decision incorporating the order of the administrative law judge in the decision upon which it is based.[60]
2. It may contain detailed findings of fact, conclusions of law, the reasons underlying the decision, and an order. The courts have held that the Board's decision must be based on explicit findings; the Board's "action cannot be upheld (by a court) merely because findings might have been made and considerations disclosed which

[53]NLRB v. Crowley's Milk Co., 208 F.2d 444, 33 LRRM 2110 (C.A. 3, 1953); Sears, Roebuck and Co. v. NLRB, 79 LRRM 2942 (D.C. D.C., 1972).
[54]NLRB v. The Item Co., 220 F.2d 956, 35 LRRM 2709 (C.A. 5, 1955); Chef Nathan Sez Eat Here, Inc., 75 LRRM 2605 (C.A. 3, 1970), *enf.* 73 LRRM 1340.
[55]Statements of Procedure Sec. 101.12.
[56]NLRB v. Oregon Worsted Co., 94 F.2d 671, 1–A LRRM 638 (C.A. 9, 1938).
[57]NLRB v. The Item Co., 220 F.2d 956, 35 LRRM 2709 (C.A. 5, 1955).
[58]NLRB v. State Center Warehouse and Cold Storage Co., 193 F.2d 156, 29 LRRM 2209 (C.A. 9, 1951); NLRB v. Champa Linen Service Co., 324 F.2d 28, 54 LRRM 2418 (C.A. 10, 1963).
[59]Retail Store Employees Union v. NLRB, 360 F.2d 494, 59 LRRM 2763 (C.A. D.C., 1965); F. W. Means and Co., 65 LRRM 2227 (C.A. 7, 1967), *denying enforcement to* 61 LRRM 1561.
[60]NLRB v. Jasper Chair Co., 138 F.2d 756, 13 LRRM 593 (C.A. 7, 1943).

would justify (the) order. . . . There must be . . . a responsible finding."[61]

The Board's decision may uphold or dismiss the entire complaint, or it may uphold and dismiss various allegations of the complaint. Where it makes a finding of unfair labor practices, the Board is authorized to frame an order in two parts:[62]

1. A negative part, ordering the party found guilty of unfair labor practices to cease and desist from such practices.
2. An affirmative part, directing the action required to remedy the violation.

Sec. 17–18. Cease-and-desist orders.

The courts have held that the Board must issue orders to "cease and desist" whenever it finds unfair labor practices,[63] and that the Board has broad power to determine the scope of its orders.[64] Thus, for example, the courts have upheld the Board's cease-and-desist orders against certain unfair labor practices in:

1. An entire territorial jurisdiction of a union district, where the Board found that the union's unfair labor practices at certain locations were committed pursuant to an areawide policy.[65]
2. All plants of a company where the Board found that the unfair labor practices at certain plants were committed pursuant to a systemwide and centrally directed company policy.[66]

However, the courts have held that the Board's cease-and-desist order may only be broad enough to restrain: (a) the specific violations; (b) any related act; and (c) other violations only where there is a finding of a threat of recurrence.[67] For example, the Board may not issue a broad cease-and-desist order where the violation consisted of an isolated act and there appears no likelihood of future unfair labor practices.[68] Thus, the Supreme Court has said:[69]

[61]S.E.C. v. Chenery Corp., 318 U.S. 80.
[62]Sec. 10(c).
[63]NLRB v. Express Publishing Co., 312 U.S. 426, 8 LRRM 415 (1941); Communication Workers v. NLRB, 376 U.S. 479, 46 LRRM 2033 (1960).
[64]NLRB v. United Mine Workers of America, District 23, 195 F.2d 961, 30 LRRM 2022 (C.A. 6, 1952).
[65]Ibid.
[66]NLRB v. Salant and Salant, Inc., 183 F.2d 462, 26 LRRM 2234 (C.A. 6, 1950).
[67]NLRB v. Express Publishing Co., 312 U.S. 426, 8 LRRM 415 (1941).
[68]Krambo Food Stores, Inc., 106 NLRB 870, 32 LRRM 1596 (1953).
[69]NLRB v. Express Publishing Co., 312 U.S. 426, 8 LRRM 415 (1941).

To justify an order restraining other violations it must appear that they bear some resemblance to that which the employer has committed or that danger in the future is to be anticipated from the course of his conduct in the past . . . The National Labor Relations Act does not contemplate that an employer who has unlawfully refused to bargain . . . shall, for the indefinite future, conduct his labor relations at the peril of a summons for contempt on the Board's allegation, for example, that he has discriminated against a labor union in the discharge of an employee. . . .

Sec. 17–19. Affirmative orders. Unlike the cease-and-desist order, which the Board must issue in every case where it finds an unfair labor practice, the Board has discretion in ordering affirmative action.[70] The courts have held that the Board has wide discretion to frame the affirmative order. The Supreme Court has said that the Board may order "such affirmative action . . . as will effectuate the Act";[71] "it is for the Board, not the courts, to determine how the effect of unfair labor practices may be expunged."[72] However, the Supreme Court has also ruled that the Board's discretion is not unlimited.[73] Thus, it has held that the Board may not issue punitive orders; its orders may be remedial only.[74]

Within this area of wide discretion the Board has fashioned a variety of affirmative orders; for example, the Board has ordered, with subsequent court approval:

1. The hiring of certain applicants for employment.[75]
2. The reimbursement of dues and initiation fees by a union.[76]
3. The refunding to employees of the amounts collected by a union for work permits.[77]
4. The reinstatement of supervisors (who were discharged because they failed to obstruct union activities).[78]
5. The payment of back pay by an employer to employees who were not ordered reinstated.[79]

[70]Eichleay Corp. v. NLRB, 206 F.2d 799, 32 LRRM 2628 (C.A. 3, 1953).
[71]Phelps Dodge Corp. v. NLRB, 313 U.S. 177, 8 LRRM 439 (1941).
[72]Franks Bros. Co. v. NLRB, 321 U.S. 702, 14 LRRM 591 (1944).
[73]Gullett Gin Co. v. NLRB, 340 U.S. 361, 27 LRRM 2230 (1951).
[74]Consolidated Edison Co. v. NLRB, 305 U.S. 197, 3 LRRM 646 (1938); Local 60, Carpenters v. NLRB, 365 U.S. 651, 47 LRRM 2900 (1961).
[75]Phelps Dodge Corp. v. NLRB, 313 U.S. 177, 8 LRRM 439 (1941).
[76]NLRB v. Local 404, International Brotherhood of Teamsters, Chauffeurs, Warehousemen and Helpers, 205 F.2d 99, 32 LRRM 2255 (C.A. 1, 1953).
[77]NLRB v. Local 420, United Association of Journeymen and Apprentices of the Plumbing and Pipefitting Industry, 239 F.2d, 39 LRRM 2173 (C.A. 3, 1956).
[78]NLRB v. Talladega Cotton Factory, Inc., 213 F.2d 209, 34 LRRM 2196 (C.A. 5, 1954).
[79]NLRB v. West Coast Casket Co., Inc., 205 F.2d 902, 32 LRRM 2353 (C.A. 9, 1953).

6. The payment of back pay for the entire period even though the trial examiner found that the discharge was not discriminatory.[80]
7. The adding of 6 percent per annum interest to back-pay awards made to employees who have been discriminatorily separated from their employment.[81]
8. The resumption of a portion of a business contracted out for discriminatory reasons.[82]
9. The choice by an employer between reading the notice that is usually posted or having it read by a Board agent.[83]

The Board likewise has exercised its wide discretion to frame orders to bring about the reinstatement of employees without prejudice to their rights and privileges; thus, for example, the courts have approved Board orders to reinstate employees and restore their seniority rights,[84] insurance rights,[85] sick benefits,[86] and retirement benefits.[87]

Sec. 17–20. Notices. Every Board order carries a requirement for the posting of notices setting forth the action taken to remedy the specific unfair labor practices. In the case of unfair labor practices committed by a labor organization, such notices may be:
1. Posted at the union's meeting hall.
2. Mailed to the employees against whom the unfair labor practices were committed.
3. If the employer is willing, posted at the place of employment.

In the case of unfair labor practices committed by an employer, the notices usually are posted prominently at the place of business. Various types of prepared notices are available at the regional offices, each notice tailored to fit the particular unfair labor practice. (See Facsimiles No. 57 through 63, pages 298 through 304.)

Sec. 17–21. Reconsideration of Board's decision. Any party to a Board proceeding may file a motion for reconsideration, rehearing, or reopening of the record. Such motion must be filed within 20 days after service of the Board's decision and order, except that, when based on newly discovered

---

[80]Reserve Supply Corp. v. NLRB, 317 F.2d 785, 53 LRRM 2374 (C.A. 2, 1963).
[81]Isis Plumbing & Heating Co., 138 NLRB 716, 51 LRRM 1122 (1962).
[82]Fibreboard Paper Products Corp., 138 NLRB 550, 51 LRRM 1101, *enf.,* 322 F.2d 411, 53 LRRM 2666 (C.A. D.C., 1963), *aff'd,* 379 U.S. 203, 215–217, 57 LRRM 2609 (1964); Town and Country Mfg. Co., Inc. v. NLRB, 316 F.2d 846, 53 LRRM 2054 (C.A. 5, 1963).
[83]J. P. Stevens and Co. v. NLRB, 388 F.2d 892, 67 LRRM 2145 (C.A. 2, 1967).
[84]NLRB v. American Mfg. Co., 106 F.2d 61, 4 LRRM 563 (C.A. 2, 1939).
[85]Continental Oil Co. v. NLRB, 113 F.2d 473, 6 LRRM 1020 (C.A. 10, 1940).
[86]Butler Bros. v. NLRB, 134 F.2d 981, 12 LRRM 620 (C.A. 7, 1943).
[87]NLRB v. Phoenix Mutual Life Insurance Co., 167 F.2d 983, 22 LRRM 2089 (C.A. 7, 1948).

FORM NLRB–4726
(4–71)

NOTICE TO MEMBERS

POSTED BY ORDER OF THE
NATIONAL LABOR RELATIONS BOARD
AN AGENCY OF THE UNITED STATES GOVERNMENT

WE WILL NOT engage in, or induce or encourage any
individual employed by CHATTANOOGA DIVISION, VULCAN
MATERIALS COMPANY, to engage in a strike or refusal in the
course of such individual's employment to use, manufacture,
process, transport, or otherwise handle or work on any goods,
articles, materials or commodities, or to perform any services,
where an object thereof is to force or require CHATTANOOGA
DIVISION, VULCAN MATERIALS COMPANY to cease doing business
with persons engaged in commerce, or in an industry affecting
commerce, or to force or require persons engaged in commerce
or an industry affecting commerce to cease doing business with
CHATTANOOGA DIVISION, VULCAN MATERIALS COMPANY.

WE WILL NOT threaten, coerce or restrain CHATTANOOGA DIVISION,
VULCAN MATERIALS COMPANY, or any other person engaged in
commerce or in an industry affecting commerce, where an object
thereof is to force or require CHATTANOOGA DIVISION, VULCAN
MATERIALS COMPANY, to cease doing business with persons engaged
in commerce or in an industry affecting commerce, or to force or
require persons engaged in commerce or in an industry affecting
commerce to cease doing business with CHATTANOOGA DIVISION,
VULCAN MATERIALS COMPANY.

LOCAL

LOCAL UNION NO. 391, INTERNATIONAL
BROTHERHOOD OF TEAMSTERS, CW & H of A
(Labor Organization)

Dated_____ By_____
                                         (Representative)   (Title)

THIS IS AN OFFICIAL NOTICE AND MUST NOT BE DEFACED BY ANYONE

This notice must remain posted for 60 consecutive days from the date of posting and must not be altered, defaced,
or covered by any other material. Any questions concerning this notice or compliance with its provisions may be directed
to the Board's Office,

FACSIMILE No. 57.
Form of notice used in a secondary boycott case

FORM NLRB–4820
(5–72)

NOTICE

TO ALL PRESENT AND FORMER EMPLOYEES OF [EMPLOYER'S NAME]

PURSUANT TO

A DECISION AND ORDER

of the National Labor Relations Board, and in order to effectuate
the policies of the National Labor Relations Act, as amended, we
hereby give notice that:

WE, [UNION NAME] WILL NOT threaten employees of
[Employer's name] with loss of employment or
other reprisals if they do not join said labor
organization.

WE, all the undersigned, WILL NOT assault, attempt
to assault, or threaten the Company's employees
with reprisals if they refuse to support a strike
at the Company's said plant; or engage in picketing
in such a manner as to bar employees from entering
or leaving the plant; or in any other manner restrain
or coerce the Company's employees in the exercise
of their right to self-organization, to form, join,
or assist labor organizations, to bargain collectively
through representatives of their own choosing, and
to engage in other concerted activities for the
purpose of collective bargaining or other mutual
aid or protection, and to refrain from any or all
of such activities as guaranteed to them by Section
7 of the Act.

　　　　　　　　　　　　　　　　_____
　　　　　　　　　　　　　　　　(Labor Organization)

　　　　　　　　　　By　_____
　　　　　　　　　　　　　　　　(Name and Title of Officer)

　　　　　　　　　　　　　　　　_____
　　　　　　　　　　　　　　　　(Labor Organization)

　　　　　　　　　　By　_____
　　　　　　　　　　　　　　　　(Name and Title of Officer)

　　　　　　　　　　　　　　　　_____
Dated _____　　　(Agent)

THIS IS AN OFFICIAL NOTICE AND MUST NOT BE DEFACED BY ANYONE

This notice must remain posted for 60 consecutive days from the date of posting and must not be altered, defaced,
or covered by any other material. Any questions concerning this notice or compliance with its provisions may be directed
to the Board's Office,

FACSIMILE No. 58.
Form of notice used in a case of coercion
by a local and international union and an agent

FORM NLRB–4820
(5–72)

NOTICE

TO ALL OFFICERS, REPRESENTATIVES, AGENTS AND
MEMBERS OF THE UNITED METAL PRODUCTS, MACHINERY,
AND RELATED EQUIPMENT WORKERS OF AMERICA

PURSUANT TO

A DECISION AND ORDER

of the National Labor Relations Board, and in order to effectuate
the policies of the National Labor Relations Act, as amended, we
hereby notify you that:

WE WILL NOT refuse to bargain collectively as the
exclusive representative of the employees in the
units found appropriate in the Intermediate Report
of the Administrative Law Judge in Cases Nos. 15-CB-
21, 15-CB-22, 15-CB-23, and 15-CB-24, with the Muntz
Machinery Corp., Cliffside Metals, Inc., Redda Metal
Products, and Carcutt Lead Pipes, Inc., respectively,
with respect to rates of pay, wages, hours of employment,
and other conditions of employment of the employees in
such units:

WE WILL NOT require, instruct, or induce our representatives
or agents to require that the above-named Companies execute
contracts which expressly, or in their performance, make
membership in UMP a condition of employment, except in
accordance with the provisos in Section 8(a)(3) of the
aforesaid Act:

WE WILL NOT direct, instigate, encourage, approve, or
ratify strike action for the purpose of requiring that the
above-named Companies execute contracts which expressly, or
in their performance, make membership in UMP a condition of
employment, except in accordance with the provisos in
Section 8(a)(3) of the aforesaid Act.

WE WILL NOT cause, or attempt to cause, the above-named
Companies to discriminate in any manner against their
respective employees, in violation of Section 8(a)(3) of
the aforesaid Act.

_____
(Labor organization)

Dated _____ By _____
                          (Representative)   (Title)

THIS IS AN OFFICIAL NOTICE AND MUST NOT BE DEFACED BY ANYONE

This notice must remain posted for 60 consecutive days from the date of posting and must not be altered, defaced,
or covered by any other material. Any questions concerning this notice or compliance with its provisions may be directed
to the Board's Office,

FACSIMILE NO. 59.
*Form of notice used in a case of a union's refusal
to bargain and insistence upon an illegal hiring clause*

FORM NLRB–4727
(9–69)

NOTICE TO EMPLOYEES

POSTED BY ORDER OF THE
NATIONAL LABOR RELATIONS BOARD
AN AGENCY OF THE UNITED STATES GOVERNMENT

WE WILL NOT in any manner interfere with, restrain, or coerce
our employees in the exercise of their right to self-organization,
to form labor organizations, to join or assist

or any other labor organization, to bargain collectively through
representatives of their own choosing, or to engage in concerted
activities for the purpose of collective bargaining or other
mutual aid or protection, or to refrain from any or all such
activities except to the extent that such right may be affected
by an agreement requiring membership in a labor organization
as a condition of employment as authorized in Section 8(a)(3)
of the Act, as modified by the Labor-Management Reporting and
Disclosure Act of 1959. All our employees are free to become
or remain members of this union, or any other labor organization.

_____
(Employer)

Dated _____ By _____
(Representative)   (Title)

THIS IS AN OFFICIAL NOTICE AND MUST NOT BE DEFACED BY ANYONE

This notice must remain posted for 60 consecutive days from the date of posting and must not be altered, defaced,
or covered by any other material. Any questions concerning this notice or compliance with its provisions may be directed
to the Board's Office,

FACSIMILE NO. 60.
Form of notice used in a case of employer interference or coercion

FORM NLRB-4727
(9-69)

NOTICE TO EMPLOYEES

POSTED BY ORDER OF THE
NATIONAL LABOR RELATIONS BOARD
AN AGENCY OF THE UNITED STATES GOVERNMENT

WE WILL NOT in any manner interfere with, restrain, or coerce
our employees in the exercise of their right to self-
organization, to form labor organizations, to join or
assist

or any other labor organization, to bargain collectively
through representatives of their own choosing, or to engage
in concerted activities for the purpose of collective
bargaining or other mutual aid or protection, or to refrain
from any or all of such activities except to the extent that
such right may be affected by an agreement requiring membership in a labor organization as a condition of employment
as authorized in Section 8(a)(3) of the Act, as modified
by the Labor-Management Reporting and Disclosure Act of
1959.

WE WILL OFFER to the employees named below immediate and full
reinstatement to their former or substantially equivalent
positions without prejudice to any seniority or other rights
and privileges previously enjoyed, and make them whole for any
loss of pay suffered as a result of the discrimination against
them, with interest thereon at 6 percent.

All our employees are free to become or remain members of the
above-named union or any other labor organization. We will not
discriminate in regard to hire or tenure of employment or any
term or condition of employment against any employee because of
membership in or activity on behalf of any such labor organization.

_____
(Employer)

Dated _____ By _____
                                      (Representative)   (Title)

THIS IS AN OFFICIAL NOTICE AND MUST NOT BE DEFACED BY ANYONE

This notice must remain posted for 60 consecutive days from the date of posting and must not be altered, defaced,
or covered by any other material. Any questions concerning this notice or compliance with its provisions may be directed
to the Board's Office,

FACSIMILE NO. 61.
Form of notice used in a case of discriminatorily discharged employees

FORM NLRB-4727
(9-69)

NOTICE TO EMPLOYEES

POSTED BY ORDER OF THE
NATIONAL LABOR RELATIONS BOARD
AN AGENCY OF THE UNITED STATES GOVERNMENT

WE WILL NOT in any manner interfere with, restrain, or coerce our employees in the exercise of their right to self-organization, to form labor organizations, to join or assist

or any other labor organization, to bargain collectively through representatives of their own choosing, or to engage in concerted activities for the purpose of collective bargaining or other mutual aid or protection, or to refrain from any or all of such activities except to the extent that such right may be affected by an agreement requiring membership in a labor organization as a condition of employment as authorized in Section 8(a)(3) of the Act, as modified by the Labor-Management Reporting and Disclosure Act of 1959. All our employees are free to become or remain members of this union, or any other labor organization.

WE WILL BARGAIN collectively upon request with the above-named union as the exclusive representative of all employees in the bargaining unit described herein with respect to rates of pay, hours of employment or other conditions of employment, and if an understanding is reached, embody such understanding in a signed agreement. The bargaining unit is:

_____
(Employer)

Dated _____ By _____
(Representative)   (Title)

THIS IS AN OFFICIAL NOTICE AND MUST NOT BE DEFACED BY ANYONE

This notice must remain posted for 60 consecutive days from the date of posting and must not be altered, defaced, or covered by any other material. Any questions concerning this notice or compliance with its provisions may be directed to the Board's Office,

FACSIMILE NO. 62.
Form of notice used in a case of an employer's refusal to bargain

FORM NLRB–4727
(9–69)

NOTICE TO EMPLOYEES

POSTED BY ORDER OF THE
NATIONAL LABOR RELATIONS BOARD
AN AGENCY OF THE UNITED STATES GOVERNMENT

WE HEREBY DISESTABLISH as the representative of any of our employees for the purpose of dealing with us concerning grievances, labor disputes, wages, rates of pay, hours of employment, or other conditions of employment, and we will not recognize it or any successor thereto for any of the above purposes.

WE WILL NOT dominate or interfere with the formation or administration of any labor organization or contribute financial or other support to it.

WE WILL NOT in any manner interfere with, restrain, or coerce our employees in the exercise of their right to self-organization, to form labor organizations, to join or assist

or any other labor organization, to bargain collectively through representatives of their own choosing, or to engage in concerted activities for the purpose of collective bargaining or other mutual aid or protection, or to refrain from any or all of such activities except to the extent that such right may be affected by an agreement requiring membership in a labor organization as a condition of employment as authorized in Section 8(a)(3) of the Act, as modified by the Labor-Management Reporting and Disclosure Act of 1959. All our employees are free to become or remain members of this union, or any other labor organization.

_____
(Employer)

Dated _____ By _____
                                 (Representative)   (Title)

THIS IS AN OFFICIAL NOTICE AND MUST NOT BE DEFACED BY ANYONE

This notice must remain posted for 60 consecutive days from the date of posting and must not be altered, defaced, or covered by any other material. Any questions concerning this notice or compliance with its provisions may be directed to the Board's Office,

FACSIMILE No. 63.
Form of notice used in a case of employer domination or interference with the formation or administration of a labor organization

evidence, it may be filed promptly on the discovery of that evidence. The motions must be based on "extraordinary circumstances" and only newly discovered evidence which has become available since the close of the hearing, or evidence which the Board believes should have been taken at the hearing, will be taken at any further hearing. The filing and pendency of such motions does not operate to stay the effectiveness of the Board's order unless so ordered.[88] This is not significant with respect to seeking review of a Board order in a court of appeals as the statute places no time limit within which an appeal must be filed.

The Board's policy has been to refer any motion for reconsideration to the same Board panel which made the decision; that panel, however, may refer such motion to the full Board for its consideration.[89]

Sec. 17–22. Compliance with the Board's decision. All communications and conferences concerning compliance with the terms of the Board's decision should be had with the regional director who issued the complaint. Immediately upon receipt of the Board's decision from Washington, the regional director sends out a letter in which he offers assistance to achieve early compliance. (See Facsimile No. 64, page 306.) Failing to obtain compliance with the Board's decision, the regional director will so report to the Board in Washington. Mere failure to comply with the Board's decision does not constitute a violation of the Act.[90] Also, the decision and order of the Board is not self-enforcing. Thus, there are no fines, jail sentences, or other sanctions for failure to submit to the Board's decision.

Sec. 17–23. Enforcement of the Board's decision. Consequently, if the party against whom the order is issued does not comply, the Board must either close the case or petition the appropriate United States court of appeals for enforcement of its order; in other words, enforcement is permissive and not mandatory upon the Board.[91] The courts have ruled that there is no time limit within which the Board must file a petition for enforcement;[92] the Board's order does not become stale because of nonenforcement.[93] (See Chart No. 8, page 307, for NLRB Order-Enforcement Chart.)

The statute requires the Board to file its petition for enforcement in the court of appeals for the circuit either: (a) where the alleged unfair labor practices occurred; or (b) where the party against whom the order issued

[88]R. and R. Sec. 102.48(d); Franklin Homes, Inc., NLRB No. 10–CA–8037, –8097, 76 LRRM 1412 (1971), *denied reconsid. en banc* 76 LRRM 1085.
[89]Enterprise Industrial Piping Co., 118 NLRB 1, 40 LRRM 1114 (1957).
[90]Harris-Woodson Co., Inc., 77 NLRB 819, 22 LRRM 1083 (1948).
[91]NLRB v. Pool Mfg. Co., 339 U.S. 577, 26 LRRM 2127 (1950); Stock Restaurant v. McLeod, 312 F.2d 105, 52 LRRM 2271 (C.A. 2, 1963).
[92]NLRB v. Todd Co., Inc., 173 F.2d 705, 23 LRRM 2534 (C.A. 2, 1949).
[93]NLRB v. Cannon Mfg. Corp., 177 F.2d 197, 25 LRRM 2001 (C.A. 9, 1949).

NATIONAL LABOR RELATIONS BOARD

Regional Office

Respondent
Address

Re: Name and no. of case

Gentlemen:

You have recently received the /Decision and Order of the Board/ /Judgment
of the Court of Appeals/ in the above case. Pursuant thereto, you are required
to notify me within 20 days of the receipt of that document what steps you
have taken or will take to comply.

Further formal action in this matter can be avoided by complying promptly and
completely with the /Decision and Order of the Board/ /Judgment of the Court
of Appeals/. Compliance Officer _____ will assist you in effecting
compliance. If you have any questions, please write or telephone Mr. _____.

I am enclosing _____copies of the notice you will need in order to comply
with the terms of the /Order/ /Judgment/. Please sign and date these; post an
appropriate number; and return three signed and dated copies with a covering
letter stating exactly where and when you posted other copies.

   /As soon as you offer reinstatement to the discriminatee(s) please
   advise us and we shall assist you in computing back pay/.

   /If and when the charging union requests bargaining meetings, it would
   be appreciated if you would keep a complete file of all correspondence
   and memoranda so that the character of the bargaining may be evaluated if
   it becomes necessary to do so./

At the end of the posting period please advise me that the notices were
continuously and conspicuously posted. If and when you have fully complied
with the affirmative terms of the /Order/ /Judgment/ and there are no
reported violations of its negative provision, we shall notify you that the
case has been "closed" on compliance.

                                        Very truly yours,

                                        Regional Director

FACSIMILE No. 64.

*Form of letter sent by regional director regarding compliance
with the decision and order of the Board or a decree of the court of appeals*

NLRB ORDER ENFORCEMENT CHART

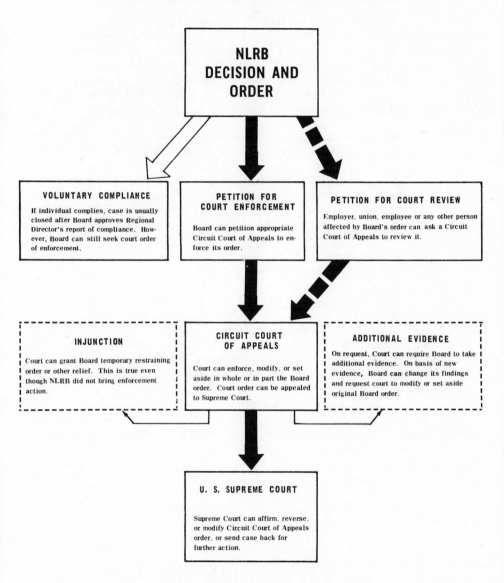

NLRB DECISION AND ORDER

VOLUNTARY COMPLIANCE

If individual complies, case is usually closed after Board approves Regional Director's report of compliance. However, Board can still seek court order of enforcement.

PETITION FOR COURT ENFORCEMENT

Board can petition appropriate Circuit Court of Appeals to enforce its order.

PETITION FOR COURT REVIEW

Employer, union, employee or any other person affected by Board's order can ask a Circuit Court of Appeals to review it.

INJUNCTION

Court can grant Board temporary restraining order or other relief. This is true even though NLRB did not bring enforcement action.

CIRCUIT COURT OF APPEALS

Court can enforce, modify, or set aside in whole or in part the Board order. Court order can be appealed to Supreme Court.

ADDITIONAL EVIDENCE

On request, Court can require Board to take additional evidence. On basis of new evidence, Board can change its findings and request court to modify or set aside original Board order.

U. S. SUPREME COURT

Supreme Court can affirm, reverse, or modify Circuit Court of Appeals order, or send case back for further action.

CHART NO. 8. *NLRB order enforcement chart*

resides or conducts business.[94] The Board uniformly files its petition in that court of appeals within whose geographical jurisdiction the alleged unfair labor practices occurred.

Sec. 17–24. Review of the Board's decision.   Parties aggrieved by a "final order" of the Board need not wait for the Board to seek enforcement of its order. The statute enables them to file a petition to review that order in the appropriate United States court of appeals.[95] A "final order" has been defined by the courts to mean an order "either dismissing a complaint . . . or directing a remedy for the unfair labor practice found."[96] Accordingly, review of a Board decision may be sought by:

1. The party against whom an order is issued.
2. The party who filed the charge, where the Board dismissed any allegation of unfair labor practice. Thus, the courts have permitted charging parties such as: (a) individual discriminatees to seek review of the Board's order dismissing the complaint;[97] and (b) an employer to seek review of that part of an order which dismissed part of a complaint alleging unfair labor practices by a labor organization.[98]
3. In petitioning for review, private parties may not seek enforcement of any part of a Board order which is favorable to them; the Board alone may seek enforcement.[99]

A party who disagrees with the Board's theory of the case may not petition for review unless aggrieved by the Board's order.[100]

If the party which seeks court review of the Board's order of dismissal of the complaint is successful in getting the court to reverse the Board, the court will not fashion a remedy for the unfair labor practices. The most that the court will do is to remand the case to the Board with instructions to issue an order in accordance with the court's decision.[101]

The statute permits parties who seek review of Board orders to file their petitions in the court of appeals for the circuit either: (a) where the alleged unfair labor practices occurred; or (b) where the parties reside or conduct business; or (c) in the District of Columbia.[102]

The statute states that the commencement of proceedings to enforce or review a Board order does not operate as a stay of that order, unless

---

[94]Sec. 10(e).
[95]Sec. 10(f).
[96]Lincourt v. NLRB, 170 F.2d 306, 23 LRRM 2015 (C.A. 1, 1948).
[97]Charles Albrecht v. NLRB, 181 F.2d 652, 26 LRRM 2158 (C.A. 7, 1950).
[98]American Newspaper Publishers Assn. v. NLRB, 190 F.2d 45, 28 LRRM 2157 (C.A. 7, 1951).
[99]*Ibid.*
[100]Deaton Truck Line, Inc. v. NLRB, 337 F.2d 697, 57 LRRM 2209 (C.A. 5, 1964).
[101]NLRB v. Kelley & Picerne, Inc., 298 F.2d 895, 49 LRRM 2663 (C.A. 1, 1962).
[102]Sec. 10(f).

specifically directed by the court.[103] Because the orders are not self-enforcing the provision is of little practical significance.

The courts have held that the Board may seek and the courts may grant enforcement of the Board's order, even though the order has been obeyed,[104] or even if changed circumstances indicate less need for the order than at the time it was originally issued by the Board.[105] In the words of the Supreme Court:[106]

> The employer's compliance with an order of the Board does not render the cause moot, depriving the Board of its opportunity to secure enforcement from an appropriate court. . . . A Board order imposes a continuing obligation; and the Board is entitled to have the resumption of the unfair labor practice barred by an enforcement decree.

The procedure to be followed in the preparation of records and handling of cases in the United States court of appeals varies from circuit to circuit. For a complete discussion see *Briefing and Arguing Federal Appeals* by Frederick Bernays Wiener (Washington: BNA Books, 1967).

If the Board's order is enforced, the Court enters a decree. This decree is in the nature of a continuing injunction; disobedience to it is punishable in a contempt proceeding. Only the Board, and no other party, can institute a contempt proceeding.[107]

[103]Sec. 10(g).
[104]NLRB v. Pennsylvania Greyhound Lines, Inc., 303 U.S. 261, 2 LRRM 599 (1938).
[105]NLRB v. Crompton-Highland Mills, Inc., 337 U.S. 217, 24 LRRM 2088 (1949).
[106]NLRB v. Mexia Textile Mills, 339 U.S. 563, 26 LRRM 2123 (1950).
[107]Amalgamated Utility Workers v. Consolidated Edison Co. of New York, 309 U.S. 261, 6 LRRM 669 (1940).

CHAPTER 18

Back-Pay Proceedings

Sec. 18–1. In general. The Board's remedy in a case of discrimination calls for "restoration of the situation, as nearly as possible, to that which would have obtained but for the illegal discrimination."[1] Accordingly, the obligation of back pay, whether imposed on an employer, a labor organization, or both, is designed only to correct the situation caused by an unfair labor practice; back pay cannot be computed either to reward an individual[2] or punish the party which committed the unfair labor practice,[3] nor does it relieve an individual from his obligation to take reasonable steps to secure work during the period of discrimination and thereby mitigate the respondent's back-pay liability.[4] Recently, however, the Board has begun to require reimbursement to parties of some expenditures resulting from unfair labor practices, e.g., litigation expenses.[5]

Sec. 18–2. Definitions of back pay. The Board has established certain procedures for cases which involve the payment of back pay. It is important to understand the definitions of the various terms which the Board uses before describing those procedures:

1. Back-pay period: The period beginning with the date of the discrimination and ending with the date a bona fide offer of reinstatement, if made.[6]
2. Gross back pay: The amount of money a back-pay claimant would have earned had he not been the subject of discrimination.[7] Included in this term are not only his wages but other sums of money or the

[1]Phelps Dodge Corp. v. NLRB, 313 U.S. 177, 8 LRRM 439 (1941).
[2]NLRB v. Stilley Plywood Co., Inc., 199 F.2d 319, 31 LRRM 2014 (C.A. 4, 1952).
[3]Republic Steel Corp. v. NLRB, 311 U.S. 7, 7 LRRM 287 (1940).
[4]NLRB v. Madison Courier, Inc., 80 LRRM 3377, 3386 (C.A. D.C., 1972); Madison Courier, Inc., 202 NLRB No. 115, 82 LRRM 1667 (1973), *suppl'g* 162 NLRB 550, 64 LRRM 1148.
[5]Heck's, Inc., 215 NLRB No. 142, 88 LRRM 1049 (1974); Gasoline Retailers Association of Metropolitan Chicago, 210 NLRM No. 58, 86 LRRM 1011 (1974); General Counsel's Memo, January 22, 1975, 88 LRRM 136.
[6]A.P.W. Products Co., Inc., 137 NLRB 25, 50 LRRM 1042 (1902); Ferrell-Hicks Chevrolet, Inc., 160 NLRB No. 134, 58 LRRM 1006 (1965).
[7]Harvest Queen Mill & Elevator Co., 90 NLRB 320, 26 LRRM 1189 (1950).

equivalent which he would have received, such as bonuses,[8] vacation pay,[9] and tips.[10]

3. Interim earnings: The money a back-pay claimant actually earned at other work during the back-pay period. Included is any money the claimant received for work performed upon federal, state, county, municipal, or other work-relief projects.[11] It does not include: money received from a "second job" held prior to the discrimination; union benefits;[12] unemployment compensation.[13]

4. Expenses: Expenses the back-pay claimant incurred in seeking and holding other employment during the back-pay period which he would not have incurred had he not been the subject of discrimination, such as transportation, room and board, and family moving expenses.[14]

5. Net interim earnings: Interim earnings less expenses.

6. Net back pay: Gross back pay less net interim earnings.[15] This is the amount which should be paid to the back-pay claimant, plus "fringe" benefits which would have been received less those received in interim employment.

7. Excepted periods: A period of time in which the back-pay claimant was not available for work, for reasons such as military service,[16] strike,[17] pregnancy,[18] or illness. However, if the discriminatee's inability to work was due to events which would not have occurred or to environmental factors which would not have existed absent the unlawful discrimination, the disability will be attributed to the discrimination, and back pay will be awarded.[19] During excepted

[8]Story Oldsmobile Inc., 145 NLRB No. 1647, 55 LRRM 1217 (1964); Hickman Garment Co., 196 NLRB No. 51, 80 LRRM 1684 (1972), suppl'g 69 LRRM 1517; Nicky Chevrolet Sales, Inc., 195 NLRB No. 76, 79 LRRM 1460 (1972), suppl'g 63 LRRM 1135.
[9]Barberton Plastics Products, Inc., 146 NLRB 54, 55 LRRM 1337 (1964).
[10]Home Restaurant Drive-In, 127 NLRB 635, 46 LRRM 1065 (1960).
[11]Republic Steel Corp. v. NLRB, 311 U.S. 7, 7 LRRM 287 (1940).
[12]NLRB v. Brashear Freight Lines, Inc., 127 F.2d 198, 10 LRRM 578 (C.A. 8, 1942); Golay and Co., Inc., Lee Cylinder Div., 184 NLRB No. 28, 76 LRRM 1110 (1970), suppl'g 61 LRRM 1239.
[13]Gullet Gin Co., Inc. v. NLRB, 340 U.S. 361, 27 LRRM 2230 (1951); Southern Household Products Co., 203 NLRB No. 138, 83 LRRM 1247 (1973), suppl'g 73 LRRM 1361.
[14]Brown & Root, Inc., 132 NLRB 486, 48 LRRM 1391, enf., 311 F.2d 447, 52 LRRM 2115 (C.A. 8, 1963); Southern Household Products Co., 203 NLRB No 138, 83 LRRM 1247 (1973), suppl'g 73 LRRM 1361.
[15]Harvest Queen Mill & Elevator Co., 90 NLRB 320, 26 LRRM 1189 (1950).
[16]NLRB v. Gluek Brewing Co., 144 F.2d 847, 14 LRRM 912 (C.A. 8, 1944).
[17]NLRB v. Globe Wireless, Ltd., 193 F.2d 748, 29 LRRM 2319 (C.A. 9, 1951).
[18]Mastro Plastics Corp., 136 NLRB 1342, 50 LRRM 1006 (1962).
[19]East Texas Steel Castings Co., 116 NLRB 1336, 38 LRRM 1470 (1956); American Mfg. Co., 167 NLRB No. 71, 66 LRRM 1123 (1967); M.F.A. Milling Co., 170 NLRB No. 111, 68 LRRM 1077 (1968); Associated Transport Co. of Texas, Inc., 194 NLRB No. 12, 78 LRRM 1678 (1971).

periods, gross back pay is not credited to the claimant; nor are net interim earnings deducted from gross back pay.

Sec. 18–3. Instructions for back-pay purposes. Upon issuance of a complaint alleging discrimination, the Board's regional office will give each employee involved:

1. A pamphlet explaining back-pay computation, records the employee should keep, and instructions that he is under an obligation to make reasonable efforts to secure other employment during the back-pay period.[20] (See Facsimile No. 65, page 314.)
2. A Social Security form to be signed and returned by the employee to the Labor Board. This form authorizes the Social Security Administration to supply the Board with a record of the worker's employment and earnings during the back-pay period. (See Facsimile No. 66, page 315.)[21]
3. A form to keep the regional office informed of where he can be reached. (See Facsimile No. 67, page 316.)

As for recordkeeping by the party who committed the unfair labor practice, the Board's back-pay order contains the following language:

Preserve and make available to the Board or its agents upon request, for examination and copying, all payroll records, social security payment records, time cards, personnel records and reports, and all other records necessary to analyze the amounts of back pay due and the rights of employment under the terms of this Order.

At the appropriate time (for example, after issuance of the Board's back-pay order), when compliance is being effectuated, the party against whom the order issued may be supplied with a form for computation of gross back pay. (See Facsimile No. 68, page 317.) This form is to be completed and returned to the Board agent.

Sec. 18–4. Computing gross back pay. There is no single formula for computing gross back pay to cover every situation. The basic aim of the computation is to reflect fairly what the claimant would have earned during the back-pay period but for the discrimination. Accordingly, the computation should take into account all normal pay-rate changes and

---

[20]Southern Silk Mills, Inc., 116 NLRB 769, 38 LRRM 1317 (1956); American Bottling Co., 116 NLRB 1303, 38 LRRM 1465 (1956); Madison Courier Inc., 202 NLRB No. 115, 82 LRRM 1667 (1973), *suppl'g* 64 LRRM 1148.
[21]Associated Transport Co. of Texas, Inc., 194 NLRB No. 12, 78 LRRM 1678 (1971).

FORM NLRB-4288
(1-68)

NATIONAL LABOR RELATIONS BOARD

INFORMATION FOR EMPLOYEES ON BACK PAY

1. PURPOSE OF THIS LEAFLET

Your name has been included in a complaint issued by the General Counsel of the National Labor Relations Board. This may result in a decision that you have been illegally discharged, laid off, demoted, or refused employment. The National Labor Relations Board may decide that you are entitled to back pay because of this. We will need your help to find out how much the back pay will be. The purpose of this leaflet is to tell you how we compute back pay and how you can help us. It is important to remember, however, that the charges concerning your discharge may be dismissed. If this happens, you will not receive back pay.

2. WHAT YOU SHOULD DO IMMEDIATELY

Fill out the enclosed forms and return them to us in the self-addressed envelope.

INSTRUCTIONS FOR FILLING OUT FORMS:

NLRB-916 - Back Pay Claimant Identification
Type or print in ink all the information asked for in the form.

NLRB-4180 - Authorization to Social Security Administration to Furnish Employment and Earnings Information
3 forms are enclosed. Sign each one, in ink, after the word "SIGNATURE", and print your full name, date of birth and Social Security number on the top line if this information does not already appear there. This form will give us authorization to get a report from the Social Security Administration of your interim earnings during your back pay period.

NOW FOLD THE ENCLOSED FOUR FORMS, PLACE IN THE ENCLOSED ENVELOPE, AND DROP IN THE MAIL. NO POSTAGE STAMP IS NEEDED.

FACSIMILE NO. 65.
Leaflet containing information for employees on back pay

FORM NLRB-4180
(9-72)

NATIONAL LABOR RELATIONS BOARD

AUTHORIZATION TO SOCIAL SECURITY ADMINISTRATION
TO FURNISH EMPLOYMENT AND EARNINGS INFORMATION

SOCIAL SECURITY NUMBER	DATE OF BIRTH	PLEASE SUPPLY THIS INFORMATION FOR THE PERIOD
NAME		FROM _____ TO _____
NLRB CASE NAME AND NUMBER		

I hereby authorize the Social Security Administration to forward to the Regional Office of the National Labor Relations Board the record (by quarters) of my places of employment, employers' addresses, and corresponding earnings.

Signature _____

N.L.R.B. REGIONAL OFFICE ADDRESS:

FACSIMILE No. 66.
*Authorization to Social Security Administration
to furnish employment and earnings information*

FORM NLRB-916
(1-65)

Form Approved
Budget Bureau No. 64-R008.11

NATIONAL LABOR RELATIONS BOARD

BACK PAY CLAIMANT IDENTIFICATION

1. NAME OF CLAIMANT (Mr., Mrs., Miss.)

2. DATE OF BIRTH

3. SOCIAL SECURITY NO.

A. MAIDEN NAME, IF MARRIED

B. OTHER NAMES USED, IF ANY

4. ADDRESS (Street and No., City, State and ZIP Code, NOTIFY REGIONAL OFFICE OF NLRB OF NEW ADDRESS IF YOU MOVE)

5. TELEPHONE NO.

6. LIST BELOW FRIENDS OR RELATIVES WHO WILL KNOW WHERE YOU ARE IN CASE YOU MOVE

NAME	ADDRESS	TELEPHONE NUMBER

7. SUPPLY THE FOLLOWING INFORMATION REGARDING YOUR EMPLOYMENT AT

_____
(Name of Company)

CASE NO.

A. NAME OF DEPARTMENT YOU WERE IN AT TIME OF UNFAIR LABOR PRACTICE

C. DATE YOU STARTED WORK-ING FOR THIS COMPANY

B. KIND OF JOB YOU HAD AT TIME OF UNFAIR LABOR PRACTICE

GPO 886-031

FACSIMILE No. 67.
Form for back-pay claimant identification

FORM NLRB-4312 (8-65)	COMPUTATION OF BACK PAY		YEAR	QUARTER
CASE NO.			EXCEPTED PERIOD(S)	
NAME		SOCIAL SECURITY NO.		
JOB TITLE AND DEPARTMENT				

BACK PAY COMPUTATION FOR CALENDAR QUARTER

1. NUMBER OF HOURS, DAYS OR WEEKS						
2. HOURLY, DAILY OR WEEKLY RATE OF PAY	$		$		$	
3. PRODUCT: ITEM 1 X ITEM 2	$		$		$	
4. BONUS AND OTHER					$	
5. QUARTERLY TOTAL GROSS BACK PAY						$

6. QUARTERLY INTERIM EARNINGS AND EXPENSES	EARNINGS	EXPENSES
TOTALS	$	$

7. QUARTERLY NET INTERIM EARNINGS		$
8. NET BACK PAY FOR QUARTER *(Item 5 minus Item 7)*		$
9. INTEREST *(See Note below)*	FROM: _____ THROUGH _____ *No. days*	$ _____ *Interest*
10. TOTAL NET BACK PAY PLUS INTEREST *(Item 8 plus Item 9)*		$

NOTE: *Interest will not be computed, usually, until a tender of the backpay due has been made or a date for payment has been agreed upon, since interest accrues until that date.*

FACSIMILE NO. 68
Form for computation of gross back pay

changes in hours worked, such as overtime,[22] seasonal shutdown,[23] layoff period,[24] or promotion.[25]

The Board order always calls for back-pay computations to be performed in accordance with the Woolworth formula, i.e., on the basis of separate calendar quarters. These quarterly periods begin with the first day of January, April, July, and October. Earnings in one particular quarter have no effect upon the back pay liability for any other quarter.[26] Payment of 6 percent interest is also required.[27]

Sec. 18–5. Computing net back pay.   The Board agent will compute the net back pay on the basis of:

1. The claimant's sworn statement, which is checked.
2. The Social Security Administration's report of interim earnings.
3. The computation of gross back pay by the party who committed the discrimination, which is checked.

After completion of his computation, the Board agent submits to the party who is to make the payment of back pay: (a) the net back-pay computation; (b) the report of the Social Security Administration; and (c) appropriate portions of the claimant's sworn statement.

The employer is required: (a) to deduct from the net back-pay bill the sums he would normally have deducted from wages for deposit with state and federal agencies on account of social security and other similar benefits; and (b) to pay the deducted sums to such agencies. This requirement does not apply to a labor organization where it is the only party against whom the back-pay order is issued; in such instance, the labor organization is required to pay the employee the entire amount of net back pay without making deductions for such benefits.[28]

Back-pay computations are rarely free from controversy, particularly if there have been extended periods of unemployment or intermittent employment on the part of the discriminatee. Formal back-pay proceedings are complicated and expensive for the Government as well as the parties. Therefore settlement possibilities should always be carefully considered.

[22]Hall Electric Co., 111 NLRB 68, 35 LRRM 1414.
[23]NLRB v. Nelson Manufacturing Co., 120 F.2d 444, 8 LRRM 837 (C.A. 8, 1941).
[24]NLRB v. Carolina Mills, Inc., 190 F.2d 675, 28 LRRM 2323 (C.A. 4, 1951).
[25]Underwood Machinery Co., 95 NLRB 1386, 28 LRRM 1447 (1951).
[26]F. W. Woolworth Co., 90 NLRB 289, 26 LRRM 1185 (1950); NLRB v. Seven-Up Bottling Co. of Miami, Inc., 344 U.S. 344, 31 LRRM 2237 (1953); Southern Household Products Co., 203 NLRB No. 138, 83 LRRM 1247 (1973), suppl'g 73 LRRM 1361.
[27]Isis Plumbing and Heating Co., 138 NLRB 716, 51 LRRM 1123 (1962); Fugua Homes Missouri, Inc., 201 NLRB No. 13, 82 LRRM 1142 (1973); Webber American, Inc., 202 NLRB No. 129, 82 LRRM 1733 (1973), suppl'g 79 LRRM 1058.
[28]Lancaster Transportation Co., 116 NLRB 399, 38 LRRM 1254 (1956); cf. Operating Engineers, Local 925 (T.L. Manta, Inc.), 180 NLRB No. 117, 76 LRRM 1856 (1970), suppl'g 60 LRRM 1009.

The Board does not consider itself bound by a compromise back-pay settlement negotiated by a regional director after issuance of an order.[29] Thus, such settlement does not become final until it is approved by the Board.

Sec. 18–6. Back-pay specification.

The Board may institute a separate and formal back-pay proceeding where:

1. An agreement as to the net back pay cannot be reached, after a court decree enforcing the Board's order.[30]
2. Enforcement of the Board's back-pay order is pending in court.[31]
3. The Board is of the opinion that a formal computation and hearing may result in compliance with its back-pay order, without the necessity of a court decree.[32]

The back-pay proceeding is started by the regional director's service of a "back-pay specification" upon the party who is liable for the back pay, as well as upon other parties in the case.[33] Attached to the specification will be a notice of hearing before an administrative law judge. The charging party may participate in the hearing.[34]

In accord with the Board's rules, the specification must "specifically and in detail show, for each employee, the back pay periods broken down by calendar quarters, the specific figures and basis of computation as to gross back pay and interim earnings, the expenses for each quarter, the net back pay due, and any other pertinent information."[35]

Sec. 18–7. Answer to specification.

The party liable for back pay has 15 days from the service of the specification to file an answer. An original and four copies should be filed with the regional director. Immediately upon filing the answer, a copy should be sent to any other party jointly liable.[36] The original copy of the answer must be signed and sworn to by the party or by his duly authorized agent.

The answer, according to the Board's rules, "shall specifically admit, deny, or explain each and every allegation of the specification, unless the respondent is without knowledge."[37] As to any matter within the party's

[29]Armstrong Tire & Rubber Co., 119 NLRB 353, 41 LRRM 1108 (1957).
[30]R. and R. Sec. 102.52.
[31]Spoon Tile Co., 117 NLRB 1596, 40 LRRM 1051(1957).
[32]*Ibid.*
[33]Statements of Procedure, Sec. 101.16.
[34]Armstrong Tire and Rubber Co., 119 NLRB 353, 41 LRRM 1108(1957).
[35]R. and R. Sec. 102.53.
[36]R. and R. Sec. 102.54(a).
[37]R. and R. Sec. 102.54(b).

knowledge, "a general denial will not suffice."[38] If the party has no knowledge of certain allegations, he should so state in his answer; such statement will operate as a denial. If the party disputes either the accuracy of the figures in the specification or the basis on which they are computed, he "shall" state the basis for his disagreement and furnish the appropriate supporting figures.[39]

Sec. 18–8. Board action.   The Board may find the specification to be true and proceed to find so in an order, where:

1. No answer is filed within the prescribed time limit;[40] or
2. The answer's denials do not satisfy the manner of presentation required in the Board's rules, as described in the above paragraph.[41]

Otherwise the Board will issue a notice of hearing before a administrative law judge. Any specification may be withdrawn by the regional director before the opening of the hearing.[42] For example, the specification and notice of hearing will be withdrawn where an agreement is reached after the filing of the answer. The procedures for unfair labor practice cases are followed insofar as applicable in back-pay proceedings after issuance of the notice of hearing.[43] (These procedures are set forth in Chapter 16.)

Sec. 18–9. Delay in locating discriminatee.   Ordinarily, back-pay checks are mailed to the discriminatee. If there is a long delay in locating the discriminatee, the respondent will be asked to replace the check made to the discriminatee with a check made out to the United States Treasurer. After two years, the amount will be returned to the respondent with the written understanding that upon instruction by the Agency, he will turn it over to the discriminatee.[44]

---

[38]*Ibid.*
[39]*Ibid.*
[40]R. and R. Sec. 102.54(c); Midland Engineering Co., NLRB Case No. 13–CA–1707 and 13–CB–311, March 30, 1956;
[41]R. and R. Sec. 102.54(c).
[42]R. and R. Sec. 102.58.
[43]R. and R. Sec. 102.59.
[44]NLRB Field Manual 10676.

CHAPTER 19

Recognition and Organizational Picketing

Sec. 19–1. In general. The 1959 amendments to the statute prohibit a labor organization, which is not currently certified as the employees' bargaining representative, from certain picketing or threatening to picket for the purpose of obtaining recognition by the employer (recognition picketing) or acceptance by his employees as their representative (organizational picketing). Sec. 8(b)(7) provides that such picketing is an unfair labor practice where:

A. The employer has lawfully recognized another union and the picketing occurs at a time when a representation election is not appropriate;[1]

B. A valid representation election has been conducted by the NLRB within the preceding 12 months;[2] or

C. The picketing has been conducted without a representation petition having been filed "within a reasonable period of time not to exceed thirty days from the commencement of such picketing."[3]

There are two provisos to subsection (C):

1. Under the first, if a timely representation petition has been filed, i.e., within a reasonable time, the NLRB is required to conduct an expedited election. (Neither a hearing by the regional director nor a showing of interest of employees by the petitioner is required.)

2. Under the second proviso, picketing or other publicity which truthfully advises the public (including consumers) that an employer does not employ members of, or have a contract with, a union shall not be regarded as unlawful unless an effect of such picketing is to cause an employee of another person not to perform services.[4]

---

[1]Section 8(b)(7)(A).
[2]Section 8(b)(7)(B).
[3]Section 8(b)(7)(C).
[4]*Ibid.*

Sec. 19–2. Injunctive relief. Implementing Section 8(b)(7) is an amendment to Section 10(*l*) which makes it mandatory for the NLRB to seek injunctive relief with respect to Section 8(b)(7) violations, except where the employer has assisted another union unlawfully in violation of Section 8(a)(2).[5]

Sec. 19–3. Violation of Section 8(b)(7). Examples of conduct which the Board has held violates Section 8(b)(7) are:

1. Picketing by a noncertified union for organizational purposes after a valid NLRB election has been held within the preceding 12 months[6] (but the union may continue to picket until the validity of the election has been determined).
2. Picketing by a union for organizational purposes shortly after the employer has entered into a lawful contract with another union.[7]
3. Picketing by a union for recognition continuing for more than 30 days without the filing of a representation petition where the picketing stops all deliveries by employees of another employer.[8]
4. Picketing where the sole object was to cause the employer to enter into a contract covering the union members currently or thereafter employed.[9]
5. Picketing for the object of recognition and bargaining to cover future employees.[10]

The statutory language is not as restrictive as might appear, however, as shown by the following examples of conduct which the Board has held does not violate Section 8(b)(7).

[5]Section 10(1).
[6]Dallas General Drivers, Warehousemen and Helpers, Local No. 745 Teamsters Union (Macatee, Inc.), 127 NLRB 683, 46 LRRM 1069 (1960); Carpenters Dist. Council of Detroit, Wayne, and Oakland Counties, United Brotherhood of Carpenters, 195 NLRB No. 97, 79 LRRM 1428 (1972); Hotel and Restaurant Employees, San Francisco, Local Joint Executive Board (Associated Union Street Restaurants), 201 NLRB No. 15, 82 LRRM 1329 (1973).
[7]Local 182, Teamsters Union (Sitrue Inc.), 129 NLRB 1459, 47 LRRM 1219 (1961); Local 363, IBEW (Whitman Electric Inc.), 201 NLRB No. 123, 82 LRRM 1423 (1973); *see also* Lane - Coos - Curry - Douglas Counties Bldg. and Construction Trades Council (Tens Worshup) v. NLRB, 415 F.2d 656, 72 LRRM 2149 (1969).
[8]Local 705, Teamsters Union (Cartage & Terminal Management Corp.), 130 NLRB 558, 47 LRRM 1325 (1961); *see also* Local 445, Teamsters Union v. NLRB, 82 LRRM 2485 (C.A. 2, 1973), *enf.* 79 LRRM 1053; Operating Engineers, Loc. 4 (Seaward Construction Co.), 193 NLRB No. 87, 78 LRRM 1475 (1971).
[9]Local 101, Operating Engineers Union (Sherwood Construction Co.), 140 NLRB 1175, 52 LRRM 1198 (1963); NLRB v. Longshoremen (Waterway Terminals Co.), 82 LRRM 2686 (C.A. 9, 1973), *enf.* 78 LRRM 1573.
[10]Local 542, Operating Engineers Union (R. W. Noonan, Inc.), 142 NLRB 1132, 53 LRRM 1205 (1963); Seeler v. Local 724, IBEW (Rondout Electric, Inc.), 81 LRRM 2878 (D.C. N.Y., 1972).

1. Picketing for recognition purposes over a 12-week period where the picket signs were not truthful but there was no "intent to deceive the public and, although there were some interruptions in deliveries, there was no proof of interference, disruption or curtailment of the employer's business."[11]

2. Picketing for recognition purposes more than 30 days where the picketing also protested a refusal to bargain or other unfair labor practice by the employer.[12]

3. Picketing where evidence apart from the picket signs showed its purpose to be recognition because the picket signs truthfully advised the public that a cafeteria employed nonunion employees, or had no contract with the union.[13]

4. Picketing to require an employer to conform to union standards of employment prevailing in the area.[14]

5. Picketing to promote a consumer boycott by urging the public to shop at named stores organized by the picketing union and not to shop at unnamed "unfair" stores.[15]

6. Picketing by a recognized union during an economic strike where the employer has permanently replaced all of the strikers and challenges the union's majority status.[16]

Sec. 19–4. Special procedures under Section 8(b)(7)—Initiation of proceedings. The Board has adopted a number of special procedures for cases arising under Section 8(b) (7).[17] A charge alleging a violation of Section 8(b)(7) is docketed by the regional office as a "CP" case. The statute requires that it be handled as a priority matter.[18] It is processed as other priority cases except, in the case of Section 8(b)(7)(C), where a

---

[11]Locals 324 and 770, Retail Clerks (Barker Bros. Corp. & Golds Inc.), 138 NLRB 478, 51 LRRM 1053 (1962); *petition to review denied sub nom.* Barker Bros. Corp. & Gold's Inc. v. NLRB, 328 F. 2d 431, 55 LRRM 2544 (C.A. 9, 1964).

[12]Local 840, Hod Carriers Union (C. A. Blinne Construction Co.), 135 NLRB 1153, 49 LRRM 1638(1962).

[13]Local 681, Hotel and Restaurant Employees Union (Smitley d/b/a/ Crown Cafeteria, 135 NLRB 1183, 49 LRRM 1648 (1962); *petition to review denied sub nom.* Smitley d/b/a/ Crown Cafeteria v. NLRB, 327 F. 2d 351, 55 LRRM 2302 (C.A. 9, 1964).

[14]Houston Building and Construction Trades Council (Claude Everett Construction Co.), 136 NLRB 321, 49 LRRM 1757(1962).

[15]Alton-Wood River Building and Construction Trades Council (Jerseyville Retail Merchants Assn.), 144 NLRB 526, 54 LRRM 1099(1963).

[16]Warehouse Employees Union Local No. 570 (Whitaker Paper Co.), 149 NLRB 731, 57 LRRM 1334 (1964); for other examples, see Painters, Local 76 (Gomez Painting and Decorating Co.), 182 NLRB No. 58, 74 LRRM 1295 (1970); Plumbers, Local 5 v. Sachs, 72 LRRM 2900 (D.C. D.C., 1969); Carpenters, Local 906 (Blankenship Builders, Inc.), 201 NLRB No. 88, 82 LRRM 1275 (1973).

[17]R. & R. Sec. 102.73–102.82.

[18]Sec. 10(1).

representation petition is pending or is filed within a reasonable time thereafter.[19]

Sec. 19–5. Special procedures under Section 8(b)(7)—"CP" charge and no petition.

If the investigation conducted by the regional office discloses merit in a Section 8(b)(7)(A) or (B) charge, or an 8(b)(7)(C) charge where no representation petition is pending, a complaint is issued and application for injunctive relief under Section 10(1) is made. Again there is an exception. A charge that the employer has assisted or dominated another labor organization, which the regional director believes is a violation of Section 8(a)(2) precludes proceedings for an injunction.[20] Where it appears that the Section 8(b)(7) charge lacks merit, the regional director requests withdrawal of the charge or dismisses it subject to an appeal to the General Counsel.[21] (See Facsimile No. 69, page 325.)

Sec. 19–6. Special procedures under Section 8(b)(7)—Expedited elections.

An outstanding election petition changes the procedure in Section 8(b)(7)(C) cases. Whether pending when the CP charge is filed or whether timely filed thereafter and the regional director finds that issuance of a Section 8(b)(7)(C) complaint would be warranted except for the pendency of the representation petition, the charge is dismissed upon issuance of the direction of election. (See Facsimile No. 70, page 326.) A petition is not timely for the purpose of an expedited election if filed more than 30 days after commencement of recognition or organizational picketing.

Sec. 19–7. Special procedures under Section 8(b)(7)—Appeal from dismissal or charge.

A request for the General Counsel to review the dismissal of the charge must be filed within three days (unlike 10 days in other cases) and must contain a complete statement setting forth the facts and reasons upon which the request is based. The request for review does not operate as a stay of any dismissal action by the regional director.[22] A pending election petition has no effect on Section 8(b)(7)(A) or (B) charges as both subsections speak to circumstances when no petition could properly be filed.

Sec. 19–8. Special procedures under Section 8(b)(7)—Petition and "CP" charge pending.

The expedited election procedure is used only when the regional office's investigation of a representation petition involving the employees of the employer named in the pending CP charge discloses that:

[19]Sec. 8(b)(7)(C).
[20]Sec. 10(1).
[21]R. & R. Sec. 102.74 and 102.19.
[22]R. & R. Sec. 102.81.

NATIONAL LABOR RELATIONS BOARD

Regional Office

Charging Party
Address

Re: Case name
      Case number

Gentlemen:

The above-captioned case charging a violation under Section 8(b)(7)
of the National Labor Relations Act has been carefully investigated and
considered.

It does not appear that further proceedings on the charge are warranted
inasmuch as

there is insufficient evidence that there was picketing of, or a
threat to picket, an employer;

there is insufficient evidence that there was picketing of, or a
threat to picket, an employer for an object proscribed by Section 8(b)(7)
of the Act;

it appears that the picketing or threat thereof described in the
charge was engaged in by a labor organization which is currently
certified pursuant to Section 9(c) of said Act;

it appears that the picketing which has been alleged in the charge is
privileged under the second proviso to Section 8(b)(7)(C) of the Act;

there is insufficient evidence that the picketing or the threat(s) of
picketing occurred under circumstances which violate Section 8(b)(7)(A)
or (B) of the Act.

I am, therefore, refusing to issue /reissue/ a complaint in this matter.

Pursuant to the National Labor Relations Board Rules and Regulations, you
may obtain a review of this action by filing an appeal with the General Counsel
addressed to the Office of Appeals, National Labor Relations Board, Washington,
D. C. 20570, and a copy with me. This appeal must contain a complete statement setting forth the facts and reasons upon which it is based. The appeal
must be received by the General Counsel in Washington, D.C., by the close of
business on (month-day-year). Upon good cause shown, however, the General
Counsel may grant special permission for longer period within which to file.
Any request for extension of time must be submitted to the Office of Appeals
in Washington, and a copy of any such request should be submitted to me.

If you file an appeal, please complete the notice forms I have enclosed with
this letter and send one copy of the form to each of the other parties. Their
names and addresses are listed below. The notice forms should be mailed at
the same time you file the appeal, but mailing the notice forms does not relieve
you of the necessity for filing the appeal itself with the General Counsel and
a copy of the appeal with the Regional Director within the time stated above.

Very truly yours,

Regional Director

cc: General Counsel
      Respondent(s)
      Attorney(s) or Representative(s) of record

FACSIMILE NO. 69.
*Sample of regional director's dismissal of CP charge
in which no direction of election is involved*

NATIONAL LABOR RELATIONS BOARD

Regional Office

Charging Party
Address

                                        Re: Case name
                                              Case number

Gentlemen:
Dear Sir:

The above-captioned case charging a violation under Section 8(b)(7) of
the National Labor Relations Act has been carefully investigated and considered.

It does not appear that further proceedings on the charge are warranted
inasmuch as a timely valid representation petition involving the employees of
the employer named in the charge has been filed within a reasonable time from
the commencement of the picketing described in said charge, and a determination
has been made that an expedited election should be conducted upon such petition in accordance with the provisions of Sections 8(b)(7)(C) and 9(c) of said
Act, and the National Labor Relations Board Rules and Regulations. A notice of
such election is being issued in Case No. _____.

I am, therefore, refusing to issue a complaint in this matter.

Pursuant to the National Labor Relations Board Rules and Regulations, you
may obtain a review of this action by filing an appeal with the General Counsel
addressed to the Office of Appeals, National Labor Relations Board, Washington,
D.C. 20570, and a copy with me. This appeal must contain a complete statement
setting forth the facts and reasons upon which it is based. The appeal must
be received by the General Counsel in Washington, D.C., the close of business
on (month-day-year). Such appeal shall not operate as a stay to any action by
the Regional Director.

If you file an appeal, please complete the notice forms I have enclosed
with this letter and send one copy of the form to each of the other parties.
Their names and addresses are listed below. The notice forms should be mailed
at the same time you file the appeal, but mailing the notice forms does not relieve
you of the necessity for filing the appeal itself with the General Counsel and
a copy of the appeal with the Regional Director within the time stated above.

                                        Very truly yours,

                                        Regional Director

cc: General Counsel
      Respondent
      Other Interested Labor
        Organization(s) (in Petition)
      Attorney(s) or Representative(s) of record

FACSIMILE NO. 70.
*Form of regional director's dismissal of CP charge
with direction of election*

1. The employer's operations come within the Board's jurisdictional dollar volume standards.
2. Picketing of the employer is being conducted for an object prohibited by Section 8(b)(7).
3. Section 8(b)(7)(C) is applicable to the picketing.
4. The petition has been filed within a reasonable period of time not to exceed 30 days from the commencement of the picketing.[23]

If these four requirements are satisfied, the petition may omit certain items normally required under Section 9(c)(1). The items which may be omitted are:

1. Petitioner is not required to allege in the petition that a claim was made upon the employer for recognition.
2. The petitioner is not required to submit the usual 30 percent showing of interest by the employees.[24]

Sec. 19–9. Election ordered without hearing. In such cases, the regional director, without a hearing, may direct that an election be held in an appropriate unit of the employees.[25] (See Facsimile No. 71, page 328.) When an election is directed without a hearing, any party aggrieved may promptly file a request with the Board for special permission to appeal that action to the Board; however, the request for review does not stay any action by the regional director unless specifically ordered by the Board.[26]

Sec. 19–10. Hearing ordered before election. On the other hand, if the regional director believes that the proceedings raise substantial issues which require determination before an election may be held, he is not required to proceed without a hearing but may order that such a hearing be held. (See Facsimile No. 72, page 329.) If held, the procedures followed in connection with such a hearing are similar to those used for regular representation election petitions pursuant to Section 9(c) except that the hearing is ordinarily directed on a shorter notice to the parties and the parties are not permitted to file briefs unless special permission is granted; however, the parties may state their respective positions fully on the record at the hearing. Any request for review of a decision of the regional director must be filed promptly after issuance of such a decision rather than within the 10 days normally permitted.[27]

[23]R. and R. Sec. 102.76 and Statements of Procedure Sec. 101.23.
[24]Sec. 8(b)(7)(C) and Statements of Procedure Sec. 101.23 fn. 1.
[25]R. & R. Sec. 102.77(b).
[26]R. & R. Sec. 102.77(b) and Statements of Procedure Sec. 101.23(b).
[27]R. and R. Sec. 102.77(b) and Statements of Procedure Sec. 101.23(c).

NATIONAL LABOR RELATIONS BOARD

Date_____

Petitioner
Employer
Unions

Re: Employer
Case No.   -R-

Gentlemen:

On the basis of the investigation made to date in the above matter, it appears appropriate now to conduct an election by secret ballot to determine whether or not the employees of _____(name of employer)_____ in the unit of employees described below wish to be represented for purposes of collective bargaining by _____(name of union)_____ or _____(names of other interested unions)_____ pursuant to section 9(c) of the National Labor Relations Act, as amended, or by no union.

Accordingly, pursuant to section 8(b) (7) (c) and 9(c) of said Act, and Section 102.77 of the National Labor Relations Board Rules and Regulations, an election by secret ballot will be conducted as provided in the enclosed Notice of Election, among the employees of the above-named employer in a unit described as follows, which is hereby found to be appropriate:

Description of Unit

Additional copies of the Notice of Election are being herewith furnished the employer for posting in conspicuous places throughout the plant (or other premises).

Your cooperation will be appreciated.

Very truly yours,

Regional Director

FACSIMILE NO. 71.
Sample of regional director's direction of election without hearing

UNITED STATES OF AMERICA
BEFORE THE NATIONAL LABOR RELATIONS BOARD
_____ Region

* * * * * * * * * * * * * *
                               *
                               *
                               *   Case No.
                               *
                               *
                               *
                               *
* * * * * * * * * * * * *

NOTICE OF REPRESENTATION HEARING

The Petitioner, above named, having heretofore filed a Petition
pursuant to section 9(c) of the National Labor Relations Act, as amended,
copy of which Petition is hereto attached, and it appearing that, pursuant to
said section and to section 8(b)(7)(c) of the said Act, a question affecting
commerce has arisen concerning whether the employees described by such
Petition desire a collective bargaining representative as defined in section
9(a) of the Act, and concerning the unit in which an election may appropriately
be conducted to resolve such question.

YOU ARE HEREBY NOTIFIED that, pursuant to section 9(c) of the Act, and
the National Labor Relations Board Rules and Regulations, on the _____ day
of _____ 1966, at _____ a hearing will be conducted
before a hearing officer of the National Labor Relations Board upon the
aforesaid question, at which time and place the parties will have the right
to appear in person or otherwise, and give testimony.

IN WITNESS WHEREOF, the undersigned has signed this Notice of Representation Hearing on this _____ day of _____, 1966.

_____
Regional Director

_____
Address

FACSIMILE NO. 72.
*Sample of regional director's notice of hearing
on petition filed under section 8(b)(7)(C)*

Sec. 19–11. Election procedure.   When a petition has been filed for an expedited election, the parties may, subject to the approval of the regional director, enter into a consent-election agreement. They may not enter into a stipulation upon consent-election agreement.[28] In the absence of a consent-election agreement, the regional director fixes the basis of eligibility of voters and the place, date, and hours of balloting. The mechanics of arranging the balloting and other procedures for the conduct of the election are the same as in the usual election conducted by the Board.[29]

Sec. 19–12. Postelection procedure.   The regional director's rulings on any objections to the conduct of the election or challenged ballots are final and binding, unless the Board, on an application by one of the parties, grants special permission to appeal from the regional director's rulings. The party requesting such review by the Board must do so promptly, in writing, and state briefly the grounds relied upon. A copy must be served on each of the other parties including the regional director. The request for the review does not stay the regional director's rulings unless so ordered by the Board.[30]

Sec. 19–13. Dismissal of petition.   If a petition seeking an expedited election is filed and there is no "CP" charge on file with the regional office but the petitioner claims an exemption from the requirements of Section 9(c)(1) of the Act because of the picketing, the claim will not be honored. However, the regional director will afford the petitioner an opportunity to furnish the necessary evidence to sustain the usual petition processed under Section 9(c)(1) of the Act. (See Facsimile No. 73, page 331.) If within a reasonable time, usually 48 hours after receipt of the letter, the petitioner does not furnish such evidence in compliance with the requirements of Section 9(c)(1), the petition is dismissed, absent withdrawal. (See Facsimile No. 74, page 332.) There is no right to appeal from the dismissal of a petition filed pursuant to Section 102.76 of the Board's Rules and Regulations in order to invoke the expedited election procedure except by special permission of the Board.[31]

---

[28]R. and R. Sec. 102.79.
[29]Statements of Procedure Sec. 101.23(b).
[30]R. & R. Sec. 102.78 and Statements of Procedure Sec. 101.23(b).
[31]R. & R. Sec. 102.80 and Statements of Procedure Sec. 101.25.

NATIONAL LABOR RELATIONS BOARD

Date _____

Petitioner

Re: Name of Employer
Case No.   -R-

Dear Sir:

The above-captioned case, arising from a petition filed pursuant to Section 9(c) and a charge filed pursuant to section 8(b)(7) of the National Labor Relations Act, as amended, has been carefully investigated and considered.

It does not appear that expedited procedures pursuant to said section of the Act are warranted inasmuch as

the petition has not been filed within a reasonable time after the commencement of picketing of the employer named in the petition, a reasonable time having been determined in the current circumstances to be _____ days.

⌐Other reason.⌐

I am therefore declining to process the petition under said expedited procedures, and am proceeding to process the petition in accordance with the provisions of Section 9(c)(1) of the National Labor Relations Act and of Subpart C of the National Labor Relations Board Rules and Regulations.

If you have not already done so, furnish evidence that

a substantial number of employees wish to be represented by a petitioner for the purposes of collective bargaining.

⌐or⌐

a substantial number of employees do not desire to be represented for collective bargaining purposes by the labor organization (individual) currently certified (recognized).

⌐or⌐

a labor organization or individual has presented a claim to the petitioner to be recognized as the representative of the petitioner's employees as defined in Section 9(a) of the Act.

Unless such evidence is submitted promptly, the petition will be dismissed.

Very truly yours,

Regional Director

FACSIMILE No. 73.
Sample of regional director's refusal to process under expedited procedure

NATIONAL LABOR RELATIONS BOARD

Date_____

Petitioner

Petitioner's representative

                                   Re: Employer Case No.   -R-

Gentlemen:

   The above-captioned case, arising from a petition filed pursuant to
Section 9(c) and a charge filed pursuant to Section 8(b)(7) of the National
Labor Relations Act, as amended, has been carefully investigated and
considered.

   It does not appear that further proceedings are warranted inasmuch as

            the picketing described in the charge is violative of
            Section 8(b)(7)(A) - (B)

                      or

      ⌐Other reason.⌐

I am therefore dismissing the petition in this matter.

                              Very truly yours,

                              Regional Director

FACSIMILE NO. 74.
Form of regional director's dismissal of petition

CHAPTER 20

Jurisdictional Dispute Cases

Sec. 20–1. In general. The settlement of jurisdictional disputes, as such, is not a function of NLRB. Instead the statute, in Section 8(b)(4)(D), includes as an unfair labor practice certain conduct which has as an object the forcing or requiring of an employer to assign work to one group of employees rather than to another. The Act makes an exception where the employer fails to conform to a Board order or certification.

The procedures used to enforce other union unfair labor practices would appear adequate to handle Section 8(b)(4)(D) charges but, because of the failure to remove Section 10(k) from the statute through a legislative oversight, it was necessary for the Board to adopt special procedures to be used in such cases. That section provides that when a charge alleging a violation of Section 8(b)(4) (D) is filed, the Board is "empowered and directed to hear and determine the dispute," unless the parties submit evidence which satisfies the Board that: (a) the dispute has been adjusted; or (b) an agreement has been reached on the methods for adjustment.[1] Such evidence should be submitted to the regional director within 10 days after notice of the filing of the charge.

The charge is filed in the same manner as other charges. (See Chapter 13.) Such charges, unlike other Section 8(b)(4) charges, receive priority treatment only if the case is one in which injunctive relief is deemed appropriate.[2] These are usually cases where there is a work stoppage of some sort.

Sec. 20–2. Notice of charge. The regional office promptly serves a copy of the charge, together with a copy of "Notice of Charge Filed," upon all parties to the dispute, including employers who are directly or indirectly responsible for the assignment of the disputed work, and unions to which the work has been assigned. (See Facsimile No. 75, page 335.)

---

[1]Sec. 10(k); see General Counsel's Memorandum 73-82, issued December 3, 1973, for concise discussion of problems in jurisdictional dispute cases. Copies may be obtained from the Division of Information, National Labor Relations Board, Washington, D.C. 20570.
[2]Sec. 10(1) and R. and R. Sec. 102. 95; for further discussion of priority, see NLRB v. Local 825, Operating Engineers (Burns and Roe, Inc.), 400 US 297, 76 LRRM 2129 (1971).

Sec. 20–3. Notice of Section 10(k) hearing. If, after investigation, it appears to the regional director that the charge has merit and that further proceedings should be instituted, he will issue a notice of hearing. (See Facsimile No. 76, page 336.) This notice must be served on all parties.[3] The notice includes:

1. A simple statement of the issues involved in the jurisdictional dispute.
2. A statement of the place and time of the hearing, which is scheduled at least 10 days after service of the notice, except that in cases involving the national defense, agreement will be sought for scheduling the hearing on less notice.[4]

The proceeding initiated by the issuance of the notice of hearing, followed by the hearing, and concluding with the determination by the Board in Washington is known as a "10(k) proceeding," named after the pertinent section of the statute. The "10(k) proceeding" is neither: (a) an unfair labor practice proceeding which may result in an order prohibiting unfair labor practices; nor (b) a representation proceeding which may result in certification. The sole object of the "10(k) proceeding" is a determination of the dispute.[5]

Sec. 20–4. Effect of agreement. The Board has no authority to determine a dispute where:

1. The parties have actually adjusted the dispute; or
2. The parties have agreed upon a method for adjustment of the dispute.[6]

Where the parties submit satisfactory evidence that a dispute has been adjusted, the regional director will:

1. Permit withdrawal of the charge, or dismiss it; and
2. Withdraw the notice of hearing, if one has issued.[7]

---

[3]Bay Counties District Council of Carpenters and Roofers, Local 40, 115 NLRB 1757, 38 LRRM 1170 (1956).
[4]Statements of Procedure Sec. 101.33.
[5]Local 68, Association of Machinists (Moore Drydock Co.), 8 NLRB 1108, 23 LRRM 1452 (1949); Transport Workers Union of America, AFL-CIO & Loc. 504 (Triangle Maintenance Corp.), 186 NLRB No. 71, 75 LRRM 1353 (1970); Local 54, Sheet Metal Workers Union (Goodyear Tire and Rubber Co.), 203 NLRB No. 21, 83 LRRM 1003 (1973).
[6]Local 46, Lathers Union (Acoustical Contractors Association of Cleveland), 119 NLRB 1658, 41 LRRM 1293 (1958); Local 627, Teamsters Union (Hoffman & Sons, Inc.), 195 NLRB No. 13, 79 LRRM 1249 (1972);. NLRB v. Plasterers' Local No. 79 (Southwestern Construction Co.), 404 U.S. 116, 78 LRRM 2897 (1971).
[7]Statements of Procedure Sec. 101.33.

UNITED STATES OF AMERICA
BEFORE THE NATIONAL LABOR RELATIONS BOARD
_____Region

* * * * * * * * * * * * * * * * *
                      *
                      *
                      *
                      *   Case No.   -CD-
                      *
                      *
                      *
                      *
* * * * * * * * * * * * * * * * *

NOTICE OF CHARGE FILED

PLEASE TAKE NOTICE that pursuant to Section 10 (b) of the National
Labor Relations Act, a Charge has been filed alleging the above-named
organization, /Insert name of respondent or respondents /_____has
engaged in an unfair labor practice within the meaning of paragraph (4) (D)
of Section 8 (b) of the Act. A copy of this Charge is attached hereto.

YOU ARE FURTHER NOTIFIED, pursuant to Section 10 (k) of the Act, that,
unless within 10 days after receipt of this Notice of Charge Filed the
parties to the dispute alleged in said Charge submit to the undersigned
satisfactory evidence that they have adjusted said dispute or have agreed
upon methods for the voluntary adjustment thereof, the Board is empowered
and directed to hear and determine the dispute out of which the said
unfair labor practice charge arose if it is determined that the said charge
has merit.

IN WITNESS WHEREOF, the undersigned Regional Director has caused this
Notice of Charge Filed to be signed at _____on this _____day_____
1966.

                                        _____
                                        Regional Director
                                        National Labor Relations Board
                                              _____Region
                                        (address)

FACSIMILE No. 75.
Sample of notice of charge filed by regional director
in jurisdictional dispute case

UNITED STATES OF AMERICA
BEFORE THE NATIONAL LABOR RELATIONS BOARD
_____ REGION

```
* * * * * * * * * * * * * * * * * * * *
                   *
                   *
                   *
                   *
                   *
                   *        Case No.     -CD-
                   *
                   *
                   *
                   *
                   *
* * * * * * * * * * * * * * * * * * * *
```

NOTICE OF HEARING

PLEASE TAKE NOTICE that on the _____ day of_____, 19___, at
(hour and place), pursuant to Section 10(k) of the National Labor Relations
Act, a hearing will be conducted before a Hearing Officer of the National Labor
Relations Board upon the dispute alleged in the Charge attached to the Notice
of Charge Filed issued in this matter on the _____ day of_____, 19___.
At said hearing, the parties will have the right to appear in person or otherwise
and give testimony.

The dispute concerns the assignment of the following work task(s):

/ When authorized as a case involving the National Defense,
insert "THIS CASE INVOLVES THE NATIONAL DEFENSE."/

IN WITNESS WHEREOF, the undersigned Regional Director on behalf of the Board,
has caused this Notice of Hearing to be signed at_____, on
this_____day of_____, 19___.

```
                              _____
                              Regional Director
                              National Labor Relations Board

                                      _____ Region
                                                (address)
```

FACSIMILE NO. 76.
*Sample of notice of hearing issued by regional director
in jurisdictional dispute case*

Where the parties submit satisfactory evidence that they have agreed upon a method for adjustment of the dispute, the regional director will:

1. Postpone issuance of the notice of the hearing, and keep the charge on file pending final adjustment of the dispute; or
2. Withdraw the notice of hearing, if issued, and keep the charge on file pending final adjustment of the dispute.[8] (If the hearing has been started, it will be recessed before the notice is withdrawn.)

If the voluntary adjustment of the dispute results in a determination that the employees of the charged union are entitled to perform the work in question, the regional director will dismiss the charge against that union whether or not the employer complies with that determination.[9]

The regional director will find satisfactory evidence of an agreed-upon method for adjustment of the dispute where the parties agree to be bound or actually are bound by some means for resolution of the dispute—such as, an understanding to submit the dispute to arbitration, or membership in a formal program for resolving jurisdictional disputes.[10] All parties, including the employer responsible for assigning the work, must be bound and not merely the disputing unions. The Board has ruled that an international union (or its local) cannot disassociate itself from the program of the National Joint Board as long as that union is a member of the AFL-CIO's Building and Construction Trades Department.[11]

The regional director can take the above actions only if the satisfactory evidence is submitted to him before the close of the hearing. After the close of the hearing, evidence of an adjustment or of an agreed-upon method for adjustment should be submitted to the Board in Washington.

Sec. 20–5. The Section 10(k) hearing. As in a representation case, the hearing is part of the investigation, except that in a hearing on a jurisdictional dispute the parties submit evidence supporting their respective claims to the work. Furthermore, as in a representation case, the hearing officer does not make any recommendations in regard to the dispute; he submits only an analysis of both the issues and the evidence to the Board.[12] (For a description of the conduct of the hearing see Chapter 7.)

[8]*Ibid.*
[9]Statements of Procedure 101.33.; NLRB v. Plasterers, Local 79, 404 U.S. 116, 78 LRRM 2897 (1971); also see Brady-Hamilton Stevedore Co., 198 NLRB No. 18, 80 LRRM 1611 (1972).
[10]Local 2, Lather's Union (Acoustical Contractors Association of Cleveland), 119 NLRB 1345, 41 LRRM 1293 (1958); for discussion of the effect of the demise and subsequent resurrection of the National Joint Board, see Bricklayers, Local 1 (Lembke Construction Co.), 194 NLRB No. 98, 79 LRRM 1025 (1971); Sheet Metal Workers, Local 312 (Morris and Sons Co.), 194 NLRB No. 100, 79 LRRM 1015 (1971); *see also* Seafarers' Intl. Union of North America (Delta Steamship Lines), 172 NLRB No. 70, 68 LRRM 1431 (1968).
[11]*Ibid.*
[12]R. and R. Sec. 102.90.

Upon the close of the hearing the case is transferred to the Board. Briefs may be filed as a matter of right within seven days after the close of the hearing, except in cases involving the national defense where prior Board approval is required.[13] Special leave of the Board is also required to file a reply brief.

Sec. 20–6. Board determination of dispute. Prior to 1961 the NLRB initially confined itself to determining whether the employer's assignment of the work violated any Board order or certification or any contract between the employer and the striking union. If not, the Board, by a negative determination, would hold that the union was not lawfully entitled to strike or picket to force the assignment of the disputed work to its members. However, early in 1961, the United States Supreme Court held that the Board's approach to Section 10(k) proceedings was wrong and henceforth the Board must decide the underlying dispute and make affirmative awards of the disputed work.[14] The court stated: "It is the Board's responsibility and duty to decide which of two or more employee groups claiming the right to perform certain work tasks is right and then specifically to award such tasks in accordance with its decision." The award is to be made on the basis of such criteria as custom, tradition, and the like "generally used by arbitrators, unions, employers, joint boards or others in wrestling with (the) problem" of jurisdictional disputes.

Following the Supreme Court's decision, the Board now makes an "affirmative" work assignment determination in accordance with the Court's ruling. The Board has held that, in making jurisdictional awards as required by the Court, it could not and would not formulate general rules and that each case would have to be decided on its own facts. The Board said it would consider all relevant factors in determining who is entitled to the work in dispute, such as, "the skills and work involved,[15] certifications by the Board, company and industry practice,[16] agreements between unions and between employers and unions,[17] awards of arbitrators, joint boards, and the AFL-CIO in the same or related cases,[18] the assignment made by the employer, and the efficient operation of the employer's business."[19] It

---

[13]*Ibid.*
[14]NLRB v. Radio & Television Broadcast Engineers Union, Local 1212, 364 U.S. 573, 47 LRRM 2332 (1961).
[15]Bakery Wagon Drivers and Salesmen Local 432 (Lucky Stores), 171 NLRB No. 141, 68 LRRM 1221 (1969); Teamsters Union, Local 612 (Brown Mechanical Contractors), 202 NLRB No. 148, 83 LRRM 1015 (1973).
[16]Asbestos Workers, Local 4 (Cowper, Inc.), 202 NLRB No. 94, 83 LRRM 1029 (1973).
[17]Teamsters Union, Local 26 (Burns Construction Co.), 203 NLRB No. 7, 83 LRRM 1007 (1973).
[18]Iron Workers, Local 465 (Hansen and Hempel, Inc.), 202 NLRB No. 158, 83 LRRM 1005 (1973).
[19]Iron Workers, Local 377 (Judson Steel Corp.), 202 NLRB No. 150, 83 LRRM 1041 (1973).

cautioned, however, that such factors would not be exclusive, but were merely illustrative and that every decision would have to be an act of judgment based on common sense and experience rather than on precedent.[20]

The Board's determination of dispute is reviewable in court upon the limited basis that it is arbitrary or that the Board has failed to perform its statutory duty.[21]

Sec. 20–7. Compliance with Board determination. The union against whom the determination is made by the Board is given 10 days to notify the regional director of the action taken to comply with the determination. If satisfied by such compliance, the regional director will dismiss the charge. (The procedure for appeal is the same as that set forth on page 239 under "Appeal from the Dismissal.")

Sec. 20–8. Issuance of complaint. If the union fails to notify the regional director of the steps taken to comply with the determination, the regional director may presume the union is engaged in either: (a) continuation of the unlawful activity; or (b) refusal to comply with the determination.[22] In this event or if the regional director is not satisfied that the union is complying with the determination, he will issue a notice of hearing and a complaint based on the original charge.[23] From this point on, the case proceeds as any other unfair labor practice case. (The applicable procedures are set forth in Chapters 15 through 17.)

An unfair labor practice complaint may also be issued whenever the regional director finds that an agreed-upon method of adjustment has failed to settle the jurisdictional dispute.[24] When this alternative procedure is used the complaint is issued without either a Section 10(k) hearing or determination. Thus, the Labor Board has ruled that a complaint may issue against any party subject to the operations of the National Joint Board if that party strikes either in anticipation of or in protest against an award of the Joint Board.[25]

[20]Lodge 1743, Machinists Union (J.A. Jones Construction Co.), 135 NLRB 1402, 49 LRRM 1684 (1962).
[21]NLRB v. Local 825, Operating Engineers, 326 F.2d 213, 55 LRRM 2112 (C.A. 3, 1964); NLRB v. Local 991, Longshoreman's Assn., 332 F.2d 66, 56 LRRM 2250 (C.A. 5, 1964); Longshoremen & Warehousemen, Local 8 (Waterway Terminals Co.), *sub nom.* Waterway Terminals Co. v. NLRB, 81 LRRM 2449 (C.A. 9, 1972), *setting aside and reman'g* 75 LRRM 1042.
[22]Local 595, Iron Workers, AFL (Bechtel Corp.), 112 NLRB 812, 36 LRRM 1105.
[23]Statements of Procedure Sec. 101.36.
[24]R. and R. Sec. 102.93.
[25]Local 2, Lathers' Union (Acoustical Contractors Association of Cleveland), 119 NLRB 1345, 41 LRRM 1293 (1958).

Sec. 20–9. The Board's decision.   The Board's decision, just as in any unfair labor practice case, is subject to court review. (The applicable procedures are set forth on page 305 under "Enforcement of the Board's Decision," and on page 308 under "Review of the Board's Decision.") Whenever a "10(k) proceeding has been held and a complaint proceeding has followed, the record of the 10(k) proceeding and the Board's determination become part of the record in the unfair labor practice case and are subject to court review if the unfair labor practice order is taken to court by either the union or the Board.[26]

Sec. 20–10. Injunctive relief.   The Act gives the NLRB authority to seek injunctions against violations of the jurisdictionaldispute provisions while the case is pending with the Board.[27] Application for an injunction in such cases is not mandatory but is discretionary with the NLRB when relief is "appropriate."[28] This has been interpreted to mean that injunctive relief will be sought in every case in which the regional director has reasonable cause to believe there has been a violation except in those cases where picketing or a work stoppage has ceased and is not likely to resume.

[26]R. and R. Sec. 102.92.
[27]Sec. 10(1).
[28]Statements of Procedure Sec. 101.37; R. & R. Sec. 102.90.

CHAPTER 21

Dispute-Settlement Procedures

Sec. 21–1. In general. Sections 8(a)(5) and 8(b)(3) of the Act make it an unfair labor practice for employers to refuse to bargain collectively. The extent of the duty to bargain is defined in Section 8(d) which requires that the parties confer ". . . in good faith with respect to wages, hours, and other terms and conditions of employment . . . ." The Act does not attempt to establish procedures to evaluate bargaining proposals or, with limited exceptions, to provide a final method for settlement of disputes between the parties. Most important of these exceptions are the statutory system for resolving questions of representation (see Chapters 4-12) and the Board's authority under section 10(k) to determine the assignment of work in a jurisdictional dispute (see Chapter 20). Dispute-settlement procedures involving the Board are also found in the Postal Reorganization Act (see Section 21-6, page 231).

The Act does contain, however, limited general provisions to aid in the settlement of contract disputes and, in certain instances, additional procedures to be used when the dispute involves national emergency strikes, Postal Service bargaining, or employees of health care institutions.

Sec. 21–2. Dispute notice requirements.—In general. When a party desires to terminate or modify an existing collective bargaining agreement, Section 8(d) requires that a written notice to this effect be served upon the other party 60-days prior to either the expiration of the contract or the time it is proposed that the termination or modification take place. No strike or lockout is permitted during this 60-day period.

If no settlement has been reached after the expiration of 30 of those 60 days, the party desiring to terminate or modify the contract must give written notification of the existence of a dispute to both the Federal Mediation and Conciliation Service and to any established state mediation agency. (The names and locations of these agencies appear in Appendix F.) In the absence of such notice a strike called for the purpose of modifying a contract's terms is unlawful.[1]

---

[1]United Furniture Workers. Local 270 v. NLRB (Fort Smith Chair Co.), 336 F.2d 738, 55 LRRM 2990 (C.A.D.C., 1964), cert. den., 379 U.S. 838, 57 LRRM 2239.

The Supreme Court has ruled that the requirements are satisfied if the required 60- and 30-day notices and waiting periods are meshed with:[2]

1. The midterm reopening date, where the contract provides for such intermediate date during its term;

2. The expiration date, where the contract contains such date; or

3. The date when it is proposed to have the modification or termination take effect, where the contract contains neither reopening nor expiration date.

Any employee who engages in a strike within the 60-day period loses status as an employee of his employer, unless he is rehired. However, there is one exception: The Supreme Court has ruled that Section 8(d) does not deprive the striker of his status if he is engaged in a strike solely against his employer's unfair labor practices.[3]

For the convenience of the parties, the Federal Mediation and Conciliation Service has prepared and makes available a form which may be used to serve notice of a dispute. (See Facsimile No. 77, page 343.) Copies may be obtained from either a regional office or the Washington office of the FMCS. The notice of dispute may be filed with either the Washington headquarters of the FMCS or with the FMCS office in whose region the dispute exists. (Locations of these offices appear in Appendix G.)

Sec. 21–3. Dispute notice requirements—Health care institutions. The 1974 amendments extending coverage of the Act to health care institutions included several special notice requirements applicable only to labor disputes at such institutions. The Board has not yet issued regulations implementing these provisions and it may be some time before the full scope of the amendments is established. Recognizing this problem, the General Counsel has issued a set of Guidelines to be used in handling cases under the amendments that is currently the best outline of procedures to be followed.[4]

The new requirements will apply to "any hospital, convalescent hospital, health maintenance organization, health clinic, nursing home, extended care facility, or other institution devoted to the care of sick, infirm or aged

[2]NLRB v. Lion Oil Co., 352 U.S. 282, 39 LRRM 2296 (1957).
[3]Mastro Plastics Corp. v. NLRB, 350 U.S. 270, 37 LRRM 2587 (1956).
[4]*Guidelines Issued by the General Counsel for Use of Board Regional Offices in Unfair Labor Practice Cases Arising Under the 1974 Nonprofit Hospital Amendments to the Taft-Hartley Act (Memorandum 74-49, August 20, 1974)*, LABOR RELATIONS YEARBOOK—1974 (Washington, D.C.: BNA Books, 1975), p. 343.

FMCS Form F-7
Revised Jan. 1962
Ch-20u3 O/M-C/H

Form Approved
Budget Bureau No. 23-R001.9

NOTICE TO MEDIATION AGENCIES

To: Regional Office, FEDERAL MEDIATION AND CONCILIATION SERVICE; and
United States Government

To:_____   Date_____
(Appropriate State or Territorial agency)

    You are hereby notified that written notice of the proposed termination or modification of the existing collective bargaining contract was served upon and that no agreement has been reached with the other party to this contract.

1. (a) Name of employer_____Phone No._____
(If more than one company or an association, submit names and addresses on separate sheet in duplicate)

    Address of establishment affected_____
(Street)   (City)   (State)
(If more than one establishment, or plant, list addresses on separate sheet)

  (b) Employer Official to communicate with_____Phone No._____
(Name and Title)

    Address_____
(Street)   (City)   (State)

2. (a) International union_____Local No._____

    AFL-CIO_____   Independent_____   Phone No._____

    Address of local union_____
(Street)   (City)   (State)

  (b) Union Official to communicate with_____Phone No._____

    Address_____
(Street)   (City)   (State)

3. (a) Number of employees in bargaining unit or units in the negotiations_____

  (b) Total number of employees in the company(ies) or establishment(s)_____

4. Nature of business of establishment affected:
    (a) Principal products, or services rendered_____

    (b) Type of establishment_____
(Factory, mine, wholesaler, over-the-road trucking, etc.)

5. (a) Expiration date of contract_____ (b) Contract date reopening_____

6. Name of official filing this notice_____Title_____

    Address_____Phone No._____

    Check on whose behalf this notice is filed: Union_____Employer_____

Signature_____

(Attach copies of any statement you wish to make to the Mediation Agencies.)

No. 1 ORIGINAL—To appropriate F. M. C. S. regional office (See list on reverse of copy 6)

FACSIMILE NO. 77
Notice to Mediation Agencies

persons."[5] According to the Guidelines, the notice requirements are as follows:

1. A party desiring to terminate or modify a labor agreement involving employees of a health care institution must serve written notice of such intention upon the other party at least 90 days prior to the actual or proposed termination or modification date.[6]

2. A party to a contract covering health care institution employees must notify the Federal Mediation and Conciliation Service and appropriate state agencies of its intention to modify or terminate that agreement at least 60 days before the contract's expiration date, i.e., within 30 days after giving the other party the Section 8(d)(1) notice.

3. Where, after certification or recognition, a union desires to bargain for an initial contract with a health care institution, it must serve upon the institution and conciliation agencies at least 30 days notice of the existence of a dispute.

4. A labor organization must generally notify the affected health care institution(s) and the Federal Mediation and Conciliation Service of whatever action it will take, at least 10-days before engaging in any form of strike or picketing (whether primary, secondary, recognitional, organizational, area standards, or sympathetic in nature) against any health care institution.[7]

5. Where a labor organization has transmitted the 10-day notices, it must also give 12 hours additional notice when it strikes or pickets within 72 hours after the previously noticed time, except when the noticed time occurs in the middle of a work shift.

6. Even if it has provided 10-day notices, a labor organization must transmit new 10-day notices when it intends to commence its strike or picketing more than 72 hours after the previously noticed time.

7. When a union engages in intermittent strike or picketing activity, it must give additional notices as follows:

    a. Where it is reasonable to assume that the activity will resume, a 12-hour notice to the institution is required if resumption is to occur more than 72 hours from the last cessation of activity.

    b. Where it is reasonable to assume that the activity will not recommence, a 12-hour notice is required if recommencement is to occur within 72 hours of the last cessation of activity but a full 8(g) 10-day notice is required if the activity is to recommence more than 72 hours from the last cessation of activity.

8. In initial contract bargaining situations, the union's 10-day notices to the health care institution and the Federal Mediation and

[5]Sec. 2(14).
[6]Trinity Lutheran Hospital, 218 NLRB No. 34, 89 LRRM 1238 (1975).
[7]Laborers Int., Local No. 1057 (Mercy Hospital of Laredo), 219 NLRB No. 154, 89 LRRM 1777 (1975).

Conciliation Service must be served after the 30-day notice period required by Section 8(d)(B).

9. Where the union plans to protest unfair labor practices by health care institutions which are not "flagrant" or "serious," it must serve the appropriate notices.

10. If a group of unrepresented employees is found to constitute a "labor organization," it must serve the appropriate 8(g) notices.

Some of these generalized principles have exceptions. Therefore, the Guidelines deserve careful study and the regional offices of the Board should be consulted if questions remain. A further source of guidance is a new series of Monthly Reports on Health Care Cases issued by the General Counsel commencing in December 1974.[8]

The Guidelines also indicate that notices apparently will not be required:

1. By a health care institution before a lockout.

2. By a union before engaging in handbilling, at least where it is not intended to induce a work stoppage.

3. By a union protesting "serious" or "flagrant" unfair labor practices committed by a health care institution.

4. By unrepresented employees not deemed to constitute a "labor organization."

Sec. 21–4. Health care institution Boards of Inquiry. The 1974 amendments also added a new Section 213 which authorizes establishment of impartial Boards of Inquiry by the Director of the Federal Mediation and Conciliation Service to investigate the issues involved in any threatened or actual strike or lockout affecting a health care institution. The Board is required to issue a written report containing findings of fact and recommendations for settling the dispute.

In contract-termination or modification situations, the Board of Inquiry is appointed within 30 days of the 60-day notice to the FMCS under section 8(d)(A). The Board makes its report within 15 days of its establishment and the parties to the dispute are required, except by mutual agreement, to maintain the status quo from the establishment of the Board until 15 days after its report is issued. In initial contract situations, the Board is established within 10 days of the section 8(d)(B) notice to the FMCS. The report is to be issued within the next 15 days and, as in the previous instance, the status quo must be maintained from establishment of the Board until 15 days after the report is issued.

Use of Boards of Inquiry is not mandatory. They are established at the discretion of the Director of the Federal Mediation and Conciliation

Service. The Board may consist of a single individual or have several members. The Board selects the time, place, and date of the proceedings it deems necessary and determines the order of the proceedings. A record is prepared but, because of time limitations, no transcript is made. Parties are entitled to present witnesses and exhibits to the Board and must be served with a copy of the Board's written findings. Failure of a party to cooperate does not preclude the Board from conducting its own investigation and issuing a report.[9]

Sec. 21–5. Dispute notice requirements—U. S. Postal Service employees. When the U. S. Postal Service was established in 1970 and the Board given jurisdiction over its employees, a number of special provisions governing both notice of disputes and contract-settlement procedures were included.[10] (See Appendix H.) Under these provisions:

1. No party to an existing collective bargaining agreement is permitted to terminate or modify the agreement without serving a written notice of its intent on the other party not less than 90 days prior to either the expiration date of the agreement or the date it is proposed that the termination or modification take place.
2. A party desiring to terminate or modify an agreement must notify the Federal Mediation and Conciliation Service of the existence of a dispute within 45 days after giving the 90-day notice if no agreement has been reached by that time.[11]

There are no notice requirements in initial contract situations.

Sec. 21–6. Dispute-settlement procedures—U. S. Postal Service employees. The Postal Reorganization Act also includes provisions to assure settlement of all contract disputes without resort to strikes or lockouts. The following procedures are used:

1. If the parties fail to reach agreement or to voluntarily agree upon a method to provide a binding resolution of a dispute by the date of either the contract expiration or the proposed termination or modification, the Director of the Federal Mediation and Conciliation Service establishes a fact-finding panel of three persons. This is done by submitting a list of 15 names to the parties. Each party, within 10-days, selects one person, and the two chosen select from the list of 15 a third member who serves as chairman. The panel makes an

---

[9]Federal Mediation and Conciliation Service Board of Inquiry Guidelines, DLR No. 238, Dec. 10, 1974, pp. A10-All.
[10]Postal Reorganization Act, §1201-1209.
[11]Postal Reorganization Act, §1207(a).

investigation of the dispute and, not later than 45 days from the date the list of names was submitted to the parties, it must issue a report of its findings. The report may contain recommendations but it is not mandatory that it do so.[12]

2. If the foregoing procedures fail to result in an agreement within 90 days after the contract expiration or termination, or the date on which the agreement became subject to modification, an arbitration board is established. The board consists of one person chosen by the Postal Service, one by the union, and the third by the two selected. Arbitration board members may not have served on the fact-finding panel.[13]

3. After a hearing at which the parties may present evidence in support of their claims, the arbitration board issues a decision which is "conclusive and binding upon the parties." The decision must be rendered within 45 days after the board's appointment.[14]

Similar procedures are followed to settle disputes where the union does not have an agreement with the Postal Service. In those instances, the fact-finding panel is established within 90 days after bargaining commences, unless the parties agree upon another binding method of resolving their differences. If final agreement is not reached in another 90 days, an arbitration board is established to provide conclusive and binding arbitration.[15]

Sec. 21–7. Dispute-settlement procedures—National emergency disputes.
Since 1947 the Act has contained provisions for dealing with threatened or actual strikes or lockouts affecting all or a substantial part of an industry. The procedures are invoked when the President believes that the strike, if permitted to occur or to continue, will "imperil the national health or safety." He may, at his discretion, appoint a board of inquiry to investigate the issues involved in the dispute and prepare a written report within whatever time he prescribes. The report must contain a statement of the facts with respect to the dispute and each party's statement of its position but it may not contain any recommendations. The report is made public.[16]

After receiving the report the President may direct the Attorney-General to seek an 80-day injunction from a federal district court to prevent or end the strike. If an injunction issues the parties are directed by the statute "to make every effort to adjust and settle their differences," but they are not required to accept any proposed settlement. Concurrently, the President

[12]Postal Reorganization Act, §1207(b).
[13]Postal Reorganization Act, §1207(c)(1).
[14]Postal Reorganization Act, §1207(c)(2), (3).
[15]Postal Reorganization Act, §1207(d).
[16]Sec. 206, 207.

reconvenes the board of inquiry and, at the end of 60 days, if the dispute has not been settled, the board again reports to the President. This report must include the current positions of the parties and a statement of the employer's last offer of settlement. This report is also made public.[17]

Within 15 days thereafter the Board is required to conduct a secret ballot to determine whether the employees affected wish to accept or reject the offer. The results must be certified to the Attorney-General within five days and the injunction is then dissolved.[18] Although the Board has conducted such ballots in a number of cases it has never adopted any regulations or formalized the procedures to be used. The Board Manual merely states that "last-offer" elections ". . . should be undertaken pursuant to advice procured from the Division of Operations on a case-by-case basis."[19] Generally, preparation for and conduct of such elections has closely resembled procedures followed in representation elections.

[17]Sec. 208, 209.
[18]Sec. 209, 210.
[19]NLRB Field Manual, Section 11520.

CHAPTER 22

Filing And Service Of Papers

Sec. 22–1. In general. During the course of an NLRB proceeding a wide variety of papers may have to be filed or served on the Board or on other parties, as well as on their attorneys or representatives of record.[1] Neither filing nor service requirements are uniform but depend on the particular document. Also, the Board strictly construes certain of the requirements but is lenient in its approach to others. To avoid procedural errors and the possibility of prejudicing their cases, parties are well advised to use great care in complying with the Board's requirements for filing and service.

The tables—one for representation cases and one for unfair labor practice cases—found at the end of this chapter tabulate the filing and service requirements for all papers likely to be encountered in a Board proceeding. Each document need not be commented upon in detail, but certain general principles which must be followed are discussed.

Sec. 22–2. Service of papers. Charges, complaints, subpoenas served by either the Board or the parties, and accompanying notices of hearing, final orders, and administrative law judge decisions issued by the Board or its agents must be served:

1. Personally;
2. By registered mail;
3. By telegraph; or
4. By leaving a copy at the principal office or place of business of the person to be served.[2]

Certified mail may be used by the Board in serving papers other than those specifically mentioned above. A party serving other parties to a proceeding may use:[3]

1. Registered or certified mail;

[1] R. and R. Sec. 102.111(b).
[2] R. and R. Sec. 102.111(a).
[3] R. and R. Sec. 102.111(c).

349

2. Any manner provided for the service of papers in a civil action by the law of the state in which the hearing is pending;
3. The same manner as that utilized in filing the paper with the Board (except for charges, petitions, exceptions, briefs, and other papers for which a time for both filing and response has been otherwise established);
4. Personal service when filing with the Board; however, the other parties should be promptly notified of the action by telephone, followed by service of a copy by mail or telegraph.[4]

Unless state law is to the contrary, service of documents may be accomplished by serving the attorney or representative of record. The Board's current instructions to its regional directors require that all service of papers (other than subpoenas), after the initial communication to the parties, is to be made upon the attorney or representative of record with copies to the party. It has been held that:

1. Service of a charge by ordinary mail, although a technical defect, does not invalidate an unfair labor practice proceeding.[5]
2. Service is effective where it is received by the person who is authorized to accept mail on behalf of the addressee.[6]
3. Service need not be made upon each member of a partnership; it is sufficient to serve the partnership in its usual business name.[7]
4. Service is effective where the registered matter is tendered to the addressee by the post office department, the addressee refuses to accept it, and it is not delivered for that reason.[8]

The date of service will be the day of depositing in the mail or delivery in person, as the case may be.[9] Proof of service will be the post office receipt, when service is made by registered or certified mail; when service is made in a manner provided by state law, the proof of service is made according to that law.

Proof of service is desirable in all cases, even though failure to show such proof does not affect the validity of the service.[10] The Board requires a person or party who serves papers on other parties to submit a written

[4]R. and R. Sec. 102.112.
[5]Olin Industries, Inc. v. NLRB, 192 F.2d 799, 29 LRRM 2117 (C.A. 5, 1951).
[6]NLRB v. McGahey, 233 F.2d 406, 38 LRRM 2142 (C.A. 5, 1956).
[7]Ibid.
[8]Pasco Packing Co., 115 NLRB 437, 37 LRRM 1323 (1956); for further examples, see Southern Colorado Contractors Assn., 65 LRRM 2615 (C.A. 10, 1967), enf. 59 LRRM 1600; Asheville-Whitney Nursing Home, sub nom. NLRB v. Clark, 81 LRRM 2353 (C.A. 5, 1972), denying enforcement to 76 LRRM 1242.
[9]R. and R. Sec. 102.113(a).
[10]R. and R. Sec. 102.113(b).

statement to the Board setting forth the names of those served and the date and manner of service. The Board will ask for proof of service only if, subsequent to the statement of service, a question is raised with respect to proper service.[11]

Sec. 22–3. Copies of documents submitted to Board. These are the requirements the Board has established to cover all formal documents— for example, motions and briefs—submitted for its consideration:[12]

1. Eight copies of the formal document must be presented.[13]
2. Such document must be either printed or legibly duplicated; carbon copies of typewritten matter will not be accepted.[14]
3. Copies must be served upon all other parties, and proof or statement of such service given to the Board.[15]

Sec. 22–4. How time is computed. In computing the period of time required by the Board in the submission of any document:[16]

1. Start counting with the day following the day on which the particular event occurs.[17] For example, in computing the five-day period allowed for the filing of objections to an election after receipt of the tally of ballots, do not count the day on which the tally is received; begin the count with the following day. Likewise, do not count the day a paper (for example, a letter of dismissal) is postmarked; begin the count with the following date.
2. Count the last day of the period unless the last day falls on a Saturday, Sunday, or legal holiday.[18] (The term "holiday," as used by the Board, refers only to federal holidays declared as such by Congressional enactment or by presidential proclamation.[19]) If the last day of the period should fall on a Saturday, Sunday, or legal holiday, the period runs until the end of the next day which is neither a Saturday, Sunday, nor legal holiday.
3. Where the allowed period of time is less than seven days, do not count Saturdays, Sundays, or legal holidays that fall within the period.[20]

---

[11]*Ibid.*
[12]R. and R. Sec. 102.46(j).
[13]Whitlock Corp., 103 NLRB 909, 31 LRRM 1597 (1953).
[14]R. and R. Sec. 102.46(j); Somerville Cream Co., 106 NLRB 1155, 32 LRRM 1638 (1956).
[15]Union Carbide Nuclear Co., 117 NLRB 1126, 39 LRRM 1386 (1957); Franklin County Sugar Co., 100 NLRB 228, 30 LRRM 1256 (1952); NLRB v. Bratten Pontiac Corp., 70 LRRM 2249 (C.A. 4, 1969), *enf. in part* 64 LRRM 1466.
[16]R. and R. Sec. 102.114(a).
[17]The Baltimore Transfer Co. of Baltimore City, Inc., 94 NLRB 1680, 28 LRRM 1241 (1951).
[18]Crosby Construction Co., 93 NLRB 28, 27 LRRM 1320 (1951).
[19]Fisher Products Co., 114 NLRB 161, 36 LRRM 1528 (1955).
[20]R. and R. Sec. 102. 114(a); "M" System, Inc., 116 NLRB 1725, 39 LRRM 1098 (1956).

This applies, for example, to the five-day period allowed for the filing of objections to the conduct of an election.

4. If the allowed period of time is seven days or more, count Saturdays, Sundays, and legal holidays falling within the allowed time. (But note that, if the final day of the period falls on a Saturday, Sunday, or holiday, the deadline is extended to the next regular working day.) An example of a period of seven days or more is the 10-day period allowed for the filing of an appeal from dismissal of a charge.

5. Count half holidays as regular days and not as holidays.

6. Where a paper is received by mail, add three days to the date of that mailing for purposes of determining the number of days allowed for action. (The three days cannot be added if any extension of time has been granted.) For example: A regional director dismisses a union's petition for certification. The regional director's letter dismissing the petition is dated Wednesday, November 16. The Board's rules and regulations allow 10 days for an appeal from a regional director's dismissal of a petition. To determine the deadline for such an appeal, add three days to the date of the regional director's letter, and start counting from the following day (November 20). This makes the end of the 10-day period Tuesday, November 29. Since the time allowed is more than seven days, Sundays and holidays are included in figuring the deadline date.

The requirement for a filing of a motion, brief, exceptions, or other paper means that the document must be received by the Board or the officer designated to receive such matter before the close of business on the last day of the allowed period.[21] Thus, the Board has rejected a filing received 17 minutes after the close of business on the day due.[22]

When a party misses its deadline, the Board and the Court will accept the matter as timely served if:

1. The party sustains the burden of showing that the matter was mailed in reasonable time for it to have been received before the deadline; and

2. The delay in delivery was attributable not to the party, but to the postal service.[23]

---

[21]R. and R. Sec. 102.114(b).

[22]Wilson-Jacobi, Inc., NLRB No. 2-RC-13100, 55 LRRM 1342 (1964).

[23]Rio de Oro Uranium Mines, Inc., 119 NLRB 153, 41 LRRM 1057 (1957); NLRB v. Marshall Maintenance Corp., 53 LRRM 2895 (C.A. 3, 1963); see also NLRB v. Local 1401, Retail Clerks (Zinke's Foods, Inc.), 79 LRRM 2984 (C.A. D.C., 1972), enf. 75 LRRM 1211; cf. KLAS-TV, 197 NLRB No. 178, 80 LRRM 1479 (1972).

Sec. 22–5. Extensions of time. Extensions of time in which to file particular documents will be granted by the Board, the General Counsel, or other appropriate official where good cause is shown. The deadline for filing a charge cannot be extended, however, as the six-month time limitation is a jurisdictional requirement of the statute.[24]

In most cases the Board is willing to grant one reasonable extension of time in which to file appeals, exceptions and briefs. Further extensions are rarely granted. The General Counsel follows a similar approach on requests for extending the time to appeal from dismissals of unfair labor practice charges by regional directors.

Postponements of hearing dates are more difficult to obtain. Such requests in both representation and unfair labor practice matters are addressed to the regional director. A week or 10 days is usually the maximum amount obtainable in representation cases and this will ordinarily be granted only if the extended date is not more than 30 days after the petition was filed. Most directors are more lenient with respect to unfair labor practice hearing dates, but extensions of more than two or three weeks are unusual.

In requesting any extension of time, the three-day limit uniformly used must be carefully observed. Time is computed according to the less-than-seven day rule. Consequently, such requests must be received by the close of business three working days prior to the due date.

[24]Sec. 10(b).

TABLE I. REPRESENTATION CASES

Document	Who Must Be Served	When It Must Be Served	How Many Copies
Petition	Regional office	. . . .	An original and four copies
Showing of interest in support of petition	Regional office	Within 48 hours of filing petition	One copy
Appeal from regional director's dismissal of petition	a. Board in Washington b. Regional director & each other party	Within 10 days of receipt of dismissal	a. Eight copies b. One copy
Pre-hearing motion (including motion to intervene)	a. Regional director b. Each other party	. . . .	a. An original and four copies b. One copy
Pre-hearing application for subpoena	Regional director	. . . .	One copy
Petition to revoke pre-hearing subpoena	Regional director	Within five days of receipt of subpoena	One copy
Notice of hearing	Each of the parties	Usually at least five days before hearing	One copy
Request for postponement of hearing	a. Regional director b. Each other party	Within three working days of scheduled date of hearing	a. One copy b. One copy

Document	Who Must Be Served	When It Must Be Served	How Many Copies
Written motion before hearing officer (including motion to intervene)	a. Hearing officer b. Each other party	a. During hearing b. Same time	a. An original and four copies b. One copy
Application for subpoena during hearing	Hearing officer	. . . .	One copy
Petition to revoke subpoena	Hearing officer	Within five days of receipt of subpoena	One copy
Request to appeal hearing officer's ruling	Regional director	Promptly	An original and four copies
Post-hearing brief	a. Regional director b. Each other party	Within seven days of close of hearing	a. An original and one copy b. One copy
Request for extension of time in which to file brief	a. Regional director b. Each other party	Three days before due date	a. One copy b. One copy
Request for oral argument before regional director's decision	Regional director	With brief	One copy
Notice of oral argument before regional director	Each of the parties	. . . .	One copy

TABLE I. REPRESENTATION CASES *(Contd.)*

Document	Who Must Be Served	When It Must Be Served	How Many Copies
Post-hearing motions	a. Regional director prior to transfer of case to Board	. . . .	An original and four copies
	b. Board after transfer of case by regional director	. . . .	Eight copies
	c. Each other party	. . . .	One copy
Request for direct appeal from ruling on motion	a. Board	Promptly	a. Eight copies
	b. Regional director and each other party		b. One copy
Request for review of regional director's decision	a. Board	Within 10 days after service	a. Eight copies
	b. Regional director and each other party		b. One copy
Opposition to request for review of regional director's decision	a. Board	Within seven days after the last day on which request for review may be filed	a. Eight copies
	b. Regional director and each other party		b. One copy
Briefs on review of regional director's decision	a. Board	Within seven days after issuance of order granting review	a. Eight copies
	b. Regional director and each other party		b. One copy

Document	Who Must Be Served	When It Must Be Served	How Many Copies
Extension of time in which to file brief on review	a. Board b. Regional director and each other party	Within three working days prior to due date of briefs	a. Eight copies b. One copy
Order transferring case to Board (after hearing and before regional director's decision)	a. Board b. Each other party	. . . .	a. One copy b. One copy
Briefs filed with Board—after transfer of case to Board by regional director	a. Board b. Regional director and each other party	Time fixed by regional director after service of order	a. Eight copies b. One copy
Extension of time in which to file briefs after transfer of case to Board by regional director	a. Board b. Regional director and each other party	Three working days before due date of briefs	a. Eight copies b. One copy
Withdrawal of petition	a. Regional director—if case before him b. Board—if case has been transferred to Board	. . . .	a. One copy b. One copy
Tally of ballots	Each designated representative of the parties	Upon completion of tally	One copy

TABLE I. REPRESENTATION CASES (*Contd.*)

Document	Who Must Be Served	When It Must Be Served	How Many Copies
Objections to election	a. Regional director b. Each other party	Within five working days after service of tally of ballots	a. An original and three copies b. One copy
Exceptions to hearing officer's report on objections and/or challenged ballots. (Hearing ordered by regional director)	a. Regional director b. Each other party	Within 10 days after service of report	a. An original and one copy b. One copy
Regional director's report on objections to conduct of election	Each of the parties	. . . . .	One copy
Regional director's report on challenged ballots	Each of the parties	. . . . .	One copy
Exceptions to the regional director's report on objections to conduct of election	a. Board b. Regional director and each other party	Within 10 days after issuance of report	a. Eight copies b. One copy
Exceptions to the regional director's report on challenged ballots	a. Board b. Regional director and each other party	Within 10 days after issuance of report	a. Eight copies b. One copy

Document	Who Must Be Served	When It Must Be Served	How Many Copies
Exceptions to hearing officer's report on objections and/or challenged ballots. (Hearing ordered by the Board on basis of regional director's report and exceptions thereto)	a. Board b. Regional director and each other party	Within 10 days after issuance of report	a. Eight copies b. One copy
Revised Tally of ballots	Each designated representative of the parties	Upon completion of revised tally	One copy
Objections to revised tally of ballots	a. Regional director b. Each other party	Within three working days after revised tally has been furnished	a. An original and three copies b. One copy
Request for hearing in expedited election cases	a. Board b. Each other party	Promptly	a. Eight copies b. One copy
Request to appeal regional director's decision in "expedited election" cases	a. Board b. Each other party	Promptly	a. Eight copies b. One copy
Request to appeal refusal to issue complaint in "expedited election" cases	a. General Counsel b. Regional director	Within three working days from service of notice of dismissal	a. One copy b. One copy

TABLE I. REPRESENTATION CASES (*Contd.*)

Document	Who Must Be Served	When It Must Be Served	How Many Copies
Petition for clarification of bargaining unit	Regional Office	. . . .	An original and four copies
Petition for amendment of certification	Regional Office	. . . .	An original and four copies
Motion to revoke certification	a. Board b. Regional director and each other party	. . . .	a. Eight copies b. One copy
Petition to rescind union shop agreement	Regional Office	Any time	An original and four copies
Petition for advisory opinion	a. Board b. Each other party	While a proceeding is pending	a. Eight copies b. One copy
Response to petition for advisory petition	a. Board b. Each other party	Within five days after service of petition	a. Eight copies b. One copy
Motion to intervene on petition for advisory opinion	a. Board b. Each other party	Promptly	a. Eight copies b. One copy
Response to petition for declaratory order and brief in support thereof	a. Board b. Each other party	Within five days after service of petition	a. Eight copies b. One copy
Motion to intervene on petition for declaratory order	a. Board b. Each other party	Promptly	a. Eight copies b. One copy

TABLE 2. UNFAIR LABOR PRACTICE CASES

Document	Who Must Be Served	When It Must Be Served	How Many Copies
Charge	a. Regional office b. Party against whom the charge is made	a. Within six months after the alleged unfair labor practice b. Same time	a. An original and four copies b. One copy
Data in support of charge	Regional office	Within 72 hours of filing charge	One copy
Appeal from regional director's dismissal of charge	a. General Counsel in Washington b. Regional director	a. Within 10 days after receipt of dismissal b. Same time	a. One copy b. One copy
Regional director's complaint	Each of the parties	. . . .	One copy
Answer to complaint	a. Regional director b. Each other party	a. Within 10 days after receipt of complaint b. Same time	a. An original and four copies b. One copy
Request for extension of time to file answer to complaint	a. Regional director	Within three working days prior to due date	One copy
Notice of hearing	Each of the parties	At least 10 days before date of hearing	One copy
Request for postponement of hearing	a. Regional director b. Each other party	Within three working days prior to hearing date	a. An original and two copies b. One copy

TABLE 2. UNFAIR LABOR PRACTICE CASES *(contd.)*

Document	Who Must Be Served	When It Must Be Served	How Many Copies
Prehearing motion	a. Regional director b. Each other party	· · · · · · · ·	a. An original and four copies b. One copy
Prehearing application for subpoena	Regional director	· · · ·	One copy
Petition to revoke prehearing subpoena	Regional director	Within five days of receipt of subpoena	One copy
Request for special permission to appeal from regional director's ruling	a. Board b. Each other party	Promptly	a. Eight copies b. One copy
Request for special permission to appeal from administrative law judge's ruling	a. Board b. Each other party c. Administrative law judge	Promptly	a. Eight copies b. One copy c. One copy
Written motion before administrative law judge	Administrative law judge	· · · ·	One copy
Motion to intervene	a. Regional director prior to hearing; administrative law judge during hearing b. Each other party	· · · ·	a. An original and four copies or orally upon the record b. One copy

Document	Who Must Be Served	When It Must Be Served	How Many Copies
Application to take depositions	a. Regional director prior to hearing; administrative law judge during hearing b. Each other party	Seven days prior to proposed date	a. An original and four copies b. One copy
Application for subpoena during hearing	Administrative law judge		One copy
Petition to revoke subpoena	Administrative law judge	Within five days of receipt of subpoena	One copy
Appeal from administrative law judge's ruling before issuance of his decision	a. Board b. Each other party	. . . .	a. Eight copies b. One copy
Motion filed with administrative law judge after close of hearing and before issuance of his decision	a. Administrative law judge, care of chief administrative law judge in Washington b. Each other party	. . . .	a. One copy b. One copy
Brief to be filed with administrative law judge after close of hearing	a. Administrative law judge b. Each other party	a. Within a maximum of 35 days after close of hearing b. Same time	a. Three copies b. One copy

TABLE 2. UNFAIR LABOR PRACTICE CASES (*contd.*)

Document	Who Must Be Served	When It Must Be Served	How Many Copies
Request made after close of hearing for extension of time in which to file brief with administrative law judge	a. Chief administrative law judge in Washington b. Each other party	a. No later than three working days before due date b. Same time	a. One copy b. One copy
Exceptions to administrative law judge's decision and brief in support of exceptions	a. Board b. Each other party	20 days from service of administrative law judge's decision	a. Eight copies b. One copy
Request for extension of time for filing exceptions to administrative law judge's decision and brief in support of exceptions	a. Board b. Each other party	Three working days prior to due date of exceptions	a. Eight copies b. One copy
Brief in support of administrative law judge's decision	a. Board b. Each other party	20 days from service of administrative law judge's decision	a. Eight copies b. One copy
Request for extension of time for filing brief in support of administrative law judge's decision	a. Board b. Each other party	Three working days prior to due date of brief in support of administrative law judge's decision	a. Eight copies b. One copy

Document	Who Must Be Served	When It Must Be Served	How Many Copies
Answering brief to the exceptions	a. Board b. Each other party	10 days from due date of exceptions	a. Eight copies b. One copy
Request for extension of time to file answering brief	a. Board b. Each other party	Three working days prior to due date of answering brief	a. Eight copies b. One copy
Cross-exceptions to administrative law judge's decision together with supporting brief	a. Board b. Each other party	10 days from due date of exceptions	a. Eight copies b. One copy
Request for extension of time to file cross-exceptions together with supporting brief	a. Board b. Each other party	Three working days prior to due date of exceptions	a. Eight copies b. One copy
Answering brief to cross-exceptions	a. Board b. Each other party	10 days from due date of cross-exceptions	a. Eight copies b. One copy
Request for extension of time to file answering brief to cross-exceptions	a. Board b. Each other party	Three working days prior to due date of answering brief to cross-exceptions	a. Eight copies b. One copy
Special permission to file further brief	a. Board b. Each other party	Promptly	a. Eight copies b. One copy
Request for oral argument before Board	a. Board b. Each other party	Time of filing of exceptions or cross-exceptions	a. Eight copies b. One copy

TABLE 2. UNFAIR LABOR PRACTICE CASES *(contd.)*

Document	Who Must Be Served	When It Must Be Served	How Many Copies
Motion for reconsideration, rehearing, or reopening of record	a. Board b. Each other party	Within 20 days after service of Board's decision	a. Eight copies b. One copy
Motion for leave to adduce additional evidence	a. Board b. Each other party	Promptly upon discovery of such evidence	a. Eight copies b. One copy
Briefs in jurisdictional-dispute (Sec. 10(k)) proceedings (except cases involving the national defense)	a. Board b. Each other party	Seven days after close of hearing	a. Eight copies b. One copy
Request for extension of time to file brief in Sec. 10(k) proceedings	a. Board b. Each other party	Three working days prior to due date	a. Eight copies b. One copy
Special permission to file reply brief in Sec. 10(k) proceedings	a. Board b. Each other party	Promptly	a. Eight copies b. One copy
Special permission to file briefs in Sec. 10(k) proceedings involving the national defense	a. Board b. Each other party	Expeditiously	a. Eight copies b. One copy
Regional director's issuance of back-pay specification	Each of the parties	. . . . .	One copy

Document	Who Must Be Served	When It Must Be Served	How Many Copies
Answer to back-pay specification	a. Regional director b. Each other party	Within 15 days of service of specification	a. An original and four copies b. One copy
Request for extension of time for filing answer to specification	Regional director	Within three working days prior to due date	One copy
Request for postponement of back-pay hearing	a. Regional director b. Each other party	Within three working days prior to hearing date	a. One copy b. One copy

CHAPTER 23

Records and Information

Sec. 23–1. In general. From its earliest days the Board has made available to the public bound volumes of its case decisions, copies of its rules and regulations, and its annual reports. It refused to supply most other records and information, however. During this period the majority of its representation case decisions were issued as "short forms" and were unpublished. After the delegation of authority over these matters to the regional directors in 1961 (see Sec. 4–2, Delegation to the regional directors, page 41), all Board decisions in representation matters were included in the bound volumes, but regional directors' decisions continued to be unpublished.

In recent years other materials have finally begun to be made available, particularly after decisions under the Freedom of Information Act generally required greater disclosure by government agencies. The public should soon have access to a wide range of internal Board memoranda and policy handbooks.

Sec. 23–2. Materials currently published on a regular basis. The Board and the General Counsel regularly publish the following:

1. Decisions and Orders of the National Labor Relations Board. These are bound volumes containing complete decisions of the Board. They may be purchased from the Superintendent of Documents, U. S. Government Printing Office, Washington, D. C. 20402. Only relatively current volumes are available and there are serious delays in publication, frequently as much as a year. Copies of individual decisions may be obtained immediately after issuance from the Division of Information, National Labor Relations Board, Washington, D. C. 20570, but the Board has declined to establish any method for distributing such decisions to the general public. They are available to the public promptly, however, through commercial services such as the *Labor Relations Reporter* (published by the Bureau of National Affairs, Washington, D. C. 20037).

2. The Annual Report of the National Labor Relations Board. After the close of each fiscal year the Board issues an annual report containing statistical material and a review of significant case decisions. These rarely appear until the following calendar year. They are available from the Superintendent of Documents, U. S. Government Printing Office, Washington, D. C. 20402.

3. *Rules and Regulations and Statements of Procedure, Series 8, As Amended.* Formerly a paperback pamphlet, the Board's rules and regulations are now issued in looseleaf form in order that amendments may be added. Copies of the current rules and a subscription to any changes are available through the Superintendent of Documents, U. S. Government Printing Office, Washington, D. C. 20402. Frequently there are long delays before changes are distributed.

4. *Weekly Summary of NLRB cases.* The Board's Division of Information issues a weekly summary of Board decisions and orders, directions of elections by the Board, decisions and certifications, decisions on review, determinations of disputes in jurisdictional dispute cases, dismissals of representation petitions by the Board and stipulated decisions. Actions of administrative law judges and regional directors are listed but not summarized. Special notices of various types are also included. Unfortunately, the summaries are so limited in nature that they are not useful as a research source. Requests to be placed on the mailing list for the summaries should be addressed to Division of Information, National Labor Relations Board, Washington, D. C. 20570.

5. *General Counsel's Report of Case Handling Developments.* Each quarter the General Counsel issues a report discussing his rulings on whether or not to issue unfair labor practice complaints in cases involving important or unusual issues. These reports are valuable sources of policy changes and developments at the earliest stages. Copies may be obtained from the Division of Information, National Labor Relations Board, Washington, D. C. 20570, and are also published by the Bureau of National Affairs on a current basis as a part of its weekly *Labor Relations Reporter* service and as a permanent reference in its *Labor Relations Yearbooks.*

6. *NLRB General Counsel's Monthly Report on Health Care Institution Cases.* After enactment in 1974 of the amendments extending the jurisdiction of the Act to include nonprofit hospitals, the General Counsel announced that he would issue monthly reports of determinations made in cases arising under the amendments. The purpose of the reports is to keep ". . . the public and affected parties as fully informed as possible with respect to the General Counsel's case dispositions under the amendments."[1] The reports receive the same distribution as the General Counsel's quarterly reports on case handling.

---

[1]LABOR RELATIONS YEARBOOK - 1974 (Washington, D. C.: BNA Books, 1975), p. 335.

7. Miscellaneous Materials. Infrequently the Board issues, through the Division of Information, general explanatory pamphlets on its function and the law it enforces. These are not in sufficient detail to be useful as research sources or procedural manuals. Statistical information, news releases, and other miscellaneous materials are also issued by the Division of Information from time to time.

Sec. 23–3. Records and information available for inspection and copying.
The Board has adopted amendments to its rules that list in some detail the Board materials and documents available for public inspection and copying.[2] The following are available to the public:

1. Final opinions and orders made by the Board.
2. Administrative staff manuals and instructions that affect any member of the public (excepting those establishing internal operating rules, guidelines, and procedures for the investigation, trial, and settlement of cases).
3. A record of the final votes of each member of the Board in every agency proceeding.
4. A current index of final opinions and orders made in the adjudication of cases (which may be relied on, used, or cited as precedent by the agency against any private party).
5. Formal documents constituting the record in a case or proceeding.

These are available for inspection and copying at the Board's Washington office and, except for the record of final votes, at the regional offices also. Final opinions and orders made by regional directors in representation cases are also available at the original office where issued. Duplicating charges are established by amendments to the rules.

The rules contemplate that records other than those listed above will also be available under the Freedom of Information Act. They establish a procedure for making written requests containing a description of the records sought and indicating that the request is made under the Freedom of Information Act. The requests must contain a specific statement assuming financial liability for the search of the records. They are to be addressed to the Freedom of Information Officer, Office of the General Counsel, if the records are in the Washington office of the General Counsel; to the Executive Secretary of the Board, if in the Washington office of the Board; and to the appropriate regional or subregional office if in that office.[3]

The scope of materials include:

1. Memoranda of decisions of the General Counsel in advice and appeal cases where the General Counsel refuses to issue an unfair labor

---

[2]R. and R. Sec. 102.117, Sec. 102.118(a).
[3]Ibid., Sec. 102.117(c)(1).

practice complaint.[4] The General Counsel has adopted the practice of disclosing advice and appeals memoranda in cases where a complaint is issued but not until the matter has been litigated.

2. An index of unpublished regional directors' decisions.[5]
3. A classification outline of advice memoranda indexing all such memoranda since 1967. (These are now available in each regional office.)

Sec. 23–4. Materials expected to be published. Recently the Board and the General Counsel advised the Committee on Practice and Procedure under the National Labor Relations Act of the American Bar Association that the following are expected to be published in 1975:

1. A classification index and litigation manual.
2. Completely revised field manuals consisting of an unfair labor practice case manual, a representation case manual, and a compliance manual. Revisions are to be published in the regular weekly summary and through a subscription service.
3. A hearing officer's guide used by hearing officers in representation cases.
4. An outline of the law in representation cases.
5. A revised administrative law judges' manual. This will replace the outdated Trial Examiner's Manual issued several years ago.

Some of these materials seem to go beyond the exceptions to disclosable material under the rules discussed above; in any event, they will be valuable sources of information for the labor law practitioner. Presumably they will be available through the Superintendent of Documents, U. S. Government Printing Office.

[4]NLRB v. Sears, Roebuck & Co., —— U.S. ——, 89 LRRM 2001 (1975).
[5]Automobile Club of Missouri v. N.L.R.B., 495 F.2d 1074, 86 LRRM 2064, (D.C. Cir. 1974).

LABOR MANAGEMENT RELATIONS ACT

Pub. L. No. 101, 80th Cong., 1st Sess. (1947), 61
Stat. 136 (1947), as amended by Pub. L. No. 257,
86th Cong., 1st Sess. (1959), 73 Stat. 541 (1959),
and by Pub. L. No. 93-360, 93rd Cong., 2nd Sess. (1974),
88 Stat. 395 (1974); 29 U.S.C. §§141 et seq.

SHORT TITLE AND DECLARATION OF POLICY

§1. (a) This Act may be cited as the "Labor Management Relations Act, 1947".

(b) Industrial strife which interferes with the normal flow of commerce and with the full production of articles and commodities for commerce, can be avoided or substantially minimized if employers, employees, and labor organizations each recognize under law one another's legitimate rights in their relations with each other, and above all recognize under law that neither party has any right in its relations with any other to engage in acts or practices which jeopardize the public health, safety, or interest.

It is the purpose and policy of this Act, in order to promote the full flow of commerce, to prescribe the legitimate rights of both employees and employers in their relations affecting commerce, to provide orderly and peaceful procedures for preventing the interference by either with the legitimate rights of the other, to protect the rights of individual employees in their relations with labor organizations whose activities affect commerce, to define and proscribe practices on the part of labor and management which affect commerce and are inimical to the general welfare, and to protect the rights of the public in connection with labor disputes affecting commerce.

TITLE I — AMENDMENT OF NATIONAL LABOR RELATIONS ACT
[49 Stat. 449 (1935)]

§101. The National Labor Relations Act is hereby amended to read as follows: *

* Section 201(d) and (e) of the Labor-Management Reporting and Disclosure Act of 1959, which repealed Section 9(f), (g), and (h) of the Labor Management Relations Act, 1947, and Section 505 amending Section 302(a), (b), and (c) of the Labor Management Relations Act, 1947, took effect upon enactment of Public Law 86-257, September 14, 1959. As to the other amendments of the Labor Management Relations Act, 1947, Section 707 of the Labor-Management Reporting and Disclosure Act provides:

"The amendments made by this title shall take effect sixty days after the date of the enactment of this Act and no provision of this title shall be deemed to make an unfair labor practice, any act which is performed prior to such effective date which did not constitute an unfair labor practice prior thereto."

The provisions of the original NLRA are in roman type; provisions added by the Labor Management Relations Act (1947) are in bold face; provisions added by the Labor-Management Reporting and Disclosure Act (1959) are in italics; provisions added by Public Law 93-360 (enacted July 26, 1974) are in bold-face italics. Material deleted by any of those statutes is enclosed by brackets.

FINDINGS AND POLICIES

§1. The denial by some employers of the right of employees to organize and the refusal by some employers to accept the procedure of collective bargaining lead to strikes and other forms of industrial strife or unrest, which have the intent or the necessary effect of burdening or obstructing commerce by (a) impairing the efficiency, safety, or operation of the instrumentalities of commerce; (b) occurring in the current of commerce; (c) materially affecting, restraining, or controlling the flow of raw materials or manufactured or processed goods from or into the channels of commerce, or the prices of such materials or goods in commerce; or (d) causing diminution of employment and wages in such volume as substantially to impair or disrupt the market for goods flowing from or into the channels of commerce.

The inequality of bargaining power between employees who do not possess full freedom of association or actual liberty of contract, and employers who are organized in the corporate or other forms of ownership association substantially burdens and affects the flow of commerce, and tends to aggravate recurrent business depressions, by depressing wage rates and the purchasing power of wage earners in industry and by preventing the stabilization of competitive wage rates and working conditions within and between industries.

Experience has proved that protection by law of the right of employees to organize and bargain collectively safeguards commerce from injury, impairment, or interruption, and promotes the flow of commerce by removing certain recognized sources of industrial strife and unrest, by encouraging practices fundamental to the friendly adjustment of industrial disputes arising out of differences as to wages, hours, or other working conditions, and by restoring equality of bargaining power between employers and employees.

Experience has further demonstrated that certain practices by some labor organizations, their officers, and members have the intent or the necessary effect of burdening or obstructing commerce by preventing the free flow of goods in such commerce through strikes and other forms of industrial unrest or through concerted activities which impair the interest of the public in the free flow of such commerce. The elimination of such practices is a necessary condition to the assurance of the rights herein guaranteed.

It is hereby declared to be the policy of the United States to eliminate the causes of certain substantial obstructions to the free flow of commerce and to mitigate and eliminate these obstructions when they have occurred by encouraging the practice and procedure of collective bargaining and by protecting the exercise by workers of full freedom of association, self-organization, and designation of representatives of their own choosing, for the purpose of negotiating the terms and conditions of their employment or other mutual aid or protection.

DEFINITIONS

§2. When used in this Act —

(1) The term "person" includes one or more individuals, labor organizations, partnerships, associations, corporations, legal representatives, trustees, trustees in bankruptcy, or receivers.

(2) The term "employer" includes any person acting [in the interest] **as an agent** of an employer, directly or indirectly, but shall not include the United States **or any wholly owned Government corporation, or any Federal Reserve Bank,** or any State or political subdivision thereof, [**or any corporation or association operating a hospital, if no part of the net earnings inures to the benefit of any private shareholder or individual,**] or any person subject to the Railway Labor Act, as amended from time to time, or any labor organization (other than when acting as an employer), or anyone acting in the capacity of officer or agent of such labor organization.

(3) The term "employee" shall include any employee, and shall not be limited to the employees of a particular employer, unless the Act explicitly states otherwise, and shall include any individual whose work has ceased as a consequence of, or in connection with, any current labor dispute or because of any unfair labor practice, and who has not obtained any other regular and substantially equivalent employment, but shall not include any individual employed as an agricultural laborer, or in the domestic service of any family or person at his home, or any individual employed by his parent or spouse, **or any individual having the status of an independent contractor, or any individual employed as a supervisor, or any individual employed by an employer subject to the Railway Labor Act, as amended from time to time, or by any other person who is not an employer as herein defined.**

(4) The term "representatives" includes any individual or labor organization.

(5) The term "labor organization" means any organization of any kind, or any agency or employee representation committee or plan, in which employees participate and which exists for the purpose, in whole or in part, of dealing with employers concerning grievances, labor disputes, wages, rates of pay, hours of employment, or conditions of work.

(6) The term "commerce" means trade, traffic, commerce, transportation, or communication among the several States, or between the District of Columbia or any Territory of the United States and any State or other Territory, or between any foreign country and any State, Territory, or the District of Columbia, or within the District of Columbia or any Territory, or between points in the same State but through any other State or any Territory or the District of Columbia or any foreign country.

(7) The term "affecting commerce" means in commerce, or burdening or obstructing commerce or the free flow of commerce, or having led or tending to lead to a labor dispute burdening or obstructing commerce or the free flow of commerce.

(8) The term "unfair labor practice" means any unfair labor practice listed in section 8.

(9) The term "labor dispute" includes any controversy concerning terms, tenure or conditions of employment, or concerning the association or representation of persons in negotiating, fixing, maintaining, changing, or seeking to arrange terms or conditions of employment, regardless of whether the disputants stand in the proximate relation of employer and employee.

(10) The term "National Labor Relations Board" means the National Labor Relations Board provided for in section 3 of this Act.

(11) The term "supervisor" means any individual having authority, in the interest of the employer, to hire, transfer, suspend, lay off, recall, promote, discharge, assign, reward, or discipline other employees, or responsibly to direct them, or to adjust their grievances, or effectively to recommend such action, if in connection with the foregoing the exercise of such authority is not of a merely routine or clerical nature, but requires the use of independent judgment.

(12) The term "professional employee" means—

(a) any employee engaged in work (i) predominantly intellectual and varied in character as opposed to routine mental, manual, mechanical, or physical work; (ii) involving the consistent exercise of discretion and judgment in its performance; (iii) of such a character that the output produced or the result accomplished cannot be standardized in relation to a given period of time; (iv) requiring knowledge of an advanced type in a field of science or learning customarily acquired by a prolonged course of specialized intellectual instruction and study in an institution of higher learning or a hospital, as distinguished from a general academic education or from an apprenticeship or from training in the performance of routine mental, manual, or physical processes; or

(b) any employee, who (i) has completed the courses of specialized intellectual instruction and study described in clause (iv) of paragraph (a), and (ii) is performing related work under the supervision of a professional person to qualify himself to become a professional employee as defined in paragraph (a).

(13) In determining whether any person is acting as an "agent" of another person so as to make such other person responsible for his acts, the question of whether the specific acts performed were actually authorized or subsequently ratified shall not be controlling.

(14) The term 'health care institution' shall include any hospital, convalescent hospital, health maintenance organization, health clinic, nursing home, extended care facility, or other institution devoted to the care of sick, infirm, or aged person.

NATIONAL LABOR RELATIONS BOARD

§3. (a) The National Labor Relations Board (hereinafter called the "Board") created by this Act prior to its amendment by the Labor Management Relations Act, 1947, is hereby continued as an agency of the United States, except that the Board shall consist of five instead of three members, appointed by the President by and with the advice and consent of the Senate. Of the two additional members so provided for, one shall be appointed for a term of five years and the other for a term of two years. Their successors, and the successors of the other members, shall be appointed for terms of five years each, excepting that any individual chosen to fill a vacancy shall be appointed only for the unexpired term of the member whom he shall succeed. The President shall designate one member to serve as Chairman of the Board. Any member of the Board may be removed by the President, upon notice and hearing, for neglect of duty or malfeasance in office, but for no other cause.

(b) The Board is authorized to delegate to any group of three or more members any or all of the powers which it may itself exercise. *The Board is also authorized to delegate to its regional directors its powers under section 9 to determine the unit appropriate for the purpose of collective bargaining, to investigate and provide for hearings, and determine whether a question of representation exists, and to direct an election or take a secret ballot under subsection (c) or (e) of section 9 and certify the results thereof, except that upon the filing of a request therefor with the Board by any interested person, the Board may review any action of a regional director delegated to him under this paragraph, but such a review shall not, unless specifically ordered by the Board, operate as a stay of any action taken by the regional director.* A vacancy in the Board shall not impair the right of the remaining members to exercise all of the powers of the Board, and three members of the Board shall, at all times, constitute a quorum of the Board, except that two members shall constitute a quorum of any group designated pursuant to the first sentence thereof. The Board shall have an official seal which shall be judicially noticed.

(c) The Board shall at the close of each fiscal year make a report in writing to Congress and to the President stating in detail the cases it has heard, the decisions it has rendered, the names, salaries, and duties of all employees and officers in the employ or under the supervision of the Board, and an account of all moneys it has disbursed.

(d) There shall be a General Counsel of the Board who shall be appointed by the President, by and with the advice and consent of the Senate, for a term of four years. The General Counsel of the Board shall exercise general supervision over all attorneys employed by the Board (other than trial examiners and legal assistants to Board members) and over the officers and employees in the regional offices. He shall have final authority, on behalf of the Board, in respect of the investigation of charges and issuance of complaints under section 10,

and in respect of the prosecution of such complaints before the Board, and shall have such other duties as the Board may prescribe or as may be provided by law. *In case of a vacancy in the office of the General Counsel the President is authorized to designate the officer or employee who shall act as General Counsel during such vacancy, but no person or persons so designated shall so act (1) for more than forty days when the Congress is in session unless a nomination to fill such vacancy shall have been submitted to the Senate, or (2) after the adjournment sine die of the session of the Senate in which such nomination was submitted.*

§4. (a) **Each member of the Board and the General Counsel of the Board shall receive a salary of $12,000 * a year, shall be eligible for reappointment, and shall not engage in any other business, vocation, or employment. The Board shall appoint an executive secretary, and such attorneys, examiners, and regional directors, and such other employees as it may from time to time find necessary for the proper performance of its duties. The Board may not employ any attorneys for the purpose of reviewing transcripts of hearings or preparing drafts of opinions except that any attorney employed for assignment as a legal assistant to any Board member may for such Board member review such transcripts and prepare such drafts. No trial examiner's report shall be reviewed, either before or after its publication, by any person other than a member of the Board or his legal assistant, and no trial examiner shall advise or consult with the Board with respect to exceptions taken to his findings, rulings, or recommendations. The Board may establish or utilize such regional, local, or other agencies, and utilize such voluntary and uncompensated services, as may from time to time be needed. Attorneys appointed under this section may, at the direction of the Board, appear for and represent the Board in any case in court. Nothing in this Act shall be construed to authorize the Board to appoint individuals for the purpose of conciliation or mediation, or for economic analysis.**

(b) **All the expenses of the Board, including all necessary traveling and subsistence expenses outside the District of Columbia incurred by the members or employees of the Board under its orders, shall be allowed and paid on the presentation of itemized vouchers therefor approved by the Board or by any individual it designates for that purpose.**

§5. The principal office of the Board shall be in the District of Columbia, but it may meet and exercise any or all of its powers at any other place. The Board may, by one or more of its members or by such agents or agencies as it may designate, prosecute any inquiry necessary to its functions in any part of the United States. A member who participates

---

* Pursuant to Pub. L. No. 426, 88th Cong., 2d Sess., Title III, approved August 14, 1964, the salary of the Chairman of the Board shall be $28,500 per year and the salaries of the general counsel and each board member shall be $27,000 per year. Pursuant to the recommendations of the President, the chairman's salary was raised to $40,000 per year and that of a board member and of the general counsel to $38,000 per year, effective February 14, 1969. See 5 U.S.C.A. §5314(25) and §5315(63) (and 1970 pocket part).

in such an inquiry shall not be disqualified from subsequently participating in a decision of the Board in the same case.

§6. The Board shall have authority from time to time to make, amend, and rescind, **in the manner prescribed by the Administrative Procedure Act,** such rules and regulations as may be necessary to carry out the provisions of this Act.

RIGHTS OF EMPLOYEES

§7. Employees shall have the right to self-organization, to form, join, or assist labor organizations, to bargain collectively through representatives of their own choosing, and to engage in **other** concerted activities for the purpose of collective bargaining or other mutual aid or protection, **and shall also have the right to refrain from any or all of such activities except to the extent that such right may be affected by an agreement requiring membership in a labor organization as a condition of employment as authorized in section 8(a)(3).**

UNFAIR LABOR PRACTICES

§8. (a) It shall be an unfair labor practice for an employer—

(1) to interfere with, restrain, or coerce employees in the exercise of the rights guaranteed in section 7;

(2) to dominate or interefere with the formation or administration of any labor organization or contribute financial or other support to it: *Provided,* That subject to rules and regulations made and published by the Board pursuant to section 6, an employer shall not be prohibited from permitting employees to confer with him during working hours without loss of time or pay;

(3) by discrimination in regard to hire or tenure of employment or any term or condition of employment to encourage or discourage membership in any labor organization: *Provided,* That nothing in this Act, or in any other statute of the United States, shall preclude an employer from making an agreement with a labor organization (not established, maintained, or assisted by any action defined in section 8(a) of this Act as an unfair labor practice) to require as a condition of employment membership therein **on or after the thirtieth day following the beginning of such employment or the effective date of such agreement, whichever is the later,** (i) if such labor organization is the representative of the employees as provided in section 9(a), in the appropriate collective-bargaining unit covered by such agreement when made **[and has at the time the agreement was made or within the preceding twelve months received from the Board a notice of compliance with section 9(f), (g), (h)], and (ii) unless following an election held as provided in section 9(e) within one year preceding the effective date of such agreement, the Board shall have certified that at least a majority of the employees eligible to vote in such election have voted to rescind the authority of such labor organization to make such an agreement:** *Provided*

further, That no employer shall justify any discrimination against an employee for nonmembership in a labor organization (A) if he has reasonable grounds for believing that such membership was not available to the employee on the same terms and conditions generally applicable to other members, or (B) if he has reasonable grounds for believing that membership was denied or terminated for reasons other than the failure of the employee to tender the periodic dues and the initiation fees uniformly required as a condition of acquiring or retaining membership;

(4) to discharge or otherwise discriminate against an employee because he has filed charges or given testimony under this Act;

(5) to refuse to bargain collectively with the representatives of his employees, subject to the provisions of section 9(a).

(b) **It shall be an unfair labor practice for a labor organization or its agents—**

(1) **to restrain or coerce (A) employees in the exercise of the rights guaranteed in section 7:** *Provided,* **That this paragraph shall not impair the right of a labor organization to prescribe its own rules with respect to the acquisition or retention of membership therein; or (B) an employer in the selection of his representatives for the purposes of collective bargaining or the adjustment of grievances;**

(2) **to cause or attempt to cause an employer to discriminate against an employee in violation of subsection (a)(3) or to discriminate against an employee with respect to whom membership in such organization has been denied or terminated on some ground other than his failure to tender the periodic dues and the initiation fees uniformly required as a condition of acquiring or retaining membership;**

(3) **to refuse to bargain collectively with an employer, provided it is the representative of his employees subject to the provisions of section 9(a);**

(4)(i) **to engage in, or to induce or encourage [the employees of any employer]** *any individual employed by any person engaged in commerce or in an industry affecting commerce* **to engage in, a strike or a [concerted] refusal in the course of [their]** *his* **employment to use, manufacture, process, transport, or otherwise handle or work on any goods, articles, materials, or commodities or to perform any services [,];** *or (ii) to threaten, coerce, or restrain any person engaged in commerce or in an industry affecting commerce,* **where** *in either case* **an object thereof is:**

(A) **forcing or requiring any employer or self-employed person to join any labor or employer organization or [any employer or other person to cease using, selling, handling, transporting, or otherwise dealing in the products of any other producer, processor, or manufacturer, or to cease doing business with any other person]** *to enter into any agreement which is prohibited by section 8(e);*

(B) *forcing or requiring any person to cease using, selling, handling, transporting, or otherwise dealing in the products of any other producer, processor, or manufacturer, or to cease doing business with any other person, or* **forcing or requiring any other employer to recognize or bargain with a labor organization as the representative of his employees unless such labor organization has been certified as the representative of such employees under the provisions of section 9 [;]:** *Provided, That nothing contained in this clause (B) shall be construed to make unlawful, where not otherwise unlawful, any primary strike or primary picketing;*

(C) **forcing or requiring any employer to recognize or bargain with a particular labor organization as the representative of his employees if another labor organization has been certified as the representative of such employees under the provisions of section 9;**

(D) **forcing or requiring any employer to assign particular work to employees in a particular labor organization or in a particular trade, craft, or class rather than to employees in another labor organization or in another trade, craft, or class, unless such employer is failing to conform to an order or certification of the Board determining the bargaining representative for employees performing such work;**

***Provided*, That nothing contained in this subsection (b) shall be construed to make unlawful a refusal by any person to enter upon the premises of any employer (other than his own employer), if the employees of such employer are engaged in a strike ratified or approved by a representative of such employees whom such employer is required to recognize under this Act [;]:** *Provided further, That for the purposes of this paragraph (4) only, nothing contained in such paragraph shall be construed to prohibit publicity, other than picketing, for the purpose of truthfully advising the public, including consumers and members of a labor organization, that a product or products are produced by an employer with whom the labor organization has a primary dispute and are distributed by another employer, as long as such publicity does not have an effect of inducing any individual employed by any person other than the primary employer in the course of his employment to refuse to pick up, deliver, or transport any goods, or not to perform any services, at the establishment of the employer engaged in such distribution;*

(5) **to require of employees covered by an agreement authorized under subsection (a)(3) the payment, as a condition precedent to becoming a member of such organization, of a fee in an amount which the Board finds excessive or discriminatory under all the circumstances. In making such a finding, the Board shall consider, among other relevant factors, the practices and customs of labor organizations in the particular industry, and the wages currently paid to the employees affected; [and]**

(6) **to cause or attempt to cause an employer to pay or deliver or agree to pay or deliver any money or other thing of value, in the nature of an exaction, for services which are not performed or not to be performed[.]; and**

(7) *to picket or cause to be picketed, or threaten to picket or cause to be picketed, any employer where an object thereof is forcing or requiring an employer to recognize or bargain with a labor organization as the representative of his employees, or forcing or requiring the employees of an employer to accept or select such labor organization as their collective bargaining representative, unless such labor organization is currently certified as the representative of such employees:*

(A) *where the employer has lawfully recognized in accordance with this Act any other labor organization and a question concerning representation may not appropriately be raised under section 9(c) of this Act,*

(B) *where within the preceding twelve months a valid election under section 9(c) of this Act has been conducted, or*

(C) *where such picketing has been conducted without a petition under section 9(c) being filed within a reasonable period of time not to exceed thirty days from the commencement of such picketing:* Provided, *That when such a petition has been filed the Board shall forthwith, without regard to the provisions of section 9(c)(1) or the absence of a showing of a substantial interest on the part of the labor organization, direct an election in such unit as the Board finds to be appropriate and shall certify the results thereof:* Provided further, *That nothing in this subparagraph (C) shall be construed to prohibit any picketing or other publicity for the purpose of truthfully advising the public (including consumers) that an employer does not employ members of, or have a contract with, a labor organization, unless an effect of such picketing is to induce any individual employed by any other person in the course of his employment, not to pick up, deliver or transport any goods or not to perform any services.*

Nothing in this paragraph (7) shall be construed to permit any act which would otherwise be an unfair labor practice under this section 8(b).

(c) **The expressing of any views, argument, or opinion, or the dissemination thereof, whether in written, printed, graphic, or visual form, shall not constitute or be evidence of an unfair labor practice under any of the provisions of this Act, if such expression contains no threat of reprisal or force or promise of benefit.**

(d) **For the purposes of this section, to bargain collectively is the performance of the mutual obligation of the employer and the representative of the employees to meet at reasonable times, and confer in good faith with respect to wages, hours, and other terms and conditions of employment, or the negotiation of an agreement, or any question aris-**

ing thereunder, and the execution of a written contract incorporating any agreement reached if requested by either party, but such obligation does not compel either party to agree to a proposal or require the making of a concession: *Provided*, That where there is in effect a collective-bargaining contract covering employees in an industry affecting commerce, the duty to bargain collectively shall also mean that no party to such contract shall terminate or modify such contract, unless the party desiring such termination or modification—

(1) serves a written notice upon the other party to the contract of the proposed termination or modification sixty days prior to the expiration date thereof, or in the event such contract contains no expiration date, sixty days prior to the time it is proposed to make such termination or modification;

(2) offers to meet and confer with the other party for the purpose of negotiating a new contract or a contract containing the proposed modifications;

(3) notifies the Federal Mediation and Conciliation Service within thirty days after such notice of the existence of a dispute, and simultaneously therewith notifies any State or Territorial agency established to mediate and conciliate disputes within the State or Territory where the dispute occurred, provided no agreement has been reached by that time; and

(4) continues in full force and effect, without resorting to strike or lockout, all the terms and conditions of the existing contract for a period of sixty days after such notice is given or until the expiration date of such contract, whichever occurs later:

The duties imposed upon employers, employees, and labor organizations by paragraphs (2), (3), and (4) shall become inapplicable upon an intervening certification of the Board, under which the labor organization or individual, which is a party to the contract, has been superseded as or ceased to be the representative of the employees subject to the provisions of section 9(a), and the duties so imposed shall not be construed as requiring either party to discuss or agree to any modification of the terms and conditions contained in a contract for a fixed period, if such modification is to become effective before such terms and conditions can be re-opened under the provisions of the contract. Any employee who engages in a strike within [the sixty-day] *any notice* period specified in this subsection, *or who engages in any strike within the appropriate period specified in subsection (g) of this section* shall lose his status as an employee of the employer engaged in the particular labor dispute, for the purposes of sections 8, 9, and 10 of this Act, as amended, but such loss of status for such employee shall terminate if and when he is reemployed by such employer. *Whenever the collective bargaining involves employees of a health care institution, the provisions of this section 8(d) shall be modified as follows:*

(A) The notice of section 8(d)(1) shall be ninety days; the notice of section 8(d)(3) shall be sixty days; and the contract period of

section 8(d)(4) shall be ninety days.

(B) Where the bargaining is for an initial agreement following certification or recognition, at least thirty days' notice of the existence of a dispute shall be given by the labor organization to the agencies set forth in section 8(d)(3).

(C) After notice is given to the Federal Mediation and Conciliation Service under either clause (A) or (B) of this sentence, the Service shall promptly communicate with the parties and use its best efforts, by mediation and conciliation, to bring them to agreement. The parties shall participate fully and promptly in such meetings as may be undertaken by the Service for the purpose of aiding in a settlement of the dispute.

(e) It shall be an unfair labor practice for any labor organization and any employer to enter into any contract or agreement, express or implied, whereby such employer ceases or refrains or agrees to cease or refrain from handling, using, selling, transporting or otherwise dealing in any of the products of any other employer, or to cease doing business with any other person, and any contract or agreement entered into heretofore or here-after containing such an agreement shall be to such extent unenforceable and void: Provided, *That nothing in this subsection (e) shall apply to an agreement between a labor organization and an employer in the construction industry relating to the contracting or subcontracting of work to be done at the site of the construction, alteration, painting, or repair of a building, structure, or other work:* Provided further, *That for the purposes of this subsection (e) and section 8(b)(4) (B) the terms "any employer", "any person engaged in commerce or in industry affecting commerce", and "any person" when used in relation to the terms "any other producer, processor, or manufacturer", "any other employer", or "any other person" shall not include persons in the relation of a jobber, manufacturer, contractor, or subcontractor working on the goods or premises of the jobber or manufacturer or performing parts of an integrated process of production in the apparel and clothing industry:* Provided further, *That nothing in this Act shall prohibit the enforcement of any agreement which is within the foregoing exception.*

(f) It shall not be an unfair labor practice under subsections (a) and (b) of this section for an employer engaged primarily in the building and construction industry to make an agreement covering employees engaged (or who, upon their employment, will be engaged) in the building and construction industry with a labor organization of which building and construction employees are members (not established, maintained, or assisted by any action defined in section 8(a) of this Act as an unfair labor practice) because (1) the majority status of such labor organization has not been established under the provisions of section 9 of this Act prior to the making of such agreement, or (2) such agreement requires as a condition of employment, membership in such labor organization after the seventh day following the beginning of such employment or the effective date of the agreement, whichever is later, or (3) such agreement requires the employer to notify such labor organization of opportunities for employ-

ment with such employer, or gives such labor organization an opportunity to refer qualified applicants for such employment, or (4) such agreement specifies minimum training or experience qualifications for employment or provides for priority in opportunities for employment based upon length of service with such employer, in the industry or in the particular geographical area: Provided, *That nothing in this subsection shall set aside the final proviso to section 8(a)(3) of this Act:* Provided further, *That any agreement which would be invalid, but for clause (1) of this subsection, shall not be a bar to a petition filed pursuant to section 9(c) or 9(e).**

(g) A labor organization before engaging in any strike, picketing, or other concerted refusal to work at any health care institution shall, not less than ten days prior to such action, notify the institution in writing and the Federal Mediation and Conciliation Service of that intention, except that in the case of bargaining for an initial agreement following certification or recognition the notice required by this subsection shall not be given until the expiration of the period specified in clause (B) of the last sentence of section 8(d) of this Act. The notice shall state the date and time that such action will commence. The notice, once given, may be extended by the written agreement of both parties.

REPRESENTATIVES AND ELECTIONS

§9. (a) Representatives designated or selected for the purposes of collective bargaining by the majority of the employees in a unit appropriate for such purposes, shall be the exclusive representatives of all the employees in such unit for the purposes of collective bargaining in respect to rates of pay, wages, hours of employment, or other conditions of employment: *Provided,* That any individual employee or a group of employees shall have the right at any time to present grievances to their employer **and to have such grievances adjusted, without the intervention of the bargaining representative, as long as the adjustment is not inconsistent with the terms of a collective-bargaining contract or agreement then in effect:** *Provided further,* **That the bargaining representative has been given opportunity to be present at such adjustment.**

(b) The Board shall decide in each case whether, in order to assure to employees the fullest freedom in exercising the rights guaranteed by this Act, the unit appropriate for the purposes of collective bargaining shall be the employer unit, craft unit, plant unit, or subdivision thereof: ***Provided,* That the Board shall not (1) decide that any unit is appropriate for such purposes if such unit includes both professional employees and employees who are not professional employees unless a majority of**

---

* Section 8 (f) was inserted in the Act by subsection (a) of Section 705 of Public Law 86-257. Section 705(b) provides: "Nothing contained in the amendment made by subsection (a) shall be construed as authorizing the execution or application of agreements requiring membership in a labor organization as a condition of employment in any State or Territory in which such execution or application is prohibited by State or Territorial law."

such professional employees vote for inclusion in such unit; or (2) decide that any craft unit is inappropriate for such purposes on the ground that a different unit has been established by a prior Board determination, unless a majority of the employees in the proposed craft unit vote against separate representation or (3) decide that any unit is appropriate for such purposes if it includes, together with other employees, any individual employed as a guard to enforce against employees and other persons rules to protect property of the employer or to protect the safety of persons on the employer's premises; but no labor organization shall be certified as the representative of employees in a bargaining unit of guards if such organization admits to membership, or is affiliated directly or indirectly with an organization which admits to membership, employees other than guards.

[(c) Whenever a question affecting commerce arises concerning the representation of employees, the Board may investigate such controversy and certify to the parties, in writing, the name or names of the representatives that have been designated or selected. In any such investigation, the Board shall provide for an appropriate hearing upon due notice, either in conjunction with a proceeding under section 10 or otherwise, and may take a secret ballot of employees, or utilize any other suitable method to ascertain such representatives.]

(c)(1) Wherever a petition shall have been filed, in accordance with such regulations as may be prescribed by the Board—

(A) by an employee or group of employees or any individual or labor organization acting in their behalf alleging that a substantial number of employees (i) wish to be represented for collective bargaining and that their employer declines to recognize their representative as the representative defined in section 9(a), or (ii) assert that the individual or labor organization, which has been certified or is being currently recognized by their employer as the bargaining representative, is no longer a representative as defined in section 9(a); or

(B) by an employer, alleging that one or more individuals or labor organizations have presented to him a claim to be recognized as the representative defined in section 9(a);

the Board shall investigate such petition and if it has reasonable cause to believe that a question of representation affecting commerce exists shall provide for an appropriate hearing upon due notice. Such hearing may be conducted by an officer or employee of the regional office, who shall not make any recommendations with respect thereto. If the Board finds upon the record of such hearing that such a question of representation exists, it shall direct an election by secret ballot and shall certify the results thereof.

(2) In determining whether or not a question of representation affecting commerce exists, the same regulations and rules of decision shall apply irrespective of the identity of the persons filing the petition or

the kind of relief sought and in no case shall the Board deny a labor organization a place on the ballot by reason of an order with respect to such labor organization or its predecessor not issued in conformity with section 10(c).

(3) No election shall be directed in any bargaining unit or any subdivision within which, in the preceding twelve-month period, a valid election shall have been held. Employees [on] *engaged in an economic* strike who are not entitled to reinstatement shall [not] be eligible to vote[.] *under such regulations as the Board shall find are consistent with the purposes and provisions of this Act in any election conducted within twelve months after the commencement of the strike.* In any election where none of the choices on the ballot receives a majority, a run-off shall be conducted, the ballot providing for a selection between the two choices receiving the largest and second largest number of valid votes cast in the election.

(4) Nothing in this section shall be construed to prohibit the waiving of hearings by stipulation for the purpose of a consent election in conformity with regulations and rules of decision of the Board.

(5) In determining whether a unit is appropriate for the purposes specified in subsection (b) the extent to which the employees have organized shall not be controlling.

(d) Whenever an order of the Board made pursuant to section 10(c) is based in whole or in part upon facts certified following an investigation pursuant to subsection (c) of this section and there is a petition for the enforcement or review of such order, such certification and the record of such investigation shall be included in the transcript of the entire record required to be filed under section 10(e) or 10(f), and thereupon the decree of the court enforcing, modifying, or setting aside in whole or in part the order of the Board shall be made and entered upon the pleadings, testimony, and proceedings set forth in such transcript.

(e)(1) Upon the filing with the Board, by 30 per centum or more of the employees in a bargaining unit covered by an agreement between their employer and a labor organization made pursuant to section 8(a)(3), of a petition alleging they desire that such authority be rescinded, the Board shall take a secret ballot of the employees in such unit and certify the results thereof to such labor organization and to the employer.

(2) No election shall be conducted pursuant to this subsection in any bargaining unit or any subdivision within which, in the preceding twelve-month period, a valid election shall have been held.

PREVENTION OF UNFAIR LABOR PRACTICES

§10. (a) The Board is empowered, as hereinafter provided, to prevent any person from engaging in any unfair labor practice (listed in section 8) affecting commerce. This power shall not be affected by any other means of adjustment or prevention that has been or may be established by agreement, law, or otherwise: *Provided*, **That the Board is empowered by agreement with any agency of any State or Territory to cede to such agency jurisdiction over any cases in any industry (other than mining, manufacturing, communications, and transportation except where predominantly local in character) even though such cases may involve labor disputes affecting commerce, unless the provision of the State or Territorial statute applicable to the determination of such cases by such agency is inconsistent with the corresponding provision of this Act or has received a construction inconsistent therewith.**

(b) Whenever it is charged that any person has engaged in or is engaging in any such unfair labor practice, the Board, or any agent or agency designated by the Board for such purposes, shall have power to issue and cause to be served upon such person a complaint stating the charges in that respect, and containing a notice of hearing before the Board or a member thereof, or before a designated agent or agency, at a place therein fixed, not less than five days after the serving of said complaint: *Provided*, **That no complaint shall issue based upon any unfair labor practice occurring more than six months prior to the filing of the charge with the Board and the service of a copy thereof upon the person against whom such charge is made, unless the person aggrieved thereby was prevented from filing such charge by reason of service in the armed forces, in which event the six-month period shall be computed from the day of his discharge.** Any such complaint may be amended by the member, agent, or agency conducting the hearing or the Board in its discretion at any time prior to the issuance of an order based thereon. The person so complained of shall have the right to file an answer to the original or amended complaint and to appear in person or otherwise and give testimony at the place and time fixed in the complaint. In the discretion of the member, agent, or agency conducting the hearing or the Board, any other person may be allowed to intervene in the said proceeding and to present testimony. [In any such proceeding the rules of evidence prevailing in courts of law or equity shall not be controlling.] **Any such proceeding shall, so far as practicable, be conducted in accordance with the rules of evidence applicable in the district courts of the United States under the rules of civil procedure for the district courts of the United States, adopted by the Supreme Court of the United States pursuant to the Act of June 19, 1934 (U.S.C., title 28, secs. 723-B, 723-C).**

(c) The testimony taken by such member, agent, or agency or the Board shall be reduced to writing and filed with the Board. Thereafter, in its discretion, the Board upon notice may take further testimony or hear argument. If upon [all] **the preponderance of** the testimony taken the Board shall be of the opinion that any person named in the complaint has engaged in or is engaging in any such unfair labor practice, then the Board shall state its findings of fact and shall issue and cause to be served on such person an order requiring such person to cease and desist from such unfair labor practice, and to take such affirmative action including reinstatement of employees with or without back pay, as will effectuate the policies of this Act: *Provided,* **That where an order directs reinstatement of an employee, back pay may be required of the employer or labor organization, as the case may be, responsible for the discrimination suffered by him:** *And provided further,* **That in determining whether a complaint shall issue alleging a violation of section 8(a)(1) or section 8(a)(2), and in deciding such cases, the same regulations and rules of decision shall apply irrespective of whether or not the labor organization affected is affiliated with a labor organization national or international in scope. Such order may further require such person to make reports from time to time showing the extent to which it has complied with the order.** If upon [all] the preponderance of the testimony taken the Board shall not be of the opinion that the person named in the complaint has engaged in or is engaging in any such unfair labor practice, then the Board shall state its findings of fact and shall issue an order dismissing the said complaint. **No order of the Board shall require the reinstatement of any individual as an employee who has been suspended or discharged, or the payment to him of any back pay, if such individual was suspended or discharged for cause. In case the evidence is presented before a member of the Board, or before an examiner or examiners thereof, such member, or such examiner or examiners, as the case may be, shall issue and cause to be served on the parties to the proceeding a proposed report, together with a recommended order, which shall be filed with the Board, and if no exceptions are filed within twenty days after service thereof upon such parties, or within such further period as the Board may authorize, such recommended order shall become the order of the Board and become effective as therein prescribed.**

(d) Until the record in a case shall have been filed in a court, as hereinafter provided, the Board may at any time, upon reasonable notice and in such manner as it shall deem proper, modify or set aside, in whole or in part, any finding or order made or issued by it.

(e) The Board shall have power to petition any court of appeals of the United States, or if all the courts of appeals to which application may be made are in vacation, any district court of the United States, within any circuit or district, respectively, wherein the unfair labor practice in question occurred or wherein such person resides or transacts business, for the enforcement of such order and for appropriate temporary relief or restraining order, and shall file in the court the record in the proceedings, as provided in section 2112 of title 28, United States Code. Upon the filing of such petition, the court shall cause notice thereof to be served upon such person, and thereupon shall have jurisdiction of the proceeding and of the question determined therein, and shall have power to grant such temporary relief or restraining order as it deems just and proper, and to make and enter a decree enforcing, modifying, and enforcing as so modified, or setting aside in whole or in part the order of the Board. No objection that has not been urged before the Board, its member, agent, or agency, shall be considered by the court, unless the failure or neglect to urge such objection shall be excused because of extraordinary circumstances. The findings of the Board with respect to questions of fact if supported by **substantial** evidence **on the record considered as a whole** shall be conclusive. If either party shall apply to the court for leave to adduce additional evidence and shall show to the satisfaction of the court that such additional evidence is material and that there were reasonable grounds for the failure to adduce such evidence in the hearing before the Board, its member, agent, or agency, the court may order such additional evidence to be taken before the Board, its member, agent, or agency, and to be made a part of the record. The Board may modify its findings as to the facts, or make new findings, by reason of additional evidence so taken and filed, and it shall file such modified or new findings, which findings with respect to questions of fact if supported by substantial evidence on the record considered as a whole shall be conclusive, and shall file its recommendations, if any, for the modification or setting aside of its original order. Upon the filing of the record with it the jurisdiction of the court shall be exclusive and its judgment and decree shall be final, except that the same shall be subject to review by the appropriate United States court of appeals if application was made to the district court as hereinabove provided, and by the Supreme Court of the United States upon writ of certiorari or certification as provided in section 1254 of title 28.

(f) Any person aggrieved by a final order of the Board granting or denying in whole or in part the relief sought may obtain a review of such order in any circuit court of appeals of the United States in the circuit wherein the unfair labor practice in question was alleged to have been engaged in or wherein such person resides or transacts business, or in the United States Court of Appeals for the District of Columbia, by filing in such court a written petition praying that the order of the Board be modified or set aside. A copy of such petition shall be forthwith transmitted by the clerk of the court to the Board, and thereupon the aggrieved party shall file in the court the record in the proceeding, certified by the Board, as provided in section 2112 of title 28, United States Code. Upon the filing of such petition, the court shall proceed in the same manner as in the case of an application by the Board under subsection (e) of this section, and shall have the same jurisdiction to grant to the Board such temporary relief or restraining order as it deems just and proper, and in like manner to make and enter a decree enforcing, modifying, and enforcing as so modified, or setting aside in whole or in part the order of the Board; the findings of the Board with respect to questions of fact if supported by **substantial** evidence **on the record considered as a whole** shall in like manner be conclusive.

(g) The commencement of proceedings under subsection (e) or (f) of this section shall not, unless specifically ordered by the court, operate as a stay of the Board's order.

(h) When granting appropriate temporary relief or a restraining order, or making and entering a decree enforcing, modifying, and enforcing as so modified, or setting aside in whole or in part an order of the Board, as provided in this section, the jurisdiction of courts sitting in equity shall not be limited by the Act entitled "An Act to amend the Judicial Code and to define and limit the jurisdiction of courts sitting in equity, and for other purposes," approved March 23, 1932 (U.S.C., Supp. VII, title 29, secs. 101-115).

(i) Petitions filed under this Act shall be heard expeditiously, and if possible within ten days after they have been docketed.

(j) **The Board shall have power, upon issuance of a complaint as provided in subsection (b) charging that any person has engaged in or is engaging in an unfair labor practice, to petition any district court of the United States (including the District Court of the United States for the District of Columbia), within any district wherein the unfair labor practice in question is alleged to have occurred or wherein such person resides or transacts business, for appropriate temporary relief or restraining order. Upon the filing of any such petition the court shall cause notice thereof to be served upon such person, and thereupon shall have jurisdiction to grant to the Board such temporary relief or restraining order as it deems just and proper.**

(k) **Whenever it is charged that any person has engaged in an unfair labor practice within the meaning of paragraph (4)(D) of section 8(b), the Board is empowered and directed to hear and determine the dispute out of which such unfair labor practice shall have arisen, unless, within ten days after notice that such charge has been filed, the parties to such dispute submit to the Board satisfactory evidence that they have adjusted, or agreed upon methods for the voluntary adjustment of, the dispute. Upon compliance by the parties to the dispute with the decision of the Board or upon such voluntary adjustment of the dispute, such charge shall be dismissed.**

(l) **Whenever it is charged that any person has engaged in an unfair labor practice within the meaning of paragraphs (4)(A), (B), or (C) of section 8(b),** *or section 8(e) or section 8(b)(7),* **the preliminary investigation of such charge shall be made forthwith and given priority over all other cases except cases of like character in the office where it is filed or to which it is referred. If, after such investigation, the officer or regional attorney to whom the matter may be referred has reasonable cause to believe such charge is true and that a complaint should issue, he shall, on behalf of the Board, petition any district court of the United States (including the District Court of the United States for the District of Columbia) within any district where the unfair labor practice in question has occurred, is alleged to have occurred, or wherein such person resides or transacts business, for appropriate injunctive relief pending the final adjudication of the Board with respect to such matter. Upon the filing of any such petition the district court shall have jurisdiction to grant such injunctive relief or temporary restraining order as it deems just and proper, notwithstanding any other provision of law:** *Provided further,* **That no temporary restraining order shall be issued** without notice unless a petition alleges that substantial and irreparable injury to the charging party will be unavoidable and such temporary restraining order shall be effective for no longer than five days and will become void at the expiration of such period [.]: *Provided further, That such officer or regional attorney shall not apply for any restraining order under section 8(b)(7) if a charge against the employer under section 8(a)(2) has been filed and after the preliminary investigation, he has reasonable cause to believe that such charge is true and that a complaint should issue.* Upon filing of any such petition the courts shall cause notice thereof to be served upon any person involved in the charge and such person, including the charging party, shall be given an opportunity to appear by counsel and present any relevant testimony: *Provided further,* That for the purposes of this subsection district courts shall be deemed to have jurisdiction of a labor organization (1) in the district in which such organization maintains its principal office, or (2) in any district in which its duly authorized officers or agents are engaged in promoting or protecting the interests of employee members. The service of legal process upon such officer or agent shall constitute service upon the labor organization and make such organization a party to the suit. In situations where such relief is appropriate the procedure specified herein shall apply to charges with respect to section 8(b)(4)(D).

(m) *Whenever it is charged that any person has engaged in an unfair labor practice within the meaning of subsection (a)(3) or (b)(2) of section 8, such charge shall be given priority over all other cases except cases of like character in the office where it is filed or to which it is referred and cases given priority under subsection (l).*

INVESTIGATORY POWERS

§11. For the purpose of all hearings and investigations, which, in the opinion of the Board, are necessary and proper for the exercise of the powers vested in it by section 9 and section 10—

(1) The Board, or its duly authorized agents or agencies, shall at all reasonable times have access to, for the purpose of examination, and the right to copy any evidence of any person being investigated or proceeded against that relates to any matter under investigation or in question. The Board, or any member thereof, shall upon application of any party to such proceedings, forthwith issue to such party subpenas requiring the attendance and testimony of witnesses or the production of any evidence in such proceeding or investigation requested in such application. Within five days after the service of a subpena on any person requiring the production of any evidence in his possession or under his control, such person may petition the Board to revoke, and the Board shall revoke, such subpena if in its opinion the evidence whose production is required does not relate to any matter under investigation, or any matter in question in such proceedings, or if in its opinion such subpena does not describe with sufficient particularity the evidence whose production is required. Any

member of the Board, or any agent or agency designated by the Board for such purposes, may administer oaths and affirmations, examine witnesses, and receive evidence. Such attendance of witnesses and the production of such evidence may be required from any place in the United States or any Territory or possession thereof, at any designated place of hearing.

(2) In case of contumacy or refusal to obey a subpena issued to any person, any district court of the United States or the United States courts of any Territory or possession, or the District Court of the United States for the District of Columbia, within the jurisdiction of which the inquiry is carried on or within the jurisdiction of which said person guilty of contumacy or refusal to obey is found or resides or transacts business, upon application by the Board shall have jurisdiction to issue to such person an order requiring such person to appeal before the Board, its member, agent, or agency, there to produce evidence if so ordered, or there to give testimony touching the matter under investigation or in question; and any failure to obey such order of the court may be punished by said court as a contempt thereof.

[(3) No person shall be excused from attending and testifying or from producing books, records, correspondence, documents, or other evidence in obedience to the subpena of the Board, on the ground that the testimony or evidence required of him may tend to incriminate him or subject him to a penalty or forfeiture; but no individual shall be prosecuted or subjected to any penalty or forfeiture for or on account of any transaction, matter, or thing concerning which he is compelled, after having claimed his privilege against self-incrimination, to testify or produce evidence, except that such individual so testifying shall not be exempt from prosecution and punishment for perjury committed in so testifying.] *

(4) Complaints, orders, and other process and papers of the Board, its member, agent, or agency, may be served either personally or by registered mail or by telegraph or by leaving a copy thereof at the principal office or place of business of the person required to be served. The verified return by the individual so serving the same setting forth the manner of such service shall be proof of the same, and the return post office receipt or telegraph receipt therefor when registered and mailed or telegraphed as aforesaid shall be proof of service of the same. Witnesses summoned before the Board, its member, agent, or agency, shall be paid the same fees and mileage that are paid witnesses in the courts of the United States, and witnesses whose depositions are taken and the persons taking the same shall severally be entitled to the same fees as are paid for like services in the courts of the United States.

(5) All process of any court to which application may be made under this Act may be served in the judicial district wherein the defendant or other person required to be served resides or may be found.

* Repealed by §259 of the Organized Crime Control Act of 1970, 18 U.S.C. §6001 n. See 18 U.S.C. §§6003-04.

(6) The several departments and agencies of the Government, when directed by the President, shall furnish the Board, upon its request, all records, papers, and information in their possession relating to any matter before the Board.

§12. Any person who shall willfully resist, prevent, impede, or interfere with any member of the Board or any of its agents or agencies in the performance of duties pursuant to this Act shall be punished by a fine of not more than $5,000 or by imprisonment for not more than one year, or both.

LIMITATIONS

§13. Nothing in this Act, **except as specifically provided for herein,** shall be construed so as either to interfere with or impede or diminish in any way the right to strike, **or to affect the limitations or qualifications on that right.**

§14. (a) **Nothing herein shall prohibit any individual employed as a supervisor from becoming or remaining a member of a labor organization, but no employer subject to this Act shall be compelled to deem individuals defined herein as supervisors as employees for the purpose of any law, either national or local, relating to collective bargaining.**

(b) **Nothing in this Act shall be construed as authorizing the execution or application of agreements requiring membership in a labor organization as a condition of employment in any State or Territory in which such execution or application is prohibited by State or Territorial law.**

(c)(1) *The Board, in its discretion, may, by rule of decision or by published rules adopted pursuant to the Administrative Procedure Act, decline to assert jurisdiction over any labor dispute involving any class or category of employers, where, in the opinion of the Board, the effect of such labor dispute on commerce is not sufficiently substantial to warrant the exercise of its jurisdiction:* Provided, *That the Board shall not decline to assert jurisdiction over any labor dispute over which it would assert jurisdiction under the standards prevailing upon August 1, 1959.*

(2) *Nothing in this Act shall be deemed to prevent or bar any agency or the courts of any State or Territory (including the Commonwealth of Puerto Rico, Guam, and the Virgin Islands), from assuming and asserting jurisdiction over labor disputes over which the Board declines, pursuant to paragraph (1) of this subsection, to assert jurisdiction.*

§15. **Wherever the application of the provisions of section 272 of chapter 10 of the Act entitled "An Act to establish a uniform system of bankruptcy throughout the United States," approved July 1, 1898, and Acts amendatory thereof and supplementary thereto (U.S.C., title 11, sec. 672), conflicts with the application of the provisions of this Act, this Act shall prevail:** *Provided,* **That in any situation where the provisions of this Act cannot be validly enforced, the provisions of such other Acts shall remain in full force and effect.**

§16. If any provision of this Act, or the application of such provision to any person or circumstances, shall be held invalid, the remainder of this Act, or the application of such provision to persons or circumstances other than those as to which it is held invalid, shall not be affected thereby.

§17. This Act may be cited as the "National Labor Relations Act."

§18. No petition entertained, no investigation made, no election held, and no certification issued by the National Labor Relations Board, under any of the provisions of section 9 of the National Labor Relations Act, as amended, shall be invalid by reason of the failure of the Congress of Industrial Organizations to have complied with the requirements of section 9(f), (g), or (h) of the aforesaid Act prior to December 22, 1949, or by reason of the failure of the American Federation of Labor to have complied with the provisions of section 9(f), (g), or (h) of the aforesaid Act prior to November 7, 1947: *Provided,* That no liability shall be imposed under any provision of this Act upon any person for failure to honor any election or certificate referred to above, prior to the effective date of this amendment: *Provided, however,* That this proviso shall not have the effect of setting aside or in any way affecting judgments or decrees heretofore entered under section 10(e) or (f) and which have become final.

INDIVIDUALS WITH RELIGIOUS CONVICTIONS

§19. Any employee of a health care institution who is a member of and adheres to established and traditional tenets or teachings of a bona fide religion, body, or sect which has historically held conscientious objections to joining or financially supporting labor organization shall not be required to join or financially support any labor organization as a condition of employment; except that such employee may be required, in lieu of periodic dues and initiation fees, to pay sums equal to such dues and initiation fees to a nonreligious charitable fund exempt from taxation under section 501(c)(3) of the Internal Revenue Code, chosen by such employee from a list of at least three such funds, designated in a contract between such institution and a labor organization, or if the contract fails to designate such funds, then to any such fund chosen by the employee.

EFFECTIVE DATE OF CERTAIN CHANGES *

§102. No provision of this title shall be deemed to make an unfair labor practice any act which was performed prior to the date of the

---

* The effective date referred to in Sections 102, 103, and 104 is August 22, 1947. For effective dates of 1959 amendments, see footnote p. 56 supra.

enactment of this Act which did not constitute an unfair labor practice prior thereto, and the provisions of section 8(a)(3) and section 8(b)(2) of the National Labor Relations Act as amended by this title shall not make an unfair labor practice the performance of any obligation under a collective bargaining agreement entered into prior to the date of the enactment of this Act, or (in the case of an agreement for a period of not more than one year) entered into on or after such date of enactment, but prior to the effective date of this title, if the performance of such obligation would not have constituted an unfair labor practice under section 8(3) of the National Labor Relations Act prior to the effective date of this title, unless such an agreement was renewed or extended subsequent thereto.

§103. No provisions of this title shall affect any certification of representatives or any determination as to the appropriate collective-bargaining unit, which was made under section 9 of the National Labor Relations Act prior to the effective date of this title until one year after the date of such certification or if, in respect of any such certification, a collective-bargaining contract was entered into prior to the effective date of this title, until the end of the contract period or until one year after such date, whichever first occurs.

§104. The amendments made by this title shall take effect sixty days after the date of the enactment of this Act, except that the authority of the President to appoint certain officers conferred upon him by section 3 of the National Labor Relations Act as amended by this title may be exercised forthwith.

TITLE II—CONCILIATION OF LABOR DISPUTES; NATIONAL EMERGENCIES

§201. It is the policy of the United States that—

(a) sound and stable industrial peace and the advancement of the general welfare, health, and safety of the Nation and of the best interests of employers and employees can most satisfactorily be secured by the settlement of issues between employers and employees through the processes of conference and collective bargaining between employers and the representatives of their employees;

(b) the settlement of issues between employers and employees through collective bargaining may be advanced by making available full and adequate governmental facilities for conciliation, mediation, and voluntary arbitration to aid and encourage employers and the representatives of their employees to reach and maintain agreements concerning rates of pay, hours, and working conditions, and to make all reasonable efforts to settle their differences by mutual agreement reached through conferences and collective bargaining or by such methods as may be provided for in any applicable agreement for the settlement of disputes; and

(c) certain controversies which arise between parties to collective-bargaining agreements may be avoided or minimized by making available full and adequate governmental facilities for furnishing assistance to employers and the representatives of their employees in formulating for inclusion within such agreements provision for adequate notice of any proposed changes in the terms of such agreements, for the final adjustment of grievances or questions regarding the application or interpretation of such agreements, and other provisions designed to prevent the subsequent arising of such controversies.

§202. (a) There is created an independent agency to be known as the Federal Mediation and Conciliation Service (herein referred to as the "Service", except that for sixty days after June 23, 1947, such term shall refer to the Conciliation Service of the Department of Labor). The Service shall be under the direction of a Federal Mediation and Conciliation Director (hereinafter referred to as the "Director"), who shall be appointed by the President by and with the advice and consent of the Senate. The Director shall not engage in any other business, vocation, or employment.

(b) The Director is authorized, subject to the civil service laws, to appoint such clerical and other personnel as may be necessary for the execution of the functions of the Service, and shall fix their compensation in accordance with the Classification Act of 1949, and may, without regard to the provisions of the civil service laws, appoint such conciliators and mediators as may be necessary to carry out the functions of the Service. The Director is authorized to make such expenditures for supplies, facilities, and services as he deems necessary. Such expenditures shall be allowed and paid upon presentation of itemized vouchers therefor approved by the Director or by any employee designated by him for that purpose.

(c) The principal office of the Service shall be in the District of Columbia, but the Director may establish regional offices convenient to localities in which labor controversies are likely to arise. The Director may by order, subject to revocation at any time, delegate any authority and discretion conferred upon him by this chapter to any regional director, or other officer or employee of the Service. The Director may establish suitable procedures for cooperation with State and local mediation agencies. The Director shall make an annual report in writing to Congress at the end of the fiscal year.

(d) All mediation and conciliation functions of the Secretary of Labor or the United States Conciliation Service under section 8 of the Act entitled "An Act to create a Department of Labor", approved March 4, 1913 (U.S.C., title 29, sec. 51), and all functions of the United States Conciliation Service under any other law are transferred to the Federal Mediation and Conciliation Service, together with the personnel and records of the United States Conciliation Service. Such transfer shall take effect upon the sixtieth day after June 23, 1947. Such transfer shall not affect any proceedings pending before the United States Conciliation Service or any certification, order, rule, or regulation theretofore made by it or by the Secretary of Labor. The Director and the Service shall not be subject in any way to the jurisdiction or authority of the Secretary of Labor or any official or division of the Department of Labor.

FUNCTIONS OF THE SERVICE

§203. (a) It shall be the duty of the Service, in order to prevent or minimize interruptions of the free flow of commerce growing out of labor disputes, to assist parties to labor disputes in industries affecting commerce to settle such disputes through conciliation and mediation.

(b) The Service may proffer its services in any labor dispute in any industry affecting commerce, either upon its own motion or upon the request of one or more of the parties to the dispute, whenever in its judgment such dispute threatens to cause a substantial interruption of commerce. The Director and the Service are directed to avoid attempting to mediate disputes which would have only a minor effect on interstate commerce if State or other conciliation services are available to the parties. Whenever the Service does proffer its services in any dispute, it shall be the duty of the Service promptly to put itself in communication with the parties and to use its best efforts, by mediation and conciliation, to bring them to agreement.

(c) If the Director is not able to bring the parties to agreement by conciliation within a reasonable time, he shall seek to induce the parties voluntarily to seek other means of settling the dispute without resort to strike, lock-out, or other coercion, including submission to the employees in the bargaining unit of the employer's last offer of settlement for approval or rejection in a secret ballot. The failure or refusal of either party to agree to any procedure suggested by the Director shall not be deemed a violation of any duty or obligation imposed by this Act.

(d) Final adjustment by a method agreed upon by the parties is declared to be the desirable method for settlement of grievance disputes arising over the application or interpretation of an existing collective-bargaining agreement. The Service is directed to make its conciliation and mediation services available in the settlement of such grievance disputes only as a last resort and in exceptional cases.

§204. (a) In order to prevent or minimize interruptions of the free flow of commerce growing out of labor disputes, employers and employees and their representatives, in any industry affecting commerce, shall—

(1) exert every reasonable effort to make and maintain agreements concerning rates of pay, hours, and working conditions, including provision for adequate notice of any proposed change in the terms of such agreements;

(2) whenever a dispute arises over the terms or application of a collective-bargaining agreement and a conference is requested by a party or prospective party thereto, arrange promptly for such a conference to be held and endeavor in such conference to settle such dispute expeditiously; and

(3) in case such dispute is not settled by conference, participate fully

and promptly in such meetings as may be undertaken by the Service under this Act for the purpose of aiding in a settlement of the dispute.

§205. (a) There is created a National Labor-Management Panel which shall be composed of twelve members appointed by the President, six of whom shall be selected from among persons outstanding in the field of management and six of whom shall be selected from among persons outstanding in the field of labor. Each member shall hold office for a term of three years, except that any member appointed to fill a vacancy occurring prior to the expiration of the term for which his predecessor was appointed shall be appointed for the remainder of such term, and the terms of office of the members first taking office shall expire, as designated by the President at the time of appointment, four at the end of the first year, four at the end of the second year, and four at the end of the third year after the date of appointment. Members of the panel, when serving on business of the panel, shall be paid compensation at the rate of $25 per day, and shall also be entitled to receive an allowance for actual and necessary travel and subsistence expenses while so serving away from their places of residence.

(b) It shall be the duty of the panel, at the request of the Director, to advise in the avoidance of industrial controversies and the manner in which mediation and voluntary adjustment shall be administered, particularly with reference to controversies affecting the general welfare of the country.

NATIONAL EMERGENCIES

§206. Whenever in the opinion of the President of the United States, a threatened or actual strike or lock-out affecting an entire industry or a substantial part thereof engaged in trade, commerce, transportation, transmission, or communication among the several States or with foreign nations, or engaged in the production of goods for commerce, will, if permitted to occur or to continue, imperil the national health or safety, he may appoint a board of inquiry to inquire into the issues involved in the dispute and to make a written report to him within such time as he shall prescribe. Such report shall include a statement of the facts with respect to the dispute, including each party's statement of its position but shall not contain any recommendations. The President shall file a copy of such report with the Service and shall make its contents available to the public.

§207. (a) A board of inquiry shall be composed of a chairman and such other members as the President shall determine, and shall have power to sit and act in any place within the United States and to conduct such hearings either in public or in private, as it may deem necessary or proper, to ascertain the facts with respect to the causes and circumstances of the dispute.

(b) Members of a board of inquiry shall receive compensation at the rate of $50 for each day actually spent by them in the work of the board, together with necessary travel and subsistence expenses.

(c) For the purpose of any hearing or inquiry conducted by any board appointed under this title, the provisions of sections 9 and 10 (relating to the attendance of witnesses and the production of books, papers, and documents) of the Federal Trade Commission Act of September 16, 1914, as amended (U.S.C. 19, title 15, secs. 49 and 50, as amended), are hereby made applicable to the powers and duties of such board.

§208. (a) Upon receiving a report from a board of inquiry the President may direct the Attorney General to petition any district court of the United States having jurisdiction of the parties to enjoin such strike or lock-out or the continuing thereof, and if the court finds that such threatened or actual strike or lock-out—

(i) affects an entire industry or a substantial part thereof engaged in trade, commerce, transportation, transmission, or communication among the several States or with foreign nations, or engaged in the production of goods for commerce; and

(ii) if permitted to occur or to continue, will imperil the national health or safety, it shall have jurisdiction to enjoin any such strike or lock-out, or the continuing thereof, and to make such other orders as may be appropriate.

(b) In any case, the provisions of the Act of March 23, 1932, entitled "An Act to amend the Judicial Code and to define and limit the jurisdiction of courts sitting in equity, and for other purposes," shall not be applicable.

(c) The order or orders of the court shall be subject to review by the appropriate United States court of appeals and by the Supreme Court upon writ of certiorari or certification as provided in sections 239 and 240 of the Judicial Code, as amended (U.S.C., title 29, secs. 346 and 347).

§209. (a) Whenever a district court has issued an order under section 208 enjoining acts or practices which imperil or threaten to imperil the national health or safety, it shall be the duty of the parties to the labor dispute giving rise to such order to make every effort to adjust and settle their differences, with the assistance of the Service created by this Act. Neither party shall be under any duty to accept, in whole or in part, any proposal of settlement made by the Service.

(b) Upon the issuance of such order, the President shall reconvene the board of inquiry which has previously reported with respect to the dispute. At the end of a sixty-day period (unless the dispute has been settled by that time, the board of inquiry shall report to the President the current position of the parties and the efforts which have been made for settlement, and shall include a statement by each party of its position and a statement of the employer's last offer of settlement. The President shall make such report available to the public. The National Labor Relations Board, within the succeeding fifteen days, shall take a secret ballot of the employees of each employer involved in the dispute on the question of whether they wish to accept the final offer of settlement made by their employer as stated by him and shall certify the results thereof to the Attorney General within five days thereafter.

§210. Upon the certification of the results of such ballot or upon a settlement being reached, whichever happens sooner, the Attorney General shall move the court to discharge the injunction, which motion shall then be granted and the injunction discharged. When such motion is granted, the President shall submit to the Congress a full and comprehensive report of the proceedings, including the findings of the board of inquiry and the ballot taken by the National Labor Relations Board, together with such recommendations as he may see fit to make for consideration and appropriate action.

COMPILATION OF COLLECTIVE-BARGAINING AGREEMENTS, ETC.

§211. (a) For the guidance and information of interested representatives of employers, employees, and the general public, the Bureau of Labor Statistics of the Department of Labor shall maintain a file of copies of all available collective bargaining agreements and other available agreements and actions thereunder settling or adjusting labor disputes. Such file shall be open to inspection under appropriate conditions prescribed by the Secretary of Labor, except that no specific information submitted in confidence shall be disclosed.

(b) The Bureau of Labor Statistics in the Department of Labor is authorized to furnish upon request of the Service, or employers, employees, or their representatives, all available data and factual information which may aid in the settlement of any labor dispute, except that no specific information submitted in confidence shall be disclosed.

EXEMPTION OF RAILWAY LABOR ACT

§212. The provisions of this title shall not be applicable with respect to any matter which is subject to the provisions of the Railway Labor Act, as amended from time to time.

CONCILIATION OF LABOR DISPUTES IN THE HEALTH CARE INDUSTRY

§213. (a) If, in the opinion of the Director of the Federal Mediation and Conciliation Service a threatened or actual strike or lockout affecting a health care institution will, if permitted to occur or to continue, substantially interrupt the delivery of health care in the locality concerned, the Director may further assist in the resolution of the impasse by establishing within 30 days after the notice to the Federal Mediation and Conciliation Service under clause (A) of the last sentence of section 8(d) (which is required by clause (3) of such section 8(d)), or within 10 days after the notice under clause B), an impartial Board of Inquiry to investigate the issues involved in the dispute and to make a written report thereon to the parties within fifteen (15) days after the establishment of such a Board. The written report shall contain the findings of fact together with the Board's recommendations for settling the dispute, with the objective of achieving a prompt, peaceful and just settlement of the dispute. Each such Board shall be composed of such number of

individuals as the Director may deem desirable. No member appointed under this section shall have any interest or involvement in the health care institutions or the employee organizations involved in the dispute.

(b)(1) Members of any board established under this section who are otherwise employed by the Federal Government shall serve without compensation but shall be reimbursed for travel, subsistence, and other necessary expenses incurred by them in carrying out its duties under this section.

(2) Members of any board established under this section who are not subject to paragraph (1) shall receive compensation at a rate prescribed by the Director but not to exceed the daily rate prescribed for GS–18 of the General Schedule under section 5332 of title 5, United States Code, including travel for each day they are engaged in the performance of their duties under this section and shall be entitled to reimbursement for travel, subsistence, and other necessary expenses incurred by them in carrying out their duties under this section.

(c) After the establishment of a board under subsection (a) of this section and for 15 days after any such board has issued its report, no change in the status quo in effect prior to the expiration of the contract in the case of negotiations for a contract renewal, or in effect prior to the time of the impasse in the case of an initial bargaining negotiation, except by agreement, shall be made by the parties to the controversy.

(d) There are authorized to be appropriated such sums as may be necessary to carry out the provisions of this section.

TITLE III
SUITS BY AND AGAINST LABOR ORGANIZATIONS

§301. (a) Suits for violation of contracts between an employer and a labor organization representing employees in an industry affecting commerce as defined in this Act, or between any such labor organizations, may be brought in any district court of the United States having jurisdiction of the parties, without respect to the amount in controversy or without regard to the citizenship of the parties.

(b) Any labor organization which represents employees in an industry affecting commerce as defined in this Act and any employer whose activities affect commerce as defined in this Act shall be bound by the acts of its agents. Any such labor organization may sue or be sued as an entity and in behalf of the employees whom it represents in the courts of the United States. Any money judgment against a labor organization in a district court of the United States shall be enforceable only against the organization as an entity and against its assets, and shall not be enforceable against any individual member or his assets.

(c) For the purposes of actions and proceedings by or against labor organizations in the district courts of the United States, district courts shall be deemed to have jurisdiction of a labor organization (1) in the district in which such organization maintains its principal office, or (2) in any district in which its duly authorized officers or agents are engaged in representing or acting for employee members.

(d) The service of summons, subpena, or other legal process of any court of the United States upon an officer or agent of a labor organization, in his capacity as such, shall constitute service upon the labor organization.

(e) For the purposes of this section, in determining whether any person is acting as an "agent" of another person so as to make such other person responsible for his acts, the question of whether the specific acts performed were actually authorized or subsequently ratified shall not be controlling.

RESTRICTIONS ON PAYMENTS TO EMPLOYEE REPRESENTATIVES *

§302. (a) It shall be unlawful for any employer *or association of employers or any person who acts as a labor relations expert, adviser, or consultant to an employer or who acts in the interest of an employer* to pay, *lend,* or deliver, or [to] agree to pay, *lend,* or deliver, any money or other thing of value—

(1) to any representative of any of his employees who are employed in an industry affecting commerce[.]; *or*

(2) *to any labor organization, or any officer or employee thereof, which represents, seeks to represent, or would admit to membership, any of the employees of such employer who are employed in an industry affecting commerce; or*

(3) *to any employee or group or committee of employees of such employer employed in an industry affecting commerce in excess of their normal compensation for the purpose of causing such employee or group or committee directly or indirectly to influence any other employees in the exercise of the right to organize and bargain collectively through representatives of their own choosing; or*

(4) *to any officer or employee of a labor organization engaged in an industry affecting commerce with intent to influence him in respect to any of his actions, decisions, or duties as a representative of employees or as such officer or employee of such labor organization,*

(b)(1) It shall be unlawful for any [representative of any employees who are employed in an industry affecting commerce] *person to request, demand,* [to] receive or accept, or [to] agree to *receive or accept* [from the employer of such employees] *any payment, loan, or delivery of any money or other thing of value* [.] *prohibited by subsection (a) of this section.*

(2) *It shall be unlawful for any labor organization, or for any person acting as an officer, agent, representative, or employee of such labor organization, to demand or accept from the operator of any motor vehicle (as defined in part II of the Interstate Commerce Act) employed in the transportation of property in commerce, or the employer of any*

* The provisions of §§302 and 303 contained in the LMRA are in roman type below; additions to those sections made by the LMRDA appear in italics; and deletions, in brackets.

such operator, any money or other thing of value payable to such organization or to an officer, agent, representative or employee thereof as a fee or charge for the unloading, or in connection with the unloading, of the cargo of such vehicle: Provided, *That nothing in this paragraph shall be construed to make unlawful any payment by an employer to any of his employees as compensation for their services as employees.*

(c) The provisions of this section shall not be applicable (1) [with] *in* respect to any money or other thing of value payable by an employer *to* any *of his employees whose established duties include acting openly for such employer in matters of labor relations or personnel administration or to any representative of his employees, or to any officer or employee of a labor organization,* who is *also* an employee or former employee of such employer, as compensation for, or by reason of, his service[s] as an employee of such employer; (2) with respect to the payment or delivery of any money or other thing of value in satisfaction of a judgment of any court or a decision or award of an arbitrator or impartial chairman or in compromise, adjustment, settlement, or release of any claim, complaint, grievance, or dispute in the absence of fraud or duress; (3) with respect to the sale or purchase of an article or commodity at the prevailing market price in the regular course of business; (4) with respect to money deducted from the wages of employees in payment of membership dues in a labor organization: Provided, That the employer has received from each employee, on whose account such deductions are made, a written assignment which shall not be irrevocable for a period of more than one year, or beyond the termination date of the applicable collective agreement, whichever occurs sooner; [or] (5) with respect to money or other thing of value paid to a trust fund established by such representative, for the sole and exclusive benefit of the employees of such employer, and their families and dependents (or of such employees, families, and dependents jointly with the employees of other employers making similar payments, and their families and dependents): Provided, That (A) such payments are held in trust for the purpose of paying, either from principal or income or both, for the benefit of employees, their families and dependents, for medical or hospital care, pensions or retirement or death of employees, compensation for injuries or illness resulting from occupational activity or insurance to provide any of the foregoing, or unemployment benefits or life insurance, disability and sickness insurance, or accident insurance; (B) the detailed basis on which such payments are to be made is specified in a written agreement with the employer, and employees and employers are equally represented in the administration of such fund, together with such neutral persons as the representatives of the employers and the representatives of [the] employees may agree upon and in the event the employer and employee groups deadlock on the administration of such fund and there are no neutral persons empowered to break such deadlock, such agreement provides that the two groups shall agree on an impartial umpire to decide such dispute, or in event of their failure to agree within a reasonable length of time, an impartial umpire to decide such dispute shall, on petition of either group, be appointed by the district court of the United States for the district where the trust fund has its principal office, and shall also contain provisions for an annual audit of the trust fund, a statement of the results of which shall be available for inspection by interested persons at the principal office of the trust fund and at such other places as may be designated in such written agreement; and (C) such payments as are intended to be used for the purpose of providing pensions or annuities for employees are made to a separate trust which provides that the funds held therein cannot be used for any purpose other than paying such pensions or annuities[.]; [or] *(6) with respect to money or other thing of value paid by any employer to a trust fund established by such representative for the purpose of pooled vacation, holiday, severance or similar benefits, or defraying costs of apprenticeship or other training programs:* Provided, *That the requirements of clause (B) of the proviso to clause (5) of this subsection shall apply to such trust funds;* [or] (7) with respect to money or other thing of value paid by any employer to a pooled or individual trust fund established by such representative for the purpose of (A) scholarships for the benefit of employees, their families, and dependents for study at educational institutions, or (B) child care centers for preschool and school age dependents of employees: *Provided,* that no labor organization or employer shall be required to bargain on the establishment of any such trust fund, and refusal to do so shall not constitute an unfair labor practice: *Provided further,* That the requirements of clause (B) of the proviso to clause (5) of this subsection shall apply to such trust funds; or (8) with respect to money or any other thing of value paid by any employer to a trust fund established by such representative for the purpose of defraying the costs of legal services for employees, their families, and dependents for counsel or plan of their choice: *Provided,* that the requirements of clause (B) of the proviso to clause (5) of this subsection shall apply to such trust funds: *Provided further,* that no such legal services shall be furnished: (A) to initiate any proceeding directed (i) against any such employer or its officers or agents except in workman's compensation cases, or (ii) against such labor organization, or its parent or subordinate bodies, or their officers or agents, or (iii) against any other employer or labor organization, or their officers or agents, in any matter arising under the National Labor Relations Act, as amended, or this Act; and (B) in any proceeding where a labor organization would be prohibited from defraying the costs of legal services by the provisions of the Labor-Management Reporting and Disclosure Act of 1959.*

(d) Any person who willfully violates any of the provisions of this section shall, upon conviction thereof, be guilty of a misdemeanor and be subject to a fine of not more than $10,000 or to imprisonment for not more than one year, or both.

---

* [Subsection (c)(7) was added by P.L. 91-86, enacted October 14, 1969. Subsection (c)(8) was added by P.L. 93-95, enacted August 15, 1973.]

(e) The district courts of the United States and the United States courts of the Territories and possessions shall have jurisdiction, for cause shown, and subject to the provisions of section 17 (relating to notice to opposite party) of the Act entitled "An Act to supplement existing laws against unlawful restraints and monopolies, and for other purposes", approved October 15, 1914, as amended (U.S.C., title 28, sec. 381), to restrain violations of this section, without regard to the provisions of sections 6 and 20 of such Act of October 15, 1914, as amended (U.S.C., title 15, sec. 17, and title 29, sec. 52), and the provisions of the Act entitled "An Act to amend the Judicial Code and to define and limit the jurisdiction of courts sitting in equity, and for other purposes", approved March 23, 1932 (U.S.C., title 29, secs. 101-115).

(f) This section shall not apply to any contract in force on June 23, 1947, until the expiration of such contract, or until July 1, 1948, whichever first occurs.

(g) Compliance with the restrictions contained in subsection (c)(5)(B) of this section upon contributions to trust funds, otherwise lawful, shall not be applicable to contributions to such trust funds established by collective agreement prior to January 1, 1946, nor shall subsection (c)(5) (A) of this section be construed as prohibiting contributions to such trust funds if prior to January 1, 1947, such funds contained provisions for pooled vacation benefits.

BOYCOTTS AND OTHER UNLAWFUL COMBINATIONS

§303. (a) It shall be unlawful, for the purpose[s] of this section only, in an industry or activity affecting commerce, for any labor organization to engage in *any activity or conduct defined as an unfair labor practice in section 8(b)(4) of the National Labor Relations Act, as amended.* [or to induce or encourage the employees of any employer to engage in, a strike or a concerted refusal in the course of their employment to use, manufacture, process, transport, or otherwise handle or work on any goods, articles, materials, or commodities or to perform any services, where an object thereof is—

(1) forcing or requiring any employer or self-employed person to join any labor or employer organization or any employer or other person to cease using, selling, handling, transporting, or otherwise dealing in the products of any other producer, processor, or manufacturer, or to cease doing business with any other person;

(2) forcing or requiring any other employer to recognize or bargain with a labor organization as the representative of his employees unless such labor organization has been certified as the representative of such employees under the provisions of section 9 of the National Labor Relations Act;

(3) forcing or requiring any employer to recognize or bargain with a particular labor organization as the representative of his employees if another labor organization has been certified as the representative of

such employees under the provisions of section 9 of the National Labor Relations Act;

(4) forcing or requiring any employer to assign particular work to employees in a particular labor organization or in a particular trade, craft, or class rather than to employees in another labor organization or in another trade, craft, or class unless such employer is failing to conform to an order or certification of the National Labor Relations Board determining the bargaining representative for employees performing such work. Nothing contained in this subsection shall be construed to make unlawful a refusal by any person to enter upon the premises of any employer (other than his own employer), if the employees of such employer are engaged in a strike ratified or approved by a representative of such employees whom such employer is required to recognize under the National Labor Relations Act.]

(b) Whoever shall be injured in his business or property by reason of any violation of subsection (a) may sue therefor in any district court of the United States subject to the limitations and provisions of section 301 hereof without respect to the amount in controversy, or in any other court having jurisdiction of the parties, and shall recover the damages by him sustained and the cost of the suit.

RESTRICTION ON POLITICAL CONTRIBUTIONS

§304. Section 313 of the Federal Corrupt Practices Act, 1925 (U.S.C., 1940 edition, title 2, sec. 251; Supp. V, title 50, App., sec. 1509), as amended, is amended to read as follows:

§313. It is unlawful for any national bank, or any corporation organized by authority of any law of Congress to make a contribution or expenditure in connection with any election to any political office, or in connection with any primary election or political convention or caucus held to select candidates for any political office, or for any corporation whatever, or any labor organization to make a contribution or expenditure in connection with any election at which Presidential and Vice Presidential electors or a Senator or Representative in, or a Delegate or Resident Commissioner to Congress are to be voted for, or in connection with any primary election or political convention or caucus held to select candidates for any of the foregoing offices, or for any candidate, political committee, or other person to accept or receive any contribution prohibited by this section. Every corporation or labor organization which makes any contribution or expenditure in violation of this section shall be fined not more than $5,000; and every officer or director of any corporation, or officer of any labor organization, who consents to any contribution or expenditure by the corporation or labor organization, as the case may be, in violation of this section shall be fined not more than $1,000 or imprisoned for not more than one year, or both. For the purposes of this section "labor organization" means any organization of any kind, or any agency or employee representation committee or plan, in which employees participate and which exists for the purpose, in whole or in part, of dealing with employers concerning grievances, labor disputes, wages, rates of pay, hours of employment, or conditions of work.

STRIKES BY GOVERNMENT EMPLOYEES

§305. It shall be unlawful for any individual employed by the United States or any agency thereof including wholly owned Government corporations to participate in any strike. Any individual employed by the United States or by any such agency who strikes shall be discharged immediately from his employment, and shall forfeit his civil-service status, if any, and shall not be eligible for reemployment for three years by the United States or any such agency.*

TITLE IV

CREATION OF JOINT COMMITTEE TO STUDY AND REPORT ON BASIC PROBLEMS AFFECTING FRIENDLY LABOR RELATIONS AND PRODUCTIVITY **

TITLE V

DEFINITIONS

§501. When used in this Act—

(1) The term "industry affecting commerce" means any industry or activity in commerce or in which a labor dispute would burden or obstruct commerce or tend to burden or obstruct commerce or the free flow of commerce.

(2) The term "strike" includes any strike or other concerted stoppage of work by employees (including a stoppage by reason of the expiration of a collective-bargaining agreement) and any concerted slow-down or other concerted interruption of operations by employees.

(3) The terms "commerce," "labor disputes," "employer," "employee," "labor organization," "representative," "person," and "supervisor" shall have the same meaning as when used in the National Labor Relations Act as amended by this Act.

SAVING PROVISION

§502. Nothing in this Act shall be construed to require an individual employee to render labor or service without his consent, nor shall anything in this Act be construed to make the quitting of his labor by an individual employee an illegal act; nor shall any court issue any process to compel the performance by an individual employee of such labor or service, without his consent; nor shall the quitting of labor by an employee or employees in good faith because of abnormally dangerous conditions for

---

* Section 305 was repealed by Pub. L. No. 330, 84th Cong., 1st Sess., approved August 9, 1955, which added 5 U.S.C. §§118p-118r, [now 5 U.S.C. §§3333, 7311, 18 U.S.C. §1918]; those provisions retain the proscription of strikes by federal employees.
** Omitted.

work at the place of employment of such employee or employees be deemed a strike under this Act.

SEPARABILITY

§503. If any provision of this Act, or the application of such provision to any person or circumstance, shall be held invalid, the remainder of this Act, or the application of such provision to persons or circumstances other than those as to which it is held invalid, shall not be affected thereby.

STATEMENTS OF PROCEDURE
SERIES 8 AS AMENDED—PART 101

SUBPART A—GENERAL STATEMENT

§ 101.1 **General statement.**—By virtue of the authority vested in it by section 6 of the National Labor Relations Act, 49 Stat. 449, as amended, the National Labor Relations Board has issued and published simultaneously herewith its Rules and Regulations, Series 8, as amended. The following statements of the general course and method by which the Board's functions are channeled and determined are issued and published pursuant to 5 U.S.C. section 552(a)(1) (B). [*As amended July 8, 1968*]

SUBPART B—UNFAIR LABOR PRACTICE CASES U N D E R SECTION 10(a) TO (i) OF THE ACT AND TELEGRAPH MERGER ACT CASES

§ 101.2 **Initiation of unfair labor practice cases.**—The investigation of an alleged violation of the National Labor Relations Act is initiated by the filing of a charge, which must be in writing and signed, and must either be notarized or must contain a declaration by the person signing it, under the penalties of the Criminal Code, that its contents are true and correct to the best of his knowledge and belief. The charge is filed with the regional director for the region in which the alleged violations have occurred or are occurring. A blank form for filing such charge is supplied by the regional office upon request. The charge contains the name and address of the person against whom the charge is made and a statement of the facts constituting the alleged unfair labor practices.

§ 101.3 **Note.** This section, which in series 7 of the Statements of Procedure related to the filing requirements of Section 9(f),(g), and (h) of the Labor Management Relations Act, was eliminated by amendments effective September 14, 1959. To avoid the renumbering of Sections 101.4 to 101.21, the Board has left this section number blank.

§ 101.4 **Investigation of charges.**— When the charge is received in the regional office it is filed, docketed, and assigned a case number. The regional director may cause a copy of the charge to be served upon the person against whom the charge is made, but timely service of a copy of the charge within the meaning of the proviso to section 10(b) of the act is the exclusive responsibility of the charging party and not of the general counsel or his agents. The regional director requests the person filing the charge to submit promptly evidence in its support. As part of the investigation hereinafter mentioned, the person against whom the charge is filed, hereinafter called the respondent, is asked to submit a statement of his position in respect to the allegations. The case is assigned for investigation to a member of the field staff for investigation, who interviews representatives of the parties and other persons who have knowledge as to the charges, as is deemed necessary. In the investigation and in all other stages of the proceedings, charges alleging violation of section 8(b)(4)(A), (B), and (C), charges alleging violation of Section 8(b)(4)(D) in which it is deemed appropriate to seek-injunctive relief under Section 10(l) of the act, and charges alleging violations of Section 8(b)(7) or 8(e) are given priority over all other cases in the office in which they are pending except cases of like character; and charges alleging violation of Section 8(a)(3) or 8(b)(2) are given priority over all other cases except cases of like character and cases under section 10(l) of the act. The regional d i r e c t o r may in his discretion dispense with any portion of the investigation described in this section as appears necessary to him in consideration of such factors as the amount of time necessary to complete a full investigation, the nature of the proceeding, and the public interest. After investigation, the case may be disposed of through informal methods such as withdrawal, dismissal, or settlement; or, the case may necessitate formal methods of disposition. Some of the informal methods of handling unfair labor practice cases will be stated first.

§ 101.5 **Withdrawal of charges.**—If investigation reveals that there has been no violation of the National Labor Relations Act or the evidence is insufficient to substantiate the charge, the regional director recommends withdrawal of the charge by the person who filed. The complainant may also, on its own initiative, request withdrawal. If the complainant accepts the recommendation of the director or requests withdrawal on its own initiative, the respondent is immediately notified of the withdrawal of the charge.

§ 101.6 **Dismissal of charges and appeals to general counsel.**—If the complainant refuses to withdraw the charge as recommended, the regional director dismisses the charge. The regional director thereupon informs the parties of his action, together with a simple statement of the grounds therefor, and the complainant of his right of appeal to the general counsel in Washington, D.C., within 10 days. If the complainant appeals to the general counsel, the entire file in the case is sent to Washington, D.C., where the case is fully reviewed by the general counsel with the assistance of his staff. Oral presentation of the appeal issues may be permitted a party on timely written request, in which event the other parties are notified and afforded a like opportunity at another appropriate time. Following such review, the general counsel may sustain the regional director's dismissal, stating the grounds of his affirmance, or may direct the regional director to take further action. [*As amended effective July 4, 1967*]

§ 101.7 **Settlements.**—Before a n y complaint is issued or other formal action taken, the regional director affords an opportunity to all parties for the submission and consideration of facts, argument, offers of settlement, or proposals of adjustment, except where time, the nature of the proceeding, and the public interest do not permit. Normally prehearing conferences are held, the principal purpose of which is to discuss and explore such submissions and proposals of adjustment. The regional office provides Board-prepared forms for such settlement agreements, as well as printed notices for posting by the respondent.

These agreements, which are subject to the approval of the regional director, provide for an appeal to the general counsel, as described in section 101.6, by a complainant who will not join in a settlement or adjustment deemed adequate by the regional director. Proof of compliance is obtained by the regional director before the case is closed. If the respondent fails to perform his obligations under the informal agreement, the regional director may determine to institute formal proceedings.

§ 101.8 **Complaints.**—If the charge appears to have merit and efforts to dispose of it by informal adjustment are unsuccessful, the regional director institutes formal action by issuance of a complaint and notice of hearing. In certain types of cases, involving novel and complex issues, the regional director, at the discretion of the general counsel, must submit the case for advice from the general counsel before issuing a complaint. The complaint, which is served on all parties, sets forth the facts upon which the Board bases its jurisdiction and the facts relating to the alleged violations of law by the respondent. The respondent must file an answer to the complaint within 10 days of its receipt, setting forth a statement of its defense.

§ 101.9 **Settlement a f t e r issuance of complaint.**—(a) Even though formal proceedings have begun, the parties again have full opportunity at every stage to dispose of the case by amicable adjustment and in compliance with the law. Thus, after the complaint has been issued and a hearing scheduled or even begun, the attorney in charge of the case and the regional director afford all parties every opportunity for the submission and consideration of facts, argument, offers of s e t t l e m e n t, or proposals of adjustment, e x c e p t where time, the nature of the proceeding, and the public interest do not permit.

(b)(1) After the issuance of a complaint, the agency favors a formal settlement agreement, which is subject to the approval of the Board in Washington, D.C. In such an agreement, the parties agree to waive their right to hearing and agree further that the Board may issue an order requiring the respondent to take action appropriate to the terms of the settlement. Ordinarily the formal settlement agreement also contains the respondent's c o n s e n t to the Board's application for the entry of a decree by the appropriate circuit court of appeals enforcing the Board's order.

(2) In some cases, however, the regional director, pursuant to his authority to withdraw the complaint before the hearing (section 102.18), may conclude that an informal settlement agreement of the type described in section 101.7 is appropriate. Such an agreement is not subject to approval by the Board and does not provide for a Board order. It provides for the withdrawal of the complaint.

(c)(1) If after issuance of complaint but before opening of the hearing, the charging party will not join in a settlement tentatively agreed upon by the regional director, the respondent, and any other parties whose consent may be required, the regional director serves a copy of the proposed settlement agreement on the charging party with a brief written statement of the reasons for proposing its approval. Within 5 days after service of these documents, the charging party may file with the regional director a written statement of any objections to the proposed settlement. Such objections will be considered by the regional director in determining whether to approve the proposed settlement. If the settlement is approved by the regional director notwithstanding the objections, the charging party is so informed and provided a brief written statement of the reasons for the approval.

(2) If the settlement agreement approved by the regional director is a formal one, providing for the entry of a Board order, the settlement agreement together with the charging party's o b j e c t i o n s and the regional director's written statements, are submitted to Washington, D.C., where they are reviewed by the general counsel. If the general counsel decides to approve the settlement agreement, he shall so inform the charging party and submit the agreement and accompanying documents to the Board, upon whose approval

the settlement is contingent. Within 7 days after service of notice of submission of the settlement agreement to the Board, the charging party may file with the Board in Washington, D.C., a further statement in support of his objections to the settlement agreement.

(3) If the settlement agreement approved by the regional director is an informal one, providing for the withdrawal of the complaint, the charging party may appeal the regional director's action to the general counsel, as provided in section 102.19 of the rules and regulations.

(d)(1) If the settlement occurs after the opening of the hearing and before issuance of the administrative law judge's decision and there is an all-party informal settlement, the request for withdrawal of the complaint must be submitted to the administrative law judge for his approval. If the all-party settlement is a formal one, final approval must come from the Board. If any party will not join in the settlement agreed to by the other parties, the administrative law judge will give such party an opportunity to state on the record or in writing its reasons for opposing the settlement. [As amended, effective August 19, 1972]

(2) If the administrative law judge decides to accept or reject the proposed settlement, any party aggrieved by such ruling may ask for leave to appeal to the Board as provided in Section 102.26

(e)(1) In the event the respondent fails to comply with the terms of a settlement stipulation, upon which a Board order and court decree are based, the Board may petition the court to adjudge the respondent in contempt. If the respondent refuses to comply with the terms of a stipulation settlement providing solely for the entry of a Board order, the Board may petition the c o u r t for enforcement of its order, pursuant to section 10 of the National Labor Relations Act.

(2) In the event the respondent fails to comply with the terms of an informal settlement agreement, the regional director may set the agree-

ment aside and institute further proceedings. [*As amended effective July 4, 1967*]

§ 101.10 **Hearings.**—(a) Except in extraordinary situations the hearing is open to the public and usually conducted in the region where the charge originated. A duly designated administrative law judge presides over the hearing. The Government's case is conducted by an attorney attached to the Board's regional office, who has the responsibility of presenting the evidence in support of the complaint. The rules of evidence applicable in the district courts of the United States under the Rules of Civil Procedure adopted by the Supreme Court are, so far as practicable, controlling. Counsel for the general counsel, all parties to the proceeding, and the administrative law judge have the power to call, examine, and cross-examine witnesses and to introduce evidence into the record. They may also submit briefs, engage in oral argument, and submit proposed findings and conclusions to the administrative law judge. The attendance and testimony of witnesses and the production of evidence material to any matter under investigation may be compelled by subpena.

(b) The functions of all administrative law judges and other Board agents or employees participating in decisions in conformity with section 8 of the Administrative Procedure Act (5 U.S.C., § 557) are conducted in an impartial manner and any such administrative law judge, agent or employee may at any time withdraw if he deems himself disqualified because of bias or prejudice. The Board's attorney has the burden of proof of violations of section 8 of the National Labor Relations Act and section 222 (f) of the Telegraph Merger Act. In connection with hearings subject to the provisions of section 7 of the Administrative Procedure Act (5 U.S.C. § 556): [*As amended, effective August 19, 1972*]

(1) No sanction is imposed or rule or order issued except upon consideration of the whole record or such portions thereof as may be cited by any party and as supported by and in accordance with the preponderance of the reliable, probative, and substantial evidence.

(2) Every party has the right to present his case or defense by oral or documentary evidence, to submit rebuttal evidence, and to conduct such cross-examination as may be required for a full and true disclosure of the facts.

(3) Where any decision rests on official notice of a material fact not appearing in the evidence in the record, any party is on timely request afforded a reasonable opportunity to show the contrary.

(4) Subject to the approval of the administrative law judge, all parties to the proceeding voluntarily may enter into a stipulation dispensing with a verbatim written transcript of record of the oral testimony adduced at the hearing and providing for the waiver by the respective parties of their right to file with the Board exceptions to the findings of fact (but not to conclusions of law or recommended orders) which the administrative law judge shall make in his decision. [*As amended effective August 19, 1972*]

§ 101.11 **Administrative law judge's decision.**—(a) At the conclusion of the hearing the administrative law judge prepares a decision stating findings of fact and conclusions, as well as the reasons for his determination on all material issues, and making recommendations as to action which should be taken in the case. The administrative law judge may recommend dismissal or sustain the complaint, in whole or in part and recommend that the respondent cease and desist from the unlawful acts found and take action to remedy their effects. [*As amended, effective August 19, 1972*]

(b) The administrative law judge's decision is filed with the Board in Washington, D.C., and copies are simultaneously served on each of the parties. At the same time the Board, through its executive secretary, issues and serves on each of the parties an order transferring the case to the Board. The parties may accept and comply with the recommendations of the administrative law judge, and thus normally conclude the entire proceedings at this point. Or, the parties or counsel for the Board may file exceptions to the administrative law judge's decision with the Board. Whenever any party files exceptions, any other party may file an answering brief limited to questions raised in the exceptions and/or may file cross-exceptions relating to any portion of the administrative law judge's decision. Cross-exceptions may be filed only by a party who has not previously filed exceptions. Whenever any party files cross-exceptions, any other party may file an answering brief to the cross-exceptions. The parties may request permission to appear and argue orally before the Board in Washington, D.C. They may also submit proposed findings and conclusions to the Board. [As amended, effective August 19, 1972]

§ 101.12 Board decision and order.—
(a) If any party files exceptions to the administrative law judge's decision, the Board with the assistance of the legal assistants to each Board member who function in much the same manner as law clerks do for judges, reviews the entire record, including the administrative law judge's report and recommendations, the exceptions thereto, the complete transcript of evidence, and the exhibits, briefs, and arguments. The Board does not consult with members of the administrative law judge staff or with any agent of the general counsel in its deliberations. It then issues its decision and order in which it may adopt, modify, or reject the findings and recommendations of the administrative law judge. The decision and order contains detailed findings of fact, conclusions of law, and basic reasons for decision on all material issues raised, and an order either dismissing the complaint in whole or in part or requiring the respondent to cease and desist from its unlawful practices and to take appropriate affirmative action. [As amended, effective August 19, 1972]

(b) If no exceptions are filed to the administrative law judge's decision, his decision and recommended order automatically become the deci-

sion and order of the Board, pursuant to section 10(c) of the Act. All objections and exceptions whether or not previously made during or after the hearing, are deemed waived for all purposes. [As amended, effective August 19, 1972]

§ 101.13 Compliance with Board decision and order.—(a) Shortly after the Board's decision and order is issued the director of the regional office in which the charge was filed communicates with the respondent for the purpose of obtaining compliance. Conferences may be held to arrange the details necessary for compliance with the terms of the order.

(b) If the respondent effects full compliance with the terms of the order, the regional director submits a report to that effect to Washington, D. C., after which the case may be closed. Despite compliance, however, the Board's order is a continuing one; therefore, the closing of a case on compliance is necessarily conditioned upon the continued observance of that order; and in some cases it is deemed desirable, notwithstanding compliance, to implement the order with an enforcing decree. Subsequent violations of the order may become the basis of further proceedings.

Sec. 101.14 Judicial review of Board decision and order.—If the respondent does not comply with the Board's order, or the Board deems it desirable to implement the order with a court decree, the Board may petition the appropriate Federal court for enforcement. Or, the respondent may petition the circuit court of appeals to review and set aside the Board's order. Upon such review or enforcement proceedings, the court reviews the record and the Board's findings and order and sustains them if they are in accordance with the requirements of law. The court may enforce, modify, or set aside in whole or in part the Board's findings and order, or it may remand the case to the Board for further proceedings as directed by the court. Following the court's decree, either the Government or the private party may petition the Supreme Court for review upon writ of certiorari. Such applications for review to the Supreme Court are handled by the Board through the Solicitor General of the United States.

Sec. 101.15 **Compliance with court decree.**—After a Board order has been enforced by a court decree, the Board has the responsibility of obtaining compliance with that decree. Investigation is made by the regional office of the respondent's efforts to comply. If it finds that the respondent has failed to live up to the terms of the court's decree the general counsel may, on behalf of the Board, petition the court to hold him in contempt of court. The court may order immediate remedial action and impose sanctions and penalties.

Sec. 101.16 **Back-pay proceedings.**— (a) After a Board order directing the **payment of back pay has been issued** or after enforcement of such order by a court decree, if informal efforts to dispose of the matter prove unsuccessful, the regional director is then authorized in his discretion to issue a "back-pay specification" in the name of the Board and a notice of hearing before an administrative law judge, both of which are served on the parties involved. The specification sets forth computations showing gross and net back pay due and any other pertinent information. The respondent must file an answer within 15 days of the receipt of the specification setting forth a particularized statement of its defense. [*As amended, effective August 19, 1972*]

(b) In the alternative and in his discretion, the regional director, under the circumstances specified above, may issue and serve upon the parties a notice of hearing only, without a specification. Such notice contains, in addition to the time and place of hearing before an administrative law judge, a brief statement of the matters in controversy. [*As amended, effective August 19, 1972*]

(c) The procedure before the administrative law judge or the Board, whether initiated by the "back pay specification" or by notice of hearing without a back-pay specification, is substantially the same as that described in sections 101.10 to 101.14 inclusive. [*As amended, effective August 19, 1972*]

SUBPART C — REPRESENTATION CASES UNDER SECTION 9(c) OF THE ACT AND PETITIONS FOR CLARIFICATION OF BARGAINING UNITS AND FOR AMENDMENT OF CERTIFICATIONS UNDER SECTION 9(b) OF THE ACT

§ 101.17 **Initiation of representation cases and petitions for clarification and amendment.**—The investigation of the question as to whether a union represents a majority of an appropriate grouping of employees is initiated by the filing of a petition by any person or labor organization acting on behalf of a substantial number of employees or by an employer when one or more individuals or labor organizations present to him a claim to be recognized as the exclusive bargaining representative. If there is a certified or currently recognized representative, any employee, or group of employees or any individual or labor organization acting in their behalf may also file decertification proceedings to test the question of whether the certified or recognized agent is still the representative of the employees. If there is a certified or currently recognized representative of a bargaining unit and there is no question concerning representation, a party may file a petition for clarification of the bargaining unit. If there is a unit covered by a certification and there is no question concerning representation, any party may file a petition for amendment to reflect changed circumstances, such as changes in the name or affiliation of the labor organization involved or in the name or location of the employer involved. The petition must be in writing and signed, and either must be notarized or must contain a declaration by the person signing it, under the penalties of the Criminal Code, that its contents are true and correct to the best of his knowledge and belief. It is filed with the regional director for the region in which the proposed or actual bargaining unit exists. Petition forms, which are supplied by the regional office upon request, provide, among other things, for a description of the contemplated or existing appropriate bargaining unit, the approximate number of employees involved, and the names of all labor organizations which claim to represent the employees. If a petition is filed by a labor organization seeking certification, or in the case of a petition to decertify a certified or recognized bargaining agent, the petitioner must supply, within 48 hours after filing but in no event later than the last day on which the petition might timely be filed, evidence of representation. Such evidence is usually in the form of cards authorizing the labor organization to represent the employees or authorizing the petitioner to file a decertification proceeding. If a petition is filed by an employer, the petitioner must supply, within 48 hours after filing, proof of demand for recognition by the labor organization named in the petition and, in the event the labor organization named is the incumbent representative of the unit involved, a statement of the objective considerations demonstrating reasonable g r o u n d s for believing that the labor organization has lost its majority status. [As amended effective July 4, 1967]

§ 101.18 **Investigation of petition.**— (a) Upon receipt of the petition in the regional office, it is docketed and assigned to a member of the staff, usually a field examiner, for investigation. He conducts an investigation to ascertain (1) whether the employer's operations affect commerce within the meaning of the act, (2) the appropriateness of the unit of employees for the purposes of collective bargaining and the existence of a bona fide question concerning representation within the meaning of the act, (3) whether the election would effectuate the policies of the act and reflect the free choice of employees in the appropriate unit, and (4) whether, if the petitioner is a labor organization seeking recognition, there is a sufficient probability, based on the evidence of representation of the petitioner, that the employees have selected it to represent them. The evidence of representation submitted by the petitioning labor organization or by the person seeking decertification is ordinarily checked to determine the number or proportion of employees who have designated the petitioner, it being the Board's administrative experience that in the absence of special factors the conduct of an election serves no purpose under the statute unless the petitioner has been designated by at least 30 percent of the employees. However, in the case of a petition by an employer, no proof of representation on the part of the labor organization claiming a majority is required and the regional director proceeds with the case if other factors require it unless the labor organization withdraws its claim to majority representation. The field examiner, or other member of the staff, attempts to ascertain from all interested parties whether or not the grouping or unit of employees described in the petition constitutes an appropriate bargaining unit. The petition may be amended at any time prior to hearing and may be amended during the hearing in the discretion of the hearing officer upon such terms as he deems just. [As amended effective July 4, 1967]

(b) The petitioner may on its own initiative request the withdrawal of the petition if the investigation discloses that no question of representation exists within the meaning of the statute, because, among other possible reasons, the unit is not appropriate, or a written contract precludes further investigation at that time, or where the petitioner is a labor organization or a person seeking decertification and the showing of representation among the employees is insufficient to warrant an election under the 30-percent principle stated in subsection (a) of this section.

(c) For the same or similar reasons the regional director may request the petitioner to withdraw its petition. If, the petitioner, despite the regional director's recommendations, refuses to withdraw the petition, the regional director then dismisses the petition, stating the grounds for his dismissal and informing the petitioner of his right of appeal to the Board in Washington, D.C. The petition may also be dismissed in the discretion of the regional director if the petitioner fails to make available necessary facts which are in its possession. The petitioner may within 10 days appeal from the regional director's dismissal by filing such request with the Board in Washington, D.C., after a full review of the file with the assistance of its staff, the Board may sustain the dismissal, stating the grounds of its affirmance, or may direct the regional director to take further action. [*As amended effective July 4, 1967*]

§ 101.19 **Consent adjustments before formal hearing.**—The Board has devised and makes available to the parties two types of informal consent procedures through which representation issues can be resolved without recourse to formal procedures. These informal arrangements are commonly referred to as (a) consent-election agreement, followed by regional director's determination, and (b) consent-election agreement, followed by Board certification. Forms for use in these informal procedures are available in the regional offices.

(a) (1) The consent-election agreement followed by the regional director's determination of representatives is the most frequently used method of informal adjustment of representation cases. The terms of the agreement providing for this form of adjustment are set forth in printed forms, which are available upon request at the Board's regional offices. Under these terms the parties agree with respect to the appropriate unit, the payroll period to be used as the basis of eligibility to vote in an election, and the place, date, and hours of balloting. A Board agent arranges the details incident to the mechanics and conduct of the election. For example, he usually arranges preelection conferences in which the parties check the list of voters and attempt to resolve any questions of eligibility. Also, prior to the date of election, the holding of such election shall be adequately publicized by the posting of official notices in the establishment whenever possible or in other places, or by the use of other means considered appropriate and effective. These notices reproduce a sample ballot and outline such election details as location of polls, time of voting, and eligibility rules.

(2) The actual polling is always conducted and supervised by Board agents. Appropriate representatives of each party may assist them and observe the election. As to the mechanics of the election, a ballot is given to each eligible voter by the Board's agents. The ballots are marked in the secrecy of a voting booth. The Board agents and authorized observers have the privilege of challenging for reasonable cause employees who apply for ballots.

(3) Customarily the Board agents, in the presence and with the assistance of the authorized observers, count and tabulate the ballots immediately after the closing of the polls. A complete tally of the ballots is served upon the parties upon the conclusion of the count.

(4) If challenged ballots are sufficient in number to affect the results of the count, the regional director conducts an investigation and rules on the challenges. Similarly, if objections to the conduct of the election are filed within 5 days of the issuance of the tally of ballots, the regional director likewise conducts an investigation and rules upon the objections. If, after investigation, the objections are found to have merit, the regional director may void the election results and conduct a new election.

(5) This form of agreement provides that the rulings of the regional director on all questions relating to the election (for example, eligibility to vote and the validity of challenges and objections) are final and binding. Also, the agreement provides for the conduct of a runoff election, in accordance with the provisions of the Board's Rules and Regulations, if two or more labor organizations appear on the ballot and no one choice receives the majority of the valid votes cast.

(6) The regional director issues to the parties a certification of the results of the election, including certification of representatives where appropriate, with the same force and effect as if issued by the Board.

(b) The consent-election agreement followed by a Board determination provides that disputed matters following the agreed-upon election, if determinative of the results, shall be the basis of a formal decision by the Board instead of an informal determination by the regional director, except that if the regional director decides that a hearing on objections or challenged ballots is necessary he may direct such a hearing before a hearing officer, or if the case is consolidated with an unfair labor practice proceeding before an administrative law judge. If a hearing is directed such action on the part of the regional director constitutes a transfer of the case to the Board. Thus, except for directing a hearing, it is provided that the Board, rather than the regional director, makes the final determination of questions raised concerning eligibility, challenged votes, and objections to the conduct of the election. Thus, if challenged ballots are sufficient in number to affect the results of the count, the regional director conducts an investigation and issues a report on the challenges instead of ruling thereon, unless he elects to hold a hearing. Similarly, if objections to the conduct of the election are filed within 5 days after issuance of the tally of ballots, the regional director likewise conducts an investigation and issues a report instead of ruling on the validity of the objections, unless he elects to hold a hearing. The regional director's report is served on the parties, who may file exceptions thereto within 10 days with the Board in Washington, D.C. The Board then reviews the entire record made and may, if a substantial issue is raised, direct a hearing on the challenged ballots or the objections to the conduct of the election. Or, the Board may, if no substantial issues are raised, affirm the regional director's report and take appropriate action in termination of the proceedings. If a hearing is ordered by the regional director or the Board on the challenged ballots or objections, all parties are heard and a report containing findings of fact and recommendations as to the disposition of the challenges or objections, or both, and resolving issues of credibility is issued by the hearing officer and served on the parties, who may file exceptions thereto within 10 days with the Board in Washington, D.C. The record made on the hearing is reviewed by the Board with the assistance of its legal assistants and a

final determination made thereon. If the objections are found to have merit, the election results may be voided and a new election conducted under the supervision of the regional director. If the union has been selected as the representative, the Board or the regional director, as the case may be, issues its certification and the proceeding is terminated. If upon a decertification or employer petition the union loses the election, the Board or the regional director, as the case may be, certifies that the union is not the chosen representative.

§ 101.20 Formal hearing.—(a) If no informal adjustment of the question concerning representation has been effected and it appears to the regional director that formal action is necessary, the regional director will institute formal proceedings by issuance of a notice of hearing on the issues, which is followed by a decision and direction of election or dismissal of the case. In certain types of cases, involving novel or complex issues, the regional director may submit the case for advice to the Board before issuing notice of hearing.

(b) The notice of hearing, together with a copy of the petition, is served upon the unions and employer filing or named in the petition and upon other known persons or labor organizations claiming to have been designated by employees involved in the proceeding.

(c) The hearing, usually open to the public, is held before a hearing officer who normally is an attorney or field examiner attached to the regional office but may be another qualified official. The hearing, which is nonadversary in character, is part of the investigation in which the primary interest of the Board's agents is to insure that the record contains as full a statement of the pertinent facts as may be necessary for determination of the case. The parties are afforded full opportunity to present their respective positions and to produce the significant facts in support of their contentions. In most cases a substantial number of the relevant facts are undisputed and stipulated. The parties are permitted to argue orally on the record before the hearing officer.

§ 101.21 Procedure after hearing.—

(a) Pursuant to section 3(b) of the act, the Board has delegated to its regional directors its powers under section 9 of the act, to determine the unit appropriate for the purpose of collective bargaining, to investigate and provide for hearings and determine whether a question of representation exists, and to direct an election or take a secret ballot under subsection (c) or (e) of section 9 and certify the results thereof. These powers include the issuance of such decisions, orders, rulings, directions, and certifications as are necessary to process any representation or deauthorization petition. Thus, by way of illustration and not of limitation, the regional director may dispose of petitions by administratve dismissal or by decision after formal hearing: pass upon rulings made at hearings and requests for extensions of time for filing of briefs; rule on objections to elections and challenged ballots in connection with elections directed by the regional director or the Board, after administrative investigation or formal hearing; rule on motions to amend or rescind any certification issued after the effective date of the delegation; and entertain motions for oral argument. The regional director may at any time transfer the case to the Board for decision, but until such action is taken, it will be presumed that the regional director will decide the case. In the event the regional director decides the issues in a case, his decision is final subject to the review procedure set forth in the Board's Rules and Regulations.

(b) Upon the close of the hearing, the entire record in the case is forwarded to the regional director or, upon issuance by the regional director of an order transferring the case, to the Board in Washington, D.C. The hearing officer also transmits an analysis of the issues and the evidence, but makes no recommendations in regard to resolution of the issues. All parties may file briefs with the regional director or, if the case is transferred to the Board at the close of the hearing, with the Board, within 7 days after the close of the hearing. If the case is transferred to the Board after the close of the hearing, briefs may be filed with the Board within the time prescribed by the regional director. The parties may also request to be heard orally. Because of the nature of the proceedings, however, permission to argue orally is rarely granted. After review of the entire case, the regional director or the Board issues a decision, either dismissing the petition or directing that an election be held. In the latter event, the election is conducted under the supervision of the regional director in the manner already described in section 101.19.

(c) With respect to objections to the conduct of the election and challenged ballots, the regional director may, in his discretion, (1) issue a report on such objections and/or challenged ballots and transmit the issues to the Board for resolution, as in cases involving consent elections to be followed by Board certifications, or (2) decide the issues on the basis of the administrative investigation or after a hearing, with the right to transfer the case to the Board for decision at any time prior to his disposition of the issues on the merits. In the event the regional director adopts the first procedure, the parties have the same rights, and the same procedure is followed, as has already been described in connection with the post election procedures in cases involving consent election to be followed by Board certification. In the event the regional director adopts the second procedure, the parties have the same rights, and the same procedure is followed, as has already been described in connection with hearings before elections.

(d) The parties have the right to request review of any final decision of the regional director, within the times set forth in the Board's Rules and Regulations, on one or more of the grounds specified therein. Any such request for review must be a self-contained document permitting the Board to rule on the basis of its contents without the necessity of recourse to the record, and must meet the other requirements of the Board's Rules and Regulations as to its contents. The regional director's action is not stayed by the filing of such a request or the granting of review, unless otherwise ordered by the Board. Thus, the regional director may proceed immediately to make any necessary arrangements for an election, including the issuance of a notice of election. However, unless a waiver is filed, he will normally not schedule an election until a date between the 20th and 30th days after the date of his decision, to permit the Board to rule on any request for review which may be filed. As to administrative dismissals prior to the close of hearing, see section 101.18(c).

(e) If the election involves two or more labor organizations and if the election results are inconclusive because no choice on the ballot received the majority of valid votes cast, a runoff election is held as provided in the Board's Rules and Regulations.

SUBPART D—UNFAIR LABOR PRACTICE AND REPRESENTATION CASES UNDER SECTIONS 8(b)(7) AND 9(c) OF THE ACT

§ 101.22 **Initiation and Investigation of a case under Section 8(b)(7).**—(a) The investigation of an alleged violation of section 8(b)(7) of the act is initiated by the filing of a charge. The manner of filing such charge and the contents thereof are the same as described in section 101.2. In some cases, at the time of the investigation of the charge, there may be pending a representation petition involving the employees of the employer named in the charge. In those cases, the results of the investigation of the charge will determine the course of the petition.

(b) The investigation of the charge is conducted in accordance with the provisions of Section 101.4, insofar as they are applicable. If the investigation reveals that there is merit in the charge, a complaint is issued as described in section 101.8, and an ap-

plication is made for an injunction under section 10(1) of the act, as described in section 101.37. If the investigation reveals that there is no merit in the charge, the regional director, absent a withdrawal of the charge, dismisses it, subject to appeal to the general counsel. However, if the investigation reveals that issuance of a complaint may be warranted but for the pendency of a representation petition involving the employees of the employer named in the charge, action on the charge is suspended pending the investigation of the petition as provided in section 101.23.

§ 101.23 **Initiation and investigation of a petition in connection with a case under section 8(b)(7).**—(a) A representation petition [1] involving the employees of the employer named in the charge is handled under an expedited procedure when the investigation of the charge has revealed that: (1) the employer's operations affect commerce within the meaning of the act; (2) picketing of the employer is being conducted for an object proscribed by section 8(b)(7) of the act; (3) subparagraph (C) of that section is applicable to the picketing; and (4) the petition has been filed within a reasonable period of time not to exceed 30 days from the commencement of the picketing. In these circumstances, the member of the regional director's staff, to whom the matter has been assigned, investigates the petition to ascertain further: (1) the unit appropriate for collective bargaining; and (2) whether an election in that unit would effectuate the policies of the act.

(b) If, based on such investigation, the regional director determines that an election is warranted, he may, without a prior hearing, direct that an election be held in an appropriate unit of employees. Any party aggrieved may file a request with the Board for special permission to appeal that action to the Board, but such review, if granted, will not, unless otherwise ordered by the Board, stay the proceed-

---

[1] The manner of filing of such petition and the contents thereof are the same as described in section 101.17, except that the petitioner is not required to allege that a claim was made upon the employer for recognition or that the union represents a substantial number of employees.

ing. If the regional director determines that an election is not warranted, he dismisses the petition or makes other disposition of the matter. Should he conclude that an election is warranted, he fixes the basis of eligibility of voters and the place, date, and hours of balloting. The mechanics of arranging the balloting, the other procedures for the conduct of the election, and the postelection proceedings are the same, insofar as appropriate, as those described in section 101.19, except that the regional director's rulings on any objections to the conduct of the election or challenged ballots are final and binding, unless the Board, on an application by one of the parties, grants such party special permission to appeal from the regional director's rulings. The party requesting such review by the Board must do so promptly, in writing, and state briefly the grounds relied on. Such party must also immediately serve a copy on each of the other parties, including the regional director. Neither the request for review by the Board nor the Board's grant of such review operates as a stay of any action taken by the regional director, unless specifically so ordered by the Board. If the Board grants permission to appeal, and it appears to the Board that substantial and material factual issues have been presented with respect to the objections to the conduct of the election or challenged ballots, it may order that a hearing be held on such issues or take other appropriate action.

(c) If the regional director believes, after preliminary investigation of the petition, that there are substantial issues which require determination before an election may be held, he may order a hearing on the issues. This hearing is followed by regional director or Board decision and direction of election, or other disposition. The procedures to be used in connection with such hearing and posthearing proceedings are the same, insofar as they are applicable, as those described in sections 101.20 and 101.21, except that the parties may not file briefs with the regional director or the Board, unless special permission therefor is granted, but may state

their respective legal positions fully on the record at the hearing, and except that any request for review must be filed promptly after issuance of the regional director's decision.

(d) Should the parties so desire, they may, with the approval of the regional director, resolve the issues as to the unit, the conduct of the balloting, and related matters pursuant to informal consent procedures, as described in section 101.19(a).

(e) If a petition has been filed which does not meet the requirements for processing under the expedited procedures the regional director may process it under the procedures set forth in subpart C.

§ 101.24 **Final disposition of a charge which has been held pending investigation of the petition.**—(a) Upon the determination that the issuance of a direction of election is warranted on the petition, the regional director, absent withdrawal of the charge, dismisses it subject to an appeal to the general counsel in Washington, D.C.

(b) If, however, the petition is dismissed or withdrawn, the investigation of the charge is resumed, and the appropriate steps described in section 101.22 are taken with respect to it.

§ 101.25 **Appeal from the dismissal of a petition, or from the refusal to process it under the expedited procedure.**—If the regional director determines after his investigation of the representation petition that further proceedings based thereon are not warranted, he, absent withdrawal of the petition, dismisses it, stating the grounds therefor. If the regional director determines that the petition does not meet the requirements for processing under the expedited procedure, he advises the petitioner of his determination to process the petition under the procedures described in subpart C. In either event, the regional director informs all the parties of his action, and such action is final, although the Board may grant an aggrieved party permission to appeal from the regional director's action. Such party must request such review promptly, in writing, and state briefly the grounds relied upon. Such party must also immediately serve a copy on each of the other parties, including the regional director. Neither the request for review by the Board, nor the Board's grant of such review, operates as a stay of the action taken by the regional director, unless specifically so ordered by the Board.

SUBPART E—REFERENDUM CASES UNDER SECTION 9(e)(1) and (2) OF THE ACT

§ 101.26 **Initiation of rescission of authority cases.** — The investigation of the question as to whether the authority of a labor organization to make an agreement requiring membership in a labor organization as a condition of employment is to be rescinded is initiated by the filing of a petition by an employee or group of employees on behalf of 30 percent or more of the employees in a bargaining unit covered by an agreement between their employer and a labor organization requiring membership in such labor organization. The petition must be in writing and signed, and either must be notarized or must contain a declaration by the person signing it, under the penalties of the Criminal Code, that its contents are true and correct to the best of his knowledge and belief. It is filed with the regional director for the region in which the alleged appropriate bargaining unit exists or, if the bargaining unit exists in two or more regions, with the regional director for any such regions. The blank form, which is supplied by the regional office upon request, provides, among other things, for a description of the bargaining unit covered by the agreement, the approximate number of employees involved, and the names of any other labor organizations which claim to represent the employees. The petitioner must supply with the petition, or within 48 hours after filing, evidence of authorization from the employees.

§ 101.27 **Investigation of petition; withdrawals and dismissals.**— (a) Upon receipt of the petition in the regional office, it is filed, docketed, and assigned to a member of the staff, usually a field examiner, for investigation. He conducts an investigation to ascertain whether (1) the employer's operations affect commerce within the meaning of the act, (2)

there is in effect an agreement requiring as a condition of employment membership in a labor organization, (3) the petitioner has been authorized by at least 30 percent of the employees to file such a petition and (4) an election would effectuate the policies of the act by providing for a free expression of choice by the employees. The evidence of designation submitted by petitioner, usually in the form of cards signed by individual employees authorizing the filing of such a petition, is checked to determine the proportion of employees who desire rescission.

(b) The petitioner may on its own initiative request the withdrawal of the petition if the investigation discloses that an election is inappropriate, because among other possible reasons, petitioner's card-showing is insufficient to meet the 30-percent statutory requirement referred to in subsection (a) of this section.

(c) For the same or similar reasons the regional director may request the petitioner to withdraw its petition. If petitioner, despite the regional director's recommendation, refuses to withdraw the petition, the regional director then dismisses the petition, stating the grounds for his dismissal and informing petitioner of his right of appeal to the Board in Washington, D.C. The petitioner may within 10 days appeal from the regional director's dismissal by filing such request with the Board in Washington, D.C. The request shall contain a complete statement setting forth the facts and reasons upon which the request is made. After a full review of the file, the Board, with the assistance of its staff, may sustain the dismissal, stating the grounds for its affirmance, or may direct the regional director to take further action.

§ 101.28 **Consent agreements providing for election.**—The Board makes available to the parties two types of informal consent procedures through which authorization issues can be resolved without resort to formal procedures. These informal agreements are commonly referred to as (a) consent-election agreement, followed by regional director's determination, and (b) consent-election agreement, followed by Board certification. Forms for use in these informal procedures are available in the regional offices.

The procedures to be used in connection with a consent-election agreement providing for regional director's determination and a consent-election agreement providing for Board certification are the same as those already described in subpart C of the Statements of Procedure in connection with similar agreements in representation cases under section 9(c) of the act, except that no provision is made for runoff elections.

§ 101.29 **Procedure respecting election conducted without hearing.**—If the regional director determines that the case is an appropriate one for election without formal hearing, an election is conducted as quickly as possible among the employees and upon the conclusion of the election the regional director furnishes to the parties a tally of the ballots. The parties, however, have an opportunity to make appropriate challenges and objections to the conduct of the election and they have the same rights, and the same procedure is followed, with respect to objections to the conduct of the election and challenged ballots, as has already been described in subpart C of the Statements of Procedure in connection with the post-election procedures in representation cases under section 9(c) of the act, except that no provision is made for a runoff election. If no such objections are filed within 5 days and if the challenged ballots are insufficient in number to affect the results of the election, the regional director issues to the parties a certification of the results of the election, with the same force and effect as if issued by the Board.

§ 101.30 **Formal hearing and procedure respecting election conducted after hearing.**—(a) The procedures are the same as those described in subpart C of the Statements of Procedure respecting representation cases arising under section 9(c) of the Act. If the preliminary investigation indicates that there are substantial issues which require determination before an appropriate election may be held, the regional director will institute formal proceedings by issuance of a notice of hearing on the issues which, after hearing, is followed by regional director or Board decision and direction of election or dismissal. The notice of hearing together with a copy of the petition is served upon petitioner, the employer, and upon any other known persons or labor organizations claming to have been designated by employees involved in the proceeding.

(b) The hearing, usually open to the public, is held before a hearing officer who normally is an attorney or field examiner attached to the regional office but may be another qualified official. The hearing, which is non-adversary in character, is part of the investigation in which the primary interest of the Board's agents is to insure that the record contains as full a statement of the pertinent facts as may be necessary for determination of the case. The parties are afforded full opportunity to present their respective positions and to produce the significant facts in support of their contentions. In most cases a substantial number of the relevant facts are undisputed and stipulated. The parties are permitted to argue orally on the record before the hearing officer.

(c) Upon the close of the hearing, the entire record in the case is then forwarded to the regional director or the Board, together with an informal analysis by the hearing officer of the issues and the evidence but without recommendations. All parties may file briefs with the regional director or the Board within 7 days after the close of the hearing. If the case is transferred to the Board after the close of the hearing, briefs may be filed with the Board within the time prescribed by the regional director. The parties may also request to be heard orally. Because of the nature of the proceeding, however, permission to argue orally is rarely granted. After review of the entire case, the regional director or the Board issues a decision either dismissing the petition or directing that an electon be held. In the latter event, the election is conducted under the supervision of the regional director in the manner already described in section 101.19.

(d) The parties have t h e s a m e rights, and the same procedure is followed, with respect to objections to the conduct of the election and challenged ballots as has already been described in connection with the postelection procedures in representation cases under section 9(c) of the act.

SUBPART F—JURISDICTIONAL DISPUTE CASES UNDER SECTION 10 (k) OF THE ACT

§ 101.31 I n i t i a t i o n of proceedings to hear and determine jurisdictional disputes under section 10(k).— The investigation of a jurisdictional dispute under section 10(k) is initiated by the filing of a charge, as described in section 101.2, by any person alleging a violation of paragraph (4)(D) of section 8(b). As soon as possible after a charge has been filed, the regional director serves upon the parties a copy of the charge together with a notice of the filing of such charge.

§ 101.32 Investigation of charges; withdrawal of charges; dismissal of charges and appeals to Board.—These matters are handled as described in sections 101.4 to 101.7, inclusive. Cases involving violation of paragraph (4)(D) of section 8(b) in which it is deemed appropriate to seek injunctive relief of a district court pursuant to section 10(l) of the act, are given priority over all other cases in the office except other cases under section 10(l) of the act and cases of like character.

§ 101.33 Initiation of formal action; settlement.—If, after investigation, it appears to the regional director that the Board should determine the dispute under section 10(k) of the act, he issues a notice of hearing which includes a simple statement of issues involved in the jurisdictional dispute and which is served on all parties to the dispute out of which the unfair labor practice is alleged to have arisen. The hearing is scheduled for not less than 10 days after service of the notice of the fil-

ing of the charge, except that in cases involving the national defense, agreement will be sought for scheduling of hearing on less notice. If the parties present to the regional director satisfactory evidence that they have adjusted the dispute, the regional director withdraws the notice of hearing and either permits the withdrawal of the charge or dismisses the charge. If the parties submit to the regional director satisfactory evidence that they have agreed upon methods for voluntary adjustment of the dispute, the regional director shall defer action upon the charge and shall withdraw the notice of hearing if issued. The parties may agree on an arbitrator, a proceeding under section 8(c) of the act, or any other satisfactory method to resolve the dispute. If the agreed-upon method for voluntary adjustment results in a determination that employees represented by a charged union are entitled to perform the work in dispute, the regional director dismisses the charge against that union irrespective of whether the employer complies with that determination. [As amended, effective June 1, 1971]

§ 101.34 Hearing.—If the parties have not adjusted the dispute or agreed upon methods of voluntary adjustment, a hearing, usually open to the public, is held before a hearing officer. The hearing is nonadversary in character, and the primary interest of the hearing officer is to insure that the record contains as full a statement of the pertinent facts as may be necessary for a determination of the issues by the Board. All parties are afforded full opportunity to present their respective positions and to produce evidence in support of their contentions. The parties are permitted to argue orally on the record before the hearing officer. At the close of the hearing, the case is transmitted to the Board for decision. The hearing officer prepares an analysis of the issues and the evidence, but makes no recommendations in regard to resolution of the dispute.

§ 101.35 P r o c e d u r e before the Board.—The parties have 7 days after the close of the hearing, subject to any extension that may have been granted, to file briefs with the Board and to request oral argument which the Board may or may not grant. However, in cases involving the national defense and so designated in the notice of hearing, the parties may not file briefs but after the close of the evidence may argue orally upon the record their respective contentions and positions, except that for good cause shown in an application expeditiously made to the Board in Washington, D.C., after the close of the hearing, the Board may grant leave to file briefs in such time as it shall specify. The Board then considers the evidence taken at the hearing and the hearing officer's analysis together with any briefs that may be filed and the oral argument, if any, and issues its determination or makes other disposition of the matter.

§ 101.36 Compliance w i t h determination; further proceedings.—After the issuance of determination by the Board, the regional director in the region in which the proceeding arose communicates with the parties for the purpose of ascertaining their intentions in regard to compliance. Conferences may be held for the purpose of working out details. If the regional director is satisfied that the parties are complying with the determination, he dismisses the charge. If the regional director is not satisfied that the parties are complying, he issues a complaint and notice of hearing, charging violation of section 8(b) (4) (D) of the act, and the proceeding follows the procedure outlined in sections 101.8 to 101.15, inclusive. However, if the Board determines that employees represented by a charged union are entitled to perform the work in dispute, the regional director dismisses the charge against that union irrespective of whether the employer complies with the determination.

SUBPART G—PROCEDURE UNDER SECTION 10(j) AND (l) OF THE ACT

§ 101.37 Application for temporary relief or restraining orders.—When-

ever it is deemed advisable to seek temporary injunctive relief under section 10(j) or whenever it is determined that a complaint should issue alleging violation of section 8(b)(4) (A), (B), or (C), or section 8(e), or section 8(b)(7), or whenever it is appropriate to seek temporary injunctive relief for a violation of section 8(b) (4)(D), the officer or regional attorney to whom the matter has been referred will make application for appropriate temporary relief or restraining order in the district court of the United States within which the unfair labor practice is alleged to have occurred or within which the party sought to be enjoined resides or transacts business, except that such officer or regional attorney will not apply for injunctive relief under section 10(l) with respect to an alleged violation of section 8(b)(7) if a charge under section 8(a)(2) has been filed and after preliminary investigation, he has reasonable cause to believe that such charge is true and that a complaint should issue.

§ 101.38 Change of circumstances. —Whenever a temporary injunction has been obtained pursuant to section 10(j) and thereafter the administrative law judge hearing the complaint, upon which the determination to seek such injunction was predicated, recomends dismissal of such complaint, in whole or in part, the officer or regional attorney handling the case for the Board suggests to the district court which issued the temporary injunction the possible change in circumstances arising out of the findings and recommendations of the administrative law judge. [As amended, effective August 19, 1972]

SUBPART H—ADVISORY OPINIONS AND DECLARATORY O R D E R S REGARDING BOARD JURISDICTION

§ 101.39 Initiation of advisory opinion case.—The question of whether the Board will assert jurisdiction over a labor dispute which is the subject of a proceeding in an agency or court of a State or territory is initiated by the filing of a petition with the Board. This petition may be filed only if (a) a proceeding is currently pending before such agency or court, and (b) the petitioner is a party to such proceedings before such agency or court, or is the agency or court itself. The petition must be in writing and signed. When a petition is filed by a private party, it shall either be sworn to or shall contain a declaration under the penalties of the Criminal Code that its contents are true and correct. It is filed with the Executive Secretary of the Board in Washington, D.C. No particular form is required, but the petition must be properly captioned and must contain the allegations required by Section 102.99 of the Rules and Regulations. None of the information sought relates to the merits of the dispute. The petition may be withdrawn at any time before the Board issues its advisory opinion determining whether it would or would not assert jurisdiction on the basis of the facts before it.

§ 101.40 **Proceedings following the filing of the petition.**—(a) A copy of the petition is served upon all other parties and the appropriate regional director by the petitioner.

(b) Interested persons may request intervention by a written motion to the Board. Such intervention may be granted at the discretion of the Board.

(c) Parties other than the petitioner may reply to the petition in writing, admitting or denying any or all of the matters asserted therein.

(d) No briefs shall be filed except upon special permission of the Board.

(e) After review of the entire record, the Board issues an advisory opinion as to whether the facts presented would or would not cause it to assert jurisdiction over the case if the case had been originally filed before it. The Board will limit its advisory opinion to the jurisdictional issue confronting it, and will not presume to render an opinion on the merits of the care or on the question of whether the subject matter of the dispute is governed by The Labor Management Relations Act of 1947, as amended.

§ 101.41 **Informal Procedures for obtaining opinions on jurisdictional questions.**—Although a formal petition is necessary to obtain an advisory opinion from the Board, other avenues are available to persons seeking in-formal and, in most cases, speedy opinions on jurisdictional issues. In discussion of jurisdiction questions informally with regional office personnel, information and advice concerning the Board's jurisdictional standards may be obtained. Such practices are not intended to be discouraged by the rules providing for formal advisory opinions by the Board, although the opinions expressed by such personnel are not to be regarded as binding upon the Board or the general counsel.

§ 101.42 **Procedures for obtaining declaratory orders of the Board.**—(a) When both an unfair labor practice charge and a representation petition are pending concurrently in a regional office, appeals from a regional director's dismissals thereof do not follow the same course. Appeal from the dismissal of a charge must be made to the general counsel, while appeal from dismissal of a representation petition may be made to the Board. To obtain uniformity in disposing of such cases on jurisdictional grounds at the same stage of each proceeding, the general counsel may file a petition for a declaratory order of the Board. Such order is intended only to remove uncertainty with respect to the question of whether the Board would assert jurisdiction over the labor dispute.

(b) A petition to obtain a declaratory Board order may be filed only by the general counsel. It must be in writing and signed. It is filed with the Executive Secretary of the Board in Washington, D.C. No particular form is required, but the petition must be properly captioned and must contain the allegations required by section 102.106 of the Rules and Regulations. None of the information sought relates to the merits of the dispute. The petition may be withdrawn any time before the Board issues its declaratory order deciding whether it would or would not assert jurisdiction over the cases.

§ 101.43 **Proceedings following the filing of the petition.**—(a) A copy of the petition is served upon all other parties.

(b) Interested persons may request intervention by a written motion to the Board. Such intervention may be granted at the discretion of the Board.

(c) All other parties may reply to the petition in writing.

(d) Briefs may be filed.

(e) After review of the record, the Board issues a declaratory order as to whether it will assert jurisdiction over the cases, but it will not render a decision on the merits at this stage of the cases.

(f) The declaratory Board order will be binding on the parties in both cases.

NATIONAL LABOR RELATIONS BOARD
RULES AND REGULATIONS
SERIES 8—PART 102

SUBPART A—DEFINITIONS

§ 102.1 **Terms defined in section 2 of the act.**—The terms "person," "employer," "employee," "representative," "labor organization," "commerce," "affecting commerce," and "unfair labor practice," as used herein, shall have the meanings set forth in section 2 of the National Labor Relations Act, as amended by title I of the Labor Management Relations Act, 1947.

§ 102.2 **Act; Board; Board agent.**—The term "act" as used herein shall mean the National Labor Relations Act, as amended. The term "Board" shall mean the National Labor Relations Board and shall include any group of three or more members designated pursuant to section 3(b) of the act. The term "Board agent" shall mean any member, agent, or agency of the Board, including its general counsel.

§ 102.3 **General counsel.**—The term "general counsel" as used herein shall mean the general counsel under section 3(d) of the act.

§ 102.4 **Region; subregion.** — The term "region" as used herein shall mean that part of the United States or any Territory thereof fixed by the Board as a particular region. The term "subregion" shall mean that area within a region fixed by the Board as a particular subregion.

§ 102.5 **Regional director; officer-in-charge; regional attorney.** — The term "regional director" as used herein shall mean the agent designated by the Board as the regional director for a particular region, and shall also include any agent designated by the Board as officer-in-charge of a subregional office, but the officer-in-charge shall have only such powers, duties, and functions appertaining to regional directors as shall have been duly delegated to such officer-in-charge. The term "regional attorney" as used herein shall mean the attorney designated as regional attorney for a particular region.

§ 102.6 **Administrative law judge; hearing officer.**—The term "administrative law judge" as used herein shall mean the agent of the Board conducting the hearing in an unfair labor practice or Telegraph Merger Act proceeding. The term "hearing officer" as used herein shall mean the agent of the Board conducting the hearing in a proceeding under section 9 or in a dispute proceeding under section 10(k) of the act. (As amended, effective August 19, 1972)

§ 102.7 **State.**—The term "State" as used herein shall include the District of Columbia and all States, Territories, and possessions of the United States.

§ 102.8 **Party.**—The term "party" as used herein shall mean the regional director in whose region the proceeding is pending and any person named or admitted as a party, or properly seeking and entitled as of right to be admitted as a party, in any Board proceeding, including, without limitation, any person filing a charge or petition under the act, any person named as respondent, as employer, or as party to a contract in any proceeding under the act, and any labor organization alleged to be dominated, assisted, or supported in violation of section 8(a)(1) or 8(a)(2) of the act; but nothing herein shall be construed to prevent the Board or its designated agent from limiting any party to participate in the proceedings to the extent of his interest only.

SUBPART B—PROCEDURE UNDER SECTION 10(a) TO (i) OF THE ACT FOR THE PREVENTION OF UNFAIR LABOR PRACTICES[1]

Charge

§ 102.9 **Who may file; withdrawal and dismissal.**—A charge that any person has engaged in or is engaging in any unfair labor practice affecting

---

1 Procedure under sec. 10(j) to (l) of the act is governed by subparts F and G of the Rules and Regulations. Procedure for unfair labor practice cases and representation cases under section 8(b)(7) of the act are governed by subpart D.

commerce may be made by any person. Any such charge may be withdrawn, prior to the hearing, only with the consent of the regional director with whom such charge was filed; at the hearing and until the case has been transferred to the Board pursuant to section 102.45, upon motion, with the consent of the administrative law judge designated to conduct the hearing; and after the case has been transferred to the Board pursuant to section 102.45, upon motion, with the consent of the Board. Upon withdrawal of any charge, any complaint based thereupon shall be dismissed by the regional director issuing the complaint, the administrative law judge designated to conduct the hearing, or the Board. (As amended, effective August 19, 1972)

§ 102.10 **Where to file.**—Except as provided in section 102.33 such charge shall be filed with the regional director for the region in which the alleged unfair labor practice has occurred or is occurring. A charge alleging that an unfair labor practice has occurred or is occurring in two or more regions may be filed with the regional director for any such regions.

§ 102.11 **Forms; jurat; or declaration.**—Such charges shall be in writing and signed, and either shall be sworn to before a notary public, Board agent, or other person duly authorized by law to administer oaths and take acknowledgments or shall contain a declaration by the person signing it, under the penalties of the Criminal Code, that its contents are true and correct to the best of his knowledge and belief. Three additional copies of such charge shall be filed together with one copy for each additional charged party named.[2]

§ 102.12 **Contents.** — Such charge shall contain the following:

(a) The full name and address of the person making the charge.

(b) If the charge is filed by a labor organization, the full name and address of any national or international labor organization of which it is an affiliate or constituent unit.

_____
[2] A blank form for making a charge will be supplied by the regional director upon request.

(c) The full name and address of the person against whom the charge is made (hereinafter referred to as the "respondent").

(d) A clear and concise statement of the facts constituting the alleged unfair labor practices affecting commerce.

§ 102.13 **Note.**—This section, which in Series 7 of the Rules and Regulations related to the filing requirements of Section 9(f), (g), and (h) of the Labor Management Relations Act, was eliminated by amendments effective September 14, 1959. To avoid the renumbering of Sections 102.14 to 102.72, the Board has left this section number blank.

§ 102.14 **Service of charge.**—Upon the filing of a charge, the charging party shall be responsible for the timely and proper service of a copy thereof upon the person against whom such charge is made. The regional director will, as a matter of course, cause a copy of such charge to be served upon the person against whom the charge is made, but he shall not be deemed to assume responsibility for such service.

Complaint

§ 102.15 **When and by whom issued; contents; service.**—After a charge has been filed, if it appears to the regional director that formal proceedings in respect thereto should be instituted, he shall issue and cause to be served upon all the other parties a formal complaint in the name of the Board stating the unfair labor practices and containing a notice of hearing before an administrative law judge at a place therein fixed and at a time not less than 10 days after the service of the complaint. The complaint shall contain (1) a clear and concise statement of the facts upon which assertion of jurisdiction by the Board is predicated, and (2) a clear and concise description of the acts which are claimed to constitute unfair labor practices, including, where known, the approximate dates and places of such acts and the names of respondent's agents or other representatives by whom committed. (As amended, effective August 19, 1972)

§ 102.16 **Hearing; change of date or place.**—Upon his own motion or upon proper cause shown by any other party, the regional director issuing the complaint may extend the date of such hearing, or may change the place at which it is to be held. [*As amended February 10, 1975, 40 F.R. 6204.*]

§ 102.17 **Amendment.**—Any such complaint may be amended upon such terms as may be deemed just, prior to the hearing, by the regional director issuing the complaint; at the hearing and until the case has been transferred to the Board pursuant to section 102.45, upon motion, by the administrative law judge designated to conduct the hearing; and after the case has been transferred to the Board pursuant to section 102.45, at any time prior to the issuance of an order based thereon, upon motion, by the Board.

§ 102.18 **Withdrawal.**—Any such complaint may be withdrawn before the hearing by the regional director on his own motion.

§ 102.19 **Appeal to the general counsel from refusal to issue or reissue.**— (a) If, after the charge has been filed, the regional director declines to issue a complaint, or having withdrawn a complaint pursuant to section 102.18, refuses to reissue it, he shall so advise the parties in writing, accompanied by a simple statement of the procedural or other grounds for his action. The person making the charge may obtain a review of such action by filing an appeal with the general counsel in Washington, D.C., and filing a copy of the appeal with the regional director, within 10 days from the service of the notice of such refusal to issue or reissue by the regional director, except as a shorter period is provided by § 102.81. If an appeal is taken the person doing so should notify all other parties of his action, but any failure to give such notice shall not affect the validity of the appeal. The appeal shall contain a complete statement setting forth the facts and reasons upon which it is based. A request for extension of time to file an appeal shall be in writing and be received by the general counsel, and a copy of such request filed with the regional

director, prior to the expiration of the filing period. Copies of the acknowledgement of the filing of an appeal and of any ruling on a request for an extension of time for the filing of an appeal shall be served on all parties. Consideration of an appeal untimely filed is within the discretion of the general counsel upon good cause shown.

(b) Oral presentation in Washington D.C., of the appeal issues may be permitted a party on written request made within 4 days after service of acknowledgement of the filing of an appeal. In the event such request is granted, the other parties shall be notified and afforded, without additional request, a like opportunity at another appropriate time.

(c) The general counsel may sustain the regional director's refusal to issue or reissue a complaint, stating the grounds of his affirmance, or may direct the regional director to take further action; the general counsel's decision shall be served on all the parties. A motion for reconsideration of the decision must be filed within 10 days of service of the decision, except as hereinafter provided, and shall state with particularity the error requiring reconsideration. A motion for reconsideration based upon newly discovered evidence which has become available only since the decision on appeal shall be filed promptly on discovery of such evidence. Motions for reconsideration of a decision previously reconsidered will not be entertained, except in unusual situations where the moving party can establish that new evidence has been discovered which could not have been discovered by diligent inquiry prior to the first reconsideration. (As amended, effective March 7, 1972)

Answer

§ 102.20 **Answer to complaint; time for filing; contents; allegations not denied deemed admitted.**—The respondent shall, within 10 days from the service of the complaint, file an answer thereto. The respondent shall specifically admit, deny, or explain each of the facts alleged in the complaint, unless the respondent is without knowledge, in which case the respondent shall so state, such statement operating as a denial. All allegations in the complaint, if no answer is filed, or any allegation in the complaint not specifically denied or explained in an answer filed, unless the respondent shall state in the answer that he is without knowledge, shall be deemed to be admitted to be true and shall be so found by the Board, unless good cause to the contrary is shown.

§ 102.21 **Where to file; service upon the parties; form.**—An original and four copies of the answer shall be filed with the regional director issuing the complaint. Immediately upon the filing of his answer, respondent shall serve a copy thereof on each of the other parties. An answer of a party represented by counsel shall be signed by at least one attorney of record in his individual name, whose address shall be stated. A party who is not represented by an attorney shall sign his answer and state his address. Except when otherwise specifically provided by rule or statute, an answer need not be verified or accompanied by affidavit. The signature of an attorney constitutes a certificate by him that he has read the answer; that to the best of his knowledge, information, and belief there is good ground to support it; and that it is not interposed for delay. If an answer is not signed or is signed with intent to defeat the purpose of this rule, it may be stricken as sham and false and the action may proceed as though the answer had not been served. For a willful violation of this rule an attorney may be subjected to appropriate disciplinary action. Similar action may be taken if scandalous or indecent matter is inserted.

§ 102.22 **Extension of time for filing.** —Upon his own motion or upon proper cause shown by any other party the regional director issuing the complaint may by written order extend the time within which the answer shall be filed.

§ 102.23 **A m e n d m e n t .**—The respondent may amend his answer at any time prior to the hearing. During the hearing of subsequent thereto, he may amend his answer in any case where the complaint has been amended, within such period as may be fixed by the administrative law judge or the Board. Whether or not the complaint has been amended, the answer may in the discretion of the administrative law judge or the Board, upon motion be amended upon such terms and within such periods as may be fixed by the administrative law judge or the Board. [*As amended, effective August 19, 1972*]

Motions

§ 102.24 **Motions; where to file; contents; service on other parties; promptness in filing and response.**— All motions under sections 102.16, 102.22, and 102.29 made prior to hearing shall be filed in writing with the regional director issuing the complaint. All motions for summary judgment made prior to hearing shall be filed in writing with the Board pursuant to the provisions of section 102.50. All other motions prior to hearing shall be filed in writing with the chief administrative law judge in Washington, D.C., or with the presiding judge in San Francisco, California, as the case may be. All motions made at the hearing shall be made in writing to the administrative law judge or stated orally on the record. All motions filed subsequent to the hearing, but before the transfer of the case to the Board pursuant to section 102.45, shall be filed with the administrative law judge, care of the chief administrative law judge in Washington, D.C., or the presiding judge, San Francisco, California, as the case may be. All motions made subsequent to transfer of the case to, and while it is pending before, the Board shall be filed with the executive secretary of the Board in Washington, D.C., as provided in section 102.47. Motions shall briefly state the order or relief applied for and the grounds therefor. All motions prior to transfer of the case to the Board shall be filed by moving party in an original and four copies and a copy thereof, shall be immediately served on the other parties. Unless otherwise provided in these rules, motions and responses thereof shall be filed promptly and within such time as not to delay the proceeding. [*As amended, effective August 19, 1972*]

§ 102.25 **Ruling on motions**—An administrative law judge designated by the chief administrative law judge, or by the presiding judge in San Francisco, California, shall rule on all prehearing motions (except as provided in sections 102.16, 102.22, 102.29, and 102.50), and all such rulings and orders shall be issued in writing and a copy served on each of the parties. The administrative law judge designated by the chief administrative law judge, or by the presiding judge in San Francisco, California, to conduct the hearing shall rule on all motions after opening of the hearing (except as provided in section 102.47), and any orders in connection therewith, if announced at the hearing, shall be stated orally on the record; in all other cases the administrative law judge shall issue such rulings and orders in writing and shall cause a copy of the same to be served on each of the parties, or shall make his ruling in his decision. Whenever the administrative law judge has reserved his ruling on any motion, and the proceeding is thereafter transferred to and continued before the Board pursuant to section 102.50, the Board shall rule on such motion. (As amended, effective August 9, 1972)

§ 102.26 **Motions; rulings and orders part of the record; rulings not to be appealed directly to Board without special permission; requests for special permission to appeal.**—All motions, rulings, and orders shall become part of the record, except that rulings on motions to revoke subpenas shall become a part of the record only upon the request of the party aggrieved thereby, as provided in section 102.31. Unless expressly authorized by the Rules and Regulations, rulings by the regional director and by the administrative law judge on motions, by the administrative law judge on objections, and orders in connection therewith, shall not be appealed directly to the Board except by special permission of the Board, but shall be considered by the Board in reviewing the record, if exception to the ruling or order is included in the statement of exceptions filed with the Board, pursuant to section 102.46. Requests to the Board for special permission to appeal from such rulings of the regional director or the administrative law judge shall be filed promptly, in writing, and shall briefly state the grounds relied on. The moving party shall immediately serve a copy thereof on each other party, and if the request involves a ruling by an administrative law judge, on that administrative law judge. [*As amended, effective August 19, 1972*]

§ 102.27 **Review of granting of motion to dismiss entire complaint; reopening of record.**—If any motion in the nature of a motion to dismiss the complaint in its entirety is granted by the administrative law judge before filing his decision, any party may obtain a review of such action by filing a request therefor with the Board in Washington, D.C., stating the grounds for review and immediately on such filing shall serve a copy thereof on the regional director and the other parties. Unless such request for review is filed within 10 days from the date of the order of dismissal, the case shall be closed. [*As amended, effective August 19, 1972*]

§ 102.28 **Filing of answer or other participation in proceedings not a waiver of rights.**—The right to make motions or to make objections to rulings upon motions shall not be deemed waived by the filing of an answer or by other participation in the proceedings before the administrative law judge.

Intervention

§ 102.29 **Intervention; requisite; rulings on motions to intervene.**—Any person desiring to intervene in any proceeding shall file a motion in writing or, if made at the hearing, may move orally on the record, stating the grounds upon which such person claims an interest. Prior to the hearing, such a motion shall be filed with the regional director issuing the complaint; during the hearing such motion shall be made to the administrative law judge. An original and four copies of written motions shall be filed. Immediately upon filing such motion, the moving party shall serve a copy thereof upon each of the other parties. The regional director shall rule upon all such motions filed prior to the hearing, and shall cause a copy of said rulings to be served upon each of the other parties, or may refer the motion to the administrative law judge for ruling. The administrative law judge shall rule upon all such motions made at the hearing or referred to him by the regional director, in the manner set forth in section 102.25. The regional director or the administrative law judge, as the case may be, may by order permit intervention in person or by counsel or other representative to such extent and upon such terms as he may deem proper.

Witnesses, Depositions, and Subpenas

§ 102.30 **Examination of witnesses; depositions.**—Witnesses shall be examined orally under oath, except that for good cause shown after the issuance of a complaint, testimony may be taken by deposition.

(a) Applications to take depositions shall be in writing setting forth the reasons why such depositions should be taken, the name and post office address of the witness, the matters concerning which it is expected the witness will testify, and the time and place proposed for the taking of the deposition, together with the name and address of the person before whom it is desired that the deposition be taken (for the purposes of this section hereinafter referred to as the "officer"). Such application shall be made to the regional director prior to the hearing, and to the administrative law judge during and subsequent to the hearing but before transfer of the case to the Board pursuant to section 102.45 or section 102.50. Such application shall be served on the regional director or the administrative law judge, as the case may be, and on all other parties not less than 7 days (when the deposition is to be taken within the continental United States) and 15 days (if the deposition is to be taken elsewhere) prior to the time when it is desired that the deposition be taken. The regional director or administrative law judge, as the case may be, shall upon receipt of the application, if in his discretion good cause has been shown, make and serve

upon the parties an order which will specify the name of the witness whose deposition is to be taken and the time the place, and the designation of the officer before whom the witness is to testify, who may or may not be the same officer so that specified in the application. S u c h order shall be served upon all the other parties by the regional director or upon all parties by the administrative law judge. (As amended, effective August 19, 1972)

(b) Such deposition may be taken before any officer authorized to administer oaths by the laws of the United States or of the place where the examination is held, including any agent of the Board authorized to administer oaths. If the examination is held in a foreign country, it may be taken before any secretary of embassy or legation, consul general, consul, vice consul, or consular agent of the United States.

(c) At the time and place specified in said order the officer designated to take such deposition shall permit the witness to be examined and cross-examined under oath by all the parties appearing, and his testimony shall be reduced to typewriting by the officer or under his direction. All objections to questions or evidence shall be deemed waived unless made at the examination. The officer shall not have power to rule upon any objections but he shall note them upon the deposition. The testimony shall be subscribed by the witness in the presence of the officer who shall attach his certificate stating that the witness was duly sworn by him, that the deposition is a true record of the testimony and exhibits given by the witness, and that said officer is not of counsel or attorney to any of the parties nor interested in the event of the proceeding or investigation. If the deposition is not signed by the witness because he is ill, dead, cannot be found, or refuses to sign it, such fact shall be included in the certificate of the officer and the deposition may then be used as fully as though signed. The officer shall immediately deliver an original and two copies of said transcript, together with his certificate, in person or by registered mail 'to the regional director or the administrative law judge, care of the chief administrative law judge in Washington, D.C., or presiding judge, San Francisco, California, as the case may be.

(d) The administrative law judge shall rule upon the admissibility of the deposition or any part thereof. (As amended, effective August 19, 1972)

(e) All errors or irregularities in compliance with the provisions of this section shall be deemed waived unless a motion to suppress the deposition or some part thereof is made with reasonable promptness after such defect is or, with due diligence, might have been ascertained.

(f) If the parties so stipulate in writing, depositions may be taken before any person at any time or place, upon any notice and in any manner, and when so taken may be used like other depositions.

§ 102.31 **Issuance of subpenas; petitions to revoke subpoenas; right to inspect and copy data.**—(a) Any member of the Board shall, on the written application of any party, forthwith issue subpenas requiring the attendance and testimony of witnesses and the production of any evidence, including books, records, correspondence, or documents, in their possession or under their control. Applications for subpenas, if filed prior to the hearing, shall be filed with the regional director. Applications for subpenas filed during the hearing shall be filed with the administrative law judge. Either the regional director or the administrative law judge, as the case may be, shall grant the application, on behalf of any member of the Board. Applications for subpenas may be made *ex parte*. The subpena shall show on its face the name and address of the party at whose request the subpena was issued. (As amended, effective August 19, 1972)

(b) Any person, served with a subpena, whether *ad testificandum* or *duces tecum*, if he does not intend to comply with the subpena, shall, within 5 days after the date of service of the subpena upon him, petition in writing to revoke the subpena. All petitions to revoke subpenas shall be served upon the party at whose request the subpena was issued. Such petition to revoke, if made prior to the hearing, shall be filed with the regional director and the regional director shall refer the petition to the administrative law judge or the Board for ruling. Petitions to revoke subpenas filed during the hearing shall be filed with the administrative law judge. Notice of the filing of petitions to revoke shall be promptly given by the regional director or the administrative law judge as the case may be, to the party at whose request the subpena was issued. The administrative law judge or the Board, as the case may, be shall revoke the subpena if in its opinion the evidence whose production is required does not relate to any matter under investigation or in question in the proceedings or the subpena is otherwise invalid. The adinistrative law judge or the Board, as the case may be, shall make a simple statement of procedural or other grounds for the ruling on the petition to revoke. The petition to revoke, any answer filed thereto, and any ruling thereon shall not become part of the official record except upon the request of the party aggrieved by the ruling. [*As amended, effective August 19, 1972*]

(c) With the approval of the Attorney General of the United States, the Board may issue an order requiring any individual to give testimony or provide other information at any proceeding before the Board if, in the judgment of the Board, (1) the testimony or other information from such individual may be necessary to the public interest, and (2) such individual has refused or is likely to refuse to testify or provide other information on the basis of his privilege against self-incrimination. Requests for the issuance of such an order by the Board may be made by any party. Prior to hearing, and after transfer of the proceeding to the Board, such requests shall be made to the Board in Washington, D.C., and the Board shall take such action thereon as it deems appropriate. During the hearing, and thereafter while the proceeding is pending before the administrative law judge, such requests shall be made to the administrative law judge. If the administrative law judge denies the requests, his ruling shall be subject to appeal to the Board in Washington, D.C., in the manner and to the extent provided in § 102.26 with respect to rulings and orders by an administrative law judge, except that requests for permission to appeal in this instance shall be filed within 24 hours of the administrative law judge's ruling. If no appeal is sought within such time, or the appeal is denied, the ruling of the administrative law judge shall become final and his denial shall become the ruling of the Board. If the administrative law judge deems the request appropriate, he shall recommend that the Board seek the approval of the Attorney General for the issuance of the order and the Board shall take such action on the administrative law judge's recommendation as it deems appropriate. Until the Board has issued the requested order no individual who claims the privilege against self-incrimination shall be required, or permitted, to testify or to give other information respecting the subject matter of the claim. [As amended, effective August 19, 1972]

(d) Upon the failure of any person to comply with a subpena issued upon the request of a private party, the general counsel shall, in the name of the Board but on relation of such private party, institute proceedings in the appropriate district court for the enforcement thereof, unless in the judgment of the Board the enforcement of such subpena would be inconsistent with law and with the policies of the act. Neither the general counsel nor the Board shall be deemed thereby to have assumed responsibility for the effective prosecution of the same before the court.

(e) Persons compelled to submit data or evidence at a public proceeding are entitled to retain or, on payment of lawfully prescribed costs, to procure copies or transcripts of the data or evidence submitted by them.

Persons compelled to submit data or evidence in the nonpublic investigative stages of proceedings may, for good cause, be limited by the regional director to inspection of the official transcript of their testimony, but shall be entitled to make copies of documentary evidence or exhibits which they have produced. [As added by amendment, effective December 14, 1970]

§ 102.32 **Payment of witness f e e s and mileage; fees of persons taking depositions.**—Witnesses summoned before the administrative law judge shall be paid the same fees and mileage that are paid witnesses in the courts of the United States, and witnesses whose depositions are taken and the persons taking the same shall severally be entitled to the same fees as are paid for like services in the courts of the United States. Witness fees and mileage shall be paid by the party at whose instance the witnesses appear and the person taking the deposition shall be paid by the party at whose instance the deposition is taken. [As amended, effective August 19, 1972]

Transfer, Consolidation, and Severance

§ 102.33 **Transfer of c h a r g e and proceeding from region to region; consolidation of proceedings in same region; severance.**—(a) Whenever the general counsel deems it necessary in order to effectuate the purposes of the act or to avoid unnecessary costs or delay, he may permit a charge to be filed with him in Washington, D.C., or may, at any time after a charge has been filed with a regional director pursuant to section 102.10, order that such charge and any proceeding which may have been initiated with respect thereto:

(1) Be transferred to and continued before him for the purpose of investigation or consolidation with any other proceeding which may have been instituted in a regional office or with him; or

(2) Be consolidated with any other proceeding which may have been instituted in the same region; or

(3) Be transferred to and continued in any other region for the purpose

of investigation or consolidation with any proceeding which may have been instituted in or transferred to such region; or

(4) Be severed from any other proceeding with which it may have been consolidated pursuant to this section.

(b) The provisions of Sections 102.9 to 102.32, inclusive, shall, insofar as applicable, govern proceedings before the general counsel pursuant to this section, and the powers granted to regional directors in such provisions shall, for the purpose of this section, be reserved to and exercised by the general counsel. After the transfer of any charge and any proceeding which may have been instituted with respect thereto from one region to another pursuant to this section, the provisions of this subpart shall, insofar as applicable, govern such charge and such proceeding as if the charge had originally been filed in the region to which the transfer is made.

(c) The regional director may, prior to hearing, exercise the powers in paragraph (a) (2) and (4) of this section with respect to proceedings in pending his region.

(d) Motions to consolidate or sever proceedings after issuance of complaint shall be filed as provided in section 102.24 and ruled upon as provided in section 102.25, except that the regional director may consolidate or sever proceedings prior to hearing upon his own motion. Rulings by the administrative law judge upon motions to consolidate or sever may be appealed to the Board as provided in section 102.26. [*As amended, effective August 19, 1972*]

Hearings

§ 102.34 **Who shall conduct; to be public unless otherwise ordered.**—The hearing for the purpose of taking evidence upon a complaint shall be conducted by an administrative law judge designated by the chief administrative law judge in Washington, D.C., or the presiding judge, San Francisco, California, as the case may be, unless the Board or any member thereof presides. At any time an administrative law judge may be designated to take the place of the administrative

law judge previously designated to conduct the hearing. Such hearings shall be public unless otherwise ordered by the Board or the administrative law judge.

§ 102.35 **Duties and powers of administrative law judges.**—It shall be the duty of the administrative law judge to inquire fully into the facts as to whether the respondent has engaged in or is engaging in an unfair labor practice affecting commerce as set forth in the complaint or amended complaint. The administrative law judge shall have authority, with respect to cases assigned to him, between the time he is designated and transfer of the case to the Board, subject to the Rules and Regulations of the Board and within its powers: [*As amended, effective August 19, 1972*]

(a) **To administer oaths and affirmations;**

(b) **To grant applications for subpenas;**

(c) **To rule upon petitions to revoke subpenas;**

(d) **To rule upon offers of proof and receive relevant evidence;**

(e) **To take or cause depositions to be taken whenever the ends of justice would be served thereby;**

(f) **To regulate the course of the hearing and, if appropriate or necessary, to exclude persons or counsel from the hearing for contemptuous conduct and to strike all related testimony of witnesses refusing to answer any proper question;**

(g) **To hold conferences for the settlement or simplification of the issues by consent of the parties, but not to adjust cases;**

(h) **To dispose of procedural requests, motions or similar matters, including motions referred to the administrative law judge by the regional director and motions for summary judgment or to amend pleadings; also to dismiss complaints or portions thereof; to order hearings reopened; and upon motion, order proceedings consolidated or severed prior to issuance of administrative law judge decisions;**

(i) **To approve a stipulation voluntarily entered into by all parties to** the case which will dispense with a verbatim written transcript of record of the oral testimony adduced at the hearing, and which will also provide for the waiver by the respective parties of their right to file with the Board exceptions to the findings of fact (but not to conclusions of law or recommended orders) which the administrative law judge shall make in his decision; [As amended, effective August 19, 1972]

(j) To make and file decisions in conformity with **Public Law 89-544, 5** U.S.C. section 557; [As amended, effective November 27, 1971]

(k) To call, examine, and cross-examine witnesses and to introduce into the record documentary or other evidence;

(l) To request the parties at any time during the hearing to state their respective positions concerning any issue in the case or theory in support thereof; [As added by amendment, effective September 3, 1963]

(m) To take any other action necessary under the foregoing and authorized by the published Rules and Regulations of the Board.

§ 102.36 **Unavailability of administrative law judges.**—In the event the administrative law judge designated to conduct the hearing becomes unavailable to the Board after the hearing has been opened, the chief administrative law judge, or the presiding judge, San Francisco, California, as the case may be, may designate another administrative law judge for the purpose of further hearing or other appropriate action. [As amended, effective May 2, 1974]

§ 102.37 **Disqualification of administrative law judges.** An administrative law judge may withdraw from a proceeding whenever he deems himself disqualified. Any party may request the administrative law judge, at any time following his designation by the chief administrative law judge or the presiding judge, San Francisco, California, and before filing of his decision, to withdraw on ground of personal bias or disqualification, by filing with him promptly upon the discovery of the alleged facts a timely affidavit setting forth in detail the matters alleged to constitute grounds for disqualification. If, in the opinion of the administrative law judge, such affidavit is filed with due diligence and is sufficient on its face, he shall forthwith disqualify himself and withdraw from the proceeding. If the administrative law judge does not disqualify himself and withdraw from the proceeding, he shall so rule upon the record, stating the grounds for his ruling and proceed with the hearing, or if the hearing has closed, he shall proceed with issuance of his decision and the provisions of section 102.26, with respect to review of rulings of administrative law judges shall thereupon apply.

§ 102.38 **Rights of parties.**—Any party shall have the right to appear at such hearing in person, by counsel, or by other representative, to call, examine, and cross-examine witnesses, and to introduce into the record documentary or other evidence, except that the participation of any party shall be limited to the extent permitted by the administrative law judge: And provided further, That documentary evidence shall be submitted in duplicate. [As amended, effective August 19, 1972]

§ 102.39 **Rules of evidence controlling so far as practicable.**—Any such proceeding shall, so far as practicable, be conducted in accordance with the rules of evidence applicable in the district courts of the United States under the rules of civil procedure for the district courts of the United States, adopted by the Supreme Court of the United States pursuant to the act of June 19, 1934 (U.S.C., Title 28, Secs. 723-B, 723-C).

§ 102.40 **Stipulations of fact admissible.**—In any such proceeding stipulations of fact may be introduced in evidence with respect to any issue.

§ 102.41 **Objection to conduct of hearing; how made; objections not waived by further participation.**—Any objection with respect to the conduct of the hearing, including any objection to the introduction of evidence, may be stated orally or in writing, accompanied by a short statement of the grounds of such objection, and included in the record. No such objection shall be deemed waived by further participation in the hearing.

§ 102.42 **Filing of briefs and proposed findings with the administrative law judge and oral argument at the hearing.**—Any party shall be entitled, upon request, to a reasonable period at the close of the hearing for oral argument, which shall be included in the stenographic report of the hearing. Any party shall be entitled, upon request made before the close of the hearing, to file a brief or proposed findings and conclusions, or both, with the administrative law judge who may fix a reasonable time for such filing, but not in excess of 35 days from the close of the hearing. Requests for further extensions of time shall be made to the chief administrative law judge in Washington, D.C., or presiding judge, San Francisco, California, as the case may be. No request will be considered unless received at least 3 days prior to the expiration of the time fixed for the filing of briefs or proposed findings and conclusions. Notice of the request for any extension shall be immediately served upon all other parties, and proof of service shall be furnished. Three copies of the brief or proposed findings and conclusions shall be filed with the administrative law judge, and copies shall be served upon each of the other parties, and proof of such service shall be furnished.

§ 102.43 **Continuance and adjournment.**—In the discretion of the administrative law judge, the hearing may be continued from day to day, or adjourned to a later date or to a different place, by announcement thereof at the hearing by the administrative law judge, or by other appropriate notice. (As amended, effective August 19, 1972)

§ 102.44 **Misconduct at hearing before an administrative law judge or the Board; refusal of witness to answer questions.** — (a) Misconduct at any hearing before an administrative

law judge or before the Board shall be ground for summary exclusion from the hearing. (As amended, effective August 19, 1972)

(b) Such misconduct of an aggravated character, when engaged in by an attorney or other representative of a party, shall be ground for suspension or disbarment by the Board from further practice before it after due notice and hearing.

(c) The refusal of a witness at any such hearing to answer any question which has been ruled to be proper shall, in the discretion of the administrative law judge, be ground for striking all testimony previously given by such witness on related matters. (As amended, effective August 19, 1972)

Administrative Law Judge's Decision and Transfer Of Case To The Board

§ 102.45 **Administrative law judge's decision; contents; service; transfer of the case to the Board; contents of record in case.**—(a) After hearing for the purpose of taking evidence upon a complaint, the administrative law judge shall prepare a decision. Such decision shall contain findings of fact, conclusions, and the reasons or basis therefor, upon all material issues of fact, law, or discretion presented on the record, and shall contain recommendations as to what disposition of the case should be made which may include, if it be found that the respondent has engaged in or is engaging in the alleged unfair labor practices, a recommendation for such affirmative action by the respondent as will effectuate the policies of the act. The administrative law judge shall file the original of his decision with the Board and cause a copy thereof to be served upon each of the parties. Upon the filing of the decision the Board shall enter an order transferring the case to the Board and shall serve copies of the order, setting forth the date of such transfer, upon all the parties. Service of the administrative law judge's decision and of the order transferring the case to the Board shall be complete upon mailing. (As amended, effective August 19, 1972)

(b) The charge upon which the

complaint was issued and any amendments thereto, the complaint and any amendments thereto, notice of hearing, answer and any amendments thereto, motions, rulings, orders, the stenographic report of the hearing, stipulations, exhibits, documentary evidence, and depositions, together with the administrative law judge's decision and exceptions and any cross-exceptions or answering briefs as provided in § 102.46, shall constitute the record in the case. [*As amended, effective August 19, 1972*]

§ 102.46 Exceptions, cross-exceptions, briefs, answering briefs; time for filing; where to file; service on parties; extension of time; effect of failure to include matter in exceptions; oral arguments.—(a) Within 20 days, or within such further period as the Board may allow, from the date of the service of the order transferring the case to the Board, pursuant to section 102.45, any party may (in accordance with section 10(c) of the act and sections 102.113 and 102.114 of these rules) file with the Board in Washington, D.C., exceptions to the administrative law judge's decision or to any other part of the record or proceedings (including rulings upon all motions or objections), together with a brief in support of said exceptions. Any party may, within the same period, file a brief in support of the administrative law judge's decision. The filing of such exceptions and briefs is subject to the provisions of subsection (j) of this section. Requests for extension of time to file exceptions or briefs shall be in writing and copies thereof shall be served promptly on the other parties. Such requests must be received by the Board 3 days prior to the due date. [*As amended, effective August 19, 1972*]

(b) Each exception (1) shall set forth specifically the questions of procedure, fact, law, or policy to which exceptions are taken; (2) shall identify that part of the administrative law judge's decision to which objection is made; (3) shall designate by precise citation of page the portions of the record relied on, and (4) shall state the grounds for the exceptions and shall include the citation of authorities unless set forth in a supporting brief. Any exception to a rul-

ing, finding, conclusion, or recommendation which is not specifically urged shall be deemed to have been waived. Any exception which fails to comply with the foregoing requirements may be disregarded.

(c) Any brief in support of exceptions shall contain no matter not included within the scope of the exceptions and shall contain, in the order indicated, the following:

(1) A clear and concise statement of the case containing all that is material to the consideration of the questions presented.

(2) A specification of the questions involved and to be argued.

(3) The a r g u m e n t, presenting clearly the points of fact and law relied upon in support of the position taken on each question, with specific page reference to the transcripts and the legal or other material relied upon.

(d)(1) Within 10 days, or such further period as the Board may allow, from the last date on which exceptions and any supporting brief may be filed, a party opposing the exceptions may file an answering brief to the exceptions, in accordance with the provisions of subsection (j) of this section. The provision for 3 additional days as contained in section 102.114 shall be applicable to this subsection.

(2) The answering brief to the exceptions shall be limited to the questions raised in the exceptions and in the brief in support thereof. It shall present clearly the points of fact and law relied upon in support of the position taken on each question. Where exception has been taken to a factual finding of the administrative law judge and it is proposed to support that finding, the answering brief should specify those pages of the record which, in the view of the party filing the brief, support the administrative law judge's finding.

(3) Requests for extension of time to file an answering brief to the exceptions shall be in writing and copies thereof shall be served promptly on the other parties. Such re-

quests must be received by the Board 3 days prior to the due date.

(e) Any party who has not previously filed exceptions may, within 10 days, or such further period as the board may allow, from the last date on which exceptions and any supporting brief may be filed, file cross-exceptions to any portion of the administrative law judge's decision, together with a supporting brief, in accordance with the provisions of subsections (b) and (j) of this section. The provision for 3 additional days as contained in section 102.114 shall be applicable to this subsection.

(f)(1) Within 10 days, or such further period as the Board may allow, from the last date on which cross-exceptions and any supporting brief may be filed, any other party may file an answering brief to such cross-exceptions in accordance with the provisions of subsections (c) and (j) of this section. Such answering brief shall be limited to the questions raised in the cross-exceptions. The provision for 3 additional days as contained in section 102.114 shall be applicable to this subsection.

(2) Requests for extension of time to file cross-exceptions, or answering brief to cross-exceptions, shall be in writing and copies thereof shall be served promptly on each of the other parties. Such requests must be received by the Board 3 days prior to the due date.

(g) No further briefs shall be filed except by special leave of the Board. Requests for such leave shall be in writing and copies thereof shall be served promptly on the other parties.

(h) No matter not included in exceptions or cross-exceptions may thereafter be urged before the Board, or in any further proceeding.

(i) Should any party desire permission to argue orally before the Board, request therefor must be made in writing to the Board simultaneously with the statement of any exceptions or cross-exceptions filed pursuant to the provisions of this section with a statement of service on the other parties. The Board shall notify the parties of the time and place of oral argument, if such permission is granted. Oral arguments are limited to 30 minutes for each party entitled to participate. No request for additional time will be granted unless timely application is made in advance of oral argument.

(j) Exceptions to administrative law judges' decisions, or to the record, briefs in support of exceptions, and briefs in support of administrative law judge's decisions, cross-exceptions, and answering briefs shall be printed or otherwise legibly duplicated: *Provided, however,* That carbon copies of typewritten matter shall not be filed and if submitted will not be accepted. Eight copies of such documents shall be filed with the Board in Washington, D.C., and copies shall also be served promptly on the other parties. Where any brief filed pursuant to this section exceeds 20 pages, it shall contain a subject index with page references and an alphabetical table of cases and other authorities cited. [*As amended, effective August 19, 1972*]

§ 102.47 **Filing of motion after transfer of case to Board.**—All motions filed after the case has been transferred to the Board pursuant to section 102.45 shall be filed with the Board in Washington, D.C., by transmitting eight copies thereof, together with an affidavit of service on the parties. Such motions shall be printed or otherwise legibly duplicated: *Provided, however,* That carbon copies of typewritten matter shall not be filed and if submitted will not be accepted.

Procedure Before the Board

§ 102.48 **Action of Board upon expiration of time to file exceptions to administrative law judge's decision; decisions by the Board; extraordinary post decisional motions.**—(a) In the event no timely or proper exceptions are filed as herein provided, the findings, conclusions, and recommendations of the administrative law judge as contained in his decision shall, pursuant to section 10(c) of the act, automatically become the decision and order of the Board and become its findings, conclusions and order, and all objections and exceptions thereto shall be deemed waived for all purposes. [*As amended, effective August 19, 1972*]

(b) Upon the filing of timely and proper exceptions, and any cross-exceptions, or answering briefs, as provided in section 102.46, the Board may decide the matter forthwith upon the record, or after oral argument, or may reopen the record and receive further evidence before a member of the Board or other Board agent or agency, or may make other disposition of the case. [*As amended September 24, 1969*]

(c) Where exception is taken to a factual finding of the administrative law judge, the Board, in determining whether the finding is contrary to a preponderance of the evidence, may limit its consideration to such portions of the record as are specified in the exception, the supporting brief, and the answering brief. [*As amended, effective August 19, 1972*]

(d)(1) A party to a proceeding before the Board may, because of extraordinary circumstances move for reconsideration, rehearing or reopening of the record after the Board decision or order. A motion for reconsideration shall state with particularity the material error claimed and with respect to any finding of material fact shall specify the page of the record relied on. A motion for rehearing shall specify the error alleged to require a hearing *de novo* and the prejudice to the movant alleged to result from such error. A motion to reopen the record shall state briefly the additional evidence sought to be adduced, why it was not presented previously, and that, if adduced and credited, it would require a different result. Only newly discovered evidence, evidence which has become available only since the close of the hearing, or evidence which the Board believes should have been taken at the hearing, will be taken at any further hearing.

(2) Any motion pursuant to this subsection shall be filed within 20 days, or such further period as the Board may allow, after the service of its decision or order, except that a motion for leave to adduce additional evidence shall be filed promptly upon discovery of such evidence. Any request for an extension of time must be received by the Board 3 days prior to the due date and copies thereof shall be served promptly on the other parties.

(3) The filing and pendency of a motion under this provision shall not operate to stay the effectiveness of the action of the Board unless so ordered. A motion for reconsideration or rehearing need not be filed to exhaust administrative remedies. [*As amended, effective September 3, 1963.*]

§ 102.49 **Modification or setting aside of order of Board before record filed in court; action thereafter.—** Within the limitations of the provisions of section 10(c) of the act, and section 102.48 of these rules, until a transcript of the record in a case shall have been filed in a court, within the meaning of section 10 of the act, the Board may at any time upon reasonable notice modify or set aside, in whole or in part, any findings of fact, conclusions of law, or order made or issued by it. Thereafter, the Board may proceed pursuant to section 102.50, insofar as applicable.

§ 102.50 **Hearings before Board or member thereof.—**Whenever the Board deems it necessary in order to effectuate the purpose of the act or to avoid unnecessary costs or delay, it may, at any time after a complaint has issued pursuant to section 102.15 or section 102.33, order that such complaint and any proceeding which may have been instituted with respect thereto be transferred to and continued before it or any member of the Board. The provisions of this subpart shall, insofar as applicable, govern proceedings before the Board or any member pursuant to this section, and the powers granted to administrative law judges in such provisions shall, for the purpose of this section, be reserved to and exercised by the Board or the member thereof who shall preside. [*As amended, effective August 19, 1972*]

§ 102.51 **Settlement or adjustment of issues.—**At any stage of a proceeding prior to hearing, where time, the nature of the proceeding, and the public interest permit, all interested parties shall have opportunity to submit to the regional director, with whom the charge was filed, for consideration facts, arguments, offers of settlement, or proposals of adjustment.

Backpay Proceedings

§ 102.52 Initiation of proceedings; issuance of backpay specification; **issuance of notice of hearing without** backpay specification. — A f t e r the entry of a Board order directing the payment of backpay or the entry of a court decree enforcing such a Board order, if it appears to the regional director that a controversy exists between the Board and a respondent concerning the amount of back pay due which cannot be resolved without a formal proceeding, the regional director may issue and serve upon all parties a backpay specification in the name of the Board. The specification shall contain or be accompanied by a notice of hearing before an administrative law judge at a place therein fixed and at a time not less than 15 days after the service of the specification. In the alternative and in his discretion, the regional director may, under the circumstances specified above, issue and serve upon the parties a notice of hearing only, without the back-pay specification, the hearing to be held before an administrative law judge, at a place therein fixed and at a time not less than 15 days after the service of the notice of hearing.

§ 102.53 Contents of backpay spec-**ification and of notice of hearing** without specification.—(a) *Contents of back-pay specification.*—Where the **specification procedure is used, the specification shall specifically and in detail show, for each employee, the back-pay periods broken down by calendar quarters, the specific figures and basis of computation as to gross back pay and interim earnings, the expenses for each quarter, the net back pay due, and any other pertinent information.**

(b) *Contents of notice of hearing without specification.*—The notice of **hearing w i t h o u t specification shall contain, in addition to the time and** place of hearing before an administrative law judge, a brief statement of the matters in controversy. [*As amended, effective August 19, 1972*]

§ 102.54 Answer to specification; no requirement for answer to notice of hearing issued without back pay specification.—(a) *Filing and service of answer to specification.*—The respondent shall, within 15 days from the service of the specification, if any, file an answer thereto; an original and four copies shall be filed with the regional director issuing the specification, and a copy thereof shall immediately be served on any other respondent jointly liable.

(b) *Contents of the answer to specification.*—The answer to the specification shall be in writing, the original being signed and sworn to by the respondent or by a duly authorized agent with appropriate power of attorney affixed, and shall contain the post office address of the respondent. The respondent shall specifically admit, deny, or explain each and every allegation of the specification, unless the respondent is without knowledge, in which case the respondent shall so state, such statement operating as a denial. Denials shall fairly meet the substance of the allegations of the specifications denied. When a respondent intends to deny only a part of an allegation, the respondent shall specify so much of it as is true and shall deny only the remainder. As to all matters within the knowledge of the respondent, including but not limited to the various factors entering into the computation of gross back pay, a general denial shall not suffice. As to such matters, if the respondent disputes either the accuracy of the figures in the specification or the premises on which they are based, he shall specifically state the basis for his disagreement, setting forth in detail his position as to the applicable premises and furnishing the appropriate supporting figures.

(c) *Effect of failure to answer or to plead specifically and in detail to the specification.*—If the respondent **fails to file any answer to the specifi-**

cation within the time prescribed by this section, the Board may, either with or without taking evidence in support of the a l l e g a t i o n s of the specification and without notice to the respondent, find the specification to be true and enter such order as may be appropriate. If the respondent files an answer to the specification but fails to deny any allegation of the specification in the manner required by paragraph (b) of this section, and the failure so to deny is not adequately explained, such allegation shall be deemed to be admitted to be true, and may be so found by the Board without the taking of evidence supporting such allegation, and the respondent shall be precluded from introducing any evidence controverting said allegation.

(d) *Answer to the notice of hearing issued without backpay specification.* —No answer need be filed by respondent to notice of hearing issued without a specification.

§ 102.55 **Extension of time for filing answer to specification.**—Upon his own motion or upon proper cause shown by any respondent, the regional director issuing the specification may be written order extend the time within which the answer to the specification shall be filed.

§ 102.56 **E x t e n s i o n of date of hearing.**—Upon his own motion or upon proper cause shown, the regional director issuing the specification or notice of hearing without specification may extend the date of hearing.

§ 102.57 **Amendment to b a c k p a y specification.**—After the issuance of the notice of hearing, but prior to the opening thereof, the regional director may amend the backpay specification and the respondent affected thereby may amend his answer thereto. After the opening of the hearing, the specification and the answer thereto may be amended upon leave of the administrative law judge or of the Board, as the case may be, good cause therefor appearing.

§ 102.58 **Withdrawal.**—Any   s u c h

specification or notice of hearing may be withdrawn before the hearing by the regional director on his own motion.

§ 102.59 **Hearing; posthearing procedure.**—After the issuance of a notice of hearing, with or without backpay specification the procedures provided in sections 102.24 to 102.51, inclusive, shall be followed insofar as applicable.

SUBPART C—PROCEDURE UNDER SECTION 9(c) OF THE ACT FOR THE DETERMINATION OF QUESTIONS CONCERNING REPRESENTATION OF EMPLOYEES[3] AND FOR CLARIFICATION OF BARGAINING UNITS AND FOR AMENDMENT O F CERTIFICATIONS UNDER SECTION 9(b) OF THE ACT

§ 102.60 **Petitions.** (a) *Petition for certification or decertification; who may file; where to file; withdrawal.* —A petition for investigation of a question concerning representation of employees under paragraphs (1) (A) (i) and (1) (B) of section 9(c) of the act (hereinafter called a petition for certification) may be filed by an employee or group of employees or any individual or labor organization acting in their behalf or by an employer. A petition under paragraph (1) (A) (ii) of section 9(c) of the act, alleging that the individual or labor organization which has been certified or is being currently recognized as the bargaining representative is no longer such representative (hereinafter called a petition for decertification), may be filed by any employee or group of employees or any individual or labor organization acting in their behalf. Petitions under this section shall be in writing and signed,[4] and either shall be sworn to before a notary public, Board agent, or other person duly authorized by law to administer oaths and take acknowledgments or shall contain a

---

3 Procedure under the first proviso to sec. 8(b)(7)(C) of the act is governed by subpart D.

4 Blank forms for filing such petitions will be supplied by the regional office upon request.

declaration by the person signing it, under the penalties of the Criminal Code, that its contents are true and correct to the best of his knowledge and belief. An original and four copies of the petition shall be filed. Except as provided in section 102.72, such petitions shall be filed with the regional director for the region wherein the bargaining unit exists, or, if the bargaining unit exists in two or more regions, with the regional director for any of such regions. Prior to the transfer of the case to the Board, pursuant to section 102.67, the petition may be withdrawn only with the consent of the regional director with whom such petition was filed. After the transfer of the case to the Board, the petition may be withdrawn only with the consent of the Board. Whenever the regional director or the Board, as the case may be, approves the withdrawal of any petition, the case shall be closed.

(b) *Petition for clarification of bargaining unit or petition for amendment of certification under section 9(b) of the act; who may file; where to file; withdrawal.*—A petition for clarification of an existing bargaining unit or a petition for amendment of certification, in the absence of a question concerning representation, may be filed by a labor organization or by an employer. Where applicable the same procedures set forth in paragraph (a) of this section shall be followed.

§ 102.61 **Contents of petition for certification; contents of petition for decertification; contents of petition for clarification of bargaining unit; contents of petition for amendment of certification.**—(a) A petition for certification, when filed by an employee or group of employees or an individual or labor organization acting in their behalf, shall contain the following:

(1) The name of the employer.

(2) The address of the establishment involved.

(3) The general nature of the employer's business.

(4) A description of the bargaining unit which the petitioner claims to be appropriate.

(5) The names and addresses of any other persons or labor organizations who claim to represent any employees in the alleged appropriate unit, and brief descriptions of the contracts, if any, covering the employees in such unit.

(6) The number of employees in the alleged appropriate unit.

(7) A statement that the employer declines to recognize the petitioner as the representative within the meaning of section 9(a) of the act or that the labor organization is currently recognized but desires certification under the act.

(8) The name, the affiliation, if and address of the petitioner.

(9) Whether a strike or picketing is in progress at the establishment involved and, if so, the approximate number of employees participating, and the date such strike or picketing commenced.

(10) Any other relevant facts.

(b) A petition for certification, when filed by an employer, shall contain the following:

(1) The name and address of the petitioner.

(2) The general nature of the petitioner's business.

(3) A brief statement setting forth that one or more individuals or labor organizations have presented to the petitioner a claim to be recognized as the exclusive representative of all employees in the unit claimed to be appropriate; a description of such unit; and the number of employees in the unit.

(4) The name or names, the affiliation, if any, and the addresses of the individuals or labor organizations making such claim for recognition.

(5) A statement whether the petitioner has contracts with any labor organization or other representatives of employees and, if so, their expiration date.

(6) Whether a strike or picketing is in progress at the establishment involved and, if so, the approximate number of employees participating, and the date such strike or picketing commenced.

(7) Any other relevant facts.

(c) A petition for decertification shall contain the following:

(1) The name of the employer.

(2) The address of the establishment and a description of the bargaining unit involved.

(3) The general nature of the employer's business.

(4) The name, the affiliation, if any, and the address of the petitioner.

(5) The name or names of the individuals or labor organizations who have been certified or are being currently recognized by the employer and who claim to represent any employees in the unit involved, and the expiration date of any contracts covering such employees.

(6) An allegation that the individuals or labor organizations who have been certified or are currently recognized by the employer are no longer the representative in the appropriate unit as defined in section 9(a) of the act.

(7) The number of employees in the unit.

(8) Whether a strike or picketing is in progress at the establishment involved and, if so, the approximate number of employees participating, and the date such strike or picketing commenced.

(9) Any other relevant facts.

(d) A petition for clarification shall contain the following:

(1) The name of the employer and the name of the recognized or certified bargaining representative.

(2) The address of the establishment involved.

(3) The general nature of the employer's business.

(4) A description of the present bargaining unit, and, if the bargaining unit is certified, an identification of the existing certification.

(5) A description of the proposed clarification.

(6) The names and addresses of any other persons or labor organizations who claim to represent any employees affected by the proposed clarifications, and brief descriptions of the contracts, if any, covering any such employees.

(7) The number of employees in the present bargaining unit and in the unit as proposed under the clarification.

(8) The job classifications of employees as to whom the issue is raised, and the number of employees in each classification.

(9) A statement by petitioner setting forth reasons why petitioner desires clarification of unit.

(10) The name, the affiliation, if any, and the address of the petitioner.

(11) Any other relevant facts.

(e) A petition for amendment of certification shall contain the following:

(1) The name of the employer and the name of the certified union involved.

(2) The address of the establishment involved.

(3) The general nature of the employer's business.

(4) Identification and description of the existing certification.

(5) A statement by petitioner setting forth the details of the desired amendment and reasons therefor.

(6) The names and addresses of any other persons or labor organizations who claim to represent any employees in the unit covered by the certification and brief descriptions of the contracts, if any, covering the employees in such unit.

(7) The name, the affiliation, if any, and the address of the petitioner.

(8) Any other relevant facts.

§ 102.62 Consent-election agreements.—(a) Where a petition has been duly filed, the employer and any individuals or labor organizations representing a substantial number of employees involved may, with the approval of the regional director, enter into a consent-election agreement leading to a determination by the regional director of the facts ascertained after such consent election. Such agreement shall include a description of the appropriate unit, the time and place of holding the election, and the payroll period to be used in determining what employees within the appropriate unit shall be eligible to vote. Such consent election shall be conducted under the direction and supervision of the regional director. The method of conducting such consent election shall be consistent with the method followed by the regional director in conducting elections pursuant to sections 102.69 and 102.70 except that the rulings and determinations by the regional director of the results thereof shall be final, and the regional director shall issue to the parties a certification of the results of the election, including certification of representatives w h e r e appropriate, with the same force and effect as if issued by the Board, provided further that rulings or determinations by the regional director in respect to any amendment of such certification shall also be final.

(b) Where a petition has been duly filed, the employer and any individuals or labor organizations representing a substantial number of the employees involved may, with the approval of the regional director, enter into an agreement providing for a waiver of hearing and a consent election leading to a determination by the Board of the facts ascertained after such consent election, if such a determination is necessary. Such agreement shall also include a description of the appropriate bargaining unit, the time and place of holding the election, and the payroll period to be used in determining which employees within the appropriate unit shall be eligible to vote. Such consent election shall be conducted under the direction and supervision of the regional director. The method of conducting such election and the postelection procedure shall be consistent with that followed by the regional director in conducting elections pursuant to sections 102.69 and 102.70.

§ 102.63 Investigation o f petition by regional director; notice of hearing; service of notice; withdrawal of notice.

(a) After a petition has been filed under § 102.61(a), (b), or (c), if no agreement such as that provided in § 102.62 is entered into and if it appears to the regional director that there is reasonable cause to believe that a question of representation affecting commerce exists, that the policies of the act will be effectuated, and that an election will reflect the free choice of employees in the appropriate unit, the regional director shall prepare and cause to be served upon the parties and upon any known individuals or labor organizations purporting to act as representatives of any employees directly affected by such investigation, a notice of hearing before a hearing officer at a time and place fixed therein. A copy of the petition shall be served with such notice of hearing. Any such notice of hearing may be amended or withdrawn before the close of the hearing by the regional director on his own motion.

(b) After a petition has been filed under § 102.61(d) or (e), the regional director shall conduct an investigation and, as appropriate, he may issue a decision without a hearing; or prepare and cause to be served upon the parties and upon any known individuals or labor organizations purporting to act as representatives of any employees directly affected by such investigation, a notice of hearing before a hearing officer at a time and place fixed therein; or take other appropriate action. If a notice of hearing is served, it shall be accompanied by a copy of the petition. Any such notice of hearing may be amended or withdrawn before the close of the hearing by the regional director of his own motion. All hearing and posthearing procedure under this subsection (b) shall be in conformance with §§ 102.64 through 102.68 whenever applicable, *except* where the unit or certification involved arises out of an agreement as provided in § 102.62(a), the regional director's action shall be final, and the provisions for review of regional director's decisions by the Board shall not apply. Dismissals of petitions without a hearing shall not be governed by § 102.71. The regional director's dismissal shall be by decision, and a request for review therefrom may be obtained under § 102.67, except where an agreement under § 102.62(a) is involved.

§ 102.64 Conduct of hearing.—(a) Hearings shall be conducted by a hearing officer and shall be open to the public unless otherwise ordered by the hearing officer. At any time, a hearing officer may be substituted for the hearing officer previously presiding. It shall be the duty of the hearing officer to inquire fully into all matters in issue and necessary to obtain a full and complete record upon which the Board or the regional director may discharge their duties under section 9(c) of the act.

(b) The hearing officer may, in his discretion, continue the hearing from day to day, or adjourn it to a later date or to a different place, by announcement thereof at the hearing or by other appropriate notice.

§ 102.65 **Motions, interventions.** — (a) All motions, including motions for intervention pursuant to subsections (b) and (e) of this section, shall be in writing or, if made at the hearing, may be stated orally on the record and shall briefly state the order or relief sought and the grounds for such motion. An original and two copies of written motions shall be filed and a copy thereof immediately shall be served on the other parties to the proceeding. Motions made prior to the transfer of the case to the Board shall be filed with the regional director, except that motions made during the hearing shall be filed with the hearing officer. After the transfer of the case to the Board, all motions shall be filed with the Board. Such motions to the Board shall be printed or otherwise legibly duplicated: *Provided, however,* That carbon copies of typewritten matter shall not be accepted. Eight copies of such motions shall be filed with the Board. The regional director may rule upon all motions filed with him, causing a copy of said ruling to be served on the parties, or he may refer the motion to the hearing officer: *Provided,* That if the regional director prior to the close of the hearing grants a motion to dismiss the petition the petitioner may obtain a review of such ruling in the manner prescribed in section 102.71. The hearing officer shall rule, either orally on the record or in writing, upon all motions filed at the hearing or referred to him as hereinabove provided, except that all motions to dismiss petitions shall be referred for appropriate

action at such time as the entire record is considered by the regional director or the Board, as the case may be.

(b) Any person desiring to intervene in any proceeding shall make a motion for intervention, stating the grounds upon which such person claims to have an interest in the proceeding. The regional director or the hearing officer, as the case may be, may by order permit intervention in person or by counsel or other representative to such extent and upon such terms as he may deem proper, and such intervenor shall thereupon become a party to the proceeding.

(c) All motions, rulings, and orders shall become a part of the record, except that rulings on motions to revoke subpenas shall become a part of the record only upon the request of the party aggrieved, as provided in section 102.66(c). Unless expressly authorized by the Rules and Regulations, rulings by the regional director or by the hearing officer shall not be appealed directly to the Board, but shall be considered by the Board on appropriate appeal pursuant to section 102.67(b), (c), and (d) or whenever the case is transferred to it for decision; *Provided, however;* That if the regional director had issued an order transferring the case to the Board for decision, such rulings may be appealed directly to the Board by special permission of the Board. Nor shall rulings by the hearing officer be appealed directly to the regional director, unless expressly authorized by the Rules and Regulations, except by special permission of the regional director, but shall be considered by the regional director when he reviews the entire record. Requests to the regional director, or to the Board in appropriate cases, for special permission to appeal from such rulings of the hearing officer shall be filed promptly, in writing, and shall briefly state the grounds relied on. The moving party shall immediately serve a copy thereof on each of the other parties and on the regional director.

(d) The right to make motions or to make objections to rulings on motions shall not be deemed waived by participation in the proceeding.

(e)(1) A party to a proceeding may,

because of extraordinary circumstances, move after the close of the hearing for reopening of the record, or move after the decision for reconsideration or rehearing, except that no motion for reconsideration or rehearing will be entertained pursuant to this subsection by the regional director with respect to any matter which can be raised before the Board pursuant to any other section of these Rules, or by the Board with respect to any matter which could have been but was not raised before it pursuant to any other section of these Rules. A motion for reconsideration shall state with particularity the material error claimed and with respect to any finding of material fact shall specify the page of the record relied on. A motion for rehearing shall specify the error alleged to require a hearing *de novo* and the prejudice to the movant alleged to result from such error. A motion to reopen the record shall state briefly the additional evidence sought to be adduced, why it was not presented previously, and what result it would require, if adduced and credited. Only newly discovered evidence, evidence which has become available only since the close of the hearing, or evidence which the regional director or the Board believes should have been taken at the hearing, will be taken at any further hearing.

(2) Any motion pursuant to this subsection shall be filed within 10 days, or such further period as may be allowed, after the service of the decision, except that a motion for leave to adduce additional evidence shall be filed promptly on discovery of such evidence. Any request for an extension of time must be received 3 days prior to the due date and copies thereof shall be served promptly on the other parties.

(3) The filing and pendency of a motion under this provision shall not unless so ordered operate to stay the effectiveness of any action taken or directed to be taken, except that if the motion states with particularity that the granting thereof will affect the eligibility to vote of specific employees, the ballots of such employees shall be challenged and impounded in any election conducted while such motion is pending. A motion for reconsideration or rehearing need not be filed to exhaust administrative remedies. [*As amended, effective June 1, 1971*]

§ 102.66 **Introduction of evidence; rights of parties at hearing; subpenas.**—(a) Any party shall have the right to appear at any hearing in person, by counsel, or by other representative, and any party and the hearing officer shall have power to call, examine, and cross-examine witnesses and to introduce into the record documentary and other evidence. Witnesses shall be examined orally under oath. The rules of evidence prevailing in courts of law or equity shall not be controlling. Stipulations of fact may be introduced in evidence with respect to any issue.

(b) Any objection with respect to the conduct of the hearing, including any objection to the introduction of evidence, may be stated orally or in writing, accompanied by a short statement of the grounds of such objection, and included in the record. No such objection shall be deemed waived by further participation in the hearing.

(c) Any part may file applications for subpenas in writing with the regional director if made prior to hearing, or with the hearing officer if made at the hearing. Applications for subpenas may be made *ex parte*. The regional director or the hearing officer, as the case may be, shall forthwith grant the subpenas requested. Any person served with a subpena, whether *ad testificandum* or *duces tecum*, if he does not intend to comply with the subpena, shall, within 5 days after the date of service of the subpena, petition in writing to revoke the subpena. Such petition shall be filed with the regional director who may either rule upon it or refer it for ruling to the hearing officer: *Provided, however,* That if the evidence called for is to be produced at a hearing and the hearing has opened, the petition to revoke shall be filed with the hearing officer. Notice of the filing of petitions to revoke shall be promptly given by the regional director or hearing officer, as the case may be, to the party at whose request the subpena was issued. The regional director or the hearing officer, as the case may be, shall revoke the subpena if, in his opinion, the evidence whose production is required does not relate to any matter under investigation or in question in the proceedings or the subpena does not describe with sufficient particularity the evidence whose production is required, or if for any other reason sufficient in law the subpena is otherwise invalid. The regional director or the hearing officer, as the case may be, shall make a simple statement of procedural or other grounds for his ruling. The petition to revoke, any answer filed thereto, and any ruling thereon shall not become part of the record except upon the request of the party aggrieved by the ruling. Persons compelled to submit data or evidence are entitled to retain or, on payment of lawfully prescribed costs, to procure copies or transcripts of the data or evidence submitted by them.

(d) (1) Misconduct at any hearing before the regional director or the Board shall be ground for summary exclusion from the hearing.

(2) Such misconduct of an aggravated character, when engaged in by an attorney or other representative of a party, shall be ground for suspension or disbarment by the Board from further practice before it after due notice and hearing.

(3) The refusal of a witness at any such hearing to answer any question which has been ruled to be proper shall, in the discretion of the hearing officer, be ground for striking all testimony previously given by such witness on related matters.

(e) Any party shall be entitled, upon request, to a reasonable period at the close of the hearing for oral argument, which shall be included in the stenographic report of the hearing.

(f) The hearing officer may submit an analysis of the record to the regional director or the Board but he shall make no recommendations.

(g) Witness fees and mileage shall be paid by the party at whose instance the witness appears.

Sec. 102.67 Proceedings before the regional director; further hearing; briefs; action by the regional director; appeals from action by the regional director; statement in opposition to appeal; transfer of case to Board; pro-ceedings before the Board; Board action.—(a) The regional director may proceed, either forthwith upon the record, or after oral argument or the submission of briefs, or further hearing, as he may deem proper, to determine the unit appropriate for the purpose of collective bargaining, to determine whether a question concerning representation exists, and to direct an election, dismiss the petition, or make other disposition of the matter. Any party desiring to submit a brief to the regional director shall file the original and one copy thereof, which may be a typed carbon copy, within 7 days after the close of the hearing: *Provided, however,* That prior to the close of the hearing and for good cause, the hearing officer may grant an extension of time not to exceed an additional 14 days. Copies thereof shall be served simultaneously on all other parties to the proceeding. Requests for additional time in which to file a brief under authority of this section not addressed to the hearing officer during the hearing shall be made to the regional director, in writing, and copies thereof shall immediately be served on the other parties. Requests for extension of time shall be made not later than 3 days before the date such briefs are due in the regional office. No reply brief may be filed except upon special leave of the regional director.

(b) A decision by the regional director upon the record shall set forth his findings, conclusions, and order or direction. The decision of the regional director shall be final: *Provided, however,* That within 10 days after service thereof any party may file eight copies of a request for review with the Board in Washington, D. C. Such request shall be printed or otherwise legibly duplicated: *Provided, however,* That carbon copies shall not be filed and if submitted will not be accepted. Simultaneously therewith, copies thereof shall be served on all other parties to the proceeding and the regional director, and a statement of such service filed with the Board. The filing of such request shall not, unless otherwise ordered by the Board, operate as a stay of any action taken or directed by the regional director: *Provided, however,* That the regional director, in the absence of a waiver, may issue a notice of election but shall not conduct any election or open and count any challenged ballots until the Board has ruled upon any request for review which may be filed. [*As amended effective June 1, 1971*]

(c) The Board will grant a request for review only where compelling reasons exist therefor. Accordingly, a request for review may be granted only upon one or more of the following grounds:

(1) That a substantial question of law or policy is raised because of (i) the absence of, or (ii) a departure from, officially reported Board precedent.

(2) That the regional director's decision on a substantial factual issue is clearly erroneous on the record and such error prejudicially affects the rights of a party.

(3) That the conduct of the hearing or any ruling made in connection with the proceeding has resulted in prejudicial error.

(4) That there are compelling reasons for reconsideration of an important Board rule or policy.

(d) Any request for review must be a self-contained document enabling the Board to rule on the basis of its contents without the necessity of recourse to the record. With respect to ground (2), and other grounds where appropriate, said request must contain a summary of all evidence or rulings bearing on the issues together with page citations from the transcript and a summary of argument. But such request may not raise any issue or allege any facts not timely presented to the regional director.

(e) Any party may, within 7 days after the last day on which the request for review must be filed, file with the Board eight copies of a statement in opposition thereto, which shall be duplicated and served in accordance with the requirements of paragraph (b) of this section; except that if personal service of the request for review is made upon the Board,

10 days will be allowed. However, 3 days will not be added to either of the aforesaid prescribed periods as provided in section 102.114. A statement of such service of opposition shall be filed simultaneously with the Board. The Board may deny the request for review without awaiting a statement in opposition thereto.

(f) The parties may, at any time, waive the right to request review. Failure to request review shall preclude such parties from relitigating, in any related subsequent unfair labor practice proceeding, any issue which was, or could have been, raised in the representation proceeding. Denial of a request for review shall constitute an affirmance of the regional director's action which shall also preclude relitigating any such issues in any related subsequent unfair labor practice proceeding.

(g) The granting of a request for review shall not stay the regional director's decision unless otherwise ordered by the Board. Within 7 days after issuance of an order granting review, the appellants and other parties may file eight copies of a brief with the Board, which shall be duplicated and served in accordance with the requirements of subsection (b) of this section. A statement of such service shall be filed simultaneously with the Board. Such briefs may be reproductions of those previously filed with the regional director and/or other briefs which shall be limited to the issues raised in the request for review. Where review has been granted, the Board will consider the entire record in the light of the grounds relied on for review. Any request for review may be withdrawn with the permission of the Board at any time prior to the issuance of the decision of the Board thereon.

(h) In any case in which it appears to the regional director that the proceeding raises questions which should be decided by the Board, he may, at any time, issue an order, to be effective after the close of the hearing and before decision, transferring the case to the Board for decision. Such an order may be served on the parties upon the record of the hearing.

(i) If any case is transferred to the Board for decision after the parties have filed briefs with the regional director, the parties may, within such time after service of the order transferring the case as is fixed by the regional director, file with the Board eight copies of the brief previously filed with the regional director. Such copies shall be printed or otherwise legibly duplicated: *Provided, however,* That carbon copies of typewritten matter shall not be filed and if submitted will not be accepted. No further briefs shall be permitted except by special permission of the Board. If the case is transferred to the Board before the time expires for the filing of briefs with the regional director and before the parties have filed briefs, such briefs shall be filed as set forth above and served in accordance with subsection (b) of this section, within the time set by the regional director. If the order transferring the case is served on the parties during the hearing, the hearing officer may, prior to the close of the hearing and for good cause, grant an extension of time within which to file a brief with the Board for a period not to exceed an additional 14 days. Requests for extension of time in which to file a brief with the Board under authority of this section not addressed to the hearing officer during the hearing shall be filed in writing with the Board and copies thereof shall immediately be served on each of the other parties and the regional director. Requests for extension of time shall be received by the Board not later than 3 days before the date such briefs are due in Washington, D. C. A copy of any such requests shall be served immediately on each of the other parties and the regional director and shall contain a statement that such service has been made. No reply brief may be filed except upon special leave of the Board.

(j) Upon transfer of the case to the Board, the Board shall proceed, either forthwith upon the record, or after oral argument or the submission of briefs, or further hearing, as it may determine, to decide the issues referred to it or to review the decision of the regional director, and shall direct a secret ballot of the employees, dismiss the petition, affirm or reverse the regional director's order in whole or in part, or make such other disposition of the matter as it deems appropriate.

§ 102.68 **Record; what constitutes; transmission to Board.**—The record in the proceeding shall consist of: the petition, notice of hearing with affidavit of service thereof, motions, rulings, orders, the stenographic report of the hearing and of any oral argument before the regional director, stipulations, exhibits, documentary evidence, affidavits of service, depositions, and any briefs or other legal memoranda submitted by the parties to the regional director or to the Board, and the decision of the regional director, if any. Immediately upon issuance by the regional director of an order transferring the case to the Board, or upon issuance of an order granting a request for review by the Board, the regional director shall transmit the record to the Board. [*As amended, February 10, 1975, 40 F.R. 6204.*]

§ 102.69 **Election procedure; tally of ballots; objections; certification by regional director; report on challenged ballots; report on objections; exceptions; action of the Board; hearing.**—(a) Unless otherwise directed by the Board, all elections shall be conducted under the supervision of the regional director in whose region the proceeding is pending. All elections shall be by secret ballot. Whenever two or more labor organizations are included as choices in an election, either participant may, upon its prompt request to and approval thereof by the regional director, whose decision shall be final, have its name removed from the ballot: *Provided, however,* That in a proceeding involving an employer-filed petition or a petition for decertification the labor organization certified, currently recognized, or found to be seeking recognition may not have its name removed from the ballot without giving timely notice in writing to all parties, and the regional director, disclaiming any representation interest among the employees in the unit. Any party may be represented by observers of his own selection, subject to such limitations as the regional director may prescribe. Any party and Board agents may challenge, for good cause, the eligibility of any person to participate in the election. The ballots of such challenged persons shall be impounded. Upon the conclusion of the election, the regional director shall cause to be furnished to the parties a tally of the ballots. Within 5 days after the tally of ballots has been furnished, any party may file with the regional director an original and three copies of objections to the conduct of the election or conduct affecting the results of the election, which shall contain a short statement of the reasons therefor. Such filing must be timely whether or not the challenged ballots are sufficient in number to affect the results of the election. Copies of such objections shall immediately be served on the other parties by the party filing them, and a statement of service shall be made. The party filing objections shall, upon request, promptly furnish to the regional director the evidence available to it to support the objections.

(b) If no objections are filed within the time set forth above, if the challenged ballots are insufficient in number to affect the result of the election, and if no runoff election is to be held pursuant to section 102.70, the regional director shall forthwith issue to the parties a certification of the result of the election, including certification of representatives where appropriate, with the same force and effect as if issued by the Board, and the proceeding will thereupon be closed.

(c) If objections are filed to the conduct of the election or conduct affecting the result of the election, or if the challenged ballots are sufficient in number to affect the result of the election, the regional director shall, consistent with the provisions of section 102.69(d), investigate such objections or challenges, or both. If a consent election has been held pursuant to section 102.62(b), the regional director shall prepare and cause to be served on the parties a report on challenged ballots or objections, or both, including his recommendations, which report, together with the tally of ballots, he shall forward to the Board in Washington, D.C. Within 10 days from the date of issuance of the report on challenged ballots or objections, or both, or within such further period as the Board may allow upon written request to the Board for an extension received not later than 3 days before such exceptions are due in Washington, D.C., with copies of such request

served on the other parties, any party may file with the Board in Washington, D.C., eight copies of exceptions to such report, with supporting brief, if desired, which shall be printed or otherwise legibly duplicated, except that carbon copies of typewritten matter shall not be filed and if submitted will not be accepted. Immediately upon the filing of such exceptions, the party filing the same shall serve a copy thereof together with a copy of any brief filed on the other parties and shall file copies with the regional director. A statement of service shall be made to the Board simultaneously with the filing of exceptions. Within 7 days from the last date on which exceptions and any supporting brief may be filed, or such further period as the Board may allow, a party opposing the exceptions may file an answering brief with the Board in Washington, D.C.; except that if personal service of the exceptions and any supporting brief is made upon the Board, 10 days will be allowed. However, 3 days as provided in § 102.114 will not be added to the prescribed time for filing an answering brief. Such brief shall be submitted in eight copies, printed or otherwise legibly duplicated, except that carbon copies shall not be filed and if submitted will not be accepted. Immediately upon the filing of such brief, the party filing the same shall serve a copy thereof on the other parties and shall file a copy with the regional director. A statement of service shall be made to the Board simultaneously with the filing of the answering brief. If no exceptions are filed to such report, the Board, upon the expiration of the period for filing such exceptions, may decide the matter forthwith upon the record or may make other disposition of the case. The report on challenged ballots may be consolidated with the report on objections in appropriate cases. If the election has been conducted pursuant to a direction of election issued following any proceeding under § 102.67, the regional director may (1) issue a report on objections or challenged ballots, or both, as in the case of a consent election pursuant to subsection (b) of this section 102.62, or (2) exercise his authority to decide the case and issue a decision disposing of the issues and directing appropriate action or certifying the results of the election.

(d) The action of the regional director in issuing a report on objections or challenged ballots, or both, following proceedings under sections 102.62(b) or 102.67, or in issuing a decision on objections or challenged ballots, or both, following proceeding under section 102.67, may be on the basis of an administrative investigation or, if it appears to the regional director that substantial and material factual issues exist which, in the exercise of his reasonable discretion, he determines may more appropriately be resolved after a hearing, he shall issue and cause to be served on the parties a notice of hearing on said issues before a hearing officer. If the regional director issues a report on objections and challenges, the parties shall have the rights set forth in subsections (c) and (f) of this section; if the regional director issues a decision, the parties shall have the rights set forth in Sec. 102.67 to the extent consistent herewith.

(e) Any hearing pursuant to this section shall be conducted in accordance with the provisions of §§ 102.64, 102.65, and 102.66, insofar as applicable, except that upon the close of such hearing, the hearing officer shall, if directed by the regional director, prepare and cause to be served on the parties a report resolving questions of credibility and containing findings of fact and recommendations as to the disposition of the issues. In any case in which the regional director has directed that a report be prepared and served, any party may, within 10 days from the date of issuance of such report, file with the regional director the original and one copy, which may be a carbon copy, of exceptions to such report, with supporting brief, if desired. A copy of such exceptions, together with a copy of any brief filed, shall immediately be served on the other parties and a statement of service filed with the regional director. Within 7 days from the last date on which exceptions and any supporting brief may be filed, or such further time as the regional director may allow, a party opposing the exceptions may file an answering brief with the regional director; except that if personal service of the exceptions and any supporting brief is made upon the regional director, 10 days will be allowed. However, 3 days as provided in § 102.114 will not be

added to the prescribed time for filing an answering brief. An original and one copy, which may be a carbon copy, shall be submitted. A copy of such answering brief shall immediately be served on the other parties and a statement of service filed with the regional director. If no exceptions are filed to such report, the regional director, upon the expiration of the period for filing such exceptions, may decide the matter forthwith upon the record or may make other disposition of the case.

(f) In a case involving a consent election held pursuant to § 102.62(b), if exceptions are filed, either to the report on challenged ballots or objections, or both if it be a consolidated report, and it appears to the Board that such exceptions do not raise substantial and material issues with respect to the conduct or results of the election, the Board may decide the matter forthwith upon the record, or may make other disposition of the case. If it appears to the Board that such exceptions raise substantial and material factual issues, the Board may direct the regional director or other agent of the Board to issue and cause to be served on the parties a notice of hearing on said exceptions before a hearing officer. The hearing shall be conducted in accordance with the provisions of §§ 102.64, 102.65, and 102.66, insofar as applicable. Upon the close of the hearing the agent conducting the hearing, if directed by the Board, shall prepare and cause to be served on the parties a report resolving questions of credibility and containing findings of fact and recommendations to the Board as to the disposition of the challenges or objections, or both if it be a consolidated report. In any case in which the Board has directed that a report be prepared and served, any party may within 10 days from the date of issuance of the report on challenged ballots or objections, or both, or within such further period as the Board may allow, upon written request to the Board for an extension received not later than 3 days before such exceptions are due in Washington, D.C., with copies of such request served on the other parties, file with the Board in Washington, D.C., eight copies of exceptions to such report, with supporting brief if desired, which shall be printed or otherwise legibly duplicated, except that carbon copies of typewritten matter shall not be filed and if submitted will not be accepted. Immediately upon the filing of such exceptions, the party filing the same shall serve a copy thereof, together with a copy of any brief filed, on the other parties and shall file copies with the regional director. A statement of service shall be made to the Board simultaneously with the filing of exceptions. Within 7 days from the last date on which exceptions and any supporting brief may be filed, or such further period as the Board may allow, a party opposing the exceptions may file an answering brief with the Board in Washington, D.C.; except that if personal service of the exceptions and any supporting brief is made upon the Board, 10 days will be allowed. However, 3 days as provided in § 102.114 will not be added to the prescribed time for filing an answering brief. Such brief shall be submitted in eight copies, printed or otherwise legibly duplicated, except that carbon copies shall not be filed and if submitted will not be accepted. Immediately upon the filing of such brief, the party filing the same shall serve a copy thereof on the other parties and shall file a copy with the regional director. A statement of service shall be made to the Board simultaneously with the filing of the answering brief. If no exceptions are filed to such report, the Board, upon the expiration of the period for filing such exceptions, may decide the matter forthwith upon the record or may make other disposition of the case. The Board shall thereupon proceed pursuant to § 102.67; *Provided, however,* That in any proceeding wherein a representation case has been consolidated with an unfair labor practice case for purposes of hearing, the provisions of § 102.46 of these rules shall govern with respect to the filing of exceptions or an answering brief to the exceptions to the administrative law judge's decision.

(g) The notice of hearing, motions, rulings, orders, stenographic report of the hearing, stipulations, exceptions, documentary evidence, together with the objections to the conduct of the election or conduct affecting the results of the election, any report on such objections, any report on challenged ballots, exceptions to any such report, any briefs or other legal memoranda submitted by the parties, the decision of the regional director, if

any, and the record previously made as described in § 102.68, shall constitute the record in the case. Materials other than those set out above shall not be a part of the record; except that in a proceeding in which no hearing is held, a party filing exceptions to a regional director's report on objections or challenges, a request for review of a regional director's decision on objections or challenges, or any opposition thereto, may append to its submission to the Board copies of documents it has timely submitted to the regional director and which were not included in the report or decision. Immediately upon issuance of a report on objections or challenges, or both, upon issuance by the regional director of an order transferring the case to the Board, or upon issuance of an order granting a request for review by the Board, the regional director shall transmit the record to the Board. [*As amended, February 10, 1975, 40 F.R. 6204.*]

(h) In any such case in which the regional director or the Board, upon a ruling on challenged ballots, has directed that such ballots be opened and counted and a revised tally of ballots issued, and no objection to such revised tally is filed by any party within 3 days after the revised tally of ballots has been furnished, the regional director shall forthwith issue to the parties certification of the results of the election, including certification of representatives where appropriate, with the same force and effect as if issued by the Board. The proceeding shall thereupon be closed.

(i)(1) The action of the regional director in issuing a notice of hearing on objections or challenged ballots, or both, following proceedings under § 102.62(b) shall constitute a transfer of the case to the Board, and the provisions of § 102.65(c) shall apply with respect to special permission to appeal to the Board from any such direction of hearing.

(2) Exceptions, if any, to the hearing officer's report or to the administrative law judge's decision, and any answering brief to such exceptions, shall be filed with the Board in Washington, D.C., in accordance with subsection (f) of this section.

§ 102.70 **Runoff election**—(a) The regional director shall conduct a runoff election, without further order of the Board, when an election in which the ballot provided for not less than three choices (i.e., at least two representatives and "neither") results in no choice receiving a majority of the valid ballots cast and no objections are filed as provided in section 102.69. Only one runoff shall be held pursuant to this section.

(b) Employees who were eligible to vote in the election and who are in an eligible category on the date of the runoff election shall be eligible to vote in the runoff election.

(c) The ballot in the runoff election shall provide for a selection between the two choices receiving the largest and second largest number of votes.

(d) In the event the number of votes cast in an inconclusive election in which the ballot provided for a choice among two or more representatives and "neither" or "none" is equally divided among the several choices; or in the event the number of ballots cast for one choice in such election is equal to the number cast for another of the choices but less than the number cast for the third choice, the regional director shall declare the first election a nullity and shall conduct another election, providing for a selection from among the three choices afforded in the original ballot; and he shall thereafter proceed in accordance with subsections (a), (b), and (c) of this section. In the event two or more choices receive the same number of ballots and another choice receives no ballots and there are no challenged ballots that would affect the results of the election, and if all eligible voters have cast valid ballots, there shall be no runoff election and a certification of results of election shall be issued. Only one such further election pursuant to this subsection may be held.

(e) Upon the conclusion of the runoff election, the provisions of section 102.69 shall govern, insofar as applicable.

§ 102.71 **Dismissal of petition; refusal to proceed with petition; requests for review by Board of action of the regional director.**—(a) If, after a petition has been filed and at any time prior to the close of hearing, it shall appear to the regional director that no further proceedings are warranted, the regional director may dismiss the petition by administrative action and shall so advise the petitioner in writing, setting forth a simple statement of the procedural or other grounds for the dismissal, with copies to the other parties to the proceeding. Any party may obtain a review of such action by filing a request therefor with the Board in Washington, D.C., in accordance with the provisions of subsection (c) of this section. A request for review from an action of a regional director pursuant to this subsection may be granted only upon one or more of the following grounds:

(1) That a substantial question of law or policy is raised because of (i) the absence of, or (ii) a departure from, officially reported Board precedent.

(2) There are compelling reasons for reconsideration of an important Board rule or policy.

(3) The request for review is accompanied by documentary evidence previously submitted to the regional director raising serious doubts as to the regional director's factual findings, thus indicating that there are factual issues which can best be resolved upon the basis of a record developed at a hearing. [*As amended, February 10, 1975, 40 F.R. 6204.*]

(4) The regional director's action is, on its face, arbitrary or capricious.

(5) The petition raises issues which can best be resolved upon the basis of a record developed at a hearing. [*As added February 10, 1975, 40 F.R. 6204.*]

(b) Where the regional director dismisses a petition or directs that the proceeding on the petition be held in abeyance, and such action is taken because of the pendency of concurrent unresolved charges of unfair labor practices, and the regional director, upon request, has so notified the parties in writing, any party may obtain a review of the regional director's action by filing a request therefor with the Board in Washington, D.C., in accordance with the provisions of subsection (c) of this section. A review of an action of a regional director pursuant to this subsection may be granted only upon one or more of the following grounds:

(1) That a substantial question of law or policy is raised because of (i)

the absence of, or (ii) a departure from, officially reported Board precedent.

(2) There are compelling reasons for reconsideration of an important Board rule or policy.

(3) The regional director's action is, on its face, arbitrary or capricious.

(c) A request for review must be filed with the Board in Washington, D.C., and a copy filed with the regional director and copies served on all the other parties within 10 days of service of the notice of dismissal or notification that the petition is to be held in abeyance. The request shall be submitted in eight copies and shall contain a complete statement setting forth facts and reasons upon which the request is based. Such request shall be printed or otherwise legibly duplicated: *Provided, however,* That carbon copies of typewritten matter shall not be filed and if submitted will not be accepted. Requests for an extension of time within which to file the request for review shall be filed with the Board in Washington, D.C., and a statement of service shall accompany such request. [*As amended, January 29, 1974*]

§ 102.72 **Filing petition with general counsel; jurisdiction upon motion of general counsel; transfer of petition and proceeding from region to general counsel or to another region; consolidation of proceedings in same region; severance; procedure before general counsel in cases over which he has assumed jurisdiction.—** (a) Whenever it appears necessary in order to effectuate the purposes of the act, or to avoid unnecessary costs or delay, the general counsel may permit a petition to be filed with him in Washington, D.C., or may, at any time after a petition has been filed with a regional director pursuant to section 102.60, order that such petition and any proceeding that may have been instituted with respect thereto:

(1) Be transferred to and continued before him, for the purpose of investigation or consolidation with any other proceeding which may have been instituted in a regional office or with him; or

(2) Be consolidated with any other proceeding which may have been instituted in the same region; or

(3) Be transferred to and continued in any other region, for the purpose of investigation or consolidation with any proceeding which may have been instituted in or transferred to such region; or

(4) Be severed from any other proceeding with which it may have been consolidated pursuant to this section.

(b) The provisions of sections 102.60 to 102.71, inclusive, shall, insofar as applicable, apply to proceedings before the general counsel pursuant to this section, and the powers granted to regional directors in such provisions shall, for the purpose of this section, be reserved to and exercised by the general counsel. After the transfer of any petition and any proceeding which may have been instituted in respect thereto from one region to another pursuant to this section, the provisions of this subpart shall, insofar as applicable, govern such petition and such proceeding as if the petition had originally been filed in the region to which the transfer was made.

(c) The regional director may exercise the powers in subsections (a)(2) and (4) of this section with respect to proceedings pending in his region.

SUBPART D—PROCEDURE FOR UNFAIR LABOR PRACTICE AND REPRESENTATION CASES UNDER SECTIONS 8(b)(7) AND 9(c) OF THE ACT.

§ 102.73 **Initiation of proceedings.—** Whenever it is charged that any person has engaged in an unfair labor practice within the meaning of section 8(b)(7) of the act, the regional director shall investigate such charge, giving it the priority specified in Subpart G of these rules.

§ 102.74 **Complaint and formal proceedings.—**If it appears to the Regional Director that the charge has merit, formal proceedings in respect thereto shall be instituted in accordance with the procedures described in sections 102.15 to 102.51, inclusive, insofar as they are applicable, and insofar as they are not inconsistent with the provisions of this subpart. If it appears to the regional director that issuance of a complaint is not warranted, he shall decline to issue a complaint, and the provisions of section 102.19, including the provisions for appeal to the general counsel, shall be applicable unless an election has been directed under sections 102.77 and 102.78, in which event the provisions of section 102.81 shall be applicable.

§ 102.75 **Suspension of proceedings on the charge where timely petition is**

filed.—If it appears to the regional director that issuance of a complaint may be warranted but for the pendency of a petition under section 9(c) of the act, which has been filed by any proper party within a reasonable time not to exceed 30 days from the commencement of picketing, the regional director shall suspend proceedings on the charge and shall proceed to investigate the petition under the expedited procedure provided below, pursuant to the first proviso to subparagraph (C) of section 8(b)(7) of the act.

§ 102.76 Petition; who may file; where to file; contents.—When picketing of an employer has been conducted for an object proscribed by section 8(b)(7) of the act, a petition for the determination of a question concerning representation of the employees of such employer may be filed in accordance with the provisions of sections 102.60 and 102.61, insofar as applicable: *Provided, however,* That if a charge under section 102.73 has been filed against the labor organization on whose behalf the picketing has been conducted, the petition shall not be required to contain a statement that the employer declines to recognize the petitioner as the representative within the meaning of section 9(a) of the act; or that the labor organization is currently recognized but desires certification under the Act; or that the individuals or labor organizations who have been certified or are curently recognized by the employer are no longer the representative; or, if the petitioner is an employer, that one or more individuals or labor organizations have presented to the petitioner a claim to be recognized as the exclusive representative of the employees in the unit claimed to be appropriate.

§ 102.77 Investigation of petition by regional director; directed election.—(a) Where a petition has been filed pursuant to section 102.76, the regional director shall make an investigation of the matters and allegations set forth therein. Any party, and any individual or labor organization purporting to act as representative of the employees involved and any labor organization on whose behalf picketing has been conducted as de-

scribed in section 8(b)(7)(C) of the act, may present documentary and other evidence relating to the matters and allegations set forth in the petition.

(b) If, after the investigation of such petition or any petition filed under subpart C of these rules, and after the investigation of the charge filed pursuant to section 102.73, it appears to the regional director that an expedited election under section 8(b)(7) (C) is warranted, and that the policies of the act would be effectuated thereby, he shall forthwith proceed to conduct an election by secret ballot of the employees in an appropriate unit, or make other disposition of the matter: *Provided, however,* That in any case in which it appears to the regional director that the proceeding raises questions which cannot be decided without a hearing, he may issue and cause to be served on the parties, individuals, and labor organizations involved a notice of hearing before a hearing officer at a time and place fixed therein. In this event, the method of conducting the hearing and the procedure following, including transfer of the case to the Board, shall be governed insofar as applicable by sections 102.63 to 102.68, inclusive, except that the parties shall not file briefs without special permission of the regional director or the Board, as the case may be, but shall, however, state their respective legal positions upon the record at the close of the hearing, and except that any request for review of a decision of the regional director shall be filed promptly after the issuance of such decision.

§ 102.78 Election procedure; method of conducting balloting; postballoting procedure.—If no agreement such as that provided in section 102.79 has been made, the regional director shall fix the time and place of the election, eligibility requirements for voting, and other arrangements for the balloting. The method of conducting the balloting and the postballoting procedure shall be governed, insofar as applicable, by the provisions of sections 102.69 and 102.70, except that the labor organization on whose behalf picketing has been conducted may not have its name removed from the ballot without the consent of the regional director and except that the regional director's rulings on any objections or challenged ballots shall be final unless the Board grants special permission to appeal from the regional director's rulings. Any request for such permission shall be filed promptly, in writing, and shall briefly state the grounds relied on. The party requesting review shall immediately serve a copy thereof on each other party. A request for review shall not operate as a stay of the regional director's rulings unless so ordered by the Board.

§ 102.79 **Consent-election a g r e e - ments.**—Where a petition has been duly filed, the parties involved may, subject to the approval of the regional director, enter into an agreement governing the method of conducting the election as provided for in section 102.62(a), insofar as applicable.

§ 102.80 **Dismissal of petition; refusal to process petition under expedited procedure.**—(a) If, after a petition has been filed pursuant to the provisions of section 102.76, and prior to the close of the hearing, it shall appear to the regional director that further proceedings in respect thereto in accordance with the provisions of section 102.77 are not warranted, he may dismiss the petition by administrative action, and the action of the regional director shall be final, subject to a prompt appeal to the Board on special permission which may be granted by the Board. Upon such appeal the provisions of section 102.71 shall govern insofar as applicable. Such appeal shall not operate as a stay unless specifically ordered by the Board.

(b) If it shall appear to the regional director that an expedited election is not warranted but that proceedings under subpart C of these rules are warranted he shall so notify the parties in writing with a simple statement of the grounds for his decision.

(c) Where the regional director, pursuant to sections 102.77 and 102.78, has determined that a hearing prior to election is not required to resolve the issues raised by the petition and has directed an expedited election, any party aggrieved may file a request with the Board for special permission to appeal from such determination.

Such request shall be filed promptly, in writing, and shall briefly state the grounds relied on. The party requesting such appeal shall immediately serve a copy thereof on each other party. Should the Board grant the requested permission to appeal such action shall not, unless specifically ordered by the Board, operate as a stay of any action by the regional director.

§ 102.81 **Review by the general counsel of refusal to proceed on charge; resumption of proceedings upon charge held during pendency of petition; review by general counsel of refusal to proceed on related charge.**—(a) Where an election has been directed by the regional director or the Board in accordance with the provisions of § § 102.77 and 102.78, the regional director shall decline to issue a complaint on the charge, and he shall so advise the parties in writing, accompanied by a simple statement of the procedural or other grounds for his action. The person making the charge may obtain a review of such action by filing an appeal with the general counsel in Washington, D.C., and filing a copy of the appeal with the regional director, within 3 days from the service of the notice of such refusal by the regional director. In all other respects the appeal shall be subject to the provisions of section 102.19. Such appeal shall not operate as a stay of any action by the regional director.

(b) Where an election has not been directed and the petition has been dismissed in accordance with the provisions of section 102.80, the regional director shall resume investigation of the charge and shall proceed in accordance with section 102.74.

(c) If in connection with a section 8(b)(7) proceeding, unfair labor practice charges under other sections of the act have been filed and the regional director upon investigation has declined to issue a complaint upon such charges, he shall so advise the parties in writing, accompanied by a simple statement of the procedural or other grounds for his action. The person making such charges may obtain a review of such action by filing an appeal with the general counsel in Washington, D.C., and filing a copy of the appeal with the regional director, within 3 days from the service of the notice of such refusal by the regional director. In all other respects the appeal shall be subject to the provisions of section 102.19.

§ 102.82 **Transfer, consolidation, and severance.**—The provisions of sections tions 102.33 and 102.72, respecting the filing of a charge or petition with the general counsel and the transfer, consolidation, and severance of proceedings, shall apply to proceedings under this subpart of these rules, except that the provisions of sections 102.73 to 102.81, inclusive, shall govern proceedings before the general counsel.

SUBPART E—PROCEDURE FOR REFERENDUM UNDER SECTION 9 (e) OF THE ACT

§ 102.83 **Petition for referendum under section 9 (e) (1) of the act; who may file; where to file; withdrawal.**— A petition to rescind the authority of a labor organization to make an agreement requiring as a condition of employment membership in such labor organization may be filed by an employee or group of employees on behalf of 30 percent or more of the employees in a bargaining unit covered by such an agreement. The petition shall be in writing and signed, and either shall be sworn to before a notary public, Board agent, or other person duly authorized by law to administer oaths and take acknowledgments or shall contain a declaration by the person signing it, under the penalties of the Criminal Code, that its contents are true and correct to the best of his knowledge and belief.[5] An original and four copies of the petition shall be filed with the regional director wherein the bargaining unit exists or, if the unit exists in two or more regions, with the regional director for any of such regions. The petition may be withdrawn only with the approval of the regional director with whom such petition was filed, except that if the

[5] Forms for filing such petitions will be supplied by the regional office upon request.

proceeding has been transferred to the Board, pursuant to section 102.67, the petition may be withdrawn only with the consent of the Board. Upon approval of the withdrawal of any petition the case shall be closed.

§ 102.84 **Contents of petition to rescind authority.**—
  (a) The name of the employer.
  (b) The address of the establishments involved.
  (c) The general nature of the employer's business.
  (d) A description of the bargaining unit involved.
  (e) The name and address of the labor organization whose authority it is desired to rescind.
  (f) The number of employees in the unit.
  (g) Whether there is a strike or picketing in progress at the establishment involved and, if so, the approximate number of employees participating, and the date such strike or picketing commenced.
  (h) The dates of execution and of expiration of any contract in effect covering the unit involved.
  (i) The name and address of the person designated to accept service of documents for petitioners.
  (j) Any other relevant facts.

§ 102.85 **Investigation of petition by regional director; consent referendum; directed referendum.**—Where a petition has been filed pursuant to section 102.83 and it appears to the regional director that the petitioner has made an appropriate showing, in such form as the regional director may determine, that 30 percent or more of the employees within a unit covered by an agreement between their employer and a labor organization requiring membership in such labor organization desire to rescind the authority of such labor organization to make such an agreement, he shall proceed to conduct a secret ballot of the employees involved on the question whether they desire to rescind the authority of the labor organization to make such an agreement with their employer: *Provided, however,* That in any case in which it appears to the regional director that the proceeding raises questions which cannot be decided without a hearing, he may issue and cause to be served on the parties a notice of hearing before a hearing officer at a time and place fixed therein. The regional director shall fix the time and place of the election, eligibility requirements for voting, and other arrangements of the balloting, but the parties may enter into an agreement, subject to the approval of the regional director, fixing such arrangements. In any such consent agreements, provision may be made for final determination of all questions arising with respect to the balloting by the regional director or by the Board.

§ 102.86 **Hearing; posthearing procedure.**—The method of conducting the hearing and the procedure following the hearing, including transfer of the case to the Board, shall be governed, insofar as applicable, by sections 102.63 to 102.68, inclusive.

§ 102.87 **Method of conducting balloting; postballoting procedure.**—The method of conducting the balloting and the postballoting procedure shall be governed by the provisions of section 102.69, insofar as applicable.

§ 102.88 **Refusal to conduct referendum; appeal to Board.**—If, after a petition has been filed, and prior to the close of the hearing, it shall appear to the regional director that no referendum should be conducted, he shall dismiss the petition by administrative action. Such dismissal shall be in writing and accompanied by a simple statement of the procedural or other grounds. The petitioner may obtain a review of such action by filing a request therefor with the Board in Washington, D.C., and filing a copy of such request with the regional director and the o t h e r parties within 10 days from the service of notice of such dismissal. The request shall contain a complete statement setting forth the facts and reasons upon which the request is based.

SUBPART F—PROCEDURE TO HEAR AND DETERMINE DISPUTES UNDER SECTION 10(k) OF THE ACT

§ 102.89 **Initiation of proceedings.**—Whenever it is charged that any person has engaged in an unfair labor practice within the meaning of paragraph (4)(D) of section 8(b) of the act, the regional director of the office in which such charge is filed or to which it is referred shall, as soon as possible after the charge has been filed, serve upon the parties a copy of the charge together with a notice of the filing of the charge and shall investigate such charge and if it is deemed appropriate to seek injunctive relief of a district court pursuant to section 10(l) of the act, he shall give it priority over all other cases in the office except other cases under section 10(l) and cases of like character.

§ 102.90 **Notice of filing of charge; notice of hearing; hearing; proceedings before the Board; briefs; determination of dispute.**—If it appears to the regional director that the charge has merit and the parties to the dispute have not submitted satisfactory evidence to the regional director that they have adjusted, or have agreed upon methods for the voluntary adjustment of, the dispute out of which such unfair labor practice shall have arisen, he shall cause to be served on all parties to such dispute a notice of hearing under section 10(k) of the act before a hearing officer at a time and place fixed therein which shall be not less than 10 days after service of the notice of the filing of said charge. The notice of hearing shall contain a simple statement of the issues involved in such dispute. Such notice shall be issued promptly, and, in cases in which it is deemed appropriate to seek injunctive relief pursuant to section 10(l) of the act, shall normally be issued within 5 days of the date upon which injunctive relief is first sought. Hearings shall be conducted by a hearing officer, and the procedure shall conform, insofar as applicable, to the procedure set forth in sections 102.64 to 102.68, inclusive. Upon the close of the hearing, the proceeding shall be transferred to the Board and the Board shall proceed either forthwith upon the record, or after oral argument, or the submission of briefs, or further hearing, to determine the dispute or make other disposition of the matter. Should any party desire to file a brief with the Board, eight copies thereof shall be filed with the Board at Washington, D.C., within 7 days after the close of the hearing: *Provided, however,* That, in cases involving the national defense and so designated in the notice of hearing, no briefs shall be filed, and the parties, after the close of the evidence, may argue orally upon the record their respective contentions and positions: *Provided further,* That, in cases involving the national defense, upon application for leave to file briefs expeditiously made to the Board in Washington, D.C., after the close of the hearing, the Board may for good cause shown grant such leave and thereupon specify the time for filing. Immediately upon such filing, a copy shall be served on the other parties. Such brief shall be printed or otherwise legibly duplicated: *Provided, however,* That carbon copies of typewritten matter shall not be accepted. Requests for extension of time in which to file a brief under authority of this section shall be in writing and received by the Board in Washington, D.C., 3 days prior to the due date with copies thereof served on the other parties. No reply brief may be filed except upon special leave of the Board.

§ 102.91 **Compliance with determination; further proceedings.**—If, after issuance of the determination by the Board, the parties submit to the regional director satisfactory evidence that they have complied with the determination, the regional director shall dismiss the charge. If no satisfactory evidence of compliance is submitted, the regional director shall proceed with the charge under paragraph (4)(D) of section 8(b) and section 10 of the act and the procedure prescribed in sections 102.9 to 102.51, inclusive, shall, insofar as applicable, govern: *Provided, however,* That if the Board determination is that employees represented by a charged union are entitled to perform the work in dispute, the regional director shall dismiss the charge as to that union irrespective of whether the employer has complied with that determination. [*As amended, effective June 1, 1971*]

§ 102.92 **Review of determination.**— The record of the proceeding under section 10(k) and the determination of the Board thereon shall become a part of the record in such unfair labor practice proceeding and shall be subject to judicial review, insofar as it is in issue, in proceedings to enforce or review the final order of the Board under section 10(e) and (f) of the act.

§ 102.93 **Alternative procedure.**—If, either before or after service of the notice of hearing, the parties submit to the regional director satisfactory evidence that they have adjusted the dispute, the regional director shall dismiss the charge and shall withdraw the notice of hearing if notice has issued. If, either before or after issuance of notice of hearing, the parties submit to the regional director satisfactory evidence that they have agreed upon methods for the voluntary adjustment of the dispute, the regional director shall defer action upon the charge and shall withdraw the notice of hearing if notice has issued. If it appears to the regional director that the dispute has not been adjusted in accordance with such agreed-upon methods and that an unfair labor practice within the meaning of section 8(b)(4)(D) of the act is occurring or has occurred, he may issue a complaint under section 102.15, and the procedure prescribed in sections 102.9 to 102.51, inclusive, shall, insofar as applicable, govern; and sections 102.90 to 102.92 inclusive, are inapplicable: *Provided, however,* That if an agreed-upon method for voluntary adjustment results in a determination that employees represented by a charged union are entitled to perform the work in dispute, the regional director shall dismiss the charge as to that union irrespective of whether the employer has complied with that determination, [*As amended, effective June 1, 1971*]

SUBPART G—PROCEDURE IN CASES UNDER SECTION 10(j), (l), AND (m) OF THE ACT

§ 102.94 **Expeditious processing of section 10(j) cases.**—(a) Whenever temporary relief or a restraining order pursuant to section 10(j) of the act has been procured by the Board, the complaint which has been the basis for such temporary relief or restraining order shall be heard expeditiously and the case shall be given priority by the Board in its successive steps following the issuance of the complaint (until ultimate enforcement or dismissal by the appropriate circuit court of appeals) over all other cases except cases of like character and cases under section 10(l) and 10(m) of the act.

(b) In the event the administrative law judge hearing a complaint, concerning which the Board has procured temporary relief or a restraining order pursuant to section 10(j), recommends a dismissal in whole or in part of such complaint, the chief law officer shall forthwith suggest to the district court which issued such temporary relief or restraining order the possible change in circumstances arising out of the findings and recommendations of the administrative law judge. [*As amended, effective August 19, 1972*]

§ 102.95—**Priority of cases pursuant to section 10(l) and 10(m) of the Act.** —(a) Whenever a charge is filed alleging the commission of an unfair labor practice within the meaning of paragraph (4)(A), (B), (C), or (7) of section 8(b) of the act, or section 8(e) of the act, the regional office in which such charge is filed or to which it is referred shall give it priority over all other cases in the office except cases of like character and cases under paragraph (4)(D) of section 8(b) of the act in which it is deemed appropriate to seek injunctive relief of a district court pursuant to section 10(l) of the act.

(b) Whenever a charge is filed alleging the commission of an unfair labor practice within the meaning of subsection (a)(3) or (b)(2) of Section 8 of the act, the regional office in which such charge is filed or to which it is referred shall give it priority over all other cases in the office except cases of like character and cases under section 10(l) of the act.

Sec. 102.96—**Issuance of complaint promptly.**—Whenever the regional attorney or other Board officer to whom the matter may be referred seeks injunctive relief of a district court pursuant to section 10 (l) of the act, a complaint against the party or parties sought to be enjoined, covering the same subject matter as such applica-

tion for injunctive relief, shall be issued promptly, normally within 5 days of the date upon which such injunctive relief is first sought, except in those cases under section 10(l) of the act in which the procedure set forth in sections 102.90 to 102.92, inclusive, is deemed applicable.

Sec. 102.97—**Expeditious processing of section 10(l) and 10(m) cases in successive stages.**—(a) Any complaint issued pursuant to section 102.95 (a) or, in a case in which it is deemed appropriate to seek injunctive relief of a district court pursuant to section 10(l) of the act, any complaint issued pursuant to section 102.93 or notice of hearing issued pursuant to section 102.90 shall be heard expeditiously and the case shall be given priority in such successive steps following its issuance (until ultimate enforcement or dismissal by the appropriate circuit court of appeals) over all cases except cases of like character.

(b) Any complaint issued pursuant to section 102.95 (b) shall be heard expeditiously and the case shall be given priority in its successive steps following its issuance (until ultimate enforcement or dismissal by the appropriate circuit court of appeals) over all cases except cases of like character and cases under section 10(l) of the act.

SUBPART H—ADVISORY OPINIONS AND DECLARATORY ORDERS REGARDING BOARD JURISDICTION

§ 102.98 **Petition for Advisory Opinion; who may file; where to file.** (a) Whenever a party to a proceeding before any agency or court of any State or territory is in doubt whether the Board would assert jurisdiction on the basis of its current jurisdictional standards, he may file a petition with the Board for an advisory opinion on whether it would assert jurisdiction on the basis of its current standards.

(b) Whenever an agency or court of any State or territory is in doubt whether the Board would assert jurisdiction over the parties in a proceeding pending before such agency or court, the agency or court may file a petition with the Board for an advisory opinion on whether the Board would decline to assert jurisdiction on the basis of its current standards.

§ 102.99 **Contents of petition for an advisory opinion.** (a) A petition for an advisory opinion, when filed by a party to a proceeding before an agency or court of a State or territory, shall allege the following:

(1) The name of the petitioner.

(2) The names of all other parties to the proceeding.

(3) The name of the agency or court.

(4) The docket number and nature of the proceeding.

(5) The general nature of the business involved in the proceeding.

(6) The commerce data relating to the operations of such business.

(7) Whether the commerce data described in this section are admitted or denied by other parties to the proceeding.

(8) The findings, if any, of the agency or court respecting the commerce data described in this section.

(9) Whether a representation or unfair labor practice proceeding involving the same labor dispute is pending before the Board, and, if so, the the case number thereof.

Petitions under this subsection shall be in writing and signed, and either shall be sworn to before a notary public, Board agent, or other person duly authorized by law to administer oaths and take acknowledgments or shall contain a declaration by the person signing it, under the penalties of the Criminal Code, that its contents are true and correct to the best of his knowledge and belief.

(b) A petition for an advisory opinion, when filed by an agency or court of a State or territory, shall allege the following:

(1) The name of the agency or court.

(2) The names of the parties to the proceeding.

(3) The docket number and nature of the proceeding.

(4) The general nature of the business involved in the proceeding.

(5) The findings of the agency or court, or, in the absence of findings, a statement of the evidence relating to the commerce operations of such business.

(c) Eight copies of such petition shall be filed with the Board in Washington, D.C. Such petition shall be printed or otherwise legibly duplicated: *Provided, however,* That carbon copies of typewritten matter shall not be filed and if submitted will not be accepted.

§ 102.100 **Notice of petition; service of petition.**—Upon the filing of a petition, the petitioner shall immediately serve in the manner provided by Section 102.112 of these rules a copy of the petition upon all parties to the proceeding and on the director of the Board's regional office having jurisdiction over the territorial area in which such agency or court is located. A statement of service shall be filed with the petition as provided by Section 102.113(b) of these rules.

§ 102.101 **Response to petition; service of response.**—Any party served with such petition may, within 5 days after service thereof, respond to the petition, admitting or denying its allegations. Eight copies of such response shall be filed with the Board in Washington, D.C. Such response shall be printed or otherwise legibly duplicated: *Provided, however,* That carbon copies of typewritten matter shall not be filed and if submitted will not be accepted. Such response shall immediately be served upon all other parties to the proceeding, and a statement of service shall be filed in accordance with the provisions of Section 102.113(b) of these Rules.

§ 102.102 **Intervention.**—Any person desiring to intervene shall make a motion for intervention, stating the grounds upon which such p e r s o n claims to have an interest in the petition. Eight copies of such motion shall be filed with the Board in Washington. D.C. Such motion shall be printed or otherwise legibly duplicated: *Provided, however,* That carbon copies of typewritten matter shall not be filed and if submitted will not be accepted.

§ 102.103 **Proceedings before the Board; briefs; advisory opinions.**—The Board shall thereupon proceed, upon the petition, responses, and submission of briefs, to determine whether, on the facts before it, the commerce operations of the employer involved are such that it would or would not assert jurisdiction. Such determination shall be in the form of an advisory opinion and shall be served upon the parties. No briefs shall be filed except upon special permission of the Board.

§ 102.104 **Withdrawal of petition.**— The petitioner may withdraw his petition at any time prior to issuance of the Board's advisory opinion.

§ 102.105 **Petitions for declaratory orders; who may file; where to file; withdrawal.**—Whenever both an unfair labor practice charge and a representation case relating to the same employer are contemporaneously on file in a regional office of the Board, and the general counsel entertains doubt whether the Board would assert jurisdiction over the employer involved, he may file a petition with the Board for a declaratory order disposing of the jurisdictional issue in the cases. Such petition may be withdrawn at any time prior to the issuance of the Board's order.

§ 102.106 **Contents of petition for declaratory order.**—A petition for a declaratory order shall allege the following:

(a) The name of the employer.

(b) The general nature of the employer's business.

(c) The case numbers of the unfair labor practice and representation cases.

(d) The commerce data relating to the operations of such business.

(e) Whether any proceeding involving the same subject matter is pending before an agency or court of a State or territory.

Eight copies of the petition shall be filed with the Board in Washington, D.C. Such petition shall be printed or otherwise legibly duplicated: *Provided, however,* That carbon copies of typewritten matter shall not be filed and if submitted will not be accepted.

§ 102.107 **Notice of petition; service of petition.**—Upon filing a petition, the general counsel shall immediately serve a copy thereof upon all parties and shall file a statement of service as provided by section 102.113(b) of these rules.

§ 102.108 **Response to petition; service of response.**—Any party to the representation or unfair labor practice case may, within 5 days after service thereof, respond to the petition, admitting or denying its allegations. Eight copies of such response shall be filed with the Board in Washington, D.C. Such response shall be printed or otherwise legibly duplicated: *Provided, however,* That carbon copies of typewritten matter shall not be filed and if submitted will not be accepted. Such response shall be served upon the General Counsel and all other parties, and a statement of service shall be filed as provided by Section 102.113(b) of these rules.

§ 102.109 **Intervention.**—Any person desiring to intervene shall make a motion for intervention, stating the grounds upon which such person claims to have an interest in the petition. Eight copies of such motion shall be filed with the Board in Washington, D.C. Such motion shall be printed or otherwise legibly duplicated: *Provided, however,* That carbon copies of typewritten matter shall not be filed and if submitted will not be accepted.

§ 102.110 **Proceedings before the Board; briefs; declaratory orders.**— The Board shall thereupon proceed, upon the petition, responses, and submission of briefs, to determine whether, on the facts before it, the commerce operations of the employer involved are such that it would or would not assert jurisdiction over them. Such determination shall be made by a declaratory order, with like effect as in the case of other orders of the Board, and shall be served on the parties. Any party desiring to file a brief shall file eight copies with the Board in Washington, D.C., with a statement that copies thereof are being served simultaneously on the other parties. Such brief shall be printed or otherwise legibly duplicated: *Provided, however,* That carbon copies shall not be submitted and if submitted will not be accepted.

SUBPART I—SERVICE AND FILING OF PAPERS

§ 102.111 **Service of process and papers; proof of service.**—(a) Charges, complaints and accompanying notices of hearing, final orders, administrative law judges' decisions, and subpenas of the Board, its member, agent, or agency, may be served personally or by registered mail or by telegraph or by leaving a copy thereof at the principal office or place of business of the person required to be served. The verified return by the individual so serving the same, setting forth the manner of such service, shall be proof of the same, and the return post office receipt or telegraph receipt therefor when registered and mailed or telegraphed as aforesaid shall be proof of service of the same.

(b) Whenever these rules require or permit the service of pleadings or other papers upon a party, a copy shall also be served on any attorney or other representative of the party who has entered a written appearance in the proceeding on behalf of the party. If a party is represented by more than one attorney or representative, service upon any one of such persons in addition to the party shall satisfy this requirement.

(c) Process and p a p e r s of the Board, other than those specifically named in subsection (a) of this section, may be forwarded by certified mail. The return post office receipt therefor shall be proof of service of the same. [As amended effective July 4, 1967]

§ 102.112 Same; by parties; proof of service.—Service of papers by a party on other parties shall be made by registered mail, or by certified mail, or in any manner provided for the service of papers in a civil action by the law of the State in which the hearing is pending. Except for charges, petitions, exceptions, briefs, and other papers for which a time for both filing and response has been otherwise established, service on all parties shall be made in the same manner as that utilized in filing the paper with the Board, or in a more expeditious manner; however, when filing with the Board is accomplished by personal service the other parties shall be promptly notified of such action by telephone, followed by service of a copy by mail or telegraph. When service is made by registered mail, or by certified mail, the return post office receipt shall be proof of service. When service is made in any manner provided by the law of a State, proof of service shall be made in accord-

ance with such law. Failure to comply with the requirements of this section relating to timeliness of service on other parties shall be a basis for either (a) a rejection of the document or (b) withholding or reconsidering any ruling on the subject matter raised by the document until after service has been made and the served party has had reasonable opportunity to respond. [As amended effective April 19, 1972]

§ 102.113 Date of service; filing of proof of service.—(a) The date of service shall be the day when the matter served is deposited in the United States mail or is delivered in person, as the case may be. In computing the time from such date, the provisions of section 102.114 apply.

(b) The person or party serving the papers or process on other parties in conformance with sections 102.111 and 102.112 shall submit a written statement of service thereof to the Board stating the names of the parties served and the date and manner of service. Proof of service as defined in section 102.112 shall be required by the Board only if subsequent to the receipt of the statement of service a question is raised with respect to proper service. Failure to make proof of service does not affect the validity of the service.

§ 102.114 T i m e; additional time after service by mail or by telegraph.—(a) In computing any period of time prescribed or allowed by these rules, the day of the act, event, or default after which the designated period of time begins to run, is not to be included. The last day of the period so computed is to be included, unless it is a Sunday or a legal holiday, in which event the period runs until the end of the next day, which is neither a Sunday nor a legal holiday. When the period of time prescribed or allowed is less than 7 days, intermediate Sundays and holidays shall be excluded in the computation. For the purpose of this section a Saturday on which the Board's offices are not open for business shall be considered as a holiday, but a half holiday shall be considered as other days and not as a holiday. Whenever a party has the right or is required to do some act or take some proceedings within a prescribed period after service of a notice or other paper upon him, and the notice or paper is served upon him by mail or by telegraph, 3 days shall be added to the perscribed period: *Provided, however,* That 3 days shall not be added if any extension of such time may have been granted.

(b) When the act or any of these rules require the filing of a motion, brief, exception, or other paper in any proceeding, such document must be received by the Board or the officer or agent designated to receive such matter before the close of business of the last day of the time limit, if any, for such filing or extension of time that may have been granted.

SUBPART J—CERTIFICATION AND SIGNATURE OF DOCUMENTS

§ 102.115 Certification of **p a p e r s and documents.**—The executive secretary of the Board or, in the event of his absence or disability, whosoever may be designated by the Board in his place and stead shall certify copies of all papers and documents which are a part of any of the files or records of the Board as may be necessary or desirable from time to time.

§ 102.116 **Signature of orders.**—The executive secretary or an associate executive secretary or, in the event of their absence or disability, whosoever may be designated by the Board in their place and stead is hereby authorized to sign all orders of the Board

SUBPART K—RECORDS AND INFORMATION

Freedom of Information Regulations

Sec. 102.117 Board materials and formal documents available for public inspection and copying; requests for described records; time limit for response; appeal from denial of request; fees for document search and duplication; files and records not subject to inspection.

(a) (1) The following materials are available to the public for inspection and copying during normal business hours: (i) All final opinions and orders made in the adjudication of cases; (ii) administrative staff manuals and instructions that affect any member of the public (excepting those establishing internal operating

rules, guidelines, and procedures for the investigation, trial, and settlement of cases); (iii) a record of the final votes of each member of the Board in every agency proceeding; and (iv) a current index of final opinions and orders made in the adjudication of cases. Items (i) through (iv) are available for inspection and copying during normal business hours at the Board's offices in Washington, D.C. Items (ii) through (iv) are also available for inspection and copying during normal business hours at each regional, subregional, and resident office of the Board. Final opinions and orders made by regional directors in the adjudication of representation cases pursuant to the delegation of authority from the Board under section 3(b) of the act are available to the public for inspection and copying in the original office where issued.

(2) Copies of forms prescribed by the Board for the filing of charges under section 10 or petitions under section 9 may be obtained without charge from any regional, subregional, or resident office of the Board.

(b) (1) The formal documents constituting the record in a case or proceeding are matters of official record and, until destroyed pursuant to applicable statutory authority, are available to the public for inspection and copying during normal business hours, at the appropriate regional office of the Board or at the Board's offices in Washington, D.C., as the case may be.

(2) The executive secretary shall certify copies of the formal documents upon request made a reasonable time in advance of need and payment of lawfully prescribed costs.

(c) (1) Requests for the inspection and copying of records other than those specified in paragraphs (a) and (b) of this section must be in writing and must reasonably describe the record in a manner to permit its identification and location. The envelope and the letter should be clearly marked to indicate that it contains a request for records under the Freedom of Information Act (FOIA). The request must contain a specific statement assuming financial liability in accordance with paragraph (c)(2)(iv) of this section, for the direct costs of the search for the requested records and their duplication. If the request is for records in a regional or subregional office of the agency, it should be made to that regional or subregional office; if for records in the office of the general counsel and located in Washington, D.C., it should be made to the Freedom of Information officer, office of the general counsel, Washington, D.C.; and if for records in the offices of the Board in Washington, D.C., to the executive secretary of the Board, Washington, D.C. Requests made to other than the appropriate office will be forwarded to that office by the receiving office, but in that event the applicable time limit for response set forth in paragraph (c)(2) of this section shall be calculated from the date of receipt by the appropriate office.

(c)(2)(i) Within 10 working days after receipt of a request by the appropriate office of the agency a determination shall be made whether to comply with such request, and the person making the request shall be notified in writing of that determination. If the determination is to comply with the request, the records shall be made promptly available to the person making the request, upon payment of any charges due in accordance with the provisions of paragraph (c)(2)(iv) of this section. If the determination is to deny the request, the notification shall set forth the reasons therefor and the name and title or position of each person responsible for the denial, and shall notify the person making the request of the right to appeal the adverse determination under the provisions of subparagraph (ii) of this subsection.

(ii) An appeal from an adverse determination made pursuant to paragraph (c)(2)(i) of this section must be filed within 20 working days of the receipt by the person of the notifica-

tion of the adverse determination where the request is denied in its entirety; or, in the case of a partial denial, within 20 working days of the receipt of any records being made available pursuant to the request. If the adverse determination was made in a regional office, a subregional office, or by the Freedom of Information officer, office of the general counsel, the appeal shall be filed with the general counsel in Washington, D.C. If the adverse determination was made by the executive secretary of the Board, the appeal shall be filed with the chairman of the Board in Washington, D.C. Within 20 working days after the receipt of an appeal the chairman of the Board or the general counsel, as the case may be, shall make a determination with respect to such appeal and shall notify the person in writing. If the determination is to comply with the request, the records shall be made promptly available to the person making the request, upon receipt of payment of any charges due in accordance with the provisions of paragraph (c)(2)(iv) of this section. If on appeal the denial of the request for records is upheld in whole or in part, the person making the request shall be notified of the reasons for the determination, the name and title or position of each person responsible for the denial, and the provisions for judicial review of that determination under the provisions of 5 U.S.C. section 552(4)(B). Even though no appeal is filed from a denial in whole or in part of a request for records by the person making the request, the chairman of the Board or the general counsel may, without regard to the time limit for filing of an appeal, sua sponte initiate consideration of an adverse determination under this appeal procedure by written notification to the person making the request. In such event the time limit for making the determination shall commence with the issuance of such notification.

(iii) In unusual circumstances as specified in this subparagraph, the time limits prescribed in either paragraphs (c) (2) (i) or (ii) of this subsection may be extended by written notice to the person requesting the record setting forth the reasons for such extension and the date on which a determination is expected to be dispatched. No such notice or notices shall specify a date or dates that would result in an extension or extensions totaling more than 10 working days with respect to a particular request. As used in this subparagraph, "unusual circumstances" means, but only to the extent reasonably necessary to the proper processing of the particular request:

(a) The need to search for and collect the requested records from field facilities or other establishments that are separate from the office processing the request;

(b) The need to search for, collect, and appropriately examine a voluminous amount of separate and distinct records which are demanded in a single request; or

(c) The need for consultation, which shall be conducted with all practicable speed, with another agency having a substantial interest in the determination of the request or among two or more components of the agency having substantial subject-matter interest therein.

(iv) Persons requesting records from this agency shall be subject to a charge of fees for the direct cost of document search and duplication in accordance with the following schedules, procedures, and conditions:

(a) Schedule of charges:

(1) For each one-quarter hour or portion thereof of clerical time $1.10

(2) For each one-quarter hour or portion thereof of professional time ... 2.85

(3) For each sheet of duplication (not to exceed 8½ x 14 inches) of requested records $0.10

(4) All other direct costs of search or duplication shall be charged to the requester in the same amount as incurred by the agency.

(b) Each request for records shall contain a specific statement assuming financial liability, in full or to a specified maximum amount, for charges, in accordance with paragraph (c) (2) (iv) (a) of this section which may be incurred by the agency in responding to the request. If the anticipated charges exceed the maximum limit stated by the person making the request or if the request contains no assumption of financial liability for charges, the person shall be notified and afforded an opportunity to assume financial liability. The request for records shall not be deemed received for purposes of the applicable time limit for response until a written assumption of financial liability is received. When the anticipated charges exceed $50, the person making the request, upon notification, shall deposit 50 percent of the anticipated charges with the agency. The request shall not be deemed received for purposes of the applicable time limit for response until such deposit has been made.

(c) Charges may be imposed even though the search discloses no records responsive to the request, or none not exempt from disclosure. The imposition of charges may be waived for the convenience of the agency, and will be reduced or waived where the agency determines that furnishing the information can be considered as primarily benefiting the general public. The agency may, by agreement with the person making the request, make arrangements with commercial firms for required services to be charged directly to the requester.

(v) "Working days," as used in this subsection, means calendar days excepting Saturdays, Sundays, and legal holidays.

(d) Subject to the provisions of §§ 102.31 (c) and 102.66 (c), all files, documents, reports, memoranda, and records of the agency, falling within the exemptions specified in 5 U.S.C. section 552 (b), shall not be made available for inspection or copying, unless specifically permitted by the Board, its chairman, or its general counsel.

(e) An individual may be informed whether a system of records maintained by this agency contains a record pertaining to such individual. An inquiry should be made in writing or in person during normal business hours to the official of this agency designated for that purpose and at the address set forth in a notice of a system of records published by this agency, in a Notice of Systems of Government-wide Personnel Records published by the Civil Service Commission, or in a Notice of Government-wide System of Records published by the Department of Labor. The inquiry should contain sufficient information, as defined in the notice, to identify the record. Reasonable verification of identity of the inquirer, as described in subsection (i) of this section, will be required to assure that information is disclosed to the proper person. The agency shall acknowledge the inquiry in writing within 10 days (excluding Saturdays, Sundays, and legal public holidays) and, wherever practicable, the acknowledgment shall supply the information requested. If, for good cause shown, the agency cannot supply the information within 10 days, the inquirer shall within that time period be notified in writing of the reasons therefor and when it is anticipated the information will be supplied. An acknowledgment will not be provided where the information is supplied within the 10-day period. If the agency refuses to inform an individual whether a system of records contains a record pertaining to an individual, the inquirer shall be notified in writing of that determination and the reasons therefor, and of the right to obtain review of that determination under the provisions of subsection (j) of this section.

(f) An individual may be permitted access to records pertaining to such individual contained in any system of records described in the notices of systems of records published by this agency. The request for access must be made in writing or in person during normal business hours, to the person designated for that purpose and at the address set forth in the published notice of systems of records. Reasonable verification of the identity of the requester, as described in subsection (i) of this section, shall be required to assure that records are disclosed to the proper person. A request for access to records shall be acknowledged in writing by the agency within 10 days of receipt (excluding Saturdays, Sundays, and legal public holidays) and, wherever practicable, the acknowledgment shall inform the requester whether or not access will be granted and, if so, the time and location at which the records will be made available. If access to the record is to be granted, the record will normally be provided within 30 days (excluding Saturdays, Sundays, and legal public holidays) of the request, unless for good cause shown the agency is unable to do so, in which case the individual will be informed in writing within that 30-day period of the reasons therefor and when it is anticipated that access will be granted. An acknowledgment of a request will not be provided if the record is made available within the 10-day period. If an individual's request for access to a record under the provisions of this subsection is denied, the notice informing the individual of the denial shall set forth the reasons therefor and advise the individual of the right to obtain a review of that determination under the provisions of subsection (j) of this section.

(g) An individual granted access to records pertaining to such individual contained in a system of records may review all such records. For that purpose the individual may be accompanied by a person of the individual's choosing, or the record may be released to the individual's representative who has the written consent of the individual, as described in subsection (i) of this section. A first copy of any such record or information will ordinarily be provided without charge to the individual or representative in a form comprehensive to the individual. Fees for any other copies of records shall be assessed in accordance with the fee schedule set forth in subsection 102.117 (c)(2)(iv)(a)(3) of this section.

(h) An individual may request amendment of a record pertaining to such individual in a system of records maintained by this agency. A request for amendment of a record must be in writing and submitted during normal business hours to the person designated for that purpose and at the address set forth in the published notice for the system of records containing the record of which amendment is sought. The requester must provide verification of identity as described in subsection (i) of this section, and the request should set forth the specific amendment requested and the reason for the requested amendment. The agency shall acknowledge in writing receipt of the request within 10 days of its receipt (excluding Saturdays, Sundays, and legal public holidays) and, wherever practicable, the acknowledgment shall advise the individual of the determination of the request. If the review of the request for amendment cannot be completed and a determination made within 10 days, the review shall be completed as soon as possible, normally within 30 days (Saturdays, Sundays, and legal public holidays excluded) of receipt of the request unless unusual circumstances preclude completing the review within that time, in which event the requester will be notified in writing within that 30-day period of the reasons for the delay and when the determination of the request may be expected. If the determination is to amend the record, the requester shall be so notified in writing and the record shall be amended in accordance with that determination. If any disclosures accountable under the provisions of 5 U.S.C. Sec. 552a(c) have been made, all previous recipients of the record which was amended shall be advised of the amendment and its substance. If it is determined that the request should not be granted, the requester shall be notified in writing of that determination and of the reasons therefor, and advised of the right to obtain review of the adverse determination under the provisions of subsection (j) of this section.

(i) Verification of the identification of individuals required under subsections (e), (f), (g), and (h) of this section to assure that records are disclosed to the proper persons shall be required by the agency to an extent consistent with the nature, location, and sensitivity of the records being disclosed. Disclosure of a record to an individual in person will normally be made upon the presentation of acceptable identification. Disclosure of records by mail may be made upon the basis of the identifying information set forth in the request. Depending upon the nature, location, and sensitivity of the requested record, a signed notarized statement verifying identity may be required by the agency. Proof of authorization as representative to have access to a record of an individual shall be in writing, and a signed notarized statement of such authorization may be required by the agency if the record requested is of a sensitive nature.

(j)(1) Review may be obtained with respect to (i) a refusal, under subsection (e) or (k) of this section, to inform an individual if a system of records contains a record concerning that individual, (ii) a refusal, under subsection (f) or (k) of this section, to grant access to a record, or (iii) a refusal, under subsection (h) of this section, to amend a record. The request for review should be made to the chairman of the Board if the system of records is maintained in the offices of a member of the Board, the office of the executive secretary, the office of the solicitor, the division of information, or the division of administrative law judges. Consonant with the provisions of section 3(d) of the National Labor Relations Act, as amended, and the delegation of authority from the Board to the general counsel, the request should be made to the general counsel if the system of records is maintained by any office of the agency other than those enumerated above. Either the chairman of the Board or the general counsel may designate in writing another officer of the agency to review the refusal of the request. Such review shall be completed within 30 days (excluding Saturdays, Sundays, and legal public holidays) from the receipt of the request for review unless the chairman of the Board or the general counsel, as the case may be, for good cause shown, shall extend such 30-day period.

(2) If, upon review of a refusal under subsection (e) or (k), the reviewing officer determines that the individual should be informed of whether a system of records contains a record pertaining to that individual, such information shall be promptly provided. If the reviewing officer determines that the information was properly denied, the individual shall be so informed in writing with a brief statement of the reasons therefor.

(3) If, upon review of a refusal under subsection (f) or (k), the reviewing officer determines that access to a record should be granted, the requester shall be so notified and the record shall be promptly made available to the requester. If the reviewing officer determines that the request for access to records was properly denied, the individual shall be so informed in writing with a brief statement of the reasons therefor.

(4) If, upon review of a refusal under subsection (h), the reviewing official grants a request to amend, the requester, shall be so notified, the record shall be amended in accordance with the determination, and, if any disclosures accountable under the provisions of 5 U.S.C. Sec. 552a (c) have been made, all previous recipients of the record which was amended shall be advised of the amendment and its substance. If the reviewing officer determines that the denial of a request for amendment should be sustained, the agency shall advise the requester of the determination and the reasons therefor, and that the individual may file with the agency a concise statement of the reasons for disagreeing with the determination, and may seek judicial review of the agency's denial of the request to amend the record. In the event a statement of disagreement is filed, that statement (i) will be made available to anyone to whom the record is subsequently disclosed together with, at the discretion of the agency, a brief statement summarizing the agency's reasons for declining to amend the record, and (ii) will be supplied, together with any agency statements, to any prior recipients of the disputed record to the extent that an accounting of disclosures was made.

(k) To the extent that portions of systems of records described in notices of governmentwide systems of records published by the Civil Service Commission are identified by those notices as being subject to the management of an officer of this agency, or an officer of this agency is designated as the official to contact for information, access or contest of those records, individual requests for access to those records, requests for their amendment, and review of denials of requests for amendment shall be in accordance with the provisions of 5 CFR Part 297, subpart A, Section 297.101 of this title, et seq., as promulgated by the Civil Service Commission. To the extent that portions of systems of records described in notices of governmentwide systems of records published by the Department of Labor are identified by those notices as being subject to the management of an officer of this agency, or an officer of this agency is designated as the official to contact for information, access or contest of those records, individual requests for access to those records, requests for their amendment, and review of denials of requests for amendment shall be in accordance with the provisions of 29 CFR part 70a as promulgated by the Department of Labor. Review of a refusal to inform an individual whether such a system of records contains a record pertaining to that individual, and review of a refusal to grant an individual's request for access to a record in such a system may be obtained in accordance with the provisions of subsection (j) of this section. [Subsections (e) through (k) added October 14, 1974, 40 F.R. 48330, effective October 14, 1975.]

Sec. 102.118 Board employees prohibited from producing files, records, etc., pursuant to subpoena ad testificandum or subpoena duces tecum; prohibited from testifying in regard thereto; production of witnesses' statements after direct testimony.

(a) (1) Except as provided in § 102. 117 of these rules respecting requests cognizable under the Freedom of Information Act, no regional director, field examiner, administrative law judge, attorney, specially designated agent, general counsel, member of the Board, or other officer or employee of the Board shall produce or present any files, documents, reports, memoranda, or records of the Board or of the general counsel, whether in response to a subpoena duces tecum or otherwise, without the written consent of the Board or the chairman of the Board if the document is in Washington, D.C., and in control of the Board; or of the general counsel if the document is in a regional office of the agency or is in Washington, D.C., and in the control of the general counsel. Nor shall any such person testify in behalf of any party to any cause pending in any court or before the Board, or any other board, commission, or other administrative agency of the United States, or of any State, territory, or the District of Columbia, or any subdivisions thereof, with respect to any information, facts, or other matter coming to his knowledge in his official

capacity or with respect to the contents of any files, documents, reports, memoranda, or records of the Board or the general counsel, whether in answer to a subpoena or otherwise, without the written consent of the Board or the chairman of the Board if the person is in Washington, D.C., and subject to the supervision or control of the Board; or of the general counsel if the person is in a regional office of the agency or is in Washington, D.C., and subject to the supervision or control of the general counsel.

A request that such consent be granted shall be in writing and shall identify the documents to be produced, or the person whose testimony is desired, the nature of the pending proceeding, and the purpose to be served by the production of the document or the testimony of the official. Whenever any subpoena ad testificandum or subpoena duces tecum, the purpose of which is to adduce testimony or require the production of records as described hereinabove, shall have been served on any such person or other officer or employee of the Board, he will, unless otherwise expressly directed by the Board or the chairman of the Board or the general counsel, as the case may be, move pursuant to the applicable procedure whether by petition to revoke, motion to quash, or otherwise, to have such subpoena invalidated on the ground that the evidence sought is privileged against disclosure by this rule. [Sections 102.117 and 102.118(a) as revised and effective February 19, 1975, 40 F.R. 7290.]

(b) (1) Notwithstanding the prohibitions of paragraph (a) of this section, after a witness called by the general counsel or by the charging party has testified in a hearing upon a complaint under section 10(c) of the act, the administrative law judge shall, upon motion of the respondent, order the production of any statement (as hereinafter defined) of such witness in the possession of the general counsel which relates to the subject matter as to which the witness has testified. If the entire contents of any such statement relate to the subject matter of the testimony of the witness, the administrative law judge shall order it to be delivered directly to the respondent for his examination and use for the purpose of cross-examination.

(2) If the general counsel claims that any statement ordered to be produced under this section contains matter which does not relate to the subject matter of the testimony of the witness, the administrative law judge shall order the general counsel to deliver such statement for the inspection of the administrative law judge in camera. Upon such delivery the administrative law judge shall excise the portions of such statement which do not relate to the subject matter of the testimony of the witness except that he may, in his discretion, decline to excise portions which, although not relating to the subject matter of the testimony of the witness, do relate to other matters raised by the pleadings. With such material excised the administrative law judge shall then direct delivery of such statement to the respondent for his use on cross-examination. If, pursuant to such procedure, any portion of such statement is withheld from the respondent and the respondent objects to such withholding, the entire text of such statement shall be preserved by the general counsel, and, in the event the respondent files exceptions with the Board based upon such withholding, shall be made available to the Board for the purpose of determining the correctness of the ruling of the administrative law judge. If the general counsel elects not to comply with an order of the administrative law judge directing delivery to the respondent of any such statement, or such portion thereof as the administrative law judge may direct, the administrative law judge shall strike from the record the testimony of the witness.

(c) The provisions of paragraph (b) of this section shall also apply after any witness has testified in any post-election hearing pursuant to § 102.69 (d) and any party has moved for the production of any statement (as hereinafter defined) of such witness in possession of any agent of the Board which relates to the subject matter as to which the witness has testified. The authority exercised by the administrative law judge under paragraph (b) of this section shall be exercised by the hearing officer presiding.

(d) The term "statement" as used in paragraphs (b) and (c) of this section means: (1) a written statement made by said witness and signed or otherwise adopted or approved by him; or (2) a stenographic, mechanical, electrical, or other recording, or a transcription thereof, which is a substantially verbatim recital of an oral statement made by said witness to an agent of the party obligated to produce the statement and recorded contemporaneously with the making of such oral statement. [*33 F.R. 9819, July 9, 1968, as amended at 35 F.R. 10658, July 1, 1970*]

SUBPART L — PRACTICE BEFORE THE BOARD OF FORMER EMPLOYEES [1]

§ 102.119 **Prohibition of practice before Board of its former regional employees in cases pending in region during employment.**—No person who has been an employee of the Board and attached to any of its regional offices shall engage in practice before the Board or its agents in any respect or in any capacity in connection with any case or proceeding which was pending in any regional office to which he was attached during the time of his employment with the Board.

§ 102.120 **Same; application to former employees of Washington staff.**—No person who has been an employee of the Board and attached to the Washington staff shall engage in practice before the Board or its agents in any respect or in any capacity in con-

---

1 Attention is directed to Public Law 87-849 (76 Stat. 1119) which amends Chapter 11 of Title 18 United States Code, entitled "Bribery, Graft and Conflicts of Interest" and which provides for the imposition of criminal sanctions under certain circumstances.

nection with any case or proceeding pending before the Board or any regional offices during the time of his employment with the Board.

SUBPART M — CONSTRUCTION OF RULES

§ 102.121 **Rules to be liberally construed.**—The rules and regulations in this part shall be liberally construed to effectuate the purposes and provisions of the act.

SUBPART N — ENFORCEMENT OF RIGHTS, PRIVILEGES, AND IMMUNITIES GRANTED OR GUARANTEED UNDER SECTION 222(f), COMMUNICATIONS ACT OF 1934, AS AMENDED, TO EMPLOYEES OF MERGED TELEGRAPH CARRIERS

§ 102.122 **Enforcement.**—All matters relating to the enforcement of rights, privileges, or immunities granted or guaranteed under section 222(f) of the Communications Act of 1934, as amended, shall be governed by the provisions of subparts A, B, I, J, K, and M of the Rules and Regulations, insofar as applicable, except that reference in subpart B of this part to "unfair labor practices" or "unfair labor practices affecting commerce" shall for the purposes of this article mean the denial of any rights, privileges, or immunities granted or guaranteed under section 222(f) of the Communications Act of 1934, as amended.

SUBPART O—AMENDMENTS

§ 102.123 **Amendment or rescission of rules.**—Any rule or regulation may be amended or rescinded by the Board at any time.

§ 102.124 **Petitions for issuance, amendment, or repeal of rules.**—Any interested person may petition the Board, in writing, for the issuance, amendment, or repeal of a rule or regulation. An original and seven copies of such petition shall be filed with the Board in Washington, D.C., and shall state the rule or regulation proposed to be issued, amended, or repealed, together with a statement of grounds in support of such petition.

§ 102.125 **Action on petition.**—Upon the filing of such petition, the Board shall consider the same and may thereupon either grant or deny the petition in whole or in part, conduct an appropriate hearing thereon, or make other disposition of the petition. Should the petition be denied in whole or in part, prompt notice shall be given of the denial, accompanied by a simple statement of the grounds unless the denial is self-explanatory.

SUBPART P—EX PARTE COMMUNICATIONS

§ 102.126 **Unauthorized communications.**——No person who is a party to, an agent of a party to, or who intercedes in, an on-the-record proceeding of the types defined in § 102.128, shall make an unauthorized *ex parte* communication to Board agents of the categories designated in that section, concerning the disposition on the merits of the substantive and procedural issues in the proceeding.

§ 102.127 **Definitions.**——When used in this subpart:

(a) The term "person who is a party," to whom the prohibitions apply, shall include any individual outside this agency (whether in public or private life), partnership, corporation, association, or other entity, who is named or admitted as a party or who seeks admission as a party, and the general counsel or his representatives when prosecuting an unfair labor practice proceeding before the Board pursuant to section 10(b) of the act.

(b) The term "person who intercedes," to whom the prohibitions apply, shall include any individual outside this agency (whether in public or private life), partnership, corporation, association, or other entity, other than a party or an agent of a party, who volunteers a communication which he may be expected to know may advance or adversely affect the interests of a particular party to the proceeding, whether or not he acts with the knowledge or consent of any party or any party's agent.

§ 102.128 **Types of on-the-record proceedings; categories of Board agents;**

and duration of prohibition.——Unless otherwise provided by specific order of the Board entered in the proceeding, the prohibition of § 102.126 shall be applicable in the following types of on-the-record proceedings to unauthorized *ex parte* communications made to the designated categories of Board agents who participate in the decision, from the stage of the proceeding specified until the issues are finally resolved by the Board for the purposes of that proceeding under prevailing rules and practices:

(a) In a preelection proceeding pursuant to section 9(c)(1) or 9(e), or in a unit clarification or certification amendment proceeding pursuant to section 9(b), of the act, in which a formal hearing is held, communications to the regional director and members of his staff who review the record and prepare a draft of his decision, and members of the Board and their legal assistants, from the time the hearing is opened.

(b) In a postelection proceeding pursuant to section 9(c)(1) or 9(e) of the act, in which a formal hearing is held, communications to the hearing officer, the regional director and members of his staff who review the record and prepare a draft of his report or decision, and members of the Board and their legal assistants, from the time the hearing is opened.

(c) In a postelection proceeding pursuant to section 9(c)(1) or 9(e), or in a unit clarification or certification amendment proceeding pursuant to section 9(b), of the act, in which no formal hearing is held, communications to members of the Board and their legal assistants, from the time the regional director's report or decision is issued.

(d) In a proceeding pursuant to section 10(k) of the act, communications to members of the Board and their legal assistants, from the time the hearing is opened.

(e) In an unfair labor practice proceeding pursuant to section 10(b) of the act, communications to the administrative law judge assigned to hear the case or to make rulings upon any motions or issues therein and members of the Board and their legal assistants, from the time the complaint is issued. [*As amended, effective August 19, 1972*]

(f) In any other proceeding to which the Board by specific order makes the prohibition applicable, to the categories of personnel and from the stage of the proceeding specified in the order.

§ 102.129 **Communications prohibited.**—Except as provided in § 102.130 *ex parte* communications prohibited by § 102.126 shall include:

(a) Such communications, when written, if copies thereof are not contemporaneously served by the communicator on all parties to the proceeding in accordance with the provisions of § 102.112.

(b) Such communications, when oral, unless advance notice thereof is given by the communicator to all parties in the proceeding and adequate opportunity afforded to them to be present.

§ 102.130 **Communications not prohibited.** — *Ex Parte* communications prohibited by § 102.126 shall not include:

(a) Oral or written communications which relate solely to matters which the hearing officer, regional director, administrative law judge, or member of the Board is authorized by law or Board rules to entertain or dispose of on an *ex parte* basis. [*As amended, effective August 19, 1972*]

(b) Oral or written requests for information solely with respect to the status of a proceeding.

(c) Oral or written communications which all the parties to the proceeding agree, or which the responsible official formally rules, may be made on an *ex parte* basis.

(d) Oral or written communications proposing settlement or an agreement for disposition of any or all issues in the proceeding.

(e) Oral or written communications which concern matters of general significance to the field of labor-management relations or administrative practice and which are not specifically related to pending on-the-record proceedings.

§ 102.131 Communications by Board agents.——No Board agent of the categories defined in § 102.128, participating in a particular proceeding as defined in that section, shall (a) request or entertain any prohibited *ex parte* communications; or (b) make any prohibited *ex parte* communications about the proceeding to any person who is a party to the proceeding, any agent of any person who is a party, or any other person, whom he has reason to know may transmit the communication to a person who is a party or to an agent of a person who is a party.

§ 102.132 Solicitation of prohibited communications.——No person shall knowingly and willfully solicit the making of an unauthorized *ex parte* communication by any other person.

§ 102.133 Receipt of prohibited communications; reporting requirements.——(a) Any Board agent of the categories defined in § 102.128 to whom a prohibited oral *ex parte* communication is attempted to be made shall refuse to listen to the communication, inform the communicator of this rule, and advise him that if he has anything to say it should be said in writing with copies to all parties. Any such Board agent who receives a written *ex parte* communication which he has reason to believe is prohibited by this subpart shall promptly forward such communication to the Office of the Executive Secretary if the proceeding is then pending before the Board, to the chief administrative law judge if the proceeding is then pending before an administrative law judge, or to the regional director involved if the proceeding is then pending before a hearing officer or the regional director. It the circumstances in which the unauthorized communication was made are not apparent from the communication itself, a statement describing those circumstances shall

also be submitted. The executive secretary, the chief administrative law judge, or the regional director to whom such a communication is forwarded shall then place the communication in the public file maintained by the agency and shall serve copies of the communication on all other parties to the proceeding and attorneys of record for the parties. Within 10 days after the mailing of such copies, any party may file with the executive secretary, the chief administrative law judge, or regional director serving the communication, and serve on all other parties, a statement setting forth facts or contentions to rebut those contained in the unauthorized communication. [*As amended, effective August 19, 1972*]

(b) Upon appropriate motion to the regional director, the administrative law judge, or the Board, before whom the proceeding is pending, under circumstances in which such presiding authority shall determine that the dictates of fairness so require, the unauthorized communication and response thereto may be made part of the record of the proceeding, and provision made for any further action, including reopening of the record, which may be required under the circumstances. No action taken pursuant to this provision shall constitute a waiver of the power of the Board to impose an appropriate penalty under § 102.134. [*As amended, effective August 19, 1972*]

§ 102.134 Penalties and enforcement.——Upon notice and hearing, the Board may censure, suspend, or revoke the privilege of practice before the agency of any person who knowingly and willfully makes or solicits the making of a prohibited *ex parte* communication. To the extent permitted by law, the Board may, under appropriate circumstances, deny or limit remedial measures otherwise available under the Act to any party who shall, directly or indirectly, knowingly and willfully make or solicit the making of an unauthorized communication. However, before the Board institutes formal proceedings under this section, it shall first advise the person or persons concerned in writing that it proposes to take such action and that they may show cause, within a period to be stated in such written advice, but not less than 7 days from the date thereof, why it should not take such action. The Board may censure, or, to the extent permitted by law, suspend, dismiss, or institute proceedings for the dismissal of, any Board agent who knowingly and willfully violates the prohibitions and requirements of this rule.

NATIONAL LABOR RELATIONS BOARD: Delegation of Powers to General Counsel

Text of Memorandum Describing the Authority and Assigned Responsibilities of the General Counsel of the NLRB effective April 1, 1955, and as last amended effective May 15, 1961.

The statutory authority and responsibility of the General Counsel of the Board are defined in Section 3(d) of the National Labor Relations Act as follows:

"There shall be a General Counsel of the Board who shall be appointed by the President, by and with the advice and consent of the Senate, for a term of four years. The General Counsel of the Board shall exercise general supervision over all attorneys employed by the Board (other than trial examiners and legal assistants to Board members) and over the officers and employees in the regional offices. He shall have final authority, on behalf of the Board, in respect of the investigation of charges and issuance of complaints under Section 10, and in respect of the prosecution of such complaints before the Board, and shall have such other duties as the Board may prescribe or as may be provided by law."

This memorandum is intended to describe the statutory authority and to set forth the prescribed duties and authority of the General Counsel of the Board, effective April 1, 1955:

I. CASE HANDLING

A. Complaint Cases. The General Counsel of the Board has full and final authority and responsibility, on behalf of the Board, to accept and investigate charges filed, to enter into and approve informal settlement of charges, to dismiss charges, to determine matters concerning consolidation and severance of cases before complaint issues, to issue complaints and notices of hearing, to appear before Trial Examiners in hearings on complaints and prosecute as provided in the Board's Rules and Regulations, and to initiate and prosecute injunction proceedings as provided for in Section 10(1) of the Act. After issuance of Intermediate Report by the Trial Examiner, the General Counsel may file exceptions and briefs and appear before the Board in oral argument, subject to the Board's Rules and Regulations.

B. Court Litigation. The General Counsel of the Board is authorized and has responsibility, on behalf of the Board, to seek and effect compliance with the Board's orders and make such compliance reports to the Board as it may from time to time require.

On behalf of the Board the General Counsel of the Board will, in full accordance with the directions of the Board, petition for enforcement and resist petitions for review of Board Orders as provided in Section 10 (e) and (f) of the Act, initiate and prosecute injunction proceedings as provided in Section 10(j), seek temporary restraining orders as provided in Section 10(e) and (f), and take appeals either by writ of error or on petition for certiorari to the Supreme Court: *Provided however,* That the General Counsel will initiate and conduct injunction proceedings under Section 10(j) or under Section 10(e) and (f) of the Act and contempt proceedings pertaining to the enforcement of or compliance with any order of the Board, and will initiate and conduct appeals to the Supreme Court by writ of error or on petition for certiorari when authorized by the Board.

C. Representation and other election cases. The General Counsel of the Board is authorized and has responsibility, on behalf of the Board, to receive and process, in accordance with the decisions of the Board and with such instructions and rules and regulations as may be issued by the Board from time to time, all petitions filed pursuant to section 9 of the National Labor Relations Act as amended. He is also authorized and has responsibility to conduct secret ballots pursuant to section 209(b) of the Labor Management Relations Act of 1947, whenever the Board is required to do so by law; and to enter into consent election agreements in accordance with section 9(c)(4) of the act.

The authority and responsibility of the General Counsel of the Board in representation cases shall extend, in accordance with the rules and regulations of the Board, to all phases of the investigation through the conclusion of the hearing provided for in section 9(c) and section 9(e) (if a hearing should be necessary to resolve disputed issues), but all matters involving decisional action after such hearing are reserved by the Board to itself.

In the event a direction of election should issue by the Board, the authority and responsibility of the General Counsel, as herein prescribed, shall attach to the conduct of the ordered election, the initial determination of the validity of challenges and objections to the conduct of the election and other similar matters; except that if appeals shall be taken from the General Counsel's action on the validity of challenges and objections, such appeals will be directed to and decided by the Board in accordance with such procedural requirements as it shall prescribe. If challenged ballots would not affect the election results and if no objections are filed within five days after the conduct of a Board-directed election under the provisions of section 9(c) of the act, the General Counsel is authorized and has responsibility, on behalf of the Board, to certify to the parties the results of the election in accordance with regulations prescribed by the Board.

Appeals from the refusal of the General Counsel of the Board to issue a notice of hearing on any petition, or from the dismissal by the General Counsel of any petition, will be directed to and decided by the Board, in accordance with such procedural requirements as it may prescribe.

In processing election petitions filed pursuant to section 9(e) of the act, the General Counsel of the Board is authorized and has responsibility, on behalf of the Board, to conduct an appropriate investigation as to the authenticity of the 30 percent showing referred to and, upon making his determination to proceed, to conduct a secret ballot. If there are no challenges or objections which require a hearing by the Board, he shall certify the results thereof as provided for in such section, with appropriate copies lodged in the Washington files of the Board.

D. Jurisdictional Dispute Cases. The General Counsel of the Board is authorized and has responsibility, on behalf of the Board, to perform all functions necessary to the accomplishment of the provisions of Section 10(k) of the Act, but in connection therewith the Board will, at the request of the General Counsel, assign to him for the purpose of conducting the hearing provided for therein, one of its administrative law judges. This authority and responsibility and the assignment of the administrative law judge to the General Counsel shall terminate with the close of the hearing. Thereafter the Board will assume full jurisdiction over the matter for the purpose of deciding the issues in such hearing on the record made and subsequent hearings or related proceedings and will also rule upon any appeals.

II. INTERNAL REGULATIONS

Procedural and operational regulations for the conduct of the internal business of the Board within the area that is under the supervision and direction of the General Counsel of the Board may be prepared and promulgated by the General Counsel.

III. STATE AGREEMENTS

When authorized by the Board, the General Counsel may initiate and conduct discussions and negotiations, on behalf of the Board, with appropriate authorities of any of the States or Territories looking to the consummation of agreements affecting any of the States or Territories as contemplated in Section 10(a) of the Act; *Provided, however,* that in no event shall the Board be committed in any respect with regard to such discussions or negotiations or the entry into of any such agreement unless and until the Board and the General Counsel have joined with the appropriate authorities of the State or Territory affected in the execution of such agreement.

IV. LIAISON WITH OTHER GOVERNMENTAL AGENCIES

The General Counsel of the Board is authorized and has responsibility, on behalf of the Board, to maintain appropriate and adequate liaison and arrangements with the office of the Secretary of Labor, with reference to the reports required to be filed pursuant to Section 9(f) and (g) of the Act and availability to the Board and the General Counsel of the contents thereof.

The General Counsel of the Board is authorized and has responsibility, on behalf of the Board, to maintain appropriate and adequate liaison with the Federal Mediation and Conciliation Service and any other appropriate Governmental Agency with respect to functions which may be performed in connection with the provisions of Section 209(b) of the Act. Any action taken pursuant to the authority and responsibility prescribed in this paragraph will be promptly reported to the Board.

V. ANTI-COMMUNIST AFFIDAVITS

The General Counsel of the Board is authorized and has responsibility, on behalf of the Board, to receive the affidavits required under Section 9(h) of the Act, to maintain an appropriate and adequate file thereof, and to make available to the public, on such terms as he may prescribe, appropriate information concerning such affidavits, but not to make such files open to unsupervised inspection.

VI. MISCELLANEOUS LITIGATION INVOLVING BOARD AND/OR OFFICIALS

The General Counsel of the Board is authorized and has responsibility, on behalf of the Board, to appear in any court to represent the Board or any of its Members or agents, unless directed otherwise by the Board.

VII. PERSONNEL

In order better to ensure the effective exercise of the duties and responsibility described above, the General Counsel of the Board, subject to applicable laws and the rules and regulations of the Civil Service Commission, is authorized and has responsibility, on behalf of the Board, to select, appoint, retain, transfer, promote, demote, discipline, discharge, and take any other necessary and appropriate personnel action with regard to, all personnel engaged in the field offices and in the Washington office (other than Administrative Law Judges, Legal Assistants to Board Members, the personnel in the Information Division, the personnel in the Division of Administration, the Solicitor of the Board and personnel in his office, the Executive Secretary of the Board and personnel in his office, including the Docket, Order and Issuance Section, and secretarial, stenographic and clerical employees assigned exclusively to the work of trial examiners and the Board Members); *Provided, however,* that no appointment, transfer, demotion or discharge of any Regional Director or Officer in

Charge shall become effective except upon the approval of the Board.

In connection with and in order to effectuate the exercise of the powers herein delegated (but not with respect to those powers herein reserved to the Board), the General Counsel is authorized, using the services of the Division of Administration, to execute such necessary requests, certifications, and other related documents, on behalf of the Board, as may be needed from time to time to meet the requirements of the Civil Service Commission, the Bureau of the Budget, or any other governmental agency. The Board will at all times provide such of the "housekeeping" functions performed by the Division of Administration as are requested by the General Counsel for the conduct of his administrative business, so as to meet the stated requirements of the General Counsel within his statutory and prescribed functions.

The establishment, transfer or elimination of any Regional or Sub-Regional Office shall require the approval of the Board.

VIII. ASSIGNMENT OF AUTHORITY

To the extent that the above-described duties, powers and authority rest by statute with the Board, the foregoing statement constitutes a prescription and assignment of such duties, powers and authority, whether or not so specified.

NATIONAL LABOR RELATIONS BOARD: Delegation of Authority to Regional Directors

Text of Statement Issued by the National Labor Relations Board May 4, 1961, Effective May 15, 1961

Pursuant to section 3(b) of the National Labor Relations Act, as amended, and subject to the amendments to the Board's Statements of Procedure, Series 8, and to its Rules and Regulations, Series 8, effective May 15, 1961 [LRX 4051] and subject to such further amendments and instructions as may be issued by the Board from time to time, the Board delegates to its Regional Directors "its powers under section 9 to determine the unit appropriate for the purpose of collective bargaining, to investigate and provide for hearings, and determine whether a question of representation exists, and to direct an election or take a secret ballot under subsection (c) or (e) of section 9 and certify the results thereof."

Such delegation shall be effective with respect to any petition filed under subsection (c) or (e) of section 9 of the Act on May 15, 1961.

NATIONAL LABOR RELATIONS BOARD
National Office

Address: 1717 Pennsylvania Ave., N.W.,

Washington, D.C. 20570. Tel.: (202) 655-4000

Office of the Chairman

Betty Southard Murphy, Chairman, term expires December 16, 1979

Helen C. Reiner, Chief Counsel

Donald R. Klenk, Deputy Chief Counsel

Earl D. Proctor, Executive Assistant

Ingrid A. Annibale, Confidential Assistant

Office of Member Fanning

John H. Fanning, term expires December 16, 1977

William C. Baisinger, Chief Counsel

Abraham Frank, Deputy Chief Counsel

Emma King, Confidential Assistant

Office of Member Jenkins

Howard Jenkins, Jr., term expires December 27, 1978

Harry M. Leet, Chief Counsel

Eugene R. Jackson, Deputy Chief Counsel

Irma E. M. Hughes, Confidential Assistant

Office of Member Penello

John A. Penello, term expires December 27, 1976

Henry I. Segal, Chief Counsel

Marvin I. Kerner, Deputy Chief Counsel

Patricia H. Polinsky, Confidential Assistant

Office of Executive Secretary

John C. Truesdale, Executive Secretary

F. Robert Volger, Deputy Executive Secretary

George A. Leet, Associate Executive Secretary

Enid W. Weber, Associate Executive Secretary

Mario A. Lauro, Assistant Executive Secretary

Division of Judges

Thomas N. Kessel, Chief Administrative Law Judge

Thomas N. Kessel, Deputy Chief Administrative Law Judge

Associate Chief Administrative Law Judges

    Arthur Leff

    Charles W. Schneider

    San Francisco

    West Coast Presiding Judge

    James T. Barker

Office of the Solicitor

Saul J. Jaffe, *Acting* Solicitor

Division of Information

Thomas W. Miller, Jr., Director

Thomas P. Healy, Associate Director

Cliff R. McMahan, Associate Director

Office of the General Counsel

John C. Miller, *Acting* General Counsel

John S. Irving, Deputy General Counsel

B. Fred Toback, Executive Assistant

Carole R. Kurata, Deputy Executive Assistant

Dorothy J. Spearman, Special Assistant

Division of Operations Management

Joseph E. DeSio, Associate General Counsel

John E. Higgins, Jr., Deputy Associate General Counsel

Eugene L. Rosenfeld, Assistant General Counsel (District I)

Michael M. Dunn, Deputy Assistant General Counsel (District I)

Thomas R. Wilks, Assistant General Counsel (District II)

James L. Ferree, Operations Examiner (District II)

Thomas M. Harvey, Assistant General Counsel (District III)

Michael M. Balsamo, Deputy Assistant General Counsel (District III)

John P. Falcone, Assistant General Counsel (District IV)

Daniel A. Silverman, Deputy Assistant General Counsel (District IV)

William Garrett Stack, Assistant General Counsel (District V)

Gerald Kobell, Deputy Assistant General Counsel (District V)

Division of Advice

Gerald Brissman, Associate General Counsel

Harold J. Datz, Deputy Associate General Counsel

Frank H. Parlier, Assistant General Counsel, Regional Advice Branch

Joseph E. Mayer, Assistant General Counsel, Injunction Litigation

Gayle C. Gearhart, Deputy Assistant General Counsel

Standau E. Weinbrecht, Assistant General Counsel, Legal Research & Policy Planning

Bronia M. R. Walsh, Chief, Legal Reference Section

Division of Enforcement Litigation

Vacant, Associate General Counsel

Norton J. Come, Deputy Associate General Counsel, Supreme Court Branch

Elliott Moore, Deputy Associate General Counsel, Appellate Court Branch

Robert A. Giannasi, Assistant General Counsel, Enforcement Litigation

Paul Elkind, Assistant General Counsel, Contempt Litigation

Abigail Cooley, Assistant General Counsel, Special Litigation

Office of Appeals

Robert E. Allen, Director

Ronald M. Slatkin, Associate Director

Mary Shanklin, Assistant Director

Division of Administration

Richard J. Shakman, Director

Paul E. Long, Deputy Director

Felix R. Brandon, Director of Personnel

Lee D. Vincent, Comptroller (Chief, Financial Management)

Mildred E. Stevens, Chief, Budget

Homer McIntyre, Chief, Finance

William V. Leaming, Chief, Management and Audit

Donald M. Probst, Chief, Facilities and Services

Jacob Stieger, Chief, Data Systems

William L. Alcorn, Chief, Security and Safety

Regional and SubRegional Offices

REGIONAL OFFICES SERVING VARIOUS STATES

Region No.	State	Region No.	State	Region No.	State
10, 15	Alabama	15	Louisiana	16	Oklahoma
19	Alaska	1	Maine	19, 36	Oregon
28	Arizona	5	Maryland	4, 6	Pennsylvania
26	Arkansas	1	Massachusetts	24	Puerto Rico
20, 21, 31	California	7, 30	Michigan	1	Rhode Island
27	Colorado	18	Minnesota	11	South Carolina
1, 2	Connecticut	15, 26	Mississippi	18	South Dakota
4, 5	Delaware	14, 17	Missouri	5, 10, 26	Tennessee
5	Dist. of Col.	19	Montana	16, 23, 28	Texas
12, 15	Florida	17	Nebraska	27	Utah
10	Georgia	20, 31	Nevada	1	Vermont
37, 20	Hawaii	1	New Hampshire	24	Virgin Islands
19	Idaho	4, 22	New Jersey	5	Virginia
13, 14, 38	Illinois	28	New Mexico	19, 36	Washington
9, 13, 25	Indiana	2, 3, 29	New York	5, 6, 9	West Virginia
18, 38	Iowa	11	North Carolina	18, 30	Wisconsin
17	Kansas	18	North Dakota	27	Wyoming
9, 25	Kentucky	8, 9	Ohio		

Region 1

Address: Boston, Mass. 02114 — 7th Floor, Bulfinch Bldg., 15 New Chardon St., Tel.: (617) 223-3300

Robert S. Fuchs, Regional Director; Robert N. Garner, Assistant Regional Director; Harold M. Kowal, Regional Attorney; William A. Hurley, Compliance Officer

Connecticut Counties:

Hartford	New London
Litchfield	Tolland
Middlesex	Windham
New Haven	

Maine
Massachusetts
New Hampshire
Rhode Island
Vermont

Region 2

Address: New York, N.Y. 10007—36th Floor, Federal Bldg., 26 Federal Plaza, Tel: (212) 264-0300

Sidney Danielson, Regional Director; Samuel Korenblatt, Assistant Regional Director; Winifred D. Morio, Regional Attorney; Robert G. Landeson, Compliance Officer

Connecticut County:
Fairfield

New York Counties:

Bronx	Putnam
New York	Rockland
Orange	Westchester

Region 3

Address: Buffalo, N.Y. 14202 — 9th Floor, Federal Bldg., 111 West Huron St., Tel. (716) 842-3100

Thomas W. Seeler, Regional Director; Norman Goldfarb, Assistant Regional Director; Richard L. DeProspero, Regional Attorney; James J. PaLermo, Compliance Officer

Resident Office *

Address: Albany, N.Y. 12207—New Federal Building, Clinton Avenue at North Pearl Street, Tel.: (518) 472-2215

Resident Officer: Thomas J. Sheridan

New York Counties:

Albany	Clinton
Allegany	Columbia
Broome	Cortland
Cattaraugus	Delaware
Cayuga	Dutchess
Chautauqua	Erie
Chemung	Essex
Chenango	Franklin

Fulton	Rensselaer
Genesee	St. Lawrence
Greene	Saratoga
Hamilton	Schenectady
Herkimer	Schoharie
Jefferson	Schuyler
Lewis	Seneca
Livingston	Steuben
Madison	Sullivan
Monroe	Tioga
Montgomery	Tompkins
Niagara	Ulster
Oneida	Warren
Onondaga	Washington
Ontario	Wayne
Orleans	Wyoming
Oswego	Yates
Otsego	

* Area served: Counties in eastern half of state, excluding counties served by New York City office.

Region 4

Address: Philadelphia, Pa. 19106— Suite 4400, William J. Green, Jr., Federal Building, 600 Arch Street, Tel.: (215) 597-7601

Peter W. Hirsch, Regional Director; Alan Zurlnick, Assistant Regional Director; Leonard Leventhal, Regional Attorney; Sarah M. Parker, Compliance Officer

Delaware County:

New Castle

New Jersey Counties:

Atlantic	Cumberland
Burlington	Gloucester
Camden	Ocean
Cape May	Salem

Pennsylvania Counties:

Adams	Monroe
Berks	Montgomery
Bradford	Montour
Bucks	Northampton
Carbon	Northumberland
Chester	Perry
Columbia	Philadelphia
Cumberland	Pike
Dauphin	Schuylkill
Delaware	Snyder
Juniata	Sullivan
Lackawanna	Susquehanna
Lancaster	Tioga
Lebanon	Union
Lehigh	Wayne
Luzerne	Wyoming
Lycoming	York

Region 5

Address: Baltimore, Md. 21201—Federal Building, Room 1019, Charles Center, Tel.: (301) 962-2822

William C. Humphrey, Regional Director; Sidney Smith, Assistant Regional Director; Charles B. Slaughter, Regional Attorney; Leonard R. Miller, Compliance Officer

Delaware Counties:

Kent	Sussex

District of Columbia

Maryland

Tennessee

City of Bristol (Sullivan County)

Virginia

West Virginia Counties:

Berkeley	Jefferson
Grant	Mineral
Hampshire	Morgan
Hardy	Pendleton

Resident Office

Address: Washington, D.C. 20570— Gelman Building, 2120 L Street, N.W. Tel.: (202) 254-7612

Resident Officer: Alexander T. Graham, Jr.

Region 6

Address: Pittsburgh, Pa. 15222—1536 Federal Bldg., 1000 Liberty Ave., Tel.: (412) 644-2977

Henry Shore, Regional Director; Herbert Schultzman, Assistant Regional Director; Edward A. Grupp, Regional Attorney; Merrill C. Embick, Compliance Officer

Pennsylvania Counties:

Allegheny	Franklin
Armstrong	Fulton
Beaver	Greene
Bedford	Huntingdon
Blair	Indiana
Butler	Jefferson
Cambria	Lawrence
Cameron	McKean
Centre	Mercer
Clarion	Mifflin
Clearfield	Potter
Clinton	Somerset
Crawford	Venango
Elk	Warren
Erie	Washington
Fayette	Westmoreland
Forest	

West Virginia Counties:

Barbour	Lewis
Brooke	Marion
Doddridge	Marshall
Hancock	Monongalia
Harrison	Ohio

Pocahontas	Tucker
Preston	Upshur
Randolph	Webster
Taylor	Wetzel

Region 7

Address: Detroit, Mich. 48226—500 Book Bldg, 1249 Washington Blvd. Tel.: (313) 226-3200

Bernard Gottfried, Regional Director; Henry L. Chiles, Jr., Assistant Regional Director; Harry D. Camp, Regional Attorney; David L. Basso, Compliance Officer

Michigan Counties:

Alcona	Lapeer
Allegan	Leelanau
Alpena	Lenawee
Antrim	Livingston
Arenac	Macomb
Barry	Manistee
Bay	Mason
Benzie	Mecosta
Berrien	Midland
Branch	Missaukee
Calhoun	Monroe
Cass	Montcalm
Charlevoix	Montmorency
Cheboygan	Muskegon
Clare	Newaygo
Clinton	Oakland
Crawford	Oceana
Eaton	Ogemaw
Emmet	Osceola
Genesee	Oscoda
Gladwin	Otsego
Grand Taverse	Ottawa
Gratiot	Presque Isle
Hillsdale	Roscommon
Huron	Saginaw
Ingham	St. Clair
Ionia	St. Joseph
Iosco	Sanilac
Isabella	Shiawassee
Jackson	Tuscola
Kalamazoo	Van Buren
Kalkaska	Washtenaw
Kent	Wayne
Lake	Wexford

Region 8

Address: Cleveland, Ohio 44199—1695 Anthony J. Celebrezze Federal Building, 1240 East 9th St., Tel.: (216) 522-3715

Bernard Levine, Regional Director; David C. Finlay, Assistant Regional Director; Carroll L. Martin, Regional Attorney; Vaughn C. Sterling, Compliance Officer

Ohio Counties:

Allen	Logan
Ashland	Lorain
Ashtabula	Lucas
Auglaize	Mahoning
Belmont	Marion
Carroll	Medina
Champaign	Mercer
Columbiana	Miami
Coshocton	Morrow
Crawford	Muskingum
Cuyahoga	Ottawa
Darke	Paulding
Defiance	Portage
Delaware	Putnam
Erie	Richland
Fulton	Sandusky
Geauga	Seneca
Guernsey	Shelby
Hancock	Stark
Hardin	Summit
Harrison	Trumbull
Henry	Tuscarawas
Holmes	Union
Huron	Van Wert
Jefferson	Wayne
Knox	Williams
Lake	Wood
Licking	Wyandot

Region 9

Address: Cincinnati, Ohio 45202— Room 3003, Federal Office Bldg., 550 Main St., Tel.: (513) 684-3686

Emil C. Farkas, Regional Director; Thomas M. Sheeran, Regional Attorney; Joseph T. Perry, Compliance Officer

Indiana Counties:

Clark	Floyd
Dearborn	

Kentucky except counties:

Daviess	Henderson

Ohio Counties:

Adams	Lawrence
Athens	Madison
Brown	Meigs
Butler	Monroe
Clark	Montgomery
Clermont	Morgan
Clinton	Noble
Fairfield	Perry
Fayette	Pickaway
Franklin	Pike
Gallia	Preble
Greene	Ross
Hamilton	Scioto
Highland	Vinton
Hocking	Warren
Jackson	Washington

West Virginia Counties:

Boone	Mingo
Braxton	Monroe
Cabell	Nicholas
Calhoun	Pleasants
Clay	Putnam
Fayette	Raleigh
Gilmer	Ritchie
Greenbrier	Roane
Jackson	Summers
Kanawha	Tyler
Lincoln	Wayne
Logan	Wirt
McDowell	Wood
Mason	Wyoming
Mercer	

Region 10

Address: Atlanta, Ga. 30308—Room 701, Peachtree Building, 730 Peachtree St., N.E., Tel.: (404) 526-5760

Walter C. Phillips, Regional Director; Aaron Z. Dixon, Assistant Regional Director; Gilbert Cohen, Regional Attorney; Charles T. Corn, Compliance Officer

Resident Office

Address: Birmingham, Ala. 35203—2102 City Federal Bldg., 2026 2nd Ave. North, Tel.: (205) 325-3877

Resident Officer: Donald E. Howard

Alabama Counties:

Autauga	Lamar
Bibb	Lauderdale
Blount	Lawrence
Calhoun	Lee
Chambers	Limestone
Cherokee	Madison
Chilton	Marion
Clay	Marshall
Cleburne	Morgan
Colbert	Perry
Coosa	Pickens
Cullman	Randolph
DeKalb	St. Clair
Elmore	Shelby
Etowah	Sumter
Fayette	Talladega
Franklin	Tallapoosa
Greene	Tuscaloosa
Hale	Walker
Jackson	Winston
Jefferson	

Georgia

Tennessee Counties:

Anderson	Campbell
Bledsoe	Carter
Blount	Clairborne
Bradley	Clay

Cocke	Morgan
Cumberland	Overton
Fentress	Pickett
Grainger	Polk
Greene	Putnam
Grundy	Rhea
Hamblen	Roane
Hamilton	Scott
Hancock	Sequatchie
Hawkins	Sevier
Jackson	Sullivan
Jefferson	(except City of
Johnson	Bristol)
Knox	Unicoi
Loudon	Union
McMinn	Van Buren
Marion	Warren
Meigs	Washington
Monroe	White

Region 11

Address: Winston-Salem, N.C. 27101—1624 Wachovia Bldg., 301 North Main St., Tel.: (919) 723-9211, Ext. 300

Reed Johnston, Regional Director; Lewis Wolberg, Assistant Regional Director; Hugh F. Malone, Regional Attorney; Martin L. Ball, Jr., Assistant Regional Attorney; Ronald Yost, Compliance Officer

North Carolina

South Carolina

Region 12

Address: Tampa, Fla. 33602—706 Federal Office Bldg., 500 Zack St., Tel.: (813) 228-2641

Harold A. Boire, Regional Director; Norman A. Cole, Assistant Regional Director; Joseph V. Moran, Regional Attorney; Jerome L. Avedon, Assistant Regional Attorney; Robert R. Morley, Compliance Officer

Resident Offices

Address: Coral Gables, Fla. 33146—Suite 410, Madruga Bldg., 1570 Madruga Ave., Tel.: (305) 350-5391

Resident Officer: James L. Jeffers

Address: Jacksonville, Fla. 32202—Federal Building, 400 West Bay Street, Tel.: (904) 791-3768

Resident Officer: John C. Wooten

Florida Counties:

Alachua	Lee
Baker	Leon
Bradford	Levy
Brevard	Madison
Broward	Manatee
Charlotte	Marion
Citrus	Martin
Clay	Monroe
Collier	Nassau
Columbia	Okeechobee
Dade	Orange
De Soto	Osceola
Dixie	Palm Beach
Duval	Pasco
Flagler	Pinellas
Gadsden	Polk
Gilchrist	Putnam
Glades	St. Johns
Hamilton	St. Lucie
Hardee	Sarasota
Hendry	Seminole
Hernando	Sumter
Highlands	Suwannee
Hillsborough	Taylor
Indian River	Union
Jefferson	Volusia
Lafayette	Wakulla
Lake	

Region 13

Address: Chicago, Ill., 60604—Rm. 881, Everett McKinley Dirksen Bldg., 219 South Dearborn St., Tel.: (312) 353 7572

Alex V. Barbour, Regional Director; Martin H. Schneid, Assistant Regional Director; Allen P. Haas, Acting Regional Attorney; Richard B. Simon, Compliance Officer

Illinois Counties:

Cook	Lake
Du Page	Will
Kane	

Indiana County:

Lake

Sub Region 38

Address: Peoria, Ill. 61602—10th Floor, Savings Center Tower, 411 Hamilton Blvd., Tel.: (309) 673-9312

Officer-in-Charge: Glenn A. Zipp, Deputy-Officer-in-Charge: Michael B. Ryan

Illinois Counties:

Boone	De Witt
Bureau	Douglas
Carroll	Ford
Cass	Fulton
Champaign	Grundy
De Kalb	Hancock

Henderson	Mercer
Henry	Morgan
Iroquois	Moultrie
Jo Daviess	Ogle
Kankakee	Peoria
Kendall	Piatt
Knox	Putnam
La Salle	Rock Island
Lee	Sangamon
Livingston	Schuyler
Logan	Stark
Macon	Stephenson
Marshall	Tazewell
Mason	Vermilion
McDonough	Warren
McHenry	Whiteside
McLean	Winnebago
Menard	Woodford

Iowa Counties:

Clinton	Lee
Des Moines	Louisa
Dubuque	Muscatine
Jackson	Scott

Region 14

Address: St. Louis, Mo. 63101—Room 448, North 12th Blvd., Tel.: (314) 622-4167

Joseph H. Solien, Regional Director; Herman W. Glaser, Assistant Regional Director; Gerard P. Fleischut, Regional Attorney; J. Robert King, Compliance Officer

Illinois Counties:

Adams	Johnson
Alexander	Lawrence
Bond	Macoupin
Brown	Madison
Calhoun	Marion
Christian	Massac
Clark	Monroe
Clay	Montgomery
Clinton	Perry
Coles	Pike
Crawford	Pope
Cumberland	Pulaski
Edgar	Randolph
Edwards	Richland
Effingham	St. Clair
Fayette	Saline
Franklin	Scott
Gallatin	Shelby
Greene	Union
Hamilton	Wabash
Hardin	Washington
Jackson	Wayne
Jasper	White
Jefferson	Williamson
Jersey	

Missouri Counties:

Audrain	Carter
Bollinger	City of St. Louis
Butler	Clark
Callaway	Crawford
Cape Girardeau	Dent

Dunklin	Perry
Franklin	Phelps
Gasconade	Pike
Iron	Ralls
Jefferson	Reynolds
Knox	Ripley
Lewis	St. Charles
Lincoln	St. Francois
Madison	St. Louis
Maries	Ste. Genevieve
Marion	Scotland
Mississippi	Scott
Monroe	Shannon
Montgomery	Shelby
New Madrid	Stoddard
Oregon	Warren
Osage	Washington
Pemiscot	Wayne

Lawrence	Scott
Leake	Sharkey
Lincoln	Simpson
Madison	Smith
Marion	Stone
Neshoba	Walthall
Newton	Warren
Pearl River	Wayne
Perry	Wilkinson
Pike	Yazoo
Rankin	

Region 16

Address: Fort Worth, Tex. 76102—
8-A-24 Federal Office Bldg., 819 Taylor Street, Tel.: (817) 334-2921
W. Edwin Youngblood, Regional Director; H. Carnie Russell, Assistant Regional Director; Hutton S. Brandon, Regional Attorney; Billy M. Gibson, Compliance Officer

Resident Office

Address: Tulsa, Okla. 74103—
Room 616, Petroleum Building,
5th and Boulder Streets, Tel.: (918)
Resident Officer: Carlos L. Moser

Oklahoma

Texas: All counties except those under jurisdiction of Regions 23 and 28

Region 15

Address: New Orleans, La. 70113—
Suite 2700, Plaza Tower, 1001 Howard Avenue, Tel.: (504) 527-6361
Charles M. Paschal, Jr., Regional Director; Fred A. Lewis, Assistant Regional Director; Fallon W. Bentz, Regional Attorney; Joseph G. Norton, Compliance Officer

Alabama Counties:

Baldwin	Geneva
Barbour	Henry
Bullock	Houston
Butler	Lowndes
Choctaw	Macon
Clarke	Marengo
Coffee	Mobile
Conecuh	Monroe
Covington	Montogomery
Crenshaw	Pike
Dale	Russell
Dallas	Washington
Escambia	Wilcox

Florida Counties:

Bay	Jackson
Calhoun	Liberty
Escambia	Okaloosa
Franklin	Santa Rosa
Gulf	Walton
Holmes	Washington

Louisiana

Mississippi Counties:

Adams	Harrison
Amite	Hinds
Claiborne	Issaquena
Clarke	Jackson
Copiah	Jasper
Covington	Jefferson
Forrest	Jefferson Davis
Franklin	Jones
George	Kemper
Greene	Lamar
Hancock	Lauderdale

Region 17

Address: Kansas City, Kan. 66101—
616 Two Gateway Center, Fourth at State, Tel.: (816) 374-4518
Thomas C. Hendrix, Regional Director; Patrick E. Rooney, Assistant Regional Director; Harry Irwig, Regional Attorney; Joseph M. Logan, Compliance Officer

Nebraska

Kansas

Missouri Counties:

Adair	Chariton
Andrew	Christian
Atchison	Clay
Barry	Clinton
Barton	Cole
Bates	Cooper
Benton	Dade
Boone	Dallas
Buchanan	Daviess
Caldwell	De Kalb
Camden	Douglas
Carroll	Gentry
Cass	Greene
Cedar	Grundy

Henry	Nodaway
Harrison	Ozark
Hickory	Pettis
Holt	Platte
Howard	Polk
Howell	Pulaski
Jackson	Putnam
Jasper	Randolph
Johnson	Ray
Laclede	St. Clair
Lafayette	Saline
Lawrence	Schuyler
Linn	Stone
Livingston	Sullivan
McDonald	Taney
Macon	Texas
Mercer	Vernon
Miller	Webster
Moniteau	Worth
Morgan	Wright
Newton	

Region 18

Address: Minneapolis, Minn. 55401—316 Federal Bldg., 110 So. 4th St. Tel.: (612) 725-2611

Robert J. Wilson, Regional Director; Kenneth W. Haan, Assistant Regional Director; Herbert S. Dawidoff, Regional Attorney

Iowa: All counties except those under jurisdiction of Sub-Region 38

Minnesota

North Dakota

South Dakota

Wisconsin Counties:

Ashland	Jackson
Barron	Pepin
Bayfield	Pierce
Buffalo	Polk
Burnett	Price
Chippewa	Rusk
Clark	St. Croix
Douglas	Sawyer
Dunn	Taylor
Eau Claire	Trempealeau
Iron	Washburn

Region 19

Address: Seattle, Wash. 98101 — 10th Floor, Republic Bldg., 1511 Third Ave., Tel.: (206) 442-4532

Charles M. Henderson, Regional Director; Dan E. Boyd, Assistant Regional Director; Walter J. Mercer, Regional Attorney

Resident Office

Address: Anchorage, Alaska 99501—409 Hill Building, 632 West 6th Avenue. Tel.: (907) 265-5271

Resident Officer: Paul H. Eggert

Sub Region 36

Address: Portland, Ore. 97205—310 Six Ten Broadway Building, 610 S.W. Broadway. Tel.: (503) 221-3085

Officer-in-Charge: Elwood G. Strumpf

Alaska

Idaho

Montana

Oregon

Washington

Region 20

Address: San Francisco, Calif., 94102 13018 Federal Building, 450 Golden Gate Ave., Box 36047. Tel.: (415) 556-3197

Natalie P. Allen, Regional Director; Michael A. Taylor, Regional Attorney; Shirley N. Bingham, Compliance Officer

California Counties:

Alameda	Nevada
Alpine	Placer
Amador	Plumas
Butte	Sacramento
Calaveras	San Benito
Colusa	San Francisco
Contra Costa	San Joaquin
Del Norte	San Mateo
Eldorado	Santa Clara
Fresno	Santa Cruz
Glenn	Shasta
Humboldt	Sierra
Kings	Siskiyou
Lake	Solano
Lasson	Sonoma
Madera	Stanislaus
Marin	Sutter
Mariposa	**Tehama**
Mendocino	Trinity
Merced	Tulare
Modoc	Tuolumne
Mono	Yolo
Monterey	Yuba
Napa	

Nevada (except Clark, Lincoln and Nye Counties)

Sub Region 37

Address: Honolulu, Hawaii 96814—Suite 308, 1311 Kapiolani Blvd., Tel.: (808) 546-5100

Officer-in-Charge: Dennis R. MacCarthy

Hawaii

Region 21

Address: Los Angeles, Calif. 90014— Eastern Columbia Bldg., 849 South Broadway, Tel.: (213) 688-5200

Wilford W. Johansen, Regional Director; Herbert C. Bumgarner, Assistant Regional Director; James S. Scott, Regional Attorney; Claude R. Marston, Compliance Officer

California Counties:

Imperial	Riverside
Los Angeles*	San Diego
Orange	

* That portion of Los Angeles County lying east of Harbor Freeway and south of Pasadena Freeway (Arroyo Boulevard, U.S. Highway 66).

Region 22

Address: Newark, N.J. 07102 — 16th Floor, Federal Bldg., 970 Broad Street, Tel.: (201) 645-2100

Arthur Eisenberg, Regional Director; William A. Pascarell, Assistant Regional Director; Bernard L. Balicer, Regional Attorney

New Jersey Counties:

Bergen	Morris
Essex	Passaic
Hudson	Somerset
Hunterdon	Sussex
Mercer	Union
Middlesex	Warren
Monmouth	

Region 23

Address: Houston, Tex., 77002 — 4th Floor, Dallas - Brazos Bldg., 1125 Brazos St., Tel.: (713) 226-4812

Louis V. Baldovin, Jr., Regional Director; Wilton Waldrop, Assistant Regional Director; Arthur Safos, Regional Attorney; Van B. Jones, Compliance Officer

Resident Office

Address: San Antonio, Tex. 78206— 509A Federal Office Buliding, 727 East Durango Boulevard, Tel.: (512) 225-5511

Resident Officer: John C. Crawford

Texas Counties:

Aransas	Bee *
Atascosa *	Bexar *
Austin	Blanco *
Bandera *	Brazoria
Bastrop	Brazos
Brooks	Kleberg
Burleson	La Salle *
Caldwell *	Lavaca
Calhoun	Lee
Cameron	Liberty
Chambers	Live Oak *
Colorado	Matagorda
Comal *	Maverick *
De Witt	McMullen *
Dimmit *	Medina *
Duval *	Montgomery
Edwards *	Newton
Fayette	Nueces
Fort Bend	Orange
Frio *	Polk
Galveston	Real *
Gillespie *	Refugio
Goliad	San Jacinto
Gonzales *	San Patricio
Grimes	Starr
Guadalupe *	Travis *
Hardin	Tyler
Harris	Uvalde *
Hays *	Val Verde *
Hidalgo	Victoria
Jackson	Walker
Jasper	Waller
Jefferson	Washington
Jim Hogg	Webb *
Jim Wells	Wharton
Karnes *	Willacy
Kendall *	Wilson *
Kenedy	Zapata
Kerr *	Zavala *
Kinney *	

* Indicates counties serviced by San Antonio Resident Office.

Region 24

Address: Hato Rey, P.R. 00917—7th Floor, Pan Am Bldg., 255 Ponce de Leon Avenue. Mailing address: P.O. Box UU 00919. Tel.: (809) 622-0247

Raymond J. Compton, Regional Director; Robert J. Canella, Assistant Regional Director; Martin M. Arlook, Regional Attorney

Puerto Rico

U.S. Virgin Islands

Region 25

Address: Indianapolis, Ind.—46204 Room 232, Federal Office Building, 575 North Pennsylvania Street, Tel.: (317) 269-7381

William T. Little, Regional Director; John W. Hines, Assistant Regional Director; George M. Dick, Regional Attorney; Arthur G. Lanker, Assistant Regional Attorney; Wayne R. Svoboda, Compliance Officer

Indiana: All counties except Lake, Clark, Dearborn, and Floyd

Kentucky Counties:

Daviess	Henderson

Region 26

Address: Memphis, Tenn. 38103—746 Clifford Davis Federal Bldg., 167 N. Main St., Tel.: (901) 534-3161

Raymond A. Jacobson, Regional Director; William K. Harvey, Assistant Regional Director; John F. Harrington, Regional Attorney; Robert H. Watson, Compliance Officer

Resident Offices

Address: Little Rock, Ark. 72201— 3511 Federal Bldg., 700 W. Capitol Ave., Tel.: (501) 378-5512

Resident Officer: Robert K. Gentry

Address: Nashville, Tenn. 37203—U.S. Courthouse and Federal Building, Room A-702, Tel.: (615) 749-5922

Resident Officer: Bernard G. Aronstam

Arkansas

Mississippi Counties:

Alcorn	Monroe
Attala	Montgomery
Benton	Noxubee
Bolivar	Oktibbeha
Calhoun	Panola
Carroll	Pontotoc
Chickasaw	Prentiss
Choctaw	Quitman
Clay	Sunflower
Coahoma	Tallahatchie
De Sota	Tate
Grenada	Tippah
Holmes	Tishomingo
Humphreys	Tunica
Itawamba	Union
Lafayette	Washington
Lee	Webster
Leflore	Winston
Lowndes	Yalobusha
Marshall	

Tennessee Counties:

Bedford	Houston
Benton	Humphreys
Cannon	Lake
Carroll	Lauderdale
Cheatham	Lawrence
Chester	Lewis
Coffee	Lincoln
Crockett	McNairy
Davidson	Macon
Decatur	Madison
De Kalb	Marshall
Dickson	Maury
Dyer	Montgomery
Fayette	Moore
Franklin	Obion
Gibson	Perry
Giles	Robertson
Hardeman	Rutherford
Hardin	Shelby
Haywood	Smith
Henderson	Stewart
Henry	Sumner
Hickman	Tipton

Trousdale	Williamson
Wayne	Wilson
Weakley	

Region 27

Address: Denver, Colo. 80202—Rm. 260, U.S. Custom House, 721 19th St., Tel.: (303) 837-3555

Francis Sperandeo, Regional Director; Jerry Cimburek, Assistant Regional Director; W. Bruce Gillis, Jr., Regional Attorney; Jerry Legler, Compliance Officer

Wyoming

Colorado

Utah

Region 28

Address: Phoenix, Ariz. 85014—LaTorre Building, 6107 North Seventh Street. Tel.: (602) 261-3717

Milo V. Price, Regional Director; Roy H. Garner, Assistant Regional Director; William L. Schmidt, Regional Attorney

Arizona

New Mexico

Texas Counties:

Culberson	Hudspeth
El Paso	

Resident Offices

Address: Albuquerque, N.M. 87110— Patio Plaza Building, 5000 Marble Avenue, N.E., Tel.: (505) 766-2508

Resident Officer: Jerry Cimburek

Address: El Paso, Tex. 79902—Suite 307, Pershing Building, Koger Executive Center, 4100 Rio Bravo Street. Tel.: (915) 543-7737

Resident Officer: Lloyd L. Porterfield

Region 29

Address: Brooklyn, N.Y. 11241—Fourth Floor, 16 Court St. Tel.: (212) 596-3535

Samuel M. Kaynard, Regional Director; Harold L. Richman, Regional Attorney; Arthur Goldberg, Assistant Regional Director; Max Schwartz, Assistant Regional Attorney; Sidney H. Levy, Compliance Officer

New York Counties:

Kings	Richmond
Nassau	Suffolk
Queens	

Region 30

Address: Milwaukee, Wis., 53203—
2nd Floor, Commerce Bldg., 744
North 4th St., Tel.: (414) 224-3861

George F. Squillacote, Regional Director; Joseph A. Szabo, Regional
Attorney; Joseph Cohen, Assistant
Regional Director; Cecil Sutphen,
Compliance Officer

Alger	Keweenaw
Baraga	Luce
Chippewa	Mackinac
Delta	Marquette
Dickinson	Menominee
Gogebic	Ontonagon
Houghton	Schoolcraft
Iron	

Wisconsin Counties:

Adams	Lafayette
Brown	Langlade
Calumet	Lincoln
Columbia	Manitowoc
Crawford	Marathon
Dane	Marinette
Dodge	Marquette
Door	Menominee
Florence	Milwaukee
Fond du Lac	Monroe
Forest	Oconto
Grant	Oneida
Green	Outagamie
Green Lake	Ozaukee
Iowa	Portage
Jefferson	Racine
Juneau	Richland
Kenosha	Rock
Kewaunee	Sauk
La Crosse	Shawano

Sheboygan	Waukesha
Vernon	Waupaca
Vilas	Waushara
Walworth	Winnebago
Washington	Wood

Region 31

Address: Los Angeles, Calif. 90024—
Room 12100, Federal Bldg., 11000
Wilshire Blvd., Tel.: (213) 824-7351

Abraham Siegel, Regional Director;
Roger W. Goubeaux, Regional Attorney; Julius N. Draznin, Assistant Regional Director; Robert Arey,
Compliance Officer

Resident Office

Address: Las Vegas, Nev. 89101—Rm.
4-503, Federal Building, 300 Las
Vegas Boulevard. Tel.: (702) 385-6416

Resident Officer: Louis S. Eberhardt

California Counties

Inyo	San Luis Obispo
Kern	Santa Barbara
Los Angeles*	Ventura
San Bernardino	

* That portion of Los Angeles County
lying west of Harbor Freeway and north
of Pasadena Freeway (Arroyo Boulevard,
U.S. Highway 66).

Nevada Counties:

Clark	Nye
Lincoln	

NLRB District Offices

District I

Baltimore (Region 5)
Boston (Region 1)
Brooklyn (Region 29)
Newark (Region 22)
New York (Region 2)
Philadelphia (Region 4)
Washington, D.C.
  Resident Office

District II

Buffalo (Region 3)
Cincinnati (Region 9)
Cleveland (Region 8)
Detroit (Region 7)
Indianapolis (Region 25)
Pittsburgh (Region 6)
Albany, N.Y.
  Resident Office

District III

Chicago (Region 13)
Kansas City, Kan.
  (Region 17)
Milwaukee (Region 30
Minneapolis (Region 18)
St. Louis (Region 14)
Peoria Sub-Regional Office

District IV

Atlanta (Region 10)
Fort Worth (Region 16)
Houston (Region 23)
Memphis (Region 26)
New Orleans (Region 15)
Tampa (Region 12)
Winston-Salem (Region 11)

Birmingham Resident Office
Jacksonville Resident Office
Little Rock Resident Office
Miami Resident Office
Nashville Resident Office
Tulsa Resident Office

District V

Denver (Region 27)
Los Angeles (Region 21)
Phoenix (Region 28)
San Francisco (Region 20
Seattle (Region 19)

Honolulu SubRegional Office
Portland SubRegional Office
Albuquerque Resident Office
Anchorage Resident Office
El Paso Resident Office
Las Vegas Resident Office

FEDERAL MEDIATION AND CONCILIATION SERVICE
National Office

Address: U.S. Customs Service Building, Constitution Avenue & 14th St., N.W., Washington, D.C., 20427. Telephone: (202) 393-7350

National Office covers District of Columbia; Montgomery and Prince George's Counties in Maryland; Arlington and Fairfax Counties and City of Alexandria in Virginia.

Director

W. J. Usery, Jr., National Director

James F. Scearce, Deputy National Director

Lawrence B. Babcock, Jr., Executive Assistant to National Director

General Counsel

Herbert Fishgold, General Counsel

John H. Martin, Assistant General Counsel

Office of Mediation Services

Kenneth E. Moffett, Director

William P. Hobgood, Associate Director

Jerome H. Ross, Assistant Director

Donald H. Doherty, Deputy Assistant Director

Nicholas A. Fidandis, National Representative

Gaylerd F. Wineriter, Special Assistant to the Director for Mediation Services

John C. Zancanaro, Special Assistant to the Director for Mediation Services

Joe L. Russell, Construction Coordinator

Office of Technical Services

Jerome T. Barrett, Director

John J. Popular, II, Assistant Director

James F. Power, Assistant Director

Harold E. Davis, Special Assistant to the Director

Lucretia D. Tanner, Labor Economist

Mary Lou Hennessy, Research Analyst

Office of Arbitration Services

L. Lawrence Schultz, Director

John Canestraight, Assistant Director for Arbitration Systems

Office of Information

Norman O. Walker, Director

Samuel F. Marshall, National Representative

Office of Administration

Stephen P. Lejko, Director

Sorine A. Preli, Associate Director

Ruth M. Wunsch, Chief, Personnel Division

Guy Marino, Chief, Budget & Finance Division

Donald W. Herring, Chief, Administrative Services Division

Gerard A. Zeller, Chief, Management Systems Division

Regional, Field and Area Offices

REGIONAL OFFICES SERVING VARIOUS STATES

Region No.	State	Region No.	State	Region No.	State
3	Alabama	1	Maine	2	Pennsylvania
7	Alaska	2	Maryland	1	Rhode Island
7	Arizona	1	Massachusetts	3	South Carolina
6, 3	Arkansas	4, 5	Michigan	5	South Dakota
7	California	5	Minnesota	3	Tennessee
7	Colorado	3	Mississippi	6, 7	Texas
1	Connecticut	6	Missouri	7	Utah
2	Delaware	7	Montana	1	Vermont
2	District of Columbia	6	Nebraska	2, 3	Virginia
3	Florida	7	Nevada	7	Washington
3	Georgia	1	New Hampshire	2	West Virginia
7	Hawaii	1, 2	New Jersey	5	Wisconsin
7	Idaho	7	New Mexico	7	Wyoming
5, 6	Illinois	1	New York		
4, 5	Indiana	3	North Carolina		*Territories and*
6	Iowa	5	North Dakota		*Possessions*
6	Kansas	2, 4	Ohio	7	Guam
3, 4	Kentucky	6	Oklahoma	3	Puerto Rico
3	Louisiana	7	Oregon	3	Virgin Islands

Region 1

New York City 10007, Room 2937 Federal Bldg., 26 Federal Plaza. Paul Yager, Regional Director. Daniel F. Fitzpatrick, Assistant Regional Director. Daniel W. Weggeland, Regional Coordinator. Robert E. Kennedy, Maritime Coordinator. T e l e p h o n e (212) 264-1000.

Connecticut	New Hampshire
Maine	New York
Massachusetts	Rhode Island

New Jersey Counties (Northern):

Bergen	Passaic
Essex	Somerset
Hudson	Sussex
Middlesex	Union
Morris	

Vermont

Field Offices

Connecticut

Hartford 06103, 703 Federal Office Bldg., 450 Main St., Tel.: (203) 244-2550.

Maine

Portland 04101, 2011 U.S. Post Office & Federal Building, 151 Forrest Avenue (Post Office Box 3587), Tel.: (207) 772-4424.

Massachusetts

Boston 02203, John F. Kennedy Federal Bldg., Government Center, Room 2400-C, Tel.: (617) 223-7343.

Worcester 01601, 320 Federal Building & Courthouse, 595 Main Street, Tel.: (617) 791-2251.

New Hampshire

Concord 03301, Room 340 Federal Bldg., 55 Pleasant St., Tel.: (603) 228-8762.

New Jersey

Newark 07102, Room 1607, New Federal Bldg., 970 Broad St., Tel.: (201) 645-2201.

New York

Albany 12201, 306 U.S. Post Office & Courthouse, Tel.: (518) 472-4223.

Buffalo 14202, 1105 New Federal Building, 111 West Huron Street, Tel.: (716) 842-3620.

Hempstead, L. I. 11550, 404 Imperial Square Bldg., 175 Fulton Ave., Tel.: (516) 538-3232.

Syracuse 13202, 610 Hunter Plaza, South Salina and East Fayette Sts., Tel.: (315) 473-3480.

Rhode Island

Lincoln 02865, Room 1, 100 Jenckes Hill Road, Tel.: (401) 528-4441.

Region 2

Address: Philadelphia, Pa. 19106—401 Mall Bldg., 4th and Chestnut Sts. Robert W. Donnahoo, Regional Director. William R. Marlowe, Assistant Regional Director. John F. McDermott, Regional Coordinator. Telephone (215) 597-7676.

Delaware

Maryland

District of Columbia

New Jersey Counties (Southern):

Atlantic	Ocean
Burlington	Warren
Camden	Hunterdon
Cape May	Mercer
Cumberland	Monmouth
Gloucester	Salem

Pennsylvania   West Virginia

Virginia Counties including and east of: Alleghany, Botetourt, Roanoke, Franklin Henry

Ohio Counties (Southeastern):

Belmont	Monroe
Guernsey	Noble
	Washington

Field Offices

District of Columbia

Washington 20548, 3152 G.A.O. Bldg., 441 G St., N.W., Tel.: (202) 961-3535.

Maryland

Baltimore 21201, 1011 Federal Office Bldg., Charles Center, 31 Hopkins Plaza, Tel.: (301) 837-2429.

New Jersey

Trenton 08608, 518 U.S. Post Office (New), 402 E. State St. Tel.: (609) 394-7195.

Pennsylvania

Allentown 18102, 301 Farr Building, 739 Hamilton Street, Tel.: (215) 433-1927.

Erie 16501, 1018 Commerce Bldg., 12th & State Sts., Tel.: (814) 455-4914.

Harrisburg 17108, Room 504, Federal Office Bldg., 228 Walnut St. (P.O. Box 848 Federal Square Station), Tel.: (717) 782-2220.

Pittsburgh 15222, 2101 Fed. Bldg., 1000 Liberty Avenue, Tel.: (412) 644-2992.

Virginia

Richmond 23240, 8225 Fed. Off. Bldg., 400 North 8th St. (Mailing Address: P.O. Box 10027). Tel.: (804) 648-6785.

West Virginia

Parkersburg 26101, 2040 Fed. Bldg., 425 Juliana St. (Mailing Address: P.O. Box 1945). Tel.: (304) 485-6329.

Region 3

Address: Atlanta, Ga. 30309—1422 West Peachtree St., N.W., Suite 400. Tally R. Livingston, Regional Director. Charles L. Bowen, Assistant Regional Director. Robert P. Baker, Regional Coordinator. Telephone (404) 526-2473.

Alabama	**Florida**
Arkansas	**Georgia**
(Crittenden County only)	

Kentucky Counties (Southwestern):

Fulton	Lyon
Hickman	Trigg
Carlisle	Caldwell
Ballard	Crittenden
McCracken	Union
Graves	Webster
Marshall	Hopkins
Calloway	Christian
Livingston	Muhlenberg
Todd	Logan
	Simpson

Louisiana	**South Carolina**
Mississippi	**Tennessee**
North Carolina	**Virginia e x c e p t** those areas under Region 2 jurisdiction
Puerto Rico	**Virgin Islands**

Field Offices

Alabama

Birmingham 35205, Rm. 428 South Twentieth Bldg. 908 South 20th St. Tel.: (205) 325-3953.

Mobile 36602, 433 Federal Bldg., 113 St. Joseph St., Tel.: (205) 690-2810.

Florida

Jacksonville 32202, 400 West Bay St. (Mailing Address: Box 35052), Tel.: (904) 791-2630.

Miami 33130, 1301 Fed. Off. Bldg., 51 S.W. First Ave., Tel.: (305) 350-5520.

Tampa 33602, 731 Fed. Off. Bldg. 500 Zack St., Tel.: (813) 228-7711.

Louisiana

New Orleans 70130, 924 Federal Office Bldg., 600 South St., Tel.: (504) 527-6112.

North Carolina

Charlotte 28282, 1115 Jefferson Standard Bldg. 307 S. Tryon St., Tel.: (704) 372-0711.

Tennessee

Chattanooga 37402. 1019 Hamilton National Bank Bldg., 7th and Market Sts., Tel.: (615) 266-3011.

Knoxville 37919, Suite 300, Building 2, 1111 North Shore Drive, Tel.: (615) 588-7911.

Memphis 38103, 471 Clifford Davis Federal Building, 167 North Main Street, Tel.: (901) 534-3276.

Nashville 37203, Suite 1203, 1808 West End Building, Tel.: (615) 749-5935.

Region 4

Address: Cleveland, Ohio 44114—1525 Superior Building, 815 Superior Avenue, N.E. James L. MacPherson, Regional Director. Edward F. O'Brien, Assistant Regional Director. David S. Tanzman (Detroit, Mich.), Special Assistant to the Regional Director. W. Kenneth Evans, Regional Coordinator. Telephone (216) 522-4800.

Indiana Counties:

Clark   Floyd

Michigan: Lower Peninsula and upper Peninsula under Region 5

Ohio (except Belmont, Monroe, Washington, Noble and Guernsey Counties)

Kentucky (except counties under Region 3 jurisdiction)

Field Offices

Kentucky

Louisville 40201, 412-A U.S. Post Office & Courthouse Bldg., Tel.: (502) 582-5204.

Michigan

Detroit 48226, 402 Federal Bldg., 231 West Lafayette, Tel.: (313) 226-7765.

Grand Rapids 49502, 250 Federal Building & U.S. Courthouse, 110 Michigan, N.W., Tel.: (616) 456-2401.

Kalamazoo 49001, Bell Building, 500 West Crosstown Parkway, Tel.: (616) 345-2409.

Saginaw 48607, 201 U.S. Post Office & Federal Office Building, 500 Federal Street, Tel.: (517) 793-2340, Ext. 428.

Ohio

Akron 44308, 436 Ohio Building Annex B, 191 South Main St., Tel.: (216) 375-2368.

Cincinnati 45202, 5106 Federal Bldg., 5th and Main Sts., Tel.: (513) 684-2951.

Columbus 43229, Room 102, Office Building One, 6600 Busch Boulevard, Tel.: (614) 469-5575.

Dayton 45402, 824 Centre City Offices, 4th & Main Streets, Tel.: (513) 461-4830.

Toledo 43604, 709 Federal Building, 234 Summit Street, Tel.: (419) 259-6400.

Region 5

Address: Chicago, Ill. 60604—1402 Dirksen Building, 219 South Dearborn Street. Richard D. Williams, Regional Director. Bernard M. O'Keefe, Assistant Regional Director. Thurman M. Sanders, Regional Coordinator. Barton L. Hess, Jr., Area Coordinator (Minneapolis, Minn.). Telephone: (312) 353-7350.

Illinois (except counties under Region 6 jurisdiction)

Indiana (except Clark and Floyd Counties under Region 4 jurisdiction)

Michigan: Upper Peninsula under Region 5 jurisdiction and Lower Peninsula

Minnesota   South Dakota

Wisconsin

Field Offices

Illinois

Peoria 61602, 225 Jefferson Bldg., 331 Fulton St., Tel.: (309) 673-6171.

Rockford 61108, Room 300, 3600 East State Street, Tel.: (815) 399-4412.

Indiana

Evansville 47708, Room 240, Federal Bldg. and U.S. Courthouse, 101 N.W. Seventh St., Tel.: (812) 423-4271.

Indianapolis 46241, Suite B-105, 2346 South Lynhurst Drive, Tel.: (317) 269-7233.

South Bend 46601, Suite 328—JMS Bldg., 108 North Main St., Tel.: (219) 232-9961.

Minnesota

Minneapolis 55401, 17 Washington Avenue, North Building, Suite 250, Tel.: (612) 725-2581.

Wisconsin

Green Bay 54301, 214 Federal Building, 325 East Walnut Street, Tel.: (414) 465-3933.

Milwaukee 53202, 350 Federal Bldg., 517 E. Wisconsin Ave., Tel.: (414) 224-3296.

Region 6

Address: St. Louis, Mo. 63103—3266 Federal Building, 1520 Market Street. Paul E. Bowers, Regional Director. William J. Meagher, Assistant Regional Director. Charles S. Riley, Regional Coordinator. Telephone (314) 425-4591.

Arkansas (except Crittenden County)

Illinois Counties:

Calhoun	Macoupin
Greene	Monroe
Jersey	Randolph
Madison	St. Clair
Iowa	Oklahoma
Kansas	Texas (except El
Missouri	Paso and Huds-
Nebraska	peth Counties)

Field Offices

Arkansas

Little Rock 72201, 5411 Federal Office Bldg., 700 W. Capitol St., Tel.: (501) 372-4361.

Iowa

Cedar Rapids 52401, 510 American Bldg., 1st Ave & 2nd St., S.E., Tel.: (319) 366-2411.

Des Moines 50309, Room 722, Federal Bldg., 210 Walnut St., Tel.: (515) 284-4110.

Kansas

Wichita 67202, 911 Beacon Bldg., 114 South Main, Tel.: (316) 267-6173.

Missouri

Kansas City 64106, Suite 1768, Fed. Bldg. 601 E. 12th St., Tel.: (816) 374-3026.

Springfield 65806, Rm. 245, Landmark Bldg., 309 N. Jefferson St., Tel.: (417) 865-3793.

Nebraska

Omaha 68102, 3406 New Federal Bldg., 215 N. 17th St., Tel.: (402) 221-3271.

Oklahoma

Oklahoma City 73102, 513 U.S. Post Office & Courthouse Bldg., 3rd & Robinson Sts., Tel.: (405) 231-4984.

Texas

Dallas 75202, Room 1809, 1114 Commerce St., Tel.: (214) 749-2917.

Houston 77002, Rm. 6016 Federal Bldg. & U.S. Courthouse. 515 Rusk Avenue, Tel.: (713) 226-4257.

Region 7

Address: San Francisco, Calif. 94102 —450 Golden Gate Ave. Box 36007. Lowell M. McGinnis, Regional Director. Harry C. O'Connell, Assistant Regional Director. Eugene J. Barry, Regional Coordinator. Samuel H. Sackman, Area Coordinator (Los Angeles, Calif.). Telephone (415) 556-4670.

Alaska	Nevada
Arizona	New Mexico
California	Oregon
Colorado	Texas Counties:
Hawaii	El Paso, Huds-
Guam	peth
Idaho	Utah
Montana	Washington
	Wyoming

Field Offices

Alaska

Anchorage 99510, U.S. Courthouse, Room 228, 4th & F Streets, Tel.: (907) 265-5204.

Arizona

Phoenix 85025, 3455 New Federal Office Bldg., 1st Ave. & Monroe St., Tel.: (602) 261-3648.

California

Los Angeles 90012, 7118 Fed. Bldg., 300 N. Los Angeles, St., Tel.: (213) 688-4012.

Sacramento 95825, New Federal Building, Room 2300, 2800 Cottage Way, Tel.: (916) 484-4534.

San Diego 92101, 936 San Diego Trust & Savings Bldg., 530 Broadway, Tel.: (714) 293-6260.

Colorado

Denver 80202, 17539 Fed. Bldg. & U.S. Courthouse, 1961 Stout St., Tel.: (303) 837-3186.

Hawaii

Honolulu 96815, Room 416, 1833 Kalakaua Avenue, Tel.: (808) 955-0258.

Montana

Great Falls 59401, Central Plaza, Suite 310, 600 Central Avenue, Tel.: (406) 452-0180.

New Mexico

Albuquerque 87101, 3002 Federal Building, 517 Gold, S.W., Tel.: (505) 766-2459.

Oregon

Portland 97205, 320 U.S. Courthouse, 620 S.W. Main St., Tel.: (503) 221-2176.

Utah

Salt Lake City 84138, 4221 Fed. Bldg., 125 South State St., Tel.: (801) 524-5250.

Washington

Seattle 98174, 644 Federal Building, 915 2nd Avenue, Tel.: (206) 442-4555.

Spokane 99201, 795 U.S. Courthouse, 920 West Riverside Avenue, Tel.: (509) 456-2516.

State & Territorial Mediation & Conciliation Agencies

Under the Taft-Hartley Act, any *state agency* "established to mediate and conciliate disputes," as well as the federal conciliation service, must be notified if there is no agreement within 30 days after one party has notified the other of desire to change the contract.

The state mediation and conciliation agencies are listed below. Presumably, where no state agency exists, notification to the federal mediation agency will be sufficient to satisfy the requirements of the law.

ALABAMA
Agency: Department of Labor
Address: Montgomery, Ala.—36104 State Administration Bldg.
Branch offices: Birmingham, Ala.— Rm. 416-17 Lyric Bldg.; Mobile, Ala.— Rm. 428-29 First National Bank Bldg.

ALASKA
Agency: Department of Labor
Address: Juneau, Alaska 99801— P.O. Box 1149

ARIZONA
Agency: Industrial Commission, State Labor Department
Address: Phoenix, Ariz.—State Office Bldg., 1601 West Jefferson St. 85005 P.O. Box 19070

ARKANSAS
Agency: Department of Labor
Address: Little Rock Ark. 72201 Capitol Hill Bldg.

CALIFORNIA
Agency: California State Conciliation Service
Address: San Francisco, Calif. 94102 —455 Golden Gate Avenue
Local offices: San Francisco, Calif. —P.O. Box 603 (Northern Calif.); Los Angeles, Calif.—107 S. Broadway

COLORADO
Agency: Department of Labor and Employment
Address: Denver, Colo. 80203—200 E. Ninth Ave.

CONNECTICUT
Agency: Board of Mediation & Arbitration in the Department of Labor
Address: Wethersfield, Conn. 06109 —200 Folly Brook Blvd.

DELAWARE
No state agency is authorized to mediate and conciliate labor disputes. The Department of Labor, however, is required to promote the voluntary arbitration, mediation, and conciliation of disputes between employers and employees.
Address: Wilmington, Del. 19899— 801 West Street

DISTRICT OF COLUMBIA
Agency: Federal Mediation and Conciliation Service
Address: Washington, D.C. 20001— Room 615, 614 H Street, N.W.

FLORIDA
Agency: Florida Mediation and Conciliation Service
Address: Tallahassee, Fla. 32304— 501 Woodward Street, Caldwell Building
Public utilities: Petition should be addressed to the Governor of Fla., who is authorized to appoint boards of arbitration for the industry.

GEORGIA
Agency: Department of Labor
Address: Atlanta, Ga. 30334—State Labor Bldg., 254 Washington Street

HAWAII
Agency: Department of Labor and Industrial Relations
Address: Honolulu, Hawaii 96813— 825 Mililani St.

IDAHO

Agency: Department of Labor
Address: Boise, Idaho 83707—317 Main St.

ILLINOIS

Agency. Conciliation and Mediation Service
Address: Chicago, Ill. 60601—160 N. La Salle St.
Local offices: Springfield, Ill.—Capitol Bldg.

INDIANA

Agency: Division of Labor
Address: Indianapolis, Ind. 46204—1013 State Office Bldg.

IOWA

Agency: Bureau of Labor
Address: Des Moines, Iowa 50319—State House, East 7th & Court Ave.

KANSAS

Agency: Department of Labor
Address: Topeka, Kan. 66603—401 Topeka Blvd.

KENTUCKY

Agency: Department of Labor
Address: Frankfort, Ky. 40601—Capital Plaza Tower

LOUISIANA

No state agency is authorized to mediate labor disputes. The Commissioner of Labor, however, is required to promote the voluntary conciliation of disputes between employers and employees.
Address: Baton Rouge, La. 70804—205 Capitol Annex, P.O. Box 44063

MAINE

Agency: Bureau of Labor and Industry
Address: Augusta, Me. 04330—Capitol Shopping Center
Panel office: Portland, Me.—132 Pleasant Ave. (Panel of Mediators)

MARYLAND

Agency: Division of Labor & Industry
Address: Baltimore, Md. 21201—203 East Baltimore Street.

MASSACHUSETTS

Agency: Board of Conciliation and Arbitration in Department of Labor & Industries
Address: Boston, Mass. 02202—State Office Bldg., Gov't Center, 100 Cambridge St.

MICHIGAN

Agency: Michigan Employment Relations Commission
Address: 300 E. Michigan Ave., Lansing. 48926
Local offices: Detroit, Mich. 48202—7310 Woodward Avenue; Grand Rapids, Mich. 49502—400 Trust Building

MINNESOTA

Agency: Bureau of Mediation Services
Address: St. Paul, Minn. 55155—110 Veterans Service Building

MISSISSIPPI

Agency: Mississippi has no legislation authorizing a State agency to mediate labor disputes.

MISSOURI

Agency: State Board of Mediation
Mediation of labor disputes in public utilities only.
Address: Jefferson City, Mo. 65101 —1904 Missouri Boulevard

MONTANA

Agency: Department of Labor & Industry
Address: Helena, Mont. 59601—1331 Helena Ave.

NEBRASKA

Agency: Court of Industrial Relations
Mediation of labor disputes in public utilities only.
Address: Lincoln, Nebr. 68509—2413 State House Station

NEVADA

Agency: Department of Labor
Address: Carson City, Nev. 89701—Rm. 214, 111 W. Telegraph St.

NEW HAMPSHIRE

Agency: Board of Conciliation and Arbitration

Address: Concord, N.H. 03301—1 Pillsbury Street

Conciliation: Portsmouth, N.H.— Board of Conciliation & Arbitration— 62 Congress St.

NEW JERSEY

Agency: State Board of Mediation, Department of Labor & Industry

Address: Trenton, N.J. 07102-1100 Raymond Boulevard, Suite 306. Tel.: (201) 648-2860.

NEW MEXICO

No state agency has been expressly authorized by law to mediate and conciliate labor disputes. In practice however, the *Labor and Industrial Commission* under its general powers assumes responsibility of mediating labor disputes.

Address: Santa Fe N. Mex. 87503— 408 Gallisteo Street, Villagra Bldg.

NEW YORK

Agency: Department of Labor

Address: Albany, N.Y., 12201—State Campus

NORTH CAROLINA

Agency: Department of Labor

Address: Raleigh, N.C. 27611—P.O. Box 27407

NORTH DAKOTA

Agency: Department of Labor

Address: Bismarck, N.D. 58501— State Capitol

OHIO

Agency: Department of Industrial Relations

Address: Columbus, Ohio 43204— 2323 West Fifth Avenue

OKLAHOMA

Agency: Department of Labor

Address: Oklahoma City, Okla. 73105 —State Capitol

OREGON

Agency: Bureau of Labor

Address: Salem, Ore. 97310—115 Labor and Industries Bldg.

Branch Office: 1400 S.W. Fifth Ave., Portland 97201

PENNSYLVANIA

Agency: Department of Labor and Industry

Address: Harrisburg, Pa. 17120— Rm. 1510 Labor & Industry Bldg.

PUERTO RICO

Agency: Department of Labor

Address: Hato Rey, P.R. 00917—414 Barbosa Ave.

RHODE ISLAND

Agency: Department of Labor

Address: Providence, R.I. 02908—235 Promenade St.

SOUTH CAROLINA

Agency: Department of Labor

Address: Columbia, S.C. 29211—3600 Forest Drive, P.O. Box 11329

SOUTH DAKOTA

Agency: Department of Manpower Affairs

Address: Pierre, S.D. 57501—State Capitol Bldg.

TENNESSEE

Though no State agency has been specifically authorized by law to mediate labor disputes, the Commissioner of Labor, under the general duties of his office, mediates labor disputes as the need arises.

Address: Nashville, Tenn. 37219— Department of Labor, C1-100 Cordell Hull Bldg.

TEXAS

No State agency is authorized to mediate or conciliate labor disputes. The Governor, however, is required, when he believes that disputes are of public concern, to refer such disputes by proclamation to industrial commission to perform fact-finding functions.

Address: Austin, Texas 78711—Department of Labor and Standards, Capitol Station, Box 12157

UTAH

Agency: Industrial Commission (Utah LRB)

Address: Salt Lake City, Utah 84114 —Rm. 438 State Capitol Building

VERMONT

Agency: Department of Labor and Industry

Address: Montpelier, Vt. 05602— State Office Bldg.

VIRGINIA

Agency: Department of Labor & Industry

Address: Richmond, Va. 23214—P.O. Box 1814, 9th Street Office Bldg.

WASHINGTON

Agency: State Mediation Service, Department of Labor & Industries

Address: Olympia, Wash. 98504— General Adm. Bldg., P.O. Box 207.

WEST VIRGINIA

Agency: Department of Labor

Address: East Charleston, W.Va. 25305—Capitol Complex, 1900 Washington Street

WISCONSIN

Agency: Wisconsin Employment Relations Commission

Address: Madison, Wis. 53703— Room 906, 30 West Mifflin Street

WYOMING

Although no State agency has been specifically authorized by law to mediate and conciliate labor disputes, in practice, the *Department of Labor and Statistics* does at times assist disputing parties in the settlement of controversies

Address: Cheyenne,Wyo. 82001—Rm. 304 Capitol Bldg.

APPENDIX G

Labor-Management Standards Enforcement
National Office

Address: Office of Labor-Management Standards Enforcement, U.S. Department of Labor, 200 Constitution Avenue, N.W., Washington, D.C. 20216. Telephone (202) 523-7377.

Office of Director

Carl H. Rolnick, Acting
Gerald G. Gotsch, Assistant to the Director

Vacant, Deputy Director

Division of Enforcement

John V. Moran, Associate Director for Enforcement

Richard G. Hunsucker, Chief, Branch of Elections & Trusteeships

John Thiede, Chief, Branch of Investigations & Audits

Daniel Gill, Chief, Branch of Special Investigations

Division of Reports Processing and Disclosure

John J. Murphy, Assistant Director
Vincent Agnelli, Deputy Division Chief
Joseph Fuchs, Chief, Branch of Labor-Management Reporting Procedures
James Cope, Acting Chief, Branch of Compliance Review & Reports Processing

Division of Program Standards

Vacant, Assistant Director
Richard Johnson, Acting Chief, Branch of Organization Liaison & Assistance
Herbert Raskin, Acting Chief, Branch of Interpretations & Standards

Regional Offices

Region 1 (New York City)

Address: 1515 Broadway, New York, N.Y. 10019

Benjamin B. Naumoff, Assistant Regional Director; Martin Stern, Associate Assistant Regional Director, Labor-Management Standards Enforcement; William O'Loughlin, Associate Regional Director, Federal Labor-Management Relations; Joseph D. Breitbart, Associate Assistant Regional Director, Veterans' Reemployment Rights; Manuel Eber, Associate Regional Director, Technical Assistant
Telephone: (212) 971-7033

Connecticut	Rhode Island
Maine	Vermont
Massachusetts	Puerto Rico
New Hampshire	Virgin Islands
New Jersey	Canal Zone
	New York

Region 2 (Philadelphia)

Address: Gateway Building, 3535 Market Street, Philadelphia, Pa. 19104

Kenneth L. Evans, Assistant Regional Director; Frank P. Willette, Associate Assistant Regional Director, Labor-Management Standards Enforcement; Eugene M. Levine, Associate Regional Director, Federal Labor-Management Relations; (*Vacant*), Associate Assistant Regional Director, Veterans' Reemployment Rights; Joseph A. Senge, Associate Assistant Regional Director, Technical Assistant
Telephone: (215) 597-7780

Delaware	Pennsylvania
District of	Virginia
Columbia	West Virginia
Maryland	

Region 3 (Atlanta)

Address: Room 300, 1371 Peachtree St., N.E., Atlanta, Ga. 30309

Lem R. Bridges, Assistant Regional Director; B. R. Withers, Jr., Associate Assistant Regional Director, Labor-Management Standards Enforcement; Seymour X. Alsher, Associate

Assistant Regional Director, Federal Labor-Management Relations; Hayden B. Clements, Jr., Associate Assistant Regional Director, Veterans' Reemployment Rights; Edwin L. Dooley Associate Assistant Regional Director, Technical Assistant

Telephone: (404) 526-5237

Alabama	Mississippi
Florida	North Carolina
Georgia	South Carolina
Kentucky	Tennessee

Region 4 (Chicago)

Address: 848 Everett-McKinley Dirksen Building, 219 S. Dearborn St., Chicago, Ill. 60604

Abraham S. Friedman, Assistant Director; Rocco C. DeMarco, Associate Assistant Regional Director, Labor-Management Standards Enforcement; Paul A. Barry, Associate Assistant Regional Director, Federal Labor-Management Relations; Wilbur T. Lindholm, Associate Assistant Regional Director, Veterans' Reemployment Rights; Stephen Jeroutek, Associate Assistant Regional Director, Technical Assistant

Telephone: (312) 353-1920

Illinois	Minnesota
Indiana	Ohio
Michigan	Wisconsin

Region 5 (Kansas City, Mo.)

Address: Rm. 2200 Federal Office Bldg., 911 Walnut St. Kansas City, Mo. 64106

Cullen P. Keough, Assistant Regional Director; Guss Zeldich, Associate Assistant Regional Director, Labor-

Management Standards Enforcement; Gordon E. Brewer, Associate Assistant Regional Director, Federal Labor-Management Relations; James W. Higgins, Associate Assistant Regional Director, Veterans' Reemployment Rights; John C. Jackson, Associate Assistant Regional Director, Technical Assistant

Telephone: (816) 374-5131

Arkansas	Nebraska
Colorado	New Mexico
Iowa	North Dakota
Kansas	Oklahoma
Louisiana	South Dakota
Missouri	Texas
Montana	Utah
	Wyoming

Region 6 (San Francisco)

Address: 9061 Federal Office Bldg., 450 Golden Gate Ave., San Francisco, Calif. 94102

Harold D. Huxley, Assistant Regional Director; Franklynn A. Elias, Associate Assistant Regional Director, Labor-Management Standards Enforcement; Gordon M. Byrholdt, Associate Assistant Regional Director, Federal Labor-Management Relations; Robert L. Shelby, Associate Assistant Regional Director, Veterans' Reemployment Rights; Walter Slater, Associate Assistant Regional Director, Technical Assistant

Telephone: (415) 556-5915

Alaska	Nevada
Arizona	Oregon
California	Samoa (American)
Guam	Wake Island
Hawaii	Washington
Idaho	

Area Offices

ATLANTA

Address: Peachtree Bldg., Room 330, 1371 Peachtree St., N.E., Atlanta, Ga., 30309

Area Director: William D. Sexton
Telephone: (404) 526-5351

Alabama	North Carolina
Georgia	South Carolina

BOSTON

Address: 211 New Studio Building, 110 Tremont Street, Boston, Mass. 02108

Area Director: Alexander R. Sutton
Telephone: (617) 223-6736

Connecticut	New Hampshire
Maine	Rhode Island
Massachusetts	Vermont

BUFFALO

Address: 616 Federal Building, 111 West Huron Street, Buffalo, N.Y. 14202

Area Director: Milton L. Dail
Telephone: (716) 842-3260

Includes New York Counties of:

Delaware	Albany
Schoharie	Rensselaer

And All Counties North and West Thereof

CHICAGO

Address: 773 Federal Office Bldg., 219 S. Dearborn St., Chicago, Ill. 60604
Area Director: John W. Beaty
Telephone: (312) 353-7264

Illinois	Indiana

Including Wisconsin Counties of:

Vernon	Dodge
Columbia	Fond Dulac
Sauk	Sheboygan

And All Counties South Thereof

CLEVELAND

Address: Room 821, Federal Office Building, 1240 E. 9th St., Cleveland, Ohio 44199
Area Director: Joseph D. Caiola
Telephone: (216) 522-3855

Ohio

DALLAS

Address: Room 301, Post Office Building, Bryan and Ervay Streets, (P. O. Box 239), Dallas, Tex. 75221
Area Director: Merle C. Rider
Telephone: (214) 749-2886

Oklahoma	New Mexico
	Texas

DENVER

Address: Suite 217, Brooks Towers, 1020 15th Street, Denver, Colo. 80202
Area Director: Alva W. Jones
Telephone: (303) 837-3203

Colorado	Utah
Montana	Wyoming

DETROIT

Address: Room 1906, Washington Blvd. Bldg., 234 State St., Detroit, Mich. 48226
Area Director: Louis H. Woiwode
Telephone: (313) 226-6200

Michigan

HONOLULU

Address: 1833 Kalakaua Avenue, Room 601, Honolulu, Hawaii 96815
Area Director: George Lee Bensley
Telephone: (808) 955-0259

Hawaii	Wake Island
Guam	American Samoa

KANSAS CITY

Address: 2200 Federal Office Bldg., 911 Walnut St., Kansas City, Mo. 64106
Area Director: Edmund L. Burke
Telephone: (816) 374-5261

Kansas	North Dakota
Nebraska	South Dakota

Including Missouri Counties of:

Mercer	Henry
Grundy	St. Clair
Livingston	Cedar
Carroll	Dade
Lafayette	Lawrence
Johnson	Barry

And All Counties West Thereof

LOS ANGELES

Address: Room 7731, Federal Bldg., 300 N. Los Angeles St., Los Angeles, Calif. 90012
Area Director: Thomas R. Stover
Telephone: (213) 688-4975

Arizona	California (Southern Half)

Nevada (Clark County)

MIAMI

Address: P.O. Box 3750, Norland Branch, 18350 N.W. 2nd Avenue, Miami, Fla. 33130
Area Director: Carl E. Crouch
Telephone: (305) 350-5125

MINNEAPOLIS

Address: 110 Federal Courts Bldg., 110 S. 4th St., Minneapolis, Minn. 55401
Area Director: David R. Dalton
Telephone: (612) 725-2292

Minnesota	Wisconsin (Northern Half)

NASHVILLE

Address: 1808 West End Building, Room 825, Nashville, Tenn. 37203
Area Director: B. R. Withers, Jr.

Telephone: (615) 749-5906
Kentucky   Mississippi
Tennessee

NEWARK

Address: 9 Clinton Street, Room 305, Newark, N.J. 07102
Area Director: Thomas B. Daly
Telephone: (201) 645-3016
New Jersey

NEW ORLEANS

Address: 940 Federal Office Building, 600 South Street, New Orleans, La. 70130
Area Director: Donald H. Williams
Telephone: (504) 527-6173
Arkansas   Louisiana

NEW YORK CITY

Address: 26 Federal Plaza, Rm. 1751, New York, N.Y. 10007
Area Director: Lawrence G. Davey
Telephone: (212) 264-1980
New York City

PHILADELPHIA

Address: Room 4256, Federal Office Building, 600 Arch Street, Philadelphia, Pa. 19107
Area Director: Robert N. Merchant
Telephone: (215) 597-4961
Delaware   Pennsylvania
**   (Eastern Half)**

PITTSBURGH

Address: Room 1436, Federal Office Bldg., 1000 Liberty Ave., Pittsburgh, Pa. 15222
Area Director: William B. Kane
Telephone: (412) 644-2925
West Virginia
Western Half of Pennsylvania Which Includes Counties of:
Potter   Mifflin
Clinton   Huntingdon
Center   Franklin
And All Counties West Thereof

SAN FRANCISCO

Address: 100 McAllister Street, Room 1604, San Francisco, Calif. 94102

Area Director: John J. Jordan
Telephone: (415) 556-2030
Utah   Nevada (Except
**   Clark County)**
California Counties of:
Monterey   Tulare
Kings   Inyo
And All Counties North Thereof

SEATTLE

Address: 3301 Smith Tower Bldg., 506 Second Ave., Seattle, Wash. 98104
Area Director: John A. LeMay
Telephone: (206) 442-5216
Alaska   Oregon
Idaho   Washington

ST. LOUIS

Address: 210 North Twelfth Boulevard, Room 570, St. Louis, Mo. 63101
Area Director: Herbert P. Krehbiel
Telephone: (314) 622-4691

Iowa, and Eastern Half of Missouri Which Includes Counties of:
Putnam   Benton
Sullivan   Greene
Linn   Hickory
Chariton   Polk
Saline   Christian
Pettis   Stone
And All Counties East Thereof

SANTURCE

Address: Condominio San Alberto, Room 704, Santurce, Puerto Rico 00907
Area Director: Juan E. Capestany
Telephone: (809) 723-8790
Puerto Rico   Virgin Islands

WASHINGTON, D.C.

Address: Post Office Box 19257, 509 Vanguard Bldg., 1111 20th St. N.W., Washington, D.C. 20210
Area Director: Dow E. Walker
Telephone: (202) 961-4417
Maryland   Virginia
**   District of Columbia**

EXCERPTS FROM POSTAL REORGANIZATION ACT*

Sec. 2, Title 39 USC §§ 1201–1209

CHAPTER 12.—EMPLOYEE-MANAGEMENT AGREEMENTS

Sec. 1201. *Definition.* As used in this chapter, "guards" means—

(1) maintenance guards who, on the effective date of this chapter, are in key position KP–5 under the provisions of former section 3514 of title 39; and

(2) security guards, who may be employed in the Postal Service and whose primary duties shall include the exercise of authority to enforce rules to protect the safety of property, mail, or persons on the premises.

Sec. 1202. *Bargaining units.* The National Labor Relations Board shall decide in each case the unit appropriate for collective bargaining in the Postal Service. The National Labor Relations Board shall not include in any bargaining unit—

(1) any management official or supervisor;

(2) any employee engaged in personnel work in other than a purely nonconfidential clerical capacity;

(3) both professional employees and employees who are not professional employees unless a majority of such professional employees vote for inclusion in such unit; or

(4) together with other employees, any individual employed as a security guard to enforce against employees and other persons, rules to protect property of the Postal Service or to protect the safety of property, mail, or persons on the premises of the Postal Service; but no labor organization shall be certified as the representative of employees in a bargaining unit of security guards if such organization admits to membership, or is affiliated directly or indirectly with an organization which admits to membership, employees other than guards.

Sec. 1203. *Recognition of labor organizations.* (a) The Postal Service shall accord exclusive recognition to a labor organization when the organization has been selected by a majority of the employees in an appropriate unit as their representative.

(b) Agreements and supplements in effect on the date of enactment of this section covering employees in the former Post Office Department shall continue to be recognized by the Postal Service until altered or amended pursuant to law.

(c) When a petition has been filed, in accordance with such regulations as may be prescribed by the National Labor Relations Board—

*Public Law 91–375, 91st Congress., H.R. 17070, August 12, 1970

(1) by an employee, a group of employees, or any labor organization acting in their behalf, alleging that (A) a substantial number of employees wish to be represented for collective bargaining by a labor organization and that the Postal Service declines to recognize such labor organization as the representative; or (B) the labor organization which has been certified or is being currently recognized by the Postal Service as the bargaining representative is no longer a representative; or

(2) by the Postal Service, alleging that one or more labor organizations has presented to it a claim to be recognized as the representative;

the National Labor Relations Board shall investigate such petition and, if it has reasonable cause to believe that a question of representation exists, shall provide for an appropriate hearing upon due notice. Such hearing may be conducted by an officer or employee of the National Labor Relations Board, who shall not make any recommendations with respect thereto. If the National Labor Relations Board finds upon the record of such hearing that such a question of representation exists, it shall direct an election by secret ballot and shall certify the results thereof.

(d) A petition filed under subsection (c)(1) of this section shall be accompanied by a statement signed by at least 30 percent of the employees in the appropriate unit stating that they desire that an election be conducted for either of the purposes set forth in such subsection.

(e) Nothing in this section shall be construed to prohibit the waiving of hearings by stipulation for the purpose of a consent election in conformity with regulations and rules of decision of the National Labor Relations Board.

Sec. 1204. *Elections.* (a) All elections authorized under this chapter shall be conducted under the supervision of the National Labor Relations Board, or persons designated by it, and shall be by secret ballot. Each employee eligible to vote shall be provided the opportunity to choose the labor organization he wishes to represent him, from among those on the ballot, or "no union."

(b) In any election where none of the choices on the ballot receives a majority, a runoff shall be conducted, the ballot providing for a selection between the 2 choices receiving the largest and second largest number of valid votes cast in the election. In the event of a tie vote, additional runoff elections shall be conducted until one of the choices has received a majority of the votes.

(c) No election shall be held in any bargaining unit within which, in the preceding 12–month period, a valid election has been held.

Sec. 1205. *Deductions of dues.* (a) When a labor organization holds exclusive recognition, or when an organization of personnel not subject to collective-bargaining agreements has consultation rights under section 1004 of this title, the Postal Service shall deduct the regular and periodic dues of the organization from the pay of all members of the organization in the unit of recognition if the Post Office Department or the Postal Service has received from each employee, on whose account such deductions are made, a written assignment which shall be irrevocable for a period of not more than one year.

(b) Any agreement in effect immediately prior to the date of enactment of the Postal Reorganization Act between the Post Office Department and any organization of postal employees which provides for deduction by the Department of the regular and periodic dues of the organization from the pay of its members, shall continue in full force and effect and the obligation for such deductions shall be assumed by the Postal Service. No such deduction shall be made from the pay of any employee except on his written assignment, which shall be irrevocable for a period of not more than one year.

Sec. 1206. *Collective-bargaining agreements.* (a) Collective-bargaining agreements between the Postal Service and bargaining representatives recognized under section 1203 of this title shall be effective for not less than 2 years.

(b) Collective-bargaining agreements between the Postal Service and bargaining representatives recognized under section 1203 may include any procedures for resolution by the parties of grievances and adverse actions arising under the agreement, including procedures culminating in binding third-party arbitration, or the parties may adopt any such procedures by mutual agreement in the event of a dispute.

(c) The Postal Service and bargaining representatives recognized under section 1203 may by mutual agreement adopt procedures for the resolution of disputes or impasses arising in the negotiation of a collective-bargaining agreement.

Sec. 1207. *Labor disputes.* (a) If there is a collective-bargaining agreement in effect, no party to such agreement shall terminate or modify such agreement unless the party desiring such termination or modification serves written notice upon the other party to the agreement of the proposed termination or modification not less than 90 days prior to the expiration date thereof, or not less than 90 days prior to the time it is proposed to make such termination or modification. The party serving such notice shall notify the Federal Mediation and Conciliation Service of the existence of a dispute within 45 days of such notice, if no agreement has been reached by that time.

(b) If the parties fail to reach agreement or to adopt a procedure providing for a binding resolution of a dispute by the expiration date of the agreement in effect, or the date of the proposed termination or modification, the Director of the Federal Mediation and Conciliation Service shall direct the establishment of a factfinding panel consisting of 3 persons. For this purpose, he shall submit to the parties a list of not less than 15 names, from which list each party, within 10 days, shall select 1 person. The 2 so selected shall then choose from the list a third person who shall serve as chairman of the factfinding panel. If either of the parties fails to select a person or if the 2 members are unable to agree on the third person within 3 days, the selection shall be made by the Director. The factfinding panel shall issue after due investigation a report of its findings, with or without recommendations, to the parties no later than 45 days from the date the list of names is submitted.

(c)(1) If no agreement is reached within 90 days after the expiration or termination of the agreement or the date on which the agreement became subject to modification under subsection (a) of this section, or if the parties decide upon arbitration but do not agree upon the procedures therefor, an arbitration board shall be established consisting of 3 members, not members of the factfinding panel, 1 of whom shall be selected by the Postal Service, 1 by the bargaining representative of the employees, and the third by the 2 thus selected. If either of the parties fails to select a member, or if the members chosen by the parties fail to agree on the third person within 5 days after their first meeting, the selection shall be made by the Director. If the parties do not agree on the framing of the issues to be submitted, the factfinding panel shall frame the issues and submit them to the arbitration board.

(2) The arbitration board shall give the parties a full and fair hearing, including an opportunity to present evidence in support of their claims, and an opportunity to present their case in person, by counsel or by other representative as they may elect. Decisions of the arbitration board shall be conclusive and binding upon the parties. The arbitration board shall render its decision within 45 days after its appointment.

(3) Costs of the arbitration board and factfinding panel shall be shared equally by the Postal Service and the bargaining representative.

(d) In the case of a bargaining unit whose recognized collective-bargaining representative does not have an agreement with the Postal Service, if the parties fail to reach agreement within 90 days of the commencement of collective bargaining, a factfinding panel will be established in accordance with the terms of subsection (b) of this section, unless the parties have previously agreed to another procedure for a binding resolution of their differences. If the parties fail to reach agreement within 180 days of the commencement of collective bargaining, and if they have not agreed to another procedure for binding resolution, an arbitration board shall be established to provide conclusive and binding arbitration in accordance with the terms of subsection (c) of this section.

Sec. 1208. *Suits.* (a) The courts of the United States shall have jurisdiction with respect to actions brought by the National Labor Relations Board under this chapter to the same extent that they have jurisdiction with respect to actions under title 29.

(b) Suits for violation of contracts between the Postal Service and a labor organization representing Postal Service employees, or between any such labor organizations, may be brought in any district court of the United States having jurisdiction of the parties, without respect to the amount in controversy.

(c) A labor organization and the Postal Service shall be bound by the authorized acts of their agents. Any labor organization may sue or be sued as an entity and in behalf of the employees whom it represents in the courts of the United States. Any money judgment against a labor organization in a district court of the United States shall be enforcible only against the organization as an entity and against its assets, and shall not be enforcible against any individual member or his assets.

(d) For the purposes of actions and proceedings by or against labor organizations in the district courts of the United States, district courts shall be deemed to have jurisdiction of a labor organization (1) in the district in which such organization maintains its principal offices, or (2) in any district in which its duly authorized officers or agents are engaged in representing or acting for employee members.

(e) The service of summons, subpena, or other legal process of any court of the United States upon an officer or agent of a labor organization, in his capacity as such, shall constitute service upon the labor organization.

Sec. 1209. *Applicability of Federal labor laws.* (a) Employee-management relations shall, to the extent not inconsistent with provisions of this title, be subject to the provisions of subchapter II of chapter 7 of title 29.

(b) The provisions of chapter 11 of title 29 shall be applicable to labor organizations that have or are seeking to attain recognition under section 1203 of this title, and to such organizations' officers, agents, shop stewards, other representatives, and members to the extent to which such provisions would be applicable if the Postal Service were an employer under section 402 of title 29. In addition to the authority conferred on him under section 438 of title 29, the Secretary of Labor shall have authority, by regulation issued with the written concurrence of the Postal Service, to prescribe simplified reports for any such labor organization. The Secretary of Labor may revoke such provision for simplified forms of any such labor organization if he determines, after such investigation as he deems proper and after due notice and opportunity for a hearing, that the purposes of this chapter and of chapter 11 of title 29 would be served thereby.

(c) Each employee of the Postal Service shall have the right, freely and without fear of penalty or reprisal, to form, join, and assist a labor organization or to refrain from any such activity, and each employee shall be protected in the exercise of this right.

Index

Numbers refer to sections
515

Numbers refer to sections

Numbers refer to sections

Numbers refer to sections

ballots)
electioneering, form of 9–13
eligibility lists 8–11; 9–2
expanding units 5–14
extension 5–13
false or misleading propaganda 9–10
filing, dates of 5–13
fluctuating workforce 5–13
invalidation of, criteria for 9–11
mailed ballots 9–20
mechanics of voting 9–17
notice of 9–8
objections to (*See* Objections to conduct of election)
observers at 9–16
place of 9–6
preelection appeals to racial prejudice 9–12
preelection conference 9–2
preelection interference 9–15
preelection propaganda 9–9
propaganda, form and timing of 9–13
reproduction of ballot 9–13
"request to proceed" 9–4
seasonal industries 9–4
settlement agreement 14–3
speeches before 9–13
state agency 5–13
statutory bar 5–13
threats or promises in campaign statements 9–11
tie votes 10–25
time of 9–4
unfair labor practice charge pending 13–19
unfair labor practice proceeding order, effect of 9–4
voting power 9–5
Election, expedited (*See* Expedited election)
Elections, last offer 21–7
Election observers (*See* Election, conduct of)
Election petition (*See* Petition for certification)
Eligible voters 8–11
strikers 8–11
Eligibility lists 9–2
checking of 9–3
not barred to challenge of voters 9–18
deauthorization proceedings 12–6
failure to furnish 9–2
observers, use of by 9–16
Eligibility of voters
observer, conduct as not barred 9–16
Eligibility of voters
rerun election 10–21

runoff election 10–23
seasonal industries 9–4
Emergency dispute 1–1
Employee rights, interference with 1–8
Employer
agent, responsibility for acts committed by 1–10
conduct during election (*See* Election, conduct of; Objections to conduct of election)
delay of election by 6–9
domination by, not grounds for objection to conduct of election 10–7
excelsior list submitted by 6–3
information, duty to furnish 1–15
injunctions against 1–14
notice to employees in certification proceedings 6–2
petition for certification 5–7
materials submitted by 6–2
showing of interest 5–18
petition for decertification, barred from filing 11–2
unfair labor practices 1–8
charge filed by 13–6
discharge pursuant to union-shop clause 1–9
responsibilities for 1–10
voluntary recognition of union 5–2
Entertainment and amusement industries, jurisdictional standards 3–4
Evidence, rules of
decertification proceedings 11–5
documentary evidence 16–7
documents in possession of Board or General Counsel 16–8
exceptions 10–13
hearing, representation case 7–12
unfair labor practice hearing 16–5; 16–6
Excelsior lists 6–3, 6–9, 9–2
Exceptions
administrative law judge, failure to file 17–3
filing of 22–4
hearing on 10–14
notice of 10–15
report on 10–16
Exceptions, representation case
content of 10–13
filing of 10–11
report of challenges 10–10
report on objections 10–10
where no filing of 10–13
who may file 10–12
Exceptions, unfair labor practice case (*See* Administrative law judge)

Numbers refer to sections

Numbers refer to sections

–G–

Numbers refer to sections

Numbers refer to sections

Numbers refer to sections

Numbers refer to sections

Numbers refer to sections

Numbers refer to sections

Numbers refer to sections

Numbers refer to sections

Numbers refer to sections

Numbers refer to sections

Numbers refer to sections

Numbers refer to sections

Numbers refer to sections